The Hope Valley Line
Dore to Chinley

Volume One

From the Dawn of the Railways to the End of the Grouping in 1947

Ted Hancock

ii

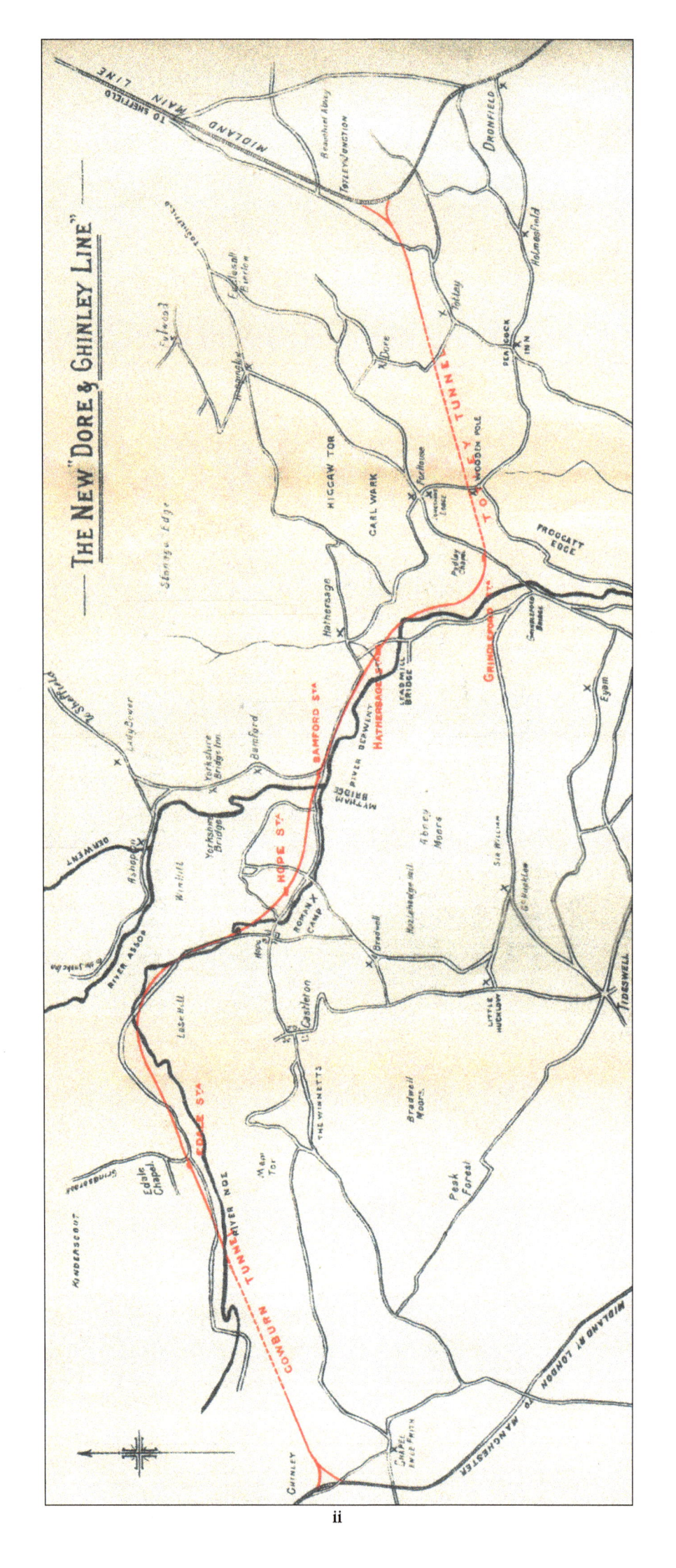

Copyright © 2019 Ted Hancock

ISBN 978-0-9562706-9-6

All rights reserved.

No part of this work may be reproduced, stored in a retrieval system, or transmitted, in any form or by any means, electronic, mechanical, photographic, electrostatic, recording, or by any storage and retrieval system without the prior written permission of the author.

First published in 2019 by Pynot Publishing on behalf of

Ted Hancock Books
127 Westwick Road
Sheffield
S8 7BW

Typesetting and graphic design by Nick Wheat

Printed by CPI Group (UK), Copland Way Ellough Beccles Suffolk NR34 7TL

Published in 2019 for Ted Hancock by
Pynot Publishing, 56 Main Road, Holmesfield, Dronfield. S18 7WT

ACKNOWLEDGEMENTS

Because of the long gestation period of the book some of the contributors are sadly no longer with us. Not all the contributors' material will appear in this volume but will in the subsequent volumes.

I would particularly like to thank those who readily helped me at the beginning when I hardly knew how to start. They are Mike Bentley, Frank Berridge, Peter Holmes, Eddie Johnson, Laurence Knighton, Roger Newman and Glynn Waite. The late Greg Fox was a civil engineer who worked on the line at various times and had a wealth of first hand knowledge and much primary source material which he readily shared. I was initially preparing the book for his excellent Foxline series but his declining health prevented this coming to fruition.

Very special thanks go to Richard Morton who volunteered to be my proof reader at the beginning. All these years later he is still working overtime to correct my 1950s English and on occasion, because he is a railway enthusiast as well, preventing me from making some elementary mistakes. He has worked out that he has contributed eighty eight hours of his time to the task for which I am extremely grateful. Also Brian Stayt, who helps me with my talks on the line and other subjects who has always been willing to help in a variety of ways and Steve Huson who has knocked the maps and diagrams into shape. The final special contributor is Nick Wheat, who produced the excellent Midland Railway Society Journal. He has designed all the artwork and completed all the typesetting.

Various organizations have been valuable sources of information and illustrations and their staff have been unfailingly helpful:-

Derbyshire Record Office at Matlock
The Local Studies Libraries at Matlock, Buxton and Chesterfield
National Archive at Kew
National Railway Museum at York
Sheffield Local Studies Library – I spent countless hours going daft and dizzy on the microfiche machines before the newspapers were digitised. The advent of the British Newspaper Archive is one technological change, among others that delayed the completion of the book. However it has allowed the content to be enriched and humanised and contributed to setting the story in the context of the time. Sheffield Libraries and Archives have also authorised the use of illustrations from the wonderful and expanding 'Picture Sheffield' collection.

Nick Tomlinson at Derbyshire Libraries 'Picture the Past' collection
Helena Robinson, John Capewell and Malcolm Andrews at Hope Construction Materials at Hope
John K. Williams of the Industrial Locomotive Society
Paul Shackcloth and his team at the Manchester Locomotive Society at Stockport
Dave Harris of the Midland Railway Society Archive at Derby which includes the Roy F. Burrows collection
The S.W.A. Newton photograph collection at Leicestershire Museums and Galleries
James Shuttleworth for access to the Shuttleworth family papers
Trevor Johnson of the Historical Model Railway Society at Butterley
Tom Robinson and Trevor Weckert at the Sheffield Transport Study Group
David Postle at Kidderminster Railway Museum
Mick Bond the Peak Rail archivist
Kevin Lane of the Industrial Railway Society
Dorne Coggins archivist to the Dore Village Society
Pauline Burnett at Totley History Group
Sally Cave and Ann Price at Hope Historical Society
Phil Rogers and Rob Lorch at the Edale Society
Malcolm Dungworth and Howard Ward at the Bamford History Society

Individual contributors were:-

Geoff Alsop, Steve Armitage, Isabel Blincow, Jack Braithwaite, Jenny Butterworth, Jane Caborn, Ian Castledine, Peter Churchman, Peter Clowes, Geoff Cooke, Chris Croft, Gary Dixon, P. Drake, Brian Edwards, Bob Essery, Keith Glossop, Brian Grandfield, Noel Hancock, Ian Howard, Glenis Howe, Bill Hudson, D.E. Jenkinson, Andrew Neale, Ken Plant, Professor Brian Robinson, Walter Rowland, Dave Sharp, James Shuttleworth, Jim Story (descendant of J. Somes and George Ernest Story), David N. Sutcliffe, Bill Taylor, Howard Turner, Roger West, Brian Wilson and John Workman.

Reminiscences from Austin Brackenbury, Derek Ashworth, Mabel Bamford, Dave Darwin, Joyce Emson, Gordon Goodwin, Dave Green, Mick Hayes, Ken Morgan, Oliver Wain, Douglas Walker and Lawrence Yeardley.

The photographers who generously allowed me to use their images:-

R.M. Casserley (H.C. Casserley collection), Barry Collins, Bryan Goodlad, Brian Green, Ken Horam, Peter Hughes, M.A. King, Michael Mensing, Bernard Mettam, John Morton (E.R. Morten collection), Tony Moyes, J.C. Naylor, Les Nixon, Geoff Parrish, Keith Pirt, David N. Sutcliffe, Howard Turner, and also Ken Boulter and Geoff Newall whose photographic collections I own.

The photograph collections I was able to draw from:-

Geoff Alsop, John Alsop, Malcolm Dungworth, John Ryan and Stephen Summerson.

I have given illustrated talks to various railway and non-railway groups on various aspects of the line; the organizers have invariably allowed me to promote the books and gather contact information from those who expressed an interest.

A DEDICATION

To my wife, Barbara, who has appreciated that this hobby, which got out of hand, has prevented me from getting under her feet and kept me mentally alert. Without her support and patience I could not have done any of it.

Those who know nothing of history make the same mistakes again.

CONTENTS

CHAPTER 1 – GETTING FROM SHEFFIELD TO MANCHESTER

The Tortuous History	1
The Pre-Railway Age	2
The Canals	6
Railways across the Peak District	26
The Pre-1830 Period	26
The Railway Mania Railways	30
The 1860s	47
The LNWR Backed Lines	48
Lines within the Peak District	51
Lines that Directly Rivalled the Dore and Chinley Railway	55
Epilogue	58

CHAPTER 2 – HOW THE RAILWAY REACHED DORE AND CHINLEY

How the Railway reached Dore and Totley	59
How the Railway reached Chinley	69

CHAPTER 3 – THE DORE AND CHINLEY RAILWAY

The Progenitors	85
The Dore & Chinley Railway Company	87
The Objectors	88
The Midland Railway Takes Over	97
Preparations for Starting the Building	99
The Engineers and Contractors	99
Memorials and Petitions	108
The Location, Dimensions and Gradients	110
Surveying the Tunnels	111
Chronology of the Building	113
Additional Information	154
The Tunnel Entrances	154
Working Practices at Cowburn Shaft	156
Machinery and Material used	159
Signalling Arrangements	159
Contractors' Locomotives	160
Transport of Equipment and Materials	168
Cost of the Total Undertaking	168
Inspections of the Line	168
The Navvies	171
Locomotives Built for the Opening	179
The Opening of the Line	183
Contemporary Reports	186

CHAPTER 4 – FROM OPENING TO NATIONALISATION 1894 TO 1947

Chronology of Events 1894 to 1947	189
Guides to the New Railway	192
From Opening to the First World War	194
New Mills and Heaton Mersey Line	197
Look Who's Coming Down the Line	202
Royal Train in the Hope Valley in 1905	209
The First World War	211
Post-War to Grouping	213
The 'Red Arrows' over Hathersage	213
The Grouping Period	215
Omnibus Services	216
The Second World War	220
Post War to Nationalisation	224
Reminiscences	224
The Winter of 1947	224
Nationalisation	230

CHAPTER 5 – OPERATIONS

Introduction to the Timetables	231
Passenger Operations	231
Oh! I do Like to be Beside the Seaside	246
Freight Operations	251
Starting and Finishing Points	251
The Working Timetables	255
Running Powers for the Great Northern Railway	272
Locomotive and Traffic Summaries	278
Motive Power	282

APPENDICES

1. Men, Horses and Engines Employed on Building the Line	288
2. Navvy Accidents and Deaths	289

Cover Photograph: Buxton's ex-Midland 2P 4-4-0 447 was originally one of the '2203' class, the first of which were built new for working the line when it opened. However this is one of a later batch which were used all over the system. In 1906 it was rebuilt with a Belpaire boiler to the '483' class which is how it is seen here. The first of the four coaches is an ex-LNWR D267 type. The train is drifting down the descent from Edale and is passing the up home signal and Norman's Bank signal box on Sat 7 Aug 1937. This is one of several photographs Ray Morten took on his visit. What a lovely way to spend a summer afternoon. *E. R. Morten*

INTRODUCTION

Having spent my formative years in the suburb of Crookes, Sheffield, which is less than three miles from the Midland station and two miles from the open country of the Rivelin valley and beyond it the Peak District I have always thought that I have enjoyed all the benefits of living in a big city and the pleasures of superb countryside.

As I have researched this book I have looked at the Hope and Noe valleys afresh. I have come to realize there is hardly a footpath that I have not walked, from the peat bogs of Kinder Scout to the gentle river walks in all seasons and all weathers. My favourite view of the Hope valley is from Longshaw where the B6054 from Owler Bar and the A625, which drops down Froggatt Edge meet. The view across to Mam Tor is always different, depending on the time of year, the light and the state of the weather. As old age beckons my last big hiking effort was to climb Lose Hill to photograph a preserved B1 on a steam special to Buxton. I reached Ward's Piece but it was so cold and windy that I could not hold my camcorder still and the result was that I only captured the smoke! As I have researched the line I have visited its entire infrastructure and had the pleasure of seeing much of it in April 2007 when the spring weather was perfect for day after day.

In the 1920s and 1930s my father, who died when I was in my twenties, was a keen walker and cyclist and was a member of the Clarion Ramblers Club. He took part in the celebrated Kinder trespass in 1932. I have a newspaper cutting from the Manchester Evening News showing a photograph of him as a wanted man. Hopefully the police have now closed the file! It was to him that I owe my love of the area.

Initially the book was to be published in the 'Scenes from the Past' series for Foxline Publishing. These books had an excellent and successful format of prolific illustrations with detailed well researched captions. However I realised that I was accumulating a considerable amount of material and that a different format would allow me to go into more detail. Unfortunately Greg Fox, the owner, who was most supportive in providing information and illustrations, became terminally ill and unable to carry on and so I decided to publish the book myself. When I had reached over 600 pages of text without the illustrations on my computer I realized that it was too much for one volume and so I decided to spread it over three volumes, this being the first.

It soon became apparent that this line was the single most important event in the lives of those who lived in the Hope and Noe valleys. This was a remote and neglected area of great beauty where the lack of decent transport links meant that it was stagnating with its agriculture, industry and tourism unable to grow and flourish. As a result I have tried to interweave the impact the coming of the railway had on the local communities into the story. I have also, I think, managed to unravel why the Midland Railway delayed for so long the building of the line given that all previous efforts had foundered because of the huge engineering costs.

Because, to my knowledge, there has been no specific book dedicated to the line published, apart from Bradbury's two guides when it first opened, this has meant that everything has been researched from scratch; surprising given the plethora of railway books published, particularly about railways in the Peak District.

Thus it has taken a very long time to bring the story to completion but I hope that those who have lost patience with the continued delays will see what a mammoth task it has been and feel that the wait has been worthwhile.

The first volume covers the canals and all the projected lines that were never built; how the connecting lines reached Dore & Totley and Chinley, the epic story of the building of the line and the contribution of the navvies and finally the period from the opening of the line to the end of the Grouping period in 1947. Volume 2 will cover the infrastructure of the line as far as Gowhole and include the widening of the lines from Sheffield to Dore and Chinley North Junction to New Mills South Junction. Also included are the railways built for the Derwent, Howden and later Ladybower reservoirs and the branch to the Hope Valley cement works of G. &. T. Earle which opened in 1929. Volume 3 will cover the British Railways period from 1948 to Privatisation between 1994 and 1997; these years were marked by a fall in passenger numbers and the decline of coal usage and the elimination of steam motive power together. The Beeching Report of 1963 seriously jeopardised the future of the line which was ultimately, and happily, reprieved. It became the only line between Derby and all places north of Sheffield to Manchester.

Sit back and enjoy the ride.

Ted Hancock, June 2019

CHAPTER 1
GETTING FROM SHEFFIELD TO MANCHESTER
THE TORTUOUS HISTORY
INTRODUCTION

Before we embark upon the story of the building of the Dore and Chinley Railway, we need to know about the pre-railway links across the Peak, specifically the canals that reached the edge of the Peak District and those canals across the Peak that would have connected to them but were never built. Also included is the line across the Pennines that was built, namely the Woodhead route, which was a long established and difficult competitor. Additionally there were many lines that were proposed but never built, some ridiculous but others of great merit. We will meet some of the great names of this heady developmental period such as John Rennie Senior, Thomas Telford, William Chapman, Thomas Brindley, John Fowler, William Jessop, George and Robert Stephenson, Charles Vignoles, Joseph Locke and later Thomas Bouch – not all of whom covered themselves in glory. It will not make any sense if the lines that connected with Dore and Totley station and Chinley station are not considered, for without them there would have been no Dore and Chinley Railway. The history of the building of these lines will also be considered.

In the next chapter, on the building of the Dore and Chinley line, I will first cover the lines that were proposed by the Midland Railway which will offer an insight into the company's thinking at the time.

Whereas further north there were east-west gaps in the Pennine chain that made canals and railways feasible, the Peak District did not easily offer these possibilities due to the high moorland immediately west of Sheffield and the bulk of Mam Tor, Colborne and Rushup Edge east of Chapel en le Frith. Further north the high moors above the Don and Etherow valleys provided obstacles that were nearly as difficult. As we shall see the promoters and surveyors eventually realised that the latter route offered the best chance, but even so this still presented formidable engineering difficulties. Added to this the area to be traversed was extremely isolated and treacherous to travellers.

The start of the railway building age began in earnest after the success of the Rainhill Trials in 1829 proved the ability of the steam locomotive. This gave the promoters of the Liverpool and Manchester Railway, the confidence to use steam power on their pioneering inter-city line which opened in 1830.

The First Railway Mania followed as the exciting future for railways became apparent and an enormous amount of energy and money was generated. Speculators and ruthless entrepreneurs set about linking the main centres of population in an orgy of competing lines that culminated in the 'Second Railway Mania' around 1845.

This inevitably led to a depression as the many losers licked their collective financial wounds. The experience gained allowed a somewhat more measured approach to railway building by the big players such as the Midland Railway, which was formed in 1844, the London and North Western Railway (LNWR) formed in 1846 and the Manchester Sheffield & Lincolnshire Railway (MSLR) formed in 1847 which emerged by amalgamation and the gobbling up of the minnows.

One would have thought that the opening of the Woodhead route between Sheffield and Manchester in 1845, with all the massive engineering problems that had to be overcome as well as the cost in life and limb, might have dampened the desire to build another line only a few miles to the south but this was not the case. The massive growth of the Victorian economy, particularly in the Lancashire, Yorkshire, north Derbyshire and Nottinghamshire areas, made the need for good rail links between the different raw material and manufacturing areas paramount for their expansion. Better access to ports like Hull and Liverpool, with its burgeoning North American trade, was also extremely important. Additionally there was a need to open up the isolated Peak District because of its mineral wealth, particularly fluorspar, lead, limestone, building stone and agricultural produce.

For 120 years from 1799 schemes were proposed, plans deposited, Acts obtained and surveys completed, to connect Sheffield and Chesterfield with Chapel en le Frith and Chinley as well as schemes to link with the Ambergate to Chinley line at Hassop. None succeeded, usually because of the inability of the promoters to raise sufficient capital and also because of the ruthless politicking of the big railway companies. Not until the Dore and Chinley Railway Co. was taken over by the Midland, which, with its enormous wealth, commercial know how and experience of building difficult lines, finally grasped the nettle, could the problem of driving a railway through the Peak District from east to west finally be solved. The route via the Hope and Edale valleys through the two long, troublesome and expensive tunnels at Totley and Cowburn was finally opened in 1894. Even after that there were further schemes to build connecting lines, the last being as recent as 1920. I found many more proposed lines than I expected but I still have a nagging concern that I might have missed one!

Much of the information has come from the deposited sections, plans and books of reference at the Derbyshire Record Office in Matlock. The reference numbers are quoted. The routes have been taken from deposited plans. It has not been possible to research every line in depth and in some cases information is sparse or incomplete. The plans, sections and books of reference always use the names of the parishes and townships across which the planned railway or canal would pass, townships being part of parishes and not vice versa as one would think.

This sometimes gives the impression of a line appearing to zig-zag rather than run in a direct line. Other sources are from the *London Gazette* which lists the Bills before Parliament and newspapers of the period particularly the *Sheffield Independent* and *Derby Mercury*.

Where I am sure of the exact location I have included an Ordnance Survey reference; for more obscure places based upon the 1:2500 sheets if this is prefixed by 'c' this indicates an approximation. The OS one inch Touring Map for the Peak District covers most of the locations and I have located or prepared maps for a few of the more important or interesting schemes. This could indeed be the subject of a book in its own right as there remains much more detailed research that could be done. However, I think that this is the first time some of this information has been published and brought together in a coherent format.

THE PRE-RAILWAY AGE

THE ROMAN ROADS

The Peak District has been criss-crossed by tracks since Mesolithic hunters and later Iron Age settlers occupied the area but it was following the arrival of the Romans in AD 43 that the first road improvements were made. The building of forts at Templeborough near Rotherham, Brough near Hope, Glossop and Manchester created deliberately planned links putting them not more than a day's march from each other on the newly constructed roads. Higher ground was favoured for look out purposes in case of attack and made for easier road building when compared with the wooded and boggy valley bottoms. The road surfaces were constructed from either rammed earth, gravel or paved fitted stones. This last method was so durable that some lengths of paved road still survive after nearly two thousand years, an example being Doctor's Gate (085935) north of the A57 Snake road.

The Roman road from Sheffield to Manchester started at Templeborough and went by Lydgate Lane in Sheffield, Lodge Moor, Redmires and over Stanage Edge to the fort at Navio (198828) and from there to the Roman spa at Buxton. The trans-Pennine route went from Navio over the shoulder of Win Hill into the Woodland valley before climbing Lady Clough and continuing to Doctor's Gate down to Melandra Camp at Glossop, a distance of twenty eight miles. The road then reached Manchester by a fairly level route of twelve miles.

PACKHORSE ROUTES

Over many centuries the Roman roads were allowed to fall into disuse. In the Middle Ages a complex network of packhorse routes developed linking towns, ports and markets. The abandoned routes survive today as eroded hollow-ways or sunken lanes. Whilst their routes were tightly defined and walled as lanes through farmland, at the moorland commons they branched out in numerous directions. Across boggy ground many packhorse routes were paved with large flat slabs and had guide stones to mark the way. Bridges were typically rebuilt in stone during the seventeenth and eighteenth centuries, to accommodate packhorses rather than wheeled vehicles.

An artist's impression of a packhorse train with the jagger at the rear.   *Author's collection*

The packhorses carried malt from Nottingham, salt from Cheshire, lead to the port of Bawtry, coal from various sources and wool, milk and lime were moved to all points of the compass. They bore the products of farms, lead mines and bell pits, lime kilns and quarries. Some of the routes were also used for driving animals to market.

However by the mid-eighteenth century the packhorse ways were in a deplorable state. They mainly used high ground and only descended into valleys to cross the rivers by bridges or at fordable places. There were sometimes fifty or sixty beasts in a packhorse train, each horse accoutred with a double crooked saddle from which panniers were suspended and each train was guided through darkness or fog by a tinkling bell that was mounted on the leading animal's collar. The whole winding procession was tended by groups of men known as jaggers, a name that survives today in our area of interest at Jaggers Lane in Hathersage (226816) and Jaggers Clough (140877) above the Edale valley.

THE TURNPIKE TRUSTS

The creation of turnpike trusts in the early eighteenth century transferred the responsibility for maintaining roads from parishes to the newly formed trusts and the costs were met by the users who paid tolls.

Most of the roads taken over in the Peak District were packhorse ways which took little account of steep hills and, in many cases, crossed unpopulated moors. Many villages that were growing as a result of water power had to wait until the end of the eighteenth century before the turnpike trustees realised that it would be more commodious and profitable for coaches and wagons to follow populous valleys even where some of the old moorland routes were more direct.

The logistics of the turnpikes are interesting. The normal distance between posting inns was about twelve miles, less in hilly districts. The working life of a horse was three years in mail coach service, four years for the crack stage coaches and up to seven years for slower passenger coaches. A four horse coach had a team of five horses, one being at rest, and the team that did a morning stage would return over the same route in the afternoon or evening. The coachman's average day was fifty miles.

This wonderful image of the entrance to the Speedwell cavern and the unmade road up the Winnats Pass shows the forbidding 1 in 5 gradient and the ruggedness of the area. It can be appreciated why most of the surveyors for canals and railways chose the Edale valley in preference to this location. The 1758 turnpike had a tollhouse here.
www.oldukphotos.com

In 1798 Samuel Coleridge had reason to travel between Sheffield and Manchester and wrote: 'Tomorrow morning I set off for Manchester at six o'clock – it is only forty eight miles distant – and the coach will not arrive until ten o'clock at night. By heavens a tortoise would out gallop us' and this was after improvements had been made! A Pickford's wagon service from Sheffield to Castleton took sixteen hours. An 1817 letter in a Sheffield newspaper noted that 'Comfort is out of the question. Annoyances include the profanities of outside passengers, the smell of putrid game and fish, the long and chilly waits for connecting coaches, and the immense loads of luggage carried on the roof to the direct danger of the passengers'.

The first part to be turnpiked between Manchester and Sheffield was the Manchester to Chapel en le Frith road in 1724. In 1749 this was extended eastwards through Sparrowpit (088887) to Peak Forest (113793) but the linking turnpike from Sparrowpit to Sheffield, was not promoted and authorized until 1758. Before improvement, the route from Sheffield went via Ringinglow to Upper Burbage Bridge (261830) and down the very steep Callow Bank (252823) into Dale Bottom and Hathersage. By 1767 this route had been superseded by making a new loop via Overstones Farm (248829). However this dale bottom way was still unsatisfactory and in 1811 was abandoned when a new road was made from Fiddler's Elbow (259827) over Booth's Edge (242807) to enter Hathersage from the south east.

The route then crossed the Derwent at Mytham Bridge (205826) where there was a smithy and tollhouse. The old bridge of four arches was washed away during a flood in 1856. From Castleton the 1758 turnpike followed the packhorse route up the 1 in 5 Winnats Pass, at the entrance of which was another tollhouse. In 1811 a new road from Castleton up the unstable flank of Mam Tor was made and continued below the line of Rushup Edge direct to Chapel en le Frith. On the old route further steep hills would be encountered at Peaslows (085808) and Eccles Pike (035812) before arriving at Sparrowpit. In 1764 this last part of the route was superseded by detours via Barmoor Clough (now the A623) and Tunstead Milton (now the A6).

However, the route via Castleton was indirect and in 1818 a new road was sanctioned over the Snake Pass. In one autobiography it is mentioned that Thomas Telford, the greatest road engineer of his day, was employed to survey the route. However the actual survey was undertaken by William Fairbank III and completed by McAdam after Fairbank's dismissal in May 1821. The road left Sheffield via the Rivelin valley and descended to the River Derwent via Cutthroat Bridge (214875). The road then passed through the village of Ashopton (192864) which stood at the confluence of the Ashop and Derwent rivers and is now below Ladybower reservoir.

As an aside it is poignant to comment that the provisional committee for the building of the Woodhead railway line had one of their meetings at the *Ashopton Hotel* only eighteen years later. From Ashopton there was a bridle road up the Woodlands valley and this was used as a basis for the Fairbank's road.

On the Glossop side of the pass an entirely new road was built which is the present day A57. Tolls were collected at Moscar, Ashopton, Broom Spring, *Snake Inn* (built 1821), Cross Poll and Woodcock Road (005943). The contemporary newspapers waxed lyrical over the benefit of the new road: they dwelt on the level gradients, the mileage lessened and the time saved, the journey time having been reduced to about ten hours. Within ten years the promoters of the Sheffield and Manchester Railway based their case largely on the tediousness and cost of transferring travellers and merchandise 'over the mountains of Derbyshire'. They claimed that 'a businessman would be able to pass to and fro in a day with six or eight hours in Manchester for attention to his affairs'.

An advertisement in the *Sheffield Independent* of 1825 describes the services leaving the General Coach Office outside the *Tontine Inn* on Haymarket in Sheffield. *The Sovereign* leaves every Monday, Wednesday and Friday at 7.00 am for the *Queen's Head Inn* at Buxton and returns the same day. The *Royal Mail* leaves every morning at 05.15 and passes through Bakewell, Ashford, Buxton, Disley, Stockport to the *Swan Inn* in Manchester at 1.00 pm in time

Not the 'wild west' but the Ashopton coach on 26 Jun 1902 when serious rail competition was threatening the coaching trade. It is rare to see a coach on the move in this early photographic period, the photographer has achieved a clear picture by showing a head on view. It brings home how revolutionary rail travel was.

*Picture Sheffield.
Sheffield Libraries*

The Snake road in the Woodlands valley beyond Ashopton, looking towards Glossop. The Alport tributary of the Ashop river runs under the road just ahead in this undated view (143896). Note the telegraph poles. It captures what a wonderful road this is as it climbs to 1,680 ft in one of the most remote and desolate areas of the Peak.

Author's collection

for the Liverpool, Chester and Holyhead mail connections. A coach returns every day at 1.00 pm. *The Norfolk* post coach, carrying four inside, leaves every morning at 7.15 am and passes over the Snake to Glossop, Mottram, Staley Bridge and Ashton under Lyne to the *Mosley Arms* and *Star Inn* in Manchester. A further service to Manchester *The Wellington* is a post coach carrying four inside and leaves every morning at 7.15 am and passes through Hathersage, Castleton, Chapel en le Frith and Stockport and arrives at *The Star* on Deansgate where it meets conveyances to Chester, Holyhead, Shrewsbury, Blackburn, Preston, Lancaster, Bolton &c. Finally *The Volunteer*, leaves at 7.15 am and passes through Warrington to the *Saracen's Head* and *Golden Lion* on Dale Street Liverpool at 8.00 pm, a 12¾ hour journey. Three coaches left within fifteen minutes of each other on three days a week'. One can imagine the scene with the sound of hoofed feet stamping in the early morning air, the passengers luggage being stored in the boot and the overflow on the roof where the outside passengers would precariously climb the steep steps to access the same area. The last minute instructions, the last check by the whip round the coach and a glance to make sure all the horses are properly harnessed before the shrill piercing note of the horn announcing that the coach was ready for off on its way across the lonely roads of the Peak whatever the weather. It was a sight well worth getting out of bed early for. When we watch a train leave a station today it glides out and nobody bothers to look. In steam days the departure of a train had the same sense of occasion that could be enjoyed with the coaches. Ah! the romance of it all.

In 1845, when traffic was already dwindling because of railway competition, the total tolls collected at the six tollhouses on the Snake road amounted to little more than £10 a week. By 1849 the trustees were in debt to the tune of £107,000, much of this huge sum being floating debts to the dukes of Devonshire and Norfolk. In short it was built too late to be profitable. Always a difficult road to maintain, particularly on the eastern side, it is still the first road in the area to be closed due to inclement weather. Yet it remains as one of the most rewarding to drive today.

The other route relevant to our area of interest is the turnpike from Buxton to Sheffield, sanctioned in 1759. Commencing from Buxton it went through Monksdale to Tideswell, where the *George Inn* welcomed travellers. At Town Head (151758) the Chesterfield to Chapel en le Frith turnpike was crossed and the road went via Great Hucklow, along Hucklow Edge, through Bretton (201799) and down the formidable Sir William Hill (this was replaced by a route through Foolow and Eyam in 1795) to Grindleford Bridge.

The route for Sheffield was via Longshaw Woods to Fox House (in 1840 the present road superseded it) and then reached 1,392 ft on Houndkirk Moor (which is still a bridleway) before reaching Ringinglow (291837), where the toll house still exists.

To gain Sheffield it passed through Banner Cross and along Psalter Lane to the town centre. In 1781 a new turnpike opened from Stoney Middleton via Owler Bar at 1,010 ft (294780) where the *Peacock Hotel* was built about 1818.

An undated view of Grindleford Bridge from an old postcard. It is looking up stream from the south side. There was a wooden bridge as early as 1359, but the present stone bridge was first mentioned in 1577. It was later widened but not sufficiently for it to carry two lanes of traffic today, traffic light control being required. A modern footbridge now partly obscures the view of the fine stonework to some extent. The toll bar cottage, still extant although with a later extension behind, peaks just above the parapet although the turnpike closed in 1884.
www.oldukphotos.com

This fine view at Fox House shows the Sheffield to Baslow coach with a full complement of passengers. Note the driver and the man holding the horses still in white top hats and a very eye catching uniform. *Picture Sheffield. Sheffield Libraries*

The toll house at Ringinglow on the left, which was always known as the 'Round House', is seen from the road from Sheffield. The turnpike for Grindleford Bridge and Buxton turned left before the tollhouse into Sheephill Road. Fulwood Lane is to the right. The road ahead up the hill, is the Chapel en le Frith road via Burbage Moor to Hathersage. The *Norfolk Arms*, to the right, was built later.
Picture Sheffield. Sheffield Libraries

In 1781 a new turnpike was opened from Buxton to Sheffield with one of the toll bars situated at Owler Bar, seven miles from and nearly a 1,000 ft above Sheffield town centre. The *Peacock Hotel* was built in this commanding and windswept location and still trades today. The toll bar was a two storey homestead located nearby built in 1781 where the stage coaches stopped and changed horses. The one for Matlock, which went via Bakewell, was yellow and called *The Enterprise* whilst the other called *Lucy Long*, was red and went to Buxton. It was said that in snow and pitch dark nights the coaches never came off the road although the only lighting was from candle lit side lamps. William H. Brougham was the landlord in this Edwardian view and shows the imitation early nineteenth century building with its porch and small paned and pointed windows. The photograph is a still from a 1903 short film called 'Robbery of the Mail Coach' by the Sheffield Photograph Company. The actors are dressed in eighteenth century costume which gives a flavour of coaching life in that period.

Picture Sheffield.
Sheffield Libraries

Local authorities became responsible for maintaining the roads from 1888 and the tollgates were then thrown open. In 1895 the last stage coach service operated in the summer for tourists only, between Sheffield, Bakewell and Buxton as an alternative to the newly opened Dore and Chinley line. Generally, most services had finished by the 1860s.

REFERENCE

Dodd A. E. & Dodd E. M – *Peakland Roads and Trackways.* Moorland Publishing 2nd rev ed 1980

THE CANALS

As industrialisation gathered pace in the eighteenth century it became clear that the turnpikes, despite the improvements that they brought to road transport, were unable to carry the increasing quantities of cotton, coal, iron, salt, lime and other merchandise. Thus the canals started to appear around the periphery of the Peak District and proved ideal for transporting in bulk. The Cromford and High Peak Railway (CHPR) was a very early railway linking the Cromford Canal, the Peak Forest Tramway and Peak Forest Canal. Both are an integral part of the development of transport across the Peak District, they deserve, together with several projected schemes, our attention.

RIVER DUN NAVIGATION AND SHEFFIELD CANAL

To begin with the new navigation used 'Dun' in its titling although the antique version of the river's name increasingly fell out of use as the eighteenth century progressed. For clarity the familiar 'Don' has been used throughout.

Sheffield canal basin in 1887, crowded with loaded keels which demonstrate that carrying bulk, where speed was not the top priority, was still providing good business for the canals once the railways had taken away their other trade.

Picture Sheffield.
Sheffield Libraries

1722. Work began to make the Don navigable from Tinsley to Goole on the River Ouse.

1751. The canal was opened throughout.

1802. The Stainforth and Keadby Canal opened providing an easier route to the River Trent at Keadby.

1814. William Chapman, canal surveyor of repute, drew up a plan for the proposed canal from Tinsley to Castle Orchards (near Sheffield Castle) which was revised to include cuts north and south of the River Don. The southerly route was eventually adopted to accommodate the Duke of Norfolk's wish that his collieries at Park and Tinsley Park should connect with it. It also linked with Chapman's plan to connect the Sheffield and Chesterfield canals at Eckington.

1815 7 Jun. The Act of Parliament was passed.

1816 Jun. Work started on the canal.

1819 22 Feb. The canal opened and over 60,000 people lined the route.

REFERENCE
Report of William Chapman Civil Engineer on the Proposed Canal from Castle Orchards, Sheffield to the River Dun below Tinsley. Sheffield 1814

CHESTERFIELD CANAL

1771 25 Mar. The Act of Parliament was passed. Construction commenced from Chesterfield via Worksop and Retford to join the River Trent at Stockwith, eight miles east of Bawtry, the first sod being cut at Norwood Hill. Thomas Brindley was appointed the engineer but died a year later.

1777. The forty five mile canal opened for business, including the 2,850 yard Norwood tunnel.

1847. The canal came into the ownership of the MSLR.

REFERENCES
www.chesterfield-canal-trust.org.uk/history
Richardson Christine / Lower John – *A Walkers' and Boaters' Guide to the Chesterfield Canal and Cuckoo Way.* 1994
The Chesterfield Canal. Chesterfield Canal Trust. 1997

CROMFORD CANAL

1789. An Act was obtained to connect Cromford wharf at the site of Arkwright's Mill, alongside the River Derwent, as far as Leawood where the canal would swing to the east to cross the river by an aqueduct. At Ambergate it turned further east and crossed the Amber valley by a second aqueduct at Bull Bridge and then went below the Butterley ironworks by means of a two mile tunnel. Finally it descended by fourteen locks to meet the Erewash Canal at Langley Mill (Great Northern basin). It was 14½ miles long and was engineered by William Jessop and Benjamin Outram who were partners in the Butterley Iron Works.

1794. The canal was completely opened and was a success from the start, although it had cost twice the estimated price.

WILLIAM JESSOP

William Jessop (1745-1814) was brought up in Devon and worked as John Smeaton's pupil and assistant on various canal schemes in Yorkshire, before increasingly working on his own. In 1790 he founded, with Benjamin Outram, the 'Butterley Iron Works' to manufacture, amongst other things, cast iron edge rails. He lived in Newark during this period where he served as mayor on two occasions. *Author's collection*

The Bullbridge aqueduct was an earthwork bank surmounted by masonry walls across the Amber valley. It was pierced by three arches, one for the river, one for the houses behind, which became the small village of Bullbridge, and one for the main road which passed through the third arch and was the original Bullbridge. In 1849 when the North Midland Railway was being built it intersected the viaduct by an iron tank, 150 ft long, which was prefabricated in sections at the Butterley Iron Works. The sections were assembled on site and floated to the spot, sunk and embedded during the night without interrupting the traffic on the canal. The canal came into the nominal ownership of the newly formed LMS in 1923 but by 1937 had become untenable yet limped on until 1944 when it closed. The aqueduct was demolished in 1968 for a road improvement scheme. This view taken in the LMS period shows a horse drawn boat and an ex-Midland 4-4-0 on a passenger train below.
Hugh Potter collection. www.crichparish.co.uk

1831. The Cromford and High Peak Railway opened to Whaley Bridge.

1852. With declining receipts due to railway competition the canal was sold to the Manchester, Buxton, Matlock & Midland Junction Railway (MBMMJR) for £103,000.

1870. The Midland Railway took full control of the canal.

REFERENCE

The Cromford Canal – A Brief History based on Peter Hardcastles' Canal Roots & Routes. 2006. www.cromfordcanal.org.uk

PEAK FOREST CANAL

1791. A scheme was proposed to link the Ashton and Cromford canals.

1794 28 Mar. The Peak Forest Canal Co. was formed and its Act was obtained on this date, with Benjamin Outram being appointed as the engineer. Its main purpose was to transport limestone from the quarries around Dove Holes. From its northern terminus, at the junction with the Ashton Canal at Portland basin in Dukinfield, it proceeded in a southerly direction through Hyde, Woodley, Romiley and Marple, where a connection with the Macclesfield Canal was made. The canal then continued to Strines and New Mills to a southerly terminus at Bugsworth, a total of over fourteen miles. It involved eight sets of locks, mainly around Marple. A short distance west of Bugsworth a short branch was built to Whaley Bridge and was originally planned to continue to Chapel Milton, although this last section was eventually reached by the Peak Forest Tramway.

1796. The canal was opened from Marple to Bugsworth, although a temporary tramway was needed at Marple because of the large amount of work still to do on the locks.

1804. The canal opened over its complete length with the completion of the Marple locks. From 1810 until the late 1820s it was to become a magnet for the promoters of canals across the Peak, since it was the obvious point at which a trans Pennine route should begin.

The canal basin at Bugsworth about 1920, with little sign of activity. This was the junction between the end of the canal and the start of the tramway. Here we see the top basin with the transfer warehouse dominating the scene. To the left is the wagon tippler wheel its integral timber pier stretching along the stone wharf to the tramway interchange. A waggon containing limestone for transhipment awaits a boat being moored when its load would be discharged between the rails and horizontal beams into the wharf deck below. Loaded limestone wagons can be seen on the right awaiting unloading and in the distance are empty wagons waiting to be returned to the quarries. In the 1840s it had forty individual tramway sidings requiring 6,000 yards of track and at its busiest in the mid nineteenth century 25,000 narrow boat journeys were made in a year carrying away 1¼ million tons of limestone and quicklime.
Picture the Past. Derbyshire Libraries

1846 27 Jul. The MSLR bought the canal as well as the connecting Ashton and Macclesfield canals.

PEAK FOREST TRAMWAY

1794 28 Mar. The Act that covered the canal also allowed for a tramway from Chapel Milton basin to Lodes Knowl quarry, the tramway's original terminus. Benjamin Outram advised that a canal to Chapel Milton would be both difficult and expensive and so the tramway started at Bugsworth.

1796 31 Aug. The completed canal and horse drawn tramway opened for business. The 4 ft 2 in gauge tramway was 3¼ miles long from Bugsworth to Lodes Knowl and required a 512 yards inclined plane at 1 in 8 to lift the line 209 ft from Chapel en le Frith. The output of the terminus quarry soon became insufficient to meet demand and so the tramway was extended to Dove Holes where it fanned out to the Gisborne, Newline, Holderness, Heathcote, Perseverance and Wainwright quarries as well as to the canal company limekilns.

1799. Plans were deposited to use the route of the tramway as part of a rail road from Bugsworth to Buxton with a branch to Sparrowpit.

1803. The tramway was made double track over most of its length.

1831. Over the seven years from 1824 an average of 1,743 tons per day was carried along the tramway to the canal.

1863. The tramway came into the ownership of the MSLR.

These men have made themselves as comfortable as they can in this view of a horse drawn high sided wagon on the Peak Forest Tramway. The iron flanged track is well seen in this view. The horse looks well groomed with a nice sheen.
Author's collection

The Stockport, Disley & Whaley Bridge Railway was opened in 1857. In 1862 the extension of this line to Buxton was opened and in 1866 it came into the ownership of the LNWR. Barmoor Clough is a narrow valley and carried the then not so busy A6 trunk road and the Buxton extension line. In between are the remains of the Peak Forest Tramway, this section having been closed twenty seven years earlier. This lovely view, taken from above the 104 yard Barmoor Clough tunnel, clearly shows the tramway track bed. A three coach Manchester to Buxton slow passenger train winds around the curves from Chapel en le Frith on 3 May 1953 and is hauled by Fowler 2-6-4T No. 42365, a 9D Buxton engine.
E. R. Morten

The canal and tramway became the Mecca for all but one of the future canal schemes from the east, although it would have required major upgrading of the system to accommodate the huge amount of new traffic generated. It was inevitably bypassed by the new railways but it remained a successful and profitable canal tramway, well into the nineteenth century, transporting limestone to the wider canal system.

REFERENCES

Q/RP2/1A

Whitehead Peter J. – *The Peak Forest Tramway.* www.brocross.com

Lamb Brian – *The Peak Forest Railway 1795-1928.* Journal of the Railway and Canal Historical Society Vol. 33 Part 7 No. 178 Mar 2001 pp466-479

Ripley David – *The Peak Forest Tramway including the Peak Forest Canal.* Oakwood Press 3rd ed 1989

Findlow Alan J. Baines Don – *The Peak Forest Tramway 1796-c1927.* Lightwood Press Archive Issue 3

ASHTON CANAL AND CONNECTIONS

1792. A group of shareholders of the Duke of Bridgwater's Canal and mine owners around Ashton and Oldham put forward a plan for a canal to be called the Manchester, Ashton under Lyne and Oldham Canal.

1794. Both the Peak Forest and Huddersfield canals were originally conceived as extensions of the Ashton Canal. They were set up as different undertakings although they had many of the same shareholders. The Huddersfield Narrow Canal was to be twenty miles in length and started at Whitelands basin in Ashton under Lyne, joining the broad Sir John Ramsden's Canal at Huddersfield.

1796. The Ashton Canal opened and ran from a large basin, which is now Piccadilly station in Manchester, climbing gradually eastwards via eighteen locks to Fairfield and Droylsden. From there one level section continued eastward to Whitelands basin in Ashton under Lyne whilst another arm headed north through what is now Daisy Nook and climbed another eight locks to Hollinwood, opening in 1797. There was also a branch running east from Daisy Nook towards Park Bridge and a short arm from the Portland basin which crossed the River Tame to Dukinfield. A further branch from Clayton to Stockport also opened.

1799. The Huddersfield Narrow Canal was completed from both ends to the entrances of the notorious Standedge tunnel which was, as yet, unfinished.

1800. The Peak Forest Canal was opened and joined the Ashton Canal by way of the Dukinfield spur across the aqueduct over the Tame at the Portland basin.

1811. The Standedge tunnel on the Huddersfield Narrow Canal was finally opened after many vicissitudes and the line was complete. This was not exactly a template of how a high level canal through the Pennines should be built.

1831. The Macclesfield Canal, linking the Peak Forest Canal to the Trent and Mersey Canal from Marple and becoming part of the Cheshire Canal Ring was begun.

1846. The Ashton, Macclesfield and Peak Forest canal all came into the ownership of the MSLR.

REFERENCE

www.pennine-waterway.co.uk

The 'Weaver's Rest' towpath bridge crosses where the Peak Forest Canal joins the Ashton Canal at Portland basin at an unknown date.
David Lawrence Brown

THE FAIRBANKS, SHEFFIELD LAND SURVEYORS

Four generations of the Fairbank family were land and property surveyors in the Sheffield area for 100 years. Records survive from 1753 to 1848 and include a unique collection of important details of agricultural improvements, coal mining, roads and buildings, canals in Sheffield and around the north midlands and, latterly, railways. The papers consist of 4,650 maps and plans, 1,026 surveyors' books as well as notebooks, letters and other papers. The Fairbanks dynasty comprised William Fairbank I (c1688-1759); his son William Fairbank II (1730-1801) and his sons William Fairbank III (1771-1846) and Josiah Fairbank (1778-1844) plus Josiah's son William Fairbank Fairbank.

As we shall now see the Fairbanks were to be involved in many of the projected but abortive trans Pennine canal and railway schemes of the early nineteenth century.

REFERENCES

www.sheffieldcitycouncil/libraries&archives/archive&localstudies/researchguides/fairbankcollection

Padfield Adrian – *Land Surveyors in the Canal Age: the Fairbank Family of Sheffield.* Journal of the Railway & Canal Historical Society. Mar 2004

HIGH PEAK JUNCTION CANAL

1810 29 Dec. A local committee was formed consisting of Messrs Waldon, Steeby, Gray, Woods, Dixon and Lumley: there were further committee's in London and Manchester. They had employed an unknown agent, who was probably Josiah Fairburn, to draw up the plans but, before submitting them to Parliament, approached the famous civil engineer John Rennie to pronounce on the feasibility of the scheme. The committees took his opinion on two imperfect plans and finally engaged him to survey the planned route and amend it. He drew up a prospectus, of which 1,000 copies were printed, some being distributed to the affected landowners. It was submitted to Parliament but subsequently abandoned.

Rennie's plan was for a thirty eight mile canal with a 149 ft rise from the Peak Forest Tramway at Chapel Milton and a fall of 530 ft to the Cromford Canal. From Chapel Milton a 2¾ mile tunnel would be required through Bowden Edge to Edale. The canal would then follow the Noe and Derwent valleys via Thornhill, Bamford, Hathersage and Padley. The Fairbank papers indicate that a branch to Tinsley from either Hathersage, Padley Mill or Grindleford Bridge was mooted. Thereafter the main canal would reach Froggatt and Calver and cross the Derwent near Baslow. It would then go through a one mile tunnel to the Wye valley near Bakewell, thus avoiding Chatsworth, and on to Rowsley with a further tunnel at Haddon Hall before following the Derwent to Matlock. Another tunnel, 1½ miles long, took the canal to Lea where it would join the Cromford Canal. Reservoirs were planned for Edale and Upper Edale. Rennie's survey as far as Padley became the bench mark for most of the future canal schemes from both Sheffield and Chesterfield.

1811 7 Oct. In an exchange of letters between James Meadows, agent of the Ashton Canal proprietors, and Josiah Fairbank, Meadows writes that because the scheme was presently suspended it would be premature to spend money on a proposed survey by Fairbank of the Padley Mill to Tinsley line.

1819 22 Oct. Eight years later Rennie's invoice of £1,221/15/6 for surveying the line had still not been paid and the litigation finished up at the Court of the King's Bench where Rennie won his case. Whether he was paid is not known!

JOHN RENNIE (1761-1821)

He was the fourth son of a prosperous farmer at East Linton twenty miles east of Edinburgh. After a rudimentary education locally he was sent to a burgh school at Dunbar before matriculating to Edinburgh University. On leaving in 1788 he worked for steam engine manufacturer Boulton and Watt at their Soho works near Birmingham. In 1791 he moved to London and set up his own business. His first works were canals, notably the Lancaster Canal (1792-1803), Kennet & Avon Canal (1794-1810) and the Royal Military Canal (1804-1809). He developed a number of docks including London (1801-1821) and Sheerness for the Royal Navy (1813-1821). The huge Plymouth breakwater, the lighthouses at Bell Rock (as an advisor), Holyhead Mail Pier and Howth in Ireland are a few more of his achievements. His bridges included Waterloo, Southwark and London bridges, the last of which was finished by his son after his death. This very brief summary does scant justice to his achievements. It is obvious why later surveyors accepted his plans for this canal almost without reservation.

This portrait by Sir Henry Raeburn of John Rennie was undertaken in 1810 when he was involved with this project. *Author's collection*

REFERENCES

Deposited Plans. Derbyshire Record Office
London Gazette 16406 18 Sep 1810
The Times Digital Archive 23 Oct 1819

NORTH EAST JUNCTION CANAL

1811 7 Mar. A meeting was held at the *Crown & Anchor Tavern* in London where the commercial advantages of building this canal were outlined. It was intended to go thirty miles from the River Don at Rotherham, following the River Rother to the Chesterfield Canal at Killamarsh and then continue southwards to join a branch of the Cromford Canal at Pinxton to complete the line from Yorkshire to London. Josiah Fairbank wrote a letter criticising the scheme and outlined the advantages of bringing goods from Liverpool and the USA to Sheffield via a branch from the High Peak Junction Canal through Hathersage and Grindleford (Padley Mill) to the River Don at Tinsley.

WILLIAM CHAPMAN'S SCHEME

1813. William Chapman (1749-1832), an eminent canal engineer from Newcastle upon Tyne, produced a flurry of reports. He was asked to consider a canal from Sheffield to Rotherham, another from Sheffield to Eckington with, or without, a connection to the Chesterfield Canal and finally a 'line up the Vale of the Sheaf across or through the ridge bounding the Vale of Derwent for as to join the projected extension of the Peak Forest Canal from near Chapel Milton to Cromford'. This last mentioned was John Rennie's High Peak Junction Canal scheme of 1810. Chapman was escorted by different gentlemen of the supporting committee and Josiah Fairbank who drew up the plans and sections.

The canal to Eckington was only surveyed as far as Attercliffe but relied on an earlier survey by the late Benjamin Outram and a letter from Josiah Jessop; the route planned was a circuitous one round the hills to Orgreave and then to Beighton before reaching Eckington, the journey distance by road was eight miles but over sixteen miles by this route.

However, Chapman thought that a tunnel of 700 yards at the north east corner of Tinsley Park Wood would shorten this length to nearly thirteen miles. The third route up the Sheaf valley was surveyed by Fairbank; starting at Castle Orchards, thus affording a connection with the Eckington proposal, it would rise 440 ft in six miles seventy chains to Strawberry Lee (298802). Passing under East Moor by a tunnel of 2¾ miles length would require a 700 ft shaft on the moor and other shafts on lower ground. The scheme crossed the Burbage Brook by a culvert before dropping a quarter of a mile by lockage to the level of the High Peak Junction Canal, whose trajectory Chapman accepted without further examination. The canal would require reservoirs above East Moor and further ones 'above the bridges of the two branches of the Burbage Brook and north of the road from Sheffield to Hathersage'.

The total length would be 29½ miles with a 503 ft rise with fifty locks and descents of 323 ft and thirty two locks down to the Peak Forest Canal. The cost was estimated at £250,000 but Chapman thought the canal would not be built immediately and, in any event, would take many years to complete.

The plan was later revised with a railway substituting for the canal but still with William Chapman as engineer.

To muddy the waters; in the Fairbank papers there is a small map headed 'Sketch of the country referred to in Mr Chapman's Report of 1813, drawn by W. & J. Fairbank, Sheffield'. The principal interest is that it shows the Ashton Canal and Peak Forest Canal from Manchester to Chapel and from there a dashed line goes via Edale to Padley Mill and continues to Calver and Stoney Middleton. A further dashed line goes from Chapel, via Castleton and Hope before joining the first line at Hathersage. There is no connection from Padley Mill to Sheffield shown or any continuation to the Cromford Canal. However, there are two larger maps; the second is titled 'A Plan of a proposed canal from the intended High Peak Junction Canal at a place near Padley Mill to the River Dun Navigation at or near Tinsley. W. & J. Fairbank 1813'. Details of the levels are dated 28 and 31 May 1813. This has sketches and columns of figures followed by several pages of distances and levels – the dimensions of the locks and the Totley tunnel are given together with some estimates of cost.

There is also a separate report on the High Peak Junction Canal from the Don Navigation at Tinsley which outlines a tunnel at Totley before descending the Sheaf valley and crossing that river by an aqueduct before another viaduct across the Don to follow the north side of the valley. The cost is estimated at £250,000 with the signature of W. & J. Fairbank and bearing the date 2 Aug 1813.

WILLIAM CHAPMAN

William Chapman was not only a canal engineer but also an important, though often overlooked, pioneer of the steam locomotive. He was a contemporary of George Stephenson, Timothy Hackworth, Matthew Murray, John Brunton and the other Northumbrian pioneers. In 1815 he built, with the last mentioned, a locomotive called *Steam Elephant*. A full size replica has been built and, at the time of writing, can be seen at the Beamish Open Air Museum. This is a painting of the original *Steam Elephant*.
Author's collection

REPORT

OF

WILLIAM CHAPMAN,

Civil Engineer,

ON

VARIOUS PROJECTED

LINES OF NAVIGATION

FROM

SHEFFIELD.

SHEFFIELD:
PRINTED BY JAMES MONTGOMERY.

1813.

This is the front cover of Chapman's report. Note that the printer is James Montgomery, the famous poet and hymn writer.

An odd document dated 1826/7 not only mentions a Peak Forest Canal reservoir but has details of lengths, rises and falls from the Peak Forest Canal at Chapel Milton via Cowburn tunnel to Edale, Hazleford Bridge and Bakewell before reaching the southerly end of the extended Matlock tunnel near Lea New Mill and the Cromford Canal. What is not clear is why the High Peak Junction Canal was still under consideration when the Cromford and High Peak Railway was making good progress and the Fairbanks were involved in surveying the Sheffield and Manchester Junction Canal for Thomas Telford.

REFERENCES

Report of William Chapman Civil Engineer on *Various Projected Lines of Navigation from Sheffield 1813*. Sheffield Local Studies Library 385.SST
Green Richard – *Locos in Profile. Finely Detailed Locomotive Illustrations. Pre 1825 Locomotives – 2 Part 4 1814-1816 and Part 5 1817-1825*. www.locos-in-profile.co.uk

The Napoleonic War and its aftermath caused a recession which lasted for several years and much dampened the appetite for further canal building.

CHESTERFIELD TO FROGGATT CANAL

1824. This proposal was sponsored by the Chesterfield Canal proprietors and surveyed by Josiah Fairbank. It was for a canal from Chesterfield towards the River Derwent near Froggatt Bridge and was surveyed in the spring and summer of 1824. The route rose 334 ft to two tunnels, with the summit level ending at the turnpike road on Froggatt Edge, 161 ft above the River Derwent. A railway link was proposed to the lime works at Calver and Stoney Middleton.

GRAND COMMERCIAL CANAL

Somewhat confusingly three different canals using this title were surveyed and competed with each other for approval.

Joseph Haslehurst had a lease on Unston colliery from at least 1815 as he was consulted by the Fairbanks on the type of rails to use on the High Peak Rail-Road which they were surveying. A year later Haslehurst employed the Fairbanks to survey a rail road from his pits to the Chesterfield Canal at Wheldon's Mill in 1816, which in the event was not built.

By this time Unston colliery was producing about 5,000 tons of coal a year ie about a hundred tons a week. That does not appear to be a great amount until the difficulties of transporting it the three miles to the Chesterfield Canal are considered, as it would all be moved by horse drawn waggons. The idea of a canal that would connect with his colliery must have seemed the passport to great wealth for Haslehurst as he would have been able to dramatically reduce his costs and also increase his output. The plan he produced would have meant that his coal would reach markets in all directions. Having said that, Haslehurst claimed that his purpose was not specifically to benefit himself, pointing out that his alternative line via Killamarsh to Sheffield was not actually in his own interest. Altruism indeed! He also had a business valuing farm tillages; these were needed when farms changed ownership and gave him an extensive knowledge of land values for compensation purposes.

In a rat-a-tat of letters in the *Sheffield Iris* during Aug 1824 with James Dean, (of whom more later) Haslehurst recalls that in the January he had mentioned to Dean, who he saw in Dronfield, that he had recently written to the Chesterfield Canal proprietors on the subject of their canal westwards. Dean expressed interest and had offered to go with him over the line. A Mr Twigg also joined them and they all met at Chapel on 30 Jan 1825. (This date cannot be correct as the report was published a week earlier.) Twigg was described by Dean as 'a very able practical mineral surveyor' relative to the working of two collieries at Dronfield and Intake, in Sheffield, for which Dean acted as agent. After looking at the terrain these men agreed that the line was feasible and Dean proposed that they should undertake the survey together. Haslehurst agreed to devote two days a week and Dean and Twigg made a similar commitment, although Dean said he could not start until he returned from a planned visit to London. In the event it took Dean five weeks after this agreement to set off for London and even longer to return. Twigg, meanwhile, withdrew because when he learned that it included a line to link with the Sheffield Canal he thought many of his friends, who were shareholders in the Chesterfield Canal, might not approve of the proposed junction.

Now Haslehurst came under pressure from Samuel Oldknow (who had financially contributed to the building of the Peak Forest Tramway and was the builder and owner of the massive Mellor cotton mill at Marple which opened in 1794 and burnt down in 1892) and the High Sheriff for Derbyshire who urged them to get on with the survey and so, in the absence of Twigg and Dean, Haslehurst pressed on by himself. He knew that he needed to start before the summer crops were sown and, because of the urgency, employed Thomas Bishop, of whom also more anon, and two others to get it done 'with perseverance and considerable expense in wages'. On returning north Dean offered the view that the line to Chesterfield only would be too expensive for the returns that could be achieved but that a junction to the Sheffield Canal would make it more feasible. Dean said that on a visit to Derby he called on 'a most respectable gentleman, of first rate talent, holding a high official position' where he outlined the three canal proposals ie links between the Peak Forest Canal, Chesterfield Canal and Sheffield Canal. He also mentioned an additional link to the Cromford Canal with two points at which it could be met. Dean told Haslehurst of this extra link who agreed with the proposal. On his return from London Dean found that Haslehurst had taken advantage of his absence by having the prospectus ready for circulation without his knowledge. He said that Haslehurst had 'cunningly duped me' by going ahead without him and using the Cromford extension suggestion without his permission.

JOSEPH HASLEHURST'S CANAL

1824 24 Jan. The first report was published, although it was printed on 10 Dec 1823, jointly by Haslehurst and Dean. In the preamble to his second report, which he titles Grand Commercial Canal, Haslehurst describes its object as 'the union of the Peak Forest, Sheffield, Chesterfield and Cromford canals'. He claims that he was appointed by meetings at Sheffield and Buxton to survey the route which suggests that, having seen the first report, those attending had sent him away to survey it properly. Haslehurst asked that the first report should be subject to 'an investigation of his views, plans and estimates by Thomas Telford or some other competent engineer to decide on its merits'. Interestingly Haslehurst admits that 'he is not supported by the experience of former projects'. It was two years since he had first addressed the proprietors of the Chesterfield Canal, and then again in December 1823, and he believed that a part of a line from Chesterfield to Middleton Dale had been surveyed by their direction but nothing had been done to bring all the canals together.

Haslehurst would have been able to consult the line that Rennie laid down in 1810, Chapman's 1813 scheme and the recent Chesterfield and Froggatt canal surveys.

The route in the first report is the same as in his second except that the line goes from Barlow Woods to Dronfield and Norton to Sheffield. The costs were estimated at £574,130 and the estimated revenue as £62,250 a year. This was all contained in a short prospectus, the routes not having been surveyed in detail, and with a promise that surveys would be laid before the public by the summer. Haslehurst started his survey for the second report at the west end in April before the summer crops of the farmers on the route became a handicap.

1824 Jun. His second report also carries the title Scarsdale and High Peak Canal and is dated 24 December and includes criticism of Dean's and Telford's reports on the Woodhead route which, as we shall see, were not published until the start of October. Yet this report was available during June, otherwise the first meeting of the GCC would not have been called on 3 Jul. Perhaps the 24 Dec report is expanded to bring matters up to date?

It is a long, rambling and repetitious document, which reflects an anxiety that he would not be taken seriously, and, unwisely, sets out to rubbish other schemes, over egging the benefits accruing to all and sundry across the kingdom if his scheme was adopted.

Haslehurst accepted the line, near enough, of Rennie's 1810 High Peak Junction Canal from Chapel Milton as far as Grindleford Bridge, from where a tunnel was required which exited at Smeecliff Woods and proceeded to Barlow Woods through the Cordwell valley. His canal then dropped, by lockage, to the Chesterfield canal basin, a total distance of twenty eight miles. There would be thirty five bridges, 120 locks of 6 ft fall each and a rise and fall of 718 ft. The tunnel under Cowburn Ridge would be 4,840 yards (2¾ miles) and under East Moor 6,188 yards (3½ miles). There would be five reservoirs; at Shireoaks, the top of Edale, Hirst Clough near Bamford, on East Moor and near Smeecliff Wood. The total cost of this section would be £365,796.

There follows a costing of a variation line from Chesterfield to Sheffield via Killamarsh. This would have used the Chesterfield Canal to the north of Killamarsh, which had five locks, leaving it near Belk Lane lock and reaching the Sheffield Canal near Greenland Engine which was 2¾ miles from the canal basin. (The Greenland

Belk Lane, Killamarsh, probably taken in the first decade of the twentieth century. It was near here that Haslehurst's canal would have left the Chesterfield Canal for Sheffield.
Picture the Past.
Derbyshire Libraries

Engine was used for pumping water from nearby mines into the Sheffield Canal.) At the same time there was a map produced by the Fairbanks titled 'Plan of the country between the Sheffield Canal at Tinsley and the Chesterfield Canal at Killamarsh 1824' which itself is based on a map by William Fairbanks II of 1792. It reappears again as the 'Sheffield Junction Canal' in Aug 1832, following a meeting at the *Tontine Inn*, Sheffield, but whether Haslehurst was aware of this map is not known.

Embankments would be required at Ballingfield colliery and Cliff Dike for ponds between the locks and the aqueduct. There would be a tunnel at Tinsley Park of 820 yards where there would be deep cuttings at both ends and near to Beighton. An aqueduct across the Rother opposite Bell Lane pond was also needed. There would be a 31 ft rise requiring lockage up to the Chesterfield Canal and the total cost of this section was estimated at £51,090.

Haslehurst's first report advocates a line to Sheffield via Dronfield and he details that there would be a deep cutting in Barlow Woods with an embankment there and also in Lounds Woods, plus a further deep cutting near Dronfield. A 2,452 yard tunnel would be required at the summit with deep cuttings at both ends at Lowages (Lowedges) and Woodseats, an embankment and aqueduct at Norton Hammer across the River Sheaf and deep cuttings at Broadfield; two reservoirs would be required at Lowages. He offers comparisons with his Killamarsh scheme – the distance would be twelve miles against 20½ miles via Killamarsh and the rise and fall 438 ft via Dronfield against 70 ft: the cost of the Dronfield route at £102,853 would be double. There would be seventy three locks on the Dronfield route and the journey time would be fifteen hours against ten hours. There is no inclusion in his costings for the very heavy expense of accessing Sheffield's canal basin from the Dronfield route because of the heavily built up nature of the area around the basin and the high attendant compensation costs.

There then comes a cost for the route from Chesterfield to the Cromford Canal, the distance being 15½ miles. This would have twenty bridges, twenty four locks with a 144 ft fall and rise, a tunnel at Clay Cross 2,640 yards (1½ miles) long and cuttings at each end of the tunnel and near to North Wingfield, with an embankment to raise the canal to join the Cromford Canal at Buckland Hollow. Reservoirs would be required at North Wingfield and two near Woodthorpe. The total cost would be £102,141. An alternative junction at Pinxton is toyed with but was not recommended. Haslehurst thought that a railroad from the proposed line of canal near to Ankerbold past Normanton to the Sutton Estate would open mining for soft and hard coal and ironstone on the estate and at Grassmoor, Normanton and North Wingfield.

Haslehurst called Dean's proposal (which we will consider next) the High Level Scheme, believing it to be error strewn from first to last, the height to be gained like a 'steeple chase' and going via Edale 'as having no minerals and being wild and nearly uninhabited country'.

He finishes by asserting that an overseeing committee should examine the schemes, two from the committees of the connecting canals and two more representing the interests of Manchester, Sheffield and Birmingham. However in the end it wasn't Telford or this proposed committee who got their teeth into these schemes but a Sheffield surveyor, Henry Sanderson.

1826 13 Dec. A report in the *Derby Mercury*, states that a man called Joseph Haslehurst, said to have formerly been a farmer, miller, coal miner and land valuer of Unstone Mill and then of Kingsley near Leek, 'is now in the Fleet Prison in London having become an insolvent debtor'. We know that Haslehurst had to employ and pay others to help him with the survey and that at least two days every week were taken up with the canal. This would have prevented him undertaking other remunerative work and because he was not employed by anybody to undertake the survey, he would have borne his own costs. There is evidence that surveys were costing over £1,000, a significant sum of money. When Haslehurst's survey was not adopted his financial demise was perhaps inevitable.

A sad end for a man who was carried away by his own enthusiasm for the project and who thought little of the consequences if it failed.

JAMES DEAN'S CANAL

1824 28 Feb. James Dean claims to have been commissioned by the Chesterfield Canal interest and gave his address as 90, High Holborn, London. Nine months later Dean placed a newspaper advert in which he describes himself as 'surveyor and civil engineer and general referee in Derbyshire and neighbouring counties'. Correspondence should be addressed to 'Dronfield near Sheffield', although for three months of the year he had business that required him to be in London. He vaguely intones that he is 'presently working on a ship canal between the Humber and the Mersey' as well as the Grand Commercial Canal scheme. Dean relates that in the spring he had business in Dronfield, it being recorded intriguingly by Henry Sanderson that 'he is known chiefly as agent for an unknown lady in Dronfield'. In a later published letter the mysterious lady is mischievously revealed as being Mrs Cecil, with the implication of mistress rather than employer! She was obviously a woman of some substance as she offered to lend £500 of the £4,000 required towards the building of the third Anglican church in the Little Sheffield area on land that she had appropriated for the purpose.

1824 30 Mar. The *Sheffield Iris* reported that the line has begun to be staked out at its western end.

1824 1 Oct. At the third meeting held to consider the GCC it was recorded that Dean's plan had been tabled for perusal by those present.

1824 24 Oct. This is the official date of Dean's report which was prepared as an alternative to Haslehurst's scheme. He states that he was employed to conduct the survey, which was undertaken by Charles Dean, his son, and John Thompson, under his direction, but his plan was sniffily described as being drawn in 'fancy colours' by Henry Sanderson, who thought 'the pictorial style, in which this map is drawn, though very suitable for the representation of a nobleman's park, is not at all proper for the purpose to which Mr Dean has applied it, because it prevents the spectator from exercising his judgement on the merits of the line, by exciting his admiration of the beautiful shades and colours with which it is enveloped'.

Dean recognized that the individual canal owners could not fund an expensive link across the Peak individually but that it might attract the necessary funding, and offer an adequate return, if the canal linked with all the existing companies allowing them to share the costs and the benefits. As a result his plan included a link to the Chesterfield, the Cromford and the Sheffield canals from the Peak Forest.

It would start at Bugsworth at the Peak Forest canal basin and rise 208 ft by lockage to a tunnel under Cowburn Ridge starting at Shireoaks (071833) and emerging just before Barber Booth (112847), 100 ft lower than Rennie's earlier proposal. It would have been built on the level to Edale End (161864) and then would descend by lockage to Yorkshire Bridge by curving round Win Hill just below Aston and Thornhill. Alternatively a three quarter mile long tunnel under the southern side of Win Hill was suggested. The line then crossed over the River Derwent and kept level at the east side of the river below Bamford and followed the hillside above Hathersage and crossed the road from Fox House just below Hathersage Booths (238809). It would then cross the Burbage Brook and enter a tunnel near Nether Padley (252781) which would emerge at Smeekley Woods (331770). From there the canal would keep the same level to above Millthorpe (318764) where a junction was proposed. The section to join the Chesterfield and Cromford canals would drop, by lockage, a short distance, to Barlow Brook and then proceed on the level through Cutthorpe (343735) where there would have been another junction. The eastward canal would descend 278 ft, by lockage, to the Chesterfield canal basin, a distance of twenty nine miles altogether. A variation from Millthorpe through Barlow Wood and under Whittington was also suggested.

To gain the Cromford Canal the southern fork at Cutthorpe would be on a level to between Woodthorpe and Tupton (c655380), via the east side of Brampton (c340718) and just west of Holymoorside (c334692). The canal would then descend 209 ft, by lockage, between the River Amber and the Derby turnpike road to the Cromford Canal at Buckland Hollow, passing to the west of Clay Cross, Stretton, Shirland and Toad Hole (390570) and then to the east of South Wingfield and west of Pentrich to Buckland Hollow (375518) which is between the junction of the present day B6013 and A610 west of Ripley. The whole distance was forty two miles.

The left northern fork at Millthorpe would pass below Holmesfield to just east of Greenhill (c348812) and then go to Norton and Gleadless, reaching Manor Farm from where a railway and inclined plane, falling 443 ft, would be used to the Sheffield Canal east of the canal basin. An alternative route would leave the above a short distance north of Greenhill down the Sheaf valley, by lockage, through Little Norton, Norton Leys (Lees) and east of Heeley to the canal basin. Dean suggests that this could be achieved by descending 449 ft through locks or by an inclined plane of 1½ miles length. He also proposed a fork, as required by the Chesterfield Canal owners, to the limestone quarries at Stoney Middleton and Calver by an inclined plane and rail-road from Padley. Dean glosses over some of the difficulties and his alternative implausible suggestion from Greenhill to the canal basin is not detailed. He thought water flowing off Cowburn Moor, reservoirs above Edale and water collected from the moors above Sheffield would be more than sufficient to satisfy all canal needs and would also supply the populations of Chesterfield and Sheffield. He estimated that the whole cost would be less than £300,000, a huge sum at that time, but in all likelihood, an incredibly optimistic total for such a mammoth undertaking.

REFERENCE
www.wordpress-com/grand-commercial-canal

THOMAS BISHOP'S CANAL

Thomas Bishop was a businessman living at 13 South Street, Sheffield who had helped Haslehurst to produce his survey.

1825 22 Dec. Bishop wrote a letter to the *Sheffield Independent*, for the attention of the gentlemen of Sheffield and Manchester and the general public, in which it is clear that he had already suggested a route but that the route had not yet been surveyed. 'I lend myself to no private interest whatever, the public good being my motto. I recommend public meetings at Sheffield and Manchester each furnishing a deputation who should compare the merits or otherwise of each scheme'. At the end of the letter the editor adds that 'some friends have wished him to make a particular survey and an accurate plan and have raised six pounds of the fifteen guineas he needs for an assistant and his own expenses'.

Bishop compares Telford's line (this is the Sheffield and Manchester Junction Canal which would have traversed the Don and Ethcrow valleys and which is described in due course) with his own and believes that Telford was premature in stating his preference for his own scheme. Another correspondent who compared the two schemes thought that Bishop's critique of Telford's contained a number of inaccuracies.

1826 23 Mar. Bishop had a second letter published on 1 Apr in response to a letter from James Dean in which Dean was trying to ascertain why Bishop had not finished his survey. Bishop replied that the inclemency of the weather had impeded his progress in pushing ahead with his survey and 'this week I have been unwell with a violent cold and plan to publish the result in May subject to the weather and the duties of my private business'. Dean had mischievously subscribed £1 to Bishop's survey costs. Bishop opined that 'Telford's plan could be sent at the same time so that the whole may be fairly and openly investigated when the public can decide on the best line'. Bishop concluded by remarking that the Manchester committee had recommended a low level for the canal and should they contribute to his costs that would entitle them to an opinion.

GRAND COMMERCIAL CANAL.

THOMAS BISHOP's proposed Line through Edale, and his variation Line by Castleton, in reference to an engraved Map contrasted with the Lines of Messrs. Dean and Haslehurst, also Mr. Haslehurst's variation Line by Killamarsh.

The heading of Bishop's proposed line and comparison map.

1826 Summer. If Bishop met his own deadline for completing his survey this undated report would have been published in this period. The preamble notes that 'In all mountainous countries the summit reservoirs cannot be altogether depended on, particularly where there are numerous water-works to satisfy; which induces me to tunnel upon the lowest possible level, alter my route, and intrude a second report on the public'. Bishop had first suggested that the route should go via Edale but then changed his mind; his new route is twenty two miles in total from Chapel Milton to Sheffield with a total descent of 477 ft and twenty three miles to Chesterfield. It would have started at Chapel Milton and on to Wash in a deep cutting of 33 ft where a tunnel would start and finish under Mam Tor, to a little below the Odin Mine (834136) near Castleton, all on the level. There was much discussion about the two mile access from Chapel Milton to Bugsworth and it was clear that there was an expectation that this would be done by canal, to save the break from canal to tramway at both ends.

There was then a descent of 60 ft in ten locks, the route passing the cotton mill on a level to near Pindale (162826) where further locks would bring the canal down to Brough. Here it would cross the River Noe on an aqueduct. The next section was level and crossed the Manchester road at Lumbley Pool (197828), near the Thornhill turn off, and proceeded below Thornhill, across the Bridge Flatts on an embankment and over the Derwent by an aqueduct below Bamford cotton mill. It would go near Hirst Clough and re-cross under the Manchester road at Sickleholme Hollow to Hill Foot, near Hathersage, and then underneath the Booths through Padley Woods to Padley Mill, after which it almost exactly follows the course of the present Totley tunnel, but on a level to near Totley. Here a descent by locks was envisaged and then, in open canal, across the Totley road, near the old lead works belonging to G. B. Greaves, and forward through Ecclesall Woods above the Abbeydale Works at Millhouses and Holt House, re-crossing the Totley road near Norton Hammer. It would then go under the Totley road again near Machon Bank and on to Broad Field crossing the Chesterfield road at Goose Green, a little below the first milestone, and go forward between the rolling mill and G. Younge's Pleasure Grounds. From there it would be in line with Mr B. Hounsfield's fence into a proposed basin in Bramall Lane. Cutting deep under the road leading from Bramall Lane it would cross the tail goit of Pond Mill and then descending down the field at the back of the Lead Mill and the gardens before crossing the River Sheaf on an aqueduct. Finally it would have proceeded, on the east side of the river, into the Sheffield canal basin. Bishop noted that Chapel Milton was 477 ft above the Sheffield canal basin.

He also proposed a branch canal or rail road to Cock Bridge (192864) for transporting limestone for the repair of the Glossop turnpike, which he thought would greatly increase the tolls collected. Finally a branch canal, or rail-road, was promulgated from Padley Woods to Calver and Middleton Dale for carrying coal, lime and limestone in return from the quarries there.

To reach the Chesterfield Canal he suggested a line from near Totley to Mickley (327793) from where a tunnel would be made to Cowley Bottoms (c335750). It would then go through Barlow Woods and over Whittington Common to the Chesterfield canal basin.

Bishop pointed out that his tunnel from Wash to Castleton would be 148 ft below the other proposed tunnel in Edale and 1½ miles longer at a cost of £35,250, saving 296 ft in lockage. It would also save a further £29,600 and would not require summit reservoirs, saving a further £16,000. The line would be 1½ miles shorter and, by decreasing the lockage, save some 2¼ hours. The report details the location of numerous reservoirs that would be needed, including ones at Wash, Castleton, near Brough, Padley Mill and an extensive one at Totley and another above it at Strawberry Lee followed by Standhills and Archer Wood. For the Chesterfield section a large reservoir would be required at Cowley Bottoms.

REFERENCES

Second Report upon the Proposed Grand Commercial Canal having for its object the Union of the Peak-Forest, Sheffield, Chesterfield and Cromford Canal by Joseph Haslehurst, civil engineer, Chesterfield 1824 including map. Sheffield Local Studies Library Pamphlets Vol 33 No. 22 042S

James Dean's first report dated 24 Oct 1824 including a map www.wordpress.com/grand-commercial-canal

Grand Commercial Canal. Thomas Bishop's proposed line through Edale, and his variation line by Castleton, in reference to an engraved map contrasted with the lines of Messrs Dean and Haslehurst, also Mr Haslehurst's variation line by Killamarsh. Sheffield Local Studies Paper 408M

GRAND COMMERCIAL CANAL

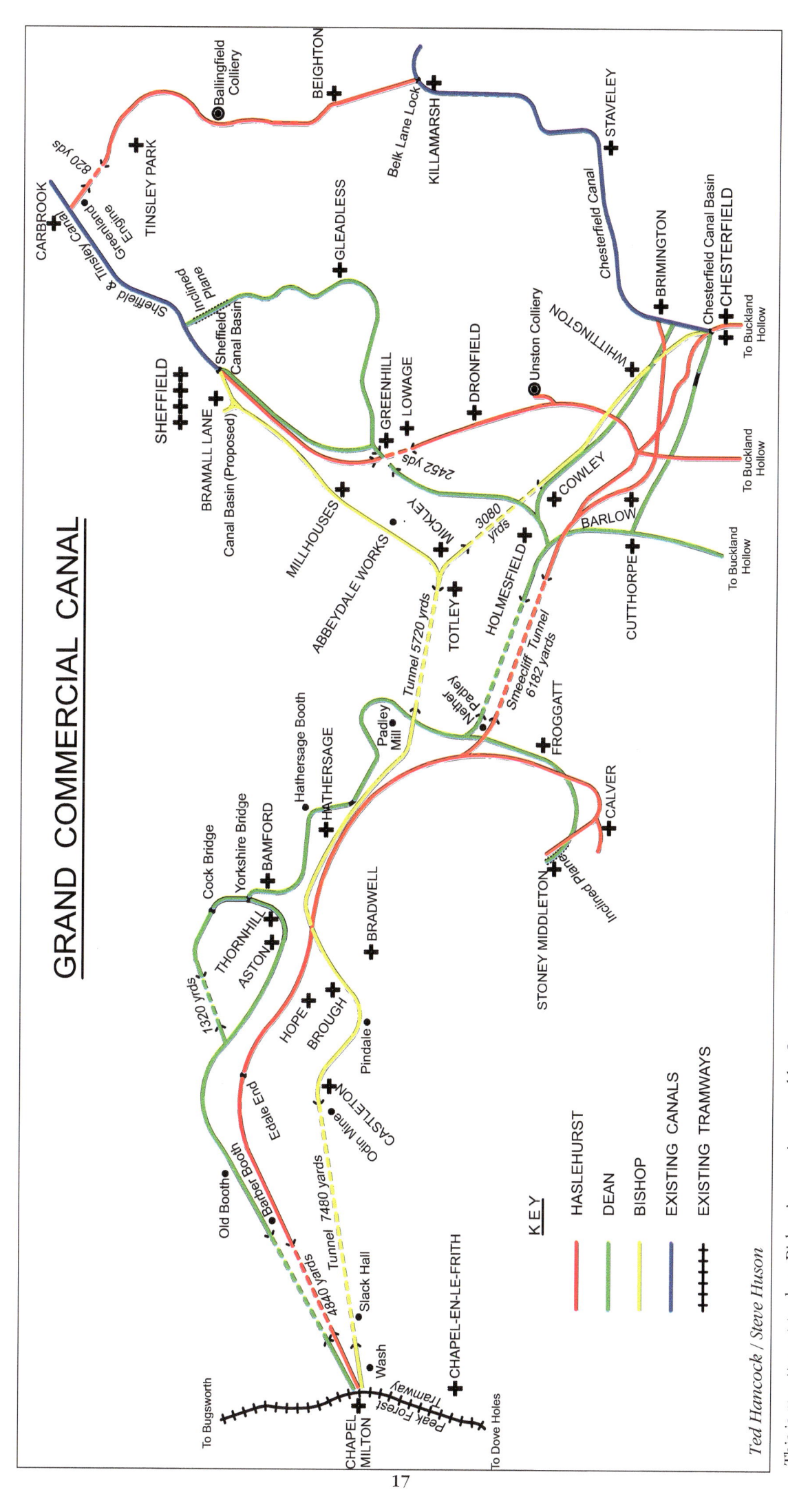

KEY

- HASLEHURST — red
- DEAN — green
- BISHOP — yellow
- EXISTING CANALS — blue
- EXISTING TRAMWAYS — +++

Ted Hancock / Steve Huson

This is my attempt to draw Bishop's map, improved by Steve Huson. On the original it is difficult to differentiate between the different routes and so here it is redrawn and, by the use of colour (not too fancy I hope!), it is made easier to follow. However I have studied Haslehurst's and Dean's separate maps and found discrepancies from the written descriptions; Bishop's map is only to be found as part of the three canals. There are some parts where the line of the canals are ill defined. To muddy the waters further in the Fairbank collection there is another version of this map dated 1826.

17

RESPONSES TO THE THREE PROPOSALS

1824 15 Jul. The first meeting to consider Joseph Haslehurst's Grand Commercial Canal proposal was held at the *Great Hotel* in Buxton. It is significant that in the month before this the first meeting to build a railway between the Cromford and the Peak Forest Canal had been held at Matlock and, a week later, a committee had been formed. From those attending it is clear that there was interest in both schemes. Philip Gell, who had taken the chair at the first meeting of the CHPR and F. G. Goodwin, a committee member, were present as was Josias Jessop, the engineer, and Andrew Brittlebank, the future CHPR solicitor. Thomas Holland and James Meadows Snr, respectively chairman and agent of the Peak Forest Canal, were also present. Representatives from Sheffield did not attend but three letters from the Cutlers' Company, the Town Trustees and the Sheffield Canal committee were read out asking that they be kept informed of developments. Twenty three attended altogether, although some additional attendees arrived late and were not recorded. It was resolved that the scheme 'is the great desideratum wanted by all the commercial men in the United Kingdom and that such a communication would not only relieve that great national want, but also contribute to the incalculable advantage of the estates through, or by the side of which, the said canal would pass'. Haslehurst's plan was read to the meeting.

James Dean turned up at the meeting, handed in a letter but did not actually attend. After the letter had been read out Dean was invited to join the meeting to speak but by then he had left. He had previously disclosed that he would not attend this meeting feeling that the matter was being rushed and that he would produce his report in due course, when a proper survey had been produced. He ventured that at that point Haslehurst's report would fade away. In the end it was resolved that 'all other plans suggested by any other person be referred to Mr Telford with instructions to him to report on those plans respectively and to suggest any improvements or alterations he shall think more eligible to effect the proposed junction'. It was also resolved that to fund this a subscription of £1 per £100 of shares should be launched, with no obligation to buy the shares if Telford's report was unfavourable.

1824 19 Aug. The second meeting of the GCC was most likely arranged at the *Tontine Inn* in Sheffield, with the Master Cutler in the chair, probably with the aim of trying to convince the sceptics of the town. Significantly it was resolved unanimously that 'the most important advantages will be conferred upon the time and trade of Sheffield and also on the Sheffield Canal by uniting that canal with the Peak Forest, Chesterfield and Cromford canals'. It was agreed a committee should be formed and that it should include Thomas Dewsnap (the Master Cutler), Hugh Parker (chairman of the Sheffield Canal), Sidney Shore (the Town Collector), Thomas Rawson, Thomas Pearson, Samuel Lucas and Ebenezer Rhodes as well as representatives from the Peak Forest and Cromford canal interests. Subscriptions to fund Telford seem to have been insufficient and so it was decided that funds should be solicited without being attached to future shares.

1824 14 Sep. Josias Jessop produced his survey of the CHPR in which he highlights the benefits of travelling steam engines for the line.

During the next two months there was a frenzy of meetings which centred round the cessation, or otherwise, of the Sheffield contingent from the GCC and the subterfuge employed in promoting the Woodhead route. In the background the CHPR was making good progress with its plans.

1824 1 Oct. The third meeting of the GCC was once more held at Buxton, where voluntary subscriptions were again sought to appoint Telford. It was at this meeting that the bombshell was dropped by Thomas Dewsnap, the Master Cutler, and Wake, the solicitor to the Sheffield Canal Company, that 'they had no confidence whatever in the individual (presumably Haslehurst) by whom the plan appeared to have been brought forward and therefore they were instructed to withdraw their further support for the measure and that Hugh Parker, the chairman of the Sheffield Canal Company wished to be struck off the committee set up at the Sheffield meeting' although he later indicated his wish to remain on the committee as a private individual. This was a body blow to the project because with the CHPR looking increasingly feasible two arms of the scheme were beginning to look untenable. Interestingly, an additional arm of the proposal included a railway from the Cromford Canal at Pinxton to Mansfield. This was the very first meeting at which both Dean's and Haslehurst's plans were on the table.

1824 4 Oct. Within three days the Sheffield Canal committee promoted a meeting which was abruptly terminated when a town meeting was arranged.

1824 9 Oct. The *Sheffield Mercury* reported that 'a communication by canal or railway is likely to be soon effected between this place and Manchester. The celebrated engineer, Thomas Telford, is employed, and has viewed the country through which the line is proposed to pass, and his surveyor, Mr Mills, is immediately to commence operations for ascertaining the usual data of calculation, and the preparatory measures for an application to Parliament in the ensuing session'.

1824 14 Oct. Hugh Parker, the chairman of the Sheffield Canal Company, called a meeting at the Sheffield Town Hall, at the request of his committee, which was attended by 'a number of respectable merchants and manufacturers of this place'. Its purpose was to 'employ an eminent engineer to take a survey of the whole area both west and south to see which existing proposals, and any new ones, should be in the best interest of Sheffield and the Sheffield Canal'. It was agreed that a subscription should be opened to secure a survey and report and a considerable sum was raised before the meeting closed. A further meeting was to be held on 4 Nov of those who might subscribe to form a committee. The *Sheffield Independent* commented that two schemes were already being pursued, namely a railway or canal from Sheffield by Bradfield to unite with the Huddersfield Narrow Canal at Stalybridge and that Telford was already engaged in making a survey for those unnamed gentlemen who had employed him together with the GCC, although the latter's attempts to raise sufficient money through subscription seemed to have failed (this proved not to be the case). The paper also commented that the meeting did not preferentially consider either of the two schemes but had the single minded aim of finding the best route for a rail-road or canal to link with the existing canals to the south and west.

1824 29 Oct. The GCC held a fourth meeting at the *Bridgwater Arms* in Manchester where it was reported that sufficient money had been raised to appoint Telford, and resolved to invite him to meet with the committee as soon as possible. The committee expressed alarm at the turn of events at the Sheffield meeting of 14 Oct and agreed that Mr Thomas, from Chesterfield, should attend the next Sheffield meeting on 4 Nov to remind them of their commitment to support the GCC. Dean was thanked for his enlarged map, sections and report. The next meeting was arranged for 15 Nov at Buxton, unless Thomas deemed it necessary to meet earlier because of a favourable response from Telford or if there was news from the Sheffield committee.

1824 4 Nov. The Sheffield canal interests, manufacturers and merchants met again at the Town Hall. It was thinly attended as it was thought that only subscribers would be admitted, which was not actually true. Four hours were spent trying to decide whether to support the GCC or to act independently but, in the end, no consensus was reached – Thomas tried to persuade the meeting to stick with the GCC. He corrected the impression that the GCC could not raise sufficient funds to employ Telford, stating that he was increasing his contribution by £100. A man called Ellison said that Telford would not throw in his lot with the GCC having, at the instigation of the Wortley family and James Rimington, undertaken a survey through the Wortley estates. Ellison was of the view that Telford would not act for both canals. A further open meeting was arranged for 12 Nov. The *Sheffield Independent* believed that the townsfolk of Sheffield should give this debate their best attention because of its importance to the future of the town.

1824 12 Nov. The above meeting reconvened at the *Tontine Inn* in Sheffield and the gloves came off as the pledging of support for the GCC, and then withdrawing that support, was discussed at length. It was commented that the gentlemen of Manchester had shaken hands with the Sheffield contingent on their support for the GCC – the two towns would give greater strength to the GCC and it would be weaker if both were not committed. Again the meeting was equally divided whether they should progress independently or combine with the GCC. Eventually it seems that a decision was made to support the GCC and await Telford's report on all the different schemes. Curiously this appears to be contradicted by a letter from Mr Tattershall, a solicitor, which was read to the meeting announcing that Telford had already decided on a scheme via Woodhead.

A letter from 'Spectator' in the *Sheffield Independent* criticised this meeting, and particularly those who had shares in the Sheffield Canal – clearly they had not realised that if they supported the GCC most of the traffic between Liverpool and Hull would pass by the Chesterfield Canal to the Trent rather than by the Sheffield Canal to the Ouse. The direct line from Sheffield to the Peak Forest Canal would allow the town to get its fair share of the business. Whilst agreeing that Telford's scrutiny of the lines was welcome 'Spectator' wondered whether an engineer was the best person to decide between the conflicting interests.

1824 15 Nov. The fifth meeting of the GCC was held at the *Great Hotel* in Buxton. A report of the meeting does not appear to have survived but it would be safe to say that it was not a happy gathering.

1824 16 Nov. Tattershall announced in the *Sheffield Independent* on 20 Nov that application was to be made to Parliament for a canal between Sheffield and Manchester via the Woodhead route. It is dated 6 Nov, before the 12 Nov meeting! This is the first recorded indication that the Sheffield and Manchester Junction Canal might be a viable proposition.

1824 1 Dec. A subscription was opened for the CHPR and, ominously for the GCC, the Duke of Devonshire became a patron and offered any of his land that the line would pass through free of charge.

THE TONTINE INN

Many of the planning meetings for the canals were held at the *Tontine Inn*, Sheffield. This is an artist's drawing of 1941 from an old lithograph, showing the size and importance of the building. It was opened in 1783, on Dixon Lane, at the side of Haymarket and became the heart of the town's municipal, cultural and economic life for more than half a century. It had an opulent 12,000 ft banqueting hall on the second floor and an on-site brewery. It had stabling for sixty horses and cottages for the footmen. When the railways arrived the coaching inns were doomed almost overnight; it closed in 1849 and demolished two years later to make way for the Norfolk Market Hall. There is now no evidence that it ever existed. *Picture Sheffield. Sheffield Libraries*

1824 7 Dec. A letter to the *Sheffield Iris* suggested that the Sheffield Canal could be extended to Killamarsh on the level and then by a new cut to Chesterfield 'as the present canal is too narrow for Sheffield boats'. The idea of the canal going by Greenhill was ridiculed as the village was 450 ft above the canal basin and would require seventy five locks of 6 ft fall in only four miles. The route via the Manor would preserve the levels but would require an appalling descent which could only be met by an inclined plane with the perpetual expense of three powerful steam engines. The Wortley projected line would be the best but the lack of limestone on the way would be averse to the agricultural interest.

1826 Apr. By this date Henry Sanderson was reporting that the GCC scheme had failed – after all it was only going to succeed if all its elements had hung together. The success of the CHPR in promoting their scheme made the canal extension to Buckland Hollow unnecessary and the withdrawal of the Sheffield interest killed the scheme; the line that was left from the Peak Forest Canal to the Chesterfield Canal was never going to be economically viable or attract the huge capital required.

Lurking menacingly in the background of all the canal proposals was the only dimly recognised threat of the travelling steam engine.

SHEFFIELD AND MANCHESTER JUNCTION CANAL

1824 24 May. In the Fairbank papers there is a letter from Telford to Josiah Fairbank expressing disappointment at not receiving a survey and hoping that it would be ready by 15 Jun. This is interesting as this was before the first recorded meeting of the GCC.

The division of opinion and contradictory information in Sheffield between the GCC and this scheme have been recorded and it becomes clear that what was going on publicly was being undermined by the decision of the Sheffield Canal Company, with the support of the town's leaders, to go ahead independently. The change of mind by the leaders of the town in withdrawing their active involvement from the GCC suggests that a decision had already been taken on which scheme would be supported irrespective of the wider opinion in the town.

1824 9 Oct. This was the date when it was publicly declared that the sixty seven year old Thomas Telford had been employed to survey this route. Further meetings in Sheffield have clearly been recorded showing how the scheme gained traction and opinion swung decisively against the GCC.

1825 7 Jan. This was the official date of the report but as we have already seen it was in the public domain a couple of months earlier. Telford, a busy man, gave his name to the survey by W. and J. Fairbank. James Mills – one of Telford's 'best men' surveyors – who was mentioned earlier was used to liaise with the Fairbanks. The large sum undoubtedly paid to Telford could have been saved by employing the talented Fairbanks for much less but it has to be said that the prestige of having Telford's name on the report gave it a status it would not have otherwise enjoyed.

The route was from Neepsend (c354800) in Sheffield along the right side of the Don, where possible, to a summit under Windleden Cross (155015), about a mile beyond Dunford Bridge. The canal would cross the Don seven times and would have eighty locks from above Kelham Wheel weir to Windleden, which is 1,203 ft above sea level. From there a tunnel of over two miles in length, with a maximum depth of 403 ft, would be dug. Three reservoirs would be required above the Don valley and three more above Saltersbrook to service the tunnel section. On emerging from the tunnel the line would follow the Etherow Vale to Tintwhistle (024973) where it would skirt around the hillside before passing under Mottram so as to reach the level of the court house at the head of a brook which ran down to Hyde (c951902) and the Peak Forest Canal. At over thirty nine miles in length a narrow canal was costed at £414,278 and a canal with width enough for two boats to pass was costed at £499,231.

1825 26 Sep. The subscribers met at the *Tontine Inn* in Sheffield with James Archibald Stuart Wortley MP in the chair. It was agreed that the plan was feasible and that a public meeting at the Town Hall in Sheffield should be held on 21 Oct. The subscribers decided that they should write to the owners of the canals in the Manchester area with whom they wished their canal to connect.

1825 27 Sep. Ominously for all these projects the Stockton and Darlington Railway was opened.

1825 11 Nov. A joint meeting was held at the *Bridgwater Arms Inn* in Manchester, chaired by Samuel Oldknow, of the committees of the Peak Forest and Manchester, Ashton under Lyne and Oldham canals where they were presented with information on the project by J. D. Skelton of Middlewood Hall and James Rimington. Mr Bradshaw of the Bridgwater Canal appointed Mr Southeran, one of his

THOMAS TELFORD (1757-1834)

Thomas Telford, the most famous of the road and canal builders, was the man who the promoters of this incredible project turned to. He was by now at the peak of his profession having become the first president of the Institution of Civil Engineers and was held in such esteem that he was buried in Westminster Abbey.

Picture Sheffield.
Sheffield Libraries

principal agents, to separately meet a deputation from the project in Manchester where they won his support.

An explanation was given of how the scheme came into existence which also sheds some light on how the committee came into being. It also highlights the thinking of both Telford and the committee. 'During the last two years various schemes have been agitated for obtaining facilities for the transit of goods by roads, canals and railways; and as previous to this project making its rise, several projects had been brought before the public for effecting a more direct communication between the towns of Manchester and Sheffield by canal. A few individuals had put down their names as subscribers to obtain from the first engineer in the country a plan to realise this important and generally desired object. Mr Telford being applied to, his first business on reaching Sheffield was to ascertain what canals at present came up to the town in order to effect a junction, if practicable, with any existing canal, which is very desirable whenever it can be accomplished. But, on viewing the only canal which exists here and then the line of country up to the summit at Windleden Cross, he decided that no junction could be formed to advantage with the Sheffield Canal, and that no engineer of eminence would venture to suggest such junction in this instance.'

Telford first drew a line across a map of the country from Sheffield to Manchester and tried to keep as near this direct line as he could; as a result his line is thirty nine miles to the Peak Forest Canal and forty eight miles to Manchester. The impracticality of forming a junction with the Sheffield Canal induced Telford to commence his line at Neepsend, thinking that the intended bridge over the River Don, near to Green Lane, would make the transfer of goods from one canal to the other as easy as possible. He felt the breaking of bulk (a term widely used then to describe cargo) was inevitable because the narrow boats on his canal would not be compatible with the boats on the Mersey and Don rivers. The shorter or longer tunnel at the summit was discussed; the adoption of the lower tunnel would result in a longer and more expensive canal but would save 200 ft of lockage on each side, the locks each having an 8 ft rise and be 80 ft in length – enough to accommodate four boats. Passing through each lock would occupy three minutes (an optimistic assumption!) which would save two hours in time. The shorter length of the higher tunnel would be preferable as it would be cheaper although involving more lockage. Since the main traffic would be lime, coal, stone, slate, paviours (paving stones) and heavy minerals the speed of transit was considered less important. The meeting held that the higher tunnel should be accepted.

The next consideration was the comparative applicability of a railway or a canal and drew on the experience of the Peak Forest Canal. This was the highest in the kingdom but had not been impeded by frosts and snow for more than ten days on average annually over some thirty years. The meeting did learn, however, that the Peak Forest Tramway required a lot more maintenance than the canal, in a ratio of £60 against £40. Telford commented on the abundance of best quality coal in the parishes of Ecclesfield, Tankersley and Silkstone. The Peak Forest Canal would be able to transfer limestone to the new canal and, although there was a great quantity of stone already available in the Manchester area transported by the Rochdale and Huddersfield canals, the market would certainly absorb this additional supply coming over the new route.

1825 17 Nov. Another meeting was held at the Town Hall in Sheffield with J. Stuart Wortley in the chair and 150 people in attendance. Wortley started by disclaiming any individual interest, despite nine miles of the canal running through his estate. A report of the *Bridgwater Arms* meeting in Manchester was given, after which a decision was taken to adopt Telford's plan, report and estimate of the narrow canal at £413,213. A provisional committee was elected whose membership was H. A. Stuart Wortley MP, John Stuart Wortley MP, Rev Stuart Corbett the Master Cutler, James Rimington, J. D. Skelton, Wm Smith, Wm Bingley, Robert Jobson and T. A. Ward. No subscription was at this stage sought because a prospectus had not been drawn up but it was agreed that the name of the project should be the Sheffield and Manchester Junction Canal.

1825 18 Nov. Two letters in the *Sheffield Independent* show that there were misgivings abroad. One thought that Telford's failure to link with the Sheffield Canal was a serious problem, whereas a canal up the Sheaf would make that link. It was also suggested that the Sheaf line would give access to coal, lime and lead from the Peak District and advocated that all the proposed canals should be considered alongside each other. The other letter writer remarks that the Sheffield to Tinsley canal was deliberately built on the south side of the Don to afford a connection with the Chesterfield Canal at Eckington and that the Peak Forest Canal link via the Sheaf went back to Chapman's proposal of 1813. There is a telling postscript – 'In the present state of perfection to which rail-roads and steam engines are brought to the County of Durham I would venture to assert that twenty tons of goods would be actually conveyed from Sheffield to the Peak Forest Canal by Chapman's line of rail-road in less than half the time that would be required to pass through the eighty locks on the intended canal'.

1825 9 Dec. An editorial in the *Manchester Gazette* remarked on the advantages of Telford's line to the population of Manchester and district. 'So great is the demand for stone, flags and slate that it cannot be supplied in sufficient quantities by the present canals. Regarding coal it is presently got in the Manchester area at depth of 200 to 300 yards and is becoming increasingly expensive. It is necessary to look for other supplies and south Yorkshire has inexhaustible amounts. When it is added to the lime over the Peak Forest Canal there will be enough business to support the cost.' The paper preferred the lower tunnel, with room for two boats passing, thus presenting a saving of forty locks at £1,000 each amounting to £40,000. The Gazette congratulated the canal interests for working together and expressed support for the scheme. It included a drawing showing the geology of the area, drawn by the 'ingenious Charles Hall of Castleton'.

The SMJC would have been the most ambitious canal ever built in Britain and certainly the most costly.

Sanderson's forensic critique of the scheme seriously undermined it and it was not proceeded with simply because there were too many locks and the projected costs were hopelessly unrealistic. The railways, with all their advantages in cheaper building costs and rapidity of transit, were starting to become viable with the example set by the Stockton and Darlington Railway which had opened earlier in the year.

REFERENCES
www.genealogistsforum.co.uk

HENRY SANDERSON

This remarkable and mostly forgotten man was born on 11 Jan 1798 in Doncaster. In 1818 he married Mary Ann Ives at Brodsworth near Doncaster. He had one daughter of this marriage who later emigrated to New Zealand where she died. His wife died in May 1830 in Doncaster. He may have had a home in Doncaster and an office in Sheffield or may have lived 'over the shop' as he records at least four addresses in Sheffield, including Porto Bello in 1826, Paradise Square, Wilkinson Street, Beale Street and the last known, 18 Westfield Terrace in 1837.

He married again in May 1831 to Elizabeth Hibberd in Sheffield and had eight children, remarkably all were sons. One of those, Albert, died in infancy. Three of his sons worked on railways in India and died there, whilst three other sons migrated to New South Wales dying there also. The last son was 'lost from the top mast' of a boat on an unknown date.

I have traced some of his other work which included preparation of a lithograph titled 'A Plan of Doncaster Race Ground, the Town Field and Part of the Town in 1829' (noted as being for sale recently at £440) and also prepared the first published plan of the town of Sheffield in 1830. In 1836 he is recorded as surveying the line of the Sheffield and Rotherham Railway which included a branch to Greasborough to serve the Earl of Wharncliffe's colliery. However George Stephenson is officially named as the surveyor, a task he would complete once he had finished the neighbouring North Midland Railway. Was the task delegated to Sanderson by Stephenson or was Wharncliffe the instigator given Sanderson's later relationship with him? If so, had Sanderson got over Stephenson's earlier poor treatment of him or had Stephenson forgiven Sanderson for savaging his survey of the doomed Sheffield and Manchester Railway?

Sanderson became recognised outside south Yorkshire for in 1837 he was employed on the Direct London and Brighton Railway, 'levelling the lines' for the branches to Lewes, Newhaven and Shoreham. By 1841 he was living at Milton Hall, the seat of Earl Fitzwilliam, in Peterborough and was buried at Marholm, near Peterborough, the burial ground of the Fitzwilliam family, on 8 Feb 1849 age 51.

SANDERSON JOINS THE FRAY

1824 Dec. The first traceable public utterance from Sanderson was a letter published in the *Sheffield Independent* of 1 Jan 1825 offering a critique of Haslehurst's second report and comparing it with his first. This is a taste of what was to come in Sanderson's pamphlet published four months later for he shows in detail the major discrepancies between the two. He begins with the rise and fall between the terminal canals and shows that within the second report there are incorrect figures in different sections eg the fall from Barlow Woods to Sheffield canal basin is given differently as 296, 264 and 294 ft. He then highlights the discrepancies in respect of the most important elements; namely the levels, estimate of expense and the figures for projected annual tonnage and income. In the last Sanderson shows that the annual tonnage swings from 340,000 tons, in the first report, to 742,800 tons in the second with income only increasing from £62,250 to £68,877. He asks 'how much confidence anybody can have in these works knowing that the two reports emanated from the same man?'

Turning to James Dean's report Sanderson observes that there are discrepancies between the two men's figures eg Dean's tunnel under Cowburn hill is about two miles whilst Haslehurst's is 2¾ miles and yet the latter's summit in his second report is 76 ft 9 in higher than Dean's. He believes that this alone makes one of the two engineers 'egregiously wrong in their reckoning' and yet finds that Haslehurst describes Dean's report regarding the distance and levels 'to be all erroneously stated and the sections erroneously laid down from first to last.' Sanderson knows not which is correct but believes that Haslehurst 'had better explain the inconsistencies of his own reports before he attacks, so severely, Dean'.

The letter concludes that the variation line via Killamarsh is very nearly the same as that recommended by the late Benjamin Outram in 1793 varying from it only in the line between Beighton and Killamarsh; yet Haslehurst's distance is over four miles longer.

1825 7 Jan. Joseph Haslehurst came back with all guns blazing and highlighted that the discrepancies between the first and second reports were because the first started at Bugsworth and the second at Chapel Milton. He had now published a supplement to his second report, correcting some of the other errors, and ends by stating 'I have to stand before authorities far more capable of detecting any inconsistencies than himself; but it would be a waste of time to attempt to give H. S. capacity to understand that which appears to be so much beyond his depth'. That comment would come back to haunt him.

1825 10 Jan. Round three finds Sanderson admitting that he had transposed two words which changed the sense of his comments on the levels. Regarding the two different starting places he believed that Haslehurst had made a mistake in naming Chapel Milton as being on the Peak Forest Canal. He still contended that this did not in itself explain the differences between Haslehurst's two reports but is pleased that his letter had caused Haslehurst to publish corrections. This letter gives Sanderson's address as being 'Wilkinson Street' whereas the first pamphlet gives his address as 'Porto Bello'. Sanderson then disappears from the public arena to prepare his superbly researched first pamphlet.

1826 Apr. Sanderson's ninety two page pamphlet, which will be further commented on later in this narrative, includes a critique of the existing canal proposals.

The preface states 'The proposed communication between Sheffield and Manchester by means of a junction canal, has been so long under discussion that one would suppose the public had by this time arrived at a tolerably just conclusion concerning the probable success of an undertaking, and that the best line for the purpose had been clearly and accurately ascertained. But this, I believe, is far from the case; and I am also persuaded, and if the relative advantages and disadvantages of canals and railways were fairly and intelligibly stated, the idea of carrying a canal across the Grand Ridge, which in any direction must be attended with an enormous expense, would not be so favourably received as it has hitherto been. Under this impression I am induced to publish my own thoughts on the subject, in the hope that I shall be able to impart some useful information, which, if I really possess it, has been gained by bestowing on the subject a more than ordinary degree of attention. In doing this it is far from being my wish to give offence to those gentlemen who have projected the intended Sheffield and Manchester Junction Canal. They can have no desire to mislead the public, but may possibly themselves entertain erroneous ideas of their own project; and if, by comparing their plan with others which appear more generally advantageous, they should become convinced of its ineligibility and discontinue to support it, my labours will have proved more useful than I dare venture to anticipate. The spirited manner, in which the business has been commenced, indicates a degree of confidence on the part of the projectors, which cannot be easily shaken; and yet, if the speculation is likely to turn out unprofitable to the subscribers generally, the sooner it is abandoned the better. If the contrary prospect can be clearly exhibited to the public, nothing which I have written can do it any injury... do not wish that a canal should be made at any expense or in any direction, but desire rather that the most beneficial line should be discovered and acted upon; or, if a canal westwards do not appear, upon close investigation, likely to pay sufficient interest to the subscribers, that a railway should be adopted as its substitute. Such a mode of conveyance as this, keeping near to the Derbyshire limestone, cannot fail to pay an ample dividend. It may be relied upon with certainty, and would be brought into operation in one third of the time required for the completion of the proposed canal...'

Considering Chapman's 1813 scheme he thought that Chapman had miscalculated the height of the Peak Forest Canal when compared with his tunnel but ventured that this could be overcome by lowering the route's trajectory. From 1813 'the idea of a junction canal remained dormant until the spring of 1824' which was when the GCC scheme emerged. Sanderson describes this 'as a much more extensive and consequently, a much less feasible project'.

His view of the Sheffield connection to the GCC outlined in Haslehurst's plan was described as follows: 'he published an eye sketch consisting of a few straight lines at the head of an ill digested report and estimate. The first report, or prospectus, was superseded by another publication which he issued soon afterwards containing a more particular eye-sketch of his line, estimates exhibited in detail, and much valuable miscellaneous information; though there appears to be a degree of amplification in his statements of the revenue to arise from the project, and the local as well as general advantages which it would present'. Sanderson comments on the Sheffield branch from Barlow Woods as follows: 'he contrived to carry the line close to his colliery at Unston, before it appeared convenient to turn towards Sheffield. But we are assured this arrangement was not caused by selfish considerations'. (An element of mischievous irony here?)

Dean's report then comes under scrutiny 'having taken the necessary levels between the four canals and formed his plan, Mr Dean caused a very inaccurate yet highly finished sketch of the country to be drawn by Mr John Thompson, of Wellington Street, Strand; upon which his line was delineated, and thus was exhibited at two public meetings held in Sheffield. In fact, to those who know the country, so many inaccuracies present themselves in Mr Dean's map, that it has every appearance of being a sketch grounded upon the old county survey published sixty years ago'.

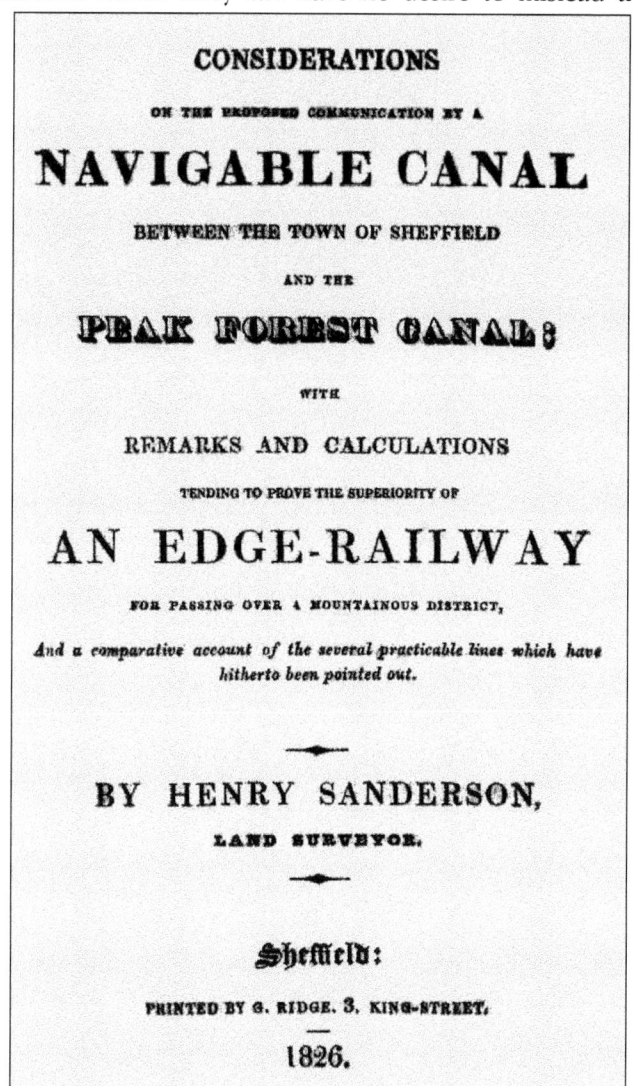

The front cover of Henry Sanderson's first pamphlet of 1826.

Sanderson continues 'however eligible the two plans might be for a fourfold union, it is very evident that the town of Sheffield would not derive that advantage from it which would accrue from a distinct and direct union of its canal with that of the Peak Forest. Another great drawback is the rapid progress being made with the Peak Forest and Cromford Railway.'

Next into his sight comes the Sheffield and Manchester Junction Canal. If Telford's instructions had been 'to examine the country between the town of Sheffield and the Peak Forest Canal' he would have recommended that the junction should be with the PFC at its eastern end. He prints Telford's report in full and comments on it by footnotes. He felt that Telford was not precise enough about the summit reservoirs, as they were crucial. Sanderson considered that Telford's description of the annual revenue as 'great' was vague because he knew that it could not possibly match the expense and so kept his thoughts to himself. Sanderson thought that coal from south Yorkshire would be so expensive after transportation that it could not possibly compete with coal mined locally in Lancashire. He also comments that the perceived access to limestone areas was handicapped by an 800 ft climb to Windleden, a 660 ft descent to Hyde Lane, a rise of 215 ft to the basin at Bugsworth and 625 ft by rail to the quarries; a distance of fifty nine miles with a rise and fall of 2,300 ft – this would have taken five days to reach Bugsworth with a load of coal and five days to return with a load of lime.

The SMJC is then compared with other canal projects, but not before he notes that the promoters had given notice that they were going to apply for an Act in the ensuing session and yet, a year later, that application was again deferred until the next Parliamentary session. He calls it the Penistone Line. Beginning by saying that the GCC has 'apparently fallen to the ground', he then describes Thomas Bishop's line, but does not offer a critique of it, obviously seeing it as being of sufficient merit to include it in his proposals and calls it the 'Castleton Line'. Almost certainly this is because he saw the possibility of converting it to a railway, surveyed as it was at such a low level.

Sanderson then puts forward three other lines which he himself had surveyed, all of which connect with Rennie's 1810 line.

EDALE No. 1 passes up the Porter valley as far as Smith Wood, by Endcliffe Hall, where it turns towards the north-west, under Rand Moor (Ranmoor) (317864) and Sandy-gate hill (c312867). A tunnel seven furlongs long brings it into the Rivelin valley which it follows to the junction of the Wyming stream with the Rivelin (274867) where a further tunnel of four miles would be required, emerging below Bamford Edge. (There are shades of the Rivelin tunnel which was built to transport water from the Derwent and Howden reservoirs to Sheffield in the early 1900s, and has the same starting point.) It would then run near the Glossop road for a short distance before crossing the Derwent by an aqueduct and proceeding along Ashop-dale to Grimber Carr (c170870). Here a short tunnel of half a mile through Win-Hill ridge into Edale would be required to meet the once intended HPJC,

'the route of which may be safely adopted, having received the united approbation of the late Mr Rennie and Messrs Brown and Meadows of Manchester; by whom, or by some assistant of Mr Rennie, it was surveyed and planned with all the attention and accuracy requisite for a formal application to parliament'.

EDALE No. 2 follows the valley of the Porter as far as the junction where another stream joins it (297846) from where a tunnel of five miles would carry it to a little beyond Hathersage. There it would continue at the same level to meet Rennie's line at the east side of his Derwent aqueduct, near Bamford cotton mill (205834).

EDALE No. 3 follows the Sheaf valley as proposed by Chapman in 1813 but, instead of joining Rennie's line near Padley Mill, Sanderson proposes to have the level of the tunnel 90 ft lower and continue at the same level along the side of the hills to meet Rennie's line near its intersection with the Castleton turnpike road. Since the tunnel is lower its length would be half a mile longer than that on Chapman's line.

With the exception of the 'Penistone Line' all the lines link directly with the Sheffield canal basin. The break of bulk was unavoidable at the canal basin because the boats on the Don were too wide for the Peak Forest Canal, whilst boats on the latter were too narrow for an open river. Transfer of cargo would be best realised by the boats being alongside each other in the canal basin, the goods would have been carried a mile in carts upon a common road from Neepsend. Sanderson then discusses the dilemma of having a canal summit level very high to avoid tunnelling but with extra time in lockage and also the problem of reservoirs at height or keeping the route low to save time and guarantee sufficient water but having the risk of ruinously expensive long tunnels. 'It has been suggested that a plan should not allow the canal to reach any higher than the difference of their respective levels at each end. Telford's rises 800 ft, Bishop's 480 ft and Rennie's 1810 plan 630 ft above the level of the Sheffield canal basin.' He then calculates the amount of time in total needed to work from Sheffield canal basin to Hyde Lane and then the actual time, based on a ten hour working day.

Sanderson outlined that the 'Castleton Line' required much less time to traverse, on account of its having so few locks compared with the 'Penistone Line', but had an excessive amount of tunnelling and might therefore be too expensive to construct when considered against the potential time saved.

Regarding income for the 'Penistone Line' he suggests that would be depressed because it did not pass through limestone country, whereas all the others would benefit from limestone traffic. The 'Castleton Line' would have the extra benefit of coal via the Smeecliff route but the extra construction costs would not compensate for the increased business; the previously suggested route via Eckington from the Sheffield to the Chesterfield Canal would be a better solution.

He then calculates what the annual income would need to be to pay a 5% dividend. Sanderson thinks that goods

	Penistone Line	Castleton Line	Edale Line No. 1	Edale Line No. 2	Edale Line No. 3
Length of new line in miles	39¼	28½	22	23½	26
Length of tunnels in miles	2½	10	8¼	7¼	6
Distance from Sheffield canal basin to Manchester	48½	51½	44¾	46	48½
Distance from canal basin to Limestone Rocks #	59	12	15½	13½	13
Greatest deviation from straight line between two towns	8¼	8½	7¾	7¾	7¾
Height of summit level above canal basin in feet *	800	480	630	630	630
No. of 10 ft locks	146	48	78	78	78
Total rise & fall bet Sheffield & Chapel Milton in feet +	1,800	480	780	780	780
Total rise & fall between Sheffield & Hyde Lane in feet +	1,460	820	1,120	1,120	1,120
Total rise between Sheffield & Piccadilly	1,620	980	1,280	1,280	1,280
Probable amount of first cost in £	410,750	488,700	394,570	417,570	357,400
Smallest annual revenue to clear 5% after deducting repairs in £	37,772	31,710	27,675	28,960	27,395
Length of time from canal basin to Hyde Lane in hours & minutes §	42.32	30.52	33.05	33.40	34.40

The limestone rocks would be those at the end of the Peak Forest Tramway at Loades Knowl.
* Summit level on the 'Penistone Line' measured from Kelham Wheel weir.
+ All the lines connected with the Peak Forest Tramway at Chapel Milton except the 'Penistone Line' which connected at Hyde Lane.
§ Assumes ten minutes to pass each lock and that a boat laden with twenty tons would be hauled by a horse at 2½ miles an hour.

on the 'Penistone Line' would be charged at 16/- per ton as against half that amount on the other routes, the higher figure being nearly as much as was currently being charged for cartage over the moors. He concluded that an income as described for the outlay in building the line would not give a sufficient return whereas a 'well constructed edge-railway of the most superior description may be formed for little more than one third of the money, and would answer every general purpose which can be possibly desired'.

This statement is the pivotal point at which Henry Sanderson recognises that the new canal building era is at an end and that the future lies with railways.

He then produces a table bringing together all his calculations for the different canals attempting to join Sheffield with Manchester.

In conclusion it can be said that the landscape we know today would have had a completely different hue had any of these schemes come to fruition. The reality was that this was the last throw of the canal planners as on 5 May 1826 the Act was passed authorising the Liverpool and Manchester Railway.

The second canal building era was coming to an end. Improvements to existing canals trying to compete with railways became the way that capital would in future reach the canals. Yet many canals continued to function profitably for many years carrying bulk traffic where speed was not of the essence but their pre-eminence was coming to an end. The 'Railway Age' was about to begin.

Even before the momentous Rainhill trials of 1829 and the opening of the Liverpool and Manchester Railway movement of goods by rail was under consideration, either to complement canals or as an alternative, with horse power and stationary steam engines on inclined planes tackling steep gradients.

REFERENCES GENERAL

Bagwell P. S. – *The Transport Revolution 1770-1985*. Routledge 1988
Hadfield C. – *The Canals of the East Midlands*. David & Charles 2nd ed 1970
Hadfield C. – *The Canals of Yorkshire and North East England Vol. 1* David & Charles 1972
As above but *Vol. 2*. David & Charles 1973
Hadfield C. & Biddle G. – *The Canals of North West England Vol. 2*. David & Charles 1970

AUTHOR'S NOTE ON UNSTON / UNSTONE

A note on the spelling of Unston(e). In general, the Midland Railway used the name *Unston* and only changed the name to *Unstone* in Jul 1911. However, earlier references to Unstone tend to include the 'e' though not exclusively. I have used the spelling I found in different documents.

RAILWAYS ACROSS THE PEAK DISTRICT

THE PRE-1830 PERIOD

WILLIAM CHAPMAN'S SCHEME

1813. As we have already seen, William Chapman (1749-1832) was much more than an eminent canal engineer as he was involved in experiments on steam locomotives in the fertile setting of the Northumberland coalfield and had taken out a patent for a steam locomotive which included the first design of the pivoted bogie. His canal scheme described earlier also included a costing showing that a rail-road up the Sheaf valley from Sheffield would be more cost effective than a canal with all its locks. He calculated that a canal would cost £87,700 and a rail-road £27,000.

He planned to use edge rails between Castle Orchards in Sheffield to where the route joined his proposed Eckington canal. It would then rise 440 ft up the Sheaf valley in 6 miles 484 yards by means of six inclined planes, three up and three down, to Strawberry Lee beyond the present Dore station. These planes would be worked by 12 horse power steam engines which he estimated could move Peak limestone traffic to the extent of 600 tons a day. The inclined plane on the Peak Forest Tramway was cited as a way of tackling seemingly insuperable hills and he proposed three inclined planes over East Moor (the old name for Big Moor and Totley Moor or Moss) rather than a canal tunnel. He also proposed a horse drawn tramway from Padley to Calver for the limestone from Stoney Middleton. He estimated that it would cost 10/6 per ton for limestone travelling between Calver and Sheffield as against the current price of 25/-. For its time Chapman's scheme was remarkably far sighted.

REFERENCE

Report of William Chapman Civil Engineer on Various Projected Lines of Navigation from Sheffield 1813. Sheffield Local Studies Library 385.SST

SPARROWPIT TO BEARD RAIL-ROAD

1815. Joel Hawkyard, a surveyor from Ashton under Lyne was employed by the Duke of Devonshire to survey an iron plateway from his quarry at Harrow Lowe, near Sparrowpit (102802) to Bar Moor Clough, there to join the Peak Forest Tramway. The incline was said to require seven full wagons going down to give it sufficient momentum to draw up seven empty ones by means of a chain weighing six tons, the chain length was at first 1,080 yards, double the length of the inclined plain. A separate rail road section would have run from the end of the Peak 'Forest Tramway' at Bugsworth to the Peak Forest Canal at Bank End near Beard in the Disley area.

1816. An Act gained the Royal Assent for this line and the High Peak Rail-Road, although both were submitted separately.

HIGH PEAK RAIL-ROAD

1815. During the Napoleonic War the increasing prices that could be demanded for agricultural produce encouraged the Duke of Devonshire to bring marginal land into agricultural use. His Woodlands estate, in the Ashop valley, of approximately 18,000 acres, was just such land and he thought about one third could be improved by adding lime to the acidic soil. In order to transport lime from his quarry at Harrow Lowe and exploit the limestone under Mam Tor a rail-road was surveyed; the success of the Peak Forest Tramway providing a model to work from.

W. & J. Fairbank, the successful Sheffield surveyors were employed to undertake a survey for a horse drawn iron plateway, their first foray into rail-roads. The first two miles from the Duke's quarries towards Rushup were not surveyed because Parliamentary sanction was not needed on land already owned by the Duke. The survey covered the rest of the eight mile route which, from Rushup, traversed the face of Mam Tor and followed just below the ridge past Hollins Cross (136845) and below Back Tor (147847) before rounding Lose Hill. From there it dropped by incline plane of 658 ft into the Edale valley (c156854 to c152863) where, after crossing the River Noe on an aqueduct, it would follow the north bank to Edale End (c162864). The line would then pass through a tunnel under the Win Hill ridge to gain the Woodlands valley at Grimber Carr, which is now lost under the Ladybower reservoir at the exact spot where Sanderson's Edale Line No. 3 would have emerged. It would then follow the River Ashop down the valley to Cock Bridge which crossed the Ashop at its confluence with the River Derwent near the now flooded Ashopton village (193863). The rail-road was to terminate 'at or near Ladybower Woods and even up Moscar if time permits', thus bringing the line within eight miles of Sheffield. In reality it would terminate at the side of the Derwent where lime kilns were to be established for converting the limestone into quicklime.

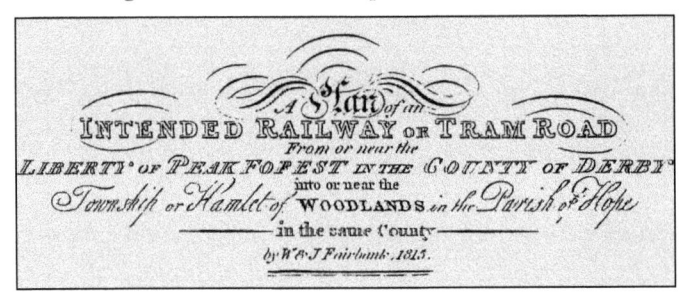

The heading of the plan of Fairbanks' proposed rail-road.

James Cropper, a Liverpool Quaker, philanthropist and anti slavery campaigner, who was later to sit on the board of the Liverpool and Manchester Railway, suggested that in conjunction with the Hawkyard line it could be the first rail-road between Manchester and Sheffield!

1816. The Act gained the Royal Assent but the work was never started.

REFERENCES

DRO Q/RP2/26

Plan of the Intended Railway or Tramroad 1815. Sheffield City Libraries Fairbank Collection Era/225S

Martin David – *The High Peak Railroad 1815.* Derbyshire Miscellany Vol 15 Part 5 Spring 2000.

Surveying a Peak Forest to Moscar Tramroad 1815. Clarion Ramblers 1932-3. Sheffield City Libraries 914.2745

HIGH PEAK RAIL-ROAD 1815

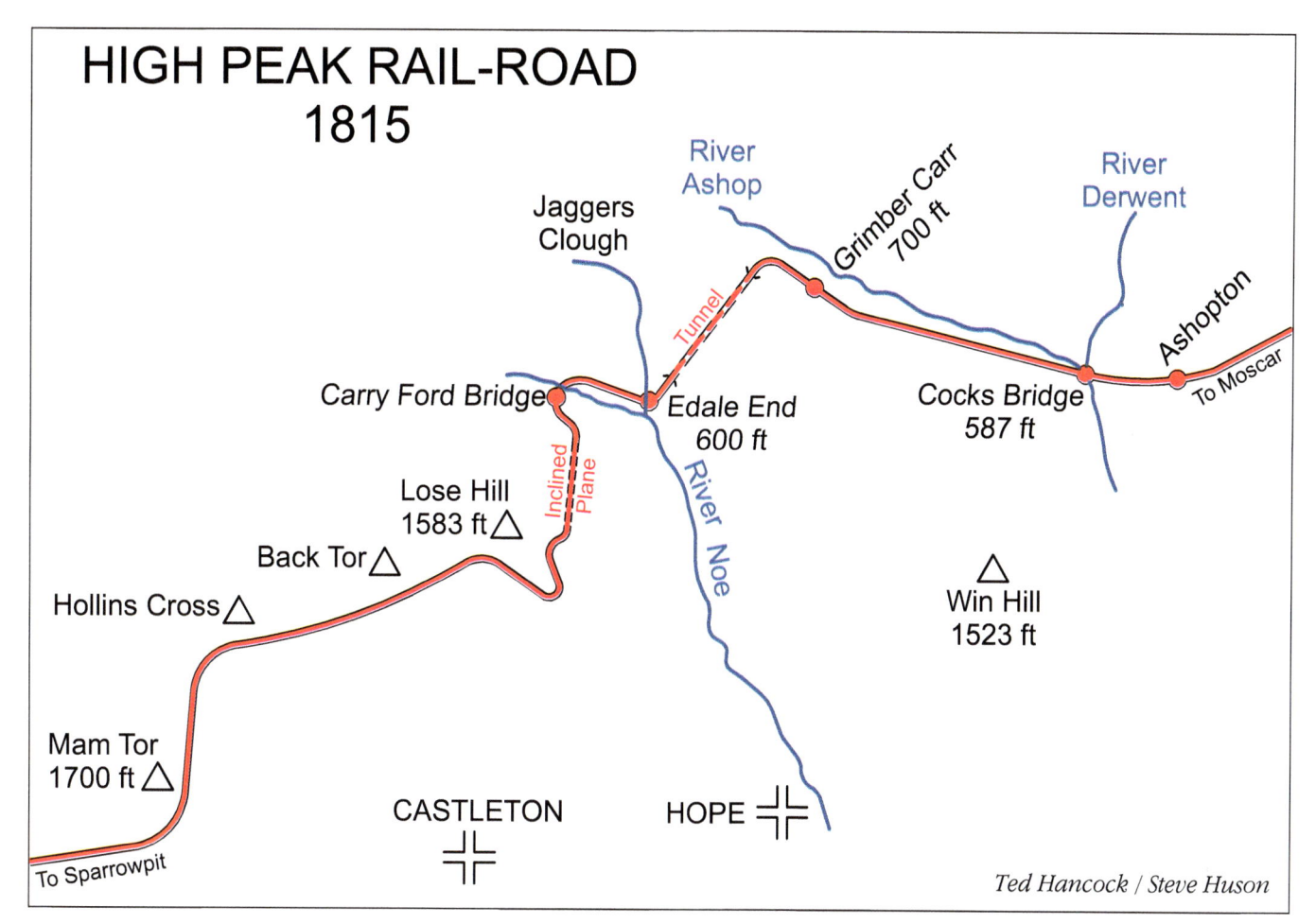

Ted Hancock / Steve Huson

A map drawn from the Fairbanks' plan of the intended rail-road.

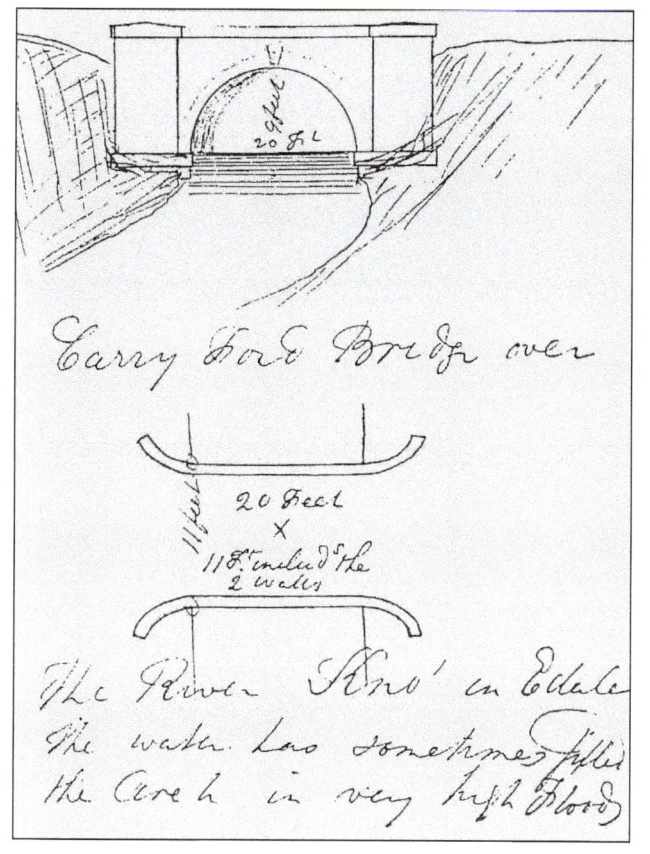

A drawing from the Fairbanks' notebooks of the Carry Ford Bridge over the River Noe.

GRAND JUNCTION RAIL ROAD

1825 8 Jan. This prospectus was published and advocated rail roads over canals and proposed to open a 'rail-road communication between the eastern and western coasts'. Lines were about to be pursued between Birmingham and the ports of Bristol and Liverpool. A further line by Derby 'passing over the mineral ports of that county to Sheffield, with a branch from that place to the eastern coast and from Sheffield through the populous and flourishing parts of the West Riding to Leeds, which had recently come forward with a plan to link itself with Hull'. There would be separate branches to bring the main line into the more important towns of Nottingham and Manchester, particularly connecting the former town with Sheffield. The country would eventually have two lines passing from London to Liverpool and from Bristol to Hull, crossing each other at Birmingham. Although no actual surveys had been made a board of management was to be formed and local boards in Sheffield and Manchester established. The engineer would be James Walker in London and William Brunton in Birmingham. The capital would be £2,000,000 in shares of £50 each.

1825 1 Feb. At a meeting in Sheffield it was learned that the iron masters of Sheffield had already thrown their lot in with this line. If this was the forerunner of the Grand Junction Railway, which was authorised in 1833 and opened in 1837 with 84 miles of line, then they were right to do so as a profitable return on their investment was likely. Sheffield would not benefit directly as the line was built from Curzon Street, Birmingham via Wolverhampton, Stafford and Warrington to join the

Liverpool and Manchester Railway via the Warrington and Newton Railway which it would absorb in 1834. The GJR became a major component of the London & North Western Railway when it was formed in 1846.

Although this line did not propose a direct connection between Manchester and Sheffield it did scupper the plans of the London Northern Rail-Road.

LONDON NORTHERN RAIL-ROAD COMPANY

1825 5 Jan. As if there wasn't enough going on with the Grand Commercial Canal and the Sheffield and Manchester Junction Canal schemes being fought over this proposal emerged to further muddy the waters. A report in the *Sheffield Independent* of 15 Jan informed its readers that a meeting of the directors had resolved to appoint competent persons to examine two lines of communication between the Metropolis and Manchester. Line one was to be via the Vale of the Lea to Ware, Cambridge, Peterborough, Oakham and near Loughborough with branches to Derby and Nottingham. From there it would join the intended Derby Peak Rail-Road (CHPR) at Cromford and then by Stockport to Manchester. Line two would go from the Metropolis to Northampton with a branch through Coventry to Birmingham, Leicester and Derby with a further branch to Nottingham and then as line one. Additionally a line would be built from Manchester to Hull with, or without, connection to other undertakings and from Derby to Sheffield and Leeds. George Stephenson is named as the engineer.

1825 31 Jan. At a meeting of the board of management it was resolved that James Walker was to take surveys and levels from Sheffield to Goole, Wakefield to Leeds and Manchester to Sheffield passing Stockport.

1825 1 Feb. Edward Wakefield, one of the deputy chairmen, called a meeting at the *Tontine Inn* in Sheffield to meet supporters of the scheme. Because of the shortness of the notice the attendance was small 'but very respectable, the majority being connected to the iron trade'. Wakefield wished to set up a committee in Sheffield to correspond with the board in London. He was told that the Grand Junction Rail Road company, of which one of Sheffield's respectable bankers was chairman, had actually received subscriptions in Sheffield to the sum of £50,000 and, as a result, 'the ground here is fully occupied' On learning this Wakefield, who had no shares to offer the town, declined to press his object and the meeting broke up without passing any resolution. However, Wakefield's parting shot was to say that 'one capitalist in London had offered to pay the whole sum required for the undertaking'.

1825 8 Feb. It was agreed that the distribution of shares should be delayed until the surveyor's reports were to hand, and were to be publicised in national and local newspapers, as there was disappointment abroad that applications for shares had not received answers.

This railway then disappears off the radar and probably died a death because it proposed schemes that would be unlikely to attract funding. It may well have been sent away with a thick ear by representatives of the other towns it was aiming to serve.

CROMFORD AND HIGH PEAK RAILWAY

1824 16 Jun. The first meeting was held in Matlock to build the railway from Cromford to Whaley Bridge.

1824 9 Jul. The first meeting of the committee was held.

1825 2 May. The Cromford and High Peak Railway was authorised with a capital of £164,000 in £100 shares together with £32,880 of loans to be raised. It was to run from Cromford Wharf to Whaley Bridge where it would link with the Peak Forest Canal. Designed as a railway, because there was insufficient water on the high plateau to make a canal viable, it followed the winding contours of the originally planned canal. The line was to be worked by stationary or travelling steam engines although it was horse drawn until 1833.

1830 29 May. This is the official date that the line was opened from Cromford Wharf to Hurdlow, with an inclined plane from the Cromford Canal to Middleton Top.

1830 16 Jun. The *Sheffield Iris* on 27 Jun stated that at the AGM at Buxton 'nearly the whole line is prepared for laying down the iron rails, several miles having already been completed, and a further length was in progress. The steam engines at the two inclined planes were nearly ready for work and those for the Middleton and Hopton planes would be ready by September. The cutting and tunnel through limestone rock at Hopton and the large embankment would also be accomplished by that time so the company would be able to open fifteen to twenty miles of the railway by the end of October. The only great work to be finished was the tunnel near Buxton, of which 460 yards are completed and a further 120 yards will be finished by the end of the year. The whole line will be finished by the date of the next AGM. It is hoped the next stage will be a junction between the line and the Liverpool and Manchester Railway for which purpose a capital has been subscribed and plans and estimates prepared.'

1831 6 Jul. The line opened throughout to Whaley Bridge.

1833. The first steam locomotive was introduced on the line.

1853 21 Feb. A physical connection with the Manchester, Buxton, Matlock & Midland Junction Railway was made at High Peak Junction.

1857 17 Aug. An extension of a quarter of a mile gave access to the Stockport, Disley & Whaley Bridge Railway at Whaley Bridge.

1862 30 Jun. The line was leased by the LNWR.

1887 19 Jun. The line came into the ownership of the LNWR.

REFERENCES

DRO Q/RP2/119

Rimmer A. – *The Cromford & High Peak Railway*. Oakwood Press 2nd ed 1985

SANDERSON'S RAILWAY PROPOSALS

1826 Apr. As we have already seen Henry Sanderson produced a ninety two page pamphlet offering a critique of the different canal schemes. On page thirty eight, in commenting on Telford's Sheffield and Manchester Junction Canal and other schemes, he observed that 'it is my opinion... that an income of £20,000 per annum is by no means certain upon any of these lines; and if this opinion be correct, I may be permitted to ask, would it be prudent to expend so large a sum as £420,000 in the construction of a narrow canal through a mountainous district, when an edge railway of the most superior description may be formed for little more than one third of the money, and would answer every general purpose which can possibly be desired? In the following part of this publication I shall endeavour to shew that a well-constructed edge railway is, in many respects, superior to such a canal; and will then leave the preceding question for the consideration of the candid reader'.

He then pontificated on the operation of railways by inclined planes, by horses and by locomotives, he being influenced by Nicholas Wood's 'Treatise upon Railroads', published in 1825. Wood was the viewer at Killingworth and other collieries near Newcastle upon Tyne and had first hand experience of steam locomotive operation in collieries in the north east, expounding the virtues of the steam locomotive and its future potential.

Sanderson's report goes on 'The line which I have suggested commences at the Sheffield canal basin and passes along the east bank of the Sheaf. After skirting the south east quarter of the town it goes a short distance up the Porter valley; then climbs up on to the high ground above Nether Green, which may be accomplished by two steam-engine inclined planes, and proceeds to Soughley Ings (269859). Thence, crossing the Wyming Brook, it ascends that side which inclines toward the Rivelin, with an easy rise, till it arrives at the division of the counties near the intersection with the Sheffield and Glossop turnpike road (232878). This point is the higher of the two summits which must necessarily be crossed by the proposed railway. (In a footnote he noted that, since the pamphlet was sent to press, it had been suggested a route via the Don and Rivelin valleys would be easier but he had discounted this because it would prove too expensive owing to the quantity of buildings which stood in its way and the bridges which would be required to cross the Don twice and the River Loxley.) After entering Derbyshire the line would begin to descend and two more steam-engine planes would be made use of, to carry it down to the level of a high bridge which would be required over the River Derwent near Ding Bank (200863). Having crossed the Derwent below the junction with the Ashop, the line would proceed along the south side of the latter river to Grimber Carr 'where a tunnel of half a mile in length may be readily opened into Edale, near the farm house called Fearney Lea. It would then ascend the vale of Edale to the foot of the Cowburn Ridge, above Barber Booth and must be carried through this ridge by another tunnel, 1¾ miles in length, which will form the second summit.' Between the west end of this proposed tunnel and the Peak Forest Tramway at Chapel Milton a fifth steam-engine plane would be required to reduce the inclination within proper bounds. 'Thus, there must necessarily be in this line five steam-engine planes, having a total rise and fall of 1,050 ft perpendicular, and two tunnels, together 2¼ miles in length in order to avoid, in those parts of the line whereon locomotive power would be used, a greater inclination than 1 in 84. This inclination is the same as that of the Peak Forest Tramway between Chapel Milton and Bugsworth and it is not too steep for the advantageous use of either horses or locomotive engines.'

The total length of the line would have been 21 miles 7½ furlongs. He estimated 'that horses would be able to draw up to four tons, excluding the weight of the wagon, and that eight ton locomotives could drag thirty six tons at six miles per hour'. Sanderson thought that both horse and steam engines could be used according to need.

He explains at length the adhesive power of a locomotive engine, calculates the resistance from friction, the size of the wheels, the force of gravity, the performance of a horse against a locomotive engine, and the velocity and superior economy of locomotive and stationary steam engines. He believed that Chapman's calculations for the power needed on an inclined plane to be understated and calculates what would actually be required. Additionally he discusses the friction of ropes.

Sanderson goes on to calculate the cost of building and maintaining the railway as against the cost of canals. 'Including a branch railway to the Castleton Road near Brough of £10,500 the total cost of the line outlined above would be £150,000. This amount is only £12,000 more than one third of Mr Telford's estimate for the Penistone Line of canal and it is a full £207,000 less than the least expensive of the lines through Edale. Consequently, the annual repairs of the proposed railway would not cost more per mile than those of the proposed canals. An income of £12,500 per annum would pay the subscribers to the railway, but £37,772 would be required on the Penistone Line and £27,395 on Edale Line No. 3 before the subscribers would enjoy a return. If, therefore, the probable annual income cannot be estimated with certainty at more than £20,000 per annum upon any of the projected lines, subscribers to a railway would stand a good chance of getting 10% for their money, and may be quite sure of 5%, while the subscribers to the Penistone Line canal must be content with a profit of less than 1%.'

He recalls that the Penistone Line subscribers rejected a railway because the cost of maintaining the Peak Forest Tramroad was a third higher than the Peak Forest Canal. He points out that the tramroad is of very inferior construction to that which he is proposing and believes that the Peak Forest Canal, if his line was built, would have to replace the tramroad with his superior edge railway or lay an edge railway alongside it from Chapel Milton to Bugsworth Basin. He then considers the maintenance costs of railway and canal, the estimated tonnage and income and the expense of carriage and locomotive engines.

Then he has an afterthought as he considers whether it would be better for the line of railway to finish at Whaley Bridge, rather than at Chapel Milton or Bugsworth. With this in mind he thought that a new line should be considered directly from the tunnel at Cowburn to Bugsworth which would allow a reduction in the incline required from 1 in 84 to 1 in 115. He believed that the extra length of three miles to Whaley Bridge would cost an extra £10,000.

Sanderson's final comment is that if it proved difficult to raise £160,000 for his twenty five mile line from Sheffield Canal to Whaley and the three mile branch from Cock's Bridge to Brough Lane Head then a horse drawn railway, in conjunction with the fixed steam engines, would reduce the cost by £38,000 to £122,000 because the rails would not have to bear so much weight and could be lighter and cheaper. This is almost as if he realises how radical the proposal is and takes a backward step to offer a fallback position should his proposals be too advanced for acceptance. Having worked so hard to persuade his readers of the efficacy of a partially locomotive worked railway this seems a retrograde step as seen from this distance in time.

However, his advocacy of rail over water came at a prescient time and attracted much criticism from the canal interests who saw it as a threat to their substantial incomes. Within a month the prospectus for the Liverpool and Manchester Railway was issued and from thereon the tide started to turn against the canals.

STOCKPORT JUNCTION RAILWAY

1828 26 Nov. A meeting was held at the *Warren Bulkeley Arms Inn*, Manchester, to raise a subscription to link the Liverpool and Manchester Railway at Water Street and the Cromford and High Peak Railway at Whaley. William Jessop was appointed the engineer. The 17⅓ miles long line would cost £165,325, with an estimated revenue of £26,000. It would run via Stockport, Goit Hall, Marple, Mellor, Strines and New Mills with a branch from the CHPR at Fernilee to Wormhill via Bradshaw and Barmoor Clough. £13,500 was subscribed by the end of the meeting.

1828 10 Dec. By this date over £70,000 had been subscribed.

1829 9 Jan. A committee was elected at a meeting at the *Albion Hotel* in Manchester.

1829 27 Jan. A further meeting was held at the *Clarendon Rooms*, South John Street, Liverpool, with Major Wilson (of Sheffield and Goole Railway notoriety) in the chair. It was reported that not all the landowners who would be affected were supporting the enterprise.

1830 9 Aug. At a meeting of subscribers in Liverpool the railway was abandoned. This was because a landowner, Mr Egerton of Tatton; had successfully opposed the Bill in Parliament, subsequently throwing his support behind the Sheffield and Manchester Railway.

1830 26 Aug. The document disbanding the undertaking was issued from Liverpool.

This line had substantial backing and at one point the shares attracted a three pound premium. However it shows that without landowner support no scheme could succeed.

REFERENCE
DRO Q/RP2/35

RAILWAY MANIA LINES
VICTORY LIMEKILN TO THE PEAK FOREST CANAL RAILWAY

1830. Plans were deposited for a line from the Victory Limekiln at Tideswell to the Peak Forest Canal at Bradshaw Edge.

REFERENCE
DRO Q/RP2/2

THOMAS BISHOP'S SCHEME

1830. When Thomas Bishop realised that the future lay with railways he proposed that his canal plan should be converted to a railway. This enjoyed some support in Sheffield. Due to the exertions of Liverpool capitalists the scheme was extended to meet the eastern extremity of the nearly completed Liverpool and Manchester Railway; the low trajectory of the canal plan made its conversion to a railway attractive.

SALFORD AND SHEFFIELD RAILWAY

Plans for this scheme were definitely drawn up but references in the contemporary newspapers are few.

1830 30 Nov. This is an almost forgotten proposal which had George Stephenson and Son as engineers on the maps and plans. It is not clear whether the line would have used incline planes but the Stephensons were prepared to use tunnels in a way that their plan for the Sheffield and Manchester Railway did not. The plans were deposited for a route starting at the canal basin in Sheffield (360877) and following the Sheaf valley with the river on the right as far as Heeley from where it would follow the present railway line to Totley. It would then rise further to enter a tunnel at Strawberry Lea, about a mile further on. It would emerge at Hathersage Booths (241807) just below the junction of the present day A625 Hathersage to Fox House road and the minor road to Ringinglow, a location high above the valley. Gaining the valley floor at Mytham Bridge below Bamford, passing north of Hathersage, and following the present day railway to Hope it would travel just behind the A625 in the village. Going to the north of Castleton it would enter another tunnel at the Odin Mine (136824), the remains of which are on the now abandoned A625 Mam Tor road. It would emerge at Peaks House (114826) on a high plain below the A625 which skirts Rushup Edge. After a short distance came another short tunnel at Rushup House (096822) which would cross under the A625 before emerging on the hill above the entrance to the western end of the present Cowburn tunnel (c077822). Next, dropping down to Wash and keeping Chapel Milton on its left, it would run adjacent to the Peak Forest Tramway and the canal to Bugsworth. To reach Manchester it would pass through Furness and New Mills from where a short tunnel would be required to Lower Hague followed by a further short tunnel. At Marple it would tunnel under where the canal crosses the River Goyt on an aqueduct. Bredbury, the northern edge of Stockport, Burnage, Demesne, Mosside and Hulme would be passed before a junction with the Liverpool and Manchester Railway would be made at a point before Water Street in Manchester.

This seems to be a mixture of William Chapman's 1813 scheme to Padley, where the first range of hills was confronted and then Thomas Bishop's line via the Odin Mine above Castleton to negotiate the second.

REFERENCE

DRO Q/RP2/161

SHEFFIELD AND MANCHESTER RAILWAY

This was a highly significant railway which, in the event, was not built but was the progenitor of the Woodhead line. It illustrates how the time scale from inception to receiving Parliamentary approval bridged the period from canal to railway with, initially, inclined planes being seen as the solution to steep gradients but very shortly afterwards nearly level railways with tunnels becoming standard practice.

1830 May. A private meeting was held in Sheffield Town Hall instigated by some Liverpool capitalists who supported any scheme that could be extended to link with the Liverpool and Manchester Railway. Henry Sanderson attended this meeting and put forward rough sketches of several possible routes. It was agreed that a deputation of Sheffield luminaries would be formed who would seek further support and guidance from the Liverpool group.

Shortly afterwards a further meeting was held at the Cutlers' Hall in Sheffield where the capital was set at £600,000, one third of the £100 shares being allotted to each of the major towns. George and Robert Stephenson were appointed engineers with Henry Sanderson to take the levels and prepare the Parliamentary sections. The Stephensons' successful collaboration with the Liverpool money men in the building of the Liverpool and Manchester Railway was clearly a prime reason why they were appointed. Although Robert is named as joint engineer with his father, Sanderson's comments were directed towards George, which suggests Robert had little, if any, input. George was very skilled at promoting the Stephenson brand by using his son and other close associates when it suited him.

Sanderson did not take up his appointment until the middle of September, by which time George had made some use of the services of Thomas Bishop. This clearly irritated Sanderson and was probably the beginning of his differences with Stephenson.

1830 26 Aug. The prospectus, which included a map, was issued from Liverpool by the chairman of the provisional committee, Nicholas Robinson. Three deputy chairmen were named, Phillip Law, the Sheffield Master Cutler, John Kennedy of Manchester and Charles Tayleur of Liverpool. (He was a shareholder and director of the Liverpool and Manchester Railway and established an engineering works at Newton le Willows which eventually became the Vulcan Foundry.) The other committee members were T. B. Barclay, William Brown, Edward Cropper (son of James Cropper who was interested in the 1815 High Peak Rail-Road), Samuel Hope (banker), Thomas Jeavons (treasurer), S. Perceval, William Rathbone and E. Roscoe from Liverpool; A. Dugdale, Joshua C. Dyer, W. H. Fairbairn, H. Houldsworth Jnr and James Lillie from Manchester; E. Barker, Joseph Read, John Rodgers, Benjamin Sayle, Jonathan Sanderson, John Shirley, William Vickers, Edward Vickers, Joseph Wilson, John Newbould, Charles Brownell and James Drabble of Sheffield.

Nicholas Robinson, the chairman, wrote 'The provisional committee of the Sheffield and Manchester Railway beg leave to lay before the public the following prospectus of that undertaking: it is proposed to open a communication by railway between the east and west coasts of the empire, to connect the German Ocean with the Irish Sea, by a continuation of the Liverpool and Manchester Railroad to the town of Sheffield, whence the connection with Hull by water is economical and convenient. To traverse the country by direct communication from east to west, through some of our principal manufacturing towns, must appear an object of vast importance and the Liverpool and Manchester Railroad assumes a new and more interesting character when considered as the commencement of a line which is to distribute so widely the industry of the country. The proposed railway, in its course through the manufacturing districts surrounding Stockport, will give new vigour to the works of that populous neighbourhood and uniting with the High Peak and Cromford Railway, at Whaley Bridge, will enable the inhabitants of the midland counties to introduce their products to new and more extensive markets. In its progress through Derbyshire it must prove of incalculable advantage; the superior quality of the limestone in those parts renders it an article of increasing demand and this road will afford the means of obtaining it on terms which must greatly extend its use. But to the town of Sheffield, this project is one of almost incalculable interest and importance. Hitherto denied by circumstances, if not by locality, those means of improvement which canals have afforded to other manufacturing towns, Sheffield has laboured under disadvantages which the perseverance and industry of its inhabitants could alone have surmounted. It will hardly be believed that, at this time, they have no other means of conveyance for their goods to Manchester, than by carting them either the whole distance of about 23 miles to the Peak Forest Canal at a rate which the nature of the country renders very expensive. Such, however, is the fact – a fact which, in itself, constitutes a claim upon the country and the legislature which will certainly not be denied. The inhabitants of the surrounding country suffer equally with the town of Sheffield from this very deficient state of their communications. Their manufactured and agricultural productions are either conveyed in a westward direction, on wagons, or by the very indirect and hardly less expensive route of the Yorkshire canals and the same difficulties, of course, occur in the conveyance from Liverpool and Manchester of the various goods required from those places.'

Robinson expressed the view that the great growth of the commerce of the country has been made possible because of the improvement in the means of communication and names the Duke of Bridgewater and Brindley as leading lights in achieving this. He celebrates the success of Liverpool as a port because of its canal links. The fifteen years of peace since the Napoleonic wars has aided the nations of Europe, and particularly the USA, to acquire many of the mechanical improvements and some of the most skilled workmen. He feels that the cheap, untaxed labour overseas is undermining the commerce of the country and feels that commerce will best be served by the advent of another invention, the railways which will give a ten fold advantage over canals.

He then issues a word of warning (which was to go unheeded) to base all railway schemes on good plans and an eye for the future good, rather than speculation for a quick profit.

Robinson's view of the Peak Forest Canal is interesting as he feels the canal's location, numerous locks and other inconveniences have made it of little benefit to Sheffield. Although its recent link to the CHPR had in some respects made it more useful it would not be sufficient to allow competition with a modern railway.

He stated that in a report from Stephenson the cost per mile would not exceed one half of the costs of the Liverpool and Manchester Railway. It was unlikely to face other competition because of the terrain and, after detailed consideration, believed that it would offer a good return for shareholders.

At almost the exact same time the prospectus of the Sheffield and Goole Railway was issued by what seems to be a different group of Liverpool capitalists. The preamble to the Sheffield and Manchester Railway prospectus never mentions it and advocated the merits of the existing canal. The chairman of this proposed line was Major Wilson from Liverpool, who seems to have behaved in a high handed manner towards the landowners beyond Doncaster, across whose land the railway would need to pass, to the point where they publicly rebelled, asking that the application to Parliament be delayed. No doubt the canal owners, who had so much to lose, encouraged the landowners in their mission but to no avail as, on 15 Feb 1831, the shareholders voted to apply to Parliament in that session. The project saw itself linking with the Sheffield and Manchester Railway but they was aware of the likelihood that their line would be completed first because of the more favourable topography through which the line would pass. It failed, when one suspects it should have succeeded. However there is an interesting letter in the *Sheffield Independent* of 5 Feb 1831 by 'Verax' advocating a line to Grimsby instead because of the limitations placed on sailing boats negotiating the Humber as far inland as Goole. (Shades of later developments.)

1830 28 Aug. The *Sheffield Independent* reported that the shares had been apportioned to Liverpool, Warrington, Manchester, Stockport and Sheffield and that a 'very great proportion are already taken... arrangements are being made for applying to Parliament for a Bill very early in the ensuing session.'

1830 15 Sep. The historic Liverpool and Manchester Railway, with which the Sheffield and Manchester planned to link, opened for business to great acclamation.

1830 25 Sep. An editorial in the *Sheffield Independent* eulogised on the benefits for Sheffield by not only this proposed railway but also the Sheffield and Goole line. It commented that while Sheffield had specialist products, Birmingham, which had a much better transport infrastructure made many of the same things but had lower transport costs, an advantage which would increase if a proposed railway between Birmingham and Liverpool was built. 'Those wild and solitary places where the trace of man is scarcely perceptible will soon be peopled and brought into profitable production by this railway.' The newspaper took the view that the success of the Liverpool and Manchester Railway, in respect of its engineering features and its motive power, had changed the mood about the future of railways irrevocably.

1831 25 Jan. Preparatory to his drawing the Parliamentary section, Henry Sanderson had been called upon only to take the levels for the eastern side of the summit, but had found a discrepancy between his and those recorded by Stephenson's assistant Gillespie on the western side. He therefore extended his observations to the Vale of Goyt and to the surface of the Peak Forest Canal, to discover that there was an error of 10 ft on the part of Gillespie. Sanderson's section for this part of the line was then adopted.

Henry Sanderson's anxieties over the route became so great that he was impelled to give expression to them in a second pamphlet, written at a third known address, Pye Bank, Sheffield. It contained a full description of Stephenson's intended line 'as it is laid down on the plan and section deposited in the office of the Clerk of the Peace' and he observed that 'contrary to the former practice with regard to canals, no report of the engineer on this line has yet been presented for public inspection.' He criticised the secrecy of the proposed route and expressed concern at the attempt to keep as much as possible in the dark 'but for what reason I cannot pretend to say – I can only surmise. Surely the directors are not desirous of avoiding public discussion on the merits of their project; nor their engineer afraid of encountering such humble critics as myself'.

Sanderson was concerned about the amount of tunnelling, which amounted to 6½ miles, and the inclined planes which were between 1 in 18 and 1 in 32 on the western side of the Cowburn ridge and 1 in 18 on the eastern side. This was on a route which involved a mean inclination of 1 in 99 on the western side of the summit and of 1 in 78 on the eastern side. He proposed an alternative route via Penistone, Woodhead, Glossop Dale and Ludworth to Stockport and Manchester, which, with two miles less tunnelling and with mean inclinations averaging 1 in 135 and 1 in 100 to attain the summit level, could be wholly worked by locomotives. He suggested that the application to Parliament be deferred until the next session so that a better route could be found.

1831 11 Feb. A lengthy letter in the *Sheffield Courant & Advertiser* by 'L.R.' expressed support for Sanderson's views. 'L.R.' strongly attacked the gradients, the inclined planes, the numerous bridges and the length of tunnels on a route of little over forty three miles which, he presumed 'must be intended for merchandise only, for no man in his senses would ever venture in a carriage on such a road; the breaking of a chain or a rope would be inevitable destruction'. He asserted that a line via Holmesfield, Calver, Middleton Dale and Peak Forest, passing close upon the Derbyshire coalfield and penetrating the best limestone districts in the country, provided an easier and more profitable route 'which it would be next to madness for the proprietors of the projected railway not to avail themselves of'.

1831 14 Feb. Despite these misgivings the provisional committee was not deterred. Nicholas Robinson's case in support of the Bill estimated that the canal and road journey times between Sheffield and Manchester would be reduced to four hours by rail and between Sheffield and Liverpool the eleven days taken by canal, and three days by horse and cart, would be cut to six hours. Goods transport charges would come down by amounts ranging from 8s to 14s per ton.

1831 23 Aug. The application was proceeded with and the determined opposition of the Duke of Bridgwater, who, contrary to custom, pursued it through the House of Lords, was overcome and the Act of Incorporation received the Royal Assent at a cost of £11,393. The capital was fixed at £530,000 with borrowing powers up to £176,000.

The seal of the Sheffield and Manchester Railway.

1831 20 Sep. George Stephenson's route was finally published and started from the Liverpool and Manchester Railway on the west side of Water Street in Manchester without bridging the River Irwell. After crossing over Water Street and the Duke of Bridgewater's canal it would tunnel below Chester Road and York Street and then proceed on a gradient of 1 in 792 the seven miles to Stockport and included a 'few cheap bridges' and a quarter mile long tunnel at Long Row. From Stockport 'after crossing the rivers Tame and Mersey by bridges of no great magnitude' the line then followed the Goyt valley for about eleven miles to the vicinity of Whaley Bridge on gradients of 1 in 307 to 1 in 119. There would be 'several short tunnels, none of them exceeding a few hundred yards in length and the River Goyt will, in some situations, be passed over by bridges, and in others the course of the river will be diverted'. From Whaley Bridge the line would proceed 3½ miles to Corn Heys, about a mile past Chapel Milton, on a 1 in 81 rising gradient, which Stephenson hoped to be able to reduce by a deviation within the prescribed limit of the plan.

Rushup Edge, the summit of the whole route, would be ascended by two inclined planes, the first being one mile rising at 1 in 18 and the second, in a tunnel, of ¾ of a mile rising at 1 in 32. At the top of the second incline there followed a level stretch of over 1¼ miles. The line then descended into the Hope valley by two more inclined planes, the first of nearly 1¼ miles falling at 1 in 18 in a tunnel and the second of ¾ of a mile on the same inclination.

Because of the proximity of limestone that could be quarried at the summit it was felt that the heavier limestone descending would far exceed any weight of general merchandise and passengers ascending and would draw up the lighter ascending trains. 'The manner in which this will be achieved is as follows: first, with respect to merchandise. As soon as a train arrives at the foot of the first inclined plane on the western side of the ridge it is attached to one end of a rope, the other end of which is attached to a train of descending limestone waggons, the number of which may be regulated according to the number of carriages that have to ascend and in this way any reasonable rate of speed may be obtained. Upon reaching the top of the first inclined plane the ascending train is attached to the end of a second rope, the other end of which, as in the first plane, is fastened to a train of limestone waggons. As I have supposed that only a single line is laid on this inclined plane (it being a tunnel) it will be necessary that the two trains should pass each other when half-way through. This may be effected without any difficulty or danger by causing the single line to diverge, for a short distance in the centre, into two lines, one of which would be taken by the ascending and the other by the descending train'.

Stephenson observed that this method of working was not only perfectly practicable and unobjectionable but was likewise used in many existing inclined planes and contended that it was equally applicable to the conveyance of passengers. 'But since it is necessary to guard against the possibility of accident where passengers are to be conveyed', he continued, 'and as on the inclined plane (the last one spoken of) there might be some danger, in case of the breakage of the rope, of one train coming into contact with another, I propose that the carriages should be raised up the second inclined plane or tunnel by a stationary engine. This will work an endless rope laid through the tunnel, and in no way be connected with the other rope or with other machinery, so that the risk of accident will be as slight as it would were the line level. It is evident that on the first or lower inclined plane there is no danger of the two trains coming in contact with each other, even if the rope should break, as there are two distinct lines along the whole length'.

To reassure subscribers who might still be feeling squeamish, Stephenson added 'to guard effectually against any chance of the carriages running away, either whilst ascending or descending the inclined planes, I propose the adoption of a variety of precautions, which cannot fail to insure safety from accident. In the first place, each carriage should be provided with a brake of such power that the necessary attendants alone would be able to stop the train, but which, at the same time, may be worked so simply, and be so placed, that any passenger may be able to handle it, and thus have his safety in his own hands. In addition to this, the last carriage in each ascending train would have a scotch, similar to that which I have applied with complete success in the Liverpool tunnel. This scotch is attached by chains to the last carriage, and slides behind it on the rails. If the rope should break, the carriages will roll back upon this scotch and be immediately stopped. In the descending trains, the scotch will hang in front of the first carriage, and being fastened to the rope by which the train is let down the incline, the moment the rope breaks the scotch falls down upon the rails in front of the carriages and eventually checks the motion'.

From the eastern side the line would continue to descend at 1 in 177 for nearly four miles and then proceed on the level for 1½ miles. An ascent of four miles at 1 in 185 would follow a section of three miles in a single line tunnel. Trains would be drawn in both directions by ropes actuated by fixed engines, one at each end.

At the eastern end of the tunnel double track would be resumed on a one mile inclined plane at 1 in 32. This would be worked by a self acting plane, on which the lines descended towards Sheffield and would raise the carriages that had to ascend. From the foot of this inclined plane there is a descent of 5½ miles at 1 in 98 into Sheffield.

After that gut wrenching proposal the report was supplemented by comprehensive supplements of income compiled by Thomas Jeavons, the treasurer. He forecast a total gross annual revenue of £136,262 of which £24,000 would be derived from passenger and parcels traffic, and an annual expenditure of £50,000. Jeavons estimated the construction costs for a double line at £526,510; the tunnels, excavations and embankments and bridges costing £274,685 of that amount. A single line would cost £424,559 and £238,943. These estimates were based on 'the rate of cost at which the Liverpool and Manchester Railway had been executed'.

Given George Stephenson's work on the easily graded line from Liverpool to Manchester and his later objections to a direct line from Chesterfield to Sheffield by comparatively modest inclines, it is completely out of character for him to recommend such an arcane line for a major trunk route. George Dow in 'Great Central' suggests that George and Robert were so busy with other contracts that they did not give the attention to this project that it deserved.

1831 26 Sep. Henry Sanderson published a third report of sixteen pages within a week of Stephenson's. He set out to simplify the issues that shareholders needed to consider by stripping the Act of its legal jargon and made a physical comparison of the Liverpool and Manchester Railway with this line and the cost of the first against the probable cost of the second. Because of the provisions and restrictions of the Act he considered 'that it is not likely the object in view will be accomplished without a considerable addition to the company's means, even if the very doubtful estimate made by Mr Stephenson may be relied upon'. No turnpike roads were to be crossed on the level; screens high enough to conceal the engines and other machinery passing along the line were to be erected and maintained by the company at any place where the railway came within 100 yards of the Sheffield and Chapel en le Frith turnpike road; the combined tare weight and load of a four wheel carriage was not to exceed four tons, nor that of a six wheeled carriage six tons.

He felt that the most damaging parts of the Act were those which stipulated that £100,000 was to be applied in making the first twenty miles out of Manchester (the most profitable section) and was to be matched by a like sum on the first twenty miles out of Sheffield; that both sums were to be expended within three years of the passing of the Act; that if the expenditure at the Sheffield end had not been incurred at the expiration of three years, the company were not to receive any rates or tolls, after such expiration, until the sum of £100,000 had been spent; and that no dividends were to be paid until the line had been completed and opened throughout for traffic.

The principal features of the physical comparison Sanderson made between the two railways were:-

	L&M	S&M
Length of line in miles	31	43
Length of tunnels in yards	1,970	11,600
Number of river bridges	5	27
Number of river diversions	0	9
Fixed engines for inclined planes in horse power	80	350
Length of inclined planes requiring fixed engines	1⅛ miles	5 miles
Mean inclination of locomotive parts of line	Nearly level	1 in 182

In making a comparison of constructional costs Sanderson took the heads of actual expenditure incurred up to Jun 1830 given him by Henry Booth, secretary and treasurer of the Liverpool and Manchester. These totalled £825,627 and, on the same scale, it was shown that the probable cost of the Sheffield and Manchester, under identical heads, would be £970,010.

In this deadly critique Sanderson had sown the seeds of its lingering death.

1831 20 Oct. The first meeting of the shareholders since the Act was obtained was held at the *York Hotel* in Manchester. Following the criticism he had received Stephenson indicated that he had revised the Rushup Edge incline by reducing the summit level by 300 ft and the inclined planes from four to two, with less steep inclines since the line would now go through Edale instead. It was revealed that the capital stock of the company was not fully subscribed but that some of the landowners were promising to subscribe. Altogether, the start of building the line should not be long delayed.

It was suggested that, because the money markets were depressed, it would be advisable to start cautiously by building the line from Manchester to Stockport first and to start the Hathersage tunnel simultaneously because of the length of time needed to complete it.

Despite this, the meeting was indecisive as doubts were abroad as to the efficacy of the scheme. The majority of those present felt it was not expedient to proceed until a special general meeting was held in six months time in Manchester. Meantime the provisional committee, strengthened by six more subscribers, were required 'to enquire into the pecuniary prospects and practicability of the undertaking'.

1831 29 Oct. The first of many subsequent advertisements appeared in relevant newspapers offering the shares at discounted prices. It was said that the Liverpool proprietors were trying to jump a sinking ship.

1832 18 Apr. At a stormy meeting of shareholders at the *York Hotel* in Manchester three propositions were tabled. The first was to abandon the scheme. The second was to shelve the scheme for three years. The third was for those who still supported the scheme to be given until June 1833 to buy shares of the dissentients at 30/- each. If they failed in that objective the scheme would then be abandoned. The last was adopted.

1833 28 May. Henry Sanderson published his final pamphlet for consideration of the shareholders. He was highly critical of the Stephenson route and costings and had become convinced that the Dun and Etherow valleys route was the best way forward. The death knell of the scheme was being sounded.

1833 5 Jun. Only twenty shareholders met at the *York Hotel* in Manchester where it was disclosed that 302 proprietors holding 2,576 shares had expressed 'no further interest in the concern' and, as nobody had come forward to take over the shares and because subscriptions were £85,000 short of the total capital required by Parliament, it was resolved that the undertaking be abandoned altogether and that the shareholders were to be refunded 25/- per share.

1833 20 Jul. It is entirely appropriate that Henry Sanderson has a last word on this story. He had a letter published in the *Mechanics Magazine* in which he includes a copy of his pamphlets (which were not printed) commenting on the sorry demise of the project. He felt that if there had been more haste and less speed many thousands of pounds would have been saved and that the line would now be being built. He described the committee as being made up of 'Liverpool speculators and Sheffield monopolists who were too much wrapped up in that chief of railway engineers, George Stephenson, and in too much haste to get rich, to listen to advice gratuitously (as in the meaning of freely) offered by a person of no note'.

Sanderson was clearly angry and embittered by his bruising experience and finished his letter expressing it thus: 'The unfortunate result of this mismanaged concern may serve as a warning to others engaged in similar projects, to find out early by any means, however cheap or humble, that a line between two extreme points, as afterwards cannot be improved upon. Even to the mere speculator, who looks only for his premium, this is a very essential object, as the real improved value of such shares is invariably denoted by the difference between common interest on the outlay, and the net amount of permanent revenue. Public opinion, as to the value of such shares, may be led astray for a time by false estimates, dishonest artifice and auctioneering puffs, but sooner or later the sterling nature of its judgement will recover itself and the shares will find their proper level in the market – if marketable they still remain. Instead of bearing the honourable premium of ten percent as some have done at their very origin, they may become so far degraded as to be advertised at a discount like stinking fish; and for want of a purchaser at any price may at last be thrown away and utterly abandoned. Some shareholders, it is true, may escape by talking to their less knowing neighbours; but then, this is undoubtedly a species of swindling – an anti social art which no honest man or true citizen would attempt to practice. Let us all endeavour to live by fair dealing and if that will not make us rich, let us be contented to remain poor under the consoling reflection so pithily expressed by Pope 'an honest man is the noblest work of God'. I had no intention of moralising when I began to write, but the subject has drawn me into it unawares'. (A moral for our times as well!)

The editor of the *Mechanics Magazine* commented that a railway between Manchester and Sheffield 'will be shelved for a time, but when it is revived the Salterbrook (Woodhead) ought to be the line and Henry Sanderson the person to execute it. Although 'but a simple surveyor as he says he evidently wants nothing to qualify him for the successful execution of that or any other similar work'. It was not to be for this line.

Dow should have the final word as he pithily concluded his account as follows: 'So died the Sheffield and Manchester Railway, hampered by the forbidding Pennine ridge, which any line having pretensions to directness must cross, hamstrung by conditions in its Act, and finally strangled by the ropes of its inclines.'

After this bruising experience the appetite for a further attempt lay fallow but by the end of 1835 the experimental period of the Railway Age was past with 337 miles of lines completed and another 970 miles authorised for construction. The locomotive operated railway was now demonstrably superior to any other form of transport.

REFERENCES

DRO Q/RP2/15

Sanderson Henry – Second pamphlet 15 Jan 1831 – Author

Third pamphlet 26 Sep 1831 – Author

Fourth pamphlet 28 May 1833 – Author

Mechanics' Magazine Vol 19 No. 519 30 Jul 1833

Dow George – *Great Central Vol 1*. Locomotive Publishing Co 1959

Hopkinson G. G. – *Railway Projection and Construction in South Yorkshire and North Derbyshire 1830-1850*. Transactions of the Hunter Archaeological Society Vol 1X part 1 1964

Three light engines at Wharncliffe Wood on the Woodhead route in 1948. The posts for the electrification of the line are in situ, the work having commenced before the war and then been suspended. Nearest to the camera is F2 2-4-2T No. 67106, with push and pull fitted. As it was withdrawn in Dec 1948 it may have been on its way to Gorton to be scrapped. Of the ten engines in the class only two received BR numbers and No. 67106 was one of those, being next to the last to be withdrawn. The two engines at the front are Robinson's O4 class 2-8-0s in rebuilt form. They provided most of the motive power for the endless freight and mineral trains on the line.
A. Brackenbury

SHEFFIELD ASHTON-UNDER-LYNE AND MANCHESTER RAILWAY

Finally there was a breakthrough. For our purposes this is only a brief headline summary since the line is covered in great depth by George Dow and those writers who came later.

1836 26 May. In this economic climate the prospects of success were infinitely better and a group of influential men from Sheffield, Manchester, Ashton under Lyne and Stalybridge emerged to build a new line from Sheffield to Manchester. Henry Sanderson's contribution in suggesting the Woodhead route was acknowledged by the promoters and a survey of the line was undertaken by Charles Vignoles, a leading civil engineer, and Joseph Locke, engineer of Grand Junction Railway fame.

1837 5 May. The Act of Incorporation was passed to build what we now know as the Woodhead line from Shore Street, Manchester, to Bridgehouses, Sheffield, via Ardwick, Ashburys, Gorton, Fairfield, Guide Bridge, Hyde, Newton, Godley, Hattersley tunnel, Mottram, Dinting, Hadfield, Valehouse, Torside, Crowden and Woodhead where a three mile tunnel would be bored allowing a maximum gradient of 1 in 120 over the route's forty one mile length. From the eastern end of the tunnel at Dunford Bridge the line would reach Sheffield via Hazel Head, Penistone, Thurgoland tunnel, Wortley, Deepcar, Oughty Bridge, Wadsley Bridge and Neepsend.

1838 1 Oct. Work started when the first sod was cut near the western end of Woodhead tunnel at Saltersbrook.

1841 17 Nov. The first section from a temporary station at Travis Street, Manchester, to Godley was opened.

1844 8 Aug. The line from Woodhead to Manchester was completed.

1845 3 May. The *Herapath Journal* reported the company as flirting with an amalgamation with the Midland but that the shareholders had firmly rejected the idea. It suggested that the two companies were playing a game of railway chess. 'Last week we mentioned the Midland directors taking up a line from Ambergate, on the North Midland (MBMMJR), to Buxton to meet the Manchester and Buxton Railway. The object of that line was clearly to abstract from the recusants all the traffic from the south over the Midland from between Manchester and London. Since then we have heard of the Sheffield and Manchester (SAMR) projecting a line from some few mile west of Sheffield to Hathersage, Bakewell and Buxton. The object of this line we suspect, is to stop the traffic from going on the Midland line, and presently to form a connection with the Churnet Valley Railway or some other line, and avoid it altogether. But we confess the object is not very palpable to us.' (We might have had GCR built 'Directors' rather than Midland 'Compounds' running on our line!).

This scene at Bullhouse, between Dunford Bridge and Penistone, epitomises the Woodhead route as it shows an empty coal train descending from Woodhead tunnel towards Wath or Sheffield hauled by an O4/8 No. 3872 on 7 Aug 1947. Another ascending coal train stands in the loop probably awaiting a passenger train to pass.
Ken Boulter © Ted Hancock

1845 24 Jul. The line from Sheffield to Dunford Bridge was opened.

1845 23 Dec. With the completion of the single line Woodhead tunnel, the whole line was opened to traffic and the dream of a Sheffield to Manchester railway came to fruition. In the same year a branch was opened to Glossop, from Dinting.

1847. By amalgamation the company became the Manchester, Sheffield and Lincolnshire Railway (MSLR).

1851. Sheffield Victoria station opened after the completion of the Wicker Arches in 1848.

1852. The second bore of the Woodhead tunnel opened.

REFERENCES

DRO Q/RP2/156

Dow George – *Great Central Vol 1*. Locomotive Publishing Co 1959

Johnson E. M. – *Woodhead Part One*. Foxline Publishing 1996.

With this great wave of railway building complete or under construction, there was a trade depression in the early 1840s which led to many bankruptcies and few proposals for new railways. This was said to be the end of the 'First Railway Mania'.

SECOND RAILWAY MANIA

The establishment of the main trunk lines, and the success that they were enjoying alerted the London capitalists, who had been sceptical of railway investment and the fortunes that could be made. This resulted in a dramatic increase in investment. It was the newly emerging middle classes, who collectively had capital to invest, together with financial speculators and the wealthy land owners, who had earlier invested in a cautious manner, who now became the driving force. This was to be a major change from the earlier schemes which, on the whole, had been carefully costed and tightly funded.

Immediately before the Second Railway Mania there were 2,235 miles of railway in operation and in 1844, 1,000 miles of railway were authorised but unbuilt. The following year more than 1,100 companies were provisionally registered to build nearly 3,000 miles of route requiring an estimated capital of £700 million, all seeking Parliamentary sanction. By 1846 270 railway Acts were passed for an additional 4,540 miles of railway. However, by 1847 the mileage authorised had dropped to 1,415 miles when the bubble burst. In the event, 5,000 miles were constructed by 1852 – even so the national rail mileage had tripled in seven years. At the peak of the mania 249,000 men were employed in the construction of railways, mainly with small contractors. By the end of 1852 nearly all of the most important lines had been constructed and yet in the following twenty years the national mileage doubled. Although the pace of enthusiasm for railways had slowed, building them continued rapidly.

Despite the undoubted, indeed unparalleled, success of the Woodhead line the Peak District did not escape this speculative frenzy, as we shall now see. What happened in our area of interest was a microcosm of what was going on all across the country.

The advertisers in the *Sheffield Independent* regularly used this drawing to show the two forms of transport on offer. The stage coach is shown as going as fast as it can, as if it is trying to keep up with the train while the train illustrates the pleasure of rail travel.

SHEFFIELD AND CHESTERFIELD JUNCTION RAILWAY

1843 25 Oct. A large and influential gathering of Sheffield residents met at the Cutlers' Hall in Sheffield, chaired by John Bagshawe, where it was resolved that the southern outlet from Sheffield be constructed. This was to replace the lengthy and inconvenient route via the Sheffield and Rotherham Railway, which had opened in 1838, to Masboro and thence by the North Midland Railway, opened in 1840, to Chesterfield. It was resolved that a provisional committee should be formed with Bagshawe in the chair and that Joseph Locke would be appointed as consulting engineer with Alfred S. Lee as the acting engineer. The capital was to be £250,000 with 10,000 shares at £25 each. A month later Locke had moved on and Lee was confirmed as engineer.

1843 28 Oct. The *Sheffield Independent* announced that the prospectus had been issued and that the line is 'now taken up in earnest' with a large number of shares having been taken up. One contractor of repute had bought a thousand shares and had started surveying the line to make it at his own expense. The effect on the Sheffield and Manchester line (Woodhead) had resulted in a jump in the value of their shares.

1843 30 Nov. The plans were lodged with the West Riding Clerk of the Peace and showed that the route would start from the terminus of the Woodhead line at Spitalfields (Bridgehouses), crossing over central Sheffield by a viaduct 960 yards in length with the Wicker 46 ft, the Don 60 ft and the Sheffield canal 45 ft below. A tunnel of 726 yards would go under the Duke of Norfolk's parkland followed by a further tunnel of 265 yards and a viaduct of 190 yards. This would take the line 80 ft above the Sheaf valley near Meersbrook, before passing within 100 yards of Meersbrook Hall on an embankment. Approaching the high ground of Beauchief and Greenhill a further tunnel of 1,540 yards would be needed to reach Dronfield and would pass the church within twenty five yards of its east end. Passing over the *White Swan Inn* it would enter a tunnel of 220 yards near Unstone before going between the *Bull's Head* and the Corn Mill at Whittington and would then reach the North Midland Railway, crossing the Chesterfield Canal 1¼ miles before Chesterfield station. The only redeeming feature was that the gradients at 1 in

105 from Sheffield to the summit at six miles and at 1in 100 from the summit to Chesterfield of five miles were reasonable, given the hilly terrain.

1844 27 Jan. The company announced that they had enough shares to comply with Parliament's standing orders and that subscribers had four days to buy shares.

1844 4 Mar. A public meeting was again held at the Cutlers' Hall in Sheffield resolving that 'the duty of the inhabitants, to the very utmost of their power, to aid the proprietors in their endeavours to obtain an Act of Parliament for making the same' and that petitions supporting the line should be presented to both houses of Parliament. Additionally, Lord Wharncliffe should be asked to present the Bill in the House of Lords with John Parker presenting to the Commons.

1844 9 Mar. An editorial in the *Sheffield Independent* supporting the line commented 'It is not to be disguised that the great railway interests are by no means friendly to Sheffield. Both in the original construction, and in the subsequent management of the North Midland, the town has been treated with great contempt: and it is quite plain that we can make ourselves respected, and create a spirit of accommodation, only by shewing that we have the power and the will to help ourselves'.

1844 18 Mar. A letter in the *Sheffield Independent* from the company stated that the line was not being opposed by the North Midland Railway who were bound by deed not to do so – the objections in Parliament were coming from the Grand Junction Railway. The hapless Charles F. Younge was now the chairman.

1844 11 May. The *Sheffield Independent* reported that the directors were settling their accounts and would shortly be making an announcement 'with renewed vigour'.

1844 12 Sep. A general meeting was held in the Cutlers' Hall without the chairman being present, although he sent a letter. It soon became clear that serious errors, some of them possibly fraudulent, had been made by the directors. At the point when they had lodged the plans they had only raised £9,000 of the £19,000 required to meet the requirements of Parliament and had secretly borrowed £10,000 to make up the total, believing that the Sheffield and Manchester Railway would buy shares to that value if the Act was passed. When the Bill failed because of inaccuracies in the schedules of property for compulsory purchase the S&M withdrew their support. Attempts were then made to link with the Sheffield and Rotherham Railway instead. The directors were seriously criticised by the shareholders who unsurprisingly wanted their money back and proposed that the project be either abandoned or merged with the proposed Gainsborough, Sheffield and Chesterfield Railway. This company was promoting a line from Chesterfield via Unstone, Dronfield, Sheffield, Canklow, Whiston, Maltby, Tickhill and Bawtry to Gainsborough. The exasperated shareholders voted to abandon the whole project.

After various negotiations a new company was born out of the ashes which was titled the Manchester, Sheffield and Midland Junction Railway.

REFERENCES

Q/RP2/156

London Gazette 20281 16 Nov 1843 page 3790

Dunstan John – *The Origins of the Sheffield and Chesterfield Railway*. Dore Village Society Occasional Pub No. 2. 1970

GREAT GRIMSBY, SHEFFIELD, THE POTTERIES AND GRAND JUNCTION RAILWAY

1845 22 Sep. The prospectus was issued for a proposal which had good intentions as there was good business potential in a link to the Grand Junction Railway, particularly in the supply of coal from the expanding south Yorkshire coalfield.

1845 4 Oct. The line was advertised and required capital of £1,750,000 with 70,000 shares available at £25 each. The chairman was Mr G. C. Holland and the engineer the young twenty eight year old John Fowler, who was born in Sheffield but had set himself up the previous year as a consulting engineer in London.

The new line would have left the Woodhead line near the Bridgehouses terminal (881358) on its fifty five mile journey by crossing the River Don and following it westward before veering left to gain the Rivelin valley at Malin Bridge. From there it kept the river on the right while traversing above the valley floor to the Sheffield to Glossop turnpike, which it kept on its right on heavy gradients to a 1,056 yard tunnel under the Moscar summit. The descent from the high moorlands into Ladybower gorge was on inclines of between 1 in 61 and 1 in 37. From there it passed down the Derwent valley, before swinging right to cross the Sheffield to Chapel en le Frith turnpike and the River Noe. Bradwell would be reached before passing between the hamlets of Little and Great Hucklow (c171876) where it would enter a 440 yard tunnel. Passing through Tideswell required a viaduct of 116 yards in length and 140 ft in depth. Four tunnels would then be built on its way to Buxton. It then proceeded to Leek, Baddeley Green, Cobridge and Newcastle under Lyme to join the Grand Junction Railway near Madeley station. There was also a branch planned to Stoke on Trent from Newton in the Moors and another from Hathersage to Calver and Stoney Middleton to Bakewell to join the proposed Manchester, Buxton, Matlock & Midland Junction Railway.

It was widely agreed that Fowler's survey was thorough and considered although, from this distance it seems to have gradients that were beyond the locomotives of the day.

1845 24 Oct. A meeting was held with representatives of the Sheffield, Buxton, Leek, Potteries and Crewe Railway to see whether common ground could be found to amalgamate the two schemes but they were unable to reach an agreement. However, the directors comment that 'negotiations are pending which hold out every prospect of success that will materially improve the value of the shares'.

It was reported that fine weather in the past week had been highly favourable for surveying and a large and efficient staff were hard at work. The engineering work required was described as 'not of an expensive character'. The atmospheric principle, as used on the Croydon line, was being considered and arrangements for the link with the Grand Junction Railway were being negotiated.

1845 3 Nov. The company announced that it was extending the time subscribers could pay their deposits by a week. Another advert included a letter from Fowler to the committee in which he stated that the plans were in a very advanced state, 'he having only that day received several lithographic sheets'. He was of the view that the section between Sheffield and Buxton would be easier to construct than the section from Buxton to Leek. On the former section he describes the works as being of a 'moderate and ordinary character except for the crossing of two narrow ravines'. Three tunnels, less than 1¼ miles in length, would be needed with the longest being three quarters of a mile.

1845 8 Nov. The national money markets were very depressed because of the huge demand of competing railways for capital but the company still felt the scheme stood a chance because it was well surveyed.

1845 2 Dec. The Bill was 115 of a staggering 568 railway bills lodged with Parliament for the next session.

1846 19 Feb. An advert was placed to abandon the line and wind up the company.

1846 17 Apr. At the winding up meeting at the *Tontine Inn* in Sheffield it was revealed that only £30,000 had actually been paid. The main expense incurred had been the survey and plans of John Fowler who some of the directors had met to negotiate a reduction in his fees. This they achieved by agreeing a figure of £8,000 which, it was said, resulted in a loss for Fowler.

REFERENCES

DRO Q/RP/2/104

Railway Magazine Vol. 93 issue 571 Sep/Oct 1947

John Fowler. *Author's collection*

JOHN FOWLER

John Fowler was born in 1817 at Wadsley Hall, near Sheffield, the son of a successful land surveyor. He was in his late twenties when he took on this commission, he having only the previous year taken the step of becoming an independent consulting engineer. As a young man he was educated privately at Whitley Hall near Ecclesfield. He trained under John Towlerton Leather, engineer of the Rivelin reservoirs and with Leather's uncle, George Leather, on the Aire and Calder Navigation. From 1837 he worked for John Urpeth Rastrick on railway projects, including the London and Brighton Railway. He then became resident engineer on the Stockton and Hartlepool Railway. In 1844 he moved to London, having already set up a practice as a consulting engineer in Yorkshire and Lincolnshire. He became engineer of the East Lincolnshire Railway, the Oxford, Worcester and Wolverhampton Railway and the Severn Valley Railway. No doubt his local contacts were useful when he applied to become the appointed engineer for this line. Despite the financial setback he experienced with this scheme, it did not deter him as he went on to have an illustrious career. He more than made up for his financial losses on his later works. Of his many assignments at home and in Egypt and India two projects are the best remembered. In 1853 he became chief engineer of the Metropolitan Railway, the world's first underground railway. Constructed in shallow cut and cover trenches the line opened between Paddington and Faringdon in 1863, for which he was paid £152,000 (£11.5 million) today. He was also engineer for the associated Metropolitan District Railway and the Hammersmith and City Railway. Of particular interest to us was his work on the Wicker Arches and Sheffield Victoria station and the impressive Manchester Central station, with its 210 ft wide train shed roof, the second widest unsupported iron arch in Britain after St Pancras. His most famous work was to design, with Benjamin Baker, the Forth railway bridge, which became the eighth wonder of the world. He was the youngest ever president of the Institution of Civil Engineers in 1865 and was made a baronet in 1890. He married Elizabeth Broadbent in 1850 by whom he had four sons. He died in 1898 at Bournemouth and is buried in London's Brompton cemetery. He was one of the towering figures of the Victorian age.

SHEFFIELD, BUXTON, LEEK, POTTERIES AND CREWE RAILWAY

This line is included because of its link with the Manchester, Sheffield and Midland Junction Railway.

1845 29 Jul. The company was provisionally registered with capital set at £800,000 with 32,000 shares at £25 each. The chairman was Thomas Carr. Committee members included a representative of the North Derbyshire Union Railway and eight committee members of the Manchester, Sheffield and Midland Junction Railway. Charles Vignoles was to be the engineer.

The object was to 'effect a most direct and comprehensive line of communication by means of existing and projected railways including the Manchester, Sheffield and Midland Junction Railway and the Manchester, Buxton and Ambergate Railway'.

1845 24 Oct. A meeting was held with representatives of the Great Grimsby, Sheffield, Potteries and Grand Junction Railway to amalgamate their schemes. But the representatives felt that going ahead would undermine their good relationship with the Manchester, Buxton, Matlock and Midland Junction Railway and the Manchester, Sheffield and Midland Junction Railway and, as a result, refused the offer. (Had the two combined I would have lost the will to live at handling a title such as the Great Grimsby, Sheffield, Buxton, Leek, Potteries, Crewe and Grand Junction Union Railway or GGSBLPC&GJUR!)

At the same time an advert was placed indicating that all the deposits had been paid, the surveys were nearly completed and that everything would then be ready to submit the application to Parliament.

1845 3 Dec. Plans were deposited with the Clerk of the Peace for Derbyshire. They showed that the line would go from Buxton to Stoke on Trent via Congleton to link with the planned North Staffordshire Railway.

1846 2 Apr. At a meeting at the Cutlers' Hall in Sheffield it was announced that because of the pressure on the money markets from all the other railway schemes, the Bill had been withdrawn and the company was to be wound up.

REFERENCES
DRO/RP2/88
London Gazette 20540 22 Nov 1845 pages 5712/3
20598 24 Apr 1846 page 1500

SHEFFIELD, MANCHESTER AND BUXTON AND MATLOCK JUNCTION RAILWAY

1845 30 Aug. An advertisement in the *Sheffield Independent* informed readers that this line required capital of £600,000 divided into 24,000 shares at £25 each with a deposit of £2.12.6 per share.

The line would have started at Sheffield (Bridgehouses) station and run via the Sheaf valley to Grindleford Bridge, Calver, Stoney Middleton, Baslow and Hassop to between Bakewell and Ashford where it would unite with the MBMMJR. The line covered seventeen miles and a prospectus was promised shortly with the names of the committee and the engineers and bankers. And there the matter appears to rest.

SHEFFIELD, BAKEWELL & WEST MIDLAND RAILWAY

This line had the following names – Sheffield, Bakewell and Ashford Railway, Sheffield Bakewell and Midland Railway and finally the above title and planned to become the North Derbyshire Union Railway by amalgamation. (No wonder it has been a struggle to make any sense of it all!)

1845 16 Aug. An advert announced the provisional registration of a line to unite the Sheffield, Ashton under Lyne & Manchester Railway, the Sheffield and Rotherham Railway (a founding member of the newly formed Midland Railway) and the Sheffield & Lincolnshire Junction Railway, to the MBMMJR at Bakewell or Buxton with a branch to Hathersage, Hope and Castleton. It saw itself as a connecting line between all these railways and planned to issue a prospectus shortly.

1845 26 Sep. An advertisement confirmed that 'the engineers have examined the country and the result of such examination, as also of further enquiries as to the objects which would be accomplished by the measure, fully justify the views of the promoters. The prospectus of the project is therefore no longer withheld.' The object would be as above but an additional branch, to Chesterfield, to join the Midland would be included 'unless the Midland Railway should decide to make it'. Applications were invited for the now registered undertaking. Capital had been fixed at £850,000 in 42,500 shares of £20 each with a deposit of two guineas per share. A provisional committee was to be appointed the following week which would include J. S. A. Shuttleworth of Hathersage and the engineers were to be George Stephenson and close confidant Frederick Swanwick with James Alexander as the surveyor.

1845 23 Nov. Plans were deposited for a line of twenty five miles from the Sheffield and Rotherham branch of the Midland at Brightside (just before Saville Street), which was then open country, to cross the River Don, before passing Effingham Street and Broad Street to where the Midland's Sheffield station would be built twenty five years later. Suffolk Road (386865) would be passed under, it being a few yards from the later Sheffield to Chesterfield line, before passing through Heeley and Millhouses as it climbed the Sheaf valley. Between the last named and Beauchief the line to Chesterfield would diverge and cross Abbey Lane and border Chancet Wood (341820), on the left, on inclines of 1 in 33 and 1 in 21, before going through the centre of Greenhill village (345812), and descending into the Drone valley at Dronfield at 1 in 40 and 1 in 44, which suggests that inclined planes would be used. Unstone would be passed on the left and the Midland Railway joined at the Newbold to Brimington road junction.

Meanwhile the main line would cross Abbey Lane at a more westerly point than that to Chesterfield and would pass Totley to Moss Road with Strawberry Lee on the right before climbing an inclined plane at 1 in 13 to a height of 1,129 ft on Totley Moss. There it would cross the the present day B6054 Owler Bar to Fox House road just to the right of its junction of the B6054 with the A625 Froggatt road (792268). From there another inclined plane of 1 in 13 would descend to Nether Padley at Grindleford

Bridge. At this point a branch would leave the main line to Castleton and follow the route of the later Dore and Chinley Railway, with Hathersage and Bamford on the right, to Hope. From there the line would pass just north of the village and cross the main road to arrive in Castleton at the point where the A625 takes a sharp left and then right into the village (151829).

Returning to the main line this would pass Froggatt on the left and Calver cross roads a hundred yards on the Grindleford side with Calver village on the left. Before reaching Hassop village the line would go through a 660 yard tunnel. Just before the village the line to Ashford would fork right and keep right of the B6020 to finish about half a mile before Ashford itself. The purpose of this branch was to form a junction with the proposed MBMMJR line from Ambergate to Buxton which, of course, eventually bypassed Ashford in favour of a short cut through Monsal Dale from Bakewell. This would not, however, be built for another twenty years.

The Bakewell branch continued on to the Baslow side of Hassop cross roads to finish, strangely, just before the junction of the B6001 and A619 roads (219698), quite a distance from Bakewell town centre.

The engineer, Frederick Swanwick, sent an invoice of £1,127.11.0 to James Alexander the surveyor, which included mention of a previously unknown branch to Eckington. Swanwick must have undertaken the survey on Alexander's behalf.

No sooner had the plans been unveiled than an amalgamation was agreed with the Manchester, Sheffield and Midland Junction Railway to become the Sheffield and North Derbyshire Union Railway with the MBMMJR also becoming party to the arrangement. This increased the capital to £1,600,000 in 40,000 shares of £40 each. It was agreed that each company would go ahead with its own plans until 30 Nov, the expenses being paid out of a consolidated fund, and both plans would be submitted to Parliament with the successful one being adopted and the other abandoned.

1846 13 Feb. Obviously all did not go well for a meeting was held to discuss the failure of the Manchester, Sheffield and Midland Junction Railway to go through with the agreed amalgamation or to meet its share of the expenses already incurred. As a result a petition was agreed to go to Parliament regarding this breach of faith and to suggest that the MSMJR Bill should be thrown out. The petition was signed by John Carr (Chairman), William Jackson, Edwin Unwin, T. B. Turton, Benjamin Vickers and Thomas Wiley.

1846 24 Oct. Winding up of the company was protracted. A demand of £4,500 in compensation from the errant MSMJR was rejected; a counter offer of £1,500 from the MSMJR was rebuffed as derisory so the company decided on court proceedings.

1848 19 Aug. Matters dragged on for a further two years before a meeting of the provisional committee resolved to make a call of £50 on each member to discharge the pending Chancery suit between themselves and the MSMJR.

REFERENCES

DRO Q/RP/2/104

Account from Frederick Swanwick. Laurence Knighton collection

Dunstan John – *The Origins of the Sheffield and Chesterfield Railway*. Dore Village Society Occasional Papers No. 2 1970

MANCHESTER, SHEFFIELD AND MIDLAND JUNCTION RAILWAY

This line was born out of the defunct Sheffield and Chesterfield Junction Railway of 1843.

1845 18 Mar. Plans were deposited with the Clerk of the Peace for the West Riding for a line which was primarily to link Sheffield from Bridgehouses to Chesterfield via Norton, Dronfield, Unstone, Newbold and Brampton to the Midland Railway at Hasland. Also included in the prospectus, was a branch from Newbold to Bakewell via Baslow and a further branch from Baslow to Calver. Additionally there were branches from Newbold to Staveley and Chesterfield to Barlow.

The following day a Parliamentary sub committee met and agreed that the standing orders had been complied with.

1845 27 Mar. A public meeting was held in Sheffield to consider the plethora of railway proposals in the area. Among those eliciting the meeting's approval was this line and the Newark and Sheffield Railway, with whom it planned to link.

1845 31 May. Over the next few days a Parliamentary committee met to consider the Bill. The capital was to be £400,000 for a line of twelve miles at a cost of £33,000 per mile. The maximum gradient would be 1 in 80 for 1½ miles. Some big hitting engineers were drafted in to support the line – John Hawkshaw (chief engineer of the Manchester and Leeds Railway) and Charles Vignoles (chief engineer on the Woodhead line 1835-1838) all said that no great difficulty in building the line was contemplated although the gradients might require the use of more powerful engines. The biggest difficulty would be crossing Sheffield via a viaduct over the hay and cattle markets: Vignoles said the piers of the viaduct would be of iron to reduce the space needed. There would be one tunnel of 2,103 yards at an inclination of 1 in 100 and two years would be needed to build it. Vignoles believed the capital proposed would be sufficient and thought it would open up the coalfields at Newbold, Unstone and Dronfield. John Urpeth Rastrick (pioneer locomotive builder and chief engineer of the Bolton and Preston Railway at this time) also supported the line as did W. Fairbank (no link to the Sheffield Fairbanks) who was said to be an engineer of twenty five years experience including work on the London and Birmingham Railway and the London and Brighton line. Fairbank had surveyed the works and had assisted Vignoles in calculating the costs, sending their estimate to William Cubitt (consulting engineer to the Great Northern Railway at this time) who had approved the figures. Jonathan Williams Nowill, a railway contractor told the committee that he could build the line within the budget calculated and all seemed to be going well. Unfortunately there were five opponents, including the influential Duke of Norfolk who thought the line would interfere with the views of woodland scenery from a number of his ornamental villas. He also thought that the gradients were too extreme. John Fowler considered the proposed line of the Sheffield and Lincolnshire Railway, from the Midland line at Woodhouse Mill to Sheffield, although 4¼ miles longer would cost less with better gradients and would avoid crossing the Sheffield markets. He reckoned that the Woodhouse line would cost £144,000 but this line's costings were grossly underestimated – £644,000 would be a more likely figure. Robert Stephenson and his cohorts Frederick Swanwick, Thomas Gooch and George Bidder supported Fowler in this. They said that the gradients would not be more than 1 in 150 on the Woodhouse line. Astonishingly Stephenson suggested that the gradients should not be greater than the Stockton and Darlington Railway, completely ignoring the engineering progress of the last twenty years. This was the same man who concurrently was working on a railway viaduct across the Menai Straits by a pioneering tubular girder method.

1845 9 Jun. The Bill was not proved and therefore rejected together with its planned partner the Newark and Sheffield Railway. It is clear that the representatives of the company were stunned by the decision. 'There was an instantaneous rush from the committee room to obtain cabs and drive with all possible speed to the share market'.

1845 20 Jun. A highly charged meeting was held at the Cutlers' Hall, Sheffield to consider the failure of the Bill. The objectors included the Dukes of Norfolk and Rutland, George Stephenson and George Hudson because of their Clay Cross coal mining interests; Frederick Swanwick, because of his close involvement with the Midland and the rival Sheffield, Bakewell and West Midland Railway. Additionally Joseph Locke (who was building the Lancaster to Carlisle line) criticised the gradients, which were not exceptional, and the Sheffield Coal Company, who did not want competition from the Unstone coal owners. Other opponents included the chairman of the meeting and the Lord Mayor, whose firm's premises would be encroached on by the line. This was opposition on a grand scale. There was no doubt that Sheffield's urgent need for an outlet to the south had been thwarted by naked self interest.

1845 14 Aug. At a special meeting of the shareholders at the Music Hall in Sheffield there was nothing to sing about as it was resolved that the acting directors could enter into any negotiations with any existing or projected company and that the North Derbyshire Union Railway would be consolidated with the company. The two projects would then be applied for during the next session of Parliament.

1845 30 Aug. The company was amalgamated with the North Derbyshire Union Railway which was promoting a line from Dronfield to Ashford to join the MBMMJR. The new chairman was named as Henry Wilkinson.

1845 7 Nov. An advertisement announced that the Manchester, Sheffield & Midland Junction Railway had amalgamated with the Sheffield, Bakewell and West Midland Railway. They thought that they had an agreement to pool their resources and for each to submit their plans to Parliament, with the unsuccessful application being abandoned. No record of the MSMJR company entering into the agreement has been traced. As the company had already amalgamated with the North Derbyshire Union Railway it is difficult to see how the agreement could be enforced.

1846 28 Jan. The Bill was deposited for a second time, to construct a railway from Sheffield to Chesterfield and from Dronfield, on that line, through Chatsworth to Bakewell, a total of 23¼ miles. The capital required would be £1,050,000 and Charles Vignoles was to be the engineer.

1846 2 Feb. Although the Bill was read a second time it did not eventually succeed.

1846 4 Apr. At a meeting called by the shareholders to meet a deputation of the board of directors in Liverpool there was a resolution to re-present the proposal to Parliament. It was argued that as the Dukes of Norfolk and Rutland had withdrawn their objections with one third of the shareholders coming from the area that the line would pass through and £85,000 being subscribed by the provisional committee, the application was now much stronger. £16,000 had been expended and no further deposit would be required to continue the Parliamentary process. A counter amendment argued that the Sheffield & Manchester line (Woodhead) was strongly objecting and was intent on retarding the passage of the Bill. Because of such opposition it was submitted that there was a need to amalgamate with other companies who were operational and if this was not possible then the company should be dissolved. The counter amendment was carried and that was the end of the line.

1846 24 Oct. Unsurprisingly the winding up of the company was just as complex as its very existence, largely because of what turned out to be a protracted dispute with the Sheffield, Bakewell and West Midland Railway. The proposed amalgamation between the two, which was probably never ratified, incurred significant winding up costs but the two could not agree on a figure. Negotiations to finalise the dispute by arbitration failed. The SBWMR wanted compensation of £4,500 while the MSMJR would only go to arbitration if the maximum that could be agreed would be £1,500. The SBWMR then decided to take the matter to court, but both companies joined the long list of proposed lines that were sucked into the frenzied vortex of the mania.

REFERENCES
DRO Q/RP2/64 & 147

London Gazette 20533 14 Nov 1845 pages 4194-6
20602 8 May 1846 page 1704

Dunstan John. – *The Origins of the Sheffield and Chesterfield Railway* Dore Village Society Occasional Papers No. 2. 1970

NORTH DERBYSHIRE UNION RAILWAY

1845 16 Aug. An advertisement showed this concern as being provisionally registered requiring a capital of £400,000 in shares of £50 each. The engineer was named as Charles Vignoles and the chairman Wilson Overend of Sheffield. Robert Younge, who was to become chairman of the Manchester, Sheffield & Midland Junction Railway was named as a potential subscriber. A proportion of the shares would be lodged with the directors of the MSMJR with an amalgamation being a possibility.

The line would start by a junction with the proposed Manchester Sheffield & Midland Junction Railway near Dronfield and go via Barlow, Bubnell, Hassop and Bakewell to Ashford near which it would unite with the unbuilt MBMMJR.

1845 24 Sep. It was announced that the line had been amalgamated with the Manchester, Sheffield & Midland Junction Railway. This date is contrary to the date of 30 Aug which was when the MSMJR announced the amalgamation. Quite where the truth lies, who can tell?

LEEDS, HUDDERSFIELD, SHEFFIELD AND SOUTH STAFFORDSHIRE (OR LEEDS AND HUDDERSFIELD TO WOLVERHAMPTON AND DUDLEY), DIRECT RAILWAY

1845 29 Sep. This scheme had a capital requirement of £1,700,000 with 85,000 shares at £1 each. The chairman was the Earl of Shrewsbury of Alton Towers. The line would be sixty five miles long from Uttoxeter, from where it would parallel the Uttoxeter and Caldon Canal, to a point near Prestwood from where it would go to Rocester, Ellaston and Mayfield to Ashbourne; then through Thorpe, Tissington, Hartington and Sheen to Buxton, Chapel en le Frith, Woodhead and Holmfirth to Huddersfield where it would join the Huddersfield and Leeds Railway. The railway would reach Sheffield by running powers over other railways. A branch from Ashbourne to Derby would require an additional £300,000 of capital.

1845 29 Oct. The *Derby Mercury* reported that an acting committee of engineers had completed a survey and this was in the hands of the engravers.

1845 3 Dec. The plans were deposited with the Derbyshire Clerk of the Peace but not surprisingly it failed considering it planned to build the line up the spine of the Pennine hills.

REFERENCE
DRO Q/RP2/107

HULL AND HOLYHEAD DIRECT RAILWAY

1845 1 Oct. The year also saw this proposal which was, at best, ill thought out, not surveyed properly and imagined it could raise a colossal £2,500,000. There were ninety four members on its provisional committee of which over half had no connection with the area. A number are named as directors of other railways never to be built. Three examples are William Fitzgibbon of the Great Welch Central and the Dorking, Arundel and Brighton Railway; John Williams of the London, Holyhead and Porthydyllaen Railway and the Rev Stephenson Isaacson of the Oxford, Cheltenham and Brighton Railway. All of them seem to have lost all reasoning when the prospect of easy money flashed before their eyes! The engineer named was William Henry Smith, although the plans have his name deleted with the note 'These plans were not completed by William Henry Smith'. (Very wise!) The notice of application stated that it would be open to being incorporated or sold to the Chester and Crewe Railway, the Sheffield and Rotherham Railway or the Great Grimsby, Sheffield, the Potteries and Grand Junction Railway companies, which is some indication of its speculative nature. The line would have started at Chester where a link to the Chester and Holyhead Railway and the Birkenhead Railway would be made. It would pass between Northwich and Middlewich to Macclesfield, Sheffield, Rotherham, Doncaster and Howden, there to connect with the Hull and Selby Railway in order to reach Hull, although there is no mention of the line east of Sheffield having being surveyed. On its route map Hathersage was located north of the Woodhead line! The passage through the Peak would have gone from Macclesfield to the townships of Taxal, Fernilee, Hope, Castleton, Derwent and Bradfield to Sheffield.

1845 14 Oct. A general meeting was held at the *London Tavern* in London to elect a committee with Lord Dunboyne in the chair. William Butcher, Sheffield's Master Cutler and J. Rowbotham, Mayor of Macclesfield had the misfortune to be elected. The secretary announced that an unnamed engineer had been engaged and had pronounced that no tunnels would be required!

1845 4 Nov. An advertisement announced that the share issue was oversubscribed and that locals would receive preferential treatment in the allocation of shares. Application to Parliament would take place for the coming session.

1845 8 Nov. At a meeting of the provisional committee in London, Lord Viscount Ingestre took the chair where a report from the engineer, now named as William H. Smith of 10 Adam Street, Adephi, was presented. Smith said that there were rumours of the impracticality of the line however, following an initial first look, he had concluded that a line might be formed without tunnels 'but the gradients would be such as could not be recommended'. Thinking that there would be less tunnelling than on the London and Birmingham Railway or the Great Western Railway to achieve this he would use what he acknowledged was the problematic atmospheric system which was gaining some traction at the time. A second report was then read, dated 6 Nov, which said that the trial levels were complete, except for a short distance between Macclesfield and Northwich 'which would be completed tomorrow'. The survey from the west side of Sheffield to Bollington was completed and also the several miles from Chester towards Northwich. The line would be sixty miles in length. There is a curious glibness about Smith's report which should have made the committee pause but they passed it without discussion.

1845 11 Nov. An advert stated that because of the depressed state of the money market it had been decided to extend the time for receiving deposits until 27 Nov.

1845 2 Dec. The plans were deposited with the Clerk to the Peace of the West Riding. These appear to be preliminary drawings with the actual line of the railway only shown on a few sheets. Very few locations are named and it is not clear where the plan commences or ends with so little detail or other geographical features being

```
PROSPECTUS
OF THE
HULL AND HOLYHEAD DIRECT RAILWAY,
VIA
SHEFFIELD, MACCLESFIELD, AND CHESTER,
Provisionally Registered.
———
CAPITAL, £2,500,000, in 100,000 Shares of £25 each.
```

The cover of the prospectus.

Glynn Waite collection.

The map of the line. Note the location of Hathersage!

shown. The book of references only covers the line from Chester as far as Sheffield and some sections are included but these are as vague as the plans. Many sheets are bound into the volume upside down!

There the trail goes cold and newspaper reports dry up. It obviously failed.

REFERENCES

Cheshire Quarter Sessions regarding Lords Deposited Plans QDP 254
www.archive.cheshire.gov.uk/dserve/dserve.exe
DRO Q/RP2/129
London Gazette 20537 19 Nov 1845 pages 5223/4
20543 26 Nov 1845 pages 6343/4

DIRECT SHEFFIELD AND MACCLESFIELD RAILWAY

This line has the same feel as the Hull and Holyhead Railway of being purely a speculators' line.

1845 17 Sep. The company was legally registered with a capital of £600,000 in 30,000 shares of £20 each.

1845 10 Oct. The line began from near Bridgehouses station in Sheffield and went up the Don valley, following its tributary, the Rivelin, on a rise of 1,000 ft in eight miles to Moscar Cross (223823) and there descends 550 ft in four miles to the Derwent valley. There was a further rise of 600 ft near Edale and the line would reach Macclesfield via Chapel en le Frith with a four mile tunnel under Goyts Moss. Atmospheric propulsion was proposed to overcome the gradients and the engineers were Messrs Sandiforth, M. F. Griffin and J. H. Taunton who had already surveyed the line. The *Morning Post* describes the supporters as being 'of that class of wealthy, yet working, men by whom the first railways were conceived and established'.

1845 1 Dec. The company advertised that the plans had been deposited with the Clerk of the Peace for Derbyshire.

1846 11 Nov. A notice was issued for a meeting of shareholders on 24 Nov 1846 at the company solicitor's office in the City of London to determine whether the company should be dissolved and whether such an action would be deemed an act of bankruptcy. It was signed by Wm. Chaplin, on behalf of the committee.

1846 24 Nov. Thirty to forty shareholders turned up at the London solicitor's office where no provision had been made for the meeting. After a long wait William Chaplin and the solicitor to the company appeared and moved the meeting to a nearby coffee house. It was shown that the advert for the meeting had not been sent to three newspapers as required and that one of the adverts announced the wrong railway. The meeting was not only illegally called but the provisional registration of the company had not been renewed after one year as required. The meeting was dissolved 'among scenes of much altercation and confusion with the directors refusing to answer any questions. The parties separated, much dissatisfied with each other'. Several actions were subsequently taken against the directors. Interestingly, one of the directors, Edward Richards, finished up in a debtors prison in connection with the debts of the company and other failed railways. A sorry tale.

REFERENCES

London Gazette 20534 15 Nov 1845 page 4423
20540 22 Nov 1845 pages 5861/2
20663 13 Nov 1846 page 4210
20746 22 Jun 1847 page 2316
Railway Magazine Vol. 93 No. 571 Sep/Oct 1947

A share certificate that became worthless.   *Laurence Knighton collection*

GREAT NORTHERN AND SOUTHERN DIRECT RAILWAY

1845 1 Nov. This railway was proposed to link Huddersfield and Derby by a junction with the proposed Huddersfield and Sheffield Junction Railway at, or near, Holmfirth and would proceed by Woodhead, Derwent, Hathersage, Nether Padley, Froggatt, Bubnell, Baslow, Bakewell, Matlock, Cromford, Wirksworth, Windley and Quarndon to, at or near, Derby by a junction with the proposed Rugby, Derby and Manchester Railway or the Midland Railway; a distance of fifty seven miles. It also proposed a branch from the Woodhead line to Glossop. The prospectus airily talks of links from Glasgow to the south coast and specifically a line from Derby to Coventry. It claimed to have the support of the landowners and claimed there were no engineering difficulties that had not been surmounted elsewhere. (Really?!).

Provisional capital required was set at £1,500,000 in 75,000 shares of £20 each. The engineer was named as Charles Blunt (who had an involvement in twelve different lines at this time) who was said to have surveyed some of the line. There was also a consulting engineer named as John Urpeth Rastrick (involved in sixteen other lines). The provisional committee consisted of over 230, many of whom were already directors of other railways that were to fail. Unsurprisingly it does not seem to have got out of the blocks.

REFERENCES
London Gazette 20534 15 Nov 1845 page 4358-9

'UNNAMED' RAILWAY

1845 8 Nov. In the *London Gazette* notice was given for an application to Parliament for the following:

1. A line from the Sheffield and Rotherham Railway in the Brightside area which would then proceed up the Sheaf valley to Totley and then to Nether Padley, Hathersage, Froggatt, Calver, Bubnell and Hassop to Bakewell and Ashford to join the not yet built MBMMJR.

2. A branch from Norton Hammer in the Sheaf valley via Dronfield was envisaged joining the Midland at the point where it crosses the River Whiting at Whittington.

3. A branch from somewhere between Dronfield and Totley to Coal Aston, Mosbrough, Renishaw, Beighton and Killamarsh to meet the west end of the tunnel on the Chesterfield Canal and also the Midland Railway at an unspecified location was also included in the notice.

4. A further branch from Nether Padley to Castleton was put forward.

Unlikely as it seems this nameless scheme disappears into the mist from whence it came! Whether it became a company it is impossible to say.

REFERENCE
London Gazette 20534 15 Nov 1845 page 4664-5

MANCHESTER, BUXTON, MATLOCK AND MIDLAND JUNCTION RAILWAY

This was a line built between Ambergate and Rowsley and was then projected to reach Stockport via Buxton. Our interest is the proposal to continue the line through the Hope and Edale valleys. Whether the line should pass through the Haddon estate of the Duke of Rutland or through the Chatsworth estate of the Duke of Devonshire was at the heart of which river valley the line should choose the Wye or the Derwent.

1845 May. A prospectus was published for the route, surveyed by George Stephenson which would leave the Manchester and Birmingham Railway a short distance south of Stockport and pass, via Whaley Bridge, to Buxton. From there it was planned to go down the valleys of the Wye and Derwent to, or near, Ashford, Bakewell, Matlock and Cromford, joining the Midland at Ambergate. The main backers were the Manchester and Birmingham Railway in the north and the recently formed Midland Railway in the south. George Henry Cavendish MP, the brother of William Cavendish, and later the seventh Duke of Devonshire, was the chairman and Joseph Paxton, the sixth duke's agent, (who had already invested £35,000 in railway ventures) was a director. In 1854 Paxton replaced Cavendish as chairman.

1845 30 Nov. The plans were deposited.

1846 16 Jul. This was the date of the Act of Incorporation and was also the same date that the Manchester and Birmingham Railway combined with two others to form the London & North Western Railway. This new company immediately developed a hostile attitude to the proposed line, not wanting the Midland to encroach on its perceived territory around Manchester. By this time the Duke of Rutland had become opposed to the line passing through his Haddon Hall estate. So the sixth Duke of Devonshire was approached for permission to build the line through his estate. This he agreed which was not surprising given the involvement of his brother and Paxton with the company.

1846 30 Nov. Plans were deposited for a deviation of the original route from Rowsley to run through Chatsworth Park and Baslow Wood where it would turn west to rejoin the line near the later Hassop station.

1847 22 Jul. The inhabitants of Bakewell, for long a significant market town, were less than happy at being excluded from the proposed new route and petitioned the Duke of Rutland to drop his opposition. The upshot was that Rutland successfully opposed the deviation in the House of Lords.

1847 30 Nov. The company did not want to give up the permission that they had gained to go through Chatsworth and so deposited plans for a revised route which would travel from Rowsley via Beeley to Chatsworth where there would be two tunnels, 1,038 yards and 767 yards long, of the arching or cut and cover type to prevent the Duke having to see trains passing his house but would allow him convenient stations at Bubnell and Beeley. The line would then go to Bubnell, near Baslow, on the north side of the River Derwent and pass through Calver Mill just beyond where there would be a 397 yard tunnel. Then by Froggatt and onwards to Curbar, Grindleford Bridge and Hathersage before crossing the River Derwent just north of Mytham Bridge, near Bamford (205827). Beyond Hope the line would travel on the north side of the River Noe to Edale. Here a 3,463 yards tunnel, with a width of 25 ft and height of 21 ft, would access Wash under Cowburn on a gradient of 1 in 187. From there a branch would run alongside the Peak Forest Tramway to Barmoor Clough, Dove Holes and Blackbrook to Buxton. Also included was a branch from between Rowsley and Beeley which involved going through the Haddon estate to a station near the former cattle market in Bakewell.

1848 13 May. Plans were deposited for an alternative branch to Bakewell from Baslow. This avoided the Haddon estate altogether.

1848 31 Aug. The alternative branch to Bakewell from Baslow, rather than Rowsley, received its Act.

1849 4 Jun. All this became much less feasible, given the continuing hostility of the LNWR and so all efforts became concentrated on building the southern section of the line from Ambergate to Rowsley, which was achieved.

It would be another twenty years before the plan to reach Buxton was revived and would be by the original line up the Wye valley which was opened in 1863. This was followed in 1867 when the extension from Blackwell Mill South Junction to New Mills South Junction was opened with a curve at Blackwell Mill to allow trains from the north and east to access Buxton.

REFERENCES
DRO/RP2/148 & 12 & 53
London Gazette 20800 27 Nov 1847 pages 4431-3
Waite Glynn / Knighton Laurence – *Rowsley: A Rural Railway Centre*. Midland Railway Society 2003
Hudson Bill – *Through Limestone Hills*. Oxford Publishing Co 1989
Warner Tim – *The Railway That Never Was*. Derbyshire Life Jan 1989
Waite Glynn – *Hassop 150*. The Rowsley Association 2012

BAKEWELL, CHESTERFIELD, STAVELEY, DRONFIELD AND SHEFFIELD JUNCTION RAILWAY

1846 6 Nov. Notice was given that an application to Parliament in the next session would be made for a line that would start at a junction with the proposed line of the MBMMJR where that line crossed the turnpike at Pine Apple beer house (218698). Then through Birchill (215716), south east of Hassop village, to Baslow and then between Curbar Edge and Ramsley and down to Millthorpe in the Cordwell valley. It would then go to Barlow, Sheepbridge, Whittington and Chesterfield to meet the Midland at about fifteen chains north of the station with a branch through Brimington to Staveley station.

Another branch from about four chains on the south side of Brierley Wood on the Duke of Devonshire's land and about twenty chains south east of Broom Bank Farm (c363753) (in the occupancy of Hannah Bargh – where the Sheepbridge trading estate is today) would pass up the Drone valley to Unstone and Dronfield; then north up to Greenhill from where it would drop down to Beauchief and then into the Sheaf valley to finish at a junction with the proposed Lincolnshire Junction Railway in property adjoining Walker Street (under the later Wicker Arches).

A further branch was also proposed starting about eight chains north of Broom Bank Farm at Sheepbridge to a junction in Brierley Wood at Unstone Green, about twenty seven chains north east of the above farm.

This gave the fledgling company a triangular arrangement right at its heart.

There was also an application for powers that the company be leased or sold to either or both of the existing Sheffield, Rotherham, Barnsley, Wakefield, Huddersfield and Goole Railway and to an unformed company called the South Yorkshire, Doncaster and Goole Railway.

The company was to deposit its plans by the end of the month.

1846 9 Nov. The last mentioned of the above companies advertised an intention to purchase the SRBWHGR in respect of all its planned lines south of Barnsley.

So here we have three companies tied up with each other, all competing with the SAMR and the Midland Railway who were also planning to extend their lines in the Barnsley area. As might be expected the big two triumphed and the triumvirate were heard of no more.

REFERENCE
London Gazette 6 Nov 1846 pages 4211/12

THE 1860s

There was a lull in interest in lines across the Peak after the traumas of the 'Second Railway Mania' but there was a new construction boom around 1863 fuelled by the emergence of the finance company. It was floated on a sea of paper, much of it of dubious worth and in 1866 a large number of contractors failed including Peto & Betts, one of the largest.

SHEFFIELD, CHESTERFIELD AND STAFFORDSHIRE RAILWAY

1863. This line was proposed as an alternative to the Midland's planned main line from Grimesthorpe Junction to Lockoford in Chesterfield. Sheffield industrialists, who felt that they had had a raw deal from the Midland, combined to float this company but were shown to have inflated the amount raised so it collapsed under Parliamentary scrutiny. The line would have left the Midland Railway near Brightside and, on reaching the north side of Beauchief, would have forked; one line going to Chesterfield on the present Midland route and the other a loop passing through a tunnel to Smeekley Wood, below Owler Bar, and on to the Cordwell valley, before joining the Chesterfield line at Newbold.

From Chesterfield, the main line would tunnel under East Moor for 2¼ miles to near Baslow, continuing via a short tunnel at Curbar and over the River Derwent by a two arch bridge, both arches being 84 ft in height with 50 ft spans. There the line would proceed to the newly opened Hassop station where a curve would link to the Midland line in the Buxton direction (217706). A left hand curve would take the line south to Bakewell where the public road, mill goit, River Wye and turnpike road (the present day A6) would be crossed on a viaduct 210 yards long. The railway would then continue to Youlgreave but before that was reached it would cross the River Lathkill by a viaduct of 267 yards with a span of 30 ft and a maximum height of 144 ft. From Youlgreave the route would pass near Winster and under Carsington Pastures to Hognaston and Ashbourne where access would be sought to the North Staffordshire Railway and onwards to the LNWR system. The two lines totalled forty four miles. A later link was announced from Ashbourne to Uttoxeter and Bramshall.

REFERENCES

DRO/RP2/120

London Gazette 22791 24 Nov 1863 pages 5776-9

Dunstan John – *The Origins of the Sheffield and Chesterfield Railway*. Dore Village Society Occasional Papers No. 2. 1970

THE LNWR BACKED LINES

Until 1857 there had been an alliance between the LNWR and MSLR with the latter being content to transfer their freight traffic from Manchester to Liverpool to the LNWR. In 1857 the MSLR's alliance was transferred to the GNR, although at that date neither had direct access into Manchester and both were dependent on the LNWR to get to Liverpool. Subsequently the MSLR gained permission to carry a line through Altrincham to Garston in Liverpool. Matters stayed like this until 1865 when the Cheshire Lines Committee (CLC) was created by the coming together of the MR, MSLR and GNR. This creation was resisted by the LNWR and the Lancashire & Yorkshire Railway (LYR) and the change in the balance of power between Manchester and Liverpool galvanised the LNWR into wanting an independent line to Sheffield – thus there would be a competing line from Sheffield to Liverpool with access to the entire LNWR system.

SHEFFIELD, BUXTON AND LIVERPOOL RAILWAY

1865 8 Nov. Plans were deposited for a twenty eight mile railway from the Stockport, Disley & Whaley Bridge Railway (a line backed by the LNWR) at New Mills station to Bugsworth and Alders Lane, Chinley. It would keep Chapel Milton on the right before entering a 1,500 yard tunnel and emerging at Ford Hall (c077823), then a further 2,810 yard tunnel to emerge near Treak Cliff Cavern (134833) above Castleton. The line would then go under the ridge between Mam Tor and Lose Hill and would cross the River Noe on a viaduct just below the later Normans Bank signal box (c164862) before regaining height to pass below Aston. After passing through Thornhill village, it would cross the River Derwent above Bamford and keep on the northern slopes of the valley to above Hathersage where a 5,120 yard tunnel would be driven, at a maximum depth of 690 ft, to a point north of the present Totley tunnel. Then through Ecclesall Woods to Nether Edge from where it would cross Cemetery Road, Ecclesall Road and Broomspring Lane to a terminus at West Street (872346) in Sheffield.

1865 29 Nov. An additional branch was added from Lansdown Road in Sheffield to a more central terminus on the corner of Division Street and Cambridge Street. Additionally, a line would be built from the northern end of Dove Holes station to Sparrowpit where there would be a short tunnel. It would then meet the previous line half a mile north east of White Lee Farm at Perryfoot (c102815), between the two tunnels.

1866 6 Jan. It was revealed that all the subscribers were LNWR directors and £600,000 of the capital was to come from the company, a third of the amount to be raised. The three tunnels would have been 1,500 yards long and 354 ft deep, 2,810 yards long and 363 ft deep and 5,120 yards long and an astonishing 690 ft deep. The viaducts were to be 672 yards and 145 ft high, 433 yards and 123 ft, 320 yards and 154 ft, 992 yards and 260 ft, 707 yards and 168 ft, 536 yards and 157 ft and finally 820 yards and 57 ft. (Phew!) The gradients would be 1 in 80 for eighteen miles and 1 in 100 for three miles.

1866 30 Jan. A meeting was held in the Council Hall, Sheffield, attended by such Sheffield luminaries as Mark Firth, F. T. Mappin, R. Leader, T. W. Cockayne and J. C. Cutler, at which Messrs Bancroft and Beecroft, who were LNWR directors, explained why the proposed line had not been deposited with Parliament as promised. They commented that the original idea had come from Sheffield interests approaching the LNWR board. He was aware that the Sheffield Company (MSLR) were denigrating the scheme and were also aware that it had been called the 'High Pique Line'. Actually they had been galvanised by the three companies gaining power to build the Cheshire Lines route between Manchester and Liverpool, cutting them off from any running powers into Sheffield. The problem was that the appointed engineer Thomas Bouch (of later Tay Bridge disaster notoriety), was so busy with his Scottish contracts that he had to use subordinates to survey the line and send the surveys to him in Edinburgh. When they had received the survey they found it 'indefensible' and, besides being very expensive the route would have taken a long time to build. The board considered it prudent to have a fresh survey undertaken by another engineer and believed, when told that it would cost about £800,000, that the cost would not deter it. The meeting approved the LNWR board's decision and were reassured that the North Western's commitment to the project still shone bright.

REFERENCES

DRO/RP2/67

London Gazette 23040 21 Nov 1865 pages 5584-6

THE MACCLESFIELD AND BUXTON AND SHEFFIELD JUNCTION RAILWAY

1865 30 Nov. Plans were deposited for this line, which was backed by the LNWR and North Staffordshire Railway, for a route from Macclesfield to Bugsworth to link in with the Sheffield, Buxton and Liverpool Railway with a branch to join the Stockport, Disley & Whaley Bridge Railway at Fernilee. This would have provided a link from Sheffield to the Potteries and beyond.

1866 25 Jan. When the Bill was examined in Parliament none of the parties responsible actually appeared. Inexplicable and also very costly.

REFERENCE

DRO/RP2/39

BUXTON, CHAPEL-EN-LE-FRITH AND SHEFFIELD RAILWAY

1867 16 Jan. The LNWR took notice of the above two schemes and deposited plans to Parliament. Despite the promise that another engineer would be found Thomas Bouch was still retained. The line was to start at Chapel en le Frith station, rather than New Mills, and would enter a 6,913 yard tunnel at Bagshaw (078881), just outside Chapel, emerging just beyond the A625 Mam Tor road at Hardhurst Farm. It would pass through the Hope valley on a more sensible lower trajectory and then follow the course of the later Dore and Chinley line, although it would gain height above the later Grindleford station to enter a tunnel half a mile above the present Totley tunnel, to emerge at Totley. This would have been 5,280 yards long, the route then running parallel with the later Midland line all the way down the Sheaf valley. However, it would have diverged slightly to the west and crossed Bramall Lane football and cricket ground (what sacrilege!) and Leadmill Road before going through a half mile tunnel below Shrewsbury Road. Here it would have had the newly planned Midland station on its left before crossing Duke Street and Blast Lane to a terminus on Cricket Inn Road, near to the present Supertram depot (373875). This area of the town was not heavily developed at this time.

1867 15 Mar. A Parliamentary committee met over the following few days to consider the Bill and hear objections. It was revealed that the cost was estimated at £1,090,000 and would be twenty two miles long with a further tramway of two miles. It would take four years to build with its tunnel and shafts and six years if tunnelling was avoided.

Objections came from the Midland Railway and Edward Watkin, the supremo of the MSLR, who commented that 'if the LNWR directors were imprudent enough to embark on such a costly undertaking he hoped the shareholders would revolt. The line would cost a million pounds and could not possibly pay'.

There was the usual opposition from the landowners, including the Duke of Norfolk, Earl Fitzwilliam and, of course, the Duke of Rutland of whom the promoter said that it was 'rather too late in the year 1867 to stop construction of an important line for a few head of cock grouse'.

A maiden lady, Miss Barnes, petitioned against the line because 'the public had a great objection to tunnels and could not dispossess themselves of the idea that darkness and danger were inseparable'.

The Bill was supported by Sheffield Town Council who wanted to encourage as much competition as possible between the railway companies. According to the council there was much dissatisfaction in the town with the Midland Railway for its extortionate charges and with the MSLR because of the unsatisfactory way goods were transferred to the LNWR in Manchester.

Also in support was Thomas Gamble, a partner of Moss & Gamble, steel, file and saw manufacturers, who said that his firm employed over 400 men and exported over 30% of its output sending large orders to Shropshire, North Wales and Liverpool. He had to send his goods by the Midland via Normanton because of delays on the MSLR. The cost of bar and pig iron cartage was very large for his firm.

J. S. A. Shuttleworth, of Hathersage Hall, said that the needle and wire manufacturers in Hathersage were carting coal from Holmesfield at 9s.0d a ton and 2,000 tons of stone was sent to Sheffield by road.

William Cameron Moore, of Bamford Mill, said that lace and thread from cotton spun in Manchester reached them from the Peak Forest Canal at Whaley Bridge from where it was carted the last eleven miles.

Thomas Somerset, of Eccles House, Bradwell, who was a farmer, timber merchant and lead mine owner said that there was limited accommodation at Sheffield for his timber.

Nathan Woodruff Ashton, a lime burner from Hope, said that he burned 900 tons of lime a year and used 300 to 400 tons of coal which cost twice as much as the pit mouth price.

Robert Ashton, of Castleton, a landowner, smelter and white lead manufacturer and lead mine owner said that he could have sent 2,620 tons of minerals by rail in the past year.

Selim Bright, a goldsmith and jeweller of Buxton, said, to laughter, that Buxton 'was good for gout … or rather the cure of gout'.

1867 2 Apr. The Bill was approved by the Commons and passed to the Lords, the LNWR having seen the objectors off.

1867 16 Apr. The Bill was withdrawn.

1867 9 May. Sheffield Town Council had learned through the press that the LNWR had withdrawn its Bill and felt that they should have been consulted before such a decision was made, although the mayor revealed that he never thought it would succeed. The fact was, that at this point, the alarmed MSLR realised that the LNWR was serious in its intent to have an independent line into Sheffield. Thus they offered the North Western through running between Ardwick Junction and Sheffield with access for the company's own staff and assistance in building the LNWR's own station and goods yard in Sheffield in return for the scheme's complete abandonment. In point of fact the LNWR already had running rights over the MSLR but had never used them because there was no infrastructure to handle the traffic. The LNWR accepted the offer with alacrity so in one fell swoop good access to a major industrial town had been achieved without having to build a hugely expensive line. The dropping of the scheme would have also been a relief to the Midland who were in the throes of building their line from Sheffield to Chesterfield via Totley and, more substantially, also from Settle to Carlisle. The Midland could not have contemplated another expensive undertaking across the Peak to thwart the LNWR.

REFERENCES
DRO/RP2/65

London Gazette 23191 27 Nov 1866 pages 6529/30

SHEFFIELD AND BUXTON NARROW GAUGE RAILWAY

1867. This proposed railway was remarkable in being a 3 ft gauge line of twenty four miles in length and is one of the more tantalising might have beens.

1871 30 Nov. Four years later plans were deposited for the 1872 Parliamentary session with the power to enter into an agreement with the LNWR to lay narrow gauge rails alongside the Stockport, Disley & Whaley Bridge Railway (SDWBR) Buxton extension line from Dove Holes station to Buxton. R. S. Norris was appointed the engineer.

Leaving the SDWBR just south of Dove Holes station and going over the turnpike road and the Midland's Dove Holes tunnel to Tideswell it then kept Smalldale (775094) and Dale Head (762126) on the right and Wheston (763133) on the left. Bending south of Crossgate Farm (760141) the descent would be between 1 in 137 and 1 in 50. A 57 ft high and 150 yards long viaduct would be crossed before passing through Tideswell at Town Head. At Tideswell Lane Head road junctions the line crossed the present A625 before descending on a gradient of 1 in 82 to an 840 yard tunnel under Windmill. Continuing its descent past Hazlebadge Hall (800171) and keeping to the right of Bradwell and the present day B6049 to Brough it then crossed the future A625 with the *Rising Sun Inn* on the left. It would then climb to below Thornhill village and keep Yorkshire Bridge on its left before crossing the River Derwent and gaining Ladybower Gorge, to the right of the present day A57 road.

Climbing on gradients of 1 in 42 and 1 in 37 and after crossing the minor road to Strines, it would enter a tunnel of 1,540 yards at a maximum depth of 128 ft to Hollow Meadows. It would then descend on gradients of 1 in 34 and 1 in 52 to Rivelin Mill Bridge, but not before crossing a viaduct over the edge of the Lower Rivelin reservoir. Further descending gradients of 1 in 42 and 1 in 90 were needed to keep the valley bottom on its left. Three more tunnels of 370, 350 and 280 yards length respectively would negotiate Bell Hagg Lane and Walkley Bank Road. A final descent between Freedom Street and Langsett Road would take the line to a terminus just below Greaves Street (890339). The site of this terminus in Hillfoot is a most curious one it being well out of the built up area of the town. There is an unsubstantiated report that it was intended to continue the route to a station at Barkers Pool.

The terrain and gradients were extreme but the amount of tunnelling was much less than other proposals because the narrow gauge would have coped with these difficult inclines and descents more easily. The *Sheffield Independent* described it as a 'cheap and useful line'. Undoubtedly the volume of merchandise carried would have been much less than a standard gauge line and the comfort of passengers would have been less than satisfactory on what must have been a slow journey; nevertheless it would have been a magnificent line to have seen and travelled on.

Although, initially, the line had LNWR support, once the North Western's own proposals were formulated, and then withdrawn, its interest in the line weakened. Finally, in order to kill off the line, the MSLR and the Midland jointly proposed to share the cost of buying out the promoters, to a maximum of £1000, to defray the costs already accrued. This was agreed and the plans and documents were surrendered to the MSLR to be securely locked away from public gaze.

The LNWR's interest in an independent line to Sheffield was at an end.

REFERENCES

DRO/RP2/170
London Gazette 23799 24 Nov 1871 pages 5002/3

SHEFFIELD & BUXTON NARROW GAUGE RAILWAY - 1871

Ted Hancock / Steve Huson

The route of the planned Sheffield and Buxton Narrow Gauge Railway. The link to the LNWR Buxton line illustrates that it was another, if unconventional, attempt by the LNWR to reach Sheffield. It would have been an enthusiast's dream and an operator's nightmare.

LINES WITHIN THE PEAK DISTRICT

A number of schemes were mooted over a period of fifty years aimed at linking the Midland Railway Peak line at Hassop to the Dore and Chinley line at Grindleford in order to reach a number of villages and their attendant industries; also to put the place with the best tourist potential, Castleton, on the railway map.

HASSOP, HATHERSAGE AND CASTLETON RAILWAY

1870 8 Sep. The promoters of this scheme convened a meeting in the committee room at the *Ordnance Arms*, Hathersage, at which it was resolved 'that all projects for the construction of a line of railway through the Castleton, Hathersage, Hope and Derwent valleys having failed mainly on account of the enormous expense and difficulty of a through undertaking, as well as through the jealousies and rivalries of the railway companies, this meeting is of the opinion that the only mode of securing railway accommodation is to commence with a short single line to be initiated, and carried through, by the landowners, commercial interests and resident population themselves'. It went on to say that 'because of the hilly nature of the area it has been denied rail access resulting in the population and industry being debarred from easy access to coal. This has adversely affected the various manufacturers of steel and iron at Hathersage, the lead mines from Peak Forest to Eyam, the lime kilns, smelting furnaces and white lead and other minerals at Hope, Brough, Bradwell and other places, in addition to mills connected with the cotton trade and various undertakings required to be worked by steam power'. Consequently the price at which coal could be brought into the area was of great importance. There was also a belief that the railway 'would encourage tourism' and noted that in the summer months Castleton attracted 'several hundred visitors a day who travelled by omnibus, coaches and vehicles of that sort'.

The capital was fixed at a modest £60,000, in £10 shares, to allow small investors the chance to purchase. Traffic returns were calculated at £6,000 a year and a provisional committee was formed. The Duke of Rutland, who had considerable land interests in the area, did not object but those of influence in Bakewell did not support the proposal which led a local journal to comment 'that it deserves all our aid is proof for all: Bakewell has a duty to perform in endeavouring to obtain her railway station as the terminus, and without that of course we shall reap very little of the advantages that are sure to accrue. Last week we made remarks to Bakewell calculated to have the effect that a red hot poker has upon a house breaker or bailiff' and described the town's inhabitants as having the 'dullness of brain' generally accorded to a stupid species of the four footed tribe'. (Pity that they didn't say what they really meant! I have noticed that writing in this period was usually more decorous than would be employed today but could descend to a level of vituperation that causes an extremely sharp intake of breath).

Under the supervision of the appointed engineers, John Sheldon Wilkinson and Thomas Smith, the single line would have started at the newly opened Hassop station and then crossed the River Derwent near Froggatt before following the course of the river to Mytham Bridge before Bamford, from where it would 'proceed nearly on a surface level along the Hope valley to Castleton'.

There was an unpleasant incident involving Thomas Smith and his assistant engineer, Arthur Pinn, when they were assaulted by three gamekeepers working for Charles Cammell of Brookfield Hall, Hathersage. They were on a leisurely walk to Stanage and had crossed Cammell's land. The gamekeepers were all fined when the matter came to court.

The population of around 10,000 failed to support the scheme sufficiently and it lapsed. I suspect that the number of people with the ability to buy shares was very small as the area was so impoverished, it being an economic backwater. So even though the proposed railway would have radically changed the economic prospects of the district sufficient financial support was not to be found.

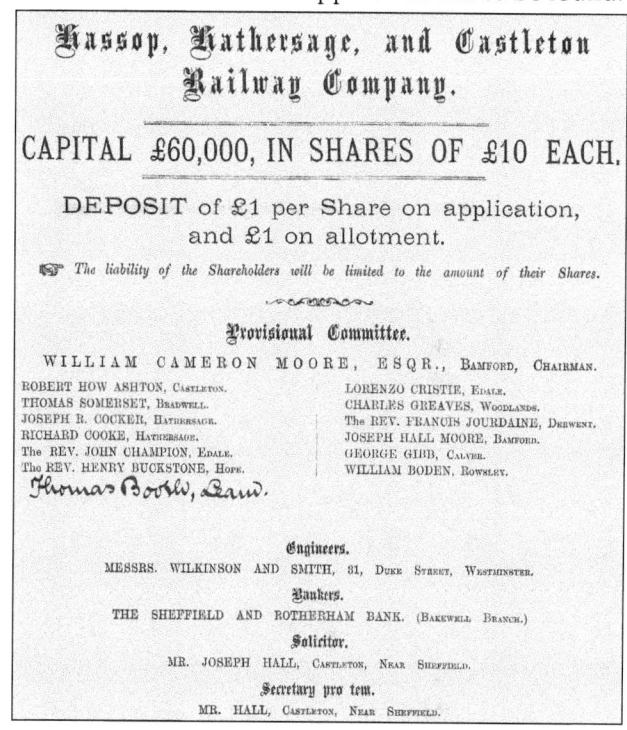

The prospectus for this eminently sensible proposal to open up the Derwent and Noe valleys to commerce and tourism failed, like the rest, because the finance could not be raised. *Laurence Knighton collection*

HASSOP AND PADLEY RAILWAY

1884 29 Nov. When the prospectus was issued the promoters had the advantage of knowing that the Dore and Chinley Railway, with the backing of the Midland, would be built and run via Padley. It was stated in the notice of intent to deposit the Bill that 'running powers would be sought over the Midland Railway's line from Hassop to Bakewell and from Hassop to Buxton'. The *Railway News* even went so far as to suggest that the line had the backing of the Midland Company.

The appointed engineer, J. N. Schoolbred, worked out that the line would have triangular junctions with the two main railways – the junctions on the Dore and Chinley line would be at Padley and Hathersage. There would be one 640 yard tunnel on a descending gradient towards Calver.

1885 26 Feb. The line was abandoned.

REFERENCES
DRO/RP2/201
London Gazette 25415 18 Nov 1884 pages 4966-8

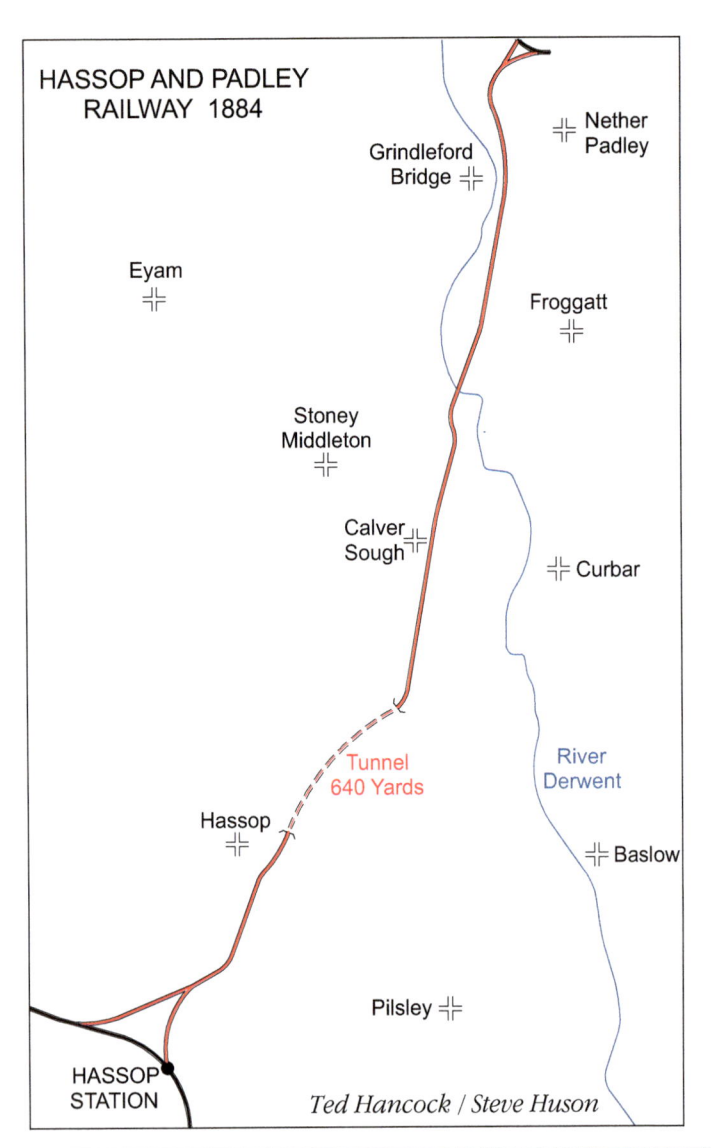

HOPE AND CASTLETON LIGHT RAILWAY

This is a might have been that firmly grips the imagination of your author had it first been built and then survived. It would have put the two major villages in the Hope valley not directly served by the Midland on the railway map. Here was the sort of line that John Betjeman would have eulogised.

1903 25 Nov. With the Dore and Chinley line well established, an application was made under the Light Railway Act of 1896 for an order to construct the line. This legislation enabled promoters to obtain grants and loans from the Treasury and local authorities for the building of cheap rural railways. It was hoped that the remainder of the shares would be taken up by the local gentry, merchants and farmers. The appointed engineers were Robert Elliott-Cooper and Fowler & Marshall.

The proposers were Robert How Ashton, Charles Bramall, Charles Castle, Herbert Hodkin, Joseph Hall Moore, Jonathan Smales and others. Ashton, who lived at Looschill Hall, had been an original director of the Dore and Chinley Railway.

1904 10 Feb. Property owners affected were notified and copies of all documents were made available for inspection at the residence of Mr Z. Walker in Bradwell. A public meeting was held at the *New Bath Hotel* in Bradwell, where the scheme won support subject to a level crossing near the station at Bradwell being made rather than a bridge.

Left: The route of the Hassop and Padley Railway. This line had the advantage of knowing that the Dore and Chinley Railway was highly likely to be built and could therefore link up Grindleford and Hassop and improve the journey times to Buxton as well as relieving the Peak line of traffic.

Below: Map of the proposed 'Hope and Castleton Light Railway'.

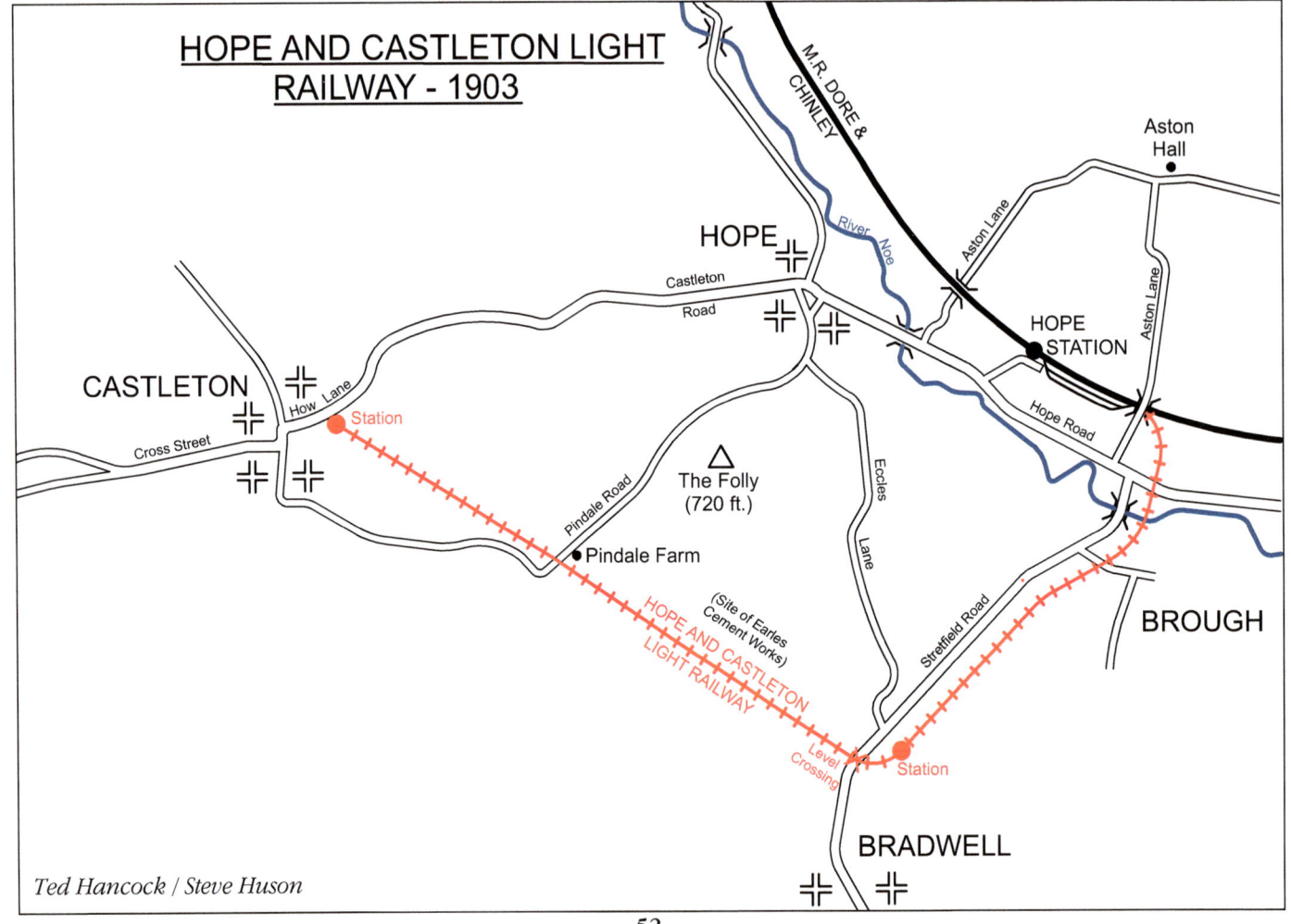

1904 26 Apr. The Light Railway Order was granted and the company was incorporated. The capital was £36,000 in £10 shares with each director being required to buy £250 of shares. The powers would lapse, unless renewed, if the line was not completed within five years. It was to be operated by either steam or electricity and was to be a standard gauge single line with additional lines at the stations. A maximum speed of 25 mph was stipulated although this was reduced to 15 mph when engines were running tender first (it would surely have been worked by small tank engines). No turntable would be permitted so presumably the turntable at Hope goods yard would have been used when required. Fares would be 3d for first, 2d for second and 1d for third class passengers.

The line was to be just short of three miles long starting from a junction with the Midland, thirty three yards east of the Aston to Bradwell road (823180). It would head in a south westerly direction over the main road and River Noe at Brough and parallel the road to Bradwell on the eastern side where a station would be built on the edge of the village. The line then headed west across the present B6049 and would skirt 'The Folly' which was 750 ft high, and terminate at Castleton on the south side of the public road called How Lane and eleven yards from the constabulary buildings (829151).

Interestingly, on the Midland Railway Distance Diagrams of 1915 the line is shown and captioned Hope and Castleton Light Railway (Proposed). On the final application the name was altered to Bradwell and Castleton Light Railway but in Apr 1904 the Light Railway Commissioners wrote about the Hope, Bradwell and Castleton Railway which offended none of the sensibilities of the villages concerned.

1910 13 Feb. The powers lapsed. Had the line been built and survived until 1929 it would have experienced a boom in traffic as, without doubt, the new cement works of G. & T. Earle would have used the line and saved themselves the expense of building a branch to the main line. The directors and shareholders would have been either bought out or seen a surge in the value of their shares. However, the journey for tourists to Castleton would have been blighted at having to run directly below the works.

Around the same time as this railway was being pursued the same promoters approached the Midland to build a similar line from Millers Dale to Tideswell and required interchange facilities with the main line. The Midland agreed, subject to the proper arrangements being entered into. Sadly this was as far as it got. The villages of Castleton, Bradwell and Tideswell were destined never to be served by a railway.

REFERENCE
DRO/Q/RP2/292

THE GRINDLEFORD, BASLOW AND BAKEWELL RAILWAY

1903 21 Jul. Starting in the same year that the Hope and Castleton Light Railway was proposed this line obtained its Act to build a 7¼ mile line from near Grindleford station to a triangular junction at Hassop. Its first directors were Joseph Wills, John Mather, William Henry Brittain (an original director of the Dore and Chinley Railway), John Henry Royce Tasker and Charles Sneath Elliot. The capital was £225,000 with 22,500 shares at £10 each.

Railway No. 1 was to be almost seven miles long. It would commence by a junction with the Dore and Chinley line near the western end of the platforms at Grindleford station to a point between Hassop village and station where the line divided. There was to be no triangular junction at Grindleford as in the Hassop and Padley Railway of twenty years earlier.

Railway No. 2 would continue towards Hassop cross roads where it turned west and passed behind the old Rowland toll bar, joining the main Manchester line near Rowland House (211788). Running powers were granted to Great Longstone station. In addition the Hassop estate gave permission for a station for passengers and local goods traffic at the Rowland toll bar (two stations right in the middle of nowhere).

Railway No. 3 was to run parallel with No. 2 for a distance before crossing the future A6020 east of Hassop station and joining the line to Bakewell at Pineapple House Farm where the Bakewell to Baslow road crossed the railway (218698): from there it would have running powers into Bakewell.

A 400 yards viaduct near Grindleford Bridge and a two span bridge to cross the River Derwent at Froggatt, to be of an ornamental design to satisfy the owners of Stoke Hall, would be built. Stoke Hall was also keen to protect its land until the line reached Calver cross roads where the owners required a station to be built, near the *Eyre Arms*, stipulating that at least two trains a day each way must stop. The route then veered left to follow the River Derwent towards Bubnell, which it passed on the left. Before Bubnell an 800 yards tunnel was required in the Townend Wood area (247733) to satisfy the Duke of Devonshire. The route onwards from Bubnell to Hassop also required a further 340 yards tunnel. Whilst the line's route would have included Baslow it was a more difficult prospect than the Hassop and Padley Railway's with the Chatsworth, Stoke Hall and Hassop estates to cross all requiring demanding and expensive protection.

1908. Like its 1884 predecessor it failed to gain sufficient financial support and its powers lapsed.

REFERENCES
DRO/Q/RP2/287
London Gazette 27496 18 Nov 1902 pages 7407/8

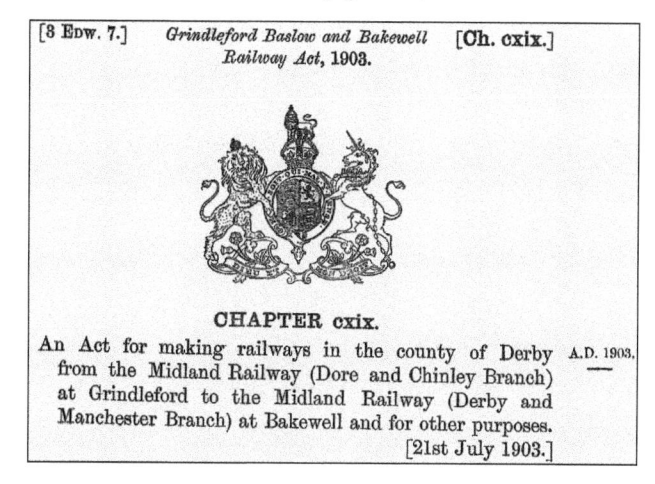

This is part of the title page of the Act authorising the line.
Glynn Waite collection

GRINDLEFORD, BASLOW & BAKEWELL RAILWAY 1903

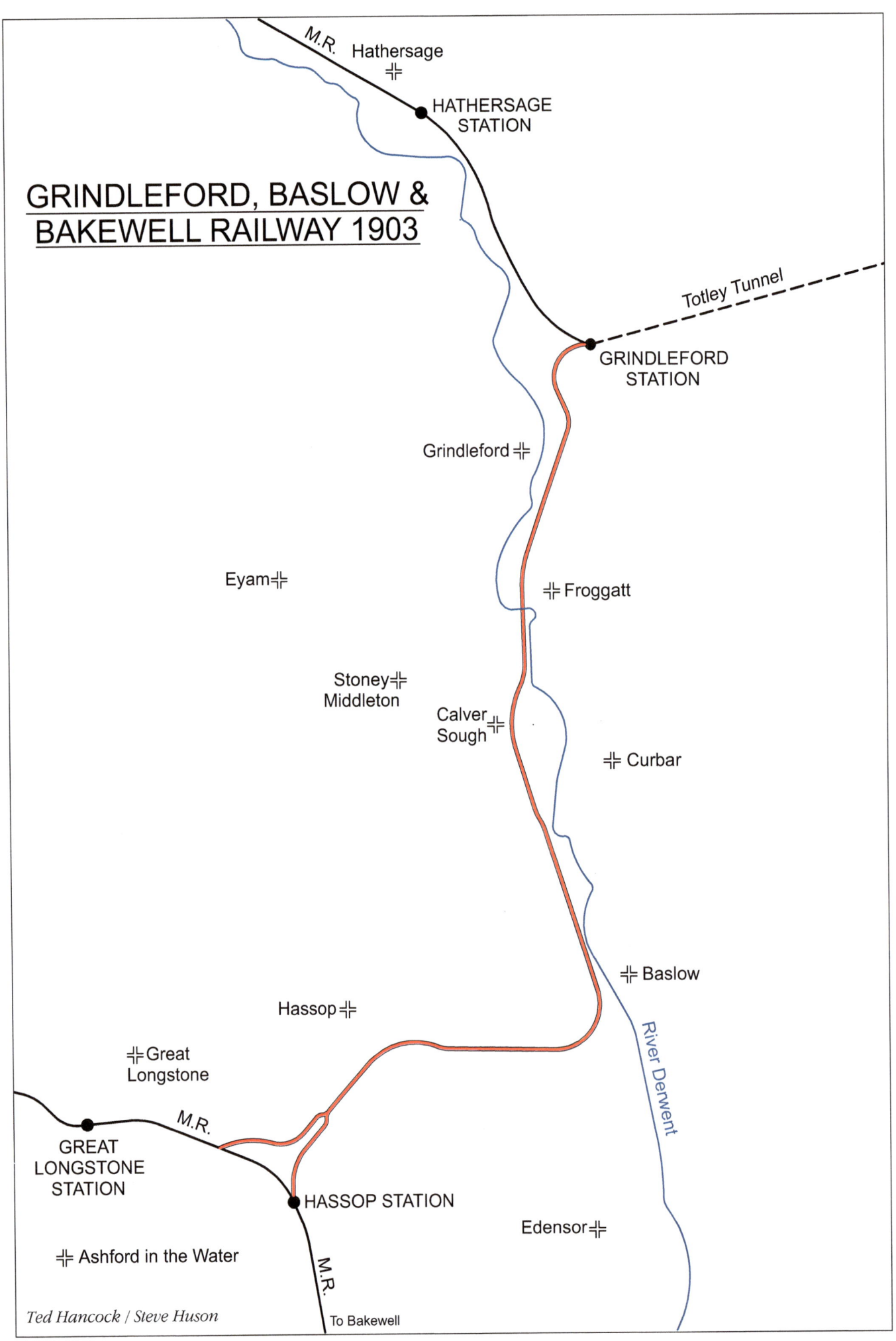

Ted Hancock / Steve Huson

The proposed route was to be a two track line whose main purpose was to connect the Midland's Dore and Chinley line with the same company's line from Ambergate to Buxton and Manchester, whilst serving villages on the way and particularly the quarries and mines of Stoney Middleton and Eyam.

THE DERWENT VALLEY, CALVER AND BAKEWELL RAILWAY

This line was the final effort to build a line between Grindleford and Hassop and did so in the difficult economic climate after the First World War. At first Bakewell UDC opposed it but later said that this was a complete misunderstanding, so even at its birth there was confusion. This was hardly an encouraging portent.

1920 4 Aug. Its Act was obtained and the first directors were Charles Paxham Markham, Sydney Jessop Robinson, Peter MacGregor, William Tozer, Herbert Barber, Herbert Brooke Taylor, Charles Henry Glossop and Percy Joseph Turner. The capital was set at £225,000 in 22,500 shares at £10 each. This was the same capital as the 1903 scheme but was cheaper in real terms because of the inflation of the intervening period. The appointed engineer was Mr Markham, although another source names Robert Elliot Cooper and whether Markham was the named director is not known. The line was also unofficially known as the Hassop Light Railway.

Railway No. 1 was to be 6¾ miles long and would start at a junction with the Dore and Chinley line 440 yards 'west from a point opposite the centre of the platform waiting-sheds at Grindleford station'. It would terminate at a junction with the Ambergate to Chinley line 'at or about the north-western face of the bridge carrying the public road between Bakewell and Baslow over the said railway, such bridge adjoining Pineapple House.' These are the same starting and finishing points as the 1903 line.

Railway No. 2 was just 280 yards long and would have a junction with the Dore and Chinley line 740 yards north west of the same point as in railway No. 1 at Grindleford station.

Railway No. 3 would be 700 yards long by a junction with railway No. 1 at a point 350 yards nearer than that of the 1903 line to Hassop cross roads and join the Midland Peak line in the same place as the 1903 scheme.

However, unlike the 1903 scheme, it proceeds roughly via the 1884 line missing out Baslow entirely. There was to be a tunnel of 767 yards between Calver and Hassop village. Although the Chatsworth, Hassop and Stoke Hall estates included conditions in the Act none were so onerous as those required in 1903.

1925. With insufficient progress made the scheme lapsed and was no more.

[10 & 11 Geo. 5.] *Derwent Valley Calver and Bakewell Railway Act, 1920.* [Ch. xcix.]

CHAPTER xcix.

An Act for incorporating the Derwent Valley Calver and Bakewell Railway Company and authorising them to construct railways in the county of Derby and for other purposes. A.D. 1920. [4th August 1920.]

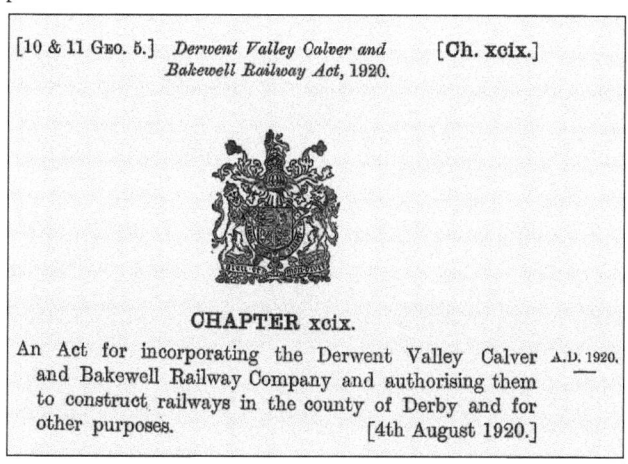

From the first page of the Act. *Glynn Waite collection*

REFERENCES

DRO/Q/RP2/313
London Gazette 31656 25 Nov 1919 pages 14454-7

As we have seen there had been a history of proposals unable to raise initial capital without the financial backing of the large companies. In this case, and other schemes between Grindleford and Hassop, the only large company that could have been interested was the Midland Railway who would, no doubt, have welcomed the shortcut. However, the company must have calculated that the returns would have hardly justified the capital outlay. In this the Midland was almost certainly right.

LINES THAT DIRECTLY RIVALLED THE DORE AND CHINLEY RAILWAY

LANCASHIRE DERBYSHIRE AND EAST COAST RAILWAY

This line was by far the most important and biggest threat to the Midland and received its Act when the building of the Dore and Chinley Railway was half way towards completion. It was partially built, but not in our area of interest, and was an extraordinary proposition at this late period of railway development. Had it been completed it would have given the Great Northern Railway direct access to Manchester and did provide the Great Eastern Railway access to the Nottinghamshire coalfields which it hardly used. William Arkwright was the first chairman with Emerson Bainbridge as the company engineer. A year later Arkwright resigned and Bainbridge took over. He was the largest lessee of the north Derbyshire coalfield, being managing director of the Bolsover Colliery Company and the principal proprietor of the Nunnery colliery in Sheffield with its annual output of half a million tons of coal. He was also an eminent engineer in his own right. The line became known as the 'East to West Line' but railwaymen called it, less respectfully, the 'Clog and Knocker'. Sir Edward Watkin, of the MSLR, thought the idea 'as ridiculous a scheme as has ever been planned'.

1891 5 Aug. The Act of incorporation was obtained and was the largest railway scheme, both in capital and mileage, to have been approved by Parliament in one go. Capital of £5,000,000 was sanctioned, with an additional £1,666,000 of borrowing for 161 miles of line despite the opposition of the MSLR, MR and LNWR. The estimated cost of the line was £4,227,522 and the time needed for the works was estimated at four years. 10,000 men would be required to build it. It enjoyed the support of many Derbyshire and Nottinghamshire coal mine owners, including the Staveley Coal and Iron Company, who between them produced 10,000,000 tons of coal annually of which the LDECR would transport a large share. A total of 100 petitions supported the enterprise.

The main line was to run from a deep water dock on the Manchester Ship Canal at Warrington to new docks at Sutton on Sea and was divided into four sections.

Section 1 started from Warrington to Knutsford, where there would be a curve to join the Cheshire Lines Committee (CLC), and on to Macclesfield with a southerly connection to the North Staffordshire Railway (NSR). At Prestbury a branch would reach Cheadle Hulme, Cheadle and Heaton Mersey where junctions would be formed with the LNWR, CLC and MR.

Section 2 took the line up to Goyts Moss, on a gradient of 1 in 72, and then through Axe Edge by a tunnel of 4,210 yards in length at 1 in 100 to a station in Buxton near to the town hall and market place, although later in the year a deviation was sought. It would then descend Ashwood Dale, at a higher level than the existing Midland Millers Dale to Buxton branch, and would cross the A6 at Topley Pike keeping at a high elevation, with the Midland main line in Chee Dale and Millers Dale on its left and Priestcliffe on its right. Passing through Brushfield, before entering a 360 yard tunnel, it would cross Monsal Dale on a high and wide viaduct. John Noble, the Midland's general manager and director, remarked 'I shall believe that viaduct when I see it'. Plunging into another tunnel of 813 yards followed by another of 340 yards, Little and Great Longstone were passed on the right and then the line would pass between Rowland and Hassop village. Swinging right over a viaduct of 554 yards in length and 122 ft in height it would cross the River Derwent and follow the river valley, keeping Calver on the left and Baslow on the right. The route to Chesterfield involved two tunnels of 2,750 yards and 750 yards respectively through East Moor. Before these it passed Robin Hood (270721) on the left and diverged to the north under the Bleak House road junction (302758) before skirting Linacre Wood reservoirs and cutting between Cutthorpe and Barlow to Four Lane Ends. Here a junction facing Chesterfield took a branch to Sheepbridge colliery and iron works, which had an annual output of 800,000 tons of coal and iron. The main line would then descend on gradients between 1 in 40 and 1 in 70 into Chesterfield keeping Newbold on its left.

This second section would have required eight tunnels, not to mention Monsal Dale viaduct costed at an incredible £73,670 all on its own.

It will scarcely come as a surprise to note that a further survey was made to avoid the Monsal Dale viaduct and to cross the Midland at Chee Dale instead. This deviation would have started at Chee Tor and gone via Tideswell Dale and through Stoney Middleton to Knouchley (750245) there joining the original line and allowing Tideswell and Eyam to be served.

Section 3 went from Chesterfield to Lincoln with stations at Arkwright Town, Bolsover, Scarcliffe and Langwith Junction from where a branch went to Beighton. From Langwith the line went on to Warsop, Edwinstowe, Ollerton, Boughton and Tuxford where a connection was made with the GNR main line. Onwards to Dukeries Junction, Clifton on Trent, Doddington and Harby and Skellingthorpe the line then reached the edge of Lincoln. A curious omission was that no passenger station was ever planned in Lincoln.

Section 4 was to have been from Lincoln, via Alford, to Mumby Road on the Sutton and Willoughby Railway, which was worked by the GNR, thence reaching a new dock at Sutton on Sea by running powers.

1892 7 Jun. Work commenced on the Chesterfield to Lincoln section.

1895 6 Jul. An Act was obtained to abandon the line west of Chesterfield which, whilst it would be a relief to the Midland, was hardly a great surprise to anybody else!

1897. The Chesterfield to Lincoln section opened for freight in its entirety.

1900. The branch to Beighton was opened for goods and the Sheffield District Railway opened from Treeton Junction to Brightside Junction.

1907. The company was bought by the GCR and took over the operation of the Sheffield District Railway.

Like many independent lines the LDECR failed in its overall objective simply because it could not raise sufficient capital and only succeeded in building the Chesterfield to Lincoln section largely because of the support of the Great Eastern Railway. Success would only have been achieved if all the colliery owners and iron barons, those who would have benefited from the line, had been prepared to finance it which, in the event, they were not.

REFERENCES

Derbyshire Record Office

Dow George – *Great Central Vol 3*. Ian Allan 1965

Cupit J. / Taylor W. – *The Lancashire Derbyshire & East Coast Railway*. Oakwood 2nd ed 1984

Wilmot David – *Lancashire, Derbyshire and East Coast Railway: Development of a New Independent Railway in the Late 19th Century*. DVM Verlag Dr Muller 2009

Booth Chris – *The Lancashire, Derbyshire and East Coast Railway: Chesterfield to Langwith Junction, the Beighton Branch and Sheffield District Railway*. Fonthill Media 2017

Gilks David – *Mr. Arkwright's Railway*. Back Track Vol 16 No. 4 Apr 2002

Hunter Zoe Elizabeth. *Tracing the Lancashire, Derbyshire & East Coast Railway Volume 4: The Abandoned Lines*. Lightning Source (2018)

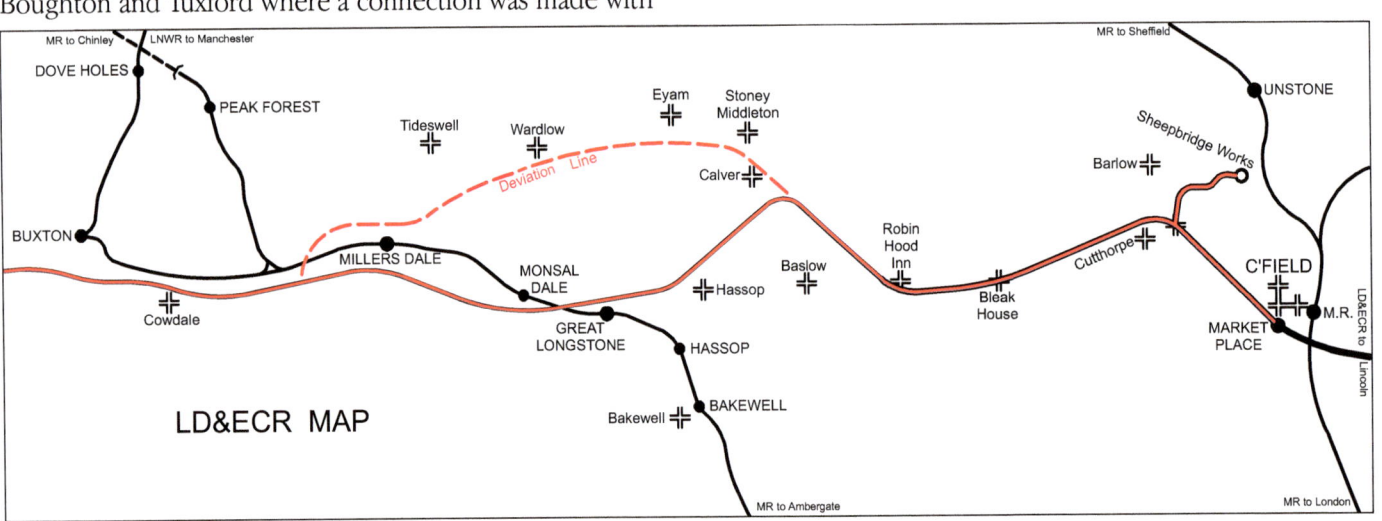

A map of the Buxton to Chesterfield section of this ambitious line. It is taken from the official one inch map which was drawn for the second section. Unfortunately it does not show the tunnels although they are alluded to in the text.

The Monsal viaduct would have been the highest viaduct in Britain it being four times higher than Headstone viaduct near it. Each span was to be 150 ft in length and 200 ft above the lower viaduct, which itself is 75 ft above the bed of the river, and 543 yards long.

It would not be built with the traditional stone arches which were considered to be too expensive, but with steel peers from the foundations and cross girders, there being other structures abroad that were higher and longer.

There were considerable concerns about the safety of this structure but the company persuaded doubters that 'the railway passage can, as a rule, easily adapt himself to circumstances, and it is probable that a few years hence travellers will hardly give danger a thought as they whisk along this viaduct – high though it may be. It is nearly as high as the clock at Westminster'.

Chesterfield Market Place station was at the eastern end of the unbuilt Section 2 and was the headquarters of the company. It was opened and named 'Chesterfield' on 8 Mar 1897. It was renamed 'Chesterfield Market Place' on 1 Jan 1907. The section from Langwith Junction to Chesterfield was closed for passengers on 3 Dec 1951 because of the high costs of maintaining Bolsover tunnel and concerns about the Doe Lea viaduct and also the limited amount of traffic. However goods services continued until 4 Mar 1957. From some point between 1951 and 1956, the station building was used by Charles Credland Ltd, a paint and wallpaper firm where they remained until the building was demolished in Apr 1973. There is now no trace that it ever existed. This photograph of the entrance was taken shortly before it was demolished. *Author's collection*

Chesterfield Market Place station's most famous occasion was the two weeks in Aug 1948 when the newly formed British Railways' mounted an exhibition to commemorate the centenary of George Stephenson's death at Tapton House in the town, he having moved there when he retired. To mark the occasion rolling stock and several locomotives were exhibited and on 14 Aug 1948 we can see ex LNER B1 4-6-0 No. 61085 when only two years old and ex GCR D10 No. 62658 *Prince George*. Behind it, not on the picture, was Rebuilt 'Patriot' No. 45529 *Stephenson*. All were lined out in British Railways' new lined black livery with its new name on the tender. Note the two boys peering at the working parts of the B1 and the toddler gazing up at the mighty machine. *Ken Boulter © Ted Hancock*

BAKEWELL AND SHEFFIELD ELECTRIC LIGHT RAILWAY

This proposal for a standard gauge tramway was not quite the same threat to the Midland hegemony as the LDECR but is of interest to record. The use of electricity for urban transportation was an exciting development at this time and the idea of tramways over longer distances seemed a logical extension of the technology and came to fruition with the eight mile Llandudno and Colwyn Bay Tramway, which was authorised in 1898 and opened in 1907. The Midland themselves, a year earlier, opened the Burton and Ashby Light Railway which was a 3ft 6in gauge line and ran over ten miles as an overhead electric tramway.

1897. An article in the *Derbyshire Times* reported a plan for an electric tramway from Bakewell to Totley which had been presented to the Bakewell and Baslow district councils for approval.

Starting at Bakewell station and running along the main road it would pass Pilsley, about 400 yards to the north, and then go to Baslow and Totley at the Sheffield boundary, which was then just north of the present Dore station, by a 600 ft climb over the moors. This would be a standard gauge single line throughout with passing places and having overhead trolley wires. The generating station would have been situated central to the route and have been consistent with the convenience of the landowners. It had to have access to a sufficient water supply to feed the boilers and for condensing purposes with the company selling in bulk the current so produced for lighting and power to the villages en route. It would be a light railway carrying merchandise, household goods and other light materials in trailers attached to the cars which would provide a half hourly service.

An application to the Light Railway Commissioners was to be submitted in May 1895 and construction would have started within twelve months. The capital required was estimated at £120,000. Intriguingly the application details that the light railway would feed the tramway at Bakewell (never built) and probably join the Sheffield tramway system, although the first electric powered route was not running until 1899 and the Abbey Lane route, which was the nearest point to Totley, was not opened until 1927.

The following week the same newspaper reported a more realistic scheme by F. Houlton Wrench AMICE of Sheffield, linking Bakewell and the newly opened station at Grindleford via Calver and Baslow. The report argued that this would save the 600 ft climb over the moors from Baslow, with the risk of snow in winter, and would allow passengers from Sheffield to reach Baslow in forty five minutes and Bakewell in an hour by train and tram.

It was proposed to construct the single line with passing places along the existing roads and to construct a new carriage road from Grindleford to Froggatt, along which the new line would run. This would shorten the existing road by about half a mile, miss the steep gradients near Stoke Hall and reduce the rise between Calver and Grindleford by about 200 ft. A new road bridge would be built nearer the church at Baslow doing away with the then existing dangerous structure.

The capital required would be a more sensible £90,000.

EPILOGUE

Had any of these schemes come to fruition what would have been the highlights for the railway enthusiast of the day? There are many, but here are a few that caught the imagination.

1: Dropping 658 ft on an inclined plane from near the summit of Lose Hill to the River Noe in the entrance to the Edale valley on the High Peak Rail-Road of 1815. One to watch, rather than travel on, I suspect.

2: The Sheffield and Manchester Railway of 1831 ascending Rushup Edge from the Chapel end by two inclined planes, the first of a mile in length with a gradient of 1 in 18 and the second, in a tunnel, of three quarters of a mile rising at 1 in 32. There then followed an even more frightening descent on two more inclined planes, one in a tunnel. Each coach had its own brakesman which could also be worked by passengers. No thank you!

3: The two cut and cover tunnels in Chatsworth Park for the alternative route via the Hope and Edale valleys of the MBMMJR to Manchester in 1846.

4: Riding into the Sheffield station of the LNWR backed Sheffield, Buxton and Liverpool Railway at the junction of Division Street and Cambridge Street.

5: Riding on a narrow gauge train on gradients of as much as 1 in 37 up Moscar from Ladybower before entering a mile long tunnel near the summit on the Sheffield and Buxton Narrow Gauge Railway of 1872.

6: Watching LNWR trains on the Buxton, Chapel-en-le-Frith and Sheffield Railway which had started at Cricket Inn Road, and Midland trains from the Sheffield Midland station race each other on parallel lines up the 1 in 100 gradient through Heeley, Millhouses and Beauchief after the completion of their respective lines in the 1870s.

7: The triangular junction at Grindleford to link the Hassop and Padley Railway with the planned Midland Railway after its completion in 1894.

8: Watching coal trains climb the 1 in 40 and 1 in 70 gradients out of Chesterfield towards Newbold on the LDECR.

9: Spending 3d to travel first class for nearly three miles on the Hope and Castleton Light Railway. The one coach train simmering in the small station at How Lane, Castleton would have added to the already rich delights of that beautiful village.

10: Riding on the Bakewell and Sheffield Electric Light Railway as it crossed the A625 road on its journey from Longshaw onto Totley Moss with the famous pole nearby.

11: And, of course, the viaduct across Monsal Dale of the LDECR.

CHAPTER 2
HOW THE RAILWAY REACHED DORE AND TOTLEY

A contemporary map of Midland Railway lines in the Peak District in 1876.

Author's collection

The first railway from central Sheffield up the Sheaf valley to Dore and Totley was proposed in 1813 by the eminent canal engineer William Chapman. He envisaged a canal and railway to link with the Peak Forest Canal by a rail road from Castle Orchards to Strawberry Lea, above the present Totley Tunnel, using edge rails and horse drawn wagons. He showed that this would be cheaper than a canal with all its locks.

This was followed by the ill fated Sheffield and Manchester Railway of 1831 which was George Stephenson's plan to build a line from Sheffield to the Peak Forest Canal using inclined planes. The line would have started at Canal Wharf in Sheffield and ascend by an inclined plane of 1 in 32 to a tunnel under East Moor to Hathersage Booths. Henry Sanderson, the Sheffield surveyor, proved that the scheme was impractical and the line was not proceeded with.

In 1838 The Sheffield and Rotherham Railway opened its line from the Wicker in Sheffield to Westgate in Rotherham. In 1840 its isolation was ended when the North Midland Railway, from Derby to Leeds, was opened with a connection at Rotherham. On 10 May 1844 the two railways became founding members of the Midland Railway.

1843 saw the proposal for the Sheffield and Chesterfield Junction Railway which would have run from a junction with the Woodhead line at Bridgehouses, Sheffield to Lockoford, near Chesterfield to join the North Midland Railway. The line would have travelled east of Totley through Greenhill to Dronfield. The line was supported by the Sheffield, Ashton under Lyne and Manchester Railway but failed because of inaccuracies in the schedules of property for compulsory purchase.

At the height of the 'Second Railway Mania' in 1845 the Manchester, Sheffield and Midland Junction Railway was promoted for a line up the Sheaf valley and down the Drone valley. However, this failed because of its steep gradients and the objections of Robert Stephenson, representing the Midland's interests, and the Duke of Norfolk, whose coal monopoly in Sheffield was threatened by the Dronfield collieries. A second attempt to gain Parliamentary approval with easier gradients also failed a year later.

Also in 1845 the Sheffield, Bakewell & West Midland Railway was proposed from the Midland's Wicker station up the Sheaf valley and over Totley Moss to Grindleford and Bakewell. There were branches to Ashford in the Water and from Millhouses to Chesterfield via Greenhill, Dronfield, Unston and the west side of the Drone to Brimington.

By the 1860s Sheffield was booming. In 1801 the population was just 31,000 but by 1851 had risen to 135,000. The second half of the century saw the population nearly treble. Alongside the Midland's Sheffield and Rotherham line Charles Cammell established the Cyclops Works in 1845, Firth's followed in 1852 and John Brown set up the Atlas Works in 1856. His was the first large works to adopt the Bessemer process in 1860 and two years later was employing 3,000 men. By the time the Sheffield to Chesterfield line was opened in 1870 Sheffield was producing 250,000 tons of steel a year, much of it in the form of steel rails for the railway industry. In spite of all this the Midland was still complacent enough to leave Sheffield on the end of a branch. The building of a line south from Sheffield came not a moment too soon and required an immense concerted effort by local industrialists and town leaders.

In 1861 the Midland Railway planned a branch to Dronfield from Chesterfield and John Crossley, the company's engineer, was instructed to make the necessary survey and plans. The following year a deputation from Sheffield town council met the Midland directors at Derby to try to persuade them to extend the line to Sheffield. A high level line to Bridgehouses and a low level line up the Sheaf valley were discussed. There was much mistrust of the Midland Railway among Sheffield's industrialists and town leaders because of the perceived neglect of Sheffield's needs by providing the town with nothing more than a branch from Rotherham. The charges for the transport of goods were also widely criticised – it was said to be cheaper to send a ton of steel to New York than it was to Birmingham via the Midland Railway. George Stephenson was also not held in high esteem due to his decision to build the North Midland Railway from Chesterfield to Rotherham via Staveley, Eckington and Beighton because of his aversion to gradients. Furthermore he followed this by poorly surveying the Sheffield and Manchester Railway which collapsed in a recriminatory atmosphere.

December of 1862 saw a large public meeting held in Sheffield, chaired by the mayor John Brown of the Atlas Works, where it was learned that the Midland planned, in the next Parliamentary session, to seek an Act for a direct line from Chesterfield to Sheffield via Dronfield. An alternative proposal for an independent line was promulgated to pressurise the Midland to follow it through. With this in mind a committee of thirty five was set up to pursue the alternative line.

Their misgivings were not misplaced because it took until the following November for the Midland to finally deposit plans for a line of 13½ miles from Lockoford, a mile north of Chesterfield, where it would form a junction with the Midland's existing Sheffield and Rotherham line at Grimesthorpe.

The route was to go via Whittington Moor, Sheepbridge, through the Broomhouse tunnel of ninety two yards and eventually up a 1 in 102 incline to Dronfield from where the summit at the Dronfield end of Bradway Tunnel was planned. The tunnel would be 2,027 yards long and emerge at Bradway where it would descend on a curve at 1 in 100 to Totley and then straighten via Beauchief, Millhouses and Heeley to a new station over the confluence of the Sheaf and Porter rivers at the Ponds. A 519 yard branch, on a 1 in 45 incline, was to be made to the MSLR from Cricket Inn Road, now Nunnery main line curve.

The committee pressed ahead with its alternative line which rejoiced in the name of the Sheffield, Chesterfield, Bakewell, Ashbourne and Stafford and Uttoxeter Junction Railway. This sonorous title was thankfully shortened a few months later to the Sheffield, Chesterfield and Staffordshire Railway. The high level

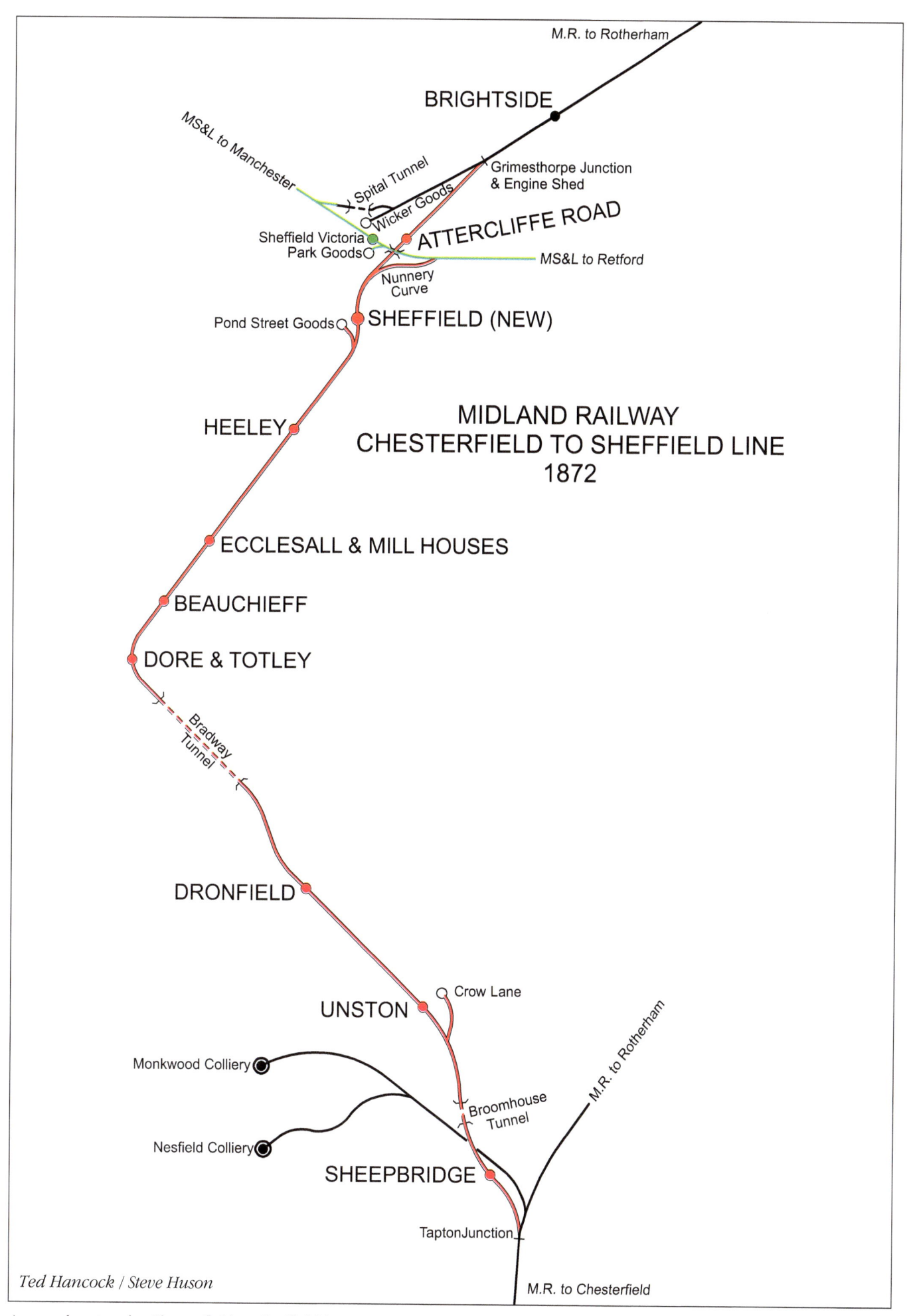

A map showing the Chesterfield to Sheffield line in 1872, two years after its opening – this date has been chosen so Dore and Totley station, which opened in that year, can be included. A number of lines and features had not yet been built, including the Unston goods loop, apart from the first section to Crow Lane, Ecclesall (later Millhouses) engine shed, Heeley carriage and coal sidings, Queens Road goods yard, the Nunnery colliery branch and Attercliffe goods yard, which became a joint undertaking with the LDECR.

Tapton Junction, where the new southbound line from Sheffield on the left, joined the original George Stephenson North Midland Railway. In this Mar 1962 view, new Derby built Type 4 locomotives Nos. D167 and D168, in green livery, head towards Gateshead to take up their duties in the north east. They were later renumbered 46030 and 46031 and designated class 46.
Geoff Newall © Ted Hancock

The first station along the line from the Chesterfield end was Sheepbridge which was just north of the junction with the Chesterfield to Rotherham line. On 8 Oct 1897 it changed its name to Sheepbridge and Whittington Moor in which guise it is seen here before reverting back to Sheepbridge in 1951.
Author's collection

The most impressive structure on the line after Bradway Tunnel was the seven arch viaduct at Unston, which is rather overblown in this lithograph from F. S. Williams' The Midland Railway; Its Rise and Progress. He comments that 'direct communication, such as it was, between the two towns had for some time been carried on by means of an extraordinary vehicle, not unlike an old fashioned diligence, which might for years afterwards be seen turned out to grass and rottenness in a field at Dronfield, and which has been faithfully depicted in the accompanying illustration'.

Dronfield station looking towards Bradway Tunnel around 1900. The Sheffield to Chesterfield road is on the right. The booking office and waiting room is on the up side and is identical to those found on Millhouses and Beauchief stations.

The footbridge is probably the one installed at the opening.

Author's collection

Looking south towards Bradway curve and the tunnel from the down platform of Dore and Totley station. Although undated the photographs were probably taken in the 1880s or early 1890s. This can be discerned because of the slotted post signals and the inside keyed rails. However, the station and bridge look new which would make the date a decade earlier. The footbridge was replaced following the widening of 1901 to 1903 and was moved to Borrowash station on the Derby to Trent line in 1903. Other known examples of this type of structure were at Ashchurch, north of Cheltenham and Berkeley Road on the Gloucester to Bristol main line. However, this one had a longer lattice girder. Note the infill panelling below the two sets of steps. The distinctive brick structure waiting room on the left did not survive the widening, it being replaced by a timbered structure on what became an island platform. Note the five examples of the graceful Midland lamps and the straight fencing which extends beyond the platforms to the railings over the River Sheaf and also the track from the road to the back of the station and the original Twenty Well Sick (later Lane) arched bridge which was to be replaced by a flat girder bridge when the Chinley line was built. *Author's collection*

This view is looking north. The station buildings on the left survived the arrival of the line to Chinley and the later quadrupling and still exists today. Note the lamps on the steps of the bridge, the bracket lamp on the station building on the right, the large station name board with an ampersand and the station master's house in the background with the signal box to its right. It was not a station of great significance at this time as it served a very small community and was not provided with goods facilities.

Author's collection

Midland Railway.

OPENING OF THE DORE & TOTLEY STATION.

The DORE and TOTLEY STATION, between Dronfield and Beauchieff, on the SHEFFIELD and CHESTERFIELD LINE, will be opened for Passenger Traffic on THURSDAY, FEBRUARY 1st, and on and from that date Trains will call there until further notice as under:—

STATIONS.	WEEK-DAYS.							SUNDAYS.		
	a.m.	a.m.	p.m.	p.m.	p.m.	p.m.	p.m.	a.m.	p.m.	p.m.
Leeds....... dep.	5.40	9.47	..	1.20	2.45	5.20	..	7. 0	..	2.15
Sheffield .... „	8. 5	11.10	1.10	2.42	4.30	7.36	8.20	9. 3	2.15	4.17
Dore and Totley .	8.23	11.28	1.28	2.59	4.48	7.54	8.38	9.22	2.33	4.35
Dronfield.... arr.	8.28	11.33	1.33	3. 4	4.53	8. 0	8.43	9.27	2.40	4.40
Chesterfield.. „	8.44	11.50	Runs on Saturdays only.	3.20	5.10	8.17	A	9.44	..	4.58
Nottingham „	10.55	1.15		5.20	7. 0	10.30	..	11.45	..	7.15
Derby....... „	9.55	12.50		4.25	7.35	9.25	..	10.55	..	6. 5
	a.m.	a.m.	a.m.	p.m.	p.m.	p.m.	p.m.	a.m.	p.m.	p.m.
Derby....... dep.	6. 0	7.30	10.20	1.30	3. 0	5.40		7. 0	..	6.35
Nottingham „	..	7. 5	9.25	Saturdays only.	12.40	3.20	4.55		6.25	..	5.40
Chesterfield.. „	7. 3	8.43	11. 7		2.35	5. 5	6.51	8. 3	..	7.35
Dronfield.... „	7.19	9. 0	11.24	2.30	2.51	5.22	7. 9	8.20	6.25	7.52
Dore and Totley .	7.24	9. 5	11.29	2.35	2.56	5.27	7.14	8.25	6.30	7.57
Sheffield..... arr.	7.42	9.25	11.46	2.55	3.15	5.45	7.33	8.43	6.50	8.18
Leeds....... „	9.45	11.55	1.38	..	5.15	..	8.50	10.45	..	10.20

A Runs through to Chesterfield on Saturdays.

JAMES ALLPORT, General-Manager.

Derby, January 29th, 1872.

Bemrose and Sons, Printers, London and Derby.

A specially published announcement and timetable to advertise the opening of Dore & Totley station on 1 Feb 1872, two years to the day after the opening of the line. Seven trains a day stopped in both directions with an additional train on Saturdays, reduced to just three on Sunday. Eighteen minutes were allowed for the five miles at 1 in 100 from Sheffield which included stops at Heeley, Ecclesall & Mill Houses and Beauchieff stations. In the other direction but with the gradients in favour the times were still the same. We are not told how many additional trains did not call. The station at this time was of little importance as it was not yet a junction and, like Beauchieff, did not serve a significant population. Thus most expresses passed it by without stopping and at considerable speed in the up direction.

Laurence Knighton collection.

Beauchief and Abbey Dale station from Abbey Lane bridge looking towards Sheffield. The Midland could not make up its mind what to call this station. At its opening on 1 Feb 1870 it was Abbey Houses; two months later it had the arcane spelling Beuchieff; on 1 May 1874 it became Beauchieff & Abbey Dale; on 1 May 1888 Beauchief and Abbey Dale before finally settling down with the abbreviated Beauchief on 19 Mar 1914, a name it carried until final closure. We are looking towards Dore and Totley station. Abbey Lane bridge, the station masters house and the waiting room can be seen. The entrance to the goods yard is to the right, behind is what became the Beauchief hotel, which was not built or owned by the Midland. The large nameboard on the down platform is not legible unfortunately. *Fotopic*

route, previously discussed at the Derby meeting, was adopted. This line was to start near Brightside, between Sheffield and Rotherham, and go via Grimesthorpe, Burngreave and Bridgehouses to a central station at Townhead Street and then proceed to Broomhall through a tunnel. Ecclesall Road would be crossed on a viaduct before tunnelling under Sharrow to Button Hill. Traversing Ecclesall woods, where a junction would be made near Beauchief, the double track line would follow the present route through a tunnel at Bradway to Dronfield, Unston and Newbold to join the Midland just north of Chesterfield station. From the Ecclesall woods junction a single line would skirt Totley and pass through a tunnel to Smeekley Wood, below Owler Bar, where there would be a branch through the Cordwell valley to the Chesterfield line at Newbold. There were additional proposals for lines around Unston and Sheepbridge. Brassey & Field, one of the largest railway contractors, would build the line and were willing to subscribe a large amount of the capital.

The Midland board were astounded when they learned of this rival scheme. The mayor, John Brown, became the first chairman and enjoyed considerable support in Sheffield but not to the extent that the towns' leaders and industrialists were prepared to pay for it. The 8% deposit was only raised by taking out a loan, from the Guardian Insurance Company, which breached company law. It had no shareholders and the necessary three names of the depositors all had the same address but, despite this, it still managed to pass Parliamentary scrutiny.

So in Mar 1864 both Bills were read for the first time but a parliamentary committee rejected the alternative proposal unanimously. Thus the Midland's Bill received the Royal Assent on 25 Jul 1864.

The first sod was cut at Bradway in 1865. The new line was to prove expensive for several reasons; the Bradway tunnel, the cost of compensating land and property owners including the owners of 1,000 newly built houses at Heeley, the Duke of Norfolk's insistence on a covered tunnel across his land and the difficulties of building a station above the confluence of the Porter and Sheaf rivers not to mention the viaduct at Unston.

On 1 Feb 1870 the line was opened without any ceremony, as far as the Midland was concerned, although it caused great excitement all along the line. The stations at Unston (Unstone), Dronfield, Abbey Houses, Ecclesall (renamed Ecclesall & Mill Houses on 1 Oct 1871), Heeley, Sheffield New station (renamed Sheffield Midland in 1876) and Attercliffe Road were all in use on the opening day. Sheepbridge opened six months later (although another source has it opening from the beginning) but Dore and Totley did not open for passengers until 1 Feb 1872.

Mention should be made of the northern exit from the Sheffield New station. F. S. Williams in 'The Midland Railway; Its Rise and Progress' (1876) comments 'We pass through heavy and difficult works, in what is called 'The Park'. This is a high hill of sandstone overlaying coal measures and clay; but the stone had been quarried, and nothing but debris left in its place: and the coal had been 'got', so that, as Mr Crossley remarked, 'We dare not tunnel. The only course left was to make an open cutting for about half a mile, with an immense number of bridges, till we came out in the valley of the Don.'

The line became part of the Midland main line although for many years a number of expresses to Leeds still followed the Old Road via Beighton. The first timetable listed ten through weekday trains from Sheffield to London, plus four stopping trains at the local stations to Chesterfield. In the other direction there were eight through trains and six local trains. The fastest trains to London took four hours ten minutes, fifteen minutes longer than the rival routes of the MSLR and GNR. However, the Midland reduced fares to London. The reporter for the *Railway News* stated that from the beginning seventy nine passenger trains used the new Sheffield station.

There were goods yards at Pond Street (1870), Queens Road (1892), Heeley station (1870) and carriage sidings and a coal depot south of Heeley (1893). Sidings to Hodkin and Jones, Black's Timber Merchants, and Laycock Engineering were also laid in later. A branch which left the main line between the Midland station and Attercliffe Road was put into Nunnery colliery during 1886. On the Chesterfield side a short branch to Broomhouse colliery (1875) was laid in. The Unston goods loop was working to Crow Lane on the opening day of the whole line and on

Heeley station looking north towards Sheffield with Havelock bridge faintly visible. It was built on the site of the old Heeley mill. This was a rapidly expanding area of the town at this time with manufacturing units surrounding the station and workmen's housing spreading up the hill to the right to the inevitable chimneys occupying the Queens Road area. It was built above the surrounding area and was on a cramped site. From Havelock bridge the line followed the River Sheaf southwards going over Cutlers Walk below Cutlers Bank, behind the Sheaf Street Primitive Methodist Chapel and over the lower end of Sheaf Street (now Gleadless Road). London Road was then crossed on a skewed bridge. This view shows a siding line at the back of the down platform, and a line to a cattle dock. The water tower partially blocks the view of the signalman. Two early forms of ground signal can be seen in the fore and middle ground. A group of female passengers stand on the up platform.

Picture Sheffield.
Sheffield Libraries

The exterior of Sheffield Midland station as built in 1870 as seen in 1896. It looks like the entrance of a station serving a medium sized market rather than a large industrial town. *C.H. Lee. Picture Sheffield. Sheffield Libraries*

Sheffield Midland station in its original form. We are looking from the north end with seven lines and five platforms visible. The overall canopy only covers the south end, whilst the near end has two distinctive types of cover. Sheaf Street is over the wall on the right. The retaining wall on the left can still be seen today. Granville Street is behind it. The train on the right is standing in the Rotherham Dock which was the place where Queen Victoria disembarked on her State visit in 1897. *Author's collection*

It is 12 Jan 1911 and this is the spot, deep in the heart of industrial Sheffield, where the new line met the original Sheffield and Rotherham Railway. The name of Grimesthorpe for the location was astonishingly apt in a way that Brightside a bit further on was the antithesis of it. Also nearby was a district called Salmon Pastures to remind one of the beauty of the Don valley before industrialisation. The eye is drawn to Grimesthorpe No. 2 signal box which was opened on 15 Jan 1899 and, although reframed twice lasted until 8 Aug 1965. The original line to the old Wicker station is behind the steam of the locomotive. To the left is the branch to Attercliffe goods depot which was jointly owned by the LDECR and Midland with the latter having running powers over the branch and the LDECR over the Midland main line to Brightside Junction. The lines emerging from the near left are from Grimesthorpe engine shed and wagon repair shops and Grimesthorpe sidings. To the right of the signal box is Cammell Laird's private siding with an industrial loco hauling some wagons. The train, headed by a Midland 0-4-4T, consists of Clayton coaches. The clerestory is an old bogie vehicle, the brake at the end a four wheeled 25 ft long van and the others are a 31 ft six wheel coaches. Disappearing into the industrial gloom next to the lamp on the left is the last coach, a clerestory, of a rake of coaches in a siding.

Author's collection

to Dronfield Silkstone colliery in 1877 – the Dronfield to Silkstone colliery line having opened by 1873. Sidings for the similar and confusingly named Dronfield colliery were opened to the north by 1891. Several other smaller sidings were laid to service factories along the route.

F. S. Williams in 'The Midland Railway; Its Rise and Progress' (1876) described the new station in Sheffield as follows. 'The station is built in the valley of the Sheaf. This site was chosen simply because almost insurmountable engineering difficulties prevented the selection of a more central position. It was not an easy work to build a railway over a river like the Sheaf. Yet it was done; and three arches of 15 ft span, and of great length cover in the river and carry the line. The station buildings stand on the solid; the rails and roof are over the water. The roof is of iron and glass and is supported by forty two iron columns. There are 1¾ miles of wrought iron girders and about 90,000 bolts and rivets in the roof; and 37,500 ft of glass. The footbridge is 105 ft long. The clear span is 90 ft, and the weight about thirty tons. The total weight of the wrought and cast iron is 630 tons. The building is of rock faced wall stone, tool dressed, and the style of architecture is Grecian, with Gothic headings. The platforms are 700 ft long, and 30 ft wide….Four lines of railway run through the station; a spacious area opens in front of it.' The *Sheffield Independent* reported that 'at the opening the booking hall, which faces the bottom of Howard Street, has four separate entrances leading through onto the platform and is lofty, spacious and well lighted. In the centre of the hall is the booking office, separate first class ladies and gentlemen's waiting rooms and a refreshment room staffed by six young ladies and a host of waiters, cellar men and servants. There is also a kitchen and second class refreshment room. At the bottom of the platform is the third class waiting room which has unpretentious furniture and fittings'. Three express and four fast trains were to run to London daily. It was anticipated that nearly all freight would go by the 'Old Road'. However, a large number of freights now trundled through the station for the Hope valley, which together with the new passenger traffic on the line made the station totally overcrowded and inadequate. (Having said that the entrance seems spacious compared with the cramped set up today where vehicle access has been forfeited for creating a good visual appearance.)

REFERENCES

Dunstan John – *The Origins of the Sheffield and Chesterfield Railway*. Dore Village Society Occasional Papers No. 2 1970

Hall Charles C. – *Rotherham & District Transport Vol. 1 to 1914*. Rotherwood Press 1996 (for Sheffield and Rotherham Railway)

Joy David – *A Regional History of the Railways of Great Britain Vol. 8: South and West Yorkshire*. David & Charles 1975

Leleux R. – As above but Vol. 9: *The East Midlands*. David & Charles 1976

Batty S. R. – *Rail Centres Sheffield*. Ian Allan 1984

Edwards Brian – *Totley and the Tunnel*. Shape Design Shop 1985

Williams F. S. – *The Midland Railway; Its Rise and Progress*. 5th ed 1888

MIDLAND RAILWAY.
National Cat Show
AT THE CRYSTAL PALACE, SEPT. 22 & 23.
INTERNATIONAL EXHIBITION.

Reduced Admission on Saturdays and Mondays. Adults 6d., Children under 14 years 3d. Other days, 1s.

On Monday, September 22nd, 1873,
THE LAST CHEAP EXCURSION FOR THE SEASON TO

LONDON
(ST. PANCRAS STATION),

BY THE MIDLAND RAILWAY COMPANY'S ROUTE,
By which Passengers will be booked from Principal Stations to

PARIS, SWITZERLAND, HOLLAND, BELGIUM, AND THE RHINE,
Will run as under:

For Through Bookings from Midland Stations to the CONTINENT, see other side.

TIMES OF STARTING AND FARES THERE AND BACK:

STATIONS.		a.m.	To LONDON & BACK. St. Pancras Station.
			FIRST CLASS / THIRD CLASS
			s. d. / s. d.
Bradford (Mid. Station)	dep.	8 40	
SHIPLEY	,,	8 45	
APPERLEY	,,	8 52	
KIRKSTALL	,,	9 2	25 0 / 15 0
Leeds (Mid. Station)	,,	9 25	
NORMANTON	,,	9 47	
SANDAL AND WALTON	,,	9 55	
Wakefield (Westgate)	,,	8 12	
Wakefield (L. & Y.)	,,	8 15	
Barnsley	,,	9 55	
CUDWORTH	,,	10 24	
SWINTON	,,	10 40	24 0 / 13 0
MASBORO'	,,	10 50	
ROTHERHAM	,,	10 20	
Sheffield (Mid. New Station)	,,	10 55	23 0 / 12 0
CHESTERFIELD	,,	11 33	

LONDON (St. Pancras), arrive about 4.25 p.m.

Returning from St. Pancras Station, on FRIDAY, SEPT. 26th, at 10.5 a.m., and Kentish Town at 10.10 a.m.

Children under 3 years of age, Free; above 3 and under 12, Half Fares. Luggage must be conveyed under the Passengers' own care, as the Company will not be responsible. The Tickets are not transferable, and will be available for returning by this Train only. Ten minutes will be allowed at Trent Station for Refreshments, both in going and returning.

TICKETS from Sheffield, Bills, and all particulars, to be obtained of Mr. Rodgers, Bookseller, Change Alley Corner, Sheffield. At all other places, Tickets to be had at Stations only.

JAMES ALLPORT, General Manager.

Derby, Sept., 1873.

Cheap Excursions from London to Brighton.—The London Brighton and South Coast Railway Company run Excursion Trains from London Bridge and Victoria Stations to Brighton and back every Monday and Tuesday.

See other Bills for DAY TRIP to LONDON the same day, Monday, Sept. 22, the Excursionists' Gala Day at the Crystal Palace.

For full particulars of above, and all Cook's Excursions and Tours to Holland, Belgium, the Rhine, Germany, Austria, the VIENNA EXHIBITION, France, Switzerland, Italy, Egypt, Palestine, &c.; apply to

THOS. COOK & SON, Tourist Offices { Ludgate Circus, Fleet St., London. / 43, Piccadilly, Manchester. / 16, Stephenson Place, Birmingham. / Temperance Hotel, Leicester.

Cook & Son, Printers, &c., London, Manchester, Birmingham, and Leicester.

This 1873 excursion leaflet to London was printed by Thomas Cook and it also included, on the reverse, holidays to the continent. It is printed on coarse poor quality paper because of its ephemeral nature which has resulted in the printing on the rear penetrating to the front. It crams in a lot of information, besides the National Cat Show. The population at large seems to have been just as animal daft as we are. (All those feral moggies who haunted the streets and alleys of Sheffield eking out a meagre existence would hardly have approved of their pampered brethren at the cat show.) The leaflet includes information on other excursions running to London on the same day, excursions from London to Brighton and notice that it would be the last cheap excursion to London of the summer season. The fares have a large price differential between first and third class but even so, third class would still have been beyond the pocket of the majority of the population. It was not until 1875 that the Midland took the radical step of formally abolishing second class and proceeded to supply upholstered seating for third class passengers to replace the four wheelers with their wooden seats. Note that Sheffield station has the nomenclature of 'Mid. New' as it could not be just 'new' indefinitely. *Author's collection*

HOW THE RAILWAY REACHED CHINLEY

The arrival of the railway at Dore and Totley was a relatively simple affair compared with the complexity of the lines eventually built between Chinley and Manchester. Whilst the Midland was reticent in providing for the booming industries of Sheffield, its drive to access the larger Manchester area is an epic of ambition, drive, ruthlessness and financial muscle which did not flinch from enormous engineering problems and had a willingness to work with competing companies to achieve its goal.

As we have seen the North Midland Railway was opened from Derby to Rotherham Masboro via Ambergate, Chesterfield and Beighton on 11 May 1840 and from Masboro to Leeds six weeks later. It became a founding member of the Midland Railway on 10 May 1844.

A year later George Hudson proposed a survey for a route from Ambergate to Manchester and George Stephenson was appointed engineer. The key decision in planning the route was whether to follow the Wye or Derwent valleys beyond Rowsley. Stephenson recommended the Wye route through the Duke of Rutlands' Haddon estate to Bakewell which was accepted and resulted in the plans being presented to Parliament.

The Manchester, Buxton, Matlock & Midland Junction Railway (MBMMJR) received its Act of incorporation on 16 Jul 1846. The Manchester and Birmingham Railway was prepared to support the company but this evaporated when it became part of the newly formed London & North Western Railway in 1846.

By this time the Duke of Rutland had changed his mind about the line crossing his Haddon estate and set his face against it so the Derwent valley route was once more considered. This would include crossing the Duke of Devonshire's Chatsworth estate. The Duke gave his consent, subject to certain conditions. There would be a branch from Rowsley to Bakewell, and also from Chapel en le Frith to Buxton.

In 1848 revised proposals were put forward for a branch from Baslow to Bakewell and on 31 Aug the new Act received the Royal Assent. By this time the 'Second Railway Mania' had passed and there was a severe lack of finance for the scheme. However, in November work began on the Ambergate to Rowsley section and on 4 Jun 1849 the line opened with locomotives and rolling stock provided by the Midland. On 17 Jul, because of the former Manchester and Birmingham Railway's involvement in the line, the LNWR flexed its muscles and forced the Midland into a joint lease to take over the MBMMJR which was fixed for nineteen years.

Matlock Bath station on 30 Sep 1903, looking south with the Willersley tunnel entrance in the distance.
Author's collection

Ambergate station was notable for being one of only three stations to be arranged in a triangular fashion. The original station was built for the North Midland Railway in 1840 and called 'Amber Gate'. It was in a symmetrical Jacobean style with an elaborate square central porch on the platform side and was designed by Francis Thompson. This station building was just north of the 129 yard Toadmoor tunnel. When the line to Rowsley opened in 1849 it left the North Midland line on a north to west curve and a station was opened on the curve. The south to west curve was opened in 1863, to give trains from Derby to Rowsley direct access. Thompsons' original station was dismantled and rebuilt in enlarged form at the south junction in the form of an 'A'. In 1876 a new station was opened on a loop from the south to the north line, the earlier station on the North Midland Railway being closed and used for storage. This view is looking north east from the station footbridge and shows the main station building on the left with the edge of the up Manchester platform (platform 2) just visible in the left foreground. Platforms 3 and 4, in the centre, were used by trains to Chesterfield and beyond and flanked the 1876 Ambergate middle curve. The original North Midland line is passing through Toadmoor tunnel behind the Midland Terrace cottages on the far right. The third side of the triangle (platforms 5 and 6) is out of sight behind the station building but the end of the platforms can just be discerned below the signals in the distance.
Picture the Past. Derbyshire Libraries

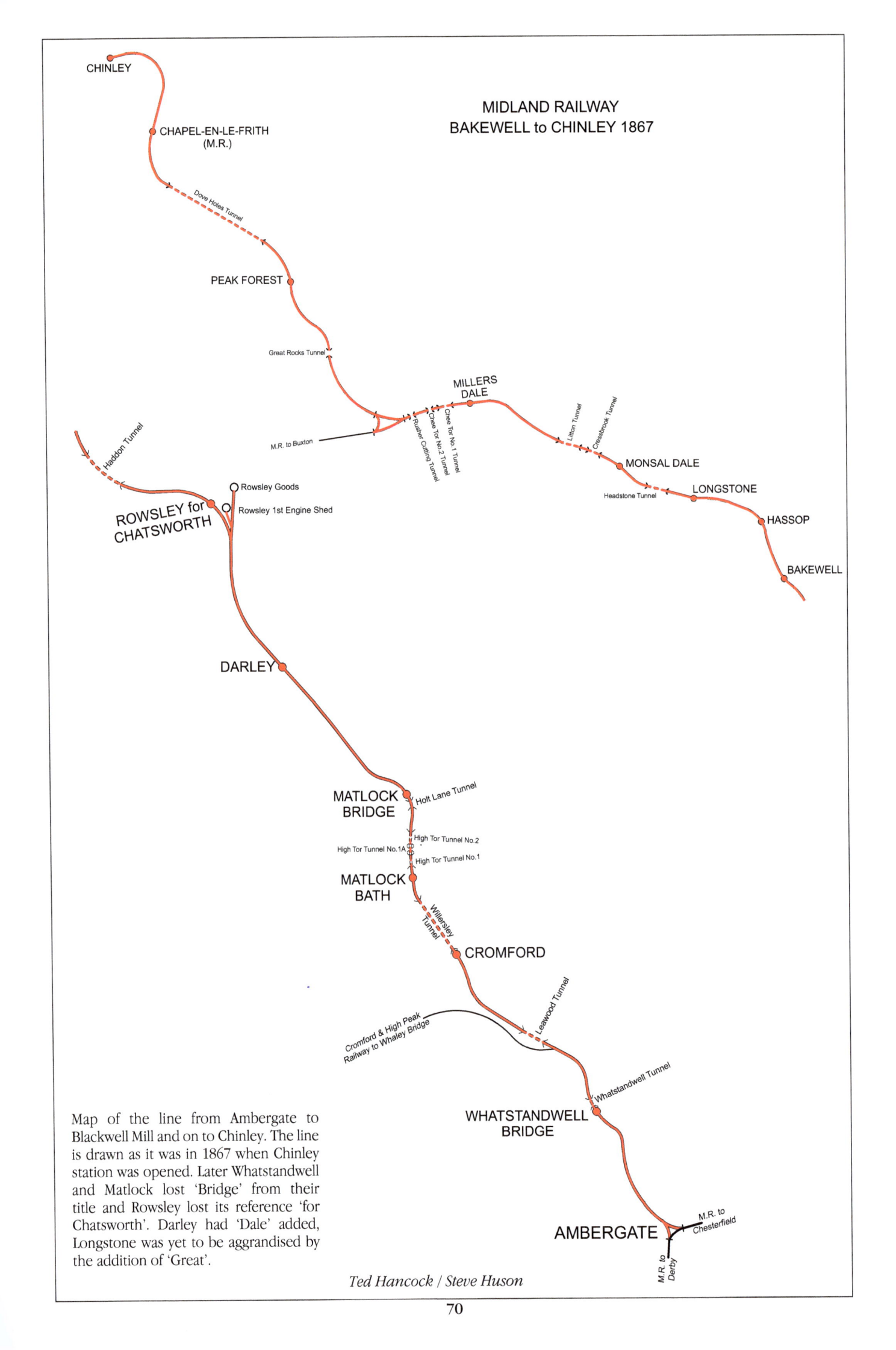

MIDLAND RAILWAY BAKEWELL to CHINLEY 1867

- CHINLEY
- CHAPEL-EN-LE-FRITH (M.R.)
  - Dove Holes Tunnel
- PEAK FOREST
  - Great Rocks Tunnel
- MILLERS DALE
  - M.R. to Buxton
  - Rusher Cutting Tunnel
  - Chee Tor No.2 Tunnel
  - Chee Tor No.1 Tunnel
  - Litton Tunnel
  - Cressbrook Tunnel
- MONSAL DALE
  - Headstone Tunnel
- LONGSTONE
- HASSOP
- BAKEWELL
- Haddon Tunnel
- ROWSLEY for CHATSWORTH
  - Rowsley Goods
  - Rowsley 1st Engine Shed
- DARLEY
- MATLOCK BRIDGE
  - Holt Lane Tunnel
  - High Tor Tunnel No.2
  - High Tor Tunnel No.1A
  - High Tor Tunnel No.1
- MATLOCK BATH
  - Willersley Tunnel
- CROMFORD
  - Leawood Tunnel
  - Cromford & High Peak Railway to Whaley Bridge
  - Whatstandwell Tunnel
- WHATSTANDWELL BRIDGE
- AMBERGATE
  - M.R. to Chesterfield
  - M.R. to Derby

Map of the line from Ambergate to Blackwell Mill and on to Chinley. The line is drawn as it was in 1867 when Chinley station was opened. Later Whatstandwell and Matlock lost 'Bridge' from their title and Rowsley lost its reference 'for Chatsworth'. Darley had 'Dale' added, Longstone was yet to be aggrandised by the addition of 'Great'.

Ted Hancock / Steve Huson

The first section from Ambergate to Matlock Bridge (Matlock from 1905) followed the River Derwent closely. It was on a long gradual ascent and involved short tunnels at Whatstandwell, Lea Wood, Cromford and four more between Matlock Bath and Matlock Bridge. The first of these three was High Tor and the last Holt Lane. This up train has just left the last of the High Tor tunnels. Near the centre of the train is the Matlock Bath up distant signal with a sighting board behind it with the down distant below sharing the same post. The photograph is undated but is before 1935. Ex-Midland 4F No. 3852 of 21 (26G after 1935) Belle Vue is hauling a train of empties and making steady progress against the incline. *Author's collection*

The northern end of the line to Manchester was planned to start from a point south of Stockport station and run via Hazel Grove and Whaley Bridge to Buxton. However in 1854 the Stockport, Disley & Whaley Bridge Railway (SDWBR), a railway backed by the rival LNWR, received its Act on 30 Jul 1854 and opened in 1857. This line closely followed the one planned by the MBMMJR nine years earlier. There followed the Buxton Extension Line from Whaley Bridge to Buxton by an Act of 30 Jul 1857. Both these undertakings were eventually taken over by the LNWR in 1863.

Under the threat of a rival scheme from the North Derbyshire Railway from Rowsley to Whaley Bridge with a branch to Buxton from Dove Holes, and the LNWR backed SDWBR the dream of a Midland line to Manchester was becoming seriously threatened. Thus at the end of 1856 the Midland proposed to the LNWR that the original MBMMJR line from Rowsley to Buxton should be constructed and that the Midland should be granted running powers from Buxton over the SDWBR and the LNWR line to Manchester. Although the LNWR agreed to accommodate local traffic, not surprisingly, it rejected the idea of through running.

The Midland managed to see off the North Derbyshire Railway but was then faced by plans deposited in Nov 1858 by another independent concern, the Rowsley, Bakewell and Buxton Railway, which would follow a similar route to the earlier schemes. Although the Midland saw this scheme fail as well it concentrated minds at Derby and resulted in the Midland giving notice of its own proposed line from Rowsley to Buxton.

The route took the Wye valley via the Bakewell route and on this occasion was not opposed by the Duke of Rutland, who never knew whether to stick or twist when it came to railways through his estate! His agreement was subject to the line not being seen from Haddon Hall which resulted in Haddon tunnel being included in the plans.

The Midland Railway's Rowsley and Buxton Act received the Royal Assent on 25 May 1860 and work on the line started by the end of the year. The line was to run through Haddon, Bakewell, Hassop, Longstone, Monsal Dale, Millers Dale, Chee Dale, Blackwell Mill and Ashwood Dale.

The building of the line from Rowsley as far as Longstone was comparatively rapid, apart from the collapse of the Haddon tunnel which involved loss of life and delays.

E. R. (Ray) Morten was, together with Harry Townley, the doyen of photographers of the Peak line in the LMS and BR steam era. Unfortunately, from our point of view, their photographic visits to the Hope valley line were infrequent. One of my favourite E. R. Morten photographs is this one on the curve looking towards Haddon tunnel. The lie by siding for 33 wagons is on the left and Haddon signal box can just be seen in the distance. No. 40520, a 17D Rowsley engine, is drifting down the gradient towards Rowsley after banking one of the endless mineral trains to the summit at Peak Forest. The telegraph poles, which always seemed to add a sense of importance to a line, the embankment with the undergrowth under control, the beautifully kept permanent way, a lovely spring day and a clean engine with a lineage going back to Midland days and with LMS still on the tender are beautifully portrayed in this view on 9 May 1953. *E. R. Morten*

Hassop station was located between the stations at Bakewell and Longstone ('Great Longstone' from 1913) and, like so many Midland stations, was nowhere near the place it purported to serve. It was the nearest station for Baslow and was one of the three stations serving Chatsworth – because of that association it was one of the larger stations and certainly more substantial than any on the Dore and Chinley line. By 1942 passenger services had been withdrawn although it had buoyant goods traffic. It opened to passengers on 1 Aug 1862 and goods three months later. This previously unpublished view from 1948, looking south from the road over bridge, shows the platform edges cut back but the signal box and goods shed still operative. The station closed in its entirety in 1964 and is now part of a walking and cycle route, the station buildings being used as a shop and tea rooms.

Ken Boulter © Ted Hancock

However, from that point seven tunnels, totalling a little over 2,000 yards, two major viaducts and eleven other bridges in the next 5½ miles were needed before Blackwell Mill was reached. Even then there was further heavy engineering work up Ashwood Dale to Buxton.

On 1 Jun 1863 the complete line was opened to Buxton, a fortnight before the LNWR line from Whaley Bridge. It was a great propaganda victory for the Midland and at the same time the south to west curve at Ambergate was opened which allowed through running from Derby for the first time.

On 1 Jul 1871, following the expiry of the joint lease of the MBMMJR, the Midland took over the company, the LNWR having surrendered its interest after the Midland threatened to build an independent line from the Wirksworth branch to Rowsley. This would have made the proposed line of no further strategic interest to the LNWR and therefore of no value.

At the point when the building of the Rowsley to Buxton line began the Midland did not know how it would break out of Buxton to reach Manchester because of the LNWR's blocking tactics. Yet within a year the Midland had pulled off a great coup when following a chance meeting between the senior officers of the Midland and the MSLR on the moors above Buxton, an agreement was reached to extend the Midland line from Blackwell Mill Junction via Peak Forest, Chapel en le Frith and Chinley to the MSLR line at

The publicists of the Midland Railway used the Monsal Dale location more than any other in advertising the scenic beauty of its various lines. This view from Monsal Head shows a Belpaire boilered Class 3 4-4-0 on a south bound train hauling a cattle truck, two LNWR and four Midland clerestory coaches across Headstone viaduct and into Headstone tunnel in the 1920s.

Roger Carpenter collection

Monsal Dale station was about half a mile north of the famous viaduct and clings to the hillside. It had a steep access road which passed under the lines, seen here in the foreground. Note the horse in the yard in this 1911 view.
Author's collection

New Mills South Junction where running powers would be granted for the Midland to run into Manchester. In return the MSLR would receive running rights from New Mills to Peak Forest to exploit the coal, limestone, lime and mineral traffic of the area which, in the event, it hardly exercised.

The line left Blackwell Mill to Peak Forest on a gradient of 1 in 90 and then was faced with difficult tunnelling under Cow Low hill. The tunnel passed through limestone, red sandstone and shales and a stream was encountered that then disappeared. This defeated the contractor and the Midland had to take the job on itself. The work took three years before the 2,860 yard Dove Holes Tunnel was finished. After that progress was made rapidly, the biggest engineering obstacle being the Chapel Milton viaduct. The line opened for goods traffic on 1 Oct 1866.

However, within a month, torrential rain caused a gigantic landslip at Bugsworth, between New Mills and Chinley. No less than sixteen acres of land slipped downhill taking with it a five arch road bridge and a neighbouring farm. Just south of the bridge was a curved viaduct which was straightened by the force of the slip. It took 400 men working night and day for ten weeks to rebuild the line which included a new timber viaduct, two skew bridges of 30 ft span with wrought iron girders and an embankment at one end and a rock cutting at the other. It was an incredible achievement.

The line was reopened for goods traffic on 24 Jan 1867 and for passengers a week later.

Even then difficulties on the line were not at an end for, on 18 Jun 1872, there was a landslip at Dove Holes Tunnel which took nearly six weeks to fix. Further problems with this difficult tunnel were to be experienced over very many years.

The stations on the line were at Peak Forest, Chapel en le Frith, Chinley and Bugsworth. Chinley was a hamlet with a population of less than 1,000 and only needed a small station west of Chinley Road bridge and was not of any strategic importance. In the early years the station was only marginally busier than Monsal Dale station further south. However once the Dore and Chinley line arrived in 1894 things were to change dramatically.

Mabel Bamford wrote 'A History of Chinley' and described Chinley around 1870 as having three paper mills, one at Whitehall, one at the Forge Mill and a paper staining mill at Bridgeholme Green which provided plentiful employment along with farming and quarrying. The row of cottages opposite Whitehall Mill were always known as 'Rag Row' because of the washing that was hung at the front. The interior of the cottages were often lime washed and most had flagged floors. Often they only had one exterior door. The earth closets were placed well away

This line from Buxton Junction to Peak Forest Junction was the northern section of the triangle at Blackwell Mill and is the link from Buxton to the extended line to New Mills South. It is still open today as a single freight only line. This view on 23 Jun 1968 captures the grandeur of the limestone landscape and illustrates the task that faced the builders. *M. A. King.*

The section from Millers Dale Junction to Dove Holes Tunnel was in limestone country and after the arrival of the line a rapid expansion of the limestone quarrying industry became possible. This 18 Aug 1951 view shows Great Rocks Junction with quarries, lime kilns and sidings in view. Jubilee No. 45620 *North Borneo*, a 16A Nottingham engine, is heading the 13.35 Manchester Central to Nottingham train. *E. R. Morten*

Midland 2-4-0 No. 258 enters Dove Holes tunnel at the southern entrance on an unknown date. This would not be the highlight of the footplate men's day! The engine was built in May 1881 and was one of the last 2-4-0s to be built. The date is probably around the Grouping as the engine had been allocated to Buxton shed by this date. The coach is probably a Bain 54 ft brake composite D519A which was non-corridor with no lavatory provision. By this time the 2-4-0s were used on secondary duties and so this is almost certainly a local train. *Author's collection*

Chapel en le Frith had become a small manufacturing and market town by the end of the nineteenth century and included the fledgling predecessor to the Ferodo works, the town's largest employer in later years, making brake shoes for the embryonic petrol engine road vehicle. The design of the station was very similar to that used at Rowsley, Bakewell and Hassop and had elaborate glass canopies fixed to a curtain wall and mounted on beautifully ornate iron spandrel supports. The station was named 'Chapel-en-le-Frith' from the opening in 1866 but was changed to 'Chapel-en-le-Frith Central' in 1924 to avoid confusion with the ex-LNWR station on the outskirts of the town. It closed to passengers in 1967. This view, looking north, in the Midland period shows a train departing at the side of the signal box and a porter, sitting on the platform edge, with some luggage, preparing to cross the line. There were signal boxes at each end of the station but these were replaced in 1905 by a single box on the up platform which dates this picture before 1905. *John Ryan collection.*

Midland Railway.

CIRCULAR No. 131.

Office of Superintendent of the Line,

Derby, August 16th, 1872.

DEAR SIR,

RE-OPENING OF THE MANCHESTER LINE.

The obstruction on the Manchester Line caused by the Land-slip near Chapel-en-le-Frith, having been removed, the Line will be Re-opened for Passenger Traffic on Tuesday next, the 20th instant (as per bills and notices sent you to-day), from which date all restrictions respecting the booking of passengers and other Coaching Traffic to Liverpool and other Stations on the Cheshire Joint Lines, and in the Manchester District, that have been in force since June 19th, will be withdrawn; and you must resume the through booking of passengers and every description of Coaching Traffic to Liverpool and all Stations in Lancashire, by the same Routes and at the same Fares as were in operation prior to that date.

The first Trains to resume working by the ordinary route, via New Mills, Woodley, and Guide Bridge, will be those leaving Manchester for Derby at 6.55 a.m., and Derby for Manchester at 8.0 a.m., on Tuesday the 20th instant.

Note, and acknowledge receipt.

Yours truly,

E. M NEEDHAM,

SUPERINTENDENT.

Mr. _____

_____ Station.

The re-opening of the Manchester Line after the landslip at Dove Holes.
Laurence Knighton collection

The first station at Chinley was opened on 1 Feb 1867 and was a modest affair. Five horse drawn carriages await passengers from the next train. The Tudor style station building, which included accommodation for the station master, is almost identical to that built at Longstone between Hassop and Monsal Dale.
Jack Braithwaite collection

The original Chinley station before 1898 when the opening of the Dore and Chinley line had greatly increased its importance, but before the rebuilding at the turn of the century. The original signal box was opened before 1 Oct 1876 but was replaced by this modern one on 5 Oct 1890 which itself was replaced in Jun 1902 with a new one further to the north. A modest shelter for passengers on the up platform, a cattle pen at the end of the down platform, a lower quadrant signal and another before the road bridge with a sighting board can be seen. A small cattle dock is at the end of the platform. The goods shed was built in 1866 and was based on the one at Chapel en le Frith. The lie by siding to the left was added in 1890 and two additional water cranes came in 1898 but are not visible.

Author's collection

The original goods shed around 1960 looking a picture of rustic charm with its course random stone exterior. In the new station set up it became located at the south end in a slightly elevated position near the turntable. From 1903 it was used for stabling the railway horses but as the use of horses declined with the arrival of motor vehicles it became a general storage facility. This is a rear end view looking north. *David Ibbotson*

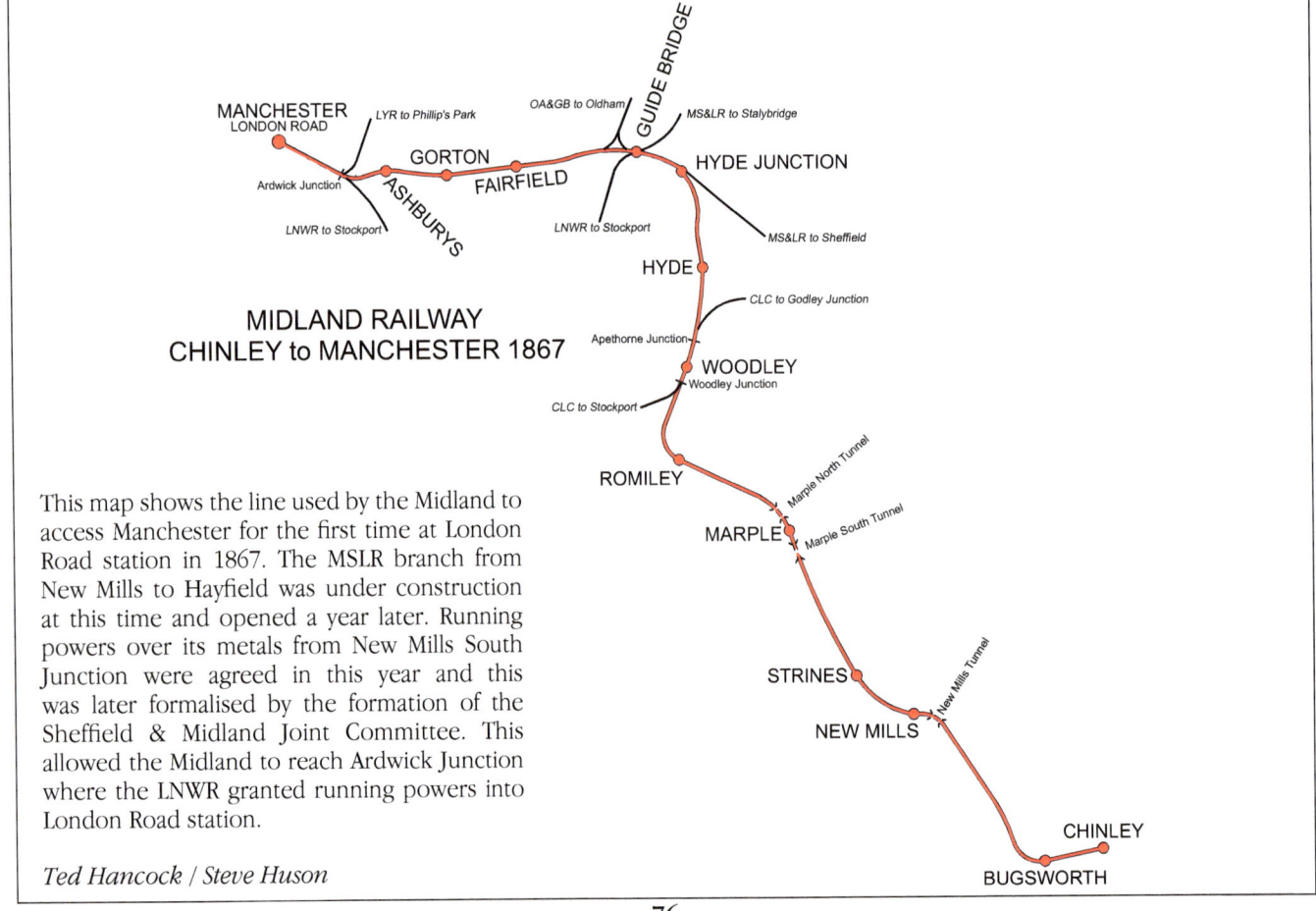

MIDLAND RAILWAY CHINLEY to MANCHESTER 1867

This map shows the line used by the Midland to access Manchester for the first time at London Road station in 1867. The MSLR branch from New Mills to Hayfield was under construction at this time and opened a year later. Running powers over its metals from New Mills South Junction were agreed in this year and this was later formalised by the formation of the Sheffield & Midland Joint Committee. This allowed the Midland to reach Ardwick Junction where the LNWR granted running powers into London Road station.

Ted Hancock / Steve Huson

from the cottages and were unlit. Candles and eventually oil lamps were used. There was a midden to throw rubbish into but most rubbish would be burnt on the open fire. The middens and closets were emptied periodically. It was not until 1923 that water closets became available. When a property was to be built the builder had first to make sure that there was a spring to supply water or sink a well. Long hours were worked, particularly on the land, and life centred round the inn, chapel or church. The *Old Squirrel Inn* was a popular place in the centre of the village kept by Mr Taylor. According to the names on an 1880 map the only houses bordering Maynestone Road, or 'Black Chinley' as it was known, were Plarr Farm (now Heatherlea), Spring Cottage, Mossley House, Clappers Gate, Oliver's Farm, Ashen Clough and The Naze, which was later rebuilt with stone from the original station.

The background to the MSLR Hyde to New Mills line was that a branch to Hyde off its Manchester to Sheffield main line was opened in Mar 1858. Later that year another Act allowed the MSLR to extend the line to Marple via Woodley and Romiley. This was followed by the Marple, New Mills and Hayfield Junction Railway Act of 1860 which authorised the line from Marple onwards to Hayfield. The line to New Mills was opened on 1 Jul 1865 and had to overcome formidable engineering difficulties including Marple viaduct and a short tunnel under the Peak Forest Canal. The branch to Hayfield opened in Mar 1868.

Buxworth station in May 1953 looking towards Chinley. The station opened in 1867, the village then being called Bugsworth, but was extensively rebuilt when the lines were widened in the early years of the century. The village was more important for the canal basin on the Peak Forest Canal than for the railway and was not important enough to have its own goods facilities. *E. R. Morten*

From Marsh Lane bridge, on the outskirts of New Mills, Trafford Park (9E) rebuilt Royal Scot No. 46158 *The Loyal Regiment*, can be seen climbing towards Chinley on the 1 in 90 gradient with the ten coach 14.10 Manchester to St Pancras relief on Easter Monday 3 Apr 1961. New Mills South Junction was an important landmark in the Midland's titanic thrust to Manchester because it was the point where the Midland obtained running powers over MSLR metals to Manchester and where the new avoiding line to Heaton Mersey through Disley tunnel left the old joint line with the MSLR. The latter can be seen crossing the River Goyt on the Newtown viaduct in the distance with the Marple line curving to the right. *J. W. Sutherland*

New Mills station at an unknown date looking towards Chinley. Beyond the footbridge can be seen the mouth of one of the tunnels driven through rock at the east end of the station. One tunnel, 242 yards long, took the line through to Hayfield; the other at 123 yards to New Mills goods, New Mills South Junction and Chinley. *Lens of Sutton*

In 1859 an Act was passed authorising the joint administration of London Road station, Manchester by the MSLR and the LNWR with the Midland having access to the MSLR part. The new London Road station was opened in 1866 and was divided in two by an iron railing. The first Midland passenger train ran into the station via New Mills, Marple and Hyde on 1 Feb 1867, although it had started at Kings Cross – its London terminus at St Pancras was eighteen months away from completion. 450 trains used London Road's platforms every twenty four hours. To consolidate its position the Midland opened the Ancoats goods station nearby in 1870 although the Midland's foothold at London Road was terminated when, in 1876, the MSLR gave the Midland three years notice to quit due to the demand for platform space being impossible to meet.

A delightful view of Strines station looking toward Marple on 30 Aug 1970. The station was located at the top of an increasingly steep road and was well away from the village it purported to serve. The overgrown goods yard is on the left. *M. A. King*

On the same visit, Michael King took this view of the up platform waiting shelter. It is a beautifully proportioned building with, unusually, the station totem above the entrance. *M. A. King*

Marple Station, looking towards Romiley showing the constricted nature of the station and the Midland's penchant for gorgeous canopies. It was congestion and delays here which contributed to the Midland deciding to build the New Mills to Heaton Mersey avoiding line. 4-4-0 No. 744 was built in 1904 as No. 834 and was renumbered in 1907. It had 6 ft 9 in driving wheels and had a G8 boiler. It was withdrawn in Jul 1936. *Author's collection*

Great Central & Midland Joint Committee.

Instructions to be observed by the Signalman on duty at Marple Station Box, with reference to the use of the Bell fixed at Marple Station.

This Bell has been provided to enable you to call the Station-master or a Porter, and to intimate to the Station Staff the approach of Passenger Trains, and it must be used in accordance with the following instructions :—

To call Station-master	One Ring.
Up Passenger Train approaching ...	Two Rings.
Down Passenger Train approaching...	Three ,,
To call Porter	Four ,,

The Bell must be rung to intimate the approach of Passenger Trains as soon as the "Is Line Clear?" signal has been received for Up Trains, and the "Train entering Section" signal has been received for Down Trains.

Should any breach of these Regulations occur, it must be immediately reported to the Superintendents of the Line.

R. HAIG BROWN,
Great Central Railway.

J ELLIOTT,
Midland Railway.

A signalling instruction for Marple station box illustrating the two companies' ability to co-operate over operational matters. I have another of these notices for Strines box dated Oct 1881 headed Sheffield & Midland Joint Railway issued by W. Bradley of the MSLR and E. M. Needham for the Midland. The titling has changed by the time this was issued because although undated, it is at a later date as the MSLR has now become the GCR.
Author's collection

Although this old postcard is captioned Romiley Viaduct, this is in fact the Marple viaduct, which is between Romiley and Marple and just before Marple Wharf Junction where the Macclesfield and Bollington Railway branched to the south. It was and still is one of the most dramatic features of the line and in this view looks very new. It has thirteen arches and one girder construction and carries the line over the Peak Forest Canal. The original MSLR signal box hides behind the telegraph pole with the signals on the right – maintenance of the signalling was taken over by the Midland in 1876. The canal itself, which by this time was owned by the MSLR, is on a magnificent aqueduct crossing over the River Goyt.
John Ryan collection

Fairfield station about 1905 looking towards Gorton. It shows work on the station as part of the Ardwick to Ashburys and Guide Bridge section being widened from two to four lines. An additional two platforms are being put in. A contractor's locomotive and wagons can be seen. The two tracks on the left served the Fallowfield line to Chorlton Junction with the central tracks being the main line. The signal box was later moved to track level at the east end of the central platform. *www.disused-stations.org.uk*

An evocative view of Manchester London Road station in 1913 over thirty years after the Midland had left. The railings between the two companies platforms are still to be seen; the LNWR on the left and the GCR on the right. I remember train spotting there in the 1950s and the railings were still in use. As a train spotter from Sheffield who had never seen a Scot the ex-LNWR side was the magnet as the many ex-GCR engines were a common site in Sheffield. *Author's collection*

We now turn our attention to developments south of Manchester. The Manchester and Stockport Railway was a scheme to build a line from Ashburys to Brinnington Junction on the CLC's Godley to Stockport Tiviot Dale route. The line was authorised in 1866, with the MSLR as its leading investor. The MSLR soon realised that, by adding a connection from Reddish Junction to Romiley, it could bring the Midland on board to share the costs. When, in 1869, the Sheffield & Midland Joint Committee was formed the Midland agreed to take over the unfinished Manchester and Stockport Railway as part of the joint line. It was also agreed to build a further line from Romiley to connect with the CLC at Bredbury Junction.

This now gave the Midland direct access to Liverpool via the CLC as well as into Manchester, avoiding the heavy congestion around Guide Bridge. The curve from Bredbury Junction to Romiley Junction, and from Ashburys to Romiley and also from Brinnington Junction to Reddish Junction were all opened in 1875. From this time all Midland main line trains ran via Reddish to Manchester although some stopping services continued to run via Hyde.

The loss of its access into London Road drove the Midland into action again and, with its CLC partners the MSLR and GNR, plans were put in place for a new Manchester station which would also cater for the CLC's Liverpool traffic. The acquisition of the six mile fourteen chain Manchester South District Railway, which opened on 1 Jan 1880, allowed a connection between Heaton Mersey East Junction and Cornbrook. It was built very quickly and was ready to access the new Manchester Central station which opened six months later on 1 Jul 1880, although an earlier station had opened in 1877, but was converted for goods use when the new station was completed. This finally provided the Midland with its own terminal, trains travelling over the SMJC between New Mills and Bredbury Junction and then using the line through Stockport Tiviot Dale although it was not until 1884 that stopping services transferred to the new route.

The final part of the Midland's fight to access Manchester was the ten mile avoiding line from New Mills South Junction to Heaton Mersey, which relieved the increasingly overloaded SMJC line. Authorisation was granted in 1897 opening in 1902. It was the fulfilment of the Midland's long and epic campaign to reach 'Cottonopolis'.

However there is more to be told when considering this last push of the Midland to reach Manchester so we will revisit the field of battle when we consider the Chinley North Junction to New Mills South Junction widening in Vol. 2.

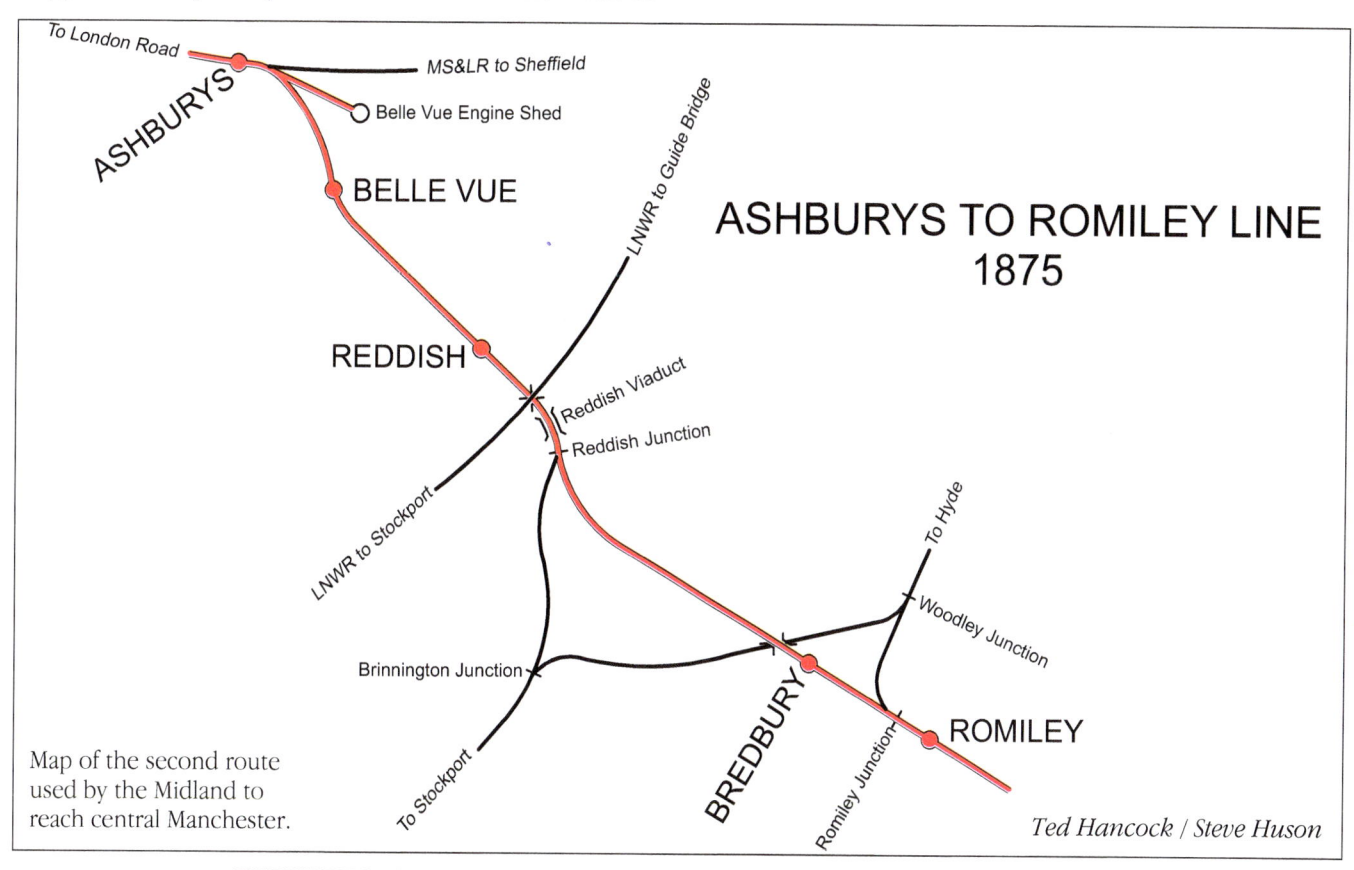

Map of the second route used by the Midland to reach central Manchester.

Ted Hancock / Steve Huson

REFERENCES

Williams F. S. – *The Midland Railway: Its Rise and Progress*. 5th ed 1888

Hudson Bill – *Through Limestone Hills: The Peak Line Ambergate to Chinley*. Oxford Publishing Co 1989

Waite Glynn – *Hassop 150: Commemorating the Opening of Hassop Station in 1st August 1862*. Rowsley Association 2012

Bentley J. M. – *Over the Peak Part 1: Chinley to Peak Forest*. Book Law/Foxline 2013

Waite G. / Knighton L. – *Rowsley: A Rural Railway Centre*. Midland Railway Society 2003

Johnson E. M. – *The Midland Route from Manchester Central to New Mills via Didsbury, Stockport & Marple Part One*. Foxline Publishing rev ed 2009

As above *Part Two: Cheadle Heath to Chinley*. Foxline Publishing rev ed 2009

Smith I. R. / Fox G. K. – *Manchester London Road to Hayfield via Reddish, Bredbury, Romiley, Marple & New Mills and including the 'Hyde Loop'*. Foxline Publications (2003)

Griffiths R. P. – *The Cheshire Lines Railway*. Oakwood 1958

Brumhead Derek – *Railways of New Mills District: Their Development and Impact, 1840-1902*. Reprint from Vol. 86 of the Transactions of the Lancashire and Cheshire Antiquarian Society 1990

Burton Warwick R. – *Railways of Marple and District from 1794*. M. T. & W. R. Burton 3rd ed 1983

Johnson E. M. – *Manchester Central*. Steam Days Feb 2005

ROMILEY to MANCHESTER CENTRAL 1880

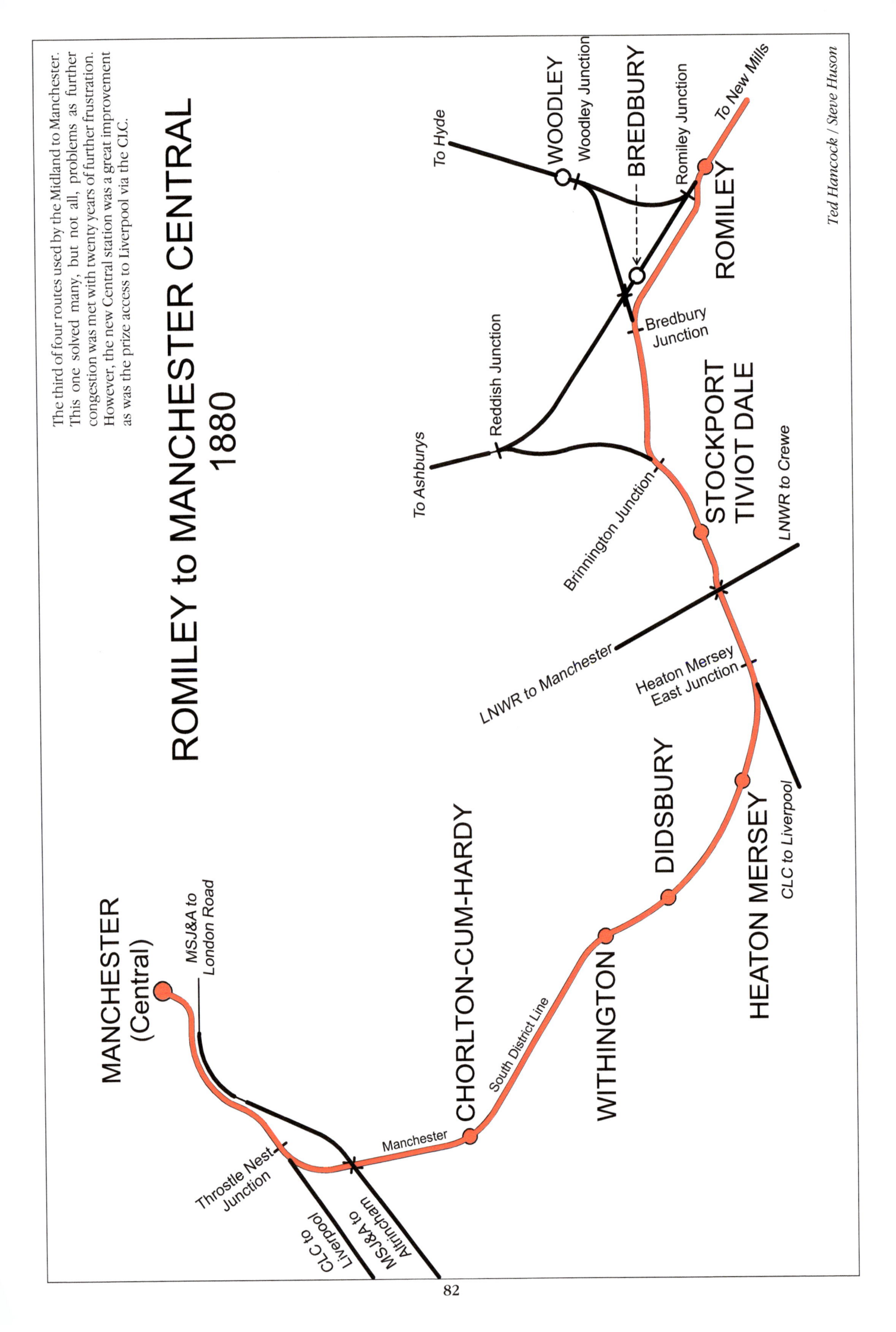

The third of four routes used by the Midland to Manchester. This one solved many, but not all, problems as further congestion was met with twenty years of further frustration. However, the new Central station was a great improvement as was the prize access to Liverpool via the CLC.

Ted Hancock / Steve Huson

Stockport Tiviot Dale station on Sat 4 Nov 1961 with the 11.45 Manchester Central to Sheffield three coach train in the platform. 'Jubilee' No. 45656 *Cochrane*, a Millhouses engine, is in charge. It was one of the class that was camera shy over the years. The train had emerged from three short sandstone tunnels – Wellington Road, Brownsword and Tiviot Dale. The station was located near the centre of the town and had an architecturally notable frontage. After its closure in Jan 1967 the frontage was demolished in the summer of 1968. The two centre lines were mostly reserved for the many freights, many from Cheadle Exchange sidings.
J. W. Sutherland

Heaton Mersey station looking toward Stockport about 1910 with the staff posing on the platform. This was the first of the stations of the Manchester South District Railway and like the others, dated from the opening of the line in Jan 1889. The engine shed of the same name was actually located in Stockport and was shared by the Midland and MSLR as members of the CLC. It was on the south side of the Cheadle and Heaton Mersey lines west of Tiviot Dale station.
Author's collection

In May 1932 Midland built Compound No. 1032 is on a Manchester Central to St Pancras express at Didsbury. The housewife with the washing on the line knew it would be safe to put it out as the wind was taking the smoke away from her house!
E. R. Morten

83

Manchester South District's last station before Manchester Central was Chorlton-cum-Hardy. The 13.04 Manchester Central to Sheffield is hauled by LMS built Compound No. 41066, a Trafford Park engine until Sep 1957. The graceful wall based lamp gives a glimpse of its ancestry, the station having opened on 1 Jan 1880. *W. A. Brown*

The magnificent Manchester Central station in its prime on 11 Apr 1911, showing 4-4-0 No. 745 setting off with a passenger train and a GCR Sacré 0-6-0. No. 745 was built in 1904 at Derby and lasted until Mar 1950. The station had a single arch roof span of 210 ft and a maximum height above rail level of 90 ft. Interestingly the roof was built by Andrew Handyside & Co of Derby, who were later to build the far more modest footbridge at Hope station. It was shared by the MSLR, GNR and the Midland and by 1897 all three company's trains were running into London stations at Marylebone, Kings Cross and St Pancras respectively. When LNWR trains from London Road to Euston are added Manchester was richly endowed with competing services to the capital.
Author's collection

CHAPTER 3
THE DORE AND CHINLEY RAILWAY

THE PROGENITORS

The Midland Railway's first attempt to cross the Peak District from east to west became possible with the completion of the Sheffield to Chesterfield line via Totley in 1870 and the extension of the Ambergate to Buxton line from Blackwell Mill South Junction to New Mills in 1867. The Midland's aim was to shorten the journey from Sheffield to Manchester which, at that time, required a lengthy detour via Ambergate.

MIDLAND HASSOP AND DORE LINE
PLANS DRAWN UP

Plans were drawn up by the Midland's chief engineer, John Sydney Crossley, who at this period was seriously challenged building the epic Settle and Carlisle line.

PLANS DEPOSITED

30 Nov 1871. The plans were deposited for a line of ten miles and two furlongs that would start four chains south east of the booking office at Hassop station. From a triangular junction the line would swing sharply away towards Hassop village, which it would pass on the left, and then needed a tunnel 957 yards in length to reach Calver cross roads away to the right. Passing Curbar, also on the right, a 5,236 yard (nearly four miles) tunnel followed climbing on a gradient of 1 in 188 to a short level section before descending at 1 in 66 to the tunnel exit at Totley (at the same location as the present Totley tunnel). Connection with the Sheffield to Chesterfield line would be made sixty four yards north east of the Twenty-well Sick Lane bridge over the Sheffield to Chesterfield line.

THE BILL WITHDRAWN

21 Dec 1871. The Bill was deposited in Parliament but later withdrawn, along with many other Bills that had been deposited at that time. The line failed for engineering and political reasons, as well as aristocratic objections. The gradients did not meet the criteria for new lines laid down by the Midland and the Duke of Rutland objected to having ventilation shafts disturbing his grouse shooting on the moors above the proposed tunnel. It was abandoned in some horse trading with the Manchester Sheffield & Lincolnshire Railway who agreed to withdraw a line from Doncaster to Nottingham and Market Harborough in return for the Midland abandoning this line plus two others.

A NEW SURVEY

1874. The Midland again had a survey undertaken to see whether the Dore to Hassop line should be resurrected or if another route should be selected. However, the matter was deferred and nothing more was done at this time. F. S. Williams in 'The Midland Railway: It's Rise and Progress' states that at the half yearly meeting of the board in Aug 1877 a line from Dore to Hassop was mentioned.

THE DORE AND HASSOP RAILWAY

18 Aug 1880. *The Times* reported a plan for an eleven mile railway from Dore and Totley station (which had opened in 1872) to Hassop station. It was described as follows:- 'After leaving Dore the line will run through a magnificent stretch of moorland belonging to the Duke of Rutland to Froggatt Edge – a high range of hills, which has hitherto been of great difficulty in opening up railway communication with that part of the country – will be cut through by a tunnel'. The line would then go via Grindleford Bridge, where there would be a station, to between Baslow and Stoney Middleton to Hassop. There would be a branch from Grindleford Bridge to Castleton. The line was reported as having been surveyed by civil engineer Mr N. Schoolbred. Unlike the Midland 1871 scheme this line had the approval of the Dukes of Rutland and Devonshire.

4 Dec 1880. The *Sheffield Independent* reported that a deputation of representatives from Buxton, Winster and Sheffield's Master Cutler, together with several landowners, met the directors to communicate that 'they were in favour of the scheme proceeding'. In reply Matthew Thompson, the Midland chairman, said 'the directors do not see their way at the present time to accede to the requests'.

22 Nov 1884. This line would not go away for four years later the *Sheffield Independent* reported that an application to Parliament in the next session was to be made to form a new company for a railway from Hassop station to Hathersage to be called the Hassop and Padley Railway. It would pass through Bradwell, Rowland and near Great Longstone to Hassop station or via Holme, Hassop village, Stoke, Calver, Froggatt, Nether Padley to Hathersage. Plans for the works were to be deposited for inspection in various parishes.

THE GENESIS OF THE
DORE & CHINLEY RAILWAY

21 Mar 1884. Mr John Noble, the general manager of the Midland, during his report to the Commons Select Committee on the Dore and Chinley Railway Bill said that 'at some time between Sep 1880 and Mar 1881 a witness was interviewed by the engineers of the present line who informed them that he had been instructed to make a report of a railway to connect the Midland line south of Sheffield with the Manchester line. They were shown plans nearly identical with the plans of the present bill for a line from Dore to somewhere near Chinley, very much as the present line was laid down. This had an advantage over the previous scheme, because it avoided ascending gradients at the points where it joined the Midland's system. So far as these plans were concerned he (Noble) dissuaded the promoters from depositing the bill. He took this step because it was clear at that time that if a line was built it could only be satisfactorily worked by the Midland company and he was not then quite prepared to recommend the board accept the proposition'.

Noble went on to say that it was made clear to the promoters, subsequently, that the Midland had not given up on the idea of building a line and if they wanted to deposit their Bill they should bear in mind that local traffic would not justify the expenditure. He also said there would be considerable summer traffic to Buxton although through traffic was the main interest of the Midland and providing an alternative route to the Ambergate line.

Herein lies the genesis of the Dore and Chinley Railway.

Although, as we have seen, the Midland flirted with the idea of a line from Dore to Hassop it is clear that they were not likely to prioritise the line even though the completion of the Sheffield to Chesterfield line and the Peak line from Rowsley to New Mills South Junction made it logistically feasible. One suspects that their enthusiasm for the undertaking and its very high engineering costs was tempered by their own financial position. The Midland had recently faced the cost of the Peak line, the extension into London, the problems of getting to Manchester from New Mills, and in the 1870s, the enormous expense and engineering challenge of building the line from Settle to Carlisle. These were not only stretching them in terms of skills and manpower; they needed to gain revenue from the new lines and then regroup before taking on what would become another major building programme.

WHY THE MIDLAND FINALLY DECIDED THE LINE SHOULD BE BUILT

The reason why the Midland reached the conclusion that, despite the expense of construction, it would be to their advantage to go ahead became clear from further evidence by John Noble to the Select Committee.

The general manager said that: 'He had discouraged independent promoters of lines in the area, as we have seen, because local traffic could never raise sufficient revenue to cover costs and only through traffic would generate sufficient business which only the Midland could take on.' He said: 'It gave the Midland an alternative route because in considering how they would best enlarge the accommodation they required for their passenger and goods traffic, they had frequently, instead of duplicating their lines, made not exactly parallel lines, but lines which would serve as alternative routes and at the same time open up a fresh piece of country'. As examples he mentioned the alternative routes between Chesterfield and Rotherham and between Nottingham and Melton.

He also commented that there had been two landslips on the Ambergate to New Mills line since 1866 (Dove Holes tunnel and Bugsworth), when an alternative line would have been very advantageous (although the Bugsworth landslip would not have been alleviated by the building of the line). He said: 'The line would be of considerable advantage to Buxton, between which place and Sheffield and places north of Sheffield, even as far as Scotland, there was a very large traffic in season'.

Continuing, he said that although the company previously had running powers since 1861 over the MSLR Woodhead line the Midland only received one third of the money they earned by their traffic and could not pick up local traffic on the route. They had tried running a passenger service from Manchester to Barnsley but it was abandoned after nineteen months because of insufficient earnings. Noble was asked whether having a route that was longer than Woodhead was economic when they already had running powers over that line. In reply he said they would serve towns and areas not reached by the Woodhead route including Liverpool, Warrington, Stockport and Buxton as well as attracting traffic from north east of Barnsley.

A month later on 18 Apr at a meeting of the Midland shareholders Mr Thompson, the chairman, said the company had in one way or another access to pretty nearly the whole of the North Eastern system. Their trains were regularly running to York and Hull and canvassing agents were at work in almost all parts of the area. Presently passenger traffic to Buxton from Edinburgh, Glasgow, Scarborough, Leeds and Bradford went by the LNWR. He also mentioned that the line would be able to attract the emigrant passengers from Hull to Liverpool (an aspiration that was achieved) and reminded the shareholders that the company was spending a large sum of money at Liverpool and Manchester to attract more traffic. Sheffield had a large traffic to America which could not be attracted via Ambergate. In speaking of this line he said it was expensive to make and to work but that the traffic they were getting from Liverpool, Manchester and other places was continually increasing and if that trend continued they would be compelled to double the lines from Ambergate to the Peak Forest tunnel.

Thompson asked for the shareholders' approval, not because the local traffic upon it would pay the cost of construction but because of its value as a through line which would shorten the distance between Sheffield and Manchester from 74 mile via Ambergate to 42 miles (45 miles in fact) via the new line. He said the distance from Nottingham to Manchester would be the same by either route but five miles longer from Derby. However, he was at pains to point out that it would provide an alternative route from London, Leicester, Peterborough and Nottingham and would save the company the expense of ever having to double the lines on the Peak route. Over the whole system the earnings averaged about £109 per mile per week. If the new line only achieved £60 a week the Midland would be able to pay the Dore and Chinley company the amount outstanding and still make a profit.

Another reason that favoured the line as described by Percy Rickard in his paper to the Institution of Civil Engineers was that the junction of the line at Dore, at an elevation of 392 ft, is on the north side of the summit of the line at 474 ft above sea level, whilst the junction at Chinley, at an elevation of 729 ft, is on the north side of the summit of the Manchester line at 982 ft above sea level. As Ambergate stands at an elevation of only 247 ft, there are two heavy inclines to be encountered in either direction by the old route. The gradients of the Dore and Chinley line rise from Dore to 548 ft at the summit level of the Totley tunnel, they then fall to 493 ft at Bamford, from where the line rises to an elevation of 863 ft at the east end of Cowburn tunnel before falling to the junction at Chinley. By comparing these figures it will be found that there is a saving each way of nearly 300 ft in rise over the route via Ambergate.

It is clear that although the Midland would still be tied in with the MSLR from New Mills onwards the running powers over the MSLR from Barnsley were too restrictive and did not allow the company to break out from Manchester to the valuable hinterland of Lancashire and Cheshire. They were to achieve this through participation in the Cheshire Lines Committee (CLC) and agreements made with the Lancashire & Yorkshire Railway (LYR) which included regular passenger services to Blackpool. There were high hopes of attracting new traffic from the north east of Sheffield and in fact it was achieved with regular goods trains from Bradford, Leeds and York running over many years. It was also thought that the Buxton seasonal passenger traffic would be substantial and so it proved to be.

However, the overarching reason for their enthusiasm was to have an alternative to the Peak line at times of engineering difficulties and to relieve the line of some of its increasing traffic. It would also prevent the heavy expense of having to widen the existing route. Although it was not said at the time it is perfectly clear that the earlier schemes to reach Hassop would not have increased the capacity problem hence the choosing of the route to Chapel en le Frith and Chinley.

THE DORE AND CHINLEY RAILWAY COMPANY

PLANS TO MAKE THE APPLICATION

14 Nov 1883. As previously noted, an application was made for an Act in the 1884 session for a railway of twenty miles nine chains and fifty links (twenty miles and 118 yards) in length starting at a junction facing Sheffield near the south end of the platform of the Dore and Totley station and terminating at a junction with the Ambergate and Manchester line of the Midland Railway at, or near, the north end of the Ambergate line's Milton viaduct. A second line at a junction with the above railway at Lower Breck Field and terminating at a junction with the Ambergate and Manchester line at a point 23 chains (506 yards) south of the junction of the main railway was also included in the application and this became known as the 'Chinley South Curve'.

Although the Act included the Chinley South Curve the Midland, when it took over the line, felt it necessary to seek a further authorisation from Parliament. The Dore South Curve was legislated for in the following year.

Originally running powers were sought to Sheffield Midland station, Buxton Midland station and to New Mills South Junction, because the D&C was a company legally independent of the Midland Railway. Further running powers were sought from the MSLR for the line from New Mills South Junction to New Mills station.

30 Nov 1883. The plans and sections were drawn up by Parry & Walker and J. Somes Story and deposited.

SHEFFIELD TOWN COUNCIL SUPPORTS THE SCHEME

14 Feb 1884. At a meeting of Sheffield Town Council chaired by the mayor Alderman W. H. Brittain, who just happened to be a director of the Dore and Chinley Railway, a motion was unanimously carried to be sent to Parliament supporting the Bill. The chairman in passing commented: 'It would also come into competition with traction engines and he hoped, would run them off the road'.

Between Mar and Jul 1884 was a period of frenetic activity.

THE SELECT COMMITTEE CONSIDER THE BILL

20 Mar 1884. Those present, many of whom gave evidence, clearly show the local industries in the valley affected and the benefits that could accrue to Chapel, Buxton, Sheffield and Chesterfield. On the first day those in favour were heard and on following days the objections were heard at length.

From **SHEFFIELD**

William Henry Brittain: Mayor and putative director of the company said that 'if a businessman wished to go to Liverpool and back in a day he would leave Sheffield at 9.00 am and arrive in Liverpool at 11.30 am. If he could not finish his business before 3.45 pm he would have a choice of two trains. One would leave at 4.45 pm which took 3¾ hours to run the seventy six miles to Sheffield or another at 8.00 pm which would arrive in Sheffield at 10.42 pm. A wait of thirty minutes occurred at Godley Junction, a terribly exposed station, with no refreshment room'. He thought it would be of great benefit to the working classes of Sheffield who could escape the smoke for the Hope valley, many being fond of fishing and other sports.

Mr Jowitt: the late Master Cutler, spoke regarding the benefit the line would bestow on those exporting to America and India. He produced a petition from most of the large firms in Sheffield who between them employed up to 20,000 workers.

Mr Bainbridge: the managing director of the Nunnery colliery, believed he could develop his trade in Derbyshire.

Alderman Leader: editor of the *Sheffield Independent*, reminded the committee that Sheffield had 'cherished the line for the past fifty to sixty years'. The ordinary road had seriously deteriorated due to the traction engines. He felt that 'though the town was not badly served it was not sufficiently well served by the MSLR'.

Others who did not speak were:

A. Wightman, Councillor T. J. Flockton, Councillor J. W. Dixon the President of the Chamber of Commerce, Councillor Aizlewood, Bernard Wake and E. Wake, solicitors.

From **CHESTERFIELD**

J. Stores Smith of Sheepbridge Ironworks told the hearing that 35,000 to 40,000 tons of limestone was transported to its works from Buxton and Worksop and that if the line was opened they would transport a large proportion of it from the Castleton area.

From the **HOPE AND EDALE VALLEYS**

Rev Francis Beresford Champion: vicar of Edale who provided information regarding the Edale valley and his land holdings. In his evidence he said he owned two farms, one of which had the line directly through it. His mother owned 720 acres in the parish and 200 acres in the Castleton parish. All the coal required was brought from Chapel en le Frith, seven miles away, over steep and bad roads at a cost of 10/- a ton which was expensive. The severity of the climate at 850 ft meant that there was a large coal usage, no wood being available as in old times. The nearest market was Sheffield, twenty miles away, which nobody went to as it was too far away. As a result the population was dependent on dealers who visited to sell cattle and dairy produce. The population had declined from about 500 to 340 due to the isolation of the area, the nearest railway station being at Chapel en le Frith. Everybody was in favour of the line. His mother owned the Speedwell and Blue John caverns which attracted 2,375 visitors the previous year (only 46 a week). The land in the valley needed draining and liming but this was not undertaken because of the high transport costs. The line would open up the milk traffic and residents would be able to get to Sheffield market. Several substantial houses which used to be occupied by gentlemen of means had now been given up to poor working farmers who only used the kitchens.

Isaac Hall of Castleton, a Manchester solicitor, said that in Manchester there was a general feeling in favour of the line.

Robert Ashton of Castleton was a smelter of iron ore and white lead until four years ago and was still the owner of several lead mines in the area. He said 'he had great difficulty working his mines because of the distance that the coal he required had to travel for pumping water and that the lead industry has been in depression for some years' and added that 'He used to get coal from Dronfield at 9/- a ton carted on roads that were in a bad condition'. He was impressed by the prospect of the railway and planned to become a director.

William Cameron Moore: son of the owner of Moore & Son, lace makers, in Bamford and attended with his father Joseph Moore. Moore Junior said they acquired 400 tons of raw materials per annum from Manchester via Chapel which was carted to Bamford from Chapel at 8/4 and 10/- a ton. The line would save the company between 6/- and 7/- a ton.

J. S. A. Shuttleworth JP of Hathersage was the deputy lieutenant of Derbyshire at this time and had a 2,500 acre estate. He echoed the view that a great reduction in the price of coal would be achieved.

J. A. Cocker of Hathersage was a manufacturer of drawing and spiral springs. He said that the line would go near his works and through his father's house. His business was not worth carrying on and he would close it down if the line was not built. He had to cart his goods the eleven miles to Sheffield at 11/3 a ton to get the best rates. He used ten to fifteen tons of coal a week which cost 7/6 a ton for cartage.

Joseph White Broomhead of Hathersage was on the board of the Guardians of the Poor and was a corn miller and grocer. He said his mill was leased from Shuttleworth. He ground forty to fifty quarters of corn and thirty quarters of oats a week. He used a quantity of flour which was ground elsewhere but chiefly in Sheffield. The cartage from Sheffield was 11/6 a ton. He received corn from Liverpool which arrived at Bakewell or Beauchief. He complained the roads had been cut up by traction engines. In commenting on the state of trade in the village he said the umbrella factory had closed down due to the cost of coal and that a good many houses in Hathersage were unoccupied.

William Johnson of Hathersage was a quarry owner producing millstones and employed twenty people. His annual production was 750 tons and he sent the stones to Liverpool, Hull and many other places for export. The cost of cartage to Beauchief was 10/6 to 12/6 a ton. He said there are ten millstone quarries in the district producing 5,000 tons annually.

From **BUXTON**

Mr Milligan: a draper and member of the local board of trustees of the hospital and spoke favourably on behalf of the trustees.

Dr Robert Bennett said that it was a great inconvenience to the town which had a population of 20,000.

From **CHAPEL EN LE FRITH**

William Henry Greaves Bagshawe JP of Ford Hall did not speak.

And

Lord Edward Cavendish said that the line would run for 1½ miles through the Duke of Devonshire's land. He added that the Duke supported the line and believed it would revive the area.

John Noble: general manager of the Midland Railway spoke later.

Mr Fowler: solicitor to the company did not speak.

Edward Parry: the chief engineer, said that stations would be built at Grindleford, Hathersage, Hope and Edale (but not Bamford). He also explained that Castleton, despite its importance, was not on the line because if the route went there and 'got an unfavourable gradient the whole purpose of the line would be destroyed'. Provision had been made for sixty four acres of ground at various points on the line to get rid of the spoil from the tunnels and cuttings.

THE OBJECTORS

THE MANCHESTER SHEFFIELD AND LINCOLNSHIRE RAILWAY

Mr Underdown, the general manager of the company, complained that the promoters were seeking to interfere with, and take considerable portions of, their property. However, an accommodation had been arrived at. Before the hearing the new Duke of Rutland had settled his differences regarding shafts on his grouse shooting land on Totley Moor but only after some considerable negotiation. This left two other objectors namely Mr Ebenezer Hall of Abbeydale Hall at Totley and Mr Edward Firth of Birchfield at Hope.

EDWARD FIRTH

Edward Firth complained that he was not consulted about the line. The proposed embankment would go straight through his estate, cutting him off from his trout stream and interfering with his views. The only access to his house was from the Hope to Aston road and the proposal to lower it to allow the line to go over it would mean that an already steep road would be impracticable for a gentleman's carriage.

The Hope to Aston bridge 35 (178834) in Oct 2006 showing the road climbing toward Aston which was changed to improve Edward Firth's carriage access to his house. *Author*

Killhill bridge No. 37 was the answer to Firth's requirement for an accommodation bridge. The Midland had to put in this bridge in any case because a public footpath already existed. This view is looking toward Edale Road in Oct 2006 (174839). *Author*

He complained that the nuisance of passing trains and the embankment would prevent him extending the park. If the station was put where proposed on the western portion of the estate it would be 430 yards from his property and 'it would be the utter and absolute ruin to his property. It would be in full view of his windows and right under the gaze of the occupants of the house when they sat down to dinner.' He thought the alternative site was just as bad. It was countered that accommodation bridges across the river would be built wherever he required them.

Regarding the proposed Hope station the company highlighted that they had selected a site at the side, rather than in front, of his house with most of the station yard being at ground level. It would be a quarter of a mile from his house and 100 ft below. However, he felt that it was just as bad as it being directly below. Either of the proposed sites would have placed the station conveniently on the edge of the village. In support of Firth Mr W. R. Blakelock JP, the managing director of the Sheffield Water Works Company, said the railway would be disastrous for the estate. 'There would be smoke, mobs of people at the station and all the dirt and annoyance that a railway from Sheffield would bring'. He thought the company had chosen this route rather than one on the other side of the valley because it would have to pass through the land of three or four large proprietors and they preferred to deal with one small one. Firth admitted that the line would bring benefits to the local economy but said that he felt he was being scapegoated by a problem he had not sought. He only wanted to be left alone. In the event Edward Firth's objections were upheld and Hope station was relocated further east to its present site, a good way from the village. His victory over the promoters of the line was well deserved because a station with a goods yard

The imposing Birchfield (178839) in Oct 2006. *Author*

would have felt like being back at the works in Sheffield and would have completely negated the tranquillity of the house and its grounds. It was bad news for the residents of Hope who for ever more had a station, in the long tradition of Midland country stations, a long way from the people it purported to serve. However, Hope's loss was Bradwell's gain as the station finally built was somewhere between the two villages. On the other hand the Midland did gain plenty of space to develop goods facilities which would have been denied them at their favoured location.

EDWARD FIRTH AND BIRCHFIELD

Edward Firth was one of the younger sons of Thomas Firth who became head smelter at Sanderson Bros & Co in Sheffield. Two of his sons, Mark and Thomas junior joined him at Sanderson's but the sons became unhappy with their wages and left to set up their own business. They started out at Charlotte Street in Sheffield in 1842 with just six crucible pot holes and then persuaded their father to join them. However, Thomas senior died in 1850 and Mark Firth became head of the firm assisted by his brothers Thomas and John. Their younger brothers Edward and Charles Henry joined the business later. The company grew quickly with the construction of the new Norfolk Gun Works. Thomas Firth junior died in 1860 at the age of 38 years but by the 1870s Thomas Firth & Sons employed over 1,000 men and had become the world's best known steel and gun forging firm. Ten years later the firm had become a limited company and doubled its workforce and the site now covered over twenty acres of land. In 1880 Mark Firth, the driving force behind the growth of the company, died age sixty one. The streets of Sheffield were lined with mourners at his funeral because of the high regard in which he was held for his creation of so many jobs and bequests to the city such as Firth Park and Firth Hall. By 1890 the complex consisted of the Norfolk steel works, shot forge, foundry, file department and the saw and edge tool section. Between them the various works produced 5,000 to 6,000 tons of crucible steel each year, this being used for general engineering work such as turning tools, twist drills, reamers, punches and hammers. Die blocks for stamping out drop forgings, parts of small arms, bicycles and sewing machines were also made in large quantities. In the rolling mills at the Norfolk works fifteen gangs of men worked day and night to produce sheets for circular and other saws, cylinder laggings, shovels and bars for tools, drills and cutlery.

The company eventually amalgamated with John Brown & Co to become Firth Browns and is now part of Sheffield Forgemasters.

From 1856 to 1881 Edward was a member of the firm. In 1881, when the firm became a limited company he became a director and a large shareholder and was in charge of the mills and forges at the Norfolk works. He was described by his old employees 'as being like a typical old English country squire. He was very neat and precise in everything he did.' When he prepared to leave the Norfolk works on horseback to go to his main home at Tapton Edge he would be seen 'sitting astride a fine horse and would carefully adjust his coat collar, flick a speck of dust off his sleeve, gently pat his horse's neck and set off'.

Edward Firth told the Select Committee that in 1874 he purchased a small property at Birchfield and from then on bought further property from twenty one freeholders round about until he had 313 acres. The price he paid for the land was £24,000. It included the buildings that were already on the ground but not his mansion house. Very little of the land was moorland. The house cost £8,000. The fishpond, drives, roads and other things cost £7,000 or more. He spent £6,000 in rebuilding and refitting the farm buildings. In total he spent £52,000 including £4,000 on pictures. The value in 1884 without the pictures and things in the house was £45,000 including the farm houses which were let out on leases. Edward is said to have been in poor health and used the property and estate for six weeks in 1882 and two months the following year, revealing that it was really a holiday home and shooting lodge. It was obviously an escape from the appalling pollution engendered by his company, and many others, in Sheffield. Enlarged several times, it had extensive grounds and is still situated on the southern slope of Win Hill with unrivalled views of the picturesque scenery in the neighbourhood. A large plain house with the palest reflection of neo Jacobean style it was lavishly appointed inside and included a porch with a modest, but delicate, Blue John window.

Edward Firth was a generous benefactor and supporter of the community and in 1887 donated £2,050 to completely restore St Peter's church in Hope and was represented at the celebrations for the opening of the line.

He died on 18 Dec 1907 and left £251,398 gross in his will, which was a very substantial sum. The estate passed to his son Edward Willoughby Firth, a bachelor who lived in the house with his sister Catherine Elizabeth until she died in 1925. The estate was auctioned and bought by Aaron Frost Hancock of Bamford, who over the following eighteen months sold significant portions of the estate in plots. The lodge was bought by Henry Stockton Evanson and his wife who turned it into a country guest house/hotel in 1926. By World War Two it had become a hostel for the Worker Travel Association until the 1950s when it was taken over by the Wood Street Mission of Manchester and subsequently the Greater Manchester Youth Association. As such it was used to accommodate youngsters from Manchester on residential courses. In 1994 it was sold to Contract Data Research Ltd, a locally based private company who restored the house as its headquarters. In 2000 it was sold again to Nash & Co who converted it into four apartments which are currently in private hands.

Edward Firth was successful in getting the projected position of the line moved to his advantage, had an accommodation bridge built for his convenience and prevented a station and attendant sidings being positioned anywhere near his house or indeed near the village.

REFERENCES

Ledingham Richard – *Birchfield Lodge and the Firth Family*. Hope Historical Society: Rediscovering Hope, research by members of the society 2011. www.hopevalleyonline.co.uk

Hamilton Christine – *Firth Brown a Sheffield Steel Company*. Tempus Pub 2000

This view, taken on 30 May 1957, shows the heightened embankment on the right, that was created to meet Ebenezer Hall's objections to the line. Hall tried to stipulate that a 600 yard tunnel should be built to protect his view. The Midland offered a landscaped cutting at a fraction of the £20,000 the tunnel would have cost. This view is taken from Twentywell Lane bridge looking towards the tunnel. To the left is Dore South Curve. The train is drifting down the gradient towards Dore and Totley station with BR standard No. 73074 in charge on 4 Aug 1962.
Geoff Newall © Ted Hancock

EBENEZER HALL

Ebenezer Hall's objections were of an even more serious nature and could have caused difficulties for the engineers and a disproportionate expense for the promoters and, ultimately, the Midland. Hall lived in retirement at Abbeydale Hall, not far from the existing Dore and Totley station, from where he could already hear trains on the Sheffield to Chesterfield line. This new line would cross his land and he objected to the noise and annoyance the trains would cause by reason of engines whistling so near his house. He wanted a six hundred yard tunnel, or covered way, to be built which would cost £20,000. Edward Parry, the engineer, offered to screen the line with an ornamental embankment but objected to a tunnel so near a junction 'because they sometimes get filled with steam and prevent lights being seen at night, and trains had occasionally to be stopped by hand lamps'. Also part of the line near Hall's estate was to be on a curve. 'If the line were in a cutting, by raising the signals, they could enable the engine drivers to see any distance, but if the line passed through a tunnel the difficulty of signalling from one point to another on the curve would be much increased. Because of its proximity to a junction trains would frequently have to stand in the tunnel, and this, besides being a cause of discomfort to passengers, would be conducive to accidents'.

Hall also objected to two reservoirs on his land being interfered with. It was pointed out by the promoters that these were mill dams and not reservoirs. The company went on to say that one of the dams would not be touched at all but there was uncertainty at this stage about the other. Hall also felt that the Old Hay trout stream would be interfered with and that the line would cross his pleasure grounds but the promoters said they would divert the line to prevent this. In the event a footbridge was built across the line for Hall's purpose and although the line was diverted it was not to the extent that Hall wanted. The bridge built was No. 4 and was half a mile from the start of the line and was named 'Hall's Private Road'. It had three arches, two of 23 ft and the centre one of 27 ft. The bridge had stone abutments, wings and piers and lattice main girders. (see page 149). The superstructure was removed and the piers taken down in Jul 1921.

The proceedings were not without some humour. Mr Hall's counsel said 'If a man wants to get away from a railway, and has bought an estate for that purpose, do you think it will be an advantage to him to have Sheffield excursionists brought under his nose'. (Laughter). The railway's counsel replied 'I do not think they would be brought under his nose. I think the railway would relieve him from a great many excursionists who at present pass close to him in vans. It has been my experience that the noisiest excursionists are those who travel on dusty roads in vans'. (More laughter).

On 26 Jun 1884 an agreement was reached with Hall that where the line would pass through his land it would be diverted to increase the distance from his residence. Furthermore the line would be in a cutting of at least 25 ft depth with shrubs or trees planted subject to the sighting of signals for the safe working of the traffic. The Midland was given three years to complete the work, these arrangements being enshrined in the first Midland Railway Act concerning the Dore and Chinley Company.

It is apparent that Hall had a rough time from the Midland Railway and its shareholders who would not brook obstacles to the building of the line or extra expense in meeting his demands. He clearly deserved more respect than he received. However he was savvy enough to realise that he might be better able to succeed in his objections by becoming a shareholder. He did get his cutting, if not the tunnel that he wanted, and also a bridge across the line to access the part of his estate that was cut off. Why it was demolished ten years after his death is not known but most probably the section of the estate beyond the railway was sold off.

EBENEZER HALL (1820-1911)

Ebenezer Hall was born in 1820, the second son and third child of Gilbert Hall and Elizabeth Slack. His father and grandfather were successful lead miners in Middleton by Wirksworth. He was a bright boy and attended Cromford school which had been founded by Richard Arkwright in 1832. His schoolmaster recommended him to John Roberts, a childless Sheffield silversmith, who wished to adopt a promising young man to succeed to his silver plating business.

Ebenezer Hall in 1896. Author's collection

So, at the age of sixteen, he moved to Sheffield and was apprenticed to the firm of Wilkinson & Roberts, living with John Roberts and his wife Sarah at their house on Shrewsbury Road. He learned quickly and became a traveller finding business for the company. In 1847 he was offered a partnership when Roberts' original partner retired, the firm becoming Roberts and Hall. The firm went from strength to strength and in 1852 amalgamated with Martin & Naylor of Fargate to became Martin, Hall & Co. The firm expanded and moved to the Shrewsbury works at Broad Street in the Park district. Around this time several of Ebenezer's brothers joined the firm.

In the mid-1850s John Roberts retired from active involvement and in 1851 purchased Abbeydale Villa at Dore, which later became Abbeydale Hall, where Ebenezer moved to live as a border. Robert's wife, Sarah, and her cousin Sarah Wilkinson (26) also lived there. The house was set in extensive grounds, in rural surroundings, on the turnpike road between Beauchief and Owler Bar. In the following six years the house was extended but was then severely fire damaged which completely destroyed Ebenezer's room. Roberts extended his estate by buying a large amount of land on both sides of Baslow Road including Greenoak House, for £10,000. After Hall had become the owner of Abbeydale Hall he bought the Totley rolling mill and land and buildings along Baslow Road at Totley Rise. It was access to this land that was at the heart of Hall's dispute with the Midland Railway.

In 1866 Martin, Hall & Co became a limited company with a capital of £150,000 and Ebenezer became a joint managing director. Ten years later he married Sarah Wilkinson and five years after that he bought Abbeydale Hall from John Roberts although the latter continued to live there until his death in 1888. John Roberts had built St John's church at a cost of £5,000 and the vicarage and its expenses were financed by Roberts, Ebenezer and the Duke of Devonshire. Ebenezer was also a benefactor of Dore church.

Ebenezer Hall had now become an important and influential figure in Sheffield and sat on the boards of Sanderson Brothers and Newbould Ltd as chairman, Sheffield and Rotherham Joint Stock Bank Co as chairman and the Sheffield United Gas – Light Co as a director. He was a generous charitable giver. Besides his major contribution to St John's church he was a trustee of the Cherrytree orphanage which had relocated to Mickley Lane. When he died in 1911, at the age of ninety one his estate was worth £194,000. After looking after his family and friends he left the residuary to the Sheffield hospitals, charity schools, Cherrytree orphanage and did not forget the needs of Middleton by Wirksworth and the Park district of Sheffield from his earlier years.

His was a typical story of a long time Peak resident moving to Sheffield in the vibrant nineteenth century boom years and through drive and entrepreneurial skill succeeding to become a trusted, respected and wealthy member of his adopted city.

Abbeydale Hall stood empty until 1923 because no buyer could be found, and it was then converted into a hotel named Abbeydale Hall. It was used to accommodate golfers and small weekend conferences. The Yorkshire and Australian cricket teams stayed there. In 1929 it was put up for sale at £7,500 or offered for rent. Norton Rural District Council eventually bought the property at less than half the asking price for £3,250 and used it as a district office and community centre in 1931. The adjacent land was sold to Abbeydale Sports Club. During the Second World War it was used as a civil defence centre and temporary buildings were put up in the car park to store gas masks for distribution. After the war it was reopened as a community, adult education and field studies centre. It has now been converted into designer apartments with an annex of additional apartments having been added.

Abbeydale Hall (318808) in its beautifully cared for rural setting. The Sheffield to Owler Bar road passes directly in front of the house. The infant River Sheaf is this side of the foreground trees. The Chinley line when built would pass in front of the stream. The Sheffield to Chesterfield line was less than a mile away to the right. Note the new villa houses in the background on New Road which is now Dore Road.
Picture Sheffield. Sheffield Libraries

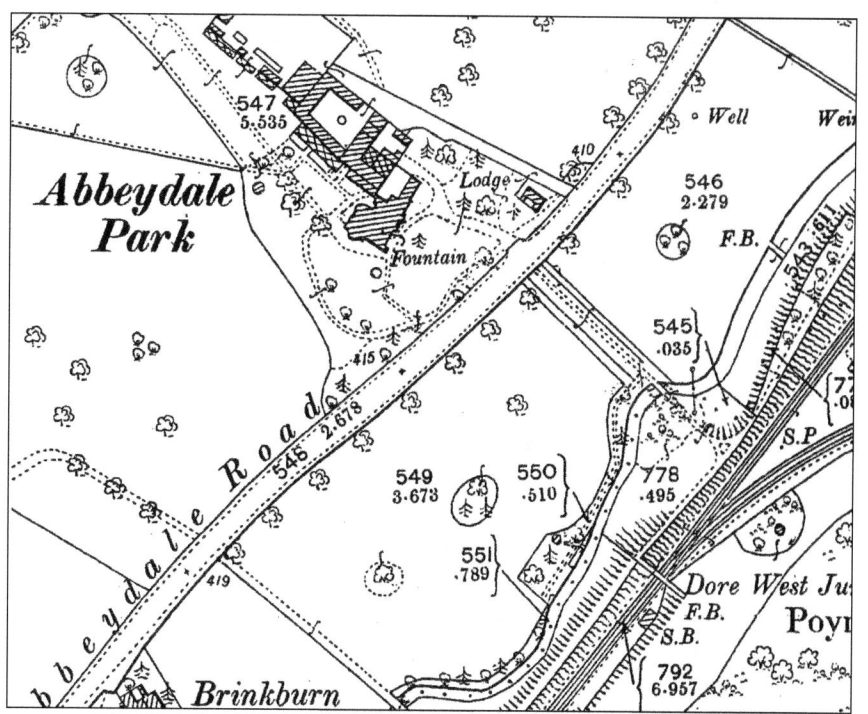

The 1898 OS map enlarged shows the location of Hall's Private Road bridge (322808) a little to the west of where his original path was located. It is situated at Dore West Junction and the signal box can be seen to its left. The bridge at 27 ft was high enough to not obscure the signalman's view of the junction. The Dore South Curve is to the right. When the Midland presented its Bill to take over the line from the Dore and Chinley Railway Co objections could not be raised again unless there was a material difference in the plans. The Dore South Curve was an addition and Hall took the opportunity to object to the curve and the tunnel without success. On the left is the line to Dore and Totley station. As can be seen the Old Hay Brook has not been diverted although it was diverted from the tunnel mouth for a few hundred yards. The size of Hall's property (322811) and the rural nature of the area are well depicted.

THE DUKES OF RUTLAND

The Midland seems to have been uncertain whether a shaft on his grouse moor was necessary but, because of the length of the tunnel, eventually realised that one was essential. Negotiations with the estate were difficult although an agreement was reached that had strict conditions as to the ventilation shafts location and size and stipulated that no work could take place during the grouse shooting season.

It took a year to complete the negotiations for the shaft on Totley Moss.

The 7th Duke of Rutland. *Author's collection*

THE DUKES OF RUTLAND

Two of the Dukes of Rutland were involved in objecting to the line. Charles Manners the sixth duke (1815 – 1888) was as the eldest son the Marquess of Granby before 1857. Educated at Eton and Trinity College, Cambridge he entered Parliament as the Conservative MP for Stamford and became known as a voluble, if not particularly talented, protectionist. He briefly held office as a Lord of the Bedchamber to Prince Albert from 1843 to 1846 (somebody had to do it!). He became leader of the party on 10 Feb 1848 but resigned within a month, feeling himself inadequate for the post. From 1849 to 1851 he became joint leader of the Conservatives in the Commons with the young Disraeli and John Charles Herries. His political career did not flourish and he declined to join the first Derby ministry in 1852, being appointed Lord Lieutenant of Lincolnshire instead. He succeeded to the dukedom of Rutland on the death of his father in 1857. He had a long cherished a passion for Mary Anne Ricketts, who later became Lady Forester, but his father forbade the two to marry.

He became known as the 'bachelor duke' and also the 'sporting duke' because of his passion for shooting. Between 1857 and 1870 he created twenty miles of roads on his Longshaw estate, including those on Totley Moor, for the benefit of his grouse shooting activities and to provide drives for his visitors and guests.

The building of the line took place under the watch of John James Robert Manners (1818-1906), the seventh Duke of Rutland, who succeeded to the dukedom on the death of his brother in 1888. He was a long serving politician and held the posts of Postmaster General twice and the Chancellorship of the Duchy of Lancaster amongst others. He was clearly a man of much more substance than his elder brother.

THE DUKES OF DEVONSHIRE

From the beginning of the railways three different Dukes supported their building and saw the long term benefits that would accrue. Their support for the building of the line from Rowsley to Buxton, including permission to build the line through Chatsworth Park, is the best illustration of that. The stipulation of the 7th Duke that a station at Hathersage should be built was not to obstruct but to provide a genuine benefit for the people of the district as well as serving ducal interests. It was already part of the planning for where the stations should be located.

The 7th Duke of Devonshire. *Author's collection*

THE DUKES OF DEVONSHIRE

William Cavendish (1808-1891) was the seventh Duke of Devonshire from 1858 until his death. Like his neighbour the sixth Duke of Rutland, he was educated at Eton and Trinity College, Cambridge. He married the celebrated Blanche Georgiana Howard (1812-1840) and had four sons, one of whom died in infancy. He was Chancellor of the University of London from 1831 to 1856 and at Cambridge endowed the building of the Cavendish Laboratory. He made large, and ultimately unsuccessful, investments in heavy industry at Barrow in Furness but inherited a considerable amount of property in Eastbourne and oversaw the development of the town into a fashionable resort. His eldest son Spencer Compton Cavendish (1833-1908) succeeded his father as the eighth Duke of Devonshire in 1891 and had a successful political career, declining to become Prime Minister on three occasions.

CONDITIONS REQUIRED OF THE COMPANY AND THE MIDLAND

Going back to the Select Committee it required the Midland to make a written agreement with the Dore and Chinley directors and this was done shortly afterwards on 18 Apr 1884. By it the Midland agreed to pay a minimum of thirty pounds a week for each mile of the line once it was opened to the Dore and Chinley Co No bridges were to be of timber and the Midland would install the signalling at the Dore and Chinley's expense. No station would be on a grade of more than 1 in 300. The permanent way was to be approved by the Midland, with the rails being of not less than 80 lbs per yard and would be properly fished and laid in chairs weighing not less than 40 lbs each. Larch or foreign wood timber would be used and covered with the best creosote, to the same standard as other Midland main lines. Maintenance of permanent way would be carried out by the Midland at its own expense with the locomotives and rolling stock also being provided by the Midland.

A Dore and Chinley fund was to be set up with the gross receipts of local traffic arising and terminating on the railway being paid into it. A mileage proportion of the through traffic and terminal allowances on through traffic terminating on the line would also be paid into the fund. Additionally tolls from other sources of revenue, including those paid by other companies, would be included. Twice yearly, at the end of June and December, the fund would be equally divided between the two companies with not less than thirty pounds per week for each mile being taken by the Dore and Chinley.

MIDLAND SHAREHOLDERS APPROVE AGREEMENT WITH THE DORE AND CHINLEY RAILWAY COMPANY

18 Apr 1884. A meeting of Midland shareholders was held at Derby which approved the agreement with the Dore and Chinley Railway. However, queries were raised by none other than Ebenezer Hall who, having failed to get his tunnel to protect his estate at Totley, had evidently decided that if you could not beat them then join them, he having become a shareholder. He asked why another company was fronting the undertaking. His question, unfortunately, went unanswered. He then argued that the company had originally guaranteed 3% in perpetuity to the Dore and Chinley Railway but were now saying that £30 per mile per week would be paid. Having felt he had received unsatisfactory answers, Hall pushed his argument to the point where he demanded a poll, to the annoyance of other shareholders present. The chairman informed Mr Hall that the directors held proxies to the value of nearly £3,000,000 and 8,136 votes whereas Mr Hall had shares to the value of £135,172 and 446 votes. On receiving this information Hall withdrew his demand!

On the same date notice was given of an application by the Dore and Chinley directors for an additional provision to be included in the Bill regarding the agreement between the promoters and the Midland Railway to the effect that the Midland would guarantee thirty pounds a mile. This also suggests that the directors had gambled on getting approval from the shareholders for the written agreement with the Dore and Chinley.

DORE AND CHINLEY RAILWAY ACT GAINS THE ROYAL ASSENT

28 Jul 1884. The Dore and Chinley Railway Act gained the Royal Assent. The first directors were Robert How Ashton of Lose Hill Hall, Castleton; William Henry Greaves Bagshawe of Ford Hall, Chapel en le Frith; William Henry Brittain (the Mayor of Sheffield); George Henry Cammell of Brookfield Manor, Hathersage (his father was the founder of Charles Cammell & Co whose huge Cyclops works in Sheffield manufactured metal products, iron wheels and rails for the railways and in 1903 amalgamated with Cammell Laird shipbuilders); Arthur Francis Pennell; John Spencer Ashton Shuttleworth of Hathersage Hall, (who profited from selling some of his land to the railway and was then further rewarded when he sold more land in the early 1900s for the opening of Bole Hill quarry – this provided the stone for the Howden and Derwent dams) and William George Thorpe of Elm Court Temple, London. The capital was to be £1,050,000 in 105,000 shares of £10 each. The company was authorised to borrow up to £350,000 and the railway was to be completed within five years.

The schedule was the same as the agreement between the Dore and Chinley Co and the Midland signed on 18 Apr and also included that no bridges would be made of timber. All the signalling would conform to Midland practice and the station facilities were to match those found on other parts of the Midland. The track was to be to the design and specification of the Midland engineer. The Dore and Chinley would maintain the structural works, embankments etc for the first year after the line's opening although the Midland would supervise the work. However, the Midland would maintain the permanent way from the date of opening. The Dore and Chinley would receive into a revenue account the gross receipts in respect of local traffic starting and finishing on the line.

The Duke of Devonshire required that a station be built in the parish of Hathersage for passengers, animals, goods and minerals. The Duke of Rutland made stipulation regarding the ventilation shaft on the moor above Totley tunnel; namely that it would be of a position that he approved and should not protrude above the level of the ground to ensure his grouse shooting was undisturbed. His Grace also required that a station be built near Grindleford Bridge. The Act stipulated that to accommodate the wishes of Edward Firth of Birchfield House the line would be thirty yards further away from his house and 5 ft lower than the deposited plans. The Hope to Aston road under the line was to be altered to ease the road gradient.

The book of reference made provision for the building of stations at Grindleford, Hathersage, Hope, Edale and the newly added Bamford.

The common seal was witnessed by Ernest Paget, director and, later, chairman, of the Midland and Messrs Ashton, Cammell and Thorpe of the Dore and Chinley Railway.

APPLICATION FOR THE DORE SOUTH CURVE

12 Nov 1884. Notice of an application for the 1885 Parliamentary session was tabled to amend the original Act to include a new line by a junction with the Sheffield to Chesterfield line, 26 chains (572 yards) south east from the booking office on Dore and Totley station to join the Dore and Chinley Railway in Poynton Woods, 20 chains (440 yards) in a south westerly direction from the junction with the Chesterfield to Sheffield line. This was to be called the 'Dore South Junction Curve'. Powers were also sought to move the proposed line a few yards south, in Totley tunnel, around Totley Bents recreation ground. Permission was requested to acquire properties and land between Killhill bridge No. 37 and the *Cheshire Cheese Inn* at Hope, this being to accommodate Edward Firth's objections. On the financial side permission was sought to raise £20,000 additional capital by shares and £6,666 by direct borrowing. Further it would empower the Midland Railway to subscribe or contribute an amount not exceeding £100,000 towards the capital of the company and to appoint two directors to the board at the expense of two of the Dore and Chinley directors. This is the first indication that the company might not raise sufficient capital to finance the project.

25 Jun 1885. The second Dore and Chinley Act came into law without any major change.

THE MIDLAND AGREES TO INVEST £100,000

6 May 1885. An agreement was made between the Dore and Chinley Railway (the owning company) and the Midland Railway (the working company) – the owning company was to construct and the working company was to maintain. The agreement altered the line's direction and its levels and sanctioned the building of the Dore South Junction Curve. The Midland agreed, subject to a special general meeting, to subscribe £100,000 to expedite the start of the two main tunnels so as to complete the railway as soon as possible. As indicated above the Midland would nominate two directors and the number of Dore and Chinley directors was consequently reduced to five.

FURTHER APPLICATION TO PAY DIVIDENDS OUT OF CAPITAL

12 Nov 1885. Notice was given of an application to Parliament for a further Act in the 1886 session to pay dividends out of capital not exceeding 3% and not to exceed £70,000 during the construction of the works and to extend the agreement between the owning company and the Midland. It was obviously thought it would be easier to attract investors if they did not have to wait five long years before receiving any return.

27 Jan 1886. The Bill was considered to have complied with standing orders.

11 Mar 1886. By this time the Bill was in trouble for although it had passed the Commons it was being opposed in the Lords. Mr A. P. Mundella, the Liberal MP for Brightside Sheffield and President of the Board of Trade, proved to be a key man in swinging opinion in Parliament. At a meeting with him he told the directors he would do what he could.

8 Apr 1886. It was reported that the Bill was experiencing some difficulty in harmonising with the standing orders of the House of Lords, which is where Mundella comes in as he was able to influence members of the Lords to refer the whole matter to a Select Committee. The arguments for this action were problematic because usually Parliament would not give approval for such a proposed course. Because of the backing of the Midland and the fact that the line would provide employment with over a million pounds in circulation for around five years it was seen to be highly advantageous at a time 'when trades were suffering from a great and protracted depression'. The Bill was at the mercy of the 'inexorable draconianism' of Lord Redesdale, but the promoters had a stroke of luck, from their point of view, for he conveniently died.

20 May 1886. The Lords Select Committee decided to report to the Commons in favour of an alteration or modification of the standing orders. The *Sheffield Independent* commented 'that the Dore and Chinley Company directors will be grateful to Mr Mundella who has extricated them from what would have been a fateful difficulty'.

19 Jun 1886. The Bill was read a third time and passed.

25 Jun 1886. The Act received the Royal Assent allowing the payment of interest out of capital subject to two thirds of the £1,050,000 share capital being raised.

THE DELAY IN PROCEEDING

18 Aug 1886. The *Sheffield Independent* reported that there was no chance of an early start on the line. Although the directors wanted to get moving since obtaining the Act the condition of trade and pressure from another quarter (the Midland) had meant no progress was likely for a considerable period. The engineers of the line and Midland officials had gone over the line recently and were sure no additional powers would be necessary. There was much disappointment in the district.

10 Dec 1886. The *Sheffield Independent* reported that speculation was rife that the company had petitioned the Midland to allow them to get started but the Midland was holding back because of the continuing depression of trade.

9 Mar 1887. The *Derby Mercury* noted that some sign of a revival in activity was reported. Landowners would shortly be approached regarding the sale of land.

23 Mar 1887. The same paper revealed that following a slight revival of trade the engineers of the line and some contractors including Thomas Oliver of Bristol and Daniel Jewitt of The Cedars, Whaley Bridge, had been making short surveys of the route to create tenders to be sent to the Midland directors.

6 Apr 1887. The *Sheffield Independent* and the *Derby Mercury* reported that the contractors who had been surveying the route had put tenders for various lengths to the Midland who were considering them. Work would commence at an early date if traffic revived which was thought to be likely. The continuing delay was because with traffic receipts falling the directors were not inclined to call on shareholders for the £100,000 they had agreed.

6 May 1887. The *Birmingham Daily Post* stated that at a special meeting of the Midland shareholders at Derby, a resolution was passed, but not unanimously, to release the £100,000 promised to the Dore and Chinley company if they were unable to raise the balance. The delay which had occurred was of their own making because the last year had been 'an anxious one for the directors and shareholders. Although trade was now improving, the progress was slow but not without encouragement'. It was the depression in the limestone and iron trades which was detrimental to Midland interests at that time. They could not wait long as the time was limited for buying the land required and having regard to the cheapness of money and the low price of materials they thought the directors of the line should be assisted to get started. They felt the railway could be built within the capital authorised.

25 May 1887. Although the prospectus of the Dore and Chinley company had not yet been issued it was expected to be circulated soon after a meeting on 3 Jun. The appointment of J. P. Edwards as contractor for the western end of the line was confirmed for the first time. He has taken Queen Anne's cottage at Chinley and would shortly take up residence. The landowners in the Hope and Edale valleys 'are not inclined to throw the least hindrance in the way of the company or delay the construction of the line by a single day and it is believed that some are willing to take up the value of their land in shares'.

The cover of the prospectus of the Dore and Chinley Railway clearly shows the Midland's footprints all over it even down to the offices of the company being at the Midland station in Derby. *Author's collection*

3 Jun 1887. At a meeting of the Dore and Chinley company at Derby, Mr G. E. Paget, deputy chairman of the Midland, was elected chair of the company and Mr Lewis Randle Starkie, another Midland director was also appointed. It was also reported that J. P. Edwards was lying seriously ill at his residence at Edgbaston, Birmingham.

20 Jun 1887. The prospectus of the Dore and Chinley Railway was finally issued.

DORE AND CHINLEY RAILWAY ABANDONED

7 Jul 1887. At a meeting of the company in London it was announced that the response to the prospectus was insufficient and as the powers of the Act would expire in three weeks time the directors saw no purpose in continuing and the proposal fell to the ground. A later newspaper report said that some unnamed private firms offered to find the necessary capital, but withdrew their offer. More than one resident in the Hope valley had remarked that 'a more disappointing wet blanket could not have been thrown upon the inhabitants'. One particular casualty was William Crossley, a farmer and landlord of the *Bull's Head Hotel* in Castleton, who filed for bankruptcy four months later. He said that the cause of his problems was the sickness of himself and his wife and bad trade but he had carried on in the hope that the new railway would revive trade.

12 Nov 1887. Notice was given to Parliament for the abandonment of the Dore and Chinley Railway in the 1888 session.

24 Jul 1888. The Dore and Chinley Railway Co, having been unable to raise the necessary capital, was dissolved and was required to repay £49,740 to the depositers. It is clear from these figures that the undertaking never really got off the ground. Potential investors were obviously not convinced that they would get a decent return.

THE MIDLAND RAILWAY TAKES OVER

17 Feb 1888. The Midland held its half yearly shareholders meeting in the board room at Derby. At it the directors recommended that the Dore and Chinley Railway Co should be taken over by the company. They had obtained powers to build the line and the Midland guaranteed the amount of traffic equal to £30 a mile per week from the time of the construction. The capital could not be raised on that guarantee and so the Dore and Chinley Railway Co had applied to the Midland directors to give them favourable terms so that they could raise the necessary capital. After consideration the directors had come to the conclusion that because of the importance of this line to the Midland company it should itself undertake the burden directly instead of indirectly and thus secure its sound and economic construction with their own, instead of borrowed money. This proposal drew applause from

The prospectus as published in the *Sheffield Independent* on 28 Jun 1887.

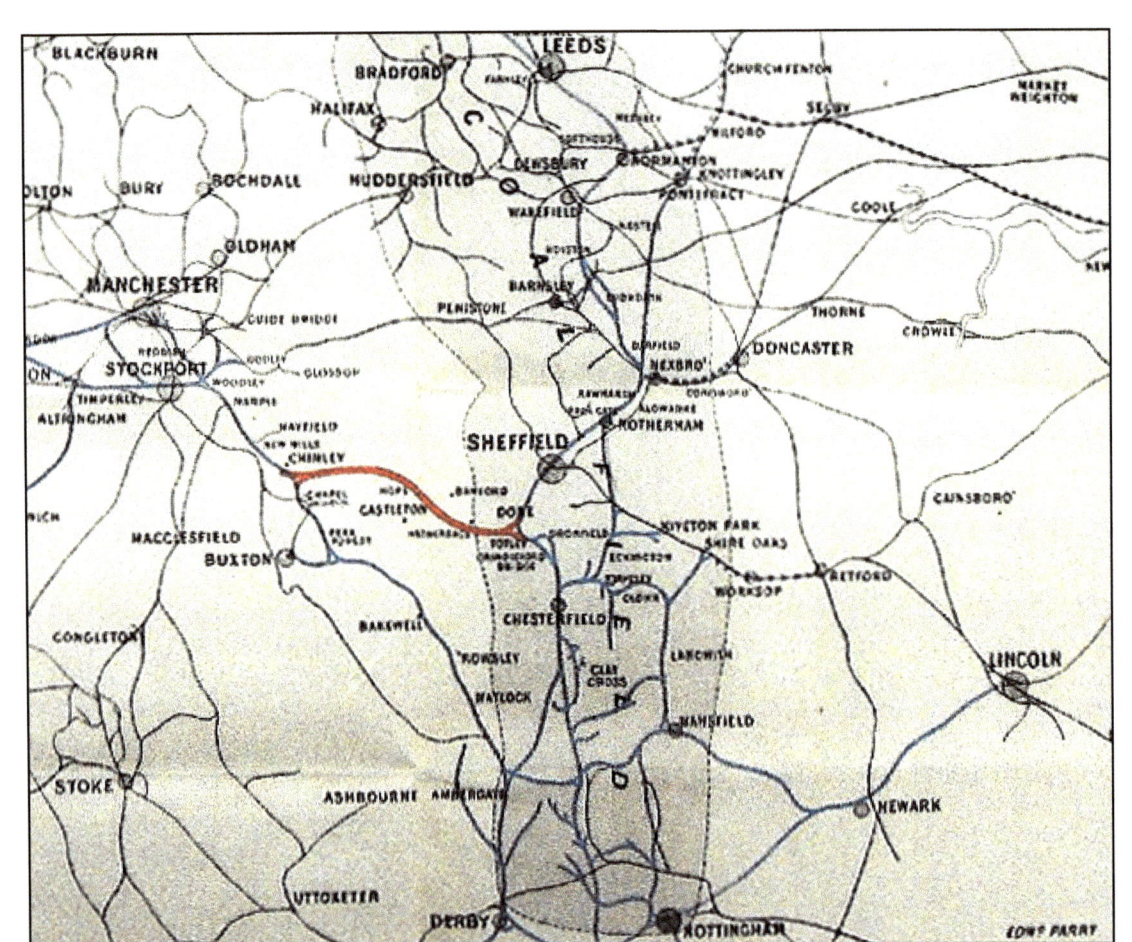

The map of the line in the prospectus showing it in the context of the rest of the Midland system.
Author's collection

the meeting. The shareholders would be asked at a further meeting to sanction an application for those powers.

The capital powers for its own Bill were £1,000,000, which it was proposed to create and issue as MR 4% preference stock. The premiums obtained were sufficient to pay interest during construction: this power of paying interest having already been specially granted to the Dore and Chinley.

The chairman said that the first resolution was 'a Bill to confer additional powers upon the Midland for the construction of works and the acquisition of lands, for raising further capital for amalgamating with their undertaking, the undertaking of the Dore and Chinley company, and for extending the time for the acquisition of lands and for the construction of the railway and for other purposes subject to such alterations as Parliament might think proper to make be approved'. The motion was carried without further discussion.

24 Jul 1888. The Act, besides dissolving the Dore and Chinley Railway, transferred its powers to the Midland Railway and the time for completion of the line, five years, was extended to start from this date and carried a penalty of £50 a day for every day after that time until the line opened. It gained the right to issue £900,000 of MR 4% preference stock as required.

THE CHINLEY SOUTH CURVE – A SECOND ACT

23 Jul 1888. Notice was given to Parliament for the 1889 session for the building of the Chinley South Curve. Although this was included in the original Dore and Chinley Railway Act of 1884 it was felt necessary to seek a second Act. The description of the line is more detailed and probably deviates from the original line.

24 Jun 1889. The Act was passed.

NEW POWERS IN EDALE VALLEY AND DORE & TOTLEY

24 Jun 1891. A notice was given to Parliament for the 1892 session for the alteration of levels and two farm road diversions around Clough Farm in the Edale valley. Application was also made for the widening of the Dore to Sheffield line from a point in the centre of Dore and Totley station by the company's own engineer J. A. McDonald. This also included the diversion of Twenty-well Sick Lane (Twentywell Lane) from where it crossed the Chinley line just south of Dore and Totley station to build a new road down to the Owler Bar main road (Abbeydale Road South) and to close the old road which curved round to the entrance to Dore and Totley station.

28 Jun 1892. The Act was passed.

CONCLUSION

The truth is plain and simple; the Midland had lost a lot of time in getting started because of the failure of the Dore and Chinley company to raise sufficient capital to begin the line. From 30 Nov 1883, when the parliamentary plans were deposited, to 11 Sep 1888 when work finally started was nearly five years. While the delay suited the Midland's purposes to some extent it was a period when the legislators and legal men were the most important players.

PREPARATIONS FOR STARTING THE BUILDING

THE ENGINEERS AND CONTRACTORS

In the deposited plans of 30 Nov 1883 for the parliamentary session of 1884 the engineers appointed are shown as Parry & Walker and J. Somes Story of Nottingham and Derby respectively. The key man was Edward Parry who drew up the plans and was the supervising engineer of the whole route with Story. Parry's partner, Walker, does not appear to have been directly involved.

The resident engineer for the first ten and a half miles from Dore and Totley station to Brough Lane Head just before Hope station was Percy Rickard with the long cutting to Totley tunnel, the cutting and short tunnel of Dore South Junction Curve, the viaduct at Hathersage, the girder bridge across the River Derwent at Mytham and, of course, Totley tunnel being the main works. The resident engineers for the western section from just before Hope station to Chinley North Junction and the Chinley South Curve was George Ernest Story and Mr Hodgson, of whom nothing is known. The main works were Cowburn tunnel, the four span Cowburn viaduct at Barber Booth and the magnificent Milton viaduct on Chinley South Curve.

The contractor for the eastern section was Thomas Oliver of Horsham, Sussex and his engineer was Joel Lean. John Price Edwards of Chester was awarded the western section and his agent was James Scott.

The contract for the stations on the line was awarded to Walker & Slater of Derby, although a number of sub-contractors were employed.

On 23 Jan 1894 a technical paper on both major tunnels and the short Dore tunnel, was prepared by the resident engineer, the late Percy Rickard (he had died three months earlier), and was presented to the Institution of Civil Engineers by Edward Parry who, with John Somes Story, was the engineer for the tunnels. Parry also surveyed the tunnels. The contractor, Thomas Oliver, was praised by Parry in the paper stating 'how admirably the work had been executed. He had under great difficulties, succeeded in carrying it out and must be heartily congratulated upon its completion'. As we will see the engineer's relationship with the contractor was not quite that rosy as the progress of Totley tunnel fell well behind schedule. Oliver does not appear to have been sufficiently hands on and his forward planning did not match that of Edwards. He was less successful than Edwards at attracting men in the early years of the work although this was primarily because of the appalling working conditions in Totley tunnel and also his tardiness in building sufficient accommodation of a good enough standard. However, with the large centres of population at nearby Sheffield and Chesterfield and a trade recession in those areas, he should have had more success than he did.

On Contract No. 2 the contractor John Price Edwards, got the job because his quote was the lowest. His tender proved to be unrealistic and the Midland knew this from the engineer's original estimate. He impresses as a man who prepared thoroughly, thought ahead as is shown by his planning for Milton viaduct and produced good quality work on time. He underestimated the cost of operating in the isolated Edale valley and the resulting costs of getting materials and machinery to the site. The dry rot in the heading timber and the cost of its replacement could not have been foreseen but the failure of the replacement timber head trees should have been anticipated. A more prudent contractor would have built into their quote an amount for unforeseen circumstances. It is clear that the costings were underestimated, which is quite surprising, given his level of experience. He comes across as being good at using local materials evidenced by his opening a quarry and brick making kilns at Edale. He was fortunate that the shorter, but still long, Cowburn tunnel did not present the same magnitude of difficulty of water ingress that bedevilled the work at Totley. Although he had problems recruiting labour at Edale he was more successful at attracting men overall than Oliver despite having to compete with the Manchester Ship Canal, under construction at the same time. His underestimate for the contract led to difficulties resulting in the work being taken from him and the Midland taking it forward in house when his bank refused him further financial support. It was an ignominious end to a long career.

EDWARD PARRY (1844-1926)

Edward Parry was born in 1844 at Hendy near Mold in Flintshire. He was educated at a private school in Chester which suggests he came from a family of some substance. In 1869 as a young man in his early twenties, he started his career with a baptism of fire (or more likely frostbite) on the Midland's Settle to Carlisle line as a resident engineer on Contract No. 2 for the seventeen miles from Dent Head, working for Benton & Woodiwiss, the contractors. It included Arten Gill viaduct, Rise Hill tunnel, Dandy Mire tunnel, Lunds viaduct, Ais Gill summit, Mallerstang, Birkett cutting and the tunnel to Smardale viaduct. It was the most difficult section on the line and became the most celebrated. He then became assistant engineer on the Nottingham to Melton Mowbray line which included four short tunnels and a viaduct across the River Trent. It was opened in 1879.

In the same year, at the age of thirty five, he became the county surveyor for Nottinghamshire and was responsible for the construction of the Nottingham Suburban Railway, an independent company but one which had a close working relationship with the Great Northern Railway. Work commenced in Jun 1887 and the line opened on 2 Dec 1889. The plans had to be constantly revised to accommodate the requirements of the Great Northern Railway, the Midland Railway and Nottingham Corporation. His estimate for the cost of the line was £194,000 which was seriously short of the eventual cost of £262,500. This three and a half mile line had four tunnels totalling 1,213 yards, the longest being 442 yards and the shortest seventy yards, eighteen bridges, steep gradients and deep cuttings. There was a fifth tunnel of 118 yards which provided a connection to the works of the Nottingham Patent Brick Company, of which he was a director from 1896 to 1903 and chairman from 1902 to 1903. The branch was so steep that it had to be worked by a stationary engine. Its most prestigious contract was the supply of ten million bricks for the building of St Pancras station and hotel. The contractor for the line was none other than J. P. Edwards, who was to win Contract No. 2 for the Dore and Chinley Railway.

Parry started his work on the construction of the Dore and Chinley Railway by August 1888 but was not resident in the area during the construction as he needed to juggle his responsibilities in Nottingham and Totley.

Edward Parry, engineer of the Dore and Chinley Railway.
Pike & Co.

After his work on the Dore and Chinley line he was resident engineer on the Great Central Railway's London extension from 1896 to 1900. His section was from Annesley to Rugby, including the tremendous earthworks around Nottingham and the Victoria station. He had three different contractors working to him. From Dec 1898 to Feb 1899 there were heavy rains and Parry recommended that fast expresses should not be run from the opening of the line because of the risk of landslips. As a result seventeen different speed slacks were imposed costing forty five minutes running time for the first three months of operation, a major blow to the prestige of the newly opened line.

From 1905 to 1909 he became engineer to the South Yorkshire Joint Railway which was used by the GCR, GNR, LYR, MR and NER to transport coal from eight newly opened collieries including Thurcroft, Maltby, Dinnington, Rossington and Harworth.

Parry was noted for the quality of his work and its durable construction which made its dismantling in the later years of railway decline and contraction difficult and expensive.

In addition to his civil engineering practice he was chairman of the Railway & Engineering Company in Nottingham and a director of the Digby collieries plus the previously mentioned Nottingham Patent Brick Company.

He lived at Woodthorpe Grange in Nottingham from 1889 until his retirement. Ironically the Nottingham Suburban Railway cut the estate in two before he bought it. It was sold to Nottingham Council in 1921 and the grounds became a well loved park which is still enjoyed today.

Parry died in Leamington in 1920, age 76 years, after a distinguished career.

JOHN SOMES STORY (1846-1927)

He was born on 26 Sep 1846 his family being from the Newcastle upon Tyne area. He first came to prominence as resident engineer along with Edward Parry, for Contract No. 2 from Dent Head to Smardale on the Midland Railway's epic Settle to Carlisle line. It was an apprenticeship like no other. He was appointed as the guide for F. S. Williams who was on a field trip researching his landmark book 'The Midland Railway: its Rise and Progress'. From 1877 to 1905 Story was the county surveyor for Derbyshire (the same post that Parry held for Nottinghamshire). One of his first designs was the imposing stone facade that marks the entrance to the Strand Arcade in Derby, which was completed in 1880. He was architect and surveyor for many of the public buildings erected in Derbyshire at this time including, in 1893, the original county council building in St Mary's Gate, Derby which cost £26,000. It was later converted into a police station and became a Grade II listed building. It has been sympathetically restored as the four star Cathedral Quarter boutique hotel. He was also involved in a large extension to the county asylum.

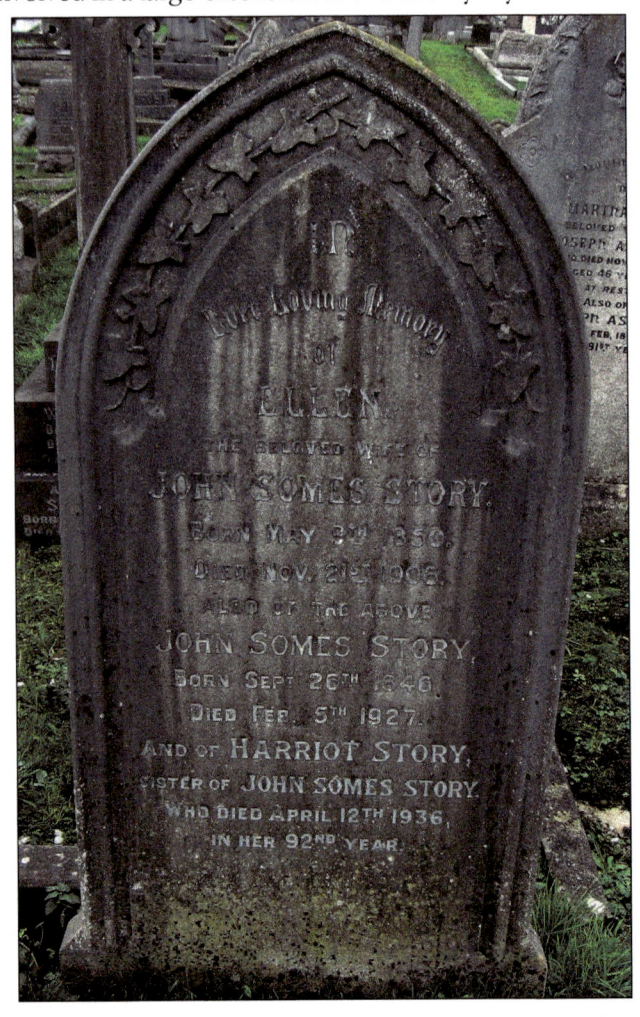

The gravestone of John Somes Story in St Giles churchyard at Matlock which he shared with his wife Ellen and sister Harriot.
Author

Story was able to combine his duties as county surveyor and take the post of overall engineer with his partner Edward Parry on the Dore and Chinley Railway. As the work drew to a close in 1895 he had a watch made to his own specification by a top watchmaker S. Smith & Son of The Strand, London for which he paid the very large sum of £85. This is an indication that here was a wealthy and successful man.

Following Story's retirement in 1905 he went to live at Bridge House at Cromford in Derbyshire where he could pursue his angling interests on the River Derwent. His wife Ellen, who was born in 1850, died in 1906 only a year after he retired. When his residence in Cromford was sold as part of the Nightingale Estate he moved to Beckenham in Kent where he died on 5 Feb 1927 age 80 years, leaving a substantial estate of £29,453 gross. At his funeral there were no flowers except a bunch of snowdrops sent by his sister Harriot. He was buried in St Giles churchyard at Matlock. His choice of burial place suggests a great love of Derbyshire and its associated country life.

PERCY RICKARD (1859-1893)

Percy Rickard was born in Derby on 12 Mar 1859 and was educated at Derby's grammar school. He gave early indication of a practical turn of mind and agreed to be placed, when not quite fifteen years of age, as a pupil in the locomotive works of the Midland Railway at Derby, under the company's locomotive superintendent S. W. Johnson. Not only did he go through the shops and drawing office with great credit, but he carefully prepared for the future by attending in his spare time the local classes held under the auspices of the science and art department. On the expiration of his pupillage he was articled, in Nov 1877, to Edward Parry, of Nottingham, who was then acting as one of the resident engineers constructing the Nottingham and Melton line of the Midland Railway.

After spending two and a half years with Parry he entered, in Apr 1880, at the age of twenty one, the service of the LYR, under William Hunt. He was first placed in the drawing office at Manchester and was entrusted with making surveys and contract drawings, the most important of those being an iron bridge carrying one of the main thoroughfares over the widening of Manchester Victoria station. He subsequently made, for Hunt, a survey of Fleetwood channel, marking the contour lines of the bottom of the channel for every fathom in depth and indicating the direction of the currents – his work was considered very well done. In Jan 1883, still only twenty four, he was appointed divisional engineer in charge of about 150 miles of line in the Yorkshire district, being responsible for the maintenance of the permanent way, station buildings and signals on that section and had charge of small contracts and extensions. In Jul 1885 the district system of organization was abolished and a permanent way engineer for the whole line was appointed with the result that Rickard left the company.

In 1886 he returned to work for Edward Parry, as resident engineer on the construction of the Nottingham Suburban Railway. This line, with its five short tunnels, proved a very valuable proving ground before he commenced his final work at Totley on the longest land tunnel in Britain. His work at Nottingham had either finished or he was released early, because it was reported, in Aug 1888, that he 'has taken up his residence in Dore, and will remain during the construction of the line'. The residence was given in 'Kelly's Directory' for 1891 as 'Grange House', Totley Brook but was in fact 'Totley Grove'. He lived there with his wife Elizabeth and young son George and two servants. He also had a gardener who lived in the grounds.

Rickard's untimely death occurred in the saddest of circumstances and can be directly attributed to the unhealthy nature of his profession. The navvy huts at the east end of the tunnel drained directly into Needham's Dyke but during the warm summer of 1893 it had run nearly dry, leaving it practically an open sewer. This brook flowed through Rickard's garden and under a corner of his residence. His doctors were of the opinion that its foul state was probably the cause of the attack of typhoid, which took his life on 31 Oct 1893 at the age of thirty four.

His qualities and experience were recognised when, on 13 Jan 1885, he was elected an associate member of the prestigious Institution of Civil Engineers and became a full member on 27 Jan 1891. Before his death he had prepared a paper for the Institution titled 'The Tunnels of the Dore and Chinley Railway' which was presented posthumously, three months later, by his employer Edward Parry, who described him as 'his late friend and assistant' and as 'a talented engineer'. In reporting his death to the Midland directors Parry commented that 'he has in every way done his utmost to watch over and secure the interests of the Company'.

Rickard had married in 1887 and, when he died, he left a wife age twenty seven and son George now age four, having lost a daughter age six months in Oct 1890. However they had two further infants age two and eleven months. By 1901 the widowed Elizabeth was living in Bakewell with her three children and a servant. After the First World War she emigrated to Canada and died in Toronto in 1951 age eighty five. Son George died at Niagara Falls in 1937 age forty eight. It is a common occurrence that the fruits of ones labours are not seen but none could have been more poignant than in this case as the line opened only days after his death. With all the responsibilities he had borne on his young shoulders in the long, fraught, wearisome and physically sapping time spent in the tunnel, together with the seemingly never ending obstacles that presented themselves as the work inched forward, it is not surprising that it may have taken a toll on his health and reduced his resistance to disease when it came. He was denied the richly deserved satisfaction of seeing the first revenue earning trains pass through the tunnel hauled by a locomotive designed and built by his first tutor, Samuel Waite Johnson.

FREDERICK HERBERT

This young man was a civil engineering assistant to Edward Parry and was no doubt a junior member of his team but is included because of his tragic death. In Aug 1889 when the work on the shafts was in full swing this twenty two year old man started work on the tunnel and a few days later, with his plan canister, he set off from Dore and Totley station for the workings. When he reached where the temporary contractor's line crossed the Abbeydale road there was a gate controlled by Edward Green, who was just about to let a train of six wagons heading for the tunnel cross the road. Green noticed that the engine overtook Herbert and he was seen to throw his canister onto the footplate and try to jump on. He missed his footing, fell to the ground and a wagon ran over his left leg, cutting it and crushing it from top to bottom and a thumb and two fingers were cut off his left hand as well. He was taken to Dore and Totley station where Dr Aldred decided he should be admitted to a Sheffield hospital. However, all was in vain, because, having lost so much blood the doctors concluded that it was too late to operate. He died without recognising his mother and sister who had arrived at his bedside that afternoon. At the inquest the engine driver, John Roberts, said that Herbert's first words after the accident were 'my address is Mapperley Road, Nottingham' which indicates that Parry had recruited him from his local community.

THOMAS OLIVER (1834-1920)

Thomas Oliver was born on 22 Mar 1834, the youngest son of Cuthbert Oliver, in Newton le Willows in Lancashire although he was baptised at nearby Lowton. It is said that his father was involved in the building of the Liverpool and Manchester Railway as a platelayer, but rose to become a railway engineer. Cuthbert was brought up in Allendale in Northumberland and it is also said that he had a close working relationship with George Stephenson. He retired to live at Hasland near Chesterfield about 1840 and died there in 1865. Was it coincidence that Cuthbert moved to live near Stephenson who retired to Tapton Hall near Chesterfield until his death in 1848?

Thomas was educated at Giggleswick, which had a notable private school, and followed his father into railway building. In 1850 at the age of sixteen he was articled to Charles Bartholomew, engineer to the South Yorkshire Railway and River Dun Company. After completing his apprenticeship he took up work with John Wignall Leather of Leeds, where he held the position of contractor's engineer working on the River Nene improvements between Wisbech and Peterborough.

His first connection with the Midland was working on the Wellingborough section of the Leicester to Hitchin line, opened in 1857. Then he worked on the Horsham to Petworth line in Sussex which opened in 1859. This was followed by the Alfreton to Clay Cross line of the Midland, opened in 1861.

Oliver was resident engineer on the Shrewsbury and Welshpool Railway and the Minsterley branch which was opened between 1861 and 1865. The original contractors fell down on the job and he took over, ensuring that the work was completed. He had set himself up in 1863, at the age of twenty nine, as an independent contractor and this would have been his first job. It was a very hard and testing beginning.

Overlapping with the above work he started a long association with the London Brighton & South Coast Railway (LBSCR). From the age of twenty three in 1857, until 1865, he worked with Edward Woods, who was involved with the ground breaking Liverpool and Manchester Railway thirty years earlier. In 1836 Woods was appointed chief engineer to the LBSCR, a post he held until 1852, when he became an independent consulting engineer in London. Oliver worked with Woods on the Mid Sussex Railway, between Horsham and Petworth, which opened in 1859 and the later Petworth to Midhurst line, which opened in 1866. At the same time they were building the Horsham and Guildford Direct Railway which also opened in 1866. In later years he independently built the line from Chichester to Midhurst and, finally, the Coulsdon, Merstham, Redhill and Earlswood line which was part of the main line from London to Brighton which opened in 1899.

In 1867 he tendered for the Blea Moor No. 2 section of the Settle and Carlisle line against six competitors which included such famous names as Brassey and Firbank. Two of the six interested the Midland board, namely Benton & Woodiwiss at £243,096 and Oliver at £242,941. However, by Nov 1867, Oliver had withdrawn his bid. Perhaps he thought that it would be more than he could cope with at this early stage of his career?

He then had the contract to build the section quadrupling the Midland main line by the Wymington curve north of Sharnbrook tunnel which allowed the ruling gradient for goods traffic to be eased from 1 in 110 to 1 in 200. It was opened in 1875.

He returned to the Midland as contractor for the Cudworth to Barnsley line which opened in 1869, followed by the Mansfield and Worksop line which was started in 1870 and opened in 1875. Further work with the Midland included the lines from Bennerley to Bulwell in 1881.

By 1884 he had a contract for part of the second line and loops of the Bristol & South Wales Union Railway between the newly opened Severn tunnel and Swindon and built Patchway station, opened in 1885. He also worked in Bristol on widening the GWR line at Lawrence Hill. The contract immediately before starting at Totley was the construction of the Barrow Gurney reservoirs for the Bristol Waterworks Company and several of the locomotives from this contract were transferred to the Dore and Chinley work site. He additionally contracted for many bridges and widenings.

Oliver's works were based in Derby and whilst living in Horsham he travelled every Monday to Derby, returning home on Friday. Like all contractors he needed to get his contracts finished on time, on budget and to the plans approved by Parliament and, above all else, handle a disparate and volatile workforce. It was reported by his descendants that he was in the habit of having a revolver handy when out on site, just in case! Legend has it that he made a lot of money on the side by accepting wagers that the tunnels he contracted for would meet exactly when the headings met!

In respect of working to budget, in the case of Totley tunnel, the Midland awarded him an extra £14,500 as recompense for the delays caused by the huge amount of water entering the headings, an almost unknown gesture by a railway company to a contractor. As an example Weetman Pearson, trading as S. Pearson & Son, obtained the contract for the South Wales Direct line of the GWR to link the new Severn tunnel with Swindon, including the tunnel at Chipping Sodbury. He was awarded the contract for £1,300,000 but because of flooding in the above tunnel it cost him £1,612,000 to complete. Despite arbitration and legal proceedings, which he lost, the GWR were not prepared to budge resulting in Pearson's vow to never again work for the GWR.

Like most contractors during this late period of railway building the engineering, design and management sides were much larger than the earlier contractors had needed and, thus, Oliver diversified his business into other building projects; there was simply not enough railway work to go round anymore.

Oliver married Caroline Gichard, a half French and half Cornish woman from Polwyn in Cornwall, in Sheffield in 1854 at the age of twenty, whilst working for Bartholomew, and they moved to live in Horsham in 1857. In 1887 he purchased the freehold of 'Tanbridge' and demolished the farm on the land to build a large neo Elizabethan house where he lived in considerable affluence and comfort for the rest of his life. They had six children, four boys and two girls.

Thomas Oliver looking every inch the country gentleman. Do I detect a steely glint in his eye which would have been required for the day job? *Author's collection*

In 1880 Oliver leased a Scottish sporting estate on an annual basis and every year transported his family and servants north in a special carriage attached to a Scotch express. One wonders if he shared his interest in shooting with the Duke of Rutland's agents and whether that helped to smooth out any difficulties with access to the Duke's land on Totley Moor. Was he perhaps invited to join the Duke's shooting parties during the season? A bit fanciful I suspect but not entirely unlikely as Thomas was an extremely clever and astute operator. There is evidence that he did not keep a close enough eye on the work in Totley tunnel and was absent from the contract more often than the resident engineers desired. He also proved to be tardy in providing hutted accommodation for the navvies and the standard of it seems to have been poor.

His wife died in 1904 but Thomas lived another sixteen years and reached the grand old age of eighty six. He was buried in Horsham. His descendants relate that his greatest boast was that he constructed the longest land tunnel in Britain.

The two eldest sons, Thomas and Frederick, joined the family contracting business and took it over when their father retired in 1900. It is difficult not to believe that Thomas senior did not get involved in a contract as prestigious as the Great Central London extension. They were awarded the fourth of seven sections from north of Rugby to Charwelton, which included the 2,987 yards Catesby tunnel. The total contract length was 15 miles 77 chains and involved the employment of 2,000 men, the use of twenty steam locomotives, eight steam navvies and 550 wagons. At the same time he had a contract to build Great Withens reservoir at Rishworth. The Olivers also secured the contract for the Northolt Junction to Neasden section of the GWR and GCR joint line from 1901 to 1905 but before that were busy with a quarry line from Stoats Nest to Earlswood for the LBSCR, the Beighton to Treeton, Thackley near Shipley, Alfreton to Clay Cross and the earthworks for the Erewash Valley widenings for the Midland. Add in a line for the Midland & Great Northern Joint Railway from Yarmouth Beach to Lowestoft Central and all were completed by 1900. In 1902/3 the Olivers worked for the Midland again on the Finchley to Welsh Harp widening. Then in 1904 they had a five year contract to build Bute docks to Pontypridd and Tongwynlais to Treforest line for the Cardiff Railway. While that was going on they were also widening the Earlswood to Horley line for the LBSCR.

Oliver & Son then obtained a major contract for a line from the Swansea and Neath Railway between Morriston and Britton Ferry, opened in 1912, and the Neath Loop line which was finished in 1914. While fulfilling these contracts they were widening the Pontardulais to Brynea and the Llandilo branch for the GWR, the Redhill widening for the LBSCR and a line from Stanton to Ripley for the Midland. In 1915 T. Oliver & Son amalgamated with J. R. Ling to become Oliver, Ling & Co. During this period they worked on Ridham Dock at Sittingbourne and the Military Camp railway at Heylesbury but by 1919 the company had gone into liquidation just before Thomas senior died.

JOEL LEAN (1859-1905)

Joel Lean was an engineer appointed by Thomas Oliver. He started his career under his father William Lean to whom he served a pupillage of three years. On its completion he worked for Charles Richardson on the construction of the Severn tunnel. Richardson had cut his engineering teeth under Marc Brunel when he was making the uncompleted Thames tunnel and succeeded the legendary Isambard Kingdom Brunel as engineer on the South Wales Union Railway following his death in 1859. Lean subsequently served as contractor's engineer on branches of the Great Western Railway and the South Devon line until he was engaged by Francis Fox of Bristol on the setting out of the Exe Valley Railway which opened in 1885 and acted as resident engineer on the Weston super Mare loop line which opened in 1884. In the same year he returned to work for Richardson on the doubling of the Bristol and South Wales Union Railway and as resident engineer on the Patchway tunnel. In 1887 he became a member of the firm of Buchholz, Lean and Metcalfe who practised as consulting engineers in London and Bristol. This company was dissolved in Dec 1890. He worked on flour milling machinery in Bristol, surveyed and devised plans for railways in the Isle of Man (the Foxdale Railway?) and worked on the widening of the Great Western main line. This included work for Lancaster Owen who was said to be resident engineer to Sir John Fowler (who we met earlier surveying a line that did not come to fruition) on the widening of Maidenhead bridge. As this took place between 1890 and 1893 it would have overlapped his work on the Dore and Chinley line. He also worked on the reservoir at Richworth for Wakefield Corporation before joining Oliver as an engineer on the Dore and Chinley line.

This information has been taken from the obituary in the minutes of the 'Proceedings of the Institution of Mechanical Engineers' in 1905 and on looking up the dates of the works he was recorded as being involved with there are overlaps and contradictions. Looking at Oliver's contract history it is almost certain their paths would have crossed in the Bristol area. Despite the reservation expressed above about Lean's CV it was such that Oliver was fortunate to get the services of such an experienced engineer who was still only around thirty years of age.

Lean was appointed as resident engineer on the Rivelin tunnel railway of 1903 to 1909, ahead of five other applicants by Sheffield Corporation. He took up post on 1 Mar 1903 and was provided accommodation at Priddock House, near the tunnel entrance at Rivelin. He persuaded the subcommittee overseeing the work that electrical plant should be acquired, this providing the necessary power for driving the four mile tunnel from Ladybower to Rivelin. However, his tenure was short for he died eighteen months after his appointment from pleurisy and pneumonia on 4 Aug 1904. His address was then Broomgrove Road, Sheffield (see Vol. 2).

It was said that his death was hastened by the nature of the work. One wonders how much his health had already been in decline, he having also worked in the Severn, Patchway and Totley tunnels. He was appointed as an associate member of the Institution of Civil Engineers in Feb 1885 and a full member on 16 Feb 1892. His obituary stated that he was a man 'who worked on the most modern lines, introducing electric traction into the tunnel'.

GEORGE DARRELL

Darrell was a subcontractor to Thomas Oliver. In Sep 1890 he was reported to have completed his contract and had a sale by auction at his home at Greenwood Farm, Millstone Edge, Hathersage. Here he had carts, chains and blocks etc and seven horses and other unnamed animals and drugs (drays) for sale.

YOUNG & WILLIAMS

In *Engineering* for Sep 1888 there is mention of this sub contractor being involved in Oliver's contract which may have involved the sinking of the Totley tunnel shafts. They were definitely involved in sinking No. 3 shaft. They had previously worked for Oliver in 1883 on the Wymington deviation.

MICHAEL FORD

Michael Ford was a Hathersage based man who gained the sub-contract to build the mighty Hathersage viaduct. He was present at the laying of the foundation stone on 29 Mar 1890 and the keystone ceremony on 20 Oct 1890 when he was presented with a purse worth £5 and commended for his workmanship. Before that on 19 Sep 1890 he ascended a ladder to examine one of the piers of the viaduct. As he descended the ladder broke and he fell 20 feet. Dr Ellison of Castleton was telegraphed to attend and found that he had only dislocated his shoulder, although he was severely shaken. Another report states that M. Hand worked with him.

ROBERT COOK

He was another Hathersage man who gained a contract under Oliver as early as Sep 1887. This is only known because he sued a man who was a publican at Intake, Sheffield at Sheffield County Court on 16 Oct 1890 for breach of warranty in respect of a horse Cook had bought to work on the line. When he tried to use it, it refused to work and a promised exchange for another horse fell through. He won his case. He is described as a manufacturer trading as R. Cook & Co Ltd, hackle pin maker.

W. IBBOTSON

This man had a contract and I can find two references to him. He was mentioned as being present at a ceremony for Hathersage viaduct and he placed an advertisement for the sale of six horses and accoutrements in Apr 1891 when his contract was completed.

WILLIAM HANCOCK

He was a local builder and was based at Sheephill Farm at Dore Moor, Sheffield and employed twenty seven men. He was awarded the contract for the portal at the east end of Totley tunnel and may have built all six tunnel entrances.

GEORGE ERNEST STORY (1860-1917)

George Ernest Story was the resident engineer on Contract No. 2. He was the younger brother of John Somes Story and was born sixteen years after his brother on 13 Sep 1860. His twin brother, Thomas Arthur, died at the age of

George Ernest Story at an unknown date.
Bedfordshire Standard

four years. He was brought up in London and was educated at the University College school and Epsom college. As an architect he was articled to the well known firm Ford and Hesketh who were based in the City of London.

George's first appointment was in the architectural department of the Midland Railway at Derby. He left after being appointed the resident engineer for No. 2 contract on the Dore and Chinley line at the age of 28 years.

On completion of the work he entered into partnership with another Derby engineer as sewerage contractors in Derby and successfully completed several sewage schemes (did his brother put a word in for him?). On the dissolution of this partnership he moved to Sheffield as assistant engineer for the corporation.

He subsequently moved to Bedford, it was said for the education of his children, where, as resident engineer, he oversaw the construction of the new waterworks on Clapham Road and also the new drainage system for the town. He remained in this post until Feb 1917, when at the age of fifty seven, a time when most men are beginning to value comfort and easier life, he volunteered to join the Army. He received a commission in the Royal Engineers. He started at Longmoor in Hampshire on 3 Feb 1917 as a Lieutenant but was sent to France three weeks later to reconstruct bridges and repair existing railway lines and lay down new ones. At the beginning of August, having always been a healthy man, he contracted dysentery. The seriousness of his condition required him to be sent home to a Wandsworth hospital but it was too late and he died on 9 Sep 1917. A full military funeral at Wandsworth was held and the mourners included his brother John Somes.

George married Evelyn Flora Marsh on 22 Aug 1893, three months after his father's death, at Alveston church in Derby. His wife died in 1937 age seventy five years at Upminster in Essex. They had three children, the eldest being Thomas Hedworth who joined the East Anglian Regiment in 1912 and at the time of his father's death was serving at the Mesopotamia front, having also served in India. His second son, John Anthony, was also in the armed forces at this time, as a cadet at Woolwich. Daughter Margaret was also involved in the war effort at a Bedford hospital. His two sons both survived the war and died in 1958 and 1956 respectively. George was an active sportsman, being a member of a rowing club in Bedford and he was also a cricket and football player.

JOHN PRICE EDWARDS (1826-1896)

John Price Edwards, the contractor responsible for No. 2 contract is always referred to as 'J. P. Edwards'. He was born at Tyddyn on a farm one mile east of Mold in Flintshire in 1826. In Oct 1847 he married Hannah Pass, age 21, at Hanley in Staffordshire and had two children, Eliza born 1850 and Thomas Edward born 1853. The 1851 census shows the family living at Elmhurst Street, Stone in Staffordshire with Edwards, then age 25, recording his profession as timekeeper and inspector of permanent railway which probably refers to permanent way maintenance. The 1861 census finds him living at Bont in Denbighshire with his wife and two children and his occupation as road contractor. The following census in 1871 finds him living at Chester Road, Tattenhall, six miles south east of Chester, working as a railway contractor. His son Thomas Edward is now 18 and described as civil engineer. This was probably his temporary home while working on the Whitchurch to Tattenhall contract. By 1875 Edwards is working on the redevelopment of Holyhead harbour and infrastructure. In 1873 there were massive dredging operations underway and a new large warehouse on the east quay was being built together with a revamped station with a five storey, sixty five bedroom, red brick station hotel which was opened in 1880. Edwards was in partnership with John Scott of Wigan and Thomas Bugbird of Caernarfon on this contract. The latter was a successful civil engineering/contracting firm in North Wales which survived until 1941. Edwards is recorded as living at Lytham at this time. On 4 Sep 1876 this partnership was dissolved by mutual agreement and does not appear to have been for financial reasons. The 1881 census records him living at Woodfield House, Pipers Ash Lane, Hoole, a village over a mile east of Chester. He married for a second time Isabella Whitehead age 37 years from Ashbourne, six miles from Melmerby, near Ripon in the late summer of 1876 and a daughter was born in 1879. What became of his first wife is not known. It suggests he met his second wife while working on the Melmerby to Masham line.

By the time Edwards was awarded the Nottingham Suburban Railway contract he was living in Birmingham but when he was awarded the Dore and Chinley No. 2 contract his address was Sibbersfield, Churton by Alford, a village eight miles south of Chester.

He worked with various partners over the years but he tendered in his own name for the Dore and Chinley contract. He worked as Smith & Edwards, Scott & Edwards, Scott, Edwards & Bugbird, Monk & Edwards and George Smith & Co.

His first contract appears to have been the building of the second station at Holyhead, which opened in 1866. He seems to have got it all wrong financially, for in Mar 1868 the *London Gazette* reported that, whilst a contractor at Holyhead, he was made bankrupt. He must have recovered quickly for a year later he had his next contract, working for no less than the LNWR. The 1870s were a very productive period for Edwards with multiple contracts running at the same time. Work was also plentiful in the 1880s. However he came unstuck for on 13 Dec 1884 the *London Gazette* reported the bankruptcy of Walter Smith of Southport and Bootle, trading with George Smith, Allan James Smith and J. P. Edwards as George Smith & Co, railway and public works contractors. This suggests that the CLC contract for the Aintree to Southport line was the problem. The bankruptcy was listed again for 21 Nov 1885.

His known contracts were:-

		Length Miles	Date Started	Date Open
LNWR	Holyhead station			1866
LNWR	Whitchurch – Tattenhall	12	1870	1872
LNWR	Frodsham Jct – Halton Jct	2		1873
NER	Melmerby – Masham branch	11	1872	1875
LYR	Lytham connecting line?		1873	1874
GWR	Alcester – Bearley North Jct	7	1873	1876
LNWR	Holyhead harbour and hotel		1873	1880
LNWR	Abersychan – Blaenavon	5	1875	1878
LYR	Burscough North West Loop, Bury?	1		1878
GVR*	Pontrilas – Dorstone	10	1876	1881
LNWR	Aston – Stechford	5	1877	1880
CLC	Sandhills & Brunswick MPD foundations		1877	1880
LNWR	Aston Gas Works branch		1878	
IWR#	Brading – Bembridge branch	4	1881	1882
CLC	Aintree – Southport line	14	1882	1884
LNWR	West Leigh branch to colliery	1	1883?	1886
NSR+	Trent Lane Jct – Daybrook	4	1887	1890
MR	Heanor Jct – Ripley line	5	1887	1890
GNR	Colwick Lane bridge		1888	
MR	Hope – Chinley North Jct	10	1888	1891
	Tyne Dock, South Shields		1890	

* Golden Valley Railway. + Nottingham Suburban Railway. # Isle of Wight Railway.

His work on the Nottingham Suburban Railway is interesting because it mirrors the Dore and Chinley contract in that his tender for the NSR of £111,501 (amended to £115,000) was the lowest whilst the highest was £151,495 and included one from Thomas Oliver. Parry had estimated the cost as £151,000, although the final cost was £262,500. He similarly underbid for the Dore and Chinley contract and got into severe difficulty as a result. Secondly, he was required to work to the engineer of the NSR, Edward Parry, and the resident engineer was the young Percy Rickard, all of whom were appointed in the same roles for the Dore and Chinley contract. There was a monetary bond required from Edwards, which was undertaken by James Scott of Scarsdale House, Ripley and Edward Price Edwards of Mold plus one other. Was this Scott his partner on previous contracts or was it the general superintendent Mr Scott of Meadow Lane, Sneinton? The former seems more likely. The latter is obviously a relative and is from the area in which Edwards was born. James Scott became the agent for Edwards on the Dore and Chinley contract.

Unlike the Dore and Chinley Railway the NSR shares were quickly sold although few were bought by the local population. As already indicated the NSR had numerous civil engineering features and vast earthworks. It cost £70,000 a mile and at the height of the contract Edwards employed 866 men, had 67 horses, seven locomotives and eleven portable engines with a maximum of 2,840 wagons.

The line was completed on 23 Nov 1889 and was opened on 2 Dec 1889 for passengers and goods but not without a controversy caused by Edwards. Although the railway inspector had sanctioned the opening Edwards refused to hand over the line to the company because he complained that outstanding financial matters had not been resolved. As the NSR had already made all the special arrangements for the opening with the GNR they were forced to seek an injunction to restrain Edwards from interfering with the opening proceedings. They were successful in obtaining an interim injunction but not in preventing Edwards from trying to sabotage the opening. The objection centred around £3,000 withheld by the company as an incentive for the contractor to fulfil his obligation of maintenance of the line for twelve months after opening. At dawn on the great day invited guests boarded the inaugural train and included Edward Parry, the engineer for the NSR, Edwards and James Scott the contractor's works agent. On arrival at Trent Lane Junction, the NSRs junction with the GNR main line, the train came to an unscheduled halt because Mr Colson, who was one of Edward's agents, was standing in the middle of the track on which the train was travelling, waving a red flag. The train was stopped within a few feet of Colson and the GNR traffic inspector alighted from the train to try and resolve matters. He was told by Colson, on behalf of Edwards, that he protested against the train going over the NSR line because the line was still in the possession of the contractor and that the train would be trespassing if it continued on its route. After an altercation in which Colson refused to move, it was decided that the train should proceed which caused Colson to jump out of the way but he left his red flag on the rails which the train ran over. On the return journey, which included a large number of fare paying passengers, it was found that Edwards and Scott did not have tickets and this was notified to the station officials. An unsavoury episode in what should have been a joyous day!

As will be seen, Edwards' contract on the Nottingham Suburban Railway, the Midland's Heanor Junction to Ripley line and the work at Tyne Dock, South Shields, overlapped the early years of the Dore and Chinley contract. There is no record of Edwards working again after he had been relieved of the Hope to Chinley contract and he died at Bourne in Cambridgeshire on 13 Aug 1896 age 70. His estate amounted to £80. It was an ignominious end to a hard working life.

JAMES SCOTT (1846-1903)

James Scott was Edwards' agent and right hand man. As we will see he was a very experienced operator.

He was born at Keighley on 20 Oct 1846. From 1862 to 1866 he was a pupil of his father Thomas Scott who was engaged on the construction of the Metropolitan Railway between Euston and Paddington, and on the MSLR Marple to New Mills and Hayfield line. Between 1866 and 1868 he was the contractor's engineer on Contract No. 1 of the Midland London extension from the North London Railway to St Pancras goods yard. On its completion he was immediately back in work on Contract No. 1 of the Midland Settle to Carlisle line from 1868 to 1873 and, then again, without a break on the LNWR widening of the Kings Langley to Bletchley section of the West Coast Main Line and on the Clydach to Brynmawr section of the LNWR Abergavenny to Merthyr line from 1873 to 1878. He was still not idle as he immediately moved on to the Weymouth to Abbotsbury Railway and the widening of the CLC at Liverpool from 1878 to 1883. From 1883 to 1888 he was busy on the Baltinglass extension of the Great Southern & Western Railway in Ireland and on the Heanor and Ripley extension of the Midland and the Nottingham Suburban Railway. He then became contractor's agent to J. P. Edwards on No. 2 contract on the Dore and Chinley line. From 1895 to 1899 he was the contractor's agent to Thomas Oliver on the GCR London extension Contract No. 4 from Rugby to Woodford which included Catesby tunnel. By 1899 he was engaged on the Midland's Thackley tunnel and widening between Keighley and Bradford and the GCR Northolt to Neasden extension line and the Midland Finchley Road to Welsh Harp line. He was elected as a member of the Institution of Civil Engineers on 1 May 1894. He died at Sudbury in Middlesex on 27 Nov 1903 age 57 years.

SUBCONTRACTORS

Edwards does not seem to have relied on subcontractors in the same way as Oliver did. He may have let the work for the portals of Cowburn tunnel to William Hancock.

ANDREW HANDYSIDE & COMPANY

The Hope station footbridge was awarded to this company following a tendering process by the Midland but was small fry compared with their other works. It was delivered on time, under budget and at a price that undercut most of the other bidders for the contract.

Andrew Handyside was born in 1805 and took over the Britannia Works in Derby in 1848, it having opened in 1820. It specialised in ornamental ironwork. By the 1840s it diversified into railway components. It had a long association with the Midland having supplied cylinder blocks and other castings for Derby works in those early years. His output ranged from garden ornaments to railway bridges. He produced lamp posts for the new gas street lighting and produced the new standard post office letter boxes. The works only occupied a small area on the banks of the River Derwent and yet produced four hundred bridges between 1840 and 1846 for the LBSCR. It manufactured the train sheds at Bradford, Middlesborough and St Enoch, Glasgow. In 1871 it built the Trent Bridge at Nottingham and a year later the Albert suspension bridge in London. Its most lasting memorial locally was the beautifully ornate Friargate bridge in Derby for the GNR which is now closed but still stands. In 1877 the CLC opened and Handysides provided the structures for the Manchester and Liverpool Central stations. Although Andrew Handyside died in 1887, the firm carried on but went into decline and closed early in the twentieth century.

WALKER & SLATER

The Midland general purposes committee considered the tenders for the stations on 15 Jun 1893. The engineers' estimate was that they would cost £11,985, and there were ten tenders ranging from £11,400 to £19,000. Walker and Slater's was the lowest bid and, after a correction from £11,400 to £11,800 was made, this was accepted. They were well established builders, having built the new Derby Royal Infirmary, the foundation stone for which was laid by Queen Victoria in 1891. They were building the stations on the line at the same time as they were finishing off the infirmary.

One commentator said that the station buildings were not much better than the signal boxes. They were not of any architectural merit and when considered alongside the stations on the Peak line, were utilitarian rather than inspiring. When the total cost of the line is considered the capital devoted to the stations was puny; this perhaps reflected how the Midland viewed the line, with the local passenger and freight traffic being considered of minor importance compared with the through traffic.

Hope station footbridge in the Pre-Grouping period looking toward Bamford. *Author's collection*

REFERENCES

Thomas Oliver of Tanbridge – Victorian Railwayman Par Excellence. The Horsham Society 2007

Thomas Oliver – A Paper by Frank D. Smith courtesy of Robin Waywell for the Industrial Railway Society collection

Hidden Horsham – Thomas Oliver. Horsham Society 2008

Cole D. & Smith F. D. – *Contractors Locomotives Part VI.* Union Publications 1982 (Oliver, Edwards)

Dow George – *Great Central Volume Two: Dominion of Watkin 1864-1899.* Locomotive Publishing Company 1962 (Parry, Oliver)

Bendall Ian – *Industrial Locomotives Nottinghamshire.* Industrial Railway Society 1999

Birch D. G. – *The Story of the Nottingham Suburban Railway Vol 1.* Book Law Publications 2010 (Parry, Edwards, Scott, Rickard)

The private papers of Jim Story descendant of John Somes and George Ernest Story

Obituary of George Ernest Story in the *Bedfordshire Standard* 14 Sep 1917

Marshall John – *Biographical Dictionary of Railway Engineers.* R&CHS 2nd revised ed. 2003 (Parry, Scott, Rickard)

West R. E. – Unpublished Research Paper. (Edwards)

Shimell Christine – *Totley Tunnel Engineer Percy Rickard.* Totley History Group, Bradway Bugle Spring 2013

MEMORIALS AND PETITIONS

As we have seen there were objections that had to be considered at the legislative stage but, additionally, there were also local requests for changes after the work was underway. These are itemised here.

NEW ROADS AT MALCOFF AND WASH

Feb 1890. Some residents at Malcoff, Bowden Head and Wash signed a memorial asking for a new road to be formed in order to avoid passing up and down certain approaches made according to the Parliamentary plans. 'Some portions of these roads currently have gradients of 1 in 5½ whereas the new roads do not exceed 1 in 12'. The estimate for acquiring the land and building the road is £350. It is not known what the company decided.

HOPE STATION – PETITION FROM BRADWELL

24 Apr 1890. The Rev H. T. Dudley, vicar of Bradwell, raised a petition 25 ft in length from the inhabitants of Bradwell and district which was sent to the Midland favouring a central station at Brough Lane Head. (NEWS) (They nearly got their way but not because of their petition.)

THE LOCATION OF BAMFORD STATION

Apr 1890. A report was submitted by the engineers on a memorial from the inhabitants of Bamford and district about the position of Bamford station. Basically, the residents wanted the station located nearer Bamford village. The engineers stated the position of the station was determined by the position of Hope and Hathersage stations, as a station at Bamford was not originally proposed. They pointed out that the station was designed to serve Bamford and the villages such as Ashopton, further up the valley, and on the south side, Brough and Bradwell which had extensive lime quarries. To move the station would be inconvenient and would cost about £5,000. However, it might be possible to construct a new road from the Bamford road, where it joined the River Derwent to the station, which would make the station exactly the same distance from the village as if placed upon the site suggested by the memorialists. The road would, however, be nearly half a mile in length and would require a bridge over the River Derwent and would cost, including the purchase of land, about £3,500. On 14 Mar 1891 the engineers report included information from the general manager John Noble that owing to the position decided on for Bamford station, and the consequent alteration in the levels of the line at this place, some additional land will be required for the station and road diversion (see page 139).

ROAD AT HATHERSAGE STATION

A letter was received from George H. Cammell of Brookfield, Hathersage and others asking for the gradient of the road near the station approach to be altered and the road widened. The general purposes committee decided the company would pay £200 and suggested that Derbyshire County Council pay the rest. The company would widen the road and the council improve the gradient.

The steep road from Grindleford approaching bridge 18 and the outskirts of Hathersage are shown in this 1950s picture (232811). The station approach is just to the right of the 30mph road sign. It shows the road as widened by the Midland and the gradient made less steep by the council.

David Ibbotson

With all the enormous trials and tribulations ahead for the builders of this epic undertaking it would have been nice to have been able to show all those involved this contemporary postcard so that they could see the result of their efforts. It shows the eastern portal between Jul 1903 and 1905. The locomotive is one of the celebrated Midland Compounds, designed and built by the revered Samuel Waite Johnson at the end of his long tenancy as locomotive superintendent of the company. With its four sisters, it was the most powerful locomotive on the Midland. The first two entered service in 1902 and were sent to Leeds to work over the Leeds to Carlisle route while bridge strengthening was taking place on the rest of the system. The following three were built in 1903 and it is likely that the one depicted here is No. 2633 as it was allocated to Nottingham when built whereas the other two went to Kentish Town and Leeds. The first two had curved framing over the outside cylinders but this shows one of the later ones with straight frames. The smokebox has the convex dished door with central locking wheel, which was replaced from 1905 with the better remembered Deeley type. An eight wheel bogie tender can be seen which was later rebuilt. The card shows the full Midland livery in all its glory, which became less elaborate after 1906. The first carriage is a matching clerestory type, probably designed by Thomas Clayton, the Midland carriage & wagon superintendent until 1901. *Locomotive Publishing Company*

DEPUTATION SEEK BRANCH FROM PADLEY WOOD TO TIDESWELL

25 Nov 1892. A deputation representing Sheffield, Buxton, Tideswell, Eyam and Grindleford Bridge waited on the directors of the Midland at Derby to ask for a branch line from Padley Wood to Millers Dale via Eyam, Hucklow and Tideswell, a total of nine miles. The proposal was presented by Lord Scarsdale and the route was described by Canon Andrew of Tideswell. John Turner, the Midland general manager, promised that an engineer would survey a route and report. (NEWS)

WATER SUPPLY TO EDALE STATION

27 Feb 1894. The engineers considered a letter from the assistant secretary of the Midland regarding the water supply at Edale station. The stream which passed under the line close to the station was contaminated by sewage from the village of Grindsbrook which had caused the engineers to seek a different supply. On the moors above the village, 1,800 yards from the railway, were some springs which in the driest weather had not been known to fail. They proposed to supply water from these springs by a three inch cast iron pipe. The pressure would be good as the source was 300 ft above the station. The pipe would be laid for 900 yards and would pass through the land of Mr W. N. Champion. He had agreed to this, subject to a supply being fed to certain houses and land belonging to him. The expenses would be trifling. A previous request had been made by a Mr Jowett, in Oct 1893, for a water supply to the village. The engineers thought that this was much needed and, as the pipe would pass through the village, it could be easily arranged. The cost of the entire water supply to the station and residents was estimated at £450 and several residents had offered to make an annual payment. Subsequently the proposal was accepted. By Jul 1895, when the work was completed, the cost was recorded as £293/14/7. (ENG)

PETITION TO REDUCE RENTS

20 Dec 1894. A petition by the residents of the cottages at Edale and Grindleford to reduce the rents from 4/- a week was declined. (GPC)

SCREENING OF THE RAILWAY BETWEEN HOPE AND NORMAN'S BANK

14 Nov 1895. A memorial was received from the ratepayers and inhabitants of Edale, Hope and Castleton to screen the railway near the highway between Hope and Edale (Norman's Bank). As trees were already being planted the memorial was refused.

On 24 Jul 1888 the Midland obtained its Act to take over from the Dore and Chinley company. It wasted no time in getting started, taking just seven weeks to start building the line.

The following section covers the overall building of the line, the two main tunnels and the other works including Chapel Milton viaduct, (it was officially called 'Milton' so as not to confuse it with the earlier viaduct but, nevertheless, was still always called 'Chapel Milton' in the reports), Cowburn viaduct at Barber Booth, Mytham viaduct, Hathersage viaduct and Dore tunnel.

The two main tunnels were the major engineering features. They were the first physical items started and the very last to be finished. They were the longest on the Midland system, the second and ninth longest in Britain with Totley being the longest land tunnel. Totley is easily the railways most famous feature and the two tunnels covered a quarter of the entire length of the line.

THE LOCATION, DIMENSIONS AND GRADIENTS

TOTLEY TUNNEL

The tunnel is located one and a half miles from Dore and Totley station and is approached by a long cutting through the river valley created by the Old Hay Brook on a rising gradient of 1 in 100, which extends for a quarter of a mile into the tunnel. The subsequent gradients are 1 in 176 followed by 1 in 150 to the summit level. The line then falls on a gradient of 1 in 1000 (which proved very useful for draining water) and emerges abruptly under the steep hill at Padley, 130 ft above the bed of the River Derwent, the difference in level between the two ends being 77 ft. The tunnel is straight, except for a curve of one hundred yards and forty chains radius which eases the alignment at the Padley end. The distance between the tunnel rails and the moor above is, at its highest, 730 ft, although the moorland is 1,250 ft above sea level. In the late summer of 1890 it was agreed that part of the 1 in 176 gradient in the tunnel could be changed to 1 in 150 to increase the length available for drilling the headings before the gradient levelled off and started to fall. Otherwise drilling would have had to stop at that point because the water could not naturally drain away. In the event the amount of water encountered significantly declined, or was completely dry, for the last part of the headings before they met so perhaps this amendment was unnecessary.

The title is something of a misnomer as the tunnel was first called Padley, after the hamlet at the western end, but it soon became known as Totley tunnel. By the time it was built experience of railway tunnelling was extensive so its construction is a conventional one and did not break new ground. What was exceptional was the length and height of the moor above the tunnel which precluded shafts to assist in the building, except on the lower ground at the Totley end. Also exceptional was the huge volume of water encountered at both ends. The only legislative condition for the building of the tunnel was the one required by the Duke of Rutland, whose grouse moors were over the path of the tunnel. He would only allow one shaft to be sunk (No. 5) and would not allow work to be undertaken between 11 Aug and 1 Oct in order to 'ensure the sanctity of the glorious twelfth'. The shaft was not to project above the ground and proper iron railings were required and the waste was to be taken away. When viewed today it is clear that these requirements were not met as the shaft head protrudes above the waste which was not removed. The shaft was not sunk until the work was nearly completed and was not used for facilitating the headings. One of the reasons for this was that a shaft of 600 ft would attract a large amount of water. As a result, headings were only possible from the Padley entrance and from Shaft No. 4 at the eastern end although headings were achieved between some of the shafts at the Totley end. Thus the length of time needed to complete the work was longer than would be normal.

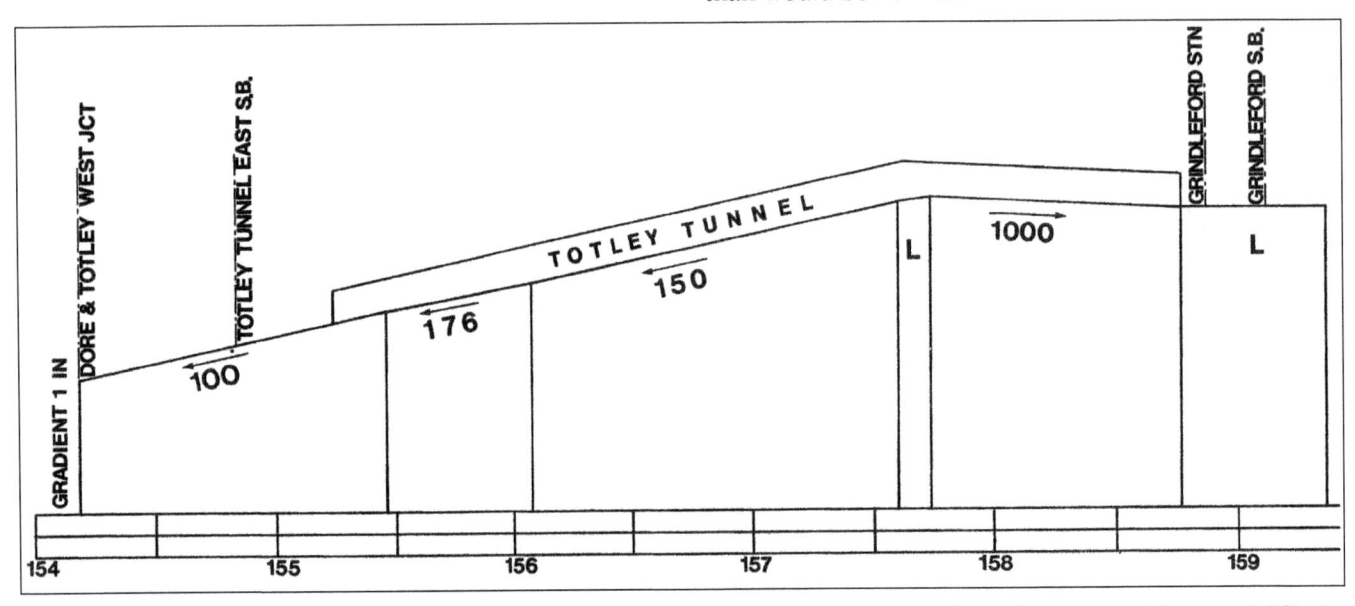

The gradient profile of Totley tunnel. It shows the shallow descent to Padley which made the flow of water out of the tunnel difficult.

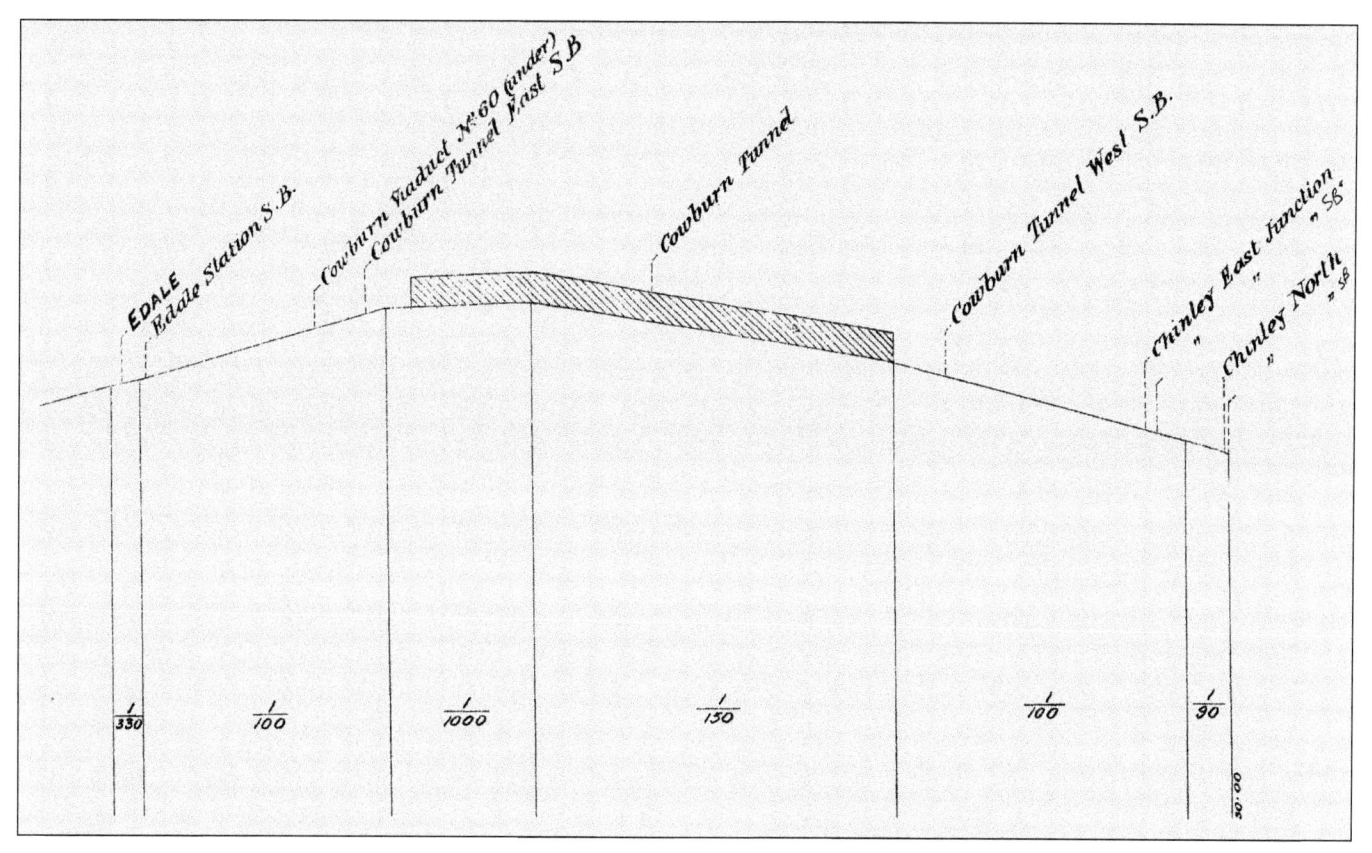

The gradient profile of Cowburn tunnel. The summit of the whole line was attained in the tunnel.

COWBURN TUNNEL

'Situated at the head of the Edale valley, out of which it springs almost perpendicularly, the arm of the Peak, known as Cowburn rises to an elevation of 1,700 ft above sea level. The tunnel cuts the axis of the hill at right angles, and lies in a west south west direction at its base. It is 3,702 yards long and is straight from end to end. The gradient rises from the Edale entrance at an inclination of 1 in 1000, for the first 913 yards, to the summit of the whole line and then falls to the Chinley entrance at 1 in 150, the difference in level between the two ends being 53 ft' so said Percy Rickard in his posthumous paper to the Institution of Civil Engineers (ICE) read on 23 Jan 1894. He was not the resident engineer for this section of the line and so the information was provided by George Ernest Story, his counterpart, and Edwards' agent James Scott.

SURVEYING THE TUNNELS

TOTLEY

Great care was taken to secure the accurate setting out of the centre line, the work being set out in detail in Rickard's paper. The profile of the land was favourable to this work because of the high ground at each end of the tunnel. Using a six inch theodolite, brick observatories were built at the extremities at Bradway (3327807), two miles to the east, and below the summit of Sir William Hill (227872), over two miles to the west. Further observatories were built at each end of the changes of the ground surface over the tunnel including one on Totley Moss near where Shaft No. 5 was later built. A further observatory was built between the entrance at Padley, at a level to command the heading on the 1 in 1,000 gradient, and a station fixed at the foot of the hill beyond to enable these two points to be seen from within the heading whenever necessary.

In setting out the line, two points in that set by the small instrument were taken as fixed, viz the summit and No. 1 West, and from the summit observatory the line was set upon the extreme observatories east and west and upon No. 1 East. The instrument was then removed to No. 2 West and, with Sir William observatory as a fixed point, the line was set on No. 2 West. The instrument was then removed to No. 2 West and the line was in the same way set upon No. 3 West and similarly on Nos. 2, 3 and 4 East. The instrument was subsequently set up at the Bradway and Sir William observatories, and the centre lines of No. 4 East and No. 3 West were checked. No. 4 West was then set out from No. 3 West, checked from No. 2 West and the external line was complete. Different sighting boards were used in the open to facilitate the view between observatories.

For transferring the centre line down the shafts a winding drum carried the wire, mounted upon an iron frame with a ratchet and pawl to secure it in position. The wire passed over an adjusting screw and was brought into line by turning the screw in either direction as required.

'Great difficulty was experienced at the outset in finding favourable weather for fixing the line upon the terminal stations, as it was essential that the atmosphere should be clear and cool to prevent aberrations due to heat, and yet still enough for the observatory to be free from vibration. It was also necessary that the time of day should be such that the sun would illuminate the front of both screens behind the objects to be sighted. The only times when the weather answered all these requirements were rare occasions in the spring and autumn, between the abatement of a high wind and a fall of rain: and these could not be predicted beforehand and, with a day's preparation being necessary, much time was wasted. The greatest difficulty was found in sighting across the Derwent valley westward, but

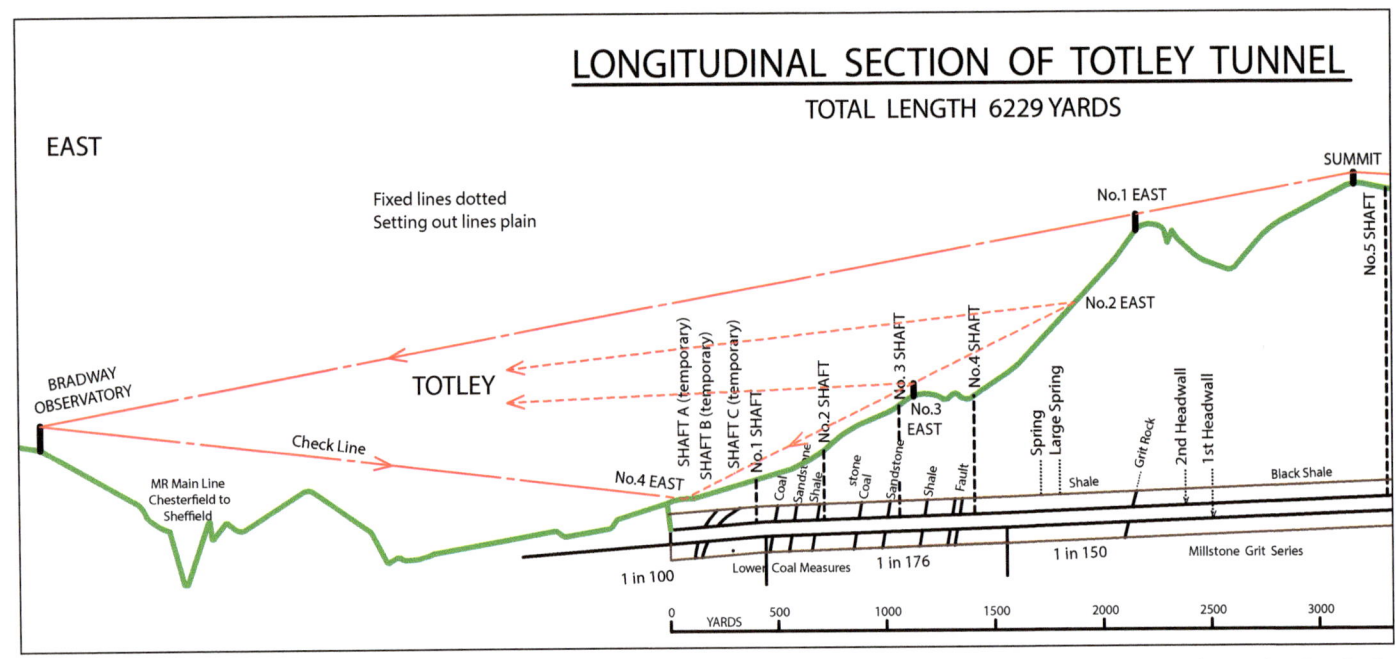

LONGITUDINAL SECTION OF TOTLEY TUNNEL
TOTAL LENGTH 6229 YARDS

excellent opportunities for sighting east could always be obtained at sunset after a warm summer's day'. After the centre line had been fixed upon the observatories at the surface, the positions of the four shafts at Totley were set out from them and, after the shafts had been sunk, the centre lines for the headings were transferred below by weighted wires suspended from the top, the lines being produced underground by a small theodolite under the headings until they met between the shafts. The brick lining was then proceeded with and the centre line was again carefully transferred below upon bats fixed securely into the brickwork at No. 4 and B shaft. With this bearing the line was produced by the large transit instrument westwards into the heading as required.

At the Padley end the line was produced into the heading direct from the observatory at that end. When used underground, the large transit instrument rested upon a balk of timber, which was supported at each end so as to clear the temporary road. The extreme range of the instrument below ground, when the air was clear, was about three quarters of a mile, but as the headings advanced, not more than 200 and 300 yards could be seen under the most favourable circumstances, and the small instrument was then used in preference. The line was marked with a file upon iron dogs and driven into the bats or head-trees in the usual way. To avoid instrumental errors the line was set out twice, the telescope being turned over transversely in the bearings between the operations. The mean of the two results was the centre line adopted. The object used for sighting underground for long distances was a large circular oil lamp of forty candle power, fitted into a circular wrought iron frame which was suspended by a wire. For short distances a carriage candle, fixed in a weighted frame, was suspended in the same way.

When built it was made of brickwork in cement and capped with stone. A large flat cast iron plate, leaving a hole six inches wide in the centre, was let into the cap and run with cement. Upon this the transit instrument rested. A brass scale, 1½ inch wide, divided into inches and twentieths of an inch, was fixed across this central hole in the plate and a plumb line from the centre of the instrument could thus be put down through the hole in the plate to touch the side of the scale. The transit instrument was of the fixed type, with a three inch object glass and a thirty inch telescope. In order to enable it to be used with facility at different observatories as required, an extra cast iron base was added resting on three levelling screws, and upon it the ordinary standard rested. The latter was pivoted at one end and was secured between two slow motion adjusting screws at the other. A hole, three inches in diameter, was made in the base plate to allow the plumbing hook to pass freely through it from the bottom of the standard to which it was attached. This extra base plate enabled the instrument to be levelled with accuracy and also provided a slow horizontal movement similar to that of an ordinary theodolite.

For signalling long distances with the large instrument an electrical signalling apparatus was employed. It consisted of two similar instruments, in each of which a seven inch single beat bell was mounted, with a battery enclosed beneath, together with three quarters of a mile of covered cable on a drum, in a portable frame. The cable was thus readily paid out from the trolley on which the instruments were conveyed every time it was used and the return was made to earth through a galvanized iron plate temporarily sunk into the ground. With this apparatus messages could be sent in either direction and, to prevent misunderstandings, all

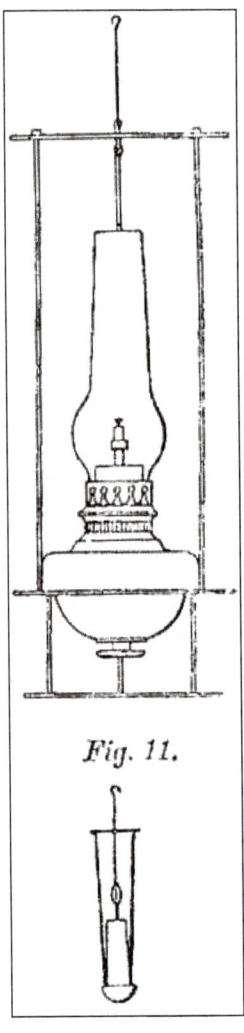

Fig. 11.

The oil lamp and carriage candle used for short distance sighting underground.
ICE Paper

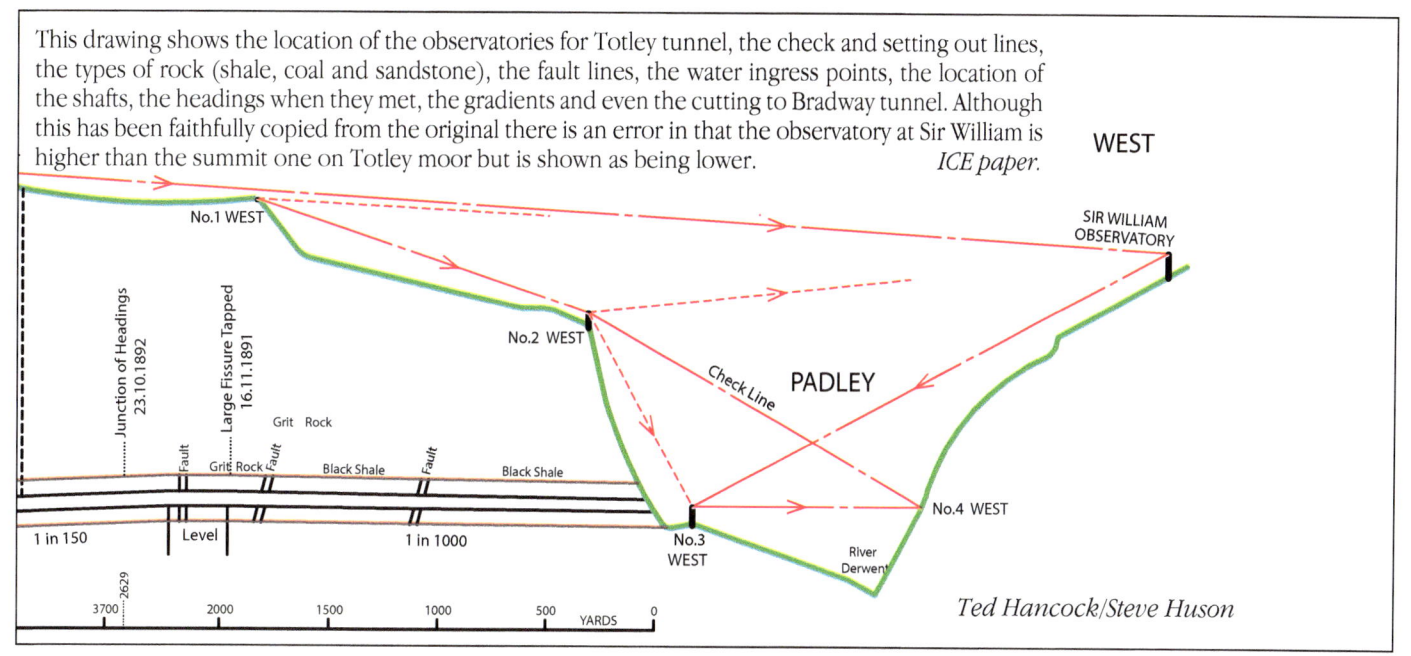

This drawing shows the location of the observatories for Totley tunnel, the check and setting out lines, the types of rock (shale, coal and sandstone), the fault lines, the water ingress points, the location of the shafts, the headings when they met, the gradients and even the cutting to Bradway tunnel. Although this has been faithfully copied from the original there is an error in that the observatory at Sir William is higher than the summit one on Totley moor but is shown as being lower. *ICE paper.*

Ted Hancock/Steve Huson

signals were repeated by the receiver and any error in transmission could then be corrected by the transmitter.

All this preparatory care and expense of time paid handsome dividends for when the headings met, the difference between the centre lines of the two headings was only four and a half inches and the difference between the levels was two and a quarter inches, although this was not better than that being achieved on other contemporary tunnels including Cowburn.

The president of the Civil Engineers remarked that when a tunnel was made at Liverpool (presumably the Liverpool and Manchester Railway of sixty years earlier) the two headings went past each other and the men working from one end heard those working from the other end behind them!

For the record the location of the observation towers are Bradway (332807), No. 1 East Wimble Holme Hill (287797), No. 2 on eastern edge of Bole Hill (291797), No. 3 East just west of present Shaft No. 2, north of the *Cricket Inn* (297799), No. 4 East directly above tunnel entrance (306801), Summit just north of Shaft No. 5 on Totley Moor (278794) No. 1 West just north of Wooden Pole (268792), No. 2 West on eastern edge of Yarncliffe Wood (254788), No. 3 West on edge of Grindleford station yard (249787), No. 4 West on west side of the Grindleford to Hathersage road (239784), Sir William Hill west of Newfoundland Nursery (230782).

REFERENCE

McGuire Stella and Nunn Stuart – *The Search for Totley Towers*. Archaeology and Conservation in Derbyshire Issue 12 Jan 2015

COWBURN

First of all the centre line was approximately set out with a six inch theodolite. A portable transit instrument, with twenty inch telescope, mounted on three legs was then employed. Two points, three quarters of a mile beyond the Chinley entrance, in the approximate line were taken as fixed. From these the line over the tunnel was set by the larger instrument on pegs driven into the ground at every change in the surface and on two pegs in the Edale valley, situated 154 yards apart beyond the eastern entrance. The operation was repeated many times until the centre line was exactly established. However, observatories of masonry, 6 ft by 4 ft, capped with ashlar, and from 6 to 8 ft in height, were built over the pegs. The two pegs beyond each end of the tunnel were surrounded with masonry to prevent them being disturbed and the centre line was then transferred from the pegs to the stone caps. From the centre line thus obtained the shafts were set out and the line produced into the headings from both ends by means of the six inch instrument only. When the headings met, at 2,305 yards from the east entrance, the difference in line between the two headings was found to be less than one inch.

CHRONOLOGY OF THE BUILDING

I have been fortunate in accessing the previously unseen monthly reports of the engineers to the Midland Railway directors, courtesy of Mr Jim Story's family papers. Mr Story is a descendant of John Somes and George Ernest Story, the main and resident engineers on the line. From this source I have selected and précised the most pertinent information keeping much of the wording and tense. It lends itself to chronological presentation and gives a real feel for the trials and tribulations ahead and the enormous time period which the project took. It also allows the progress on other parts of the line to be seen in the correct time frame eg the rapid progress of Cowburn against the tortuous progress in Totley tunnel. Although the real heroes were the men who laboured in such difficult conditions, and lodged in equally insanitary circumstances they are only mentioned in terms of recruitment statistics and the effect that this had on progress. The health and welfare of the men is hardly ever mentioned although we know that at least fourteen men were killed and twenty eight injured on Contract No. 1 and eighteen killed and seventeen injured on Contract No. 2. This is information gleaned from trawling newspapers and studying burial records. Considering that the Hathersage burial records have sixteen additional navvies who died, almost all probably in the line of duty, it indicates that if the number of additional deaths at the Totley end of the tunnel were similar, or probably more, then the number of deaths on Contract No. 1 were two thirds higher than the number reported.

All the known deaths of navvies are included and additionally listed in Appendix 2. In that same index is information of all known accidents. A few are also mentioned in this section where they are significant in the context of the events on the line. It is almost certain that there were many more accidents, probably of a more minor nature that were not reported. No deaths or injuries have been found in respect of the works on Shaft No. 5 at Totley and Shaft No. 2 at Cowburn, most likely because interest in the line had ceased once it was open. We only have an incomplete picture. No accident books seem to have been kept. I have used in describing injuries the gory language of the day.

There are five primary sources that have been drawn on:-

The engineer's monthly reports to the directors of the Midland Railway from 14 Nov 1888 to 16 Mar 1896 (ENG)

Proceedings of the Institution of Civil Engineers paper No. 2744 of 23 Jan 1894. Tunnels on the Dore and Chinley Railway by the late Percy Rickard M. Inst. C.E. (ICE)

Board of Trade inspector's reports (BT)

Minutes of various Midland Railway committee meetings but mainly the general purposes committee and, to a lesser extent, the traffic committee (GPC)

Midland Railway engineer's instructions (MRENG)

Midland Railway Chronology – John Gough. RCHS 1989 (GOUGH)

Contemporary newspaper reports, the most fertile for information being the *Sheffield Independent* and *Derby Mercury*. The date of the event rather than the date it was reported is given (NEWS)

Comments in brackets are the author's.

SURVEYING THE LAND

31 Jul 1886. A number of men are staking out the land. Negotiations with landowners will start soon. (NEWS)

23 Mar 1887. The *Derby Mercury* reported 'There are signs that construction of the line may be happening. During the week the engineers of the line including Daniel Jewitt of The Cedars, Whalley Bridge and Oliver of Bristol and others have been taking short surveys of the route and tenders of the probable cost of the different sections are to be sent to the directors of the Midland'. (NEWS)

1 Apr 1887. Contractors have been surveying the line and have sent in tenders for consideration. (NEWS)

16 Apr 1887. Edwards men have been in the district for some time surveying the line. Edwards tender is less than the company's estimate. (NEWS)

AWARDING OF CONTRACTS

16 Jan 1888. Contract No. 1 was awarded to Thomas Oliver at £451,520/11/7 and John Price Edwards was awarded No. 2 at £318,118/0/0, both of which were to be completed by 1 Sep 1892. (GPC)

DEATH OF THE DUKE OF RUTLAND

3 Mar 1888. The 6th Duke of Rutland, the 'sporting Duke', dies.

REPORT ON THE PREPARATIONS

13 Aug 1888. The *Sheffield Independent* reported 'Our readers will be pleased to learn that preparations are being made for the construction of the long talked of Dore and Chinley Railway at the Dore end of the route. The assistant (Percy Rickard) of Mr Parry, chief engineer of the line, has taken up his residence at Dore (Totley Grove) and will remain during the construction of the line. He will be assisted by Mr Parry occasionally'. The article similarly comments that Thomas Oliver is taking up residence at Dore (Oak Villa, New Road later Dore Road) and that the solicitors have served notice for purchase of the land required for the construction of the line. (NEWS)

THE ROCK MINING COMPANY

25 Aug 1888. The *Derbyshire Times* reported that 'the Rock Mining Company Ltd of London have sunk a 6 ft shaft in a field at Totley Bents. The shaft, which is 20 ft deep, is on the level of the line. A 24 ft heading extending both ways has been driven to admit some newly invented rock boring machinery for a series of experiments in rock boring. The machine is made to work by compressed air but because of the short time the company had to test the machine they were unable to put down the air compressing machine. As a result they had to test the machine by steam. Two large 25 hp boilers are fixed near the mouth of the shaft and are connected together. The steam is conveyed down the shaft in a six inch pipe to work the boring machine which is calculated to bore the holes farther and in less time than any other machine yet invented. The drills are 20 ft long and 3½ in diameter. When in motion three holes, 3½ in diameter are bored at one time. The drills strike the rock at a velocity of 350 blows per minute. The force of the blow on the rock from each drill is over four tons. A highly satisfactory trial

Totley Grove (306800) was the home of the Doncaster family but they sold the property and land to the Midland. It became the epicentre of operations on the tunnel and was used as Oliver's administrative headquarters and the home of Percy Rickard and his family. It was a fine property and is thought to have been converted into two houses around 1850. The stables and outbuildings are much earlier, suggesting an older house was built on the site in the 17th or 18th centuries. Hillfoot Road is to the left and the entrance to Totley tunnel is just off the bottom of the picture. *C. Connelly, Picture Sheffield. Sheffield Libraries*

has been made by the machine. Each drill penetrates the rock at the rate of 1 ft a minute. It is the intention of the Rock Mining Co to penetrate the holes to the extent of the drills, when they will place in explosives and try and blow out the rock. Oliver has inspected the machine which meets his approval and it will no doubt be used in making the tunnel.' (NEWS) (This is not reported in any of the primary sources and, in spite of what is stated, was not in the event used.)

4 Sep 1888. These works were not without consequences for the *Sheffield Independent* reported that Samuel Weir an engineer was engaged in removing the machinery out of the shaft. Having fixed a large chain to remove the steam pump from the bottom of the shaft, the tub which was being drawn up with some small casting in caught the large chain and took it up the shaft a distance of several feet, when it fell and severely injured Weir, and rendered him unconscious. One of his fellow workmen immediately descended the shaft and after putting him in the tub he was drawn to the surface. (NEWS)

PREPARATIONS CONTINUE

31 Aug 1888. The *Sheffield Independent* reported that 'Edwards has taken possession of some of the land. Mr Gratton, a director of the Midland, G. E. Story, Mr Hudson, the Midland's Chief Engineer and others went over the route to make preparations for starting the work.'

There are a number of navvies at Chinley waiting to be engaged on the work. (NEWS)

10 Sep 1888. The *Sheffield Independent* reported that 'the contractor has acquired rooms at Chapel en le Frith Town Hall as offices'. (NEWS)

WORKS FINALLY START ON TOTLEY SHAFTS

(After seventy eight years of high hopes and crushing failure, of hard, laborious planning and financial loss for many people, of reputations for sound judgement ruined, for hopes raised and then dashed in the impoverished Hope and Edale valleys the day most thought would never arrive finally did.)

11 Sep 1888. The works start with the sinking of permanent Shaft No. 1 at the east end of Totley tunnel on the land of Mr John Stones. (NEWS)

15 Sep 1888. Oliver & Son and subcontractor Williams & Young have this week entered a field at Totley Bents and have commenced a shaft 12 ft in diameter. The contractors then proceeded in the direction of the moors, and set out three other shafts. The shafts at Totley Bents will be about twenty five yards deep to the level of the line and will be used for drawing the refuse out of the tunnel. The building of the stables and workshops adjoining Dore and Totley station is being pushed forward. Oliver's horses are occupying stables at Twentywell Brick works until they are completed. At the tunnel mouth at Padley Wood, operations for driving a level of the line under the moors have commenced. Several tons of rail and sleepers have been carted there from Hassop station during the present work. (NEWS)

Details of the permanent and temporary shafts

Shaft	Date started	Date finished	Depth in feet	Time taken in weeks
1	11.09.1888	03.10.1888	87	3
2	17.09.1888	01.12.1888	141	10
3	24.09.1888	27.03.1889	235	22
4	20.09.1888	19.06.1889	280	37
A	24.09.1888	05.02.1889	60	8
B	28.11.1888	n/k	n/k	n/k
C	03.01.1889	n/k	n/k	n/k

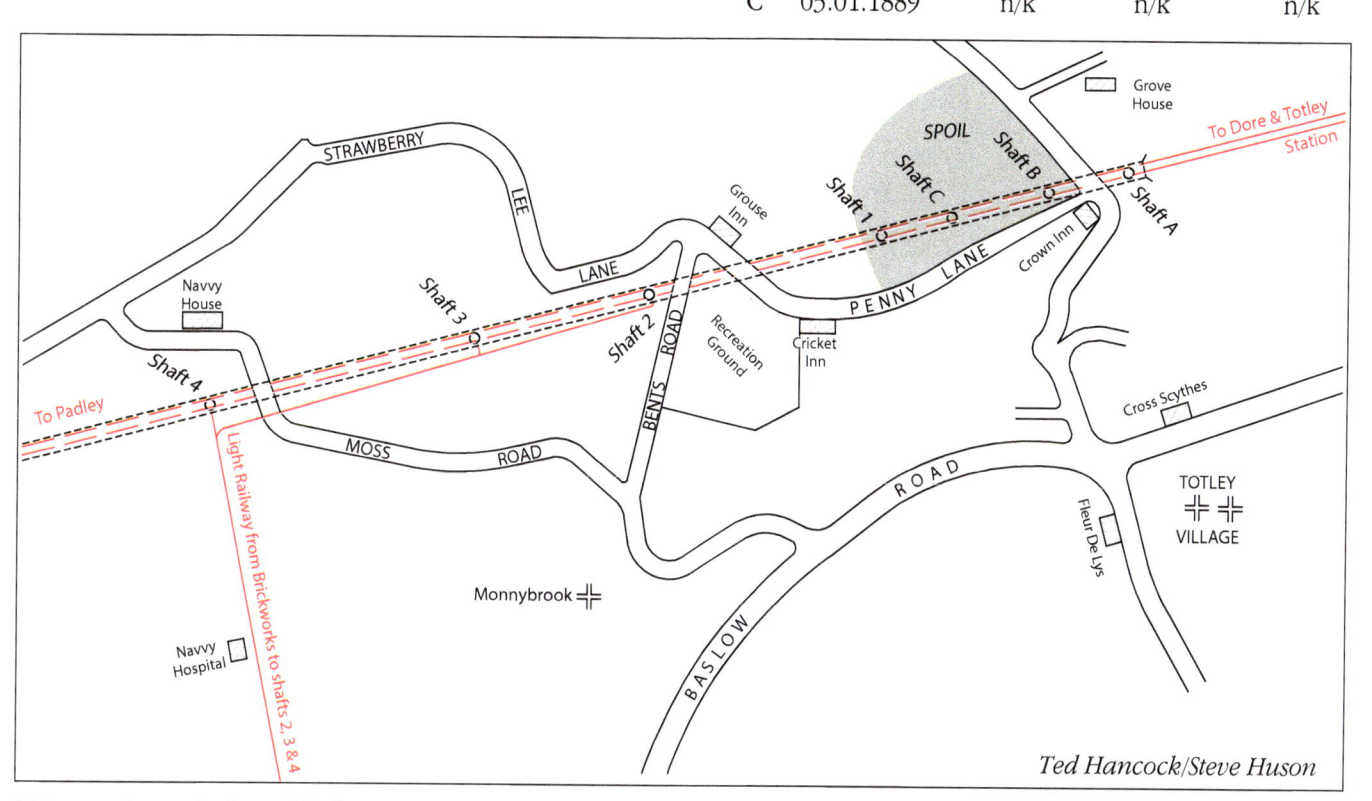

Ted Hancock/Steve Huson

This map shows the line of Totley tunnel and the location of the shafts. The location of temporary shaft C is uncertain and this is an estimate of its position. Also shown are the site of the navvy hut encampment and the navvy isolation hospital which was built later. The line from the brickworks was extended to Shaft No. 3 and No. 2 at the end of Oct 1889.

This is Shaft No. 3 from Strawberry Lee Lane on 15 Aug 2011. This is the one that became drowned and, thus, of no use until the headings reached it, when the accumulated water could be drained away.   *Author*

WHERE WILL THE NAVVIES LIVE?

22 Sep 1888. Taking into account the nearness of winter and the nature of the work to be done, it will be impossible to give employment to a great number of men, say before next spring, by which time the necessary land for the works will have been secured. Where are the workers to take up their lodgings? The Dronfield Local Board has asked Oliver to send them to Dronfield. Oliver declined the offer of the house mentioned as Dronfield was too far distant and also thought it would be difficult to organize a workmen's train, although John Noble, general manager of the Midland, thought a workmen's train should be considered. On the other hand, the Totley Garden Company have made an offer to use their range of buildings but no decision has as yet been made. A number of old hands at railway construction are daily visiting the locality, in search of work. (NEWS)

WORK STARTS ON CONTRACT NO. 2

18 Sep 1888. The Midland land agent, resident engineer G. E. Story and others went over part of the route at the Chinley end to revalue land following disagreement with its owner. Stabling for a large number of horses has been obtained at Chapel en le Frith and an office in the Town Hall has been provided for the contractor and engineers. The first sod was cut by the contractor. Workmen are passing through Chapel on their way to the works. (NEWS)

3 Oct 1888. At Cowburn tunnel ground rises steeply at both ends so there is only one permanent shaft situated 355 yards from the Edale entrance. It has a diameter of 10 ft. It is sunk through shale and several bands of rock, the quantity of water yielded amounting to 24,000 gallons an hour. A temporary shaft has also been sunk. In sinking it successive beds of shale and rock were passed through, which brought in large quantities of water, the quantities being discharged by the pumps reaching over 20,000 gallons an hour at its peak. (ICE) (This report is in advance of the work and is probably a wrongly recorded date. See 14 Nov 1888.)

WORK STARTS AT PADLEY END OF TOTLEY TUNNEL

27 Sep 1888. The heading is 10 ft by 9 ft, sufficient to take a fully loaded wagon. The first 530 yards were driven by hand power only. After a few yards water was encountered from the roof which increased as the heading proceeded. (NEWS)

29 Sep 1888. The *Derbyshire Times* reported that 'large numbers of navvies are seeking work on the railway and that two of their class have been apprehended at Stoney Middleton for larceny'. (NEWS)

ACTIVITY INCREASES AT CHINLEY AND CHAPEL

6 Oct 1888. A report in the *Derbyshire Times* stated that at Chinley 'activity increases each day. It is estimated that several thousand (an exaggeration) navvies will be needed. The contractors, surveyors and engineers have taken up residence in the neighbourhood of Chinley and Chapel en le Frith and many navvies are now seeking cottages. Material and plant arrive daily. At Chinley station many truck loads of timber and sleepers and boilers and machinery for boring are arriving. A number of horses have arrived and are stabled at Chapel. The Midland have not yet reached agreement with all the landowners and one lady's objection may need to go to arbitration. The contractors and engineers have recently offered to take the British School at Chinley on a five year lease or purchase it, but, as the school is parish property, unoccupied and in the hands of the Charity Commissioners nothing has yet been done. The line will go so close to the school that it may have to be demolished'. (NEWS)

TOTLEY BECOMES A CONSTRUCTION SITE

13 Oct 1888. On a visit to the Totley site the *Sheffield Independent* reported that 'at Dore and Totley station the whole of the land lying between the top half of the up platform and the road is littered with railway contractors wagons, sleepers, rails and chairs, baulks of timber and carts. The finishing touches are being given to a long brick building with a corrugated zinc roof, a number of men are engaged in joinery work, and a portable engine is stationed there. This is where the sidings will be and when they are constructed a start is to be made in making a temporary line to the first shaft of the tunnel. This line will turn up to the right at the lower part of Totley and run in an almost straight direction to the field opposite the pretty, ivy covered house, formerly occupied by Mrs Charles Doncaster (Totley Grove)'. In the same report a request was made to put on a workmen's train between Dronfield and Dore and Totley station. This was agreed to, provided there was sufficient custom. (NEWS)

16 Oct 1888. An anonymous letter to the *Sheffield Independent* asked why Thomas Oliver is allowed by the Inspector of Nuisances to fix an engine within a few

It is 1888 and Dore and Totley station is in its original condition with a train at the up platform with a large gathering of passengers. Of particular interest is the not very clear view in the left background of the temporary contractor's yard. In the foreground is the first view of the start of the line. The bridge over the River Sheaf is in the last stages of construction and the route of the line has been cleared.
Picture Sheffield. Sheffield Libraries

feet of the public road belching forth dense volumes of black smoke all day, enough to poison the occupants of those pretty villas opposite Dore station? No less than three horses have already taken fright at the monster and endangered life and limb.' (NEWS)

15 Nov 1888. Plans and estimates for the sidings at Dore and Totley station for the contractor were submitted for £1,180. It was agreed the contractor should pay the whole cost and all maintenance and signalling costs.

7 Dec 1888. The plans and estimates for the contractor's sidings were approved although one section will be built by the Midland. (GPC)

ACTIVITY AT BOTH ENDS OF COWBURN TUNNEL

20 Oct 1888. The *Derbyshire Times* reported that the sinking of the permanent shaft at the east end of Cowburn tunnel was the only one permitted and is located at Cartledge Meadow. At the west end the navvies are working in three gangs diverting a stream. A number of joiners are constructing a wooden house for the foreman of the navvies and a large number of huts are shortly to be built here and in the Edale valley. (NEWS)

3 Nov 1888. The *Derbyshire Courier* reported that there is now quite a sense of activity at the Chinley end. At the head of the Edale valley, at the entrance to the tunnel, large quantities of plant are being conveyed to the spot

This view, in the early 1900s, shows the contractor's line to the tunnel still extant crossing the entrance to Totley Grove. In the background are the last houses on Totley Brook Road, and, not visible in the picture, the Totley Brook Estate reservoir.
Author's collection

daily and on Wednesday (17 Oct) seven engines were brought to the place. A number of men are engaged in sinking a shaft in what is known as Cartledge Meadow, on a farm occupied by Mr R. Robinson and belonging to Mr John Moult of New Mills, who readily granted the company permission to enter upon his land pending negotiations as to its sale. This will be the only shaft on the length of moors known as Cowburn, the owner of which objects to having any shafts upon his game reserves. At the other end of the proposed tunnel, at Malcoff, near Chapel en le Frith, about seventy navvies are employed in three sets. One of these is engaged in sinking a shaft known as a 'shoot hole', the top of which will be about 60 ft from the level of the line (at the tunnel entrance) and the other two sets are constructing a culvert about 200 yards in length for the purpose of diverting the course of the Oakbrook, a stream which flows down the valley, by the side of the proposed line. A number of joiners are constructing a house of wood for the foreman over the works, and a large number of huts will shortly be built for the navvies both here and in the Edale valley. At Malcoff there is a field belonging to the MSLR through which the line will have to pass, but the contractors cannot yet enter, as no agreement has yet been arrived at between the two companies (presumably the crossing over the Peak Forest Tramway at Chapel Milton). Between this place and Chinley there will be a shorter tunnel of about 500 yards in length constructed (not correct). From the highest point on the Cowburn moors to the level of the line in the tunnel is 1,100 ft (an exaggeration). Large numbers of unemployed navvies visit the place daily in search of employment. (NEWS)

3 Nov 1888. J. P. Edwards has not yet taken up residence and rumour has it that he wants to acquire White Hall, which is located south west of Chinley at the side of the Black Brook. 'The number of men employed at the Wash is not so great as a few weeks ago owing to the completion of the culvert which conducts the Oakbrook water some distance by the side of the railway.' There is a considerable increase in the number of men at the head of the Edale valley sinking a shaft at Cartledge Meadow, above where the tunnel will be. Each day brings truckloads of railway plant and machinery to the station at Chinley and it is being brought to the spot much faster than it can be conveyed to the scene of operations. There are several engines at work and another stands on the premises of the Midland company at Chapel en le Frith awaiting conveyance to the tunnel mouth. There is to be a loop line at New Smithy towards Chapel. Through the influence of a number of inhabitants of Chapel a navvies' mission has been formed for the purpose of providing suitable recreation for the men. Premises have been secured and arrangements are being made for the opening of the institution at an early date. The number of wooden erections for the navvies will be numerous as there is a sparse population. Property will be materially enhanced in value and already there seems to be signs of extensive building operations. Now that the work is underway, businessmen in the neighbourhood of Manchester look upon the Hope valley as a desirable locality for villa residences. A new police station at Hathersage is being created. (NEWS)

14 Nov 1888. In the first report of the engineers to the general purposes committee it is stated that at the west end of Cowburn tunnel a temporary shaft has been sunk and the diversion of streams is underway as the cuttings cannot be commenced until this work is completed. At the east end, permanent Shaft No. 1 has been sunk about 70 ft and now that machinery has been erected, the shaft will be completed and the headings started. (ENG)

26 Nov 1888. Tunnelling started at the western end of Cowburn tunnel. The size of the tunnel entrance is 10 ft by 9 ft clear of timber, and is being driven at formation level. (ICE)

18 Dec 1888. The contractor has been carting material, erecting huts and laying temporary roads at the Edale end. On the permanent shaft at the east end work has had to stop due to the amount of water met and will be resumed when suitable pumping machinery is fixed. Another temporary shaft has been started. At the west end the driving of the heading is being proceeded with. (ENG)

Permanent Shaft No. 2 above Totley tunnel is surrounded by the growing amount of waste being hauled to the surface. The drum house can be seen and the winding wheel at the top and the crude ladder up the side. A contractor's spoil truck is visible half way up the structure and another one is visible on the top. Is there a rough track along the deposited waste?
Author's collection

TUNNEL HEADINGS START AT TOTLEY

14 Nov 1888. The engineer's first report to the general purposes committee stated that at the Totley end of the tunnel the contractor has been engaged in sinking four permanent shafts, one of which (No. 1) reached formation level on 3 Oct as has temporary shaft A. The tunnel heading has been commenced and has been driven about twelve yards each way from Shaft No. 1 and about thirty yards from the open end at Padley. (ENG)

Permanent Shaft No. 2 on the corner of the present Lane Head Road and Strawberry Lee Lane in 2007. *Author*

18 Dec 1888. The engineers reported that permanent shafts Nos. 1 and 2 are now sunk to formation level at the east end of Totley tunnel and the deeper shafts Nos. 3 and 4 are being proceeded with. The heading has been driven from shafts Nos. 1 and 2 and from the open end at Padley and a total of 283 yards has been achieved. Excavations for the stream diversions and cutting at the east end have also commenced. (ENG)

Rickard reported that the material pierced was rock with a little water for the first 1,300 yards the remaining distance until the headings met was dry. The strata throughout the tunnel dipped towards the west at about 1 in 16. 234 yards was driven through rock by hand but only 8.6 yards a week was achieved. Compressed air machinery was then brought into use and progress nearly doubled. (ICE)

VIOLENT GALE BLOWS DOWN CHIMNEY

30 Nov 1888. During Friday night and Saturday morning a violent gale blew down a portion of a large chimney at the Totley Moor Brick Works. The wind got under the roof of the building used in connection with the construction of the railway and completely lifted it off, carrying it a considerable distance. (NEWS)

FIRST DEATH AT TOTLEY

13 Dec 1888. George Griffiths, age 35, from Whittington Moor, Chesterfield and **James Bembridge** of Woodhouse Hill were charging some holes with gelignite while sinking Shaft No. 4. Griffiths was pressing down the gelignite with a stick because it had become hard due to frost when an explosion occurred. He was struck on the forehead and part of his scalp was blown away by a quantity of rock and he died shortly afterwards. Bembridge escaped with a black eye. At the inquest on 15 Dec it was stated the shaft where the accident happened was No. 3 not 4 and the engineer in charge was F. Cappin and subcontractor G. Young of Young and Williams. Ten days later the miners and sinkers working on Shaft No. 4 had a collection for his widow and children presenting her with £4 and said they would make another gift on pay day. Further assistance for his widow was provided three months later from the proceeds of a concert in the schoolroom at Dore presided over by the Rev Allred the vicar. The Dore brass band played, Dore minstrels sang and a pianoforte recital was played. (NEWS)

ENGINEER'S HALF YEARLY REPORT

31 Dec 1888. The engineer recorded in his first half yearly report 'the contractors have possession of nearly all the land they at present require, which is now being fenced off, and a considerable amount of preliminary work has been done at both ends of the line. Fair progress has been made with the works at the Totley and Cowburn tunnels; the five (four of the five) permanent shafts have been commenced at Totley, two of which are sunk to foundation level, and 500 yards of heading have been driven. Several of the cuttings and smaller works – such as stream diversions and culverts – are being proceeded with'. (ENG)

16 Jan 1889. The principal work on Contract No. 1 has been the excavation of the cutting at the east end of Totley tunnel. In the tunnel 243 yards of heading has been driven. The sinking of shafts No. 3 and No. 4 has been delayed by the quantities of water met necessitating larger pumps, the changing of which has taken some time. (ENG)

OPENING OF DORE & TOTLEY STATION SIGNAL BOX

6 Jan 1889. Commencing at 08.30 the new Dore & Totley Station signal box opened as an intermediate block telegraph box. (MRENG).

14 Jan 1889. At Totley, Major F. J. Marindin, the Board of Trade inspector, reported that a new siding to connect with the down line and main line crossover has been put in. A new signal box with nine working levers has been completed and the interlocking approved. (BT) (This is a temporary box to control access to the contractor's yard and line to the tunnel entrance.)

FOUR TEMPORARY SHAFTS AT EDALE

16 Jan 1889. At Cowburn east, four temporary shafts have been sunk, from two of which the headings have commenced. Winding gear has been fixed at two of these shafts, the fixing of the pumps at the permanent shaft has been completed and the sinking has started again. (ENG)

18 Jan 1889. The *Sheffield Daily Telegraph* reported 'on Contract No. 2 the purchase of some portions of the land is not settled and the need of a short Act for the construction of a portion of the work is causing some delay in getting started. In Edale there is a shortage of accommodation for the navvies and some more substantial dwellings may be erected'. (NEWS)

30 Jan 1889. A report stated that 'large amounts of coal have been carted to the Edale end from Chapel en le Frith in case of wintry weather setting in'. (NEWS)

BUSY SCENES AT TOTLEY

5 Feb 1889. A report on progress in the *Sheffield Daily Telegraph* stated that 'delay has been caused by a landowner (Ebenezer Hall) not giving up some land to the contractors. Since they gained possession which was only a fortnight ago considerable progress has been made. A new signal box has been erected and sidings put in off the main line, which runs into a field adjoining Dore station and which is now being used by the contractors as a store yard. An overland line has been started which goes from the store yard and crosses the highway opposite. Should the favourable weather continue the line should be completed in a week and be able to take an amount of heavy traffic off the roads. (An optimistic hope, in the event, as there were ferocious gales and blizzards which caused structural damage and much loss of life at sea.) There are upwards of 200 navvies working on the open cutting to the tunnel mouth at Totley Brook. The soil which has been removed from the cutting has been deposited in raising the ground around Totley Brook for the overland line. At the tunnel mouth a shaft (A) has been sunk upwards of 60 ft deep to the level of the line. A 10 ft heading has been driven 300 yards in the tunnel, which goes in a north easterly direction from the Padley end. After eighty yards had been driven another shaft had to be sunk owing to the quantity of water that had been met and shaft (A) is now used only for pumping operations. A 25 hp boiler has been fixed and is now used solely to provide steam to work the pump. It is operating non-stop but at times is unable to keep down the water sufficiently for the miners to continue. About 100 yards further on is a second shaft B which is used for the miners to descend. A steam crane is here employed to draw out the bind. It runs on rails which allows it to deposit the waste where required which is saving a lot of manual labour. About 200 yards further on is temporary shaft 3 (C). The miners here have sunk the shaft and have started driving a heading. A number of navvies huts are being erected near to Shaft No. 4 and will be used by the men employed, when they are ready. Huts have also been erected at Totley Bents and some of them which are completed are now occupied. Provision stores were opened on Saturday. At present there are 400 men employed and in the next few weeks they will be augmented by several hundred more. The Totley Moor Brick Works has now completed the tramway from the brickyard along the foot of Totley Moor to Shaft No. 4 and have commenced delivering bricks'. (NEWS) (Four days later the *Derbyshire Times* repeated the story word for word!)

12 Feb 1889. Oliver has been given possession of Ebenezer Hall's land and has now laid down a temporary line from Dore station to the tunnel entrance. 368 yards of heading has been achieved in Totley tunnel making a total so far of 894 yards. A junction has been effected between two portions of the heading and the mining of the full size tunnel is about to commence. Water is still being met in the headings at both ends. (ENG)

PEACE OF EDALE VALLEY SHATTERED

The permanent shaft at the east end of Cowburn tunnel has now been sunk to formation level and the headings are being driven from two of the temporary shafts. At the west end 204 yards of heading has now been completed. (ENG)

2 Mar 1889. The *Derbyshire Times* reported that 'in the Edale valley the contractor is employing several hundred navvies to build Cowburn tunnel and the line through the valley. Joiners are building wooden houses for the navvies as there is no accommodation in the valley. 80 to 100 men are excavating at the surface lower down the valley. A massive bridge of timber is being constructed across the river at Barber Booth and across the Edale road over which a temporary railway will be extended further down the valley for the convenience of the contractor. At Chinley operations are being pushed forward with much vigour'. (NEWS)

The *Derbyshire Courier* noted 'the scene of operations in the Edale valley gets busier as the days get longer, and several hundred men are now employed by the contractor for this portion of the line. Four shafts have been sunk to the level of the line, and as they are on rising ground, the respective depths of each from the surface are No. 1 180 ft, No. 2 60 ft, No. 3 40 ft and No. 4 30 ft. Nos. 3 and 4 are connected by a headway that has been driven and when this has been through the other shafts more engines and wagons can be used and the number of workmen will be largely increased. The shafts are about 200 yards apart from each other. Lower down the valley about eighty or a hundred men are employed in excavating at the surface, and many joiners are engaged in erecting wooden houses for the navvies, there being no house property to be got in the neighbourhood (there are limited lodgings). Operations in the shafts are carried on day and night by means of three shifts of men, who work eight hours each. A massive bridge of timber is being constructed across the river and the Edale Road at Barber Booth, over which a

Here is Cowburn shaft on the edge of a spoil heap. It is located just to the north of Dalehead Farm, which is now an outdoor pursuit centre (101846). A look through the entrance door shows a round shaft inside. There is evidence that the shaft was not used for ventilation and the top is sealed. In this 15 Aug 2011 view from left to right can be seen Lose Hill (1,563 ft), Back Tor and to the right of the trees Mam Tor (1,700 ft) which dips down to Mam Nick from where the contractor had to bring down all his materials on a 1 in 5 hill until the headings met. The slope from Mam Nick is leading on to Rushup Edge. *Author*

temporary railway will be extended so that excavators may get lower down the valley. At Chinley operations are being pushed ahead with much vigour'. (NEWS)

DRAMATIC LOWERING OF CONTRACTOR'S ENGINE INTO EDALE VALLEY

Mar 1889. There is an oft repeated story that a contractors engine, thought to be *Cocker*, was brought from Chapel by road. It went from Chapel via Rushup Edge to Mam Nick where it descended the precipitous road into the valley. It was steamed all the way using two lengths of track, the rear length being leapfrogged over to the front and the engine being driven forward. A team of horses towed the short length of track on a low loader. It is remembered that crowds gathered at a safe distance to watch the perilous 650 ft descent into the valley.

NEW PARTS OF THE WORK START

12 Mar 1889. The engineers reported 'at Totley the lining with bricks of the full size tunnel has been started. A large quantity of very good bricks has been found to aid progress but a large quantity of water is still being met within the headings especially at the face but after a time it drains off. A commencement has been made with the earthwork between the west end of the tunnel and Hathersage. A junction has now been made between two of the temporary shafts at the east end of Cowburn and at the completed permanent shaft the heading has been driven some way in both directions. Possession of all the land has now been obtained at the Chinley end of Cowburn. This will allow the contractor to lay a temporary road between what became Chinley North Junction and the tunnel. (ENG)

Heavy snowstorms were experienced during March. (NEWS)

9 Apr 1889. Permanent Shaft No. 4 at Totley has been widened to where sinking has been suspended. (ICE)

FIRST FATALITY IN COWBURN TUNNEL

Mar 1889. James Lane who lived at Hathersage was leading a horse drawn wagon loaded with bricks. On entering Cowburn tunnel the horse bolted and Lane was found dead, with his left arm smashed and his head nearly severed from his body. (NEWS)

EBENEZER DIGS HIS HEELS IN

13 Apr 1889. 151 yards of heading has been driven from two faces at Totley tunnel and thirty three yards of tunnelling has been completed. This work is now proceeding from six faces. There is a large supply of bricks on the ground at the Totley end. The works are in coal measures consisting of strong shale with occasional beds of hard stone, a thin bed of coal and about 3 ft of fire clay and requires lining throughout. A steam navvy has been started in the cutting at the east end. Progress in obtaining possession of Ebenezer Hall's land foundered when it came to the final arrangements, as under the agreement with him, the plans had to be submitted to his surveyor and while some agreement has been reached possession has still not been obtained. At the west end the drilling is through shale and no millstone grit has yet been met. (ENG)

11 May 1889. 105 yards of heading has been driven from two faces and fifty four yards of tunnelling has been completed at the east end. Preparations are being made for starting the full size tunnel at the Padley end, the mining for the break up length being now in progress. The masonry for the bridges between Dore and the tunnel has now been started. (ENG)

26 May 1889. At Totley tunnel east the temporarily abandoned permanent Shaft No. 3 has been reached by the miners and the water liberated. (NEWS)

CONTRACTOR AND MIDLAND IN CONFLICT

13 Apr 1889. At Cowburn tunnel the greater part of the material is being tipped to spoil, access to the land being obtained by erecting temporary bridges. A junction has been made between two other temporary shafts at the east end. A large quantity of water has been met at the west end. The large cutting at the west end has been commenced from which good durable building stone is being obtained. Masonry has been commenced on one of the public road bridges. (ENG)

11 May 1889. Some differences have arisen between the contractor and the Midland regarding the nature and the cost of the proposed temporary junction with the main line at Chinley North Junction. Until it is resolved it will delay the lining of Cowburn tunnel at the west end. 143 yards of heading has been driven at the Edale end from three faces but no break up has been started due to the difficulty of getting materials to the site. It is intended to put down brick making machinery and make bricks from the shale and clay excavated from the cuttings. Air compressing plant is being fixed for the working of the headings by machinery. (ENG)

TOTLEY BECOMES A BUILDING SITE

8 Jun 1889. The *Sheffield Independent* reported 'the residents in the beautiful valley of Abbeydale, of Totley, of Totley Grove and the district are to be commiserated with. They have erected there, in the midst of the most charming scenery, their villa residences, hoping to escape from the rush and noise and smoke and turmoil of their busy lives in Sheffield; but so far their expectations have by no means been realized. They have had to carry on perpetual warfare to ensure some form of peace and privacy and when prospects of success were before them a whole army of strangers and foreigners have come down upon them and turned their attractive surroundings into a veritable wilderness… where once were tasteful gardens, where sheep lazily browsed, where the air was filled with the melody of sweet songsters; where the sparkling brook noisily flowed (writers of this period can't resist going completely over the top!) – where was all this and much more a year ago are now to be seen cuttings and embankments, are to be heard the shrill whistling of engines, the whirr of machinery and other signs of modern activity… What the effect of the opening of this line will be upon Dore and the district and the residents are by no means agreed. There are those who anticipate that with increased railway facilities more strangers will be drawn there and that a disposition will be shown by capitalists to pass through the tunnel and build there residences in the Hope valley and beyond.'

This is an 1894 view looking towards Sheffield from bridge No. 6 which carries Abbeydale Road over the line. This is the main road from Sheffield to Owler Bar. The nearest feature is bridge No. 5 (319805) which carries the line over the River Sheaf by a girder bridge and bridge No. 4 which is called 'Bradway Bank' in the distance. On the right is West View cottage before it was extended. The bridge has five spans of 24 ft each on a skew of 27 ft 7¼ in with stone abutments and wings and two have main girders with lattice parapets. It crosses the railway, a water course which can be seen to the left of the line carrying water from the tunnel, land and the River Sheaf. The bridge carries an ancient footpath and road access to the cottage. Poynton Wood can be seen in the distance and to the right above the cottage is where Prospect Road would be developed for housing fifteen years later.

Brian Edwards collection

The article then describes the works. 'The new line swings right from Dore station and runs between the hill and the Abbeydale road. After crossing the Sheaf the line runs across several fields, and taking off the corner of the grounds attached to West View cottage, belonging to Joseph Hall, it strikes the turnpike road. At this point a good deal of work is being done. Instead of the footpath which leads from the turnpike to Bradway Bank a new road will be made and from this an entrance will be gained to West View cottage instead of, as now, from the main road.

The line here will pass through a cutting, but not of sufficient depth to interfere with the turnpike. The road has been diverted and men are engaged upon the tunnel which will be under the road, and are raising the ground on either side of it. The gradient on both sides will be 1 in 50. Gates have been thrown across the turnpike, which are closed on the approach of the engines employed to bring up materials or trucks of earth.

After crossing the road the line runs through the Totley Brook Estate, the cutting being about mid way between the foot of the hill and Grove Road. Two lines of rails have been temporarily laid, one on the flat by the side of the cutting and the other in the cutting itself. A great deal of work in the way of excavating, and men are still engaged upon it. For some 700 yards before reaching the tunnel, the entrance to which is about opposite Totley Grove Hall, the cutting gradually deepens until about 54 ft will be reached. All around here is a scene of much activity, and the whole face of the district is entirely changed. 'We cannot deny' observed one official 'that we have spoiled the beauty of this grove – at least for a while'. The Totley Brook (Old Hay) has been diverted and runs down a new cutting, much closer to the road than formerly, but when the railway is completed, it will pass along a bed yet to be made on the other side of the line, and nearer its former course. (NEWS)

Two streams of water come to the surface here from the tunnel, one of which flows out at the level and the other is pumped by a powerful engine in a shed. A great deal of the excavating in the cutting has been done by the means of a 'steam navvy' and thousands of people have been there to see it at work. The bucket which will hold 1½ yards of earth weighing 1½ tons is provided with powerful steel teeth and as the bucket is drawn up the face of the cutting, the teeth claw away the soil, which drops into the bucket. It is then swung over a truck, the bottom opens and the earth falls into it. Two buckets will fill a contractor's wagon.

The Old Hay Brook had to be diverted and this required crossing the line on aqueduct No. 8 (309802), which is located between Totley Tunnel East signal box and the tunnel entrance. The span is 27 ft and the skew 31 ft. 23 Mar 2005. *Author*

The diverted river runs at the back of Grove Road in a cascade of small waterfalls. 23 Mar 2005.
Author

The water draining down the culvert as seen from footbridge No. 7 which connects Totley Brook Road and Grove Road. Note the overgrown lie by siding with its catch point on the right. Totley Tunnel East signal box is behind the photographer. 23 Mar 2005.
Author

This is a Dunbar & Ruston machine of 1889. It claims it can excavate 400 to 600 cubic yards of material a day whereas a larger amount is claimed for Oliver's machine.
www.gracesguide.co.uk

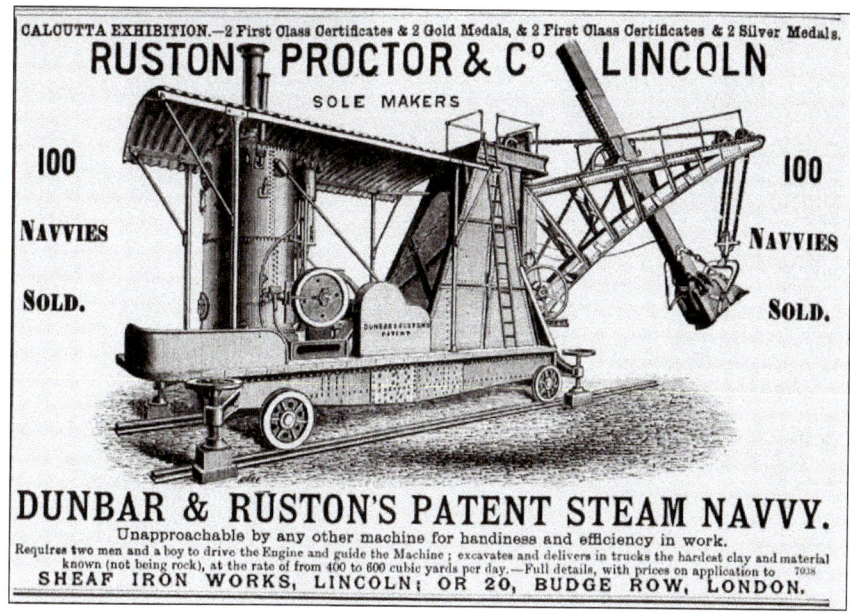

CALCUTTA EXHIBITION.—2 First Class Certificates & 2 Gold Medals, & 2 First Class Certificates & 2 Silver Medals.

RUSTON, PROCTOR & C° LINCOLN
SOLE MAKERS

100 NAVVIES SOLD. 100 NAVVIES SOLD.

DUNBAR & RUSTON'S PATENT STEAM NAVVY.
Unapproachable by any other machine for handiness and efficiency in work.
Requires two men and a boy to drive the Engine and guide the Machine; excavates and delivers in trucks the hardest clay and material known (not being rock), at the rate of from 400 to 600 cubic yards per day.—Full details, with prices on application to
SHEAF IRON WORKS, LINCOLN; OR 20, BUDGE ROW, LONDON.

The 'navvy' will excavate from 600 to 700 square yards of earth per day, and it has already advanced 600 yards or nearly up to the mouth of the tunnel. (NEWS)

There is no embankment anywhere near where the earth thrown out is required, so it is being conveyed to a tip on the other side of the road beyond Totley Grove.

Ten acres have been purchased there for the purpose and a large hill it promises to be before the last truck load is placed upon it. The new line runs through grounds in front of Totley Grove Hall. The house is now unoccupied, but is being done up, and it is stated that Mr Oliver, the contractor intends to reside there.

In constructing the tunnel the contractors have been somewhat hampered by the stipulations laid down by the Duke of Rutland in parting with his land. They were that the work should be done from the Padley Wood end of the tunnel, or within a thousand yards of the entrance at Totley, and that for the other 5,000 yards there should be no disturbance at the surface whatever. A good part of the distance is moorland, and His Grace was apprehensive that the sinking of the shafts upon it, and the throwing out of earth, would disturb the grouse, and hence the stipulation.'

The report then covers the work on the six shafts and the work at the Padley end. 'About 600 men are engaged on this part of the line, by far the larger portion of them are working in the Totley valley. The influx of so many has not, as yet caused problems. Mr Oliver, the contractor, has provided accommodation by erecting picturesque (sic) looking wooden huts at Totley Bents and elsewhere; he has enlarged the village school, so that the children may attend and be educated, and he has provided a mission hall for the adults.'

On our rambles at Totley we met with the Rev J. T. F. Allred the kind and courteous vicar at Dore and we ventured to ask about his experience amongst the workmen on the line 'we can do with the railwaymen well enough, it is your Sheffield roughs we cannot tolerate. Through them Sunday has become the worst day of the week. They come in groups – fellows with black pipes in their mouths. They describe themselves as travellers, and beginning at the *Bridge Inn*, they go around all the public houses in the parish and make a day of drunkenness of it. I only wish all who visit us from Sheffield were as well conducted as the navvies'. He also mentions that 'some of those who attended the Mission Hall have very good voices and among the children attending school there are some very amusing characters who talk in many varying dialects which makes them difficult to understand. They are very well behaved and better than some of the local children.'

It is also mentioned in this article that Oliver's son Mr T. W. N. Oliver is representing him on the spot and Mr Caffin (this is a name that occurs rarely) is acting as his engineer. (NEWS)

Shaft No. 4 on a spring day in 2009. Although it is not apparent, this shaft was wider than the others to allow machinery and wagons to be lowered down it. The main Totley to Owler Bar road can be seen in the background. *Author*

WATER IN BOTH TUNNELS BRINGS WORK TO A HALT

15 Jun 1889. 117 yards of heading has been driven from two faces at Totley and 54 yards of tunnelling has been completed. A break up length of full size tunnel has been completed at the Padley end but such large amounts of water are being dealt with that all work on the heading, driving and tunnelling has been suspended to get a twelve inch pipe drain under the invert level to draw off the water from the bottom of the lengths. A quantity of stone is being dressed for the side walls and bricks are being delivered for the arch. At Cowburn 222 yards of heading has been achieved from three faces mainly at the east end. At the west end progress is slow due to the large amounts of water being encountered and the heavy nature of the ground. A breakup has been commenced for which the excavation is nearly complete. The air compressing machinery is now fixed and the heading is well ventilated. (ENG)

19 Jun 1889. Permanent Shaft No. 4 at the east end of Totley tunnel reached rail level at 280 ft. (ICE)

16 Jul 1889. At Totley 112 yards of heading has been driven from shafts No. 3 and No. 4 and sixty yards of tunnelling has been completed. The drain under the invert at the Padley end has reached the breakup and has improved the condition of the heading. The water at the east end has still to be pumped up one of the temporary shafts. The open cutting at the east end of Totley tunnel is being assisted by the use of a steam navvy. (ENG)

6 Aug 1889. The *Sheffield Daily Telegraph* reported complaints claiming that Oliver's traction engines were seriously damaging the roads. In one case a complaint from Bakewell RDC resulted in Oliver offering to repair the roads at his own expense. These machines, which were considered an abomination by many, were being used to get material to the Padley end of Totley tunnel. (NEWS)

The drain at the Padley end is now complete and the driving and widening of the tunnel has been recommenced. (ENG)

Burrell and Sons of Thetford were manufacturing this traction engine in 1889. It is representative of what they looked like around this time. Sheffield Cycling Club complained that the road over Dore Moor was in an abominable condition and a risk to their members due to machines like this one.
www.gracesguide.co.uk

ENGINEER'S SIX MONTHLY REPORT

30 Jun 1889. Fair progress has been made. At the two tunnels all the permanent shafts are now sunk to their full depths, 2,307 yards of heading has been driven and 232 yards of tunnelling has been completed. 218,000 cubic yards of excavation has been removed from the cuttings and 4,300 cubic yards of masonry has been executed in bridges and culverts. (ENG)

EDWARDS TO START CHAPEL MILTON VIADUCT EARLY

16 Jul 1889. Progress has not been as good due to the number of men leaving to work on the hay harvest and the difficulty in finding replacements. At the west end of Cowburn two more break ups have been commenced. Brick making plant is being set up in Edale and when it becomes operative lining will start on the east end. (ENG)

Around this time the cabins and huts etc were moved from the Nottingham Suburban Railway contract to a site at Chapel en le Frith.

6 Aug 1889. During this month sidings for Edwards were agreed at a location between Chapel en le Frith and Chinley at a cost of £430 to be met by the contractor. (GPC)

At Edale the contractor has found a large quantity of stone within half a mile of the line. This will allow him to proceed with the viaducts and bridges without waiting for the headings to meet in the tunnel. Possession of land for a further 2½ miles of line has been given to Edwards. On the Chinley South Curve, the Act had just been obtained. The contractor asked for permission to start the work, which includes the substantial Chapel Milton viaduct, at once. He reasoned that when the tunnel headings have met, in an anticipated two years time, a very large gang of masons and bricklayers would be required for the tunnel work and considerable difficulty would be experienced recruiting sufficient men if the viaduct and the tunnel are proceeded with at the same time. He believed the viaduct would take between two and three years to build which would allow him to get together a good gang of men who he could then draft into the tunnel when required. The cutting at the west end of the tunnel was yielding first class stone which could be used for the viaduct but would not be available when the cutting was completed. The engineers supported Edwards' request which was subsequently agreed to by the company. (ENG)

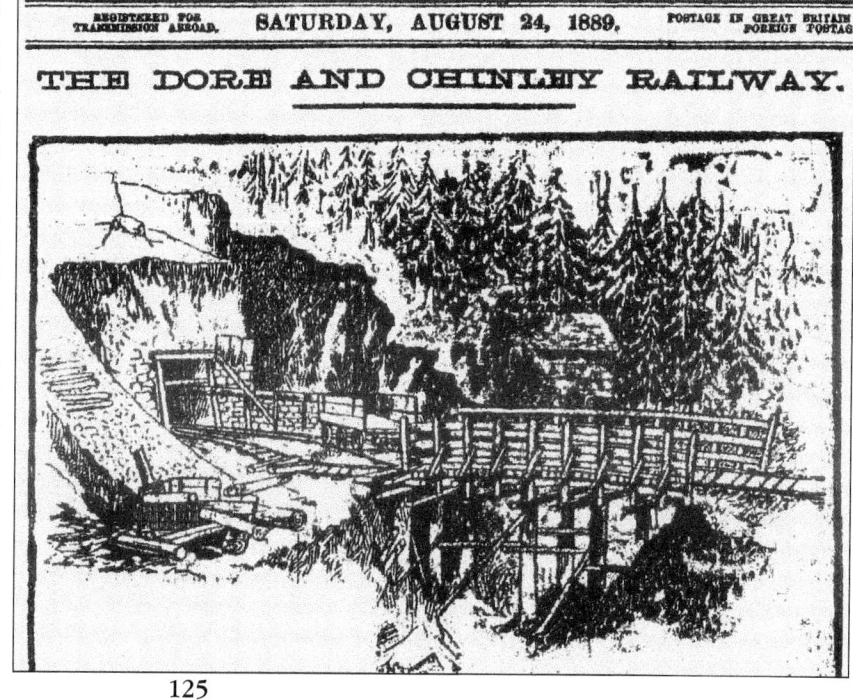

A drawing in a newspaper of the Padley end of the tunnel under construction in Aug 1889. Drilling had begun eleven months earlier and was suspended in June of that year whilst improved drains were built to remove the water which prevented further work being undertaken. The works had either just restarted, or were about to, when this sketch was made. It shows the 10 ft by 9 ft entrance that was sufficient for a fully loaded wagon to be worked. In fact a six wheeled wagon can be seen together with two lines of track and a temporary wooden bridge over the Burbage Brook. On the left is a ramp which was later to become a tramway with wagons attached by a steel cable to a stationary engine on the road above.

14 Aug 1889. The committee instructed the engineers to prepare a plan and schedule of process for the Chinley South Curve and obtain a tender from Edwards for its construction. (GPC)

ENGINEER KILLED AT TOTLEY

14 Aug 1889. Frederick William Herbert age 22 was killed when trying to get on an engine that was moving (see page 101).

CUTTING TO TOTLEY TUNNEL COMPLETED
WATER RELEASED

4 Sep 1889. The lifting of water at temporary shaft A is finished. In the six months from 15 Feb to now 1,167 yards was driven and all the water discharged from the headings was lifted at shaft A and amounted to (a staggering) 2,250,000 gallons a day. (ICE)

12 Sep 1889. At the Totley end pumping has now ceased, the heading having been driven to the open cutting which allows the water from the tunnel to drain away by gravitation. 167 yards of heading and seventy one yards of tunnelling has been completed which is the best achieved so far. 23,378 yards of excavation has been removed from the cuttings and six bridges are now in hand. (ENG)

EDWARDS GETS CONTRACT
FOR CHINLEY SOUTH CURVE

12 Sep 1889. The temporary junction with the main line at Chinley North Junction will be brought into use during the following week. For the Chinley South Curve Edwards tendered £27,950/12/1, about £2,000 below the engineers estimate. If the contract is awarded he would commence work at once as all the bridges and culverts to the west end of the tunnel are virtually completed. (ENG)

19 Sep 1889. Edwards tender was accepted. Fowler, the solicitor, is charged with acquiring and paying for the land, and gained approval to spend £108,045 (this must be an error – £18,045 is more like it). Negotiations with the main landowner, Joseph Lingard, are protracted. The only other landowner was the MSLR who owned the Peak Forest Tramway plus some other land and a plantation. On the plans and sections the engineer is named as Alf A. Langley. (GPC)

(Apart from the tunnels this was the most significant piece of engineering on the line. The main Peak line had required a similar viaduct, completed in 1865, and was 245 yards long consisting of fifteen spans of 42 ft width. One span is walled up with a 12 ft opening. It is 104 ft from the bed of Black Brook at its highest.)

The Chinley South Curve is 666 yards long in total with the viaduct being marginally shorter than its neighbour at 234 yards. It was to have thirteen masonry arches of 45 ft width and at its highest it would be 104 ft above the Black Brook. There are two less arches but each arch is 3 ft wider. The radius of the curve is one furlong seven chains (374 yards) and is on a falling gradient of 1 in 375 from Chinley East Junction. (GPC)

(Both bridges crossed Black Brook, the main Derby to Manchester road and the Peak Forest Tramway. The connection at Chinley South Junction was achieved after the Peak line was widened and was single line where it joined the Peak's down line. It was later made a double line junction. Reports observe that there were no accidents in the course of its construction, except for a mason breaking his leg. This compared well against the first viaduct where a newspaper report casually stated 'each arch cost a couple of lives'. In fact a steam navvy boiler explosion killed one man (see page 129).

The viaduct when new, towering over Chapel Milton village. In the foreground is the Peak Forest Tramway. The Ambergate to Chinley viaduct can just about be discerned through the first arch. Hayfield Road is on the right. The Chinley South Curve viaduct was called 'Milton' whereas the Peak line viaduct was called 'Chapel Milton' although the engineers confusingly insisted on the new viaduct being 'Chapel Milton'.

Mike Bentley collection

This magnificent view of the bifurcating viaducts was taken in 1894 and shows the new south curve on the left. The wall of the Hayfield road can just be discerned below the black wall in the foreground. Chinley South Junction box can be seen and a light engine is at the side of it. The signals on both viaducts can be well seen and also on the Peak line on the other side of the bridge. Another feature are the telegraph poles fastened to the side of the viaducts. The buildings of the Chinley Independent chapel, which was opened in 1711, are in the foreground.

Peter Clowes collection

MUCH ACTIVITY ON BOTH SIDES OF COWBURN

19 Sep 1889. Major Marinder approved the connection at Chinley for Edwards siding. (BT) (It was just to the north of bridge No. 105, the overbridge at New Chapel Road, on the Peak line side of the triangle.)

30 Sep 1889. The *Sheffield Independent* reported 'On the length about a mile from New Smith(y) to the entrance to the tunnel several hundred men are employed, a long cutting of considerable depth being made. It is impracticable for any more men to be employed on this portion of the works. In the Edale valley the scene is of a still busier description. Considerable progress is being made with the tunnel, the bricks for which are made in the works, so that one portion resembles a huge brickyard. There are about 300 persons living in wooden huts at the top end of the Edale valley. The traction engine which is used for conveying coal &c from the station to Chapel en le Frith to the works, is capable of managing about thirty five tons a day. It is expected that another engine will be procured shortly for the purpose of conveying material to construct a bridge at Hope……At Chapel en le Frith and Chinley there is a great demand for cottage property. The navvy mission have decided to re-open the smoke room and reading room at Chinley for the winter. Mr F. Tongue, who has laboured as a missionary since the commencement of the works, has resigned his position, with the intention of entering the Wesleyan ministry in Canada. His successor has not yet been appointed.' (NEWS)

10 Oct 1889. At Cowburn the heading at the east end is making good progress as the material is good sound shale with no water ingress. At the west end the heading is now in solid rock and requires no timbering. The work at Chinley South Curve has commenced. (ENG)

TOTLEY HEADING MEETS SHAFT No. 4

21 Sep 1889. At Totley tunnel east the heading met Shaft No. 4 where the pump located there was stopped, became disabled and then finally drowned. (ICE)

EDWARDS SELLS SOME HORSES

24 Sep 1889. The *Sheffield Daily Telegraph* carried an advertisement for the 'sale of forty six draught and two useful nag horses'. They were described as being 'between five and seven years old, sixteen to seventeen hands high and thoroughly honest and staunch workers'. There were also 'fifteen strong carts and forty sets of gears'. They could be seen working on the contract or in stables the day before the Wed 9 Oct sale date at Chapel Milton. They had been purchased in the previous twelve months but because of the adoption of steam power on the overland route and traction engines on the highway they were no longer required. (NEWS)

11 Oct 1889. The *Sheffield Independent* reported that there were an unusually large number of buyers from far and wide at Edwards' auction. Fifty one horses were sold at an average of forty six guineas each. The highest price for the nag horses was eighty guineas by Mr J. S. Adamson of Sibbersfield, Chester. The result was considered to be highly satisfactory. (NEWS) (By this time Edwards was living at Sibbersfield.)

(The reported number of horses show a drop from sixty six to fifty horses on the contract which suggests that Edwards might not have sold them all. The wording of the advert also suggests that he was using horses to carry materials by the direct route to the Edale valley and using traction engines on the road from Chapel to Mam Nick thence down the steep hill into the valley.)

DEVELOPMENTS AT HATHERSAGE

30 Sep 1889. The *Sheffield Independent* reported that 'works at Hathersage are being pushed on with great energy and, as they are in great proximity to the millstone quarries, the masonry here will be of the most massive kind. Some of the blocks of stone weigh several tons. There are to be four bridges, all of which, it is expected, will be erected before next spring… There is a great demand for cottage property'. (NEWS)

REPORT ON THE LINE FROM DORE STATION

28 Sep 1889. The *Derbyshire Times* noted that new offices have been erected by the contractor near Dore station. The cutting through the spoil bank to the main line is in progress and a great number of navvies are being employed there. It is believed that a short tunnel 100-150 yards long under the corner of the woods and two or three stone bridges have been erected for the accommodation of land owners and are ready for girders. The large bridge on Abbeydale Road is also ready for girders but little work has been done between Abbeydale Road and Totley Brook. The steam navvy will be employed around the tunnel for a long time yet. The position of the new line is 12 ft below where it now stands. Tunnelling is in active progress with miners taking out lengths and bricklayers will then be sent in to arch the tunnel. No. 4 shaft has water that is mastering the pumps. It has been decided to let the No. 4 shaft stand until the heading is driven through from No. 3 shaft when shot will be put in and a hole blown through. (NEWS) (The reporter was not up to speed!).

10 Oct 1889. Large quantities of water are reported in Totley tunnel which has held up the work but two large lengths for shafts No. 3 and No. 4 have been completed and also work has been ongoing on the inverts and drains. 22,000 cubic yards of excavation in the cuttings and a considerable quantity of masonry on the bridges has been completed. Several small culverts and the stream diversion at Totley Brook (Old Hay Brook) are making good progress. (ENG)

12 Nov 1889. At Totley the lining of No. 4 shaft is starting and when this is finished a powerful set of winding engines and machinery for the removal of the spoil and lowering of the materials into the central portion of the tunnel will start. (ENG)

MORE TUNNEL DEATHS

2 Nov 1889. Hamar Lane or **James Lane** was an unmarried man who was fairly new on the job and was living at Town End, Chapel. He was employed as a pony driver. While working in Cowburn tunnel he was knocked down by a wagon load of bricks and run over. He was mutilated and his head was nearly severed from his body. His mangled remains were picked up and removed to a shed on the works to await the coroner's enquiry. A verdict of 'accidental death' was recorded. (NEWS)

5 Nov 1889. Richard Green, age 43, who was in charge of the miners was killed by a fall of earth at the Padley end. At the inquest at the *Old Red Lion Inn* at Grindleford a verdict of 'accidental death' was recorded. He left a wife and five children. (NEWS)

NAVVIES WALKING LONG DISTANCES TO EDALE

1 Dec 1889. *The Engineer* reported that 'over 200 workmen are now employed at the Chinley and Edale ends of the tunnel. Four shafts have been sunk at the Edale end, one of which has reached the level of the line, at a depth of 150 ft. Four engines are being used for boring and pumping purposes. Temporary buildings are being erected for the accommodation of workmen and others will have to be put up. Many navvies have already taken up lodgings at the farmhouses and some are walking long distances to and from work. Large quantities of coal have been carted to the spot from Chapel en le Frith in case of wintry weather setting in.' (NEWS).

17 Dec 1889. At Cowburn 180 yards of heading has been driven from two faces, the best achieved so far. Additionally sixty nine yards of lining has been completed. The tunnel remains dry. The excavation for the foundation to the abutment of Chapel Milton viaduct has been commenced and temporary roads are being laid and other preparations made to aid the work. (ENG)

9 Jan 1890. The Edale quarry is being opened out and stone is being prepared for the bridges on the line. The brick making plant is reaching completion and will have eight kilns. At Chapel Milton viaduct masonry has been started to the abutment of the viaduct and the excavation for the foundation of two of the piers is in progress. (ENG)

LOCAL BRICKS TO BE USED FOR LINING

31 Oct 1889. A two year contract has recently been entered into between the Totley Moor Brick Works and Thomas Oliver to supply bricks to Padley Wood tunnel mouth. Prior to this considerable alterations and progress has been made in the past few weeks to meet the needs of the contractor. The tramway to Shaft No. 4 has been extended to pass shafts Nos. 3 and 2. This enables the brick company to take its bricks by the tramway to each of the shafts and dispenses with horses and carts and a traction engine. Upwards of 100 tons of coal slack per week is being moved by this new tramway to the brickyard as well as all plant and material required at the three shafts by the contractor. 90,000 to 95,000 bricks leave the brickyard every week. (NEWS)

17 Dec 1889. After slow progress in Totley tunnel better progress has been made, in that seventy yards of heading and ninety six yards of tunnelling have been achieved. This is in part due to a reduction in the amount of water encountered at the Padley end. Frost has handicapped the bridge work and there is also a shortage of facing bricks which are supplied from Staffordshire. The contractor has sourced suitable clay near the tunnel for the making of brindle bricks, for use on the arches of bridges and in the tunnel. The engineers and the Midland's representative Mr McDonald are of the view they are as good if not better. (ENG) (The GPC had stipulated that only Staffordshire bricks should be used but once it was pointed out the local bricks were for the inside lining the committee changed its mind.)

9 Jan 1890. At Totley tunnel work has stopped at the east end while new hoisting gear is being erected in Shaft No. 4. The twelve inch drainage pipe has now been laid from the entrance as far as Shaft No. 4, an open grip sufficing beyond that point. (ENG)

WORK STARTS ON DORE SOUTH JUNCTION CURVE

31 Dec 1889. The works have commenced on Dore South Junction Curve. (ENG)

(In the Parliamentary session of 1885, Parry & Story introduced Deviation No. 1 which became the 'Dore South Junction Curve' and included a tunnel of 190 yards, later reduced to ninety one yards.)

Rickard states 'this tunnel, although only four chains in length, is worthy of notice on account of a certain peculiarity possessed by it. It passes under very steep side-long ground, at no great depth, and is on a curve of twelve chains (264 yards) radius. In order to allow for the necessary canting of the vehicles on so sharp a curve, and at the same time to enable the tunnel to sustain the unequal load upon it, the cross section is inclined from the vertical towards the inside of the curve, to fit the super elevation of the outer rails of the permanent way'. (ICE)

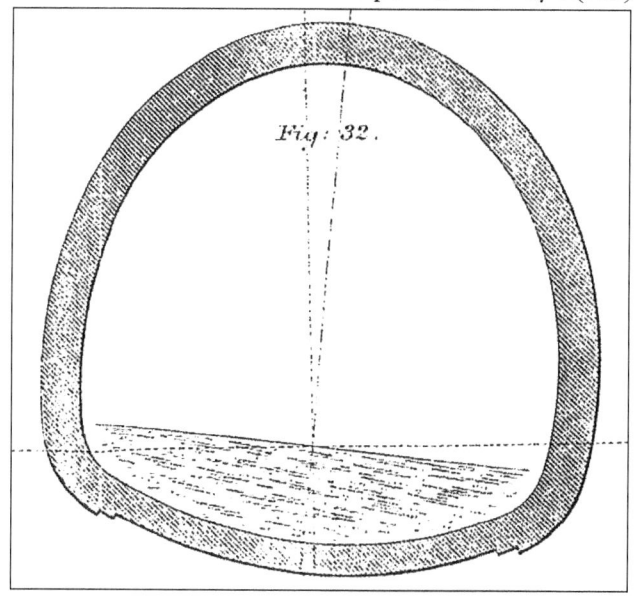

The inclination from the vertical of Dore tunnel. *ICE Paper*

ENGINEERS SIX MONTHLY REPORT

31 Dec 1889. In the two tunnels 3,551 yards of heading has been driven and 924 yards of tunnelling completed. 490,000 yards of excavation has been moved from the cuttings and 10,000 yards of masonry in viaducts, bridges and culverts has been executed. (ENG)

LETHAL WORKING CONDITIONS

8 Jan 1890. William Carey, a married Irishman age 45, was killed at 02.30 when the roof fell in on him and he was buried by rock and crushed to death at the Chinley end of Cowburn tunnel. He was removed to his home at Chapel Milton. Two other men survived but were seriously injured. After his death William's widow Mary set up a lodging house at Chapel. Eighteen months later a navvy called William Evans, from Eyam, became a boarder and two years later, in May 1893, married her. He had left his first wife because of her bad conduct and did not tell Mary about it. Evans was charged with bigamy and in his defence said that he needed to provide a home for his three children. (NEWS)

11 Jan 1890. (This was a bad day in Totley tunnel. The working conditions can only be described as lethal.) On this Saturday at 06.00 **Harry Sloper** was working at No. 1 shaft when a large piece of wood used as a prop fell and struck him on the head, cutting the scalp a considerable length and also damaging his shoulder. A medical man was summoned and stitched the head wound. At 14.00 in the crane shaft near the tunnel mouth a piece of bind fell and struck an unnamed man on the head. He received 'a nasty cut but nothing of a serious nature. After putting a handkerchief round his head he was able to walk home'. (NEWS)

A third accident befell a man known as **'Little Punch'**, a Norfolk man, who was working in the tunnel at No. 3 shaft. 'A scaffold had been erected near the head of the tunnel and several shots fired. Upon the men resuming work a large piece of bind which had been resting on the scaffold from the shots fell down 10 ft and caught him on his head, cutting a gash from which blood flowed freely. He was taken to his home, where he grew weak from loss of blood and became unconscious. A medical man was sent for and found he was 'suffering from a fractured skull and he was given little chance of recovery'. (NEWS)

Three days earlier a man named **Williams** was working in No. 3 shaft when a huge piece of wood fell and cut off two of his toes. (NEWS)

27 Jan 1890. John Hall, an engine driver, James Dyer, a rope runner, and another young man were taking an engine from the shed in the contractor's yard, near Dore and Totley station, along the temporary line to Shaft No. 2. While crossing a strong wooden bridge across the River Sheaf the bridge gave way. The engine fell into the river. James Dyer and the unnamed young man jumped into the river which was 4 ft deep. The driver, seeing the danger, opened the valves of his engine and blew the steam off, and, with great risk to his own life, stayed with the engine. He fortunately escaped with only one arm scalded. (NEWS)

STEAM CRANE BOILER EXPLOSION AT CHAPEL MILTON

12 Feb 1890. During the afternoon, at Chapel Milton viaduct, a huge steam crane's boiler exploded. It was being used for winding large blocks of stone. The machine was smashed and the jib fell. **Joseph Allen** who was below was knocked down and received cuts about the head and face. He was scalded by boiling water and steam. Nobody else was injured. (NEWS)

MEN DON'T WANT TO WORK

20 Feb 1890. At Dore tunnel the first length of brick lining has been completed but owing to a lack of drainage the work could not proceed until the heading is driven up to the completed length from the open end but it should not take too long. In Totley tunnel while progress is being made at the east end at Padley the driving of the heading is being seriously interfered with by a great quantity of water. The men seem reluctant to work under the present conditions and the gangs are only about a half their required strength, although the number of men on the contract has not fallen. (ENG)

13 Mar 1890. At Totley only ninety seven yards of heading was driven of which only twenty nine yards was at the Padley end, the main reason being the large amount of water at the face. The contractor complains of difficulty in getting a sufficient number of miners and keeping them at the Padley end, although 100 extra men have been taken on. He has not yet been able to arrange for a trial of Beaumont's boring machine in the heading. At Dore tunnel the heading has been driven to the open end which has allowed work to resume. Ironwork to two of the bridges at the Dore end has been fixed. 'We are endeavouring to impress on him the necessity of making progress in the headings, as this is the key to the whole work'. (This is the first recorded criticism of Thomas Oliver and reflects a growing concern of the engineer at the slow progress.) (ENG)

20 Mar 1890. The committee asked the engineers to report on how the works on Totley tunnel can be accelerated and the cost. (GPC)

COWBURN HEADINGS REACH HALF WAY

20 Feb 1890. At Cowburn 144 yards of heading and seventy two yards of lining has been completed from two faces. At the Chapel Milton viaduct good progress is being made. The masonry has been commenced to two piers and the foundation for two more piers has been completed. (ENG)

13 Mar 1890. At Cowburn the headings have reached the half way point. The Chapel Milton viaduct now has six piers built and the springers are set on one abutment. Edwards has appointed a fresh set of men to take charge of the Hope end of Contract No. 2 and active operations all along the line will now be started. There is a recorded increase of 222 men on the contract. (ENG)

UPDATE AT TOTLEY

3 Apr 1890. The *Sheffield Independent* had a story about a footpath, which started about a hundred yards from Dore and Totley station, before going up Bradway Lane, where there was a stile which gave access to a footpath. It then passed through a portion of Ebenezer Hall's land known as the 'Spoil Bank' (presumably a remnant of the cutting to Bradway tunnel from the late 1860s) before proceeding through the little wood beyond where a couple of stiles were crossed before passing through Tinker's brickyard. It then split, one path going to Bradway and the other to Holmesfield. When the Dore South Junction Curve was started, the footpath was severed and a notice was placed by the contractors stating that 'trespassers will be prosecuted'. The paper commented that this is how footpaths are lost. (NEWS)

5 Apr 1890. The *Sheffield Independent* reported that the men are busily engaged on the Dore South Curve. 'Opposite to Ebenezer Hall's Abbeydale Hall a high screen bank is being thrown up to hide passing trains from the view. The bed of the river has been straightened here to avoid having to construct two bridges to carry the line over it. Near to the house of Joseph Hall, West View cottage there is fast approaching completion a five arch bridge to carry the footpath up to Bradway Bank and the road to Mr. Hall's house. The walls are up and the ironwork is being fixed….The cutting to the tunnel gradually deepens. The steam navvy is working about half way up at a depth of 21 ft having been cut across the Totley Brook Road. A temporary bridge has been thrown across it. The excavations have come very near to the houses on the right hand side, but whether they will be swept away is not yet quite settled. Just before Totley Grove an aqueduct is in the course of construction for carrying the river across the line.' It is thought the line will reach the tunnel entrance by the end of the year. (NEWS)

10 Apr 1890. Totley tunnel has only progressed by seventy seven yards of heading in the last month owing to the increase in water at the east end and the very hard rock being encountered. At the Padley end water intrusion has been reduced which has allowed sixty yards of full size tunnel to be completed. The number of men working at the tunnel has improved, which is attributed to an increase in the miner's wages but there is still a shortage although the number of men on the total contract had not increased. (ENG)

The *Derbyshire Courier* recorded that the 'large bridge (No. 6 Abbeydale Road) has opened for traffic. The substantial structure is comprised of Whatstandwell stone abutments on either side of the line with the road carried on riveted wrought iron girders and patented corrugated steel floor plates'. During this period the bridge (No. 4) giving access to West View cottage was also completed. (NEWS)

HATHERSAGE VIADUCT STARTED

29 Mar 1890. Mr J. S. A. Shuttleworth of Hathersage Hall, original director of the Dore and Chinley Railway, laid the foundation stone of Hathersage viaduct and gave a small gift to each of the workers. The seven arch structure is to be built almost entirely of stone from Millstone Edge. (NEWS)

5 Apr 1890. From the tunnel forward to Hathersage 'cuttings and embankments are being made and six bridges constructed of which the largest is at Hathersage. Beyond Hathersage nothing at present has been done'. (NEWS)

10 Apr 1890. The masonry of the Hathersage viaduct has been commenced. (ENG)

TRAIN ACCIDENT IN COWBURN

9 Apr 1890. John Dunn, age 19, was caught between the buffers of two wagons in Cowburn tunnel. He was taken on an ambulance stretcher to Chapel workhouse infirmary with a fractured pelvis and it was reported that he died the next day 'but this was not so'. (NEWS)

MISGUIDED PLAN FOR TWO EXTRA SHAFTS AT TOTLEY

10 Apr 1890. The engineers indicated that they had been giving the question of the line's progress some thought. They felt there was nothing to fear with Contract No. 2. Cowburn tunnel was making good progress and should be through in about a year and the whole of this contract should be finished within three years. On Contract No. 1 the big difficulty is Totley tunnel. So much water had been met that the progress of the heading has been retarded and only twenty yards a week of heading can be relied on. Owing to the gradients in the tunnel this can only be maintained for a short time because if the same amount of water was to be met in the future, the work could only continue from the Padley end because on a descending gradient there would be nowhere for the water to go. Parry and Story, (two very experienced and senior men, had been sound in their judgement until this moment) in what begins to feel like an act of desperation suggested the sinking of two additional shafts to increase the number of faces to work from. The shafts would be a costly and tedious process as they would be over 600 ft from the moor above but would allow the headings to be completed in two and a half years as against five years at the present rate of progress with the rest of the work taking a further year. The cost would be about £25,000 and would also assist the ventilation of the tunnel. The shaft might have to be put down in any case. (ENG) (If this was felt to be desirable there was still the tricky business of negotiating with the Duke of Rutland for permission, as the enabling Act stipulated only one shaft could be sunk. Additionally there was the problem of the continuity of the work during the grouse shooting season.)

17 Apr 1890. The committee received the engineers report and asked Mr Beale (solicitor) to open negotiations with the Duke of Rutland. (GPC)

SURPRISING REJECTION OF BEAUMONT ROCK DRILL

17 Apr 1890. The Beaumont boring machine has been rejected because it was not up to drilling through hard rock. (ENG)

(This is surprising because 'Captain Beaumont's Diamond Rock Drill', as it was known, was hailed as the greatest ever contribution to tunnelling equipment in this country when it was introduced for the first time in 1874. It was a compressed air operated machine that increased the rate of progress to three and a half times the rate of hand labour. Perhaps it had been overtaken by better machines in the subsequent sixteen years?)

WORK AT A STANDSTILL AT TOTLEY

8 May 1890. At Totley the progress was even poorer owing to a stoppage of the entire works at the east end because of the influx of a further quantity of water while passing a fault in the strata. The drain has now been brought up to the face which has allowed the heading to recommence. At Padley a continuing reduction in water encountered has allowed better progress to be made. (ENG)

CUTTINGS AT EDALE START

8 May 1890. Several cuttings in Edale have started and a temporary road is being laid throughout. At the east end of Cowburn drilling is in hard rock and arrangements are being made to introduce machinery to help. At the west end shale has now been encountered which is improving progress. At Chapel Milton viaduct springers are fixed on two piers and one abutment and the foundations of all but three piers are now in. (ENG)

DIRECTORS INSPECT THE LINE

23 May 1890. The directors went over the line to inspect the works. They afterwards dined at the Castle Hotel in Castleton. (NEWS)

TEMPORARY LINE LAID IN EDALE VALLEY

12 Jun 1890. At both ends of Cowburn it is solid rock, the shales at the west end having been left behind. As a result drilling machinery has been installed at both ends. A temporary road, about three and a half miles long, has been laid in the Edale valley to get materials to the viaducts and bridges. (ENG)

MORE DEATHS IN TUNNELS

May 1890. Thomas Spencer Cook, age 51, was seen by his workmate Robert Bradley hit in the chest by a 20 ft long length of wood falling down No. 1 shaft at Totley. He could have got out of the way on hearing a warning shout from above but tripped over a stone and fell backward. On being released he gave a gasp and died. (NEWS)

18 Jun 1890. Sidney John Rosewall, age 28, who originated from New Passage near the entrance to the Severn tunnel, was killed at Cowburn tunnel mouth at the Edale end. The afternoon was wet and when a group of men had finished their dinners some of them stood about within the mouth of the tunnel to take shelter from the rain. They had been there for only a few minutes when the roof above them, which was supported by timber, fell in and the amount of the debris was so much that two men were completely buried. 'Although plenty of assistance was available on the spot it took some time to remove the debris and release the men. At last the lifeless body of Rosewell was got out and another man named **Lawrence**, although alive had received such serious injuries that his life was at first despaired of and he is still in a precarious state. The body of Rosewall was removed to his home near the works. He was buried three days later in Edale churchyard. (NEWS) (A memorial stone was later erected by his parents. It can still be seen.)

8 Jul 1890. Edward Bishop, age 19, while working in Cowburn tunnel, was walking on the track to have breakfast. The men misread a signal and a train knocked one of the men off the line, he being badly hurt. Bishop fell with his head across the rail and was killed instantly, his body having been fearfully mangled. He lived with his married sister in the railway huts at Chapel. (NEWS)

ENGINEERS SIX MONTHLY REPORT

30 Jun 1890. Owing to the large quantity of water in Totley tunnel and the scarcity of labour progress has not been as rapid as desired, despite an extra 200 men having been recruited in the two previous months. At the two tunnels 4,752 yards of heading has been driven and 1,758 yards of tunnelling has been completed out of a total of 9,900 yards. 695,000 cubic yards of excavation has been removed from the cuttings and 24,700 yards of masonry has been executed on the viaducts, bridges and culverts. (ENG)

WORK STOPPED AT TOTLEY FOR SIX WEEKS

12 Jun 1890. 117 yards of heading has been driven in the Totley tunnel which is an improvement but water still flows in large quantities at both ends which resulted in only half the rate that is required being achieved. (ENG)

10 Jul 1890. At the Totley end of the tunnel work has stopped in order to dam back the water due to a further increase in the volume encountered. The inadequate pipe is to be replaced by a grip 2 ft 6 in square which will be cut along the bottom of the heading and will require four to six weeks to complete. (ENG)

SINKING TWO NEW SHAFTS SCRAPPED

10 Jul 1890. Mr Beale has ascertained the conditions that the Duke of Rutland's estate would impose if the two shafts were to go ahead (not detailed but obviously not favourable). The engineers had reached the view that with

The first four of six arches from the east end of Chapel Milton viaduct (016819) are seen in this view from the north with Hayfield Road below, and the curve of the bridge going away. The crane is precariously located on the temporary track with tipping wagons behind it.
Author's collection

the continued problems with water in the headings 'we think the advantages to be derived from the shafts would be so doubtful as scarcely to warrant the very large expenditure' (a major volte-face). They had given the problem further consideration and suggested an alternative solution – they felt that because the Duke of Rutland's conditions would have to be met and the large quantities of water that would be tapped in the shafts the cost would at least double that quoted. They were doubtful if the shafts could be sunk in a fifteen to eighteen month timescale, which if exceeded would negate any benefit. They suggested that a portion of the sum could be allowed to the contractor to be distributed to his men working in the heading – eg if fifteen yards a week at each face was achieved an increased bonus would be paid for each extra yard. Because a falling gradient would soon be met at the east end they asked for a change in the gradient from 1 in 176 to 1 in 150. This would save about eight or nine month's time because driving from the east end could continue further before the descending gradient was met. (ENG)

17 Jul 1890. The committee accepted both proposals. (GPC)

THE BONUS CULTURE TAKES ROOT

5 Aug 1890. The drain is nearly complete at the Totley end and forty six yards of heading has been achieved at the Padley end. Arrangements for bonuses to the men working at the Totley tunnel headings is being formalised with the contractor. (ENG)

13 Sep 1890. Progress on Totley tunnel has significantly improved, despite losing some men who temporarily left to get the harvest in. It was thought that the increased premiums paid to the miners had caused this improvement despite it not being possible to recruit complete gangs. These cost £99/5/- (this seems a paltry amount when compared with other costs). Less water is being encountered at both ends but at Padley hard rock has been met which is slowing progress. (ENG)

STEAM EXCAVATOR LOWERED INTO EDALE VALLEY

5 Aug 1890. Large quantities of material are being carted into Edale by horses and traction engines for which Edwards has been paid an additional £1,284. Edwards wrote that the tunnelling costs were exceeding what he was being paid but the engineers believed that this would change as he reached easier strata and when the headings met his costs would reduce dramatically. They recommended a temporary monthly increase, which would be recalculated when the tunnel work was completed. (ENG)

The committee agreed to pay Edwards an increased contract price of £16/15/0 per linear yard of tunnel mining through hard rock and an increased price of £3/10/0 per linear yard for bottom heading through hard rock only until the headings met. If he failed to complete the contract the money paid would be treated as an advance. (GPC)

13 Sep 1890. Because of the continuing difficulties in getting navvies to work in Edale a steam excavator has recently been carted over from Chapel (a dramatic spectacle as it was lowered down the 1 in 5 road from Mam Nick) and is working in a cutting. Any quantity of stone can now be obtained from the quarry in Edale and masons for the viaducts and bridges are being advertised for. At Chapel Milton viaduct five piers and two abutments are up to springing level and arching will start shortly. (ENG)

5 Oct 1890. A new replacement signal box opened at Chinley station. (GOUGH)

TWO MEN KILLED IN TOTLEY TUNNEL

6 Aug 1890. William Farmer, age 22, was an engine driver from Wroughton in Wiltshire. Whilst working on No. 4 shaft he was trying to start an air compressing engine when he slipped into the flywheel. He was taken to his lodgings on a stretcher in a critical condition where he received medical aid. He lingered in terrible agony for four days before he succumbed. The inquest at the *Crown Inn* at Totley returned a verdict of 'accidental death'. (NEWS)

16 Aug 1890. Henry Stephen Wilcox, age 24, and another man named Brown were at work in the heading of Totley tunnel putting up props to support the roof, which was composed of shale. The head trees were from 3 to 4 ft apart. A quantity of shale from between the head trees fell on Wilcox who was passing at the time. Both his legs were broken and he was taken to the hospital where he died later in the day. At the inquest Oliver was represented by F. C. Caffin, his engineer. A verdict of 'accidental death' was returned. (NEWS)

TWICE AS MANY MEN AT COWBURN

11 Oct 1890. At Totley a large amount of water has again been tapped at the Padley end but the water in the face at Shaft No. 4 is now much reduced. The premium to the miners amounted to £127 last month. The engineers complained that Oliver was failing to complete sufficient lining which was put down to his inability to recruit sufficient masons. On Contract No. 2 (where one would think it would be more difficult to recruit men) there were twice as many men employed (1350 against 725) and the engineers remarked that the greater need for men was on Contract No. 1. Despite the hard rock very good progress was being made at Cowburn. A large stock of materials has been accumulated in Edale which is sufficient for the winter and carting has now been suspended for the winter months. (ENG)

FIFTY YOUNG DRAUGHT HORSES FOR SALE

15 Oct 1890. Hepper and Sons held an auction at the works at Chapel Milton of 'fifty grand young draught horses, all of which had been bought in the last twelve months, and two useful cobs, fifteen strong carts and wagons and forty sets of gears'. They were being sold because there was not much carting during the winter months. The advertisement for the event said that 'Edwards' judgement in the selection of horses is well known'. The animals could be seen working on the contract at any time and in the stables at Chapel Milton on the day before and also on the morning of the auction. There was a large gathering from all over the country. The draught horses sold for between twenty four and seventy guineas and were principally bought by Pickford & Co railway carriers. One of the buyers was a Mr Perkins from Hathersage.

OLIVER – PLEASE SIR I WANT SOME MORE

16 Oct 1890. A letter from Oliver asking for more favourable terms was considered by the committee. They replied that 'although they were not insensitive to the difficulties of the contract they were not agreeable with work not meeting the terms of the contract'. (GPC)

KEYSTONE SET ON HATHERSAGE VIADUCT

20 Oct 1890. A ceremony took place to set the keystone of Hathersage viaduct. Mr Shuttleworth JP of Hathersage Hall bravely ascended to the top of the arch and performed the ceremony. With mallet in hand he struck the key stone saying:

*'This stone I set fast and long may it last,
This bridge to maintain, for the railway train'.*
(A bit short of Tennyson!)

He considered the work was done in a most expeditious and substantial manner and being built of their famous millstone grit would be a lasting memorial to the skill and workmanship of Mr Michael Ford, the subcontractor to Oliver, and his men. A purse containing £5 was presented to him to commemorate the event, he having completed the work in eight months. Others present were Mr Barnes, the agent of Oliver, and a party of ladies and others. (NEWS)

KNEES UP AT HATHERSAGE AND CHAPEL

25 Oct 1890. About sixty of the inspectors and workmen dined together at the *Butcher's Arms* at Hathersage. Mr Barnes, superintendent of the line, took the chair. Among those present were Mr Thorp, the Midland inspector, Mr Michael Ford, subcontractor for Hathersage viaduct and Mr Sykes, district missionary. A pleasant evening was spent. (NEWS)

29 Oct 1890. Within four days another knees up was held at the *King's Arms Hotel* at Chapel for foremen and workmen. Mr Gudgeon on behalf of the subscribers presented a gold watch and chain costing £37 and a purse of sovereigns to Mr Barker, contractor's engineer who was leaving to work on a railway in the course of construction by the government in Galway. (NEWS)

MEN DON'T WANT TO WORK FOR OLIVER

15 Nov 1890. In Totley tunnel 127 yards of heading and seventy seven yards of lining has been completed, a slight increase on the previous month. The engineers stated 'we cannot consider this as satisfactory but having had one or two interviews (a more formal tone) with Mr Oliver who, since the meeting in October, has again been able to make a more direct personal supervision of the works, and having learnt from him what steps he is taking to further the progress of the tunnel, we think there is reason to expect a better result will be seen in another month, barely sufficient time having yet elapsed for the intended arrangement to take effect'. Oliver has commenced to increase and improve the living accommodation at Padley and has altered the system of working at that end. He is advertising in labour papers. He is also providing additional ventilation appliances for the working of machine drills which together with other unspecified changes improved

Part of Hathersage viaduct on 22 Mar 2012 (229813). It is a very difficult structure to photograph because of its length and the trees that have grown up in front of it over the years. *Author*

performance and recruitment would be achieved, 861 men are working on the contract as a whole, 263 more than in January. This compared poorly with Contract No. 2 where a record 1,406 men are employed. The premiums paid for the miners at the face of the headings is £111/4/0. (ENG)

LINGARD'S LAND AT CHAPEL MILTON OBTAINED

15 Nov 1890. At Chapel Milton viaduct one arch has been keyed in and two more are in progress. Possession of Lingard's land has been obtained at last and the excavation for the foundations of the two remaining piers has started. (ENG)

13 Dec 1890. At Cowburn 150 yards of heading and sixty two yards of tunnelling has been achieved. The two headings are now 828 yards from each other and it was estimated they would meet within six months. The two remaining foundations at Milton viaduct are being sunk but the severe weather has delayed the cuttings and the masonry. (ENG)

18 Dec 1890. The committee considered a letter from Edwards asking for a further advance of £15,000 either on plant or retention (the money held back until a certain piece of work was completed) and stating that the cost of plant was already over £70,000. It was agreed to pay the £15,000 against the security of his plant and £10,000 was to bear interest. (GPC)

(This is an illustration of Edwards continually asking for advances or loans.)

FIVE YEARS TO FINISH TOTLEY TUNNEL

13 Dec 1890. Although an improvement in the length of heading achieved in Totley tunnel was noted the lining of the tunnel was lagging well behind, 3,035 yards of heading against the 1,372 yards of lining achieved. If there was not an improvement it would take another five years before the lining would be complete against two years for the tunnelling. The engineers set a target of forty yards of lining a week to halve the length of time needed. Further discussion with Oliver revealed that new air compressors and engines had been ordered in line with the engineers' suggestion. This plant will be in duplicate at each end of the heading. It is hoped this will prevent any delay in future owing to stoppages from breakdowns etc. Oliver had complained in a letter to the GPC on 7 Oct that in the past four months his costs have been £36 per yard as against the £28 which he has been paid, and in some cases as much as £40. The east face at Totley is presently dry although at Padley there is still a considerable amount of water. The pipes laid down are finding it difficult to cope and a stoppage may be required to improve them. The work on Hathersage viaduct, bridges and culverts has been delayed by frost. (ENG)

18 Dec 1890. The committee asked the engineers and solicitor in the light of Oliver's letter of 7 Oct to make a plan to accelerate progress. (GPC)

ENGINEERS SIX MONTHLY REPORT

31 Dec 1890. Fair progress has been made on the greater part of the line and in the past two or three months there has been considerable improvement in the work at the Totley tunnel, which as previously reported had been much delayed by water met in the headings. At both tunnels 6,139 yards of heading has now been driven and 2,575 yards of tunnelling has been completed out of a total of 9,900 yards. 836,000 yards of excavation has been removed from the cuttings and 37,226 yards of masonry has been executed in the viaducts, bridges and culverts. The works on the Dore South Junction Curve and Chinley South Curve is making satisfactory progress. (ENG)

PLANS FOR LIE BY SIDINGS

10 Jan 1891. The general manager indicated that lie by sidings would be required. An intermediate block post with down lie by sidings and cross over road at about a quarter of a mile from the east end of Totley and at the east end of Cowburn tunnel and an up lie by siding, at the west end of Cowburn tunnel. Additionally an up and down lie by siding, with cross over road from one main line to the other, at all the stations would be needed. For the tunnel sidings the cost was estimated at £4,000. The station sidings could not be calculated until the station plans are completed. (ENG)

SERIOUS EXPLOSION IN COWBURN TUNNEL

10 Jan 1891. At 02.00 at the Edale end of Cowburn tunnel six men were engaged in the bottom heading. One of the men was preparing a charge and was in the act of placing a gelatine cartridge in a hole which was too large when it exploded. **Walter Mosby** or **Mosley**, age 28, was killed instantly and found to be terribly mutilated. Three others **Joseph** or **James Boyle**, age 31, **Edward Anthony** and **John James** were injured. Surgical aid was procured from Castleton and the works stopped for the rest of the day. Mosby was only recently married and his wife 'is almost overwhelmed with grief'. The internment took place at Edale church. (NEWS)

Excavation for pier nine of Chapel Milton viaduct has started. The borings show that it will be necessary to go down 45 ft, to obtain a solid foundation for this pier. (ENG)

NEW SIDINGS AND SIGNAL BOX AT DORE STATION

14 Jan 1891. The Board of Trade inspectors reported that new sidings have been connected to the main line at Dore and Totley station and, to control this, a new signal box has been sanctioned and built with nine working levers. (BT)

14 Feb 1891. 181 yards of heading has been completed, the best yet, and 110 yards of lining which although an improvement is only twenty two yards per week as against the target of forty yards. To remedy this, Oliver has started several new breakup lengths and if he can obtain the proper number of men then the target could be met. The east heading has been dry and for a few days at the Padley end also. However there is again considerable water at both headings. (ENG)

14 Mar 1891. Similar progress in Totley tunnel as last month is recorded (which leaves the engineers frustrated with the lack of progress on the lining). Pressure on Oliver causes him to complain that he cannot recruit sufficient men due to the wet condition of the tunnel, particularly at the Padley end. He has 926 men on the total contract, although it had broken the 1,000 mark for the first time at 1,001 in January. (ENG)

LITTLE HUCKLOW MAN KILLED IN TUNNEL

19 Feb 1891. Roger Hall, age about 50, from Little Hucklow was engaged in blasting operations at Norman's bridge when a gelignite cartridge exploded, blowing him up in the air. He died while being removed in a cart. The inquest was held at the *Bull's Head Inn* at Little Hucklow where it was revealed that he was a farmer and miner. He was married with no children and well known locally. (NEWS)

DOUBLE CULVERTS STARTED IN EDALE VALLEY

14 Feb 1891. At Cowburn both headings continue to be dry but the rock is still very hard. With an improvement in the weather it has been possible to proceed with the masonry on Contract No. 2 and the two large double culverts for the River Noe at 12 miles 17 chains (43 Norman's Farm) and 13 miles 17 chains (54 Grindsbrook) have been commenced. At Chapel Milton viaduct the foundation for pier eight has been sunk to a depth of 38 ft where a bed of gravel has been reached containing so much water that the pumps are unable to deal with it. Further progress is awaiting the arrival of larger pumps. (ENG)

14 Mar 1891. Progress at Cowburn continues satisfactorily with only 400 yards of heading to go. At Chapel Milton the foundations for pier nine are good, the bottom having been gained at a depth of 45 ft. (ENG)

DIRECTORS INSPECT THE LINE

24 Mar 1891. George Ernest Paget, the chairman, and directors of the Midland visited Hathersage to inspect the line. They looked at the site of Hathersage station and the viaduct which was described as nearing completion and then travelled down the line to Padley tunnel. They later examined the work at Hope and Edale. (NEWS)

SUBCONTRACTOR SELLS HORSES

7 Apr 1891. W. Ibbotson, a subcontractor on the line, sold at Smithfield Market, Sheffield, six horses and three sets of tip harness. The horses are described as being 'staunch drawn and will be at work until three days before the sale'. (NEWS)

OLIVER LAUNCHES NATIONAL RECRUITMENT DRIVE

9 Apr 1891. Oliver has been making strenuous efforts to obtain a considerable increase in the number of men for the Padley end. He has advertised in ten or twelve newspapers in various parts of the country offering high wages for miners. He has sent a man to Wales to find a number of suitable men and is paying their railway fare and sending them from Sheffield by brakes to Hathersage. (The advertisements were in the Welsh language which suggests the men would not have spoken English.)

On the Dore tunnel the fronts are being started. (ENG)

20 Apr 1891. The *Sheffield Independent* reported that a large percentage of the population at Dore and Totley are suffering from flu, especially those employed on the railway where nearly 200 are affected. (NEWS)

7 May 1891. An improvement in the lining and headings achieved in Totley tunnel was welcomed but the lining is still well short of the target set. The increased wages advertised brought a larger number of men into the tunnel but due to the quantity of water in the lengths several of the men have left. Oliver broke the 1,000 barrier for good with 1,057 men on the whole contract. After a spell of dry conditions at the Padley end water has been encountered again. Pressure is being put on Oliver to increase the number of machine drills at work in the lengths to make up for the shortage of men. (ENG)

During the month permanent Shaft No. 4 has had a double cage installed to replace the single cage and at the Totley end the narrow gauge line has been replaced by a standard gauge line. (ICE)

16 May 1891. In an advertisement in the *Sheffield Independent* Oliver offered for sale 'fifteen excellent ponies' which have been in regular work on the line, by auction at The Repository, Castle Hill, Sheffield. The sale was being made because of an alteration to the mode of working on the tunnel. (NEWS)

PROBLEM WITH LAST PIER AT CHAPEL MILTON

9 Apr 1891. At Cowburn only 308 yards of headings are still to be drilled. A large number of masons are working in Edale and good progress is being made. The foundations for the remaining piers have commenced on the Chapel Milton viaduct. Borings have found that no sound bottom can be obtained at less than 50 ft and as the sinking is so deep a hole might endanger the stability of the existing viaduct and so it has been decided to build this pier (No. 10) on piles. (ENG)

7 May 1891. At Cowburn the two headings are only 170 yards apart. At Chapel Milton viaduct one half of the foundation for the remaining pier is in. There is now a large gang of men in Edale and good progress is being made with the excavation and masonry. A record 1,506 men are employed on the whole contract. (ENG)

EXASPERATED ENGINEERS AT TOTLEY

11 Jun 1891. Two (exasperated) engineers reported that progress on Totley tunnel is again below expectations, 132 yards of heading against a target of 175 yards and 103 yards of lining as against a target 200 yards has been achieved. The reasons given this month, added to those given in previous months led them to comment (wearily) 'but as with every month something occurs to prevent the proper amount of work being done, we cannot say that the delays have been exceptional'. The engineers were asked to consider shortening the working hours from twelve to eight hours. The increased cost would have added at least a quarter to the costs and they were not convinced it would be a productive recruitment incentive as it was not attracting men to the heading faces where eight hour shifts are already in place. (For the only time in the engineers reports the number of men working in the tunnel as against those working outside is recorded, there being 608 in the tunnel and 448 on the rest of the work.) (ENG)

18 Jun 1891. The chairman of the GPC and his deputy met Oliver who asked for a further £15,000 which was agreed. (GPC) (Oliver never missed a trick!)

DRY ROT IN TIMBER CAUSES DELAY

11 Jun 1891. Breakthrough of the headings at Cowburn has not been achieved because a large quantity of timbering in the heading has been attacked by dry rot and become insecure. The men have been engaged in re-timbering this portion and have nearly finished it. (How frustrating this must have been when they had only 100 yards still to drive.) At Chapel Milton viaduct the last foundation is now in. (ENG)

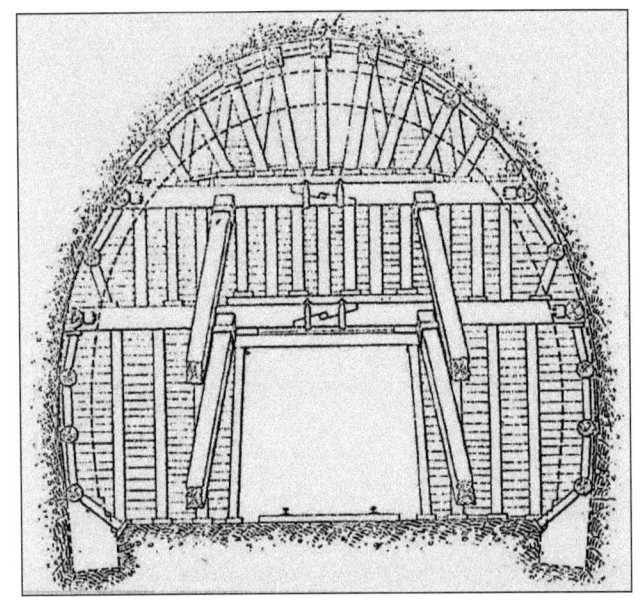

A drawing of the timbering in Totley tunnel showing how extensive it was. It would have been the same or similar in Cowburn. *ICE Paper*

ENGINEERS SIX MONTHLY REPORT

30 Jun 1891. The amount of work in Totley tunnel is slowly increasing and the amount of water decreasing. At Cowburn the heading has been driven through. At both tunnels 3,488 yards of tunnelling and 7,696 yards of heading has been completed out of a total of 9,900 yards. (ENG)

LUCKY ESCAPE AS BURST DAM FLOODS BURBAGE BROOK

8 Jul 1891. The *Derby Mercury* reported that a reservoir, the property of the Duke of Rutland on the Longshaw estate burst it banks. The water went into the Yarncliffe ravine and reached Padley Saw Mill and the temporary bridge connecting with the railway works. Fortunately the flood did not reach the mouth of the tunnel. (NEWS) (It would have been the last straw if the workings had been flooded from an outside source)

BETTER NEWS FROM TOTLEY AT LAST

9 Jul 1891. The Totley headings are finally dry and good progress has been made, the number of men engaged has improved, 1,230 against 1,056 last month. The target of forty yards of heading per week is not being met which is therefore not triggering the agreed additional price. Due to labour recruitment and retention, together with water problems at Padley, the engineers recommended a revised weekly target of thirty three yards to give the contractor a chance of earning the bonus. (ENG)

16 Jul 1891. The committee did not agree to the engineers' suggestion of reducing the target to thirty three yards of heading in Totley tunnel before the contractor could be paid a bonus. (GPC)

1 Aug 1891. At both ends of Totley tunnel the material encountered is grey shale and both faces are dry. One front of Dore tunnel is now complete and the other has been commenced. (ENG)

HEADINGS AT COWBURN MEET

9 Jul 1891. At Cowburn it is expected that every shot fired will connect the headings. (The half yearly report of the previous month had clearly jumped the gun!) Edwards complains that miners are extremely difficult to get and that the high wages being paid at Totley are drawing his men away. The figures support this for 1,230 were on No. 1 contract, an increase of 174 over the previous month and 1,179 on No. 2 contract a decrease of 129. It was also the first month since Jul 1889 that Oliver had more men than Edwards. A very useful agreement was made with Edwards to allow the Midland to convey materials through Cowburn tunnel to Contract No. 1. (ENG)

18 Jul 1891. At 02.00 the headings at Cowburn tunnel met with the traditional cheery handshakes between men who were unlikely to have met each other before. The location was 2,305 yards from the Edale end, the difference in line was less than one inch. (ICE & ENG)

1 Aug 1891. At Cowburn a temporary line of rails is being laid throughout marking the end of carting material between Chapel and Edale. The piers at Chapel Milton viaduct are up to springing level and three arches are keyed in. (ENG)

12 Aug 1891. Edwards commissioned an auction at Chapel Milton, at which he was present, to sell sixty six grand draught horses, five very useful nags, twenty very strong carts and a Fowler of Leeds 8 hp road traction engine. Because material can now go through the tunnel they had become surplus to requirements. The horses fetched £3,176 guineas. (NEWS)

Aug 1891. A horse driver named **Johnson** was killed in Cowburn tunnel.

STILL TWO YEARS TO COMPLETE TOTLEY TUNNEL

10 Sep 1891. At Totley the work continues satisfactorily in dry conditions and with an enlarged workforce, 1,339 are employed on the whole contract, the highest number so far. There are now 1,898 yards of heading and 3,942 yards of lining to be completed. If the present progress is maintained then the headings will be through in one year and the lining in two. (ENG)

17 Sep 1891. It was agreed that Oliver should be paid an additional £8,993 (presumably for his improved performance). (GPC)

DOUBLE CULVERTS IN EDALE COMPLETED

10 Sep 1891. At Cowburn lining has been below normal due to the miners being engaged on bottoming and cleaning up the heading to enable a road to be laid through it for the transport of materials. The two large double culverts for the diversion of the River Noe in Edale are now complete and several other bridges have been commenced. (ENG)

15 Oct 1891. The chairman of the GPC met Edwards. It was agreed to continue to pay the increased price for the

Here is one of two double culverts, No. 43, carrying the River Noe under the line at Norman's Farm, when nearly completed (368858). It shows the north entrance looking towards the Lose Hill, Back Tor and Hollins Cross ridge in the background. It can still be accessed by a public footpath just after going under the line at Norman's Road bridge on the right hand side. It is on the left of the footpath in a deep ravine and is difficult to see due to the foliation that has grown in the intervening years. This is a very good example of the quality work and the beauty of design that is a feature of all the bridges, viaducts and culverts on the line.
Jim Story collection

tunnelling and also the increase in price for each breakup length to £80 per yard, this to be met by a reduction of £1/10/0 per yard in the running length. (GPC)

A MILLION TONS OF ROCK REMOVED

26 Sep 1891. A 'high carnival' supper was held in the Town Hall at Chapel organized by Edwards for the men to celebrate the completion of the bottom heading. In his speech James Scott, Edwards agent, gave some statistics. 142,000 lbs of gelignite had been used and 190,000 shots fired; 576,000 holes were drilled; 246,000 lineal yards of fuse to fire the shots was required; the number of candles used if laid end to end would be about 270 miles and burned for 4,903,000 hours or 559 years. There had been about half a million tons of rock removed in 70,000 truck loads and 100,000 bricks were used to line the tunnel. (NEWS)

MYTHAM GIRDER BRIDGE STARTED

10 Oct 1891. The improved progress in Totley tunnel has been maintained. Wet conditions at Padley have again been encountered. A comparison with the progress of a year ago shows an 80% increase at the heading and a doubling of the lining due to drier conditions and an increased workforce. The bridge over the River Derwent at Mytham has commenced. Dore tunnel is very nearly completed. (ENG)

A recent picture shows that it has worn well. *Author*

A recent image of Mytham bridge No. 28 which carries the line over the River Derwent (207826). *Author*

NEGLECT LEADS TO FATALITY

6 Oct 1891. At Cowburn there was a custom that no shots should be fired when wagons were moving down the tunnel. Ganger Edwards disobeyed this and ordered nine shots should be fired simultaneously when he new a laden wagon was arriving. The other men managed to get out of the way of the wagon except **Joseph Hynds** who was run over and his right leg and arm were crushed to pulp. He was moved to Chapel workhouse hospital where both limbs were amputated. He died four hours later. Ganger Edwards was found guilty by the jury at the inquest of 'gross carelessness'. In passing a verdict of 'accidental death' Edwards was severely censured by the coroner who commented that if this kind of carelessness carried on someone would be sent for trial. Hynds who was age 50 was an experienced navvy having worked on railways in Egypt and India previously. He left a wife and four children. (NEWS)

(It is not known whether Ganger Edwards was sacked by his namesake J. P. Edwards. One could imagine today that all sorts of litigation would be commenced on the Hynds' family's behalf against the contractor, ganger Edwards and the Midland. Additionally the Health & Safety Executive would use their powers to close the whole operation down pending a review of working practices. The 'custom' mentioned in the first sentence would certainly have become a 'rule'.)

JOURNALIST VISIT TO TOTLEY TUNNEL

11 Nov 1891. J. Pendleton a journalist and author visited Totley tunnel. (See page 186 for his dramatic account).

VERY SERIOUS FLOODING AT PADLEY

12 Nov 1891. At the east end of Totley tunnel good progress has continued but big problems at the Padley end have been encountered with a large inrush of water at the face on Monday night last. This was at a change of strata from shale to millstone grit. Work has stopped and a dam has been created while improved drainage is put in. (ENG)

This inrush of water dwarfed anything previously met with. A round of holes had been drilled in the rock, and were about to be charged, when a plug of soft earth was forced out of a fissure in the roof, about a yard from the face. A stream of water was released which rapidly increased from a few square inches in area to the full width of the heading by 2 ft across. Tons of sand, silt and stones were hurled down the fissure and carried far down the heading by the torrent. A natural reservoir was discharging itself. The water rushing down was impounded where the level dipped and eventually cut off all access to the face. Inspections had to be carried out by raft and it was decided to replace the twelve inch pipes with a covered grip and a permanent drain. A puddle dam was constructed in the lined portion and a large air shoot, which had been used for ventilation, was lined with felt and made available to carry away the water which was found to be flowing at 5,000 gallons a minute. This allowed the construction of a permanent drain to start. (ICE)

(A scouring of the relevant newspapers failed to find a report of this dramatic event and no information on the fate of the men is known unless Schofield, Turner and Lynch who were buried at Hathersage in the first two weeks of December were involved and died of their injuries later (see Appendix 2). It is difficult to believe that some of them would not have been injured, killed or drowned.

EDWARDS GOES BUST

19 Nov 1891. Edwards' bankers refused to finance his debt against payment when the works were completed unless the Midland would guarantee payment of interest and charges on his overdraft and half of the unsecured capital sum. The committee refused the bank ultimatum but put forward an alternative proposal – if the bank agreed not to enforce payment until completion of the work the Midland would guarantee any increase in his overdraft. Practical control for the works would be vested in James Scott (Edwards' agent) under the supervision of the engineer. If the bank go ahead, the company solicitor will give notice to Edwards to take the work out of his hands. The engineers were to make interim arrangements to carry out the works. (GPC)

PROPERTY OWNER WINS CASE AGAINST MIDLAND

3 Dec 1891. An arbitration case was heard at the Stephenson Memorial Hall in Chesterfield. Mr T. Oates, a retired general smith, owned two houses which had cost £2,000 to build. They were situated near a cutting on the line. He claimed subsidence damage for the period when the cutting was being made. He said that the engines and wagons passing shook the buildings and even damaged the crockery and the smoke and water tank were a great nuisance. Evidence was given by several architects and engineers. At 13.45 a special train took everybody from Chesterfield to Dore where an examination was made of the location and the alleged damage. After a long deliberation the jury found for Oates and assessed the damages at £175. (NEWS)

SEVEN MILLION GALLONS A DAY AT PADLEY

10 Dec 1891. Very good progress is reported at the Totley end but work is still stopped at Padley as seven million gallons of water a day are contended with. The improved drain is expected to take another six to eight weeks to finish. Good progress in lining Cowburn tunnel is reported. At Chapel Milton viaduct nine arches are keyed in and three more are in a forward state. A number of men have been recently discharged from the Edale valley because with the short days and bad weather the costs of the works were exceeding the contract price. The figures show 134 men less, although by April through to August the figures peak at over 1,600 altogether. The amount of work to be completed is small and will be finished in the coming summer and the whole contract should be finished by the end of the year. (ENG)

SCOTT TAKES OVER FROM EDWARDS

10 Dec 1891. A special report by the engineers which was requested by Mr Beale, the Midland's solicitor, on the position of James Scott, Edwards' second in command, was presented. Under the new agreement between the company and Edwards it is suggested that he be paid £250 quarterly and that Scott should enter the service of the

The western entrance to Cowburn tunnel in 1891, with the portal in a finished state. Temporary track is still in place with both standard and narrow gauge on the up line and narrow gauge on the down line. Lifting gear is in place on a platform. The locomotive just peeping out of the entrance is not easily identifiable as there seems to be a wagon in front of it. However, it is standard gauge. The man standing on the right is possibly the one who was to be seen on the photograph of the men at the Totley tunnel entrance (see page 154). He looks to have the same type of attire and stance. Was Hancock awarded the contract for all six tunnel entrances? Information on the sub contractors is rather sketchy as the engineers do not comment on such matters.
Author's collection

company and have the entire management of Contract No. 2 under the engineers' directions. He is willing to accept this position on a salary of £800 per annum, £100 more than he was receiving from Edwards. They feel that the works have been carried out by him in an exceedingly able manner and think the company would act wisely in retaining his services. Scott reminded the engineers that Edwards owed him £1,000 for the purchase of plant for the contract and Mr Roberts, the cashier, £800. The engineers recommended that they should be paid from the proceeds of the sale of the plant at the end of the contract. It was noted that, apart from this and some debt to the bank, all Edwards' creditors have been satisfied. (ENG)

17 Dec 1891. The committee considered the proposals from the engineers. The solicitor submitted an agreement between Edwards, his bank and the company. (GPC).

14 Jan 1892. The committee agreed to pay Edwards' overdraft of £9,000 to the Wigan branch of the Manchester District Banking Company. (GPC)

OLIVER NEGOTIATES INCREASED RATES

17 Dec 1891. The committee agreed that Oliver should be paid an increased amount of £40 per lineal yard in Totley tunnel from 1 Jan 1891, together with an allowance of 10% to meet advances in the price of outdoor labour and materials since the contract started. This was subject to Oliver making the utmost effort to achieve the minimum rate of progress as previously agreed. (GPC)

14 Jan 1892. Oliver wrote to thank the committee for their help. (GPC)

ENGINEERS SIX MONTHLY REPORT

31 Dec 1891. Good progress has been made. At Totley 4,805 yards of heading and 2,805 yards of lining has been achieved out of a total of 6,218 yards. At Cowburn, with the headings completed, 2,073 yards of lining out of 3,702 yards has been completed. The Dore South Junction Curve and the Chinley South Curve are nearly completed. (ENG)

LARGE WAGONS TO BRING SPOIL UP SHAFT 4

9 Jan 1892. Further good progress at the Dore end of the tunnel is recorded. The invert and drain are nearly completed at the Padley end and the amount of water is about a third of a month ago. During Christmas week alterations have been made to the winding gear of Shaft No. 4 to enable large wagons now in use for bringing the spoil out of the tunnel to be raised there. This will be instead of it being taken out at the open end of the tunnel, thus allowing locomotives to run up to the spoil ground. Electric lighting is also being put in at the bottom of the shaft, at the pit mouth and at the spoil tip. (ENG)

BEST EVER MONTH FOR LINING

9 Jan 1892. At Cowburn the best ever month for lining was reported and one more arch has been keyed in at Chapel Milton viaduct. The rest of the work is at a standstill due to the bad weather. (ENG)

27 Jan 1892. Since the frost disappeared a large number of men have resumed work at Chinley and Edale and new men have replaced those who have left. The number of men is expected to increase further once spring arrives. (NEWS)

26 Feb 1892. At Cowburn the good progress is being maintained and at the Chapel Milton viaduct work is so far advanced that with a week's fine weather all the arches will be turned. (ENG)

'LINCOLN JOE' KILLED

15 Jan 1892. Joseph King better known as **'Lincoln Joe'**, age 45, was a horse driver. He was bringing several loaded wagons out of the Padley end when he slipped and was run over and killed. He was buried in Hathersage churchyard. It was said that he narrowly escaped being killed a few weeks previously. (NEWS)

COST OF DEVIATIONS OF LINE AROUND BAMFORD

11 Feb 1892. The *Sheffield Independent* reported that 'the deviation and alterations of the levels for a distance of two miles two furlongs between Hathersage and Hope, are estimated to cost £51,107; but against this sum is set off the estimated cost of works for which these deviations are in substitution, thus bringing the net cost down to £4,901. The quantity of land required is thirty five acres, and the estimated cost of acquiring it is £7,000 (see page 108). (NEWS)

DRILLING AT PADLEY RESUMES

11 Feb 1892. At the east end of Totley the good progress has been maintained but at Padley the expected restart at the heading has not taken place because it is necessary for the drain to be brought up to the face of the work. (ENG)

26 Feb 1892. The work on the headings at the Padley end has restarted. (ICE)

10 Mar 1892. Bad weather since the New Year has seriously affected the outside work on both contracts. At the east end of Totley a record amount of lining has been completed. At the Padley end the new drain is complete and drilling has recommenced in drier conditions. (ENG)

NEW SHAFT AT TOTLEY TO BE SUNK

17 Mar 1892. Mr McDonald, the Midland engineer, reported that the line through the tunnels will be ballasted shortly. Gritstone from the excavations is to be used and should be laid six to eight inches below the finished levels. After the aborted plan to sink two shafts from Totley moor the question of a ventilation shaft is raised again. McDonald commented that both tunnels are longer than any other tunnel not artificially ventilated and longer than any other tunnels on the Midland system, the longest being 1¾ miles, and further comments that the permanent way needs regularly relaying in badly ventilated tunnels. With no provision in place for an additional shaft in the centre of Totley tunnel it was resolved that Mr Beale (solicitor) should reopen negotiations with the Duke of Rutland. (GPC)

LAST ARCH ON CHAPEL MILTON VIADUCT KEYED IN

26 Mar 1892. The *Sheffield Independent* reported on the progress of the works. It describes the work on No. 2 contract as being 'one of remarkable activity, a large number of additional men having been engaged on the works'. The officials of the works and others watched Mr G. E. Story the resident engineer key in the last of the thirteen arches on the Chapel Milton viaduct. The massive works are coming to a completion although work has been at a standstill for a great portion of the winter. In the Edale valley several good sized viaducts are in course of construction. One of these is 265 ft long and over 15 ft high. 'Perhaps on no similar length of railway in England are there so many small bridges and culverts as on this length.' (NEWS)

7 Apr 1892. All the arches at Chapel Milton viaduct are keyed in and several more bridges in Edale have been commenced. (ENG)

12 May 1892. Work in Cowburn tunnel was delayed by a fire at a tunnel mouth which destroyed the shedding and damaged the air compressing machinery preventing the use of the drills. Fortunately the loss was covered by insurance (today's insurance companies would not consider insuring anything to do with this enterprise I suspect!). (ENG)

RAPID PROGRESS WITH HEADINGS AND LINING AT TOTLEY

7 Apr 1892. At the Totley end rapid progress is being made with the headings and lining but at the Padley end progress is handicapped by hard rock, ever present water in the lengths although the face is dry, and the difficulty of keeping men. (ENG)

12 May 1892. During the past three months 494 yards of lining has been completed at Totley with 2,787 yards still to go which, if progress is maintained, will mean that the tunnel should be finished by autumn next year. Only 901 yards of heading is left and it is thought it would meet in October or November. A good deal of water is still being met with in the full size tunnel particularly in the breakups, but the headings at both faces are still dry. (ENG)

SIX MEN KILLED IN TWO MONTHS

15 Apr 1892. Charles Ronksley, age 21, lived at Hathersage and was working near Padley Wood on Good Friday. Some wagons containing earth were being shunted and Ronksley was coupling the wagons by hand when he fell onto the line and was run over. After receiving medical assistance he was moved to Sheffield Infirmary where he died. The jury at the inquest at the Infirmary returned a verdict of 'accidentally killed' and observed that it was 'dangerous coupling wagons by hand when a pole should be used'. The Coroner replied 'the making of a new railway is always attended with difficulty and danger, and it was difficult to adhere to hard and fast rules. It was, however, possible to increase or diminish the danger by adopting different means of accomplishing the work'. (NEWS)

7 May 1892. John Morley, of no fixed abode, was killed by an engine, driven by John Hall, near the *Crown Inn* at Totley Bents where the temporary line crosses the highway. (This is the temporary line from the brickworks to shafts No. 4, No. 3 and No. 2.) Morley was going in the direction of Dore where he was employed and being very deaf did not hear the engine and wagons approaching. The man in charge of the gates, John Gardner, shouted at the man, who did not hear him and had a narrow escape himself, he also being nearly knocked down. The coroner later praised Gardner on his 'plucky attempt to save the deceased'. The left hand buffer of the engine struck Morley hurling him about six yards. His body fell across the rails and the engine and three wagons passed over it, completely severing it. The remains were removed to the *Crown Inn* to await the coroner's enquiry, at which it was decided that the deceased alone was responsible for his own death. (NEWS)

30 May 1892. Anthony Potter, age 27, a married man with two children of Goosehill, Castleton had been a horse driver for two years at the Edale end of Cowburn tunnel. At 22.30 he was taking a wagon with three tons of bricks up the tunnel when he slipped or stumbled and the wagon went over him and also left the rails causing the contents to fall on him. Whilst nearby men were removing the rubble he told them he dreamt the previous day that this would happen and that he had also shared the dream with his wife. His right leg was nearly severed and the other leg was broken in several places. He died before he could be removed from the tunnel. The inquest was held at Castleton where a verdict of 'accidental death' was returned. (NEWS)

15 Jun 1892. Whitfield Watson, age 30, a platelayer, was run over by an engine at Edale. He had been drinking at the *Nag's Head* at Edale until closing time and half an hour later was observed by the driver of a train lying on the rails as if asleep. Before he could stop, his engine and following wagons ran over him cutting off both legs, badly cutting his head and causing other injuries. He was admitted to Chapel Workhouse Infirmary where he died. He had been taking a short cut from the pub, where he had been drinking for several hours, to his lodgings. A verdict of 'accidental death' was recorded. (NEWS)

15 Jun 1892. John Watson from Skipton, who was not employed on the line, was killed while trespassing on the railway at Edale. Soon after an engine with wagons had passed on its way to the tunnel he was found lying on the rails with his legs totally severed. They were found some distance away still in his boots. When he was found he said he was not dead but drunk. His remains were removed to the infirmary. (NEWS)

17 Jun 1892. Frederick Walter Spafford, age 30, from Lincoln was killed in Totley tunnel while, with another man, he was 'taking down the centres on which the arch of the tunnel is built. One of the heavy ribs fell over, striking Spafford on the back of the head, smashing his skull and jamming him against a heavy cross beam where he was suspended by the head until he was liberated by some men who were summoned to the scene'. He was removed to the surface but died within a short time. His body was moved to the *Cricketers' Arms (Cricket Inn)* at Totley Bents. (NEWS)

THROUGH LINE FROM CHINLEY TO PADLEY OPENED

9 Jun 1892. At Totley bottom, ballasting has started with stone in the tunnel being used for the purpose. There is now a temporary line from Padley to the boundary of the contract just before Hope station where by a junction with Edwards' line a through communication is now possible between Padley and Chinley. (ENG)

The committee heard that Edwards' overdraft at his bank was £18,408 on 7 Jun. They agreed to pay £10,000. (GPC)

ENGINEERS SIX MONTHLY REPORT

30 Jun 1892. Good progress has been made with the long tunnels, they having been pressed forward more rapidly than hitherto. At Totley 5,659 yards of heading and 3,738 yards of lining, out of a total of 6,218 yards, has now been completed whilst at Cowburn only 672 yards, out of a total of 3,702 yards, of lining remains to be done. Dore tunnel and the Chapel Milton viaduct are practically finished, as is the rest of the work. (ENG)

THREE BRIDGES LEFT TO BUILD

9 Jul 1892. At Totley, 192 yards of heading and 170 yards of lining have been achieved, a record leaving 559 yards of heading and 2,480 yards of lining to finish. The total quantity of water running from the tunnel is still considerable but is gradually decreasing. Only three bridges on Contract No. 1 need to be commenced. As the tunnel is making such good progress the engineers are pressing the contractor to put more men on the outdoor work for trimming and ballasting (this is a real turnaround). Oliver has asked for a length of ballasting to be supplied to him by the company. (ENG)

2 Aug 1892. The *Sheffield Independent* reported on 5 Aug 1892 the death of **Samuel Slater**, age 14. He was working as a point turner in Totley tunnel. He missed his way in the smoke as a train passed and was crushed between the trucks and the engine. He died within a few hours. Although the tunnel was lit by electricity at this point a verdict of 'accidental death' was returned at the inquest. (NEWS)

One of only two identifiable gravestones of railway workers in Dore churchyard. The headstone is dwarfed by those nearby. *Author*

The ninety one yard Dore tunnel on Dore South Curve in 1952 looking at the western portal. The west junction which connects with the Dore and Chinley line is behind and beyond the tunnel is the junction with the Sheffield to Chesterfield main line. Note the date '1891' and the same Midland armorial device as on the Totley entrances. The tight curvature is apparent although it did not preclude Garratts from working over the curve. *David Ibbotson*

LOW BAROMETRIC PRESSURE AT PADLEY

6 Aug 1892. Continued good progress on both tunnels and on the outside work was reported. (ENG)

1 Sep 1892. This was the date when both contracts should have been completed.

15 Sep 1892. 298 yards of lining in Totley tunnel is reported which is another record. Difficulty, due to low barometric pressure, has been experienced in properly ventilating the heading at Padley on one or two occasions which has reduced the amount of heading driven. Only about two hundred yards of heading remain to be completed and the sound of the blasting at one face can now be heard from the other. A considerable length of the line between Padley and Hope is being trimmed and a commencement has been made with the bottom ballasting and laying of permanent way. At Cowburn only 339 yards of lining has to be done before the tunnel will be completed. (ENG)

GO AHEAD FOR NEW SHAFT

10 Oct 1892. The engineers were instructed to prepare an estimate and, if possible, arrange a tender for the ventilation shaft at Totley. (GPC)

13 Oct 1892. At Totley only about thirty yards of heading remain to be done with the daily expectation that a junction will be achieved. A little over a mile of lining remains to be done and ten months should see it completed. The number of men on Contract No. 1 peaked at 1,841 with the assistance of twenty nine engines and 105 horses. (ENG)

CASTLETON ROAD TO BE IMPROVED

18 Oct 1892. The *Sheffield Independent* reported that following a petition from some of the principal ratepayers of Castleton to Derbyshire County Council improvements to the narrow approach road to Castleton from Sheffield and Chesterfield are to be carried out. (NEWS)

SHOT FIRING FATALITY AT COWBURN

10 Oct 1892. William Buck, age 49, was working in the tunnel. A shot was fired and Buck and other men went into a heading for safety. He was found lying twelve yards away from where the shot was fired with a stone weighing five cwt. on his legs and body. He was removed to Chapel Workhouse infirmary and died a few hours later. A verdict of 'accidental death' was returned. (NEWS)

HEADINGS FINALLY MEET IN TOTLEY TUNNEL

19 Oct 1892. The headings meet in Totley Tunnel 'with loud shouts and shaking of hands.' (NEWS)

23 Oct 1892. This is the official date that the Totley headings met (ENG, ICE).

It was also the day a gang headed by Percy Rickard, resident engineer, first went through. (NEWS) (The proceeding days had been spent widening the heading to the same width and height as the rest of the tunnel.)

'A very good junction both of line and level has been achieved. (ENG) (It was four years since the work first began.)

16 Dec 1892. The first wagons passed through the tunnel with a load of bricks drawn by horses.

NAVVY KILLED BY TRAIN

14 Nov 1892. John Evans missed the workmen's train on his way to work in Cowburn tunnel and so set off on foot into the tunnel. Sometime afterwards he was found unconscious and fearfully injured having been knocked down by the workmen's train returning. Death was caused by 'inflammation of the stomach'. A verdict of 'accidental death' was returned at the inquest at Chapel Union workhouse. (NEWS)

SHAFT ON TOTLEY MOOR MOVING AHEAD

10 Nov 1892. Since the headings at Totley met four new breakups have been commenced. The contract engineers and the Midland engineer Mr McDonald have been instructed to further consider the question of a ventilation shaft at Totley. From information gathered from the experience of other tunnels and, after taking into consideration the probable amount and nature of the traffic likely to pass through, the engineers have arrived at the conclusion that a 16 ft diameter shaft with a ventilating fan with some form of motive power will be required. Oliver has tendered £19,710 for a 16 ft shaft with an eighteen inch brick lining. For a 30 ft shaft with the same brick lining £30,393 is quoted and for the same width with 22½ in brick lining £32,472. They think the 16 ft shaft will be sufficient and are of the view that, although the tender is high, it is acceptable because the amount of water that will be encountered will handicap the work. They did not want a new contractor to be introduced at this late stage. (ENG) (Better the devil you know!)

8 Dec 1892. At Totley 180 yards of lining has been completed making a total of 4,763 yards with 1,506 yards left to do. It is expected to take a further eight months to finish. The line west of Padley is being rapidly trimmed and completed ready for ballasting and the laying of permanent way which is being sent to the contractor through Cowburn tunnel. (ENG)

LINING OF COWBURN TUNNEL COMPLETED

10 Nov 1892. At Cowburn only ninety seven yards of lining remains to be done. (ENG)

9 Dec 1892. At Cowburn only twelve yards of lining is unfinished. (ENG)

The *Sheffield Independent* reported that work has almost come to a standstill and few men are working between Chinley and Hope. Large numbers have been discharged due to the advanced state of the work and are leaving with their families. (NEWS)

23 Dec 1892. The lining of Cowburn tunnel is completed, (ENG)

19 Jan 1893. The committee agrees to pay Edward's overdraft to his bank of £6,872. (GPC)

PLANS TO EXTRACT SMOKE

10 Jan 1893. The *Sheffield Daily Telegraph* reported that 'the Cowburn tunnel is now practically completed and the workmen are almost daily leaving the neighbourhood with their families. It is very difficult to get the smoke out of the tunnel and unless something is done to remedy this it is feared the health of the men who will have to work in the tunnel will be endangered. It is said the Midland intend to cut a heading along the side of the tunnel from end to end by means of which the smoke will escape. This will be a work of some magnitude and it is expected a number of men will be employed for twelve months carrying out the work. It is considered this would not be as expensive a process as sinking more ventilating shafts from the summit of the Cowburn hills. Something of the kind may also be done at Totley tunnel.' (NEWS) (No other reference to this has been found)

12 Jan 1893. Lining of Totley tunnel continues apace, and permanent way materials are being delivered to the Hope valley through Cowburn tunnel. Ballasting and platelaying will start in the valley as soon as the weather improves. The same circumstances pertain on Contract No. 2. The engineers have been talking to Mr McDonald about the ventilation of the tunnels. (ENG)

DESPERATE TIMES FOR NAVVY FAMILIES

16 Jan 1893. The *Sheffield Independent* reported the melancholy news that 'owing to severe weather the greater part of the outside work is at a standstill throwing a large number of men out. Agricultural work is also at a standstill. Many families are feeling the want of both food and fire.' (NEWS) (On top of that smallpox was haunting the neighbourhood.)

TRAGIC DEATH OF THIRTEEN YEAR OLD BOY

28 Jan 1893. The *Sheffield Independent* reported (reproduced above right) the inquest on **George Hunt** age 13. This was one of the few occasions that a coroner questioned working practices on the line. George was employed as a rope runner in which capacity he was responsible for hitching wagons on to the rope used to haul them up steep inclines by a stationary or moving engine.

OLIVER AWARDED TOTLEY SHAFT CONTRACT

9 Feb 1893. 1,020 yards of lining remains in Totley tunnel, which equates to about five months work. Although the weather has delayed the outdoor work the line will be ready by the time the rails are laid through the tunnel. The engineers alerted the board that nothing has yet been done with regard to the stations or signalling. They also reported their conclusions on the ventilation shafts, having drawn on the experience of working other long tunnels on other railways and have concluded that some form of mechanical ventilation will be necessary. From observations made in Cowburn tunnel since contractors engines have been running through it they have found that 'on some days smoke is cleared out remarkably quickly while there are others when the atmosphere remains so thick the men can hardly stay in it'. As a result they believe that in both tunnels the vitiated air should be extracted from a point near the centre of the tunnel to allow the fresh air to flow in from the open ends. This can be achieved by either sinking shafts or by driving a heading parallel to the tunnel. The latter idea was thought to be too expensive and so they recommended the sinking of a shaft at both tunnels and extract the vitiated air by fans. They believe there would be no difficulty in changing the air in the whole length of the tunnels once in twenty minutes which would be sufficient for the heaviest traffic

FATAL ACCIDENT ON THE DORE AND CHINLEY RAILWAY.

Mr. D. Wightman held an inquest, yesterday, at the Sheffield Hospital, on the body of George Hunt, 13 years of age, who lived with his mother at Dore. The deceased assisted on the engines which were working on the new Dore and Chinley Railway, and on Wednesday he was endeavouring to climb up an engine which was pulling three trucks, but owing to the speed at which it was travelling—about 10 miles an hour—he was unable to obtain a foothold. He fell on an embankment, and the guard of the axle box of one of the trucks caught him and dragged him underneath, two of the wheels going over his legs.—Richard Smith, who witnessed the accident, warned the deceased not to attempt to board the engine whilst it was in motion, but he took no notice. Smith could not say whether more than one truck passed over the deceased. He was conveyed to the Hospital, where he died the following morning.—The Coroner (to Richard Smith): Is it usual to employ boys of that age upon engines?—Witness: I can't say what i usual, sir.—The Coroner remarked that it was difficult to know what was usual in making new railways. Contractors seemed to do as they liked and to go at what pace they could with the engines on a road which was hardly made, but which was quite good enough to pull soil and rubbish on. Of course they were bound to use proper precautions to prevent loss of life and accident, and if they did that they seemed to act in a way which was most convenient to themselves. To Mr. Joel Lean, engineer, who was present as representing the contractors: You are not bound by any regulation except the ordinary and proper precaution against loss of life and accident.—Mr. Lean: That is so, I think. I might explain that on locomotives used in the construction of railways there are always three persons employed—the driver, a rope runner, and a boy to assist.—A verdict of "Accidental death" was returned.

likely to pass through them. The shaft at Totley should be 20 ft in diameter and at Cowburn 16 ft and they estimate the cost of sinking both is £42,500. The position of the fans is still under consideration. (ENG)

16 Feb 1893. The tender from Oliver of £24,329 for the Totley shaft is accepted (this is nearly £5,000 more than originally quoted) and work should start as soon as the land is acquired from the Duke of Rutland. (It is a year since the solicitor was asked to enter into negotiations and it was another three months before his agreement was finally obtained.) Oliver was awarded an increased price of 6/- per cubic yard for brickwork in Totley tunnel until the headings meet. (GPC)

OLIVER PAYS FOR TRACTION ENGINE DAMAGE

27 Mar 1893. At the Dore Vestry meeting the Rev J. T. F. Allred presided, and it was noted he had undertaken the task for forty one of the previous forty three years. The damage caused by Oliver's traction engines between Abbeydale Road and Dore Moor Road resulted in him paying £650 compensation last year. Negotiations for this year's damage is ongoing. (NEWS)

OLIVER BUILDING THE LAST BRIDGE

9 Mar 1893. After some bad weather in January good progress has been made with the trimming, forming and ballasting and about two miles of permanent way has been laid. (ENG)

13 Apr 1893. The earthworks in the cuttings and embankments are almost completed. The last bridge is being built and one or two approaches that were delayed by bad weather are progressing rapidly. (ENG)

SCOTT TO SINK COWBURN SHAFT

16 Feb 1893. The engineers were asked to obtain an estimate for the Cowburn shaft from the contractor. (GPC)

13 Apr 1893. The GPC request for Mr Scott to provide an estimate for the shaft above Cowburn tunnel has been received at £17,500 which agrees with the engineers estimate. They recommend acceptance and permission to start as soon as the negotiations with the landowners have been completed. (ENG)

20 Apr 1893. Despite the engineers recommending acceptance of Scott's tender the committee decided to throw the bidding for Cowburn shaft open to all comers. (GPC)

18 May 1893. The committee agreed that the Cowburn tunnel shaft will be built in house under the supervision of Scott. Edwards has been paid another £4,135. (GPC)

CHAPEL MILTON VIADUCT COMPLETED

15 Mar 1893. Following the completion of Cowburn tunnel all the men have been dispensed with. In the Edale and Hope valleys the whole line is in a very forward state and all bridges etc are finished except two small occupation bridges. The viaduct at Chapel Milton is finished and building the stations is about to start. (NEWS)

13 Apr 1893. Good progress is reported on all the work left. (ENG)

11 May 1893. On Contract No. 2 the laying of the permanent way is being carried on rapidly. (ENG)

13 May 1893. The *Sheffield Independent* reported that 'most of the navvies have disappeared from the Chapel and Chinley district and several of the local engineers and officials have moved to other spheres of labour. At Chinley a signal box is being erected (presumably Chinley South Junction) and some connections with the main line have been made. The rails have been laid over the great viaduct at Chapel Milton. (NEWS)

21 May 1893. A new intermediate block temporary signal post at the junction of the south curve with the up main line will be opened and named 'Chinley South Junction'. (MRENG)

10 Jun 1893. The excavations are nearly complete as is the masonry on the bridges and thirteen miles of permanent way (single road) has been laid and partially ballasted. (ENG)

DUKE OF RUTLAND FINALLY GIVES CONSENT FOR SHAFT

11 May 1893. The Duke of Rutland has now given his sanction for the sinking of the Totley ventilation shaft. Of several contractors invited to tender all but one would only tender to supply the labour with the company supplying the machinery, temporary tramway etc. The engineers were very unhappy at this arrangement. (This contradicts the report that Oliver had been awarded the contract.) Tenders for the stations are being obtained. (ENG).

ANOTHER TRAIN FATALITY

16 May 1893. William Wainwright, while in the tunnel at the Padley end, was carrying explosives to the men at the headings and jumped on a passing train to ride to his destination. He was jolted off and fell under the wheels of a truck sustaining considerable injuries to his head. Death was instantaneous. (NEWS)

SINKING TOTLEY SHAFT STARTS

10 Jun 1893. Since the last report permission to allow Oliver to start on the shaft contract must have been given because 'the sinking of the shaft has started. 50 ft has been achieved and it is still dry'. (ENG)

15 Jul 1893. The sinking of the ventilation shaft has been suspended due to water ingress. A nine inch bore hole is being put down to drain the water into the tunnel below. The works underground forming the connection between the tunnel and the shaft has started and is expected to take about six weeks. (ENG)

LINING OF TOTLEY TUNNEL COMPLETED

11 May 1893. The lining of Totley tunnel has been handicapped by the difficulty of ventilating the works in the past few weeks due to the prevalence of easterly winds and warm weather. (ENG)

10 Jun 1893. Only 200 yards of lining remain at Totley. It is anticipated, that the double line will be laid throughout from Padley to the end of No. 1 contract by the end of next month leaving only the permanent way through the tunnel and in the station yards to be completed. (ENG)

15 Jul 1893. The lining at Totley should be finished in the next month. The permanent drain, ballasting and laying the permanent way through the tunnel is under way and the line should be ready for goods traffic by the end of September. (ENG)

The height and graceful proportions of the two viaducts are caught in this 1954 image. Chinley South Curve viaduct is in the background.   *Eric de Mare*

Shaft No. 5 high on Totley Moor shows the more substantial winding gear for drawing up the large amount of spoil. The shaft finally sat on this spoil, contrary to the agreement with the Duke of Rutland. *Author's collection*

Here are the remains of an explosives store about 200 yards from Shaft No. 5 taken in 2009. Recently, the Eastern Moors Partnership have rebuilt it to what it may have looked like originally. *Author*

4 Aug 1893. The lining of Totley tunnel is completed. (ICE, ENG)

The Totley tunnel drain is now being rapidly pushed forward and will probably be completed in about three weeks time. The permanent way is being laid and partly ballasted throughout the line leaving only the stations and approaches to finish. The shaft bore hole has reached 450 ft. (ENG)

5 Aug 1893. The *Sheffield Independent* reported 'Another stage in this costly undertaking was finished yesterday when the last junction in the costly stone and brick work of the Padley tunnel was affected. The roof is now actually completed, the difficulties all overcome. With the staff of masons out of the way rapid progress will be made on the permanent way while the culvert to drain the water will be finished quickly. The line is now as straight and orderly as contractors and navvies can be expected to leave it between Dore and the tunnel entrance. At the Padley end work is not so well marked but what was in a chaotic state a few months ago is now being prepared for the opening of the line. Signal boxes have been erected and telegraphic communication is being made and the work of erecting the stations is to be pushed on with. Contracts for the work have been let to Michael Ford and M. Hand of Hathersage' (NEWS) (Ford built Hathersage viaduct as a subcontractor to Oliver and with Hand became a subcontractor to Walker & Slater).

PREPARATIONS FOR COWBURN SHAFT

15 Jul 1893. Preliminary work on the Cowburn shaft has commenced. (ENG)

5 Aug 1893. The incline road to be used for the haulage of materials to the Cowburn shaft site has been laid and the sinking of the shaft will start very soon. The ballasting and laying of the permanent way is making good progress. (ENG)

SALE OF THOMAS OLIVER'S HORSES

15 Aug 1893. An advertisement for a sale at The Repository, Castle Hill, Sheffield of the 'fourth portion of these powerful horses' commented that all are in good hard condition.

NAME	DESCRIPTION	AGE YEARS	HANDS
Traveller	Dark bay	7	14.2
Slavin	Dark brown	7	16.2
Jack	Chestnut	7	17.0
Doctor	Chestnut	7	15.2
Bretton	Bay	6	16.2
Prince	Black	5	13.0
Bounce	Bay	6	16.0

INSPECTOR OF WORKS KILLED

18 Aug 1893. Herbert Hall, age 34, a married man, had recently moved from Edale to live at Cromwell cottage, Chapel and was an inspector of works. He was well known in the locality and had been employed on the works from the beginning. He entered Cowburn tunnel at the Chinley end and was walking on the up line and was advised to walk on the down line but ignored the warning. He was knocked down by a train and found unconscious. He was taken to Manchester Royal Infirmary but died on arrival. A verdict of 'accidental death' was returned. (NEWS)

THE WORK IS NEARLY COMPLETED

2 Sep 1893. The track work is completed except in Totley tunnel. (ICE)

14 Sep 1893. The works in Totley tunnel are practically completed, the drain having been finished and the permanent way is expected to be laid throughout the tunnel by the end of the week. The double line of permanent way on Contract No. 1 is all laid and partly ballasted with the exception of two or three very short lengths which the contractor has had to defer until the last moment for his own temporary purposes.

Mr McDonald has sent a large quantity of ballast for the tunnel and the boxing up of the road. The Totley shaft bore hole has reached the bottom and the water has been released into the tunnel drain. On Contract No. 2 the laying of the permanent way is practically completed. The bridges, viaducts and culverts are finished and all that remains to be done is a small amount of excavation, some ballasting and trimming of slopes.

On the Cowburn shaft the connection with the tunnel below has been made. The date for opening for goods traffic of the second or third week in October still holds good. (ENG)

It is 29 Aug 1893, three days before the tunnel was officially completed. Temporary contractors track with a turn off to a siding to the right is still in place and the building of Grindleford station is not yet started. The fine bridge, No. 10, which gives access from the main road to the hamlet of Padley, is finished but work around the completed tunnel portal is still ongoing. In the foreground, on the left, is the start of culvert No. 11 which carries the beautiful Burbage Brook under the line and station platforms. A detailed examination shows that there are at least ten men working at different points on the site and near the two wagons are four men who are not navvies and are either contractors engineers and/or Midland engineers or maybe official inspectors eg Board of Trade or even Midland officials. The lack of tidiness renders the site dangerous. There is left over spoil, pipes, wood which has been hewed and not hewed and discarded sections of rail. At the top left is an upturned flat horse dray. There is smoke at the tunnel mouth which suggests there is a contractor's locomotive working in the tunnel. A steam crane is located at the mouth with a man working at the foot of it and an unidentified wheeled vehicle is just in the tunnel. At the top of the path is the winding house for the supply of material from the road above. Just on the edge on the left hand side is possibly a navvy hut. On the right hand side there are two huts, the higher one could possibly be a navvy hut. It would be another ten months before the station was ready to open.

PLAN FOR TRIANGULAR STATION AT TOTLEY?

29 Sep 1893. The *Sheffield Independent* reported that the opening of the line for through goods traffic on Sun 1 Oct has been delayed until 15 Oct and until 1 Nov for through and ordinary goods. At present the track contains several incomplete lengths and the connection with the main line at Dore has not yet been made. A gang of men are at work on this and not much remains to be done. In putting down the rails which form the junction it has been necessary to cut off a slice of the southern end of the down platform. It is protected by a new signal box between the new and old lines to the south of the station. The stations on the line are not yet started. No alterations to Dore and Totley station have been decided on yet but it is very possible that it will be removed altogether and placed within the triangle formed by the old and new lines on two sides and the new curve to become an 'island station' similar to Ambergate. (NEWS) (There is nothing in the engineers' reports that support this)

AUCTION OF HORSES AT CHAPEL MILTON

9 Oct 1893. The *Sheffield Independent* carried an advert for an auction at Chapel Milton of forty six young draught horses, two useful nag horses, fifteen strong carts and forty sets of gears by Edwards because of the adoption of steam power and a traction engine on the overland route to Edale. (NEWS)

SMALLPOX HUTS AT PADLEY TO BE DEMOLISHED

12 Oct 1893. On Contract No. 1 the station yards and approaches require finishing. The double line is sufficiently ballasted for goods trains to be run. The remainder of the ballast is to be laid by Mr McDonald after the line is opened for goods traffic as already agreed. The Totley shaft has now been sunk to a depth of 171 ft. The committee asked the engineers to see Oliver regarding the navvy huts at Padley and other places on the line which have been infected by smallpox to avoid the danger of spreading the disease by the materials being distributed and used for other purposes after they are pulled down. There are altogether fifty eight huts on Oliver's contract most of which are of timber but eleven are built with brick walls. About seven or eight of them have not been infected. Oliver ultimately offered to hand them to the company for £1,000, the original cost having being £3,594. (ENG) (I bet he did!)

19 Oct 1893. The committee agreed to pay Oliver £1,000 for the smallpox infected huts. (ENG) (They must have had an aberration!)

LINE INSPECTIONS

30 Sep 1893. The *Derbyshire Times* of 7 Oct explains that the target date of opening the line for goods traffic has not been met and reported an inspection trip on the line. 'From Dore and Totley a company of gentlemen embarked on a primitive train with uncompromising ventilation. When they emerged from the tunnel at Padley the engine only delayed sufficiently to give the passengers a glimpse of the works in progress in and about the station. (See page 146) Very much remains to be done. The contractor has not only to build the line but also to build up the ground for the station accommodation'. At Hathersage 'the station has been started and extensive provision has been made for a goods yard'. At Bamford the journey concludes just before the iron bridge over the Derwent (Mytham). 'At Hope and Edale the platforms have nearly been completed and the connection of the new line at Dore has also been completed. The block signalling system is complete as are all the signal boxes. The station buildings are not yet started'. (NEWS)

2 Oct 1893. The *Sheffield Independent* reported that the contractors organized a small party to inspect the workings. It consisted of Inspector Wilson of the Midland; Mr A. S. Jarvis, goods manager of the Midland; Mr Walker of Wharncliffe Silkstone Colliery; Mr W. B. Burdekin of W. Jessop and Sons; Mr Baguley of Charles Cammell & Co and representatives of the Sheffield press. The train consisted of an engine and two open trucks and started from Dore and went through the tunnel for a couple of miles where a halt was made to inspect the large ventilation shaft. The vertical drain was discharging an enormous force of water into a culvert on the south side of the tunnel. The tunnel is remarkable dry and well ventilated. The party then were taken as far as Bamford and on the way saw the work being done on Grindleford and Hathersage stations. The return journey to Dore took about half an hour including ten minutes to pass through the tunnel. (NEWS)

12 Oct 1893. H. J. Bell, Board of Trade inspector, who was temporarily resident in the area undertook a tour of inspection and charged the company £22/2/7. (BT)

The *Derbyshire Times* reported that in preparing for the general opening for goods traffic, the heads of department on the Midland Railway embarked on a careful inspection of the line. On the day before about 250 men were engaged in completing the connection at the Chinley South Curve in readiness for the Monday visit. (NEWS)

(See 'Inspections of the Line' section (page 168) where the three well known photographs are discussed.)

BALLASTING NEARLY COMPLETED ON CONTRACT No. 2

12 Oct 1893. On Contract No. 2 every effort is being made to get the ballasting finished. (ENG)

19 Oct 1893. The accounts are to be audited since the company took over the two contracts from Edwards. (GPC)

TOTLEY SHAFT BLOCKED AND FLOODED

21 Oct 1893. The *Derbyshire Courier* reported that 'another temporary stoppage has taken place at the new shaft which is being sunk near Fox House on the moors into the tunnel. Some time ago boring operations commenced and a depth of about 200 ft of the 700 ft had been reached. A few days ago, however, a brick or some hard substance fell into the hole and blocked it up, so that water has accumulated to a depth of about 90 ft and stopped the work.' (NEWS)

9 Nov 1893. Due to an unfortunate accident at the Totley shaft, (the nature of which is not reported), which occurred nearly a month ago, the recently sunk bore hole has become blocked. Every effort to dislodge the obstruction has so far failed. The engineers (who rightly sound very annoyed) have told Oliver to put down a second bore hole at his own expense, which will delay the work for another six weeks. (ENG)

MIDLAND TAKES POSSESSION OF THE LINE SIGNAL BOXES OPEN

28 Oct 1893. The connection with the main line at Dore and Totley is completed and the Midland has taken over possession of the line from the contractors. (MRENG)

The *Sheffield Independent* explained 'that the running lines have been taken over from the contractors. The new route is practically ready for the first through goods train next Monday. An effort will be made to get the stations and the line opened for passengers by 1 Apr next, or at the latest by Whitsuntide, and it is thought that it will be in a condition to deal with intermediate and local goods traffic before that time'. (NEWS)

29 Oct 1893. The signalling arrangements have become operative which includes all the signal boxes, except Normans Bank which opened much later. At Dore and Totley station the old signal box is to be closed and a new box named 'Dore and Totley Station Junction' opened. 'Dore South Junction Curve', junction with the main line, has not yet been laid in and the curve could, if necessary, be used for standing trains on. (MRENG)

DEATH OF PERCY RICKARD

31 Oct 1893. The death of Percy Rickard was reported (see page 101.)

PILOT ENGINE AND GUARD FOR TOTLEY TUNNEL WORKING

3 Nov 1893. Working through Totley tunnel requires a pilot engine and guard. (MRENG)

19 Nov 1893. Block telegraph working in place of working by pilot engine and guard is introduced between Totley Tunnel East and Grindleford. (MRENG)

LINE OPENED FOR THROUGH GOODS TRAFFIC

6 Nov 1893. The line opened for through goods, livestock and minerals including Chinley South Curve. (Sighs of relief all round!) (ENG)

Midland trains will cease running between Barnsley and Godley on the MSLR. (NEWS)

MIDLAND TO FINISH BALLASTING

9 Nov 1893. On the line only a few minor works connected with the station yards and the quick set planting remains to be done. As the contractor's engines are not now allowed to run down the line any more it has been arranged for Mr McDonald to finish the ballasting that is still to do. Cowburn shaft has now reached 200 ft. (ENG)

14 Nov 1893. Oliver wrote to the GPC asking for an increase in prices and other privileges of nearly £60,000. The engineers and solicitor felt it should be considered when settling the final account. (GPC)

VISIT TO GERMANY TO EXAMINE TUNNEL VENTILATION FANS
ELECTRIC PLANT AT HOPE FOR BOTH TUNNELS

9 Nov 1893. The engineers in a separate report described their ideas regarding the best method of securing the efficient ventilation of the tunnels and the cheapest and most satisfactory means of working them. So that the air could be changed every twenty minutes, Capell fans at Totley that would be 15 ft diameter and 13 ft wide and at Cowburn, 12 ft 6 in diameter and 11 ft 6 in wide, working at 200 revolutions a minute, would be required. The cheapest and best way of driving the fans would be attained by erecting engines at the top of each shaft. However when they considered the position of such engines on the top of bleak and exposed moors, particularly the Colborne Moor with no road nearby, and the cost of supplying the engine with coal and water and getting somebody to live on the moor permanently, they thought better of it. Two methods seemed possible to drive the fans, these being either compressed air or electricity. The cost of the former and the loss of power in working such plant rendered it unsuitable. The alternative, electricity, required large installations for transmitting power long distances and satisfactory working examples were already in place in Switzerland, Germany and America. It would be possible to put down such plants at Grindleford and Edale, the two nearest stations to the shafts, where coal could be obtained at low cost but having two would be expensive in labour and plant. Thus they suggested that a central plant for both shafts, somewhere near Hope station, would be best. Their estimate of the cost of the work, including buildings, boilers, steam and electrical machinery, fans, line and other apparatus was £22,000 and the annual cost of coal, oil, waste and the wages of five men at an average of 30/- a week would be about £1,150. The fans would be self starting and would only be employed when the level of smoke required it and could safely be run with only occasional attention. The engineers have submitted the whole scheme to Mr Gilbert Kapp MICE of Westminster, who is one of the highest authorities in this country on electrical transmission of power, and he has endorsed the system selected. They have obtained a tender from a firm of reliable electrical engineers. To further their knowledge the engineers visited a colliery near Essen in Germany where a similar system, though not on so large a scale, is in successful operation. (ENG)

(Little more is heard of this proposal although there is a newspaper report which states 'that a fan is used to draw off the vitiated air at Cowburn'. As late as Feb 1894 a decision had still not been made to go ahead.)

BOARD OF TRADE INSPECTION OF THE LINE

Nov 1893. During the month H. J. Bell from the Board of Trade inspected the works and charged £20/13/0. (BT) (As resident inspector he would have pre-empted his superior's visit by making sure that everything was in order.)

16 Nov 1893. The *Derbyshire Courier* and the *Derby Mercury* reported that Major F. A. Marindin, Board of Trade group inspector, aided by Mr Muglington, Midland superintendent, and a number of permanent officials of the Midland passed over the line, in between the goods trains on the line, in a saloon carriage and made an inspection of the entire length of the line starting at Chinley at 11.00. They returned to Derby from Sheffield. (NEWS)

MIDLAND DAMAGED BY BITTER COAL STRIKE

16 Nov 1893. In a separate report the *Derbyshire Courier* had a main headline on the bitter coal strike which had paralysed the industry for the previous six months being at an end, an agreement having been reached. (NEWS)

(This dispute seriously affected the Midland's traffic returns and income but more importantly created appalling hardship for the miners and their families. One shocking newspaper report said that 2,000 children were starving in Attercliffe, Sheffield.)

EXPLOSION AT THE BOTTOM OF TOTLEY SHAFT

8 Dec 1893. The *Sheffield Independent* reported an explosion of gas. The bore hole which had been put down Shaft No. 5 to release the water accumulating in the shaft above became blocked. Attempts to velar (cover) the obstruction above the heading having failed, the fireman of the gang of men working at the heading conceived the idea of pushing rods from the bottom. The idea was attempted and was partially successful and allowed some water to be released. However a large quantity of gas had accumulated in the bore hole which escaped into the heading. It came into contact with the men's candles and caused an explosion. The heading was temporarily illuminated with great brilliancy and then the workers were thrown and rendered insensible. A huge stone hit one man and his side was hurt and all the men received burns to their hands and faces. The balcony and ladder under the bore were blown away. Dr Allred had one of the men removed to Sheffield Infirmary and others who were suffering from burns and shock were sent home and one or two were able to return to work later in the day. There was considerable alarm in the neighbourhood but the consequences were not as bad as first feared. None of the men involved were named. (The engineers do not report this). (NEWS)

OLIVER'S STUBBORNNESS DELAYS WORK ON SHAFT

9 Dec 1893. On Contract No. 1 the contractor is being pressed to complete the small amount of unfinished work on the line. On the Totley shaft Oliver had originally ignored the engineers expressed wish for another bore hole but had now commenced it having spent another fruitless month trying to unblock the obstruction. While waiting for this to be completed lining of the shaft will commence. (ENG)

NEW GOODS LINE AND SIGNALLING AROUND CHAPEL

10 Dec 1893. A new up goods line from Chapel en le Frith North Junction to Chinley South Junction was brought into use. The Chapel en le Frith station signal box will be closed to be replaced by two new boxes, the first on the up side at the south end of the station is to be named 'Chapel-en-le-Frith South' and the second, on the down side of the line near the north end of the station, is to be named 'Chapel-en-le-Frith North'. To accommodate this, the levers in Chinley South Junction box were altered the week before. (MRENG, GOUGH)

7 Mar 1894. The Chapel en le Frith down goods line to down passenger line has been brought into use together with the Chapel en le Frith North to Chinley South Junction down goods line. (MRENG, GOUGH)

COTTAGES AT HOPE TO BE BUILT

20 Dec 1893. The Midland way and works committee recorded that three cottages are to be built at Hope, one for the permanent way inspector and two for lengthmen, at an estimated cost of £725. (GPC)

The Hayfield Board of Guardians decided to buy a large quantity of sleepers from Edwards for chopping into firewood by tramps at the workhouse as a labour test. (NEWS) (Not much sign of a rehabilitation programme here)

WORK DELAYED BY BAD WEATHER

11 Jan 1894. The station yards and the few other works still to be done have been delayed by the Christmas holidays and the inclement weather. The weather has also seriously delayed the Totley shaft as has a large quantity of water in the bottom of the shaft. The new bore hole is down 200 ft and lining is underway. (The engineers are now adopting a more emollient tone!) The Cowburn shaft has reached 301 ft but unfortunately water has been met and a bore hole in this shaft may be needed as well. (ENG)

RICKARD'S PAPER TO I.C.E. READ

23 Jan 1894. Edward Parry read the paper written by the late Percy Rickard to the Institution of Civil Engineers.

BORE HOLE TO BE PUT DOWN COWBURN SHAFT

8 Feb 1894. Completing the bridges, station yards and approaches and the finishing off of a few occupation bridges and other works has been the main focus on the line. The lining of the shaft at Totley is within a short distance of the top but will not be proceeded with further until a decision has been made about the fans. The sinking of the second bore hole has reached the bottom and sinking the shaft is due to resume. The shaft at Cowburn has reached 331 ft but the water is increasing and so a bore hole is to be sunk. (ENG)

8 Mar 1894. At Cowburn the bore hole has been started and no other work is possible. (ENG)

STATION YARDS AND BUILDINGS – SOME WAY TO GO

10 Feb 1894. It was reported that 'a considerable amount of work is still to be done on the line before it can be opened for passengers. Large numbers of stone masons are employed on building the station houses, booking offices etc at Edale, Hope, Bamford and Hathersage. Navvies have made an almost complete exodus from Totley although 'a few have pitched tent on Cowburn summit'. (NEWS)

J. Butler & Co charged £365/17/11 for the steelworks for the lattice main girders on bridge 3 Hall's Private Road at Dore West Junction. (GPC) (See page 91.)

8 Mar 1894. The station yards and approaches are very nearly completed. Better progress is reported on the station buildings but there is still a lot to be done. It is felt that the target date of 1 Jun will be difficult to meet. (ENG)

MIDLAND DIRECTOR'S INSPECTION

21 & 22 Mar 1894. The Midland directors inspected the line. They went from Derby to Manchester via Bakewell and then returned to Chinley and went over the Dore and Chinley line to Sheffield. (NEWS)

ACCIDENTS TO MACHINERY IN BOTH SHAFTS

8 Mar 1894. Totley shaft is now down to 230 ft of which 150 ft is lined. (ENG)

4 Apr 1894. In the Totley shaft an accident to lighting apparatus for night working caused the pit frame etc to be set on fire delaying the work for nearly a week. Cowburn shaft also experienced an accident to the boring tackle, which has now been made good, and a fresh start has been made to finish the bore hole. Notice of the line being ready for inspection has been given to the Board of Trade and the inspector has arranged to go over it on Thursday and Friday next. (ENG)

7 Apr 1894. The junction with the main line at Dore has been made. (MRENG)

TENDERS FOR HOPE COTTAGES

5 Apr 1894. Tenders were received for three cottages at Hope. Walker & Slater bid £885 but the contract was awarded to J. Walker & Sons for £688/10/7.

The cost of the Twentywell Sick Lane diversion is estimated to be £1,550.

200 Austrian pines for screening at Normans Bank were ordered by C. Smith at a cost of £6. (GPC) (See page 152.)

BOARD OF TRADE INSPECTOR KEEPS DOING HIS STUFF

19 & 20 Apr 1894. Inspecting officer H. J. Bell, following a visit for which he charged £4/16/4, comments;

Grindleford: Lettering and painting to be completed. The station is sanctioned for opening on 18 Jun, which was confirmed on a later inspection.

Hathersage: Station buildings require painting, lettering etc and a handrail on a girder bridge is to be fixed.

Bamford: Station building to be completed and painted. Lamps and door to be fixed.

Hope: Name board and lamps to be fixed and doors lettered.

Edale: Name board and lamps to be fixed, doors to be lettered and fencing painted. (BT) (I suspect the subcontractor was becoming irritated by this nit picking after all they had been through.)

28 Apr 1894. Major F. A. Marindin, the senior Board of Trade inspector responsible for the overall line inspection, reported that the speed of trains at Totley South Junction (Dore South Junction Curve) would be restricted to 30 mph over the 23.24 chain curve. He reported on the dimensions of Chapel Milton viaduct, Hathersage viaduct, Edale (Cowburn) viaduct and Derwent (Mytham) viaduct. He stated that there were twenty three culverts, four footpath crossings and that the deepest cuttings were 70, 62 and 57 ft. The highest embankments were 68, 50 and 40 ft and were not problematic. He considered the stations to be 'sufficient' and the overall masonry to be of a 'very high class'. He then itemises the signal boxes and their capacities. (BT)

29 Apr 1894. Chinley East Junction box raised. (GOUGH)

HANDYSIDES TO ERECT HOPE STATION FOOTBRIDGE

4 May 1894. Tenders were received for the footbridge (No. 33) at Hope station and ranged from £252 to £387 but Handysides of Derby, who tendered £271/11/1, was the one accepted. In the event Handysides were paid £255/7/-.

FIRST PASSENGER SERVICES

10 May 1894. An engineering notice stated that 'The line with both curves will be opened for through passenger traffic. The sidings at all stations are to be used only by Midland men and vehicles sent to these stations must be worked direct to them. The use of Dore South Junction Curve for stabling wagons is to cease. The stations are not to be opened to passengers for the time being. (MRENG)

15 May 1894. The first excursion train on the line ran from Rotherham Westgate to Southport and return. (NEWS)

16 May 1894. The line officially opened for excursion traffic including Chinley South Curve.

1 Jun 1894. The line opened for through passenger traffic (see page 184).

WORK ON COWBURN SHAFT RESUMES

12 May 1894. Totley shaft has been sunk 312 ft out of a total 722 ft, and following the completion of the bore hole at Cowburn the shaft sinking has restarted. The ground where the sinking is taking place is practically dry but a continuous flow of water is falling from the upper portion. (ENG)

FINAL CERTIFICATES ISSUED TO CONTRACTORS

16 May 1894. The engineers reported that the final certificate was issued for the completion of the works on both contracts. Another letter from Oliver was received seeking an increase in prices on which no decision was taken. (GPC)

29 May 1894. Cowburn Tunnel East box opened. (GOUGH)

LAND FOR HOPE COTTAGES TO BE BOUGHT

7 Jun 1894. The committee learned that the land for the building of the cottages at Hope is not available. It was agreed that land should be bought from Edward Firth for £25, a transaction which the estate agent completed on 5 Jul. The final bill for the land and walls was £82/16/7, the buildings £985/8/9, making a total of £1,068/5/4. (GPC)

STATION BUILDINGS ALL BUT FINISHED

9 Jun 1894. The engineers reported that the station buildings, booking offices and waiting sheds are all but ready for use but the station masters houses and cottages will not be ready for another three months. (ENG)

WATER PROBLEMS IN COWBURN SHAFT

9 Jun 1894. The Totley shaft has now reached 387 ft. A very large quantity of water in the borehole has been met in the Cowburn shaft which will necessitate a larger side drain being laid in the tunnel to carry the water away. (ENG)

STATIONS AND CURVES OPENED

11 Jun 1894. The Dore South Junction Curve is opened for goods traffic. (GOUGH)

25 Jun 1894. The stations and Chinley South Curve are opened for local passenger services.

FINAL FINANCIAL SETTLEMENT WITH CONTRACTORS

14 Jun 1894. The final financial settlement of No. 1 contract was completed. £13,000 was awarded to Oliver which was then raised to £14,500 with £2,000 being retained for maintenance in the following year. On Contract No. 2 the final settlement showed that the cost of the works since the Midland took over had exceeded the contract price. Edward's loss in carrying out the first half of the contract was to a great extent inevitable, the company having got the benefit of that loss. Edwards owes £11,500 to his bank and other creditors, principally his family, who are owed £1,200. It was suggested that Edwards should be released from his debt on payment of £4,000 from the company and £4,000 more to Edwards, out of which he would pay his family £1,200 and Scott £2,000. The bank would only accept £5,000 so the company would sell the plant and from the proceeds pay Scott £1,000 and Roberts £800 as previously agreed. All the other suggestions were accepted including the £5,000 payment to the bank. (GPC)

ALL INFRASTRUCTURE COMPLETED

19 Jul 1894. All the inspecting officers requirements have been complied with, except that the handrailings above the girders of the under bridges at Edale and Hathersage were not yet in place. (BT)

27 Jul 1894. All these tasks are completed. (BT)

3 Aug 1894. The station master's houses and cottages are being proceeded with rapidly and should be finished in the next two weeks. (ENG)

16 Aug 1894. Inspector Bell declared that the line was completed (thank goodness) except for the ventilation shafts at Totley and Cowburn. For that information he charged expenses of £5/17/3. (BT)

SHAFTS TO BE SUNK TO RAIL LEVEL

19 Jul 1894. The engineers recommended that the shafts should be sunk to rail level which will be 16 ft lower than originally planned. The heading connecting them with the tunnels should be carried to the same depth. The additional cost of between £4,000 and £5,000 was agreed. (GPC)

3 Aug 1894. Work at both shafts has made good progress, Totley having been sunk 100 ft and Cowburn, where the rock is very hard, 46 ft. (ENG)

TOTLEY GROVE HOUSE TO LET

15 Aug 1894. (The house became empty because of the huge intrusion by the works on it and was used as the contractors headquarters. With the work nearly at an end it became surplus to requirements). G. S. McCullum, estate agent of the Midland at Derby, advertised in the *Derby Mercury* that Totley Grove house is to let. (NEWS).

14 Sep 1894. Samuel Stone was paid £70/18/6 for alterations to Totley Grove. (GPC)

17 Jul 1895. Samuel Stone was paid £237/8/4 for alterations and additions to Totley Grove. (GPC)

GOOD PROGRESS ON BOTH SHAFTS

14 Sep 1894. At Cowburn 452 ft has been sunk, out of a total of 791 ft, whilst the Totley shaft has been sunk 615 ft, out of a total of 717 ft and 538 ft has been lined. The various station masters houses are practically complete, only a little painting requiring to be done while the cottages at Grindleford and Edale are making better progress and should soon be ready for occupation. (ENG)

10 Oct 1894. The Board of Trade inspector reported that 'the ventilation shaft at Cowburn will be complete in two months' (this proved wildly optimistic). His tour of inspection cost £3/5/10. (BT)

13 Oct 1894. All the station buildings, with the exception of the cottages, are now complete. (ENG)

FOOTBRIDGE AT HOPE COMPLETED

14 Sep 1894. Handysides of Derby fixed a handrail for the bridge at Hathersage for £12/9/1.

Oct 1894. During this month the footbridge at Hope was completed and bridge No. 55, over the road to Edale village, had its wooden parapets added.

George Longden & Son erected machine offices at Bamford and at all the stations in the valleys for £447/5/10. (BT) (Longdens were to have a major role in the Dore to Sheffield widening a few years later)

TOTLEY SHAFT MEETS THE TUNNEL

13 Oct 1894. The Totley ventilation shaft is now excavated to the level of the cross heading from the tunnel and preparations are being made for the excavation of the chamber connecting the tunnel to the shaft. The lining is complete within 60 ft of the bottom. Cowburn shaft has been delayed for the past two months by large quantities of water and arrangements are being made to clear it by means of water curls. The lining of the shaft is beginning and the necessary materials are already on the ground. (ENG)

9 Nov 1894. The excavation of the chamber at the Totley shaft is underway and requires considerable care owing to its size and position. Lining has started on the Cowburn shaft. (ENG)

13 Dec 1894. The lining of Totley shaft has been completed and over a half of the chamber is finished. The Cowburn shaft has made fair progress and 330 ft has been lined. (ENG)

MISCELLANEOUS NEWS

9 Nov 1894. It is now twelve months since the line opened for goods traffic so the £2,000 withheld from Oliver for maintenance had now expired and payment to him was requested. (ENG)

A safe was fixed at Hope and the WC at Edale was altered. (GPC)

13 Dec 1894. The cottages at Grindleford are now practically complete and those at Edale will be finished in about ten days. (ENG)

20 Dec 1894. The cost of acquiring the land for the Chinley South Curve was reported by Fowler, the solicitor, at £108,045 (more probably £18,045) and was agreed. (GPC)

The Board of Trade inspector H. J. Bell toured the works and charged £3/9/0. (BT) (Surely not much left to inspect by this time!)

ENGINEERS SIX MONTHLY REPORT

31 Dec 1894. The Totley shaft would be completed in about a month's time and the Cowburn shaft is about two thirds complete. The station masters houses and labourers cottages are finished. (ENG)

SIGNAL BOX IN TOTLEY TUNNEL OPENED

13 Jan 1895. The engineering notices stated that a 'new signal box in the tunnel (Totley) on the down side of the line on the Grindleford side of the central ventilation shaft is to be opened as 'Totley Tunnel Box' in order to protect engineering operations at the shaft.' (MRENG)

14 Mar 1895. The temporary signal box in Totley tunnel is removed. (BT)

SCOTT'S SALARY HALVED

9 Mar 1895. Owing to severe weather very little work has been done over the past two months, although an improvement in the weather over the last ten days has allowed work to resume. With the present state of the work at the Cowburn shaft it was not thought to be necessary for James Scott to devote the whole of his time to the work. However, as he has arranged the whole of the plant and machinery for the sinking of the shaft the engineers thought it advisable that he should continue to superintend the work until completion, especially as the most difficult part has yet to be done. Scott thought he should be paid at the rate of £400 per annum, instead of £800, which was agreed by the GPC. (ENG)

TOTLEY SHAFT COMPLETED

14 Mar 1895. The ventilation shaft at Totley is completed. The shaft at Cowburn 'will not be ready for some time'.

18 Apr 1895. Oliver asks for an additional £1,850 for the Totley shaft but is refused. (GPC)

It took five visits to Shaft No. 5 before the air was clear enough and the light bright enough to get this image with the wireless mast at the top of Sir William Hill on the horizon, which was the area where the brick observatory for the sightings for the tunnel was built. I hope it shows up after all that trouble! It is a grim, bleak, forbidding place. *Author*

MISCELLANEOUS NEWS

18 Apr 1895. C. Smith was paid £35/1/3 for planting 600 Austrian pine trees at Normans Bank (see page 149). (GPC)

FIRE AT COWBURN SHAFT

13 May 1895. The Cowburn shaft is now sunk to a depth of 606 ft which leaves 150 ft still to do. It is now lined as far as it can be. (ENG)

17 Jun 1895. A further 69 ft has been sunk on the Cowburn shaft. Because of the hard rock machine drills are being used. (ENG)

17 Jul 1895. On Sun 23 Jun a fire broke out at Cowburn shaft which damaged most of the machinery and completely destroyed part of it. The winding gear fortunately escaped and the work at the shaft, though delayed, has not been stopped for a day. Some of the damage has been repaired and the hauling engines will be at work next Wednesday. The whole of the damage amounting to £760 is covered by insurance. The shaft is now sunk 729 ft and a connection has been made with the cross heading of the tunnel. (ENG)

17 Sep 1895. The sinking and lining of Cowburn shaft is now complete and a start has been made on the excavation of the large chamber connecting the shaft and the tunnel. (ENG)

12 Oct 1895. Progress with the chamber at Cowburn is proceeding as well as can be expected considering the hardness of the rock. (ENG)

DISPOSAL OF PLANT

12 Oct 1895. The engineers were asked by the chairman to report upon the disposal of the plant on Contract No. 2 and have learned that Mr Williams has written to James Scott and has received full particulars of the plant sold and the amounts realised. As the plant has always been in Scott's charge the engineers are relying on him to provide the information required via Mr Williams. (ENG)

STATION BUILDERS ACCOUNT SETTLED

12 Oct 1895. Walker & Slater presented their final account for work done. The contract was agreed at £11,800 of which £11,500 has been paid. Their account had an additional £3323, all but £300 of which was for the cost of foundations, drainage, water supply and fittings to the various stations which were not included in the original contract. (ENG)

ELECTRIC COMMUNICATION THROUGH BOTH TUNNELS

1 Nov 1895. The installation of electric communication through both tunnels is approved at a cost of £300. (GPC)

COWBURN SHAFT PROGRESS

11 Nov 1895. The large chamber of the Cowburn shaft has proceeded 40 ft and is now complete and the masons have commenced the side walling. The work is being pushed forward as fast as possible and is kept going night and day. (ENG)

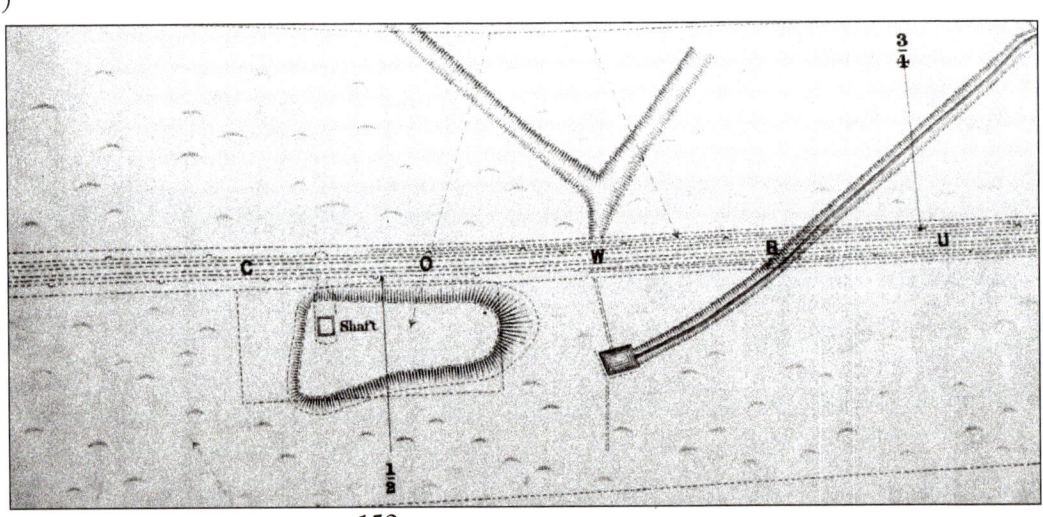

The MR two chain map of the Cowburn shaft with the spoil around it showing the location just to the south of the line with the outline of the entrance from the chamber to the tunnel.

13 Jan 1896. 102 men are engaged at the Cowburn shaft working night and day in three shifts of eight hours. The whole of the excavation for the large chamber will be out in about a week and the total work should be finished in three months time. (ENG)

16 Mar 1896. The large chamber is now completed at Cowburn as far as the excavation, masonry and brickwork are concerned. The removal of the timbering, the laying of the necessary drains and the concreting of the floor of the chamber will be finished in a few days. The winding gear will then be removed and a start made on the tower at the top of the shaft and the levelling down of the spoil heap. (ENG)

COWBURN SHAFT COMPLETED

11 Jun 1896. A letter from the Midland General Manager's office to the Board of Trade reports that 'Cowburn ventilation shaft is now complete'. The Sectional Appendix for 1893 stated that there was a hut in the middle of the tunnel with a brazier for the workmen.

MISCELLANEOUS NEWS

11 Nov 1895. £6/2/0 was paid for labour altering a dam at Chapel Milton. (GPC)

ENGINEERS FINAL REPORT TO THE DIRECTORS

The final report of the engineers (below) illustrating the way the reports were laid out and the understated and measured manner in which they were presented. The address in Nottingham, which is not usually shown, proves that the report originated from Edward Parry's office for throughout this process he was still the county surveyor for Nottinghamshire.

SALE OF CONTRACTOR'S LOCOMOTIVES

23/24 July 1896. There was a sale by George N. Dixon, auctioneers of Liverpool, a month after Cowburn shaft was completed. I have included all the items listed for sale because it illustrates the range of equipment needed to sink the Cowburn shaft and some other parts of the work which had not been sold off earlier.

LOCOMOTIVES AND OTHER VEHICLES

LNWR built standard gauge 14 in cylinders 4 coupled engine (this was probably *Cocker* although it could have been *St Helens* which was built in 1855)
Kitson built standard gauge 12 in cylinders 4 coupled engine (of which no other information is known)
10 hp standard gauge portable engine and axles
3 ft gauge 10 in cylinders 6 coupled wheels (which would be either *Union Jack* or *Jack Tar*)
3 ft gauge engineers carriage of pitch pine with wrought iron wheels, steel tyres and axles and with a corrugated iron cover
60 3 ft gauge three ton end tip wagons
3 ft gauge excellent vertical engine and winch
3 ton flat lurry (lorry), a dog cart and a timber drag
5 ton travelling gantry 50 ft span

HORSE RELATED ITEMS

A magnificent Brougham horse drawn carriage (would have had a roof, four wheels and an open driver's seat in front and was named after the designer)
A Stanhope phaeton (a light open 4 wheeled horse drawn carriage)
One set of double harness
Stable stencils

MACHINERY

Two air compressor by Fawcett Preston & Co and Kirk & Co
Large Larmuths 'Hirmant' rock drills with tripods and stretcher bars
One 3 in McKean rock drill
5 Elliot's patent hand boring machines
One pulsometer pump No. 5
One Dean's patent sinking pump and two Tangyres universal pumps
Donkey pumps
One large inclined road drum 9 ft diameter, 6 in axle with brake

BUILDINGS

A good number of wood, brick and slated buildings

MISCELLANEOUS

Large iron skip and water tanks
Pithead gearing and several large drums
Large quantity steel wire rope
Brass and iron tubes
Immense quantity of pitch pine, timber batons and firewood. Contents of various stores and workshops

---

28 Park Row. Nottingham.
June 15th 1896.

Engineers report upon the progress of the Works during the month ended June 15th 1896.

Dore & Chinley Railway

To the Chairman & Directors of the Midland Railway Company.

Gentlemen,

We have pleasure in reporting that the Cowburn Shaft is finished, & that the whole of the works on this line are now completed.

As this is our final report we wish to take the opportunity of thanking the Board for the courtesy that has been extended to us during the long period the work has been in progress, & also the officials of the Company for the assistance they have so freely rendered us on every occasion. The work has been a long & arduous one, & it is a source of gratification to us to know that it has been brought to a successful termination. No efforts have been spared on our part to construct the line in a thoroughly sound & substantial manner. We venture to hope we have attained that object, & that the result has met with your approval.

We remain Gentlemen
Your obedient Servants

ADDITIONAL INFORMATION
THE TUNNEL ENTRANCES

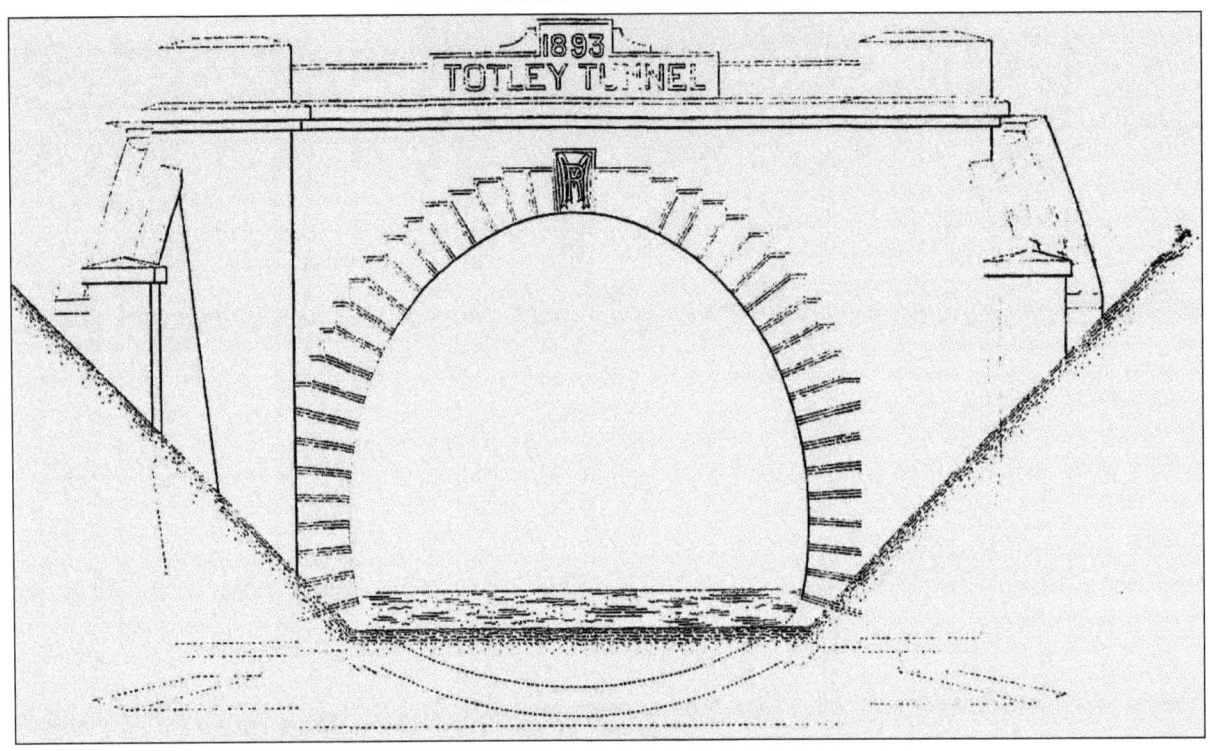

This is the official drawing of the Totley tunnel entrance at the Padley end. *ICE Paper*

A local builder, William Hancock, was awarded the contract for the stone work on one of the portals. Because he was based on the eastern side I have presumed that this is the eastern portal but it could be at the Padley end. Whether he had the contract for both entrances or indeed for all six is not known. Hancock is said to have employed twenty seven men at the time of which seventeen are pictured, including a juvenile and his dog. The dog may have been a ratter. Mr Hancock, the owner, is possibly the man standing in front of the boiler of the steam crane with his hands on his hips, but it has also been suggested he was the man in the middle row with the bowler hat. However in the picture of Cowburn tunnel entrance (see page 139) there is a man who looks similar to the man in front of the boiler. This does not mean that he is William Hancock for he may have been employed to work on the entrance or indeed inside the tunnel. However his presence on both photographs does lend credence to the idea that he may have built all six portals. I am grateful to his grandson, Noel Hancock of Sheephill Farm near Ringinglow, for supplying this splendid image and some information.

Noel Hancock collection

This view of Totley tunnel east entrance was taken when it was brand new. The entrance is horseshoe shaped, 27 ft wide and 22½ ft from rail to crown. It is of coarse masonry with millstone grit arch quoins (cornerstones) and tooled ashlar (large square cut stones), has a cornice and parapet with the name and date of opening above the parapet. The gulleys in the wing parapets are to collect water from above the tunnel and the telegraph pole is at a ninety degree angle because of the limited clearance at the entrance. Note the steps leading up the embankment on the left, these provided the shortest access for the tunnel workers from Hillfoot Road.
Locomotive Publishing Company

This view was taken on 31 Oct 2007 from bridge No. 10 at Grindleford and shows the titling above the parapet. The weeds growing out of the stonework would not have been tolerated in Midland days. The monogram at the crown of the arch is not the usual Midland wyvern. The occasion of the photograph provided the opportunity to sample the delights of the world famous Grindleford café next door with its strictures towards achieving better behaviour by its customers, particularly social workers in charge of unruly children!
Author

The entrance to the east end of Cowburn tunnel in the early 1950s. Note the spoil heap behind the entrance and the 1,800 ft ridge of Colborne behind it. Note also the signal with a sighting board.
David Ibbotson

155

The west end of Cowburn tunnel in the late 1950s. There is no embellishment above the parapet with date or crest at either end. Observe the original Midland distant lower bracket signal which must have been very difficult to spot for the driver emerging from the gloom. *David Ibbotson*

WORKING PRACTICES AT COWBURN SHAFT

These men, unsung in their day and forgotten now, were heroic in every sense of the word. They lived for two years at 1,700 ft in the bleakest conditions and were subject to the wet, wind, fog, snow and frost and everything else that the weather could throw at them at this very exposed location. To escape it they then had the courage to descend increasing depths down a hole to lay gelignite and fire it and then clear the debris. Here we have four men about to descend in a tub that was hardly big enough for all of them, with nothing apparent to light the way down and no safety equipment. The crude surrounding boards would have prevented the wind from blowing the tub about. Note the man on the left hanging onto the iron hand grips which were an aid to keeping the tub steady.
Author's collection

We have seen some hair raising working practices, particularly in the tunnels, but none beat this. The men must have had nerves of steel. John L. Waterhouse's father worked in the tunnel and, in 1962, he related that 'pumping and winding gear for the sinking of the shaft was dragged up the Castleton road from Chapel en le Frith by horse teams. When men were to descend into the shaft the skip was raised till it reached the pulley above. There it was held, until the motion ceased, when it was released and allowed to drop hundreds of feet before the brake was applied by the winder. There were no guide ropes and the above procedure was necessary to prevent an accumulated pendulum effect from generating during its descent that could have had tragic results. When the skip had bottomed it was filled with stone and sent up. No telephones were installed and signalling to the surface was done by hitting the skip or taut rope with an iron bar. The sound was transmitted to the engine house and heard by the winder. When shot firing was to take place below, the skip was slightly raised to make the rope taut, and all the men climbed in except the shot firer, who went round lighting the fuses, often a dozen. He then hastened to the skip and gave the up signal. On one occasion one of the men slipped when his iron shod boots met a smooth object and he accidentally signalled the winder. The shot firer stumbled over the debris below and grasped the skip with his fingers as it began to rise, reaching the surface with shots already exploding below'.

Later, water was struck and collected in the shaft to a depth of 90 ft so a diving bell was brought in to enable the men to drive holes into the tunnel below to drain the water away. The bottom of the shaft opened into a large chamber which was located just to the north of the line. It was described as 'having the feel of a cathedral'.

REMAINS AT COWBURN SHAFT SUMMIT

A 1962 account of the summit described it as the remains of a 'ghost camp'. There were moss covered foundations and traces of the huts where the men worked and slept and had their meals. There were a few strips of weathered concrete, planks of wood, lengths of iron, a drain pipe sticking out of the ground, and a hundred yards away, over a gully, there was part of a bridge across which the men probably hauled their machinery. (When I visited the site in Oct 2010, forty eight years later, I found the iron foundations of the bridge, a few bits of iron and the foundations of a small concrete building next to the shaft, although this may have been a more recent addition. The land where the machinery and accommodation was probably located was on a levelled area of built up spoil and is quite distinct in appearance. Most interest was at the western end of the site where a track passes through a very wet gulley and can be traced down to the Perryfoot to Hayfield bridleway. This was probably the route of the tramway. On the way down I found what may have been the remains of a sleeper although it did not look weathered enough to be authentic. The steepness of the incline would suggest that the wagons would have been rope worked or horse drawn.

Cowburn tunnel's west entrance, after the line was opened. The contractor's buildings for the shaft can be seen on the left. The line to Shaft No. 5 running up the steep incline tops the highest visible point at about 400 ft above the starting point and directly over the course of the tunnel. It appears to be of standard gauge. At the bottom is a fork to the left and, just above, a catch point. Note that two of the buildings are built of stone. One of these is to be seen in a later picture so perhaps they were built with a long term use in mind as a platelayer's store. *Author's collection*

Above: Your author sheltering from the wind. Note it is named 'SHAFT No 2'. *Author*

Above Left: Might this be the route of the tramway running up to the shaft? *Author*

Below Left: A section of lightweight rail, nearly 120 years after the contract was completed, near the shaft. *Author*

The castellated shaft, with my wife Barbara, illustrating the size of the structure. *Author*

Looking through the gated access to the shaft with droplets of water rising into the air creating a mist. The railings are a modern safety installation. All 20 Oct 2010. *Author*

We are possibly looking towards Rushup Edge in this view of the machinery at the summit. A boiler and winding gear is prominent. The deserted scene suggests that it may have been taken after the work was finished but before the site was cleared. Intriguingly there is narrow gauge track in the foreground. Could this have been laid for moving spoil and materials around the site or was it linked to the tramway from the tunnel mouth? The difference of gauge suggests not. *Author's collection*

MACHINERY AND MATERIALS USED

Two drills were typically used at the tunnel heading and were worked by four men. A further eight men were used for filling the debris from the previous round of drilling, fixing timber and laying the road. Later the number of men used increased to twenty as more filling was required at Totley and further drains were put in at Padley. Twenty four hour working with three eight hour shifts was required of the men with one eight hour shift on Sundays. After 1891 two additional Sunday shifts were introduced.

Gelignite was the only explosive used and, as the progress of the headings was of so much importance unlimited supplies were available, resulting in the excessive amount of 163 tons being used. Beyond Shaft No. 4 air compressors were used but impure air was frequently encountered and stopped work. The navvies immediately knew this had happened when the candles, which were the main form of lighting, were extinguished. The sudden experience of total darkness, together with the acute concern of whether it would be possible to breathe must have been very frightening.

PROVISION FOR PLATELAYERS AND SIGNALLING IN TOTLEY TUNNEL

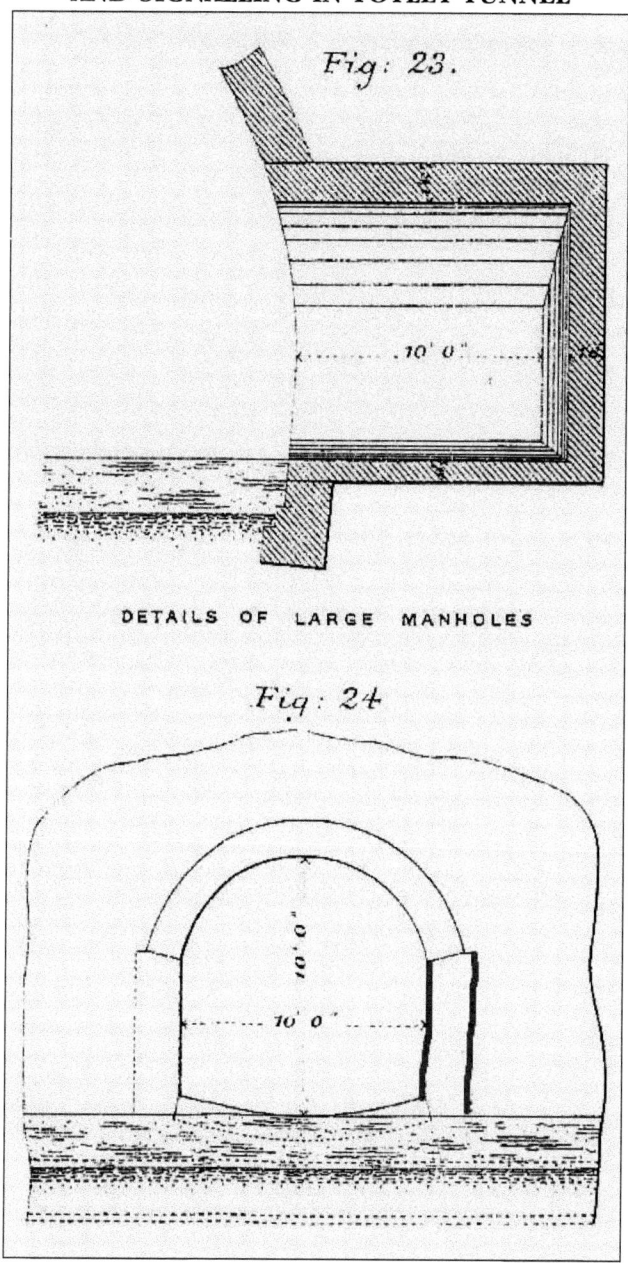

Drawings of the large manholes in Totley tunnel. *ICE Paper*

Manholes 7 ft by 3 ft 6 in by 1 ft 6 in are built every twenty two yards on alternate sides of the tunnel and large manholes 10 ft each way are constructed at every half mile for the use of plate layers. This provision was favourably commented on by one of the Institution's members, he remarking of the difficulties encountered by platelayers in the even longer Severn tunnel where none were provided. Eight platelayers' cabins were provided and three had telephones connected to the adjacent signal boxes with one used as an intermediate signal box. Two signals were provided at the western end, one being attached to a treadle gong to warn a driver of his location in adverse conditions.

SIGNALLING ARRANGEMENTS

A word about Midland signalling practices would be appropriate at this juncture.

The Midland was reluctant to incorporate interlocking, which was a mechanical means of ensuring that when a signal or point lever is moved to admit a train on to a section of line, all other signals and points which might allow conflicting movements are locked. This system also prevented signals from being cleared from the 'on' or danger indication until the points to which they apply were correctly set and facing points locked. There was overwhelming evidence that this prevented accidents. The Board of Trade forced the Midland's hand and required it to incorporate interlocking into its designs. By the 1870s the Midland had produced its own unique system which, with minor adjustments, survived for a hundred years. Each lever was pivoted in a separate casing any number of which could be positioned on a base plate and fastened together with a pair of tie rods. None of the frame's mechanism had to be positioned below the operating room floor and the locking was neatly housed immediately behind the levers and was readily accessible by removing the cast cover plates.

In 1872 the Midland opened its own signal works at Derby and soon became self sufficient in the manufacture and repair of its mechanical signalling equipment. Semaphores began to replace the slotted post signals and in line with Board of Trade requirements, from the mid 1870s became distinguished from stop signals (home and starting) by the V-shaped section cut from the end of the arms. This design remained the standard until the end of the 1880s by which time a new lower quadrant semaphore arm with integral cast spectacle pivoting on the front face of the posts was brought into use. They not only worked well but like all things Midland looked stylish – the posts being topped off with decorative spike finials and were mostly identical to those used on the boxes. After 1893 the Midland was required to adopt green as the all clear night time indication, the previous one having only circular coloured glass – red for danger.

The Midland produced its own successful frames, which were usually made up in multiples of four levers and an early standard was the twelve lever frame, which was built up on a one piece cast iron base plate. The frame was christened a 'tumbler' because the locking was activated by rotating tubes called 'tumblers'. With small modifications the basic design survived into British Railways days.

Standard, all wood, type 1 signal boxes started to appear after 1869 to accommodate block working and interlocking. From 1884 the type 2 was introduced, still all wood, and became generally longer to accommodate the increased sized lever frames which could control more signals and more complex track layouts. These were sub divided into '2a' and '2b' although the difference between them was minimal.

All the boxes on the line were type 2b. To improve visibility for the signalman the windows on the front were enlarged, by the addition of another row of glass panes at the bottom of the sashes making six in all. Four windows were fitted at the front but on the longer boxes there was a gap between each set of four windows. The side windows were smaller with less depth and were of equal size. Every other pane had an angled chamfer at the top which helped to make Midland boxes so distinctive. Three fixed windows were usual on the side and an access door and four on the other side. All could be opened. A walkway was added to the front and sometimes to the sides to facilitate maintenance and window cleaning. Iron support brackets were bolted to the horizontal frame member at floor level and two planks were laid side by side on them. A metal handrail was fitted to the top of the iron uprights which were attached to the end of the brackets. The steps were located to either the right or left of the door and were usually on the side of the box, facing the traffic, although, where room was at a premium access was gained from the rear. On the side, where the steps were located, it was usual for a door on one side and a single window to be located for the under floor locking lever room. On the opposite side two smaller windows were normal. The roofs were hipped and slated with attractive wooden finials at each end. Two or more water buckets were hung on the sides, usually under the steps. The name boards were located at the top of the lower front panel from the opening until the LMS period when they were located beneath the gutter on the backing board at the side. Depending on the location they were sometimes on both ends of the box.

At the time of opening the basic colour would be chrome yellow which was applied to all the planking on the panels between the frames. The framing was picked out in Venetian red, a rich chocolate brown colour, which was also used for the doors, down pipes, guttering and finials. The window frames were white, whilst the box name board would be painted Oxford blue with the edge and letters picked out in white. It was a very eye catching scheme when newly applied, although the yellow is said to have weathered to a 'Cotswold stone' shade quite quickly. This was all done because it was important that the box could be easily seen by train crews. The signal post and finials were painted in banana yellow. The bottom 4 ft of the post was painted Venetian red.

From the opening, the line was worked on the block telegraph system with block posts. All the boxes opened on 29 Oct 1893, unless mentioned otherwise.

The signal boxes from new were; Dore & Totley Station Junction, Dore & Totley South Junction, Dore & Totley West Junction, Totley Tunnel East, Grindleford, Hathersage, Bamford, Hope, Edale, Cowburn Tunnel East, Cowburn Tunnel West, Chinley East Junction, Chinley South Junction and Chinley North Junction.

The Water Works (1902), Norman's Bank (1904), Earle's Sidings (1929), Water Board (1935) boxes were opened later. Details of all these are included in Vol. 2.

REFERENCES

Midland Railway Engineering Notices
Dow George – *Midland Style*. Historical Model Railway Society 1975
Smith Peter – *Midland Railway Signal Boxes*. Midland Record No. 2. Wild Swan Publications 1995
Harris Dave – *Railway Signalling History of the Derby Area. Midland Railway Signal Box Types*. www.derby-signalling.org.uk
Vanns Michael A. – *Traditional Signalling: A Brief Design History*. Ian Allan 2001

CONTRACTOR'S LOCOMOTIVES

It has required an immense amount of detective work to identify which locomotives worked on the two contracts. Contractors commonly brought locomotives with them from previous jobs and then took the engines to their next contract. The locomotives carried out a number of duties as part of their daily routine. For the most part they were seen hauling short trains of freshly excavated earth and rock and returning with ballast, stone and hard core for foundations. Photographs of them are rare, but fortunately several of the locomotives on the Oliver contract moved to the London extension of the MSLR, later the Great Central Railway. Oliver obtained MSLR Contract No. 4 from Rugby to Woodford. S. W. A. Newton extensively photographed the building works, including many of the ninety four locomotives used on the total extension and prints from his glass plates are shown here. Photographs on J. P. Edwards section have proved harder to find.

THOMAS OLIVER'S CONTRACT No. 1

The engineer's monthly reports to the Midland directors indicated the number of engines and horses at work on the building. The numbers far exceed the ten or eleven locomotives known which suggest that the figures included other machinery such as steam navvies, stationary engines and pumping engines. Until shortly after the work started on 12 Feb 1889 Oliver had sixteen engines and eight horses. By the end of the year he had twenty nine engines and fourteen horses. At the end of the following year he had forty engines and eighty horses. In the first half of 1891 these numbers were maintained but in the second half of the year fell despite taking delivery of two locomotives *Gibbon* and *Lenn*, to a low point of twenty six engines on 10 Sep although there was a small increase in the number of horses. In 1892 the number of engines stabilised at an average of twenty nine whilst the number of horses increased dramatically to a peak of 155 in January and then fell away before again reaching 145 by the end of the year. By 1893 the number of engines fell from twenty eight in January to sixteen in November when the work, except shaft five, was nearly complete. After that date the numbers ceased to be reported (see Appendix 1).

STANDARD GAUGE LOCOMOTIVES

FRED: Built Hunslet Engine Co of Leeds 1875, works No. 137, 0-4-0ST, outside cylinders, 2 ft 9 in driving wheels.

After it worked on the Alfreton to Clay Cross widening it moved to the GW/GC Joint line followed by the GWR Swansea District lines when it was sold. It was previously known as *Stanley*.

ANNIE: Built Hunslet 1866, works No. 17. 0-4-0ST, outside cylinders, 2 ft 9 in driving wheels.

Annie had previously worked as the only engine on the Midland's Cudworth to Barnsley line back in 1869 before being reunited with Oliver twenty years later. After working on the GCR line it moved on to work on Oliver's LBSCR Stoats Nest to Eastwood contract and GW/GC Joint line in Buckinghamshire after which nothing further is known.

NELLIE: Built Hunslet 2 Nov 1868, works No. 29, 0-4-0ST, outside cylinders, 2 ft 9 in driving wheels.

Rumour has it that *Nellie* finished up being buried on the site at Totley. This photograph proves it was not true. It was delivered new to J. Clay for the Woodlesford Colliery, near Leeds, where it was named *Waterloo*. It was bought by Oliver in 1879 to join four other Hunslets on the Chichester to Midhurst line of the LBSCR. It was still owned by Oliver in 1898 when it was sold.

Annie at a location between Rugby and Willoughby in 1896. It was the oldest locomotive on Oliver's contract and it shows, the most obvious feature being the absence of a weatherboard. (Drivers of thirty years previously must have thought loco men had gone soft with their comfortable cabs!) The eight navvies who have packed themselves onto the photograph could well have worked the Dore and Chinley line as many moved around with individual contractors. The boy second from the left looks as if he is about fourteen years of age.
S. W. A. Newton, Leicestershire Museums

Nellie is at Rugby on the London extension about 1897. It is very like *Willie* but had outside cylinders and a different cab with square spectacle plates and large dumb buffers.
S. W. A. Newton, Leicestershire Museums

This is the only known photograph of a contractor's locomotive at work on the Dore and Chinley construction. Sources suggest that it is *Nellie* working on the construction of Totley tunnel but the lack of any background makes identifying the location impossible. However, it is of interest because it shows the wooden bodied tipping wagons, the second of which appears to be in the process of being tipped. The rough temporary nature of the track, which had lightweight rails laid on split log sleepers, can be seen. Note the precarious situation over the temporary small bridge. Unsurprisingly derailments were common. *Author's collection*

All three of the above locomotives were transferred from Oliver's contract for the construction of the Barrow Gurney reservoirs for the Bristol Waterworks Co. On completion of the D&C contract they were transferred to Oliver's contract for the Rugby to Woodford and Hinton line of the MSLR.

WILLIE: Built Hunslet 1871, works No. 65, 0-6-0ST, inside cylinders, 3 ft 1 in driving wheels.

Willie was bought new and delivered to Oliver of Stanton Gate, Derby on 26 Sep 1871. It worked for Oliver on the Stantongate quarry branch at Wellingborough in 1874.

On completion of this contract, *Willie* worked on the Midland's Alfreton to Clay Cross widening in 1899 and the GW/GC Joint line at Denham in Buckinghamshire followed by the Finchley to Welsh Harp widening in London. During 1907 to 1915 it worked on the Swansea District lines before finishing at Ridham Dock, Sittingbourne in the First World War. It then left Oliver's service to work at Austin Motors in 1919.

Willie is seen here on the MSLR London extension near Braunston siding at Willoughby in the late 1890s.
S. W. A. Newton, Leicestershire Museums

Frank is seen here on the London extension at Willoughby in Warwickshire about 1897. The chimneys of the early Hunslet locomotives were usually built up from four pieces of wrought iron plate: a chimney base, barrel and top in two parts. This later example has a cast iron top and the same weatherboard and attractive fluted safety valve as *Nellie*.
S. W. A. Newton, Leicestershire Museums

Nene is seen among piles of spoil near Newbold Grounds in Northamptonshire. Although it is ten years newer than *Willie* the design appears to be identical. *Nene* also features in the photographs of the inspection train (see page 169.)
S. W. A. Newton, Leicestershire Museums

FRANK: Built Hunslet 1876, works No. 161, 0-6-0ST, inside cylinders, 3 ft 1 in driving wheels.

Frank was bought new by Oliver as the only engine on his Bennerley to Bulwell and Watnall Colliery branch for the Midland. After working on Oliver's Contract No. 2 it worked on the Midland's Thackley widening near Shipley in 1898 before moving to his GW/GC joint line contract from Neasden to Northolt Junction between 1901 and 1905 after which it was sold.

NENE: Built Hunslet 1881, works No. 242, 0-6-0ST, inside cylinders, 3 ft 1 in driving wheels.

Nene moved on to the Midland's Beighton to Treeton and Alfreton to Clay Cross widenings after its work on the MSLR extension. It also worked on the GWR widening at Lawrence Hill, Bristol and then appears on the GW/GC joint line contract and later on the Cardiff Railway Bute docks lines before finishing its service with Oliver on the Coulsdon to Earlswood, Redhill avoiding line of the LBSCR when it was sold after 1909.

FLORENCE: Built Black Hawthorn Gateshead 1878, works No. 466, 0-6-0ST, outside cylinders.

Florence was transferred from Oliver's contract for the construction of the Barrow Gurney reservoirs for the Bristol Waterworks Co. On completion of the D&C contract it was said to have transferred to Oliver's contract for the widening of the GWR at Lawrence Hill, Bristol. After the MSLR widening it was sold to contractor Walter Scott & Co in 1898.

GIBBON: Built Hunslet 1891, works No. 545, 0-6-0ST, inside cylinders, 3 ft 1 in driving wheels.

In 1898 *Gibbon* was on Oliver's Alfreton to Clay Cross widening for the Midland before moving to the GW/GC joint line near London. It was then on the Cardiff Railway Bute docks lines contract and the Swansea district lines through to 1915. By 1917 it had been sold to W. Alban Richards.

LENN: Built Hunslet 1891, works No. 549, 0-6-0ST, inside cylinders, 3 ft 1 in driving wheels.

It was delivered new ex-works on 20 Oct and with *Gibbon* was the only one bought new for the contract. It moved to the London Extension contract and then the Midland Beighton to Treeton and Alfreton to Clay Cross widenings. It was then on the GW/GC joint line before finishing on the Cardiff Railway Bute docks lines contract. It finished in the ownership of T. Hall & Sons at Llansamlet, near Swansea, about 1918.

SHEFFIELD: Built Hunslet, date and works number not known, 0-6-0ST.

Its history and further ownership is unknown.

Florence is seen at Catesby on the GCR London extension about 1897. This Black Hawthorn example has a more modern appearance with its outside cylinders and attractive covered cab with neat dumb buffers.
S. W. A. Newton, Leicestershire Museums

Gibbon was delivered new ex-works on 26 Jun. On completion of the D&C contract it was transferred to Oliver's works for the line from Rugby to Woodford & Hinton and worked at Catesby tunnel. This view shows that it has a longer six wheel coupled wheelbase, has a more civilized covered cab and is much newer than *Nellie* or *Willie* but is still built to the same basic design of thirty years previous.
S. W. A. Newton, Leicestershire Museums

Veteran *Cowburn* at the North Warwickshire colliery (the NCB's name for Pooley Hall colliery) on 1 Mar 1959. Here it provided over sixty years of continuous service, with its original name intact until it went for scrap seven years later. *Keith Buckle*

In 1963 Brian Stayt, a Sheffield based enthusiast and important contributor to this book, but then a schoolboy in Stratford on Avon, acquired the nameplate from Bird's scrap yard for its scrap value of £10. In the late 1980s he sold it only for it to reappear in Nov 2004 where it fetched £4,200 at auction.
Brian Stayt

3 FT 6 IN NARROW GAUGE LOCOMOTIVES

Oliver had three locomotives for tunnel work which became redundant when the headings were widened and standard gauge engines could be used. On 23 Nov 1892 Oliver advertised in the *Contracts Journal* for a 3 ft 6 ins gauge locomotive. It looks as if he got two.

VIOLET: Built Hunslet 1884, works No. 348, 0-4-0ST.

Violet was bought from Rixson's Iron & Brick Co in 1892. It moved to Oliver's Great Withen's reservoir contract between 1894 and 1899 before being sold to J. H. Hope, Penmon Park in 1904.

IRIS: Built Hunslet 1887, works No. 405, 0-4-0ST.

Iris was also bought from Rixson's and was sold to the Lagos Railway in 1897.

JACK TAR: Built Manning Wardle 1889, works No. 1159, 0-6-0ST, outside cylinders.

Jack Tar was transferred from Edwards' No. 2 contract. It may have run on 3 ft 0 in track rather than being re gauged to 3ft 6in. Its later exotic history is described below.

J. P. EDWARDS CONTRACT No. 2

Thanks to the engineers reports the number of engines and horses used on the contract is known and these show that in 1891 there were, on average, twenty nine engines and ninety horses. In 1892 on average eighteen engines and forty eight horses were used. Interestingly the number of horses dropped during the harvest season. In 1893, with the tunnelling and large viaduct complete, the number of engines and horses declined, averaging twelve and sixteen respectively (see Appendix 1).

STANDARD GAUGE LOCOMOTIVES

(UNNAMED): Built St Helens 1855, 0-4-0ST.

It was LNWR engine No. 1979 by 1871 but was for sale in 1889.

DEWSBURY: Built Hunslet 1878, works No. 196, 0-6-0ST, inside cylinders.

It was delivered new to Baker & Firbank for the Dewsbury to Batley line of the GNR where it worked from 1877 to 1880. It was then probably transferred to their Ruskington to Lincoln contract of the GNR/GER joint line between 1880 and 1883. It then went possibly to Scott & Edwards on the Soho, Handsworth & Perry Barr Junction Railway of 1885 to 1888. In Sep 1887 it was up for sale but was seemingly withdrawn and transferred to the D&C contract. About 1893 it was sold to John H. Gartside & Co Ltd at Stalybridge. It was last heard of at Bennerley ironworks before 1908.

COWBURN: Built Hunslet Engine Co 1891, works No. 544, 0-4-0ST, outside cylinders, driving wheels 3 ft 1 in.

Cowburn was delivered new to Edwards. When the D&C contract finished it was sold in 1896 from Chapel en le Frith to Pooley Hall colliery, Polesworth. It remained there and was taken over by the NCB in 1947. It was sent to Bird's Commercial Motors Ltd at Birmingham Road, Stratford on Avon by 1963 but was then transferred to the company's yard at Long Marston, Worcestershire where it was cut up after Jan 1966.

COCKER: Built William & Albert Kitching of Darlington 1846, works No. 15, 0-4-2ST, inside cylinders, driving wheels 4 ft 9 in.

Nearly all Kitching locomotives were built for the Stockton & Darlington Railway but this was one of a handful built for other customers. Supplied to the Cockermouth & Workington Railway it was immediately loaned to the contractor J. & W. Ritson during the completion and ballasting of the line. It was rebuilt in early 1857 as an 0-4-0 with a lengthened coupled wheelbase, lengthened firebox and enlarged cylinders. It was derailed on 31 Mar of that year when hauling a 'special' of eleven carriages and a van and carrying about 300 passengers. It 'split the road' just beyond the Salmon Hill viaducts near Workington, rolled over the right hand bank and came to rest facing the wrong way. The fireman was injured and the company secretary, John Mayson, was severely injured but passengers in the carriages appear to have escaped. The Board of Trade inspector was scathing about the design of the engine, the condition of the viaduct involved and the permanent way. It was promptly rebuilt again as an 0-4-2. More misfortune followed when it broke its crank axle in 1858. It was again rebuilt by the LNWR at Crewe in Mar 1866 with new lengthened inside frames, enlarged cylinders and a new boiler. In December of the same year it was taken into the LNWR capital list and allotted LNWR No. 1550 in 1866, which it did not carry, and

Union Jack reincarnated as *Kettering Furnaces No. 6* outside one of the two sheds at Kettering Furnaces at an unknown date.
J. T. Clewley. Transport Treasury

Here is a copy of an original postcard showing the blondin, which was erected to span 870 ft of the Zambesi River and land on either side. The cable weighed five tons and consisted of nineteen steel wires surrounding a hemp core, with a circumference of 8½ in and a breaking strain of 270 tons. It had to be flung across the gorge by means of a rocket carrying a light cord. The cord was then used to haul a wire across attached in turn to a light rope. A traveller or carrier carrying the end of the main cable was then rigged on the rope and hauled across the gorge by a second rope and a winch. On the opposite bank the cable was attached to the top of a pair of sheer legs, 80 ft long, hinged to massive foundation plates embedded in concrete. The sheer legs were arranged to lean away from the gorge at an angle of 45° and from the top of this enormous jib was suspended a counterweight of 60 tons. The blondin was operated electrically, carrying its own driver and power lines from a generating station on the cliff top. Despite many difficulties the cable and conveyor lasted just for the duration of the job. All the material for the northern half of the bridge and beyond was duly carried along the cable in loads of ten tons and included many miles of rails, thousands of sleepers, quantities of stores, contractor's locomotive, wagons and the workmen, some 15,000 tons in all. It was said that when the atmosphere was highly charged with electricity the conveyor would sometimes be enveloped, high over the gorge, in a blaze of lightning.
Geoff Cooke collection

then No. 1577 in Apr 1867, No. 1259 in the duplicate list in Jul 1867 and No. 1821 in Nov 1871. It was sold in Mar 1874 to Joseph Firbanks where it probably initially worked at Camden. It was resold to Edwards and was rebuilt for him at Crewe in Jan 1886. The tender was removed and a saddle tank substituted but it remained as an 0-4-2 with inside cylinders. It was hired to Henry Jackson for the Brighton and Dyke railway contract during 1886 and 1887 and was in the LBSCR Brighton works in Mar and Apr 1887 for repairs and the fitting of a wooden cab and windows to the contractor's instructions. It moved with Edwards to the Nottingham Suburban Railway. In June 1889 it was overhauled and was listed for auction at a sale in Nottingham on 26 Feb 1890 but must have been withdrawn as it was transferred to Contract No. 2. On 23 and 24 Jul 1896 George N. Dixon, auctioneers, had locomotives and plant for sale at Chapel en le Frith including a '14 in four-wheeled coupled LNWR built locomotive'. This remarkable locomotive, which had more facelifts than an ageing American actor, appears in the photograph depicting the director's inspection special near Norman's Bank (see page 170).

3 FT 0 IN NARROW GAUGE LOCOMOTIVES

LIZZIE: Built Manning Wardle 1887, works No. 1038, Class E 0-4-0ST, outside cylinders, driving wheels 2 ft 6 in.

Lizzie was delivered new to Edwards for the Nottingham Suburban Railway contract on 19 Aug 1888 although it may have been stored while awaiting transfer to Contract No. 2 which probably took place by the end of Nov 1889. It was sold to H. M. Nowell, contractor, after which it had various further owners, the last being Stanton ironworks at their Nuthall sand pits site near Kimberley, Nottingham where it was named *Stanton No. 9*. It was rebuilt by the Stanton Co at Holwell ironworks in 1931. It went for scrap to T. W. Ward in May 1949.

JACK TAR: Built Manning Wardle 1889, works No. 1159, 0-6-0ST, outside cylinders, driving wheels 2 ft 9 in.

This locomotive was ex-works on 14 Nov and delivered new to this contract. It was transferred to Thomas Oliver on the No. 1 contract although it was the wrong gauge. It was returned to Edwards when either this engine or *Union Jack* was sold at auction on 23 or 24 Jul 1896 to an unknown buyer, although one of them might have been sold following adverts in the *Contracts Journal* of 31 Oct and 21 Nov 1894. However it was sold to Paulings & Co Ltd, a contractor, for £1,372 and was said to have been re-gauged to 3 ft 6 in by an unknown workshop but not the manufacturer in 1899 and sent to Rhodesia to work on their Beira to Umptali railway contract, before being sold to the Marshonaland Railway in 1901. Around 1904 and 1905 it worked on ballast trains on both sides of the bridge at the Victoria Falls. So that it could work on the other side of the bridge it was dismantled and carried across the falls by a blondin cable.

When *Jack Tar* was moved across the Zambesi Gorge it was dismantled. The frames, which weighed twelve tons, were the heaviest single load to cross on the blondin and much anxiety was experienced as the cable sagged to an extent that prevented the truck from climbing up the cable and extra counterweights had to be added to the cable end. This is said to be that anxious moment. Impressive as Chapel Milton viaducts are they fade into insignificance when set alongside this fantastic example of the imperial ambitions of Britain in Africa exemplified by Cecil Rhodes unfulfilled Cairo to Cape railway of which this was a spectacular part.
Geoff Cooke collection

This is taken from a postcard showing *Jack Tar* pulling the first train across the Victoria Falls bridge on 12 Sep 1905. It is amazing that a humble contractor's engine on our railway could achieve such fame.

Geoff Cooke collection

Jack Tar numbered as *Mashonaland No. 7* prior to rebuilding in 1935. It is shown here with a long boiler which is its distinguishing feature. It has outside cylinders and a fluted safety valve. *Geoff Cooke collection*

It then worked at Beira docks until 1929 when it was moved to the Bulawayo workshops where it was re-boilered and given an enclosed cab in 1935. From 1942 it was at the Umtali workshops and then stored.

Jack Tar was officially preserved from 1972 and is seen in the newly opened Bulawayo Museum. *Geoff Cooke collection*

EDALE: Built Manning Wardle 1889, works No. 1110, Class E 0-4-0ST, outside cylinders, driving wheels 2 ft 6 in.

Again this came new to Edwards for the Nottingham Suburban Railway contract and transferred to this contract at an unknown date. It was sold to John M. Gartside Co Ltd at Stalybridge along with standard gauge *Dewsbury* and it then went to the Heywood & Middleton Water Board on the Naden higher reservoir contract, still named *Edale*. In 1913 it was bought by J. C. Staton & Co Ltd for the Scropton Tramway, Tutbury via R. Hudson of Leeds, where it was unnamed. It was sold for scrap about 1948.

UNION JACK: Built Manning Wardle 1889, works No. 1123, 0-6-0ST, outside cylinders, driving wheels 2 ft 9 in.

Union Jack was ordered by Edwards on 9 Jan 1889 and despatched by the manufacturer on 8 May 1889 to the Nottingham Suburban Railway. This railway opened on 2 Dec 1889 and so it could have only been useful in laying the permanent way etc. by this time. It was transferred to Chapel en le Frith on 15 Nov 1889. Either this engine or *Jack Tar* was sold at auction on 23 or 24 Jul 1896 to an unknown buyer although it was bought by Kettering Iron & Coal Co Ltd at this or a later date. It was still named *Union Jack* in 1934 but was later renamed *Kettering Furnaces No. 6*. It was rebuilt in 1949 and scrapped in Apr 1963 after the furnaces closed.

(UNNAMED): Built Andrew Barclay but building date and works number are not recorded. However, it was probably delivered new on 21 Nov 1894. It was for sale along with *Jack Tar* and *Union Jack* on 23 Jul 1896 but by 5 Dec 1896 only this engine was being advertised.

REFERENCES

Cole D. and Smith F. D. – *Contractors Locomotives: Part VI*. Union Publications 1981

Bendall Ian – *Industrial Locomotives of Nottinghamshire*. Industrial Railway Society 1999

Cossons N. – *Contractors' Locomotives GCR* Leicester Museums 1963

A Contractor's locomotives list. Industrial Locomotive Society

Bowtell Harold D. – *Rails through Lakeland*. Silver Link Publishing 1989 (*Cocker*)

Baxter Bertram and David – *British Locomotive Catalogue 1825-1923 Part 2A: LNWR*. Moorland Publishing 1978. (*Cocker*)

Hamer – *Locomotives of Zimbabwe*. (*Jack Tar*)

www.geoffs-trains.com (*Jack Tar*)

West Roger – Unpublished research paper (*Union Jack*)

THE TRANSPORT OF EQUIPMENT AND MATERIALS

For the commencement of work at Padley a standard gauge road, with three cubic yard end tip wagons, was employed to remove the debris from the face. At Totley the size of the wagons was limited by the winding cages in the pit and a double road of 2 ft gauge was laid down. Here side tip wagons were used holding three quarters of a yard and the trains of wagons were drawn by ponies. The break of gauge to the standard gauge at the tunnel entrance was a handicap. The narrow gauge was eventually abandoned in favour of standard gauge because it was impossible to remove the spoil fast enough, there being too many interruptions switching between gauges.

For the lining work the contractor was fortunate in having the Totley Moor Brick Works close at hand, where very good common bricks were obtained. The brickyard was about half a mile from No. 4 shaft and at a slightly higher elevation. A light tramway was laid down and the bricks, after being examined, passed and counted, were lowered down the shaft to the workings below. From Oct 1889 the tramway was extended to shafts No. 2 and No. 3 (see page 115). The brindled bricks were forwarded from Staffordshire to Dore and Totley station. Until the headings met all the bricks for the lining at Padley had to be carted, or sent by traction engine, from Totley. As the lining of the tunnel proceeded locomotives were taken further in and employed for haulage, although horses continued to be used in the headings.

THE COST OF THE TOTAL UNDERTAKING

On 12 May 1894 the engineers reported on the final accounts for the two contracts, excluding the station buildings and the shafts. On Contract No. 1, Oliver claimed £724,806 against payments made of £653,407, a difference of £71,399. The engineers had disallowed this amount. The largest amount within this difference was £59,304 for the tunnel mining. Oliver was claiming £45/10/- per yard against the schedule price of £18/10/-, he already having been allowed £40 per yard for a portion of the work. These claims were referred to the board. Smaller amounts totalling £8,632 were for the carting of materials to Padley, before the junction of the headings, the charges by the road authorities for extraordinary traffic, an allowance for lining the tunnel with blue bricks and the amount paid to the company for the siding at Dore Junction.

On Contract No. 2, Edwards claimed £507,491 against payments of £461,799, a difference of £45,692. He wanted an additional price of £4,158 at £3/10/- per cubic yard on 1,188 yards of heading in shale, this being the price he was paid for the portion through rock. Also, Edwards claimed an additional payment of £12,797 at £16/15/0 per yard on 764 yards of tunnel mining in shale, this being the price paid for the portion through rock. He also wanted a further £23,507, a 12½% increase on all the prices for outside work.

Oliver was paid £24,329 for Shaft No. 5 but a claim for an additional payment of £1,850 was refused. The Midland, who had taken over the works following Edwards' financial difficulties, incurred a cost of £17,500 for the Cowburn Shaft No. 2. Edwards was paid £27,950 for Chinley South Curve which included Chapel Milton viaduct. Walker & Slater were paid £15,123 for the stations and cottages, The preparations of the land for the stations and yards and the lie by sidings was £46,000, the permanent way £73,000 and other sundry materials £63,856. Signalling and telegraphs added £25,000.

To summarise:

Purchase of land	£108,045
Contract No. 1 (Oliver)	£653,407
Contract No. 2 (Edwards)	£461,799
Totley shaft (Oliver)	£24,329
Cowburn shaft (MR)	£17,500
Chinley South Curve (Edwards)	£27,950
Stations & cottages (Walker & Slater)	£15,123
Preparations for stations & lie bys	£46,000
Sundry materials	£63,856
Permanent way	£73,000
Signalling and telegraphs	£25,000
Labour*	£18,165
Total	£1,534,174 (£1.7 billion today)

*This included the cost to the Midland of Edwards' workforce after they had taken over his contract.

Considered against the original costing of £1,050,000 this was a significant over spend. It is interesting to put the cost of the line in the context of the Midland's wider finances. In 1893 overall revenue was approximately £8,600,000 against expenses of about £4,800,000 leaving an overall operating profit of about £3,800,000 (£4.2 billion today). The building costs were, of course, spread over an eight year period.

INSPECTIONS OF THE LINE

Inspections of the line happened at various levels. The Board of Trade inspections were the most important because without their approval the line could not open. H. J. Bell seems to have been the resident inspector and with his team was regularly out on the line. This was in preparation for the more formal visits of the head of the inspectorate, Major F. A. Marindin, who incidentally was still inspecting changes on the line ten years later. Apart from minor comments he was always satisfied with the work and particularly commented on the high quality of the masonry.

John Noble, the general manager of the Midland, would have been a frequent visitor as well and was most likely the official who met both Oliver and Edwards to discuss particular difficulties. The best known visit was what is always described as the directors' inspection train because it had the Midland official photographer on board and there are three known photographs included here. Unfortunately, he was unlike S. W. A. Newton, who profusely photographed the works on the GCR London extension only a few years later. Illustrations of the line are few or have not survived. The passengers dress suggests that they are men of stature and status and yet I have a doubt whether these photographs are of the directors as we shall see.

All previous published references to the director's visit give the date as 10 Aug 1893 which is problematic. The engineers August report stated that on Contract No. 1

This is the best known image of the so called directors' visit at the Totley tunnel east entrance. The locomotive is Oliver's Hunslet built 0-6-0 saddle tank *Nene*, which was twelve years old at this time. Everything appears to be complete including the permanent way (see page 162).
Author's collection

the lining of Totley tunnel was finished on 4 Aug and 'the permanent way is being laid and partly ballasted throughout the line' and on Contract No. 2 'the permanent way is making good progress' which suggests that it is not completed and therefore not ready for 10 Aug.

On 14 Sep they report 'the permanent way is expected to be laid throughout Totley tunnel by the end of this week. Mr McDonald has been sending in a large quantity of ballast for the tunnel and for the boxing up of the road, which has not yet been delivered. The double line of permanent way is being all laid and partly ballasted with the exception of two or three very short lengths which the contractor has had to defer until the last moment for his own temporary purposes'. On Contract No. 2 'the laying of the permanent way is practically completed and there only remains to be done a small amount of excavation, some ballasting and soiling and trimming of slopes'. Although everything is nearly ready, was it sufficiently finished to allow an inspection train to go through?

On 29 Sep the *Sheffield Independent* reporting on the plans to open the line said that it was originally planned to open the line for goods traffic on 1 Sep but 'unforeseen difficulties arose'... 'Other obstacles have since been encountered and overcome, and there now remains only about a week's work to render the track safe and complete'. They understood the first goods train would be run on 15 Oct and by 1 Nov through and ordinary goods trains would be running (the actual date was 6 Nov). 'At the present time the track contains several incomplete lengths and the connection with the main line at Dore has not been made. A gang of men are, however, at work on the latter task, and not much remains to be done.' This suggests that the 30 Sep train could be run. The photograph on Contract No. 2 shows the ballasting to be complete. The tunnel entrance image suggests the ballasting is adequate but not complete and the one with the house in the background suggests the line is probably the rough contractor's line and much work needs to be done. This confirms that the train was run before all the track and ballasting work was complete.

On 12 Oct the engineers report on Contract No. 1 states 'very little needs to be done excepting a quantity of ballasting... The double line is laid and sufficiently ballasted to admit of goods trains being run at any time... The remainder of the ballast will be put down by Mr McDonald

The track appears to be only temporary and is at an unknown location. Two of the wagons have the initials 'TO' for Thomas Oliver the contractor. Seats have been specially made for the occasion. The engine is garlanded round the boiler and bunker and the letters 'DC' in flowers has been added to designate 'Dore Chinley', the two extremities of the line.
Author's collection

after the line is opened for goods traffic'. On Contract No. 2 'every effort is being made to get the ballasting finished'. This tells us that an inspection would not be a problem.

The newspapers do not report an inspection on 10 Aug but do on 30 Sep and 16 Oct. None of the reports specifically say they were directors' visits.

The 30 Sep visit is described in the *Derbyshire Times* as 'a company of gentlemen embarked in a primitive train, the greatest feature of which was its uncompromising ventilation'. The *Sheffield Independent* reported 'through the kindness of the contractors, a small party including Inspector Wilson, Midland Railway Company; Mr A. S. Jarvis, goods manager Midland Railway; Mr Walker, Wharncliffe Silkstone Colliery Co Ltd; Mr W. B. Burdekin, W. Jessop and Sons Ltd; Mr Baguley, Charles Cammell and Co Ltd and representatives of the Sheffield press visited and inspected the workings. A special train consisting of an engine and a couple of open trucks was arranged to convey the party from Dore'. The purpose seems to have been three fold; for the Midland men to inspect the works and the suitability for goods traffic to start; important customers and users of the line and the press to see the completed railway.

The 16 Oct inspection was described by the *Derbyshire Courier* as 'a number of officials and heads of department on the Midland system travelled over the new Dore and Chinley line to make a formal inspection before the opening for goods traffic. They left Chinley about 11.00 in two saloon carriages and proceeded along the line to Dore, carefully inspecting the work on the way. The return journey was made by way of Chinley'. The *Sheffield Independent* described the occasion as 'a number of chief officers and heads of departments on the Midland system travelled over the line to make a formal inspection before the opening of the line to goods traffic. They repeat the information about the journey arrangements. The *Derby Mercury* only said that there was 'an official tour of inspection over the line'.

If the newspaper reports are accurate then the photographs are not depicting the 16 Oct inspection as the men were travelling in 'two saloon carriages'. However, the train ran from Chinley to Dore and back which would allow the location and direction of the train in the photographs to be in either direction. The train could not have run on the two different dates because the men on the wagons are the same in each picture.

This, then, suggests that the pictures depict the 30 Sep train. However this proposition has its problems. The *Sheffield Independent* described the train as being an engine and a 'couple of trucks' which is not quite right as there were three wagons. Much more significant is the fact that the train is described as starting at Dore and terminating at Bamford, a hundred yards before Mytham Bridge. (The *Derbyshire Times* used the *Sheffield Independent* as its source so the story cannot be corroborated). The return journey from Bamford to Dore is described as taking about half an hour, including ten minutes to pass through the tunnel. This does not hold up as the image at the water point is on Contract No. 2 and the contractor's locomotive was one of Edwards' engines. It more easily fits with the 16 Oct trip which went from Chinley to Dore and back!

So what can we conclude? There are two major conflicts of information between the two trains, one regarding the nature of the train and the other the route. My hunch is that the correct date is 16 Oct 1893.

Five months later, on 21 and 22 Mar 1894, the Midland directors did inspect the line again travelling from Derby to Manchester via the Peak line and then returned to Chinley and then travelled over the line to Sheffield, before returning to Derby. Sadly, the Midland's minutes recording the event have been lost.

The train is now on Edwards' contract. The location is always described as being between Edale and Cowburn tunnel. However I have acquired an original print which was too faded to use and a later reprint is shown here. Both show a road behind the fence but the original shows a hill rising steeply to the left. That suggests the location is at Norman's Bank, between Hope and Edale, where the road runs parallel to the line with Jaggers Clough rising to Crookestone Hill behind, which means the train is travelling towards Hope from Edale at somewhere around where Normans Bank signal box would be erected later (c162862). The most noticeable difference from the two previous images is the change of engine to Edwards' *Cocker*, the locomotive with the colourful antecedents. It is ironic that the passengers are being pulled by what was a LNWR engine before it became a contractor's locomotive. The train has stopped to take water at a temporary watering point.
Jim Story collection

THE NAVVIES

THE PROBLEMS OF RECRUITMENT

Recruitment of labour was a constant problem for both contractors. They had competition for labour with other projects that were underway at the same period. At the eastern end a start was made on building the Chesterfield to Warsop section of the LDECR in Jun 1892 and included some heavy engineering features, the heaviest being the one mile 864 yard Bolsover tunnel. However, at this time Oliver's workforce had reached healthy proportions and did not decrease in the subsequent months. At the western end a much more substantial work was beginning, namely the Manchester Ship Canal. It was commenced in Nov 1887 and opened on 1 Jan 1894 so was in direct competition for labour. On average it employed 12,000 men, reaching a maximum of 17,000. Nevertheless there is no record that this competition was the cause of Edward's less problematic recruitment difficulties.

One of the reasons for the difficulties was that the contracts were unusual in that a high proportion of men were needed for the tunnels. It was considered to be a specialist job and when the exceptional water ingress problems were added at both ends of Totley tunnel it was seen as a difficult, dangerous and unhealthy occupation. It is interesting that Edwards, despite not having large centres of population nearby, was more successful in attracting men in the earlier years, probably because his tunnel was mostly dry. It was not until increased wages were offered to the men working at Totley that Oliver's recruitment problems eased, although this had the effect of drawing men away from Cowburn. Despite there being a trade recession nationally, which caused much hardship in the Sheffield area for example, recruitment of workers was still a problem. In May 1889 eighty men employed by Mr Hughes, a subcontractor, building a section of the cutting from Dore to the tunnel, demanded a four penny rise on the 3/2d daily wage (equivalent to £11 a day or £66 for a six day week in today's money. On the Manchester Ship Canal the workers were being paid 4/6d for a ten hour day.) When this was refused they walked out. Several fresh hands who had been seeking work in the neighbourhood were taken on but Hughes, thinking he could easily recruit the rest of the men he needed, advertised for replacements yet a week later was still advertising. Nationally there was a bitter dispute between the coal miners and the coal owners in 1893 over pay and conditions which caused terrible hardships for the miners and their families – they had no other form of income. A headline in a Sheffield newspaper of the time read '2,000 children dying of starvation at Attercliffe'. It recorded how the better off in Sheffield were organising soup kitchens and other aid. Yet he still could not find enough men.

Another challenge that confronted the contractors was that many local men left to get the hay in and, later, the harvest as it meant severe hardship if this was not done. (The harvest festival thanksgiving service at the local church or chapel had real meaning then.) Interestingly the works always came to a standstill for holidays such as Easter, Whitsuntide and Christmas.

During late 1892 and early 1893, an outbreak of smallpox caused some of the more itinerant men to leave for less risky locations.

It is interesting that the number of men on Oliver's contract during the latter half of 1892 improved significantly and that this coincided with drier working conditions in the tunnel.

THE EFFECT ON LOCAL COMMUNITIES

Whilst some of the workforce was recruited locally and some came from the immediate surrounding areas a high proportion were itinerant workers who followed construction works around the country. Many had previously worked for the contractors in other places but there is no evidence that Irish navvies were present in any large numbers. The arrival of this influx of more than three thousand men at its peak, and in some cases their families, into mainly rural locations was an experience the local populations were quite unprepared for. In the Hope and Edale valleys the populations had lived in considerable isolation for centuries but on the peripheries at Chapel en le Frith, Chinley and Totley there was previous experience of railway building some thirty years earlier.

The navvies arrival presented both opportunity and risk. The opportunities were for enhanced trade by providing accommodation and for retail outlets, drinking houses and other services to meet the needs of the newcomers. The risks were a breakdown of law and order and the threat to public health from an influx of large numbers of labourers and their dependants, housed in temporary accommodation with inadequate facilities in rural areas with limited law enforcement and health services. The response of the host communities varied from reacting adversely to the risks or relishing the new opportunities.

Most of the accommodation was required at the end of the tunnels ie at Totley, Padley, Edale, Chinley, Chapel Milton and Chapel en le Frith. J. P. Edwards set up his base in the Town Hall at Chapel (although he found accommodation for himself at Chinley) which had an impact on the community with nearly 700 men taking up residence in the town. There was an overflow to places like Dronfield for the Totley end of the tunnel and Stoney Middleton, Bradwell and Hathersage which absorbed some of the men working at the Padley end – these were larger places than either Padley or Grindleford Bridge. Bradwell and Castleton also supplied men for the Edale area.

At Totley, a community of 650, had to cope with an influx of over 700 navvies and their families, while a further 100 lived at Dore. At Edale the population rose from 335 to 955 by 1891, although when dependants were added the number was well over a thousand incomers. By 1901 the population had subsided back to 336. Whilst at Chapel two thirds of the incomers were under forty there was a tendency in this late period of railway building for the workforce to have an older profile because, by this time, railway construction had lost its attraction for young men. There was a growth in the number of navvies who worked with some degree of permanence and grew old in the trade.

The oldest man employed at the Edale end was a seventy two year old labourer and the youngest a twelve year old who worked with his father. Around 20% were craftsmen which included stonemasons, brick makers, bricklayers and engine drivers. These tended to be stable people who were loyal to the contractor and presented few difficulties. It was the unskilled itinerant labourers who had no loyalty and were here today and gone tomorrow who could be a problem.

ACCOMMODATION

As we have seen, a constant difficulty for the contractors was their inability to attract sufficient men to work on the line. Men recruited locally would go home at night but many had to walk long distances. A man who lived at Abbeydale walked nine miles every day to Padley.

For the itinerant workers accommodation was required and the inability of local communities to house so many incomers meant that the contractors needed to provide. The works started in Sep 1888, although preparatory work was going on before this and as early as Oct 1888, many navvies were seeking cottages in the Chapel and Chinley areas. It was not until December that Edwards started erecting huts at Edale and the following month it was reported that there was a shortage of accommodation and that more substantial dwellings were required. Oliver seems to have given little thought to the issue and it was not until Feb 1889 that he got moving, it being reported that a number of huts had been erected at Totley Bents, near No. 2 shaft. These huts were for the workforce sinking the shafts and digging the cutting to the eastern end of the tunnel and also for the tunnellers themselves. Some of the huts that were completed were occupied and a provision store had opened. However, at Shaft No. 4, a start had been made but none of the huts were ready for occupation. Another 400 men were expected in the following four weeks. Huts were eventually built at the side of Moss Road, about half a mile from the shaft. What was called a workmen's house was also built alongside the contractor's yard at Dore and Totley station.

Because of the acute difficulty in attracting men to work at Padley in Nov 1890 Oliver increased the accommodation and significantly improved the living conditions. For the tunnelling at the Padley end, and for the line from there to Hope, Oliver built twenty five huts at Hathersage in 1891 where 104 workmen and nine dependants were counted in the census of that year, which suggests that the census had not 'captured' all the men in the huts. Around eighty or so found accommodation at inns and lodging houses in the village and surrounding hamlets. By Mar 1889 Edwards was still building wooden houses in Edale. By July the cabins and huts used on the Nottingham Suburban Railway were moved to Chapel but it is not known whether any were for accommodation. As late as Dec 1889 it was reported that Edwards was still erecting temporary accommodation in Edale and some navvies were still walking long distances to reach the works. The final number of huts on Oliver's contract was fifty eight, all of which were made of wood except eleven which had brick walls. By Oct 1893 only seven or eight of these huts had not been infected by smallpox and all of them were pulled down and burned.

At Stoney Middleton a lodging house was licensed for thirty five workers and it was reported that the beds were in use for twenty four hours with day and night workers occupying the same bed. An inspector of public health, six months later, expressed his disgust that liquid from a pig sty was soaking into ground adjacent to the lodging house, with a 'nasty, filthy urinal' discharging into the open ground.

A newspaper sketch of one of the navvy huts at Padley. The outside midden would have been a breeding place for disease.

The 1891 census found that those who could find no accommodation were in the brickyard at Totley where

'Bricky Row' at Totley Rise in earlier years. Seen here before the modern deviation made the original Baslow Road into a lay by with parking spaces for the shops that now front the buildings. It was initially thought they were built for the navvies but it is now known that was not the case although some navvies would have lodged in them.
Picture Sheffield. Sheffield Libraries

two were found, while one was sleeping in a barn and another was sleeping by the roadside. Many more would have eluded the enumerators. The *Grouse Inn* at Totley, which was part farm and part drinking house, was described as 'a doss house for navvies'. At 'Bricky Row', it was reported that 'ill smelling slops and sewage was flowing into a sluggish stream from the back doors. Some of the dwellings were in a state of filthiness which cannot be described in a newspaper'. Another report observed that in one house at Totley, consisting of two bedrooms, an attic and two downstairs rooms, forty one navvies lodged with the landlord, his wife and family and in another house of the same character, nineteen adults and eight dogs were found.

The 1891 census shows 600 navvies were living in the Edale valley. Of these 147 men and 111 dependants lived in an encampment of twenty nine huts near the tunnel entrance. Another sixty or so workers lived in Hope, Castleton and other villages on the line of the railway. Those who could find no place in lodgings or the huts were discovered in places such as the brickyard at Edale, where forty eight were found and not recorded. In Edale William Alderman headed a household at Nether Meadow which comprised his wife, two children and thirteen lodgers. In a hut headed by Robert Whitfield, an overlooker lived his wife, two young children, thirteen boarders and seventeen others described as 'casual' not 'regular'. More typically Emily Mosley, a widow, her baby son, a girl cousin from Cumberland, age 9 years, and three male boarders lived together. Her husband had been killed in an explosion in the tunnel in Jan 1891 (his name was given as Mosby, see page 177). Although this was an extreme case it was not uncommon for five to eight lodgers to be with one family. At Padley, Robert Astill a foreman, had a family of six and gave room for nine boarders.

HEALTH

The lack of sanitation in the accommodations was a continuing concern. In Aug 1889 there was an outbreak of typhoid amongst the railway workers at Chinley and bad cases of overcrowding in some houses were reported. In one home there were thirteen people, including five who were sleeping in the same room as typhoid victims. Several fatal cases were reported that summer.

However it was not all bad news. In 1889, following an outbreak of enteric (intestinal) fever in cottages at Chapel Milton, the Chapel Rural Sanitary Authority (RSA) took action to reduce overcrowding by serving notices to reduce the number of lodgers. In Nov 1889 the inspector of nuisances for the Chapel RSA reported that the huts (probably at Chinley) were substantially built, dry, well ventilated and had a reasonable amount of accommodation.

SMALLPOX

Smallpox first occurred at Totley in 1888, just as the work was getting under way but did not originate from the workers. The pavilion of the Victoria Gardens Pleasure Ground was converted into a smallpox convalescent hospital.

However, it was the 1892/1893 outbreak that most affected the navvies.

It was present in areas away from the railway, there being for instance, 541 cases in the wider Chesterfield area and 121 in Bakewell during 1893. Smallpox became a serious problem at all the main railway building sites and at Totley there were 222 reported cases but only nineteen cases in the Edale valley.

The first outbreak among the navvies was in Nov 1892 in a house at Green Oak, Totley, when five cases were identified. Dr Aldred, the local doctor, reported that the disease had been contracted at a lodging house in Dronfield and 'evidently followed the line of march of the navvies to and from the great centres of their employment'. The following month three more cases were reported to the authority, two of which were imported from Chesterfield and Wigan. The number of cases increased steadily over the next four months, with fifteen cases reported in Jan 1893 rising to eighty, with nine deaths in April. By May numbers had fallen to forty and the last reported cases were in Jul 1893.

The disregard for hygiene is highlighted by a case in Apr 1893 at Eckington Magistrates court where Maria West, a married woman, was summoned for 'wilfully exposing without disinfection certain clothing which had been exposed to smallpox at Totley'. It was said that the woman had a lodger with smallpox at her lodging house and had thrown his infected clothing into the lane. It was then taken back to the house but again she threw it out. She was fined £2 plus 25/- costs with a month in prison in default of payment.

Of the forty navvy houses at Green Oak (probably on Lemont Road), only one was free from smallpox. At Totley an isolation hospital was built at Oliver's expense at the later rifle range, about two hundred yards from the navvy camp at Shaft No. 4. The Midland agreed to pay £200 for another isolation hut next to the original one. By Aug 1893 only one patient, a boy, remained. The Sheffield

One of six tiny headstones in Dore churchyard with the inscription 'S.P. (for small pox) Full Up 1893'. It sums up the prevalent view of navvies and their families and the fear and abhorrence of the disease. *Author*

The later and unreported death of Thomas Lavers records that he died working in Totley tunnel and the headstone in Dore churchyard is small when compared with those round it. *Author*

Town Council decided that smallpox patients should be temporarily admitted to the Lodge Moor Isolation Hospital on payment, by the Dore District, of £2/10/- a week to the local authority (Totley was in Derbyshire at this time). The council had concluded that the disease had assumed an epidemic character among the navvies. There are seventeen entries in the register of burials at Dore Parish Church between Mar and Jul 1893. Of these eleven were infants and children (see Appendix 2).

Seven died at the smallpox hospital at Green Oak, some of whom are buried in Dore churchyard. It was only a matter of weeks before the disease spread from Totley to Hathersage, with the illness 'being kept secret for five or six weeks'. Dr Fentem, the doctor for the north of Derbyshire arranged for immediate vaccination and isolation, when he was finally told of the outbreak. The doctor was pessimistic about the effectiveness of any precautions due to the reckless attitude among the navvies. He asked the Board of Guardians for an isolation hut to be built, which they agreed to. The disease quickly spread among the huts at Padley Wood and then to a lodging house at Stoney Middleton. The first fatality in Jan 1893 was a forty three year old man living at Padley, followed the next month by nine week old Albert Bird from Hathersage. At the beginning of February Benjamin Thompson and Myers Tym were found with the disease in the Padley huts. Thompson was too ill to walk to the workhouse at Bakewell and so a conveyance had to be found to take him whereas Tym was fit enough and had to walk the nine miles. (Could they not, for pity's sake have both been transported in the same conveyance?) When they reached the workhouse they found the four bed isolation part was full and so they all had to be crammed in. After a further death in February the disease reached its peak in the two months from the middle of March. At the Bakewell Board of Guardians meeting on 10 Apr 1893 it was reported that there had been two deaths on the railway. The bodies were conveyed in a bread cart which was afterwards used to carry bread! During March and April Hathersage Parish Church saw the burials of eight more victims, five of whom were children under five. Overall sixty nine cases had been identified in the area in the first four months of 1893, with an additional fifty two reported in May and June. In May 1893 it was reported that twenty nine cases had occurred in the past month, fifteen of these in seven different huts at Padley and eight at Hathersage. Forty eight patients were admitted to the isolation hospital at Hathersage Booths, the opening of which was delayed by the ineptitude of the Bakewell RSA in the three months from Mar 1893. However, by the beginning of July the worst was over and the last patient was discharged on 20 Jul. Forty eight patients were admitted of which three died. The incumbent of Hathersage related, chillingly, that he had buried 'fifty six navvies and railway people since work began' not all of whom would have been smallpox victims. Another source states that the same vicar recorded the word 'navvy' against fifty eight entries in the burial register. Over the period 1889 to 1894 twenty nine males, five females, three children and eighteen infants under two years of age are recorded. The last statistic should be set against high infant mortality rates among the wider population at this time.

On 26 Apr 1893 the *Sheffield Independent* let rip about the situation and lambasted the Ecclesall Bierlow Sanitary Authority regarding the overcrowded and insanitary conditions in the accommodations at Totley. To quote 'It cannot be said that the epidemic shows signs of dying out, or that the sanitary authority, which is responsible for the health of the inhabitants, are adopting measures calculated to achieve that end. They are, it is true, taking certain steps which ought to have been taken three months ago, but at no time in the history of the visitation do they appear to have once risen to the gravity of the state of affairs or to a full sense of their responsibility. To their default in this respect the spread of the infection is undoubtedly due. Needless to say the authority are coming in for severe castigation. A chorus of indignation, both loud and deep, is going up from the inhabitants of Totley and Dore at the alleged apathy and neglect of the authority, and some of them do not hesitate to lay at the door of the authority responsible for the deaths which have occurred. So serious are the complaints of negligence, and so grave have been the consequences of the infection, that in the interests of the public and of the sanitary authority we think the whole circumstances ought to be fully and impartially inquired into by the Local Government Board'.

At the height of the epidemic the sanitary authority of Ecclesall Bierlow and the medical officer of Derbyshire each applied to the Midland for £200 towards funeral help at Totley and Hathersage which the company paid.

At the end of Jan 1893 the *Glossop Times* reported that a navvy suffering from smallpox had travelled from Padley to Chapel where he had been taken to the isolation hospital at the Union workhouse where it was felt there was adequate provision. Within two more weeks five patients were in the isolation hospital. The Ecclesall Board of Guardians at their March meeting, reported that Thomas Oliver had offered to build a wooden hospital on rough ground (the later rifle range) belonging to the chairman of the board and vicar of Dore, the Rev J. T. F. Aldred, and promised to have it finished in two weeks. The navvies collected £20 towards the furnishing of the hut. Although the vaccination officer had visited the Dore and Totley vaccination stations for five successive weeks the uptake had been poor.

At their May meeting, the Bakewell Workhouse Board of Guardians thought the outbreak was under control. Although a further case was identified at Edale in May the outbreak in the Chapel district never reached the crisis levels of the Bakewell and Ecclesall Sanitary Authority areas. The Chapel RSA was more active in taking action against overcrowding in the huts and was quick to create an area next to the workhouse as an isolation hospital which was successful in containing the disease. Allied to this was the fact that Edwards provided better accommodation than Oliver.

It is interesting to note that by the time the Howden and Derwent dam construction started ten years later a model village at Birchinlee was built and that it included an isolation hospital. In 1904 all but one of twelve smallpox cases were recorded at Bole Hill quarry, Grindleford whilst there were none at Birchinlee.

ACCIDENTS

In Sep 1938 David Green, age 77, celebrated his golden wedding and in a newspaper report of the event he said he had been an inspector of the works in Totley tunnel. A local doctor offered him the opinion that 'he doubted whether any man engaged on the work at the beginning would live to see it finished'. Whilst the fatalities and injuries in both tunnels were not in the event that bad and were said to be about average for this type of construction, what will not have been factored in was the longer term toll on the health of the men working in the high temperatures with the sapping exposure to continued flows of water and the stress of knowing that life threatening injury was possible every day they went to work. The fatalities reported in the local newspapers give a feel of the conditions endured and, by today's standards, most would have been preventable. See Appendix 2 for the record of those who are known to have died or were injured in both tunnels and on the open areas. The deaths are also detailed in the chronology of the building of the line. Tunnelling work was generally acknowledged as being far more dangerous than anything else in railway construction. There were thought to be nineteen major accidents in Cowburn tunnel (excluding the main shaft), all but one being fatal. Another fourteen were reported across the rest of Edwards' contract but only one was fatal. As all of the above have been ascertained from newspaper reports, it is certain that there were many more less serious accidents that went unreported.

CRIME AND DISORDER

The incidence of serious crime in the navvy community was not as prevalent as has been widely assumed. Much of it was nuisance and low level which, even so, must have been distressing to the host villages and hamlets in, what was then, a remote and isolated part of the world.

The local courts had a regular flow of navvies and their wives before them, mainly for minor offences such as petty theft, assault and drunkenness. The police were often the subject of violence and regularly showed considerable bravery in trying to deal with offences, usually on their own. The first requisite any police recruiter would look for would be brawn. A petition by Grindleford Bridge residents was raised to protest against 'frequent disgraceful scenes' by the navvies. Police Constable Pentlow was moved to the village and no doubt some heads were quickly knocked together.

After scouring the relevant newspapers, here are some reports of criminal behaviour.

During Nov 1888 **Edward Harris**, tunnel labourer at Totley, stole a basket and sixteen eggs, the property of Mrs Thorpe a local grocer. Her son Benjamin called at 19.00 at the *Cricketers Inn* on his rounds and passed Harris coming out. Afterwards it was found the goods worth 3/6d, were gone. Ben's brother, William, saw Harris in the *Cross Scythes* pub and noticed him with the basket. PC Burford was called and apprehended Harris but received kicks to the legs. The constable stated that navvies went around in gangs and the police needed protection. Harris was sentenced to six weeks hard labour.

BOXING DAY 1888 AT TOTLEY
HOW THE NAVVIES AND THEIR WIVES ENJOYED THEMSELVES

In the cold and dark about 5.00 pm 'a great number of navvies and their wives met at Totley Bents where an altercation took place between two of the men respecting a journey from Sheffield when they got to words and then went to the cricket ground to fight and settle the dispute. The women interfered and two of them turned their dress sleeves up and fought. The spectators, first one, then another commenced to fight and there was a general fracas among the men and women. One woman bit a man through the chin. Another woman had her head cut open. Several men showed signs of rough usage. After this had been settled the parties dispersed. They afterwards met at Totley village, where another fracas occurred, both men and women fighting. One woman had two front teeth knocked out, a man had his head cut and others were roughly used. One of the navvies who had been fighting went to his home at Totley Bents and after ill using his wife, who is in a delicate state of health, commenced to smash the windows in the house.' It was remarked that the navvies did not allow their dispute to interfere with other residents of the area.   *Derby Mercury* 2 Jan 1889

On 23 Feb 1889, **George Thynne**, a miner of Totley, was charged at Dronfield Petty Sessions with stealing from John Royles, a tailor, on the highway at Totley, two waistcoats on 9 Feb. Royles had offered the waistcoats for sale at the *Cricketers Inn* and then went on to the

Crown Inn where one man tried one on and walked out but was stopped. Royles, not having sold them, put them in a bundle attached to a stick and put it over his shoulder. Twenty to thirty yards along the road to Dore he heard someone running behind him, then a man took the bundle off the stick and ran away. He was identified and PC Burford went to Thynne's house at Totley Bents and saw him wearing one of the waistcoats. The defendant said he was drunk and had a mother and father to keep. What became of him is not known.

On 2 Aug 1889, **William Cox** a navvy, violently assaulted Mrs Sarah Ann Williams, the licensee of the *Grapes Inn* at Chapel. He was sentenced to five weeks hard labour.

Eli Robins, age 17, a navvy who lived at Chapel was convicted of highway robbery with violence on Mrs Annie Tirrell of Chinley. She was returning on foot from Chapel when Robins demanded her money and said 'when I have got what I want I want something else'. He grabbed her, threw her down, stole her purse and was threatening her with a pen knife but was then disturbed and ran off. He was also convicted of an indecent assault on Esther Dexter, who is the daughter of a foreman on the works. At the same place he threw Miss Dexter on to the floor and assaulted her. When arrested he was wearing women's clothing and said he was trying to escape. He was sentenced to five years in a reformatory but came out of Derby gaol after serving only four months. *Sheffield Independent* 25 Aug 1890

Within a week of his release on 25 Feb 1891 Robins was charged with feloniously wounding Sarah Gregory with intent to do her grievous bodily harm. 'On Monday evening about 7 pm Sarah, age 16, who lives with her uncle, a farmer, in Chinley was walking along a road near the Board schools having been sent to buy an evening paper at a newsagents shop, some distance away, when Robins, who was concealed behind a wall, seized hold of her from behind and tried to force her over the wall into an adjoining field. She struggled with him and managed to get away from him twice, and failing to accomplish his purpose, he pulled out a pocket knife and during a struggle inflicted no fewer than seventeen stab wounds on her arms, hands and head. One wound on her neck is of great depth. Her cries were heard and some people at a distance ran to her assistance and Robins made his escape. *Sheffield Independent* 25 Feb 1891

(It is noteworthy that somebody as disturbed as this could readily find employment on the railway.)

RAID ON ILLICIT HUTS – HEAVY PENALTIES

'At the New Mills Petty Sessions yesterday, charges of selling liquors without a licence were heard, the cases having created a great deal of interest all over the district. The court was crowded. The Chief Constable of Derbyshire was also present. **Richard Cooper**, a farmer, of Norman's Bridge and **Charles Philpot**, **Elisabeth Ann Wilson**, wife of David Wilson, **Robert Whitfield**, **John Fawcett** all of Edale, **Ann Jane Pownall**, wife of Charles Pownall of Chinley, pleaded guilty to selling beer without a licence. **William Titmarsh** and **Harriet Millward** both of Edale pleaded guilty to selling beer and whisky. The prosecutor said 'that for a long time past complaints had been made to the police that a large amount of illicit drinking had been going on in the huts'. Two officers were instructed to procure work on the railway, and during the fortnight they were employed had every opportunity of seeing what was going on. Following their report on 11 Mar twenty officers (nearly all those serving in the Buxton, Chapel and New Mills districts) were conveyed to Edale in a furniture van in the early hours of the morning. A raid was made on the huts, where they found a large number of appliances for drinking and a great quantity of intoxicating liquors and beer. On this line of railway systematic drinking had been going on a long time, and people went into these huts and sat drinking as they would in a public house, so that the keepers in these huts must have made a considerable amount of money. Cooper occupied a farmhouse within fifty yards of the railway and had distinctly opened his house as a public house. Three hours was spent hearing the evidence. The worst cases were those of Cooper and Mrs Pownall. 'In her house there being several barrels of beer and large bottles of wine, gin, whisky, rum, brandy &c in every room'. Fines were imposed from £5 to £30 with costs and all the property seized was forfeited. Another report said that another raid was made on a hut at Wash at the same time. *Sheffield Independent* 26 Mar 1891

EXTRAORDINARY PROCEEDINGS AT EDALE

At Chapel Magistrates Court **Alfred Wood**, a ganger on the works at Edale, was summoned for assaulting William Johnson a miner of Edale on 1 Jun. While emptying wagons at 21.15 Johnson assaulted and beat Wood on the face with his fist until he was 'silly' without provocation. Wood's defence was that he struck out in self defence. Witnesses said Johnson was seen walking about the railway works at midnight carrying a gun saying he would put a shot through Wood if he could find him. The case was dismissed. *Sheffield Independent* 3 Jul 1891

PILFERING COAL ON THE DORE & CHINLEY RAILWAY

On the same day **Sarah Parrott** the wife of a hut keeper at Edale was charged with stealing 45 lbs of coal value 4d and **Mary Parrott**, her six year old daughter, with 6 lbs of coal value 1d from J. P. Edwards, the contractor. James Scott, the contractor's agent, prosecuting said many tons of coal were lost due to pilfering. The defendants were fined 1/- with costs. *Sheffield Independent* 3 Jul 1891

On the cold winter night of 2 Feb 1892, **William Baker** a navvy, was charged with assaulting PC Jones at Totley. The officer went to a cabin at Totley Bents which had been broken into and found thirty tramps (navvies looking for work) sleeping there. He told them to clear out but the defendant picked up stones and threatened him. One of them then ran at him and butted him with his head to the stomach. Baker was gaoled for a month.

MURDEROUS ASSAULT ON THE POLICE AT HOPE PRISONERS ARRESTED WHILE ASLEEP

At a special session at Chapel on 22 Apr 1892 two rough looking navvies named **Thomas Grant** and **Charles Taylor,** who were employed on the works at Hope, were brought up in custody on a charge of violently assaulting PC Pett whilst in the execution of his duty, at Hope on

Monday evening. The landlady of the *Cheshire Cheese* called to the constable to eject the men from her house when Taylor said 'I shall not go for any xxxxx policeman' and picked up a poker. When the officer had turned Taylor out of the house Grant followed and said to Taylor 'Go for the xxxxxx if you don't I'll go for you. I'll kill the xxxxxx if I die for it.' Grant struck the policeman a violent blow on the head with his fist, knocking his helmet off and struggled with him on the ground. During the struggle, Taylor took his belt off his waist (a soldier's belt), wrapped it round his hand and exclaimed 'I'll crash your xxxxxxx skull in' whilst jumping up and striking him with all his might on the head with the buckle causing a scalp wound 1½ inches long which penetrated to the bone, and rendered the officer unconscious. He lost a great deal of blood, and was still under the care of Dr Watts, of Castleton. The prisoners ran away, but were tracked by Sgt Pack of Castleton and PC Brown of Bradwell for a distance of nine miles in the direction of Sheffield until they were found in a stone quarry at Moscar at 23.00 the same night. Both men were fast asleep and were quietly handcuffed by the officers in their sleep. When they were aroused with the handcuffs on them, Taylor said 'You have been xxxxxxx quick after us, if it had not been for my pal, you would not have found us yet.' They were taken in a cart to Castleton lock up. Superintendent Hallam informed the Bench that many assaults had been committed on the police since the works were started, but this was the most violent of them all. P. C. Pett was not yet out of danger. He would have to put double the number of policemen on duty where the navvies were located, as they were such a set of ruffians to deal with, and unless the Bench made an example of them it would not be safe for a policeman to act alone. Each prisoner was sentenced to four months with hard labour.

POACHING

At Bakewell Petty Sessions on Friday **Richard Green** and **William Weaver** living in the huts at Padley were charged with trespassing on 17 Oct on the Duke of Rutland's land. They had guns. No shots were fired. P.C. Pentelow said that Weaver earned 5/- a week and Green 3/-. Each was fined 1/- and costs. Green did not appear but Weaver paid his fine on the spot. *Derby Mercury* 26 Oct 1892

ROBBERY IN EDALE

Thomas Davis, an army pensioner working on the railway at Edale, was charged at New Mills with stealing 15/- in money, a pipe and a belt belonging to John George who was the deputy of the hut where he lodged. He was fined 20/- and costs or one month in gaol. He was concerned that the offence might cause him to lose his army pension.
Sheffield Independent 23 Feb 1893

During Apr 1893 two **unnamed** navvies were sentenced to fourteen days imprisonment for sleeping in an outhouse at Grindleford Bridge (vagrancy was a criminal offence until comparatively recent times). The court was also told of 'numerous complaints about navvies sleeping in farm and other buildings' which the owners were afraid would be set on fire.

On 27 May 1893, William Booker a gamekeeper for the Duke of Rutland, saw four navvies with two dogs beating for game near the Wooden Pole. He ordered them off and they went towards Owler Bar followed by Booker. One man, **Henry Turner**, took up a cinder and threw it striking Booker in the face whereby he fell to the ground and the navvy kicked him. As he got back to his feet three cyclists came along and one fetched a police officer who handcuffed the navvy and took him to Dronfield police station. Booker was badly bruised from the top of his forehead and down the side of his face and was not at work for some time.

THE RECENT FATAL EXPLOSION ON THE DORE AND CHINLEY RAILWAY – THE CONTRACTOR FINED

It wasn't just some of the navvies who brought their calling into disrepute. One of the contractors also flouted the law. 'At the Chapel Petty Sessions yesterday **John Price Edwards**, the contractor for the Dore and Chinley Railway, was summoned and pleaded guilty through his agent for having on 10 Jan in a wooden building at Edale, unlawfully kept 100 lbs of gunpowder, 150 gelignite cartridges and 300 detonators. It was said that on that date at 02.00 a number of men were working in the tunnel at Edale with some of the cartridges, when an explosion took place and one of them, Walter Mosby, was killed on the spot (see page 173). On hearing of the explanation the police went over to Edale and found a wooden building several hundred yards from the entrance to the tunnel. When entrance was eventually obtained by the police they found there were also barrels of oil, candles, fuse and a large fire in the midst (this is not a misprint!). Its location was close to the public road and about eighty yards from the workmen's huts. The explosives were seized and the Secretary of State was informed who ordered a prosecution. The store was not registered. James Scott in defence said that the explosives were conveyed from Chapel to the tunnel daily as required, but the works were stopped in consequence of the accident and so the explosives were placed in the building. The Bench ordered the forfeiture of the explosives and imposed a fine of £5 and costs and recommended a registered store should be provided.   *Sheffield Independent* 13 Feb 1891

PLAYING WITH FIREARMS. THE SAME OLD STORY

On 27 Sep 1893 three or four lads aged between twelve and fourteen, sons of miners on the line, were playing at Totley when one of them produced a revolver belonging to his father. Not knowing it was loaded he playfully pointed it at a companion and pulled the trigger. The weapon went off and a lad named **Russell** received a bullet in his head. 'The injury, it is feared will be fatal'.

THE SPIRITUAL AND TEMPORAL WELLBEING OF THE NAVVIES

An influential committee was formed in Sep 1889 to oversee the Christian and educational needs of the navvy community. It included George H. Cammell, Mr Bagshawe, Ebenezer Hall and J. S. A. Shuttleworth among others. The largest contributors were the Midland Railway £200, J. P. Edwards and Thomas Oliver £50 each, the Duke of Devonshire £30, Mr T. S. Furniss and Mr J. S. A. Shuttleworth £10 each and a miserly £10 from the Duke of Rutland. Voluntary schools for the navvy children from the huts at Totley, Edale and other places to the value of £120 were erected and staffed, and

A navvy not bothering anybody fast asleep at the side of the road around Totley after possibly imbibing too much lunchtime alcohol.
Author's collection

furthermore, four scripture readers were employed at a cost of £325. Four mission rooms were built by the contractors which, with other provision, totalled £505. At Edale the navvy mission established day and Sunday schools and reading rooms. At Totley, All Saints school had to cope with a large influx of navvy children, some of whom were accommodated in a wooden hut erected in the school yard. On Sunday mornings temperance meetings were held at Totley Bents recreation ground and up to 250 were known to attend.

ON A MORE CHEERFUL NOTE

On 25 Feb 1889, the first wedding among the navvies took place at Dore church when **Thomas Colther**, a navvy of Totley, married **Ellen Jane Oxenham**, the daughter of a navvy and hut keeper at Totley. A number of presents were sent by inhabitants in the neighbourhood. The local butcher sent a large piece of meat, the baker made the cake and the local publican sent spirits.

During Apr 1899, athletic sports for the men took place at the Cross Scythes at Totley. A large number of spectators paid for admission to the field, the proceeds of which will be devoted to providing a tea for the children of Totley on the occasion of the opening of a new schoolroom which has been erected by the contractor.

At Chapel en le Frith, in Dec 1889, an exhibition of carved work by the navvies and sewing, knitting and baking by their wives was held followed by an entertainment of songs, readings, recitations and dialogues.

Here are three navvy children at an unknown location in Totley. Did they specially get ready in their best clothes for the photographer as all of them look healthy, clean, well dressed and are wearing shoes?
Picture the Past. Sheffield City Libraries

In May 1892, a deputation of navvies made a presentation of an illuminated address and a purse containing twenty guineas to the matron and the nurse at Chinley 'for the kind treatment and constant attention their comrades had received'. The nurse, Miss Palmer, remarked that every patient had been 'most respectful and grateful'.

When the building of Totley tunnel was finished some of the bricks left over were used to build pig sties behind a cottage close to the Crown Inn. The sties were built by a group of navvies who had lodged with the lady who owned the cottage. This was their way of thanking her for the way they had been looked after whilst lodging with her.

So not everything that involved the navvy centred around drink, violence and licentiousness. Far from it.

A notable navvy was being buried.
Six of his comrades carried him to his grave.
'Reverse the corpse' said the parson.
'What's he say?' said the unlettered navvies.
The ganger said 'Slew the miserable old bugger round'.
And they slewed him round quick.

In Jul 1891 the wife of Edward Jones a miner employed in one of the tunnels gave birth to twins. The girl was christened 'Dore' and the boy 'Chinley'. A lovely story with a tragic twist because sadly Dore died but hopes were entertained that Chinley might survive. Did Chinley Jones get a bit of stick in the school playground when he grew older?

REFERENCES

Rickard Percy – *Tunnels on the Dore and Chinley Railway*. Proceedings of the Institution of Civil Engineers Paper No. 2744 23 Jan 1894

The Engineers Reports to the Directors of the Midland Railway 14 Nov 1888 to 15 Jun 1896

Leivers Clive – *The Human Cost of Building Cowburn Tunnel*. Journal of the Railway & Canal Historical Society Vol. 35 No. 194 Mar 2006

Leivers Clive – *The Modern Ishmaels? Navvy communities in the High Peak*. Family & Community History Vol. 9 2 Nov 2006

Leivers Clive – *Smallpox among the Navvies: The Response of Bakewell Rural Sanitary Authority*. Derbyshire Miscellany Vol. 17 Part 3 Spring 2005

Edwards Brian – *Totley and the Tunnel*. Shape Designs 1985

Buxton Barbara A. – *Hathersage in the Peak*. Phillimore 2005

Sullivan Dick – *Navvyman*. Coracle Books 1983

Various newspaper reports.

Minutes of various committees of the Midland Railway. National Archive Kew.

LOCOMOTIVES BUILT FOR THE OPENING

For those not familiar with the locomotives of the Midland Railway at the time of the opening of the line a mention must be made of the celebrated Samuel Waite Johnson, the locomotive superintendent at Derby works from Jul 1873 until the end of 1903, when he retired. He was in office during the unprecedented growth of the company and on one occasion received authority to build, or have built, one hundred goods engines in one go.

Johnson not only designed and built very successful locomotives but he created an aesthetic quality which was not equalled by many, or reached by most. Through the introduction of the famous crimson lake livery in place of the previous olive green he, together with Thomas Clayton the carriage and wagon superintendent, helped to establish a public image of the Midland which exuded graciousness, comfort, beauty and style. Even John Ruskin might have conceded that a Johnson engine, with Clayton carriages behind, would have complimented the exquisite scenery of the Hope and Edale valleys as the trains travelled through at the sedate speeds which were the hallmark of the Midland.

This breathtaking painting by Graham Lee, who was a loco driver in Sheffield until his untimely death, shows a representative example of Johnson's designs of the period. Apart from the larger driving wheels the engine is identical with the engines ordered for the Dore and Chinley line. This was one of the '2183' class of 4-4-0s built in Jul 1892 by Sharp Stewart which carried numbers 2183 to 2202. They had the D type boiler, and 7 ft driving wheels and 18½ × 26 in cylinders with a 3,250 gallon capacity tender. It is fully turned out in the crimson lake livery with the company crest on the leading splasher and the 'MR' initials on the tender sides. It survived in this form until Jan 1906 when it was rebuilt. It was a Bedford engine throughout most of its life.

Graham Lee

The first of the class, No. 2203, after its transfer from Leeds to Sheffield for the opening of the line to passenger traffic on 1 Jun 1894. It is standing in Dore and Totley station before the widening of the lines from the station into Sheffield in 1902. The headlamps, with a lamp on the top of the smokebox door and the other on the right hand side but inset on the buffer beam, are for an express train, an identification system that was in use until 1897. There are six carriages attached, the first one is probably a 25 ft four wheel full brake and the rest six wheeled arc roofed non-corridor ordinary stock, typical of the period.

Roy F. Burrows. Midland Collection Trust.

No. 2209 is on its home shed at Belle Vue, known then as 'Manchester', and if it were not for the burning of the smokebox door it would look ex works. This demonstrates the standard of cleanliness maintained on the front line engines. The only difference from No. 2201 is the reduced size 6 ft 6 in driving wheels, a size probably chosen because Johnson was aware of the gradients on the Dore and Chinley line and knew that an engine with smaller wheels would be more sure footed. *Author's collection*

No. 2217, the last of the series, received its H boiler in Mar 1905 and was to be renumbered 442 in Nov 1907. It is between Chinley station, at the point where Buxton Road reaches its nearest point to the line (042847). There were two identical bracket signals at this point, the one in the view being for the Ambergate line and the other pair for the Hope valley line are obscured by the smoke. No. 2217 was a Trafford Park engine, this shed provided the engines for the Ambergate line. The train consists of a Bain and Clayton horse box and then a 43 ft bogie arc roofed Clayton brake third, followed by a 48 ft bogie Clayton clerestory lavatory third; a 54 ft bogie Bain clerestory square light brake composite; 48 ft bogie clerestory Clayton lavatory composite and probably a 48 ft bogie Clayton clerestory lavatory brake third.
H.Gordon Tidey

On 17 Dec 1891 the construction of the Dore and Chinley line was under way and Johnson applied for additional engines including 'fifteen four coupled passenger engines and tenders for the Dore and Chinley line at £2,500 apiece'. Tenders were sought on 13 Apr 1892 and, as for the '2183' class, Sharp Stewart submitted the lowest tender at £2,800 each. They were designated 'O' class and numbered from 2203 to 2217, being delivered between January and April 1893.

The opening of the Dore and Chinley line was later than planned so the engines became available early and so the first four went to Leeds for trial on the Carlisle line. The rest went to Manchester (Belle Vue). However, by the time of the opening of the line for through services on 1 Jun 1894, the engines had been allocated as intended with 2203 – 2206 from Leeds and 2207 – 2212 from Manchester transferring to Sheffield (Grimesthorpe). 2213 – 2217 remained at Manchester. The Sheffield engines also worked to Nottingham and Leeds. At Belle Vue the engines were considered too good for short runs to Sheffield and were used on the London expresses as far as Leicester for several years.

In Jun 1904, six months after Richard Deeley had taken over from Johnson, the first of the '2203' class was rebuilt with a larger H class boiler to accommodate the heavier trains now running. The rebuilding of the class was completed in May 1908. The driving wheels remained 6ft 6ins and the coupled wheelbase 9 ft. Whilst the graceful curves of the splashers suggest that Johnson's legacy had not been entirely lost the low running plate makes it appear out of proportion, which would never have been allowed under his predecessor. The period of Johnson 4-4-0 passenger elegance was to last on the Dore and Chinley line for only ten years although his equally superb 4-2-2 singles would continue to grace the line into LMS days.

No. 2212 is seen here at Sheffield Midland station. *Jack Braithwaite collection*

The last of the series, No. 2217, is on the turntable at Manchester Central around 1899, possibly having come off a London express given the lack of coal showing above the tender rails. Ahrons comments that 'generally speaking, the engines of this class never seemed to me to run as freely as other 4-4-0 engines of the Midland; they gave one the impression of having their legs tied together. Nevertheless, there were occasions when they asserted themselves'. Two things make these comments surprising, the first being that they would not have been used on the London services if not considered superior to other Belle Vue 4-4-0s and secondly, the Midland would not have ultimately authorised the building of another thirty of the class. *Stephen Summerson collection*

According to Ahrons, Belle Vue decided to use their '2203' class on the London expresses and substituted two older engines for the Sheffield turns. One of these was No. 1666, the last to be built of the '1562' class. It came into service in Nov 1883 and was a Manchester engine until at least 1921, by which time it had been rebuilt. The second was No. 1342, which was built in Oct 1877 by Dubs, and was a member of the '1346' class of slim boiler 4-4-0s. The illustration shows No. 1346 at Skipton.
Author's collection

Between Sep 1888 and Aug 1922, 575 0-6-0 goods engines were built to supplement the 290 0-6-0s that Johnson had previously designed. They were known as the 'standard goods'. On 17 Dec 1891 ten additional engines and tenders were requested for the Dore and Chinley line at £2,285 each. Approval was forthcoming and Dubs successfully tendered. The Dore and Chinley line opened for goods on 6 Nov 1893, nearly two years later, with Dubs having failed to honour its delivery date. As a result, on 21 May 1894, an order was placed for 'ten new standard goods', the only batch of the whole series to be constructed at Derby. They entered service, numbered 361 to 370, between Oct 1894 and Jan 1895, about a year after the line opened. In the 1907 renumbering they became Nos. 3460 to 3469. After various re-buildings they all survived into the LMS period and five survived into British Railways ownership.

One of the veterans was Grimesthorpe's No. 3464 (originally No. 365), which is seen here on 7 Jun 1949, still without its BR number. It is on its original stamping ground, leaving Dore West Junction on the climb to Totley tunnel and the Hope valley. After a flat bottomed wagon is a Midland clerestory coach incongruously ahead of some loaded mineral wagons and a brake van. The coach is possibly being taken to the goods yard at Hope as one was located there in the 1950s as a tools and mess vehicle. *Peter J. Hughes*

REFERENCES

Summerson Stephen – *Midland Railway Locomotives Volume Three: The Johnson Classes Part 1*. Irwell Press 2002

Braithwaite Jack – *S. W. Johnson Midland Railway Locomotive Engineer Artist*. Wyvern Publications 1985

Ahrons E. L. – *Locomotive & Train Working in the Latter Part of the Nineteeth Century Vol. 2*. Heffer 1952

Howard Ian – *Midland Expresses through the Peak*. Midland Railway Society Journal No. 38 Autumn 2008

THE OPENING OF THE LINE

The line was opened in four parts starting with goods trains, then through excursions followed by through passenger trains and finally local services.

28 Oct 1893. The Midland Railway engineers took over the line from the contractors and the Midland notice stated 'that no vehicle belonging to the contractors must be upon the running lines without being attached to a Midland train'.

29 Oct 1893. The Midland issued a notice to all operating staff and platelayers regarding the opening. Nothing in it suggests that anything was being left to chance. After all, the Midland had vast experience of opening new lines and must have developed a well tried procedure. It starts with the information that at 07.00 the block telegraph system will become operational and that most of the signal boxes will come into use. However, it was another three weeks before the system became operational through Totley tunnel, a pilot engine and guard having been needed in the interim period. Dore to Chinley was designated the 'down' line and Chinley to Dore the 'up' line. The line was to be considered as always open. The line from Dore to the west end of Hope station was to be in the Sheffield brake down van district and the line from Hope to Chinley North and South junctions was to be in the Belle Vue district. 'Trains were not to be driven at more than 25 mph and must run through all facing points and crossings at junctions at a moderate speed and with judgement and care' – this was a temporary measure whilst the embankments etc settled. The Dore South Curve junction with the main line was not laid in and the curve could, if necessary, be used for standing trains on. At Dore and Totley station the old signal box was to be closed and the new box named 'Dore and Totley Station Junction' opened.

6 Nov 1893. The first goods train ran over the line. The *Sheffield Independent* the following day recorded the event as follows; 'Twenty trains a day are booked over it in either direction. Sheffield had the honour of despatching the first of those trains, which left Grimesthorpe sidings at 13.30. Its destination was Peak Forest, and it returned to Sheffield at night. The first from the Chinley end was a cattle train from Liverpool to Leeds, which left at 13.50 and entered the new line at 14.30 (It would take more than forty minutes!) The work of preparing the line for passenger traffic – erecting stations and so forth – will now be proceeded with, and the hope is entertained that it will be completed by the spring of next year.'

11 Jan 1894. The *Derbyshire Times* reported that 'the limestone etc traffic from Buxton, Millers Dale, Peak Forest and the neighbouring quarries will be forwarded by the new route for Sheffield and places north – an improvement on the old route via Ambergate... the coal traffic from Westhouses, Blackwell, Clay Cross and the Chesterfield district for Manchester, Liverpool etc will be conveyed by this route on completion of the Dore South Junction Curve. Commodious sidings are being provided at Edale for the marshalling of goods trains, so as to admit of those from Manchester being divided for Sheffield and Chesterfield, whilst those from the north district will be separated into trains for Buxton, Manchester and Liverpool. A service of ten goods trains daily will be run over the line as a commencement.'

THROUGH CARRIAGES
BETWEEN
SHEFFIELD
AND
MANCHESTER
(CENTRAL AND VICTORIA STATIONS),
AND
LIVERPOOL
(CENTRAL).

A SERVICE OF LOCAL TRAINS
will shortly be run to and from the Stations on the New Line, particulars of which will be duly announced.

GOODS & MERCHANDISE TRAFFIC.
THE OPENING OF THE NEW LINE BETWEEN DORE AND CHINLEY affords a new and quick route for Goods and Merchandise Traffic between LEEDS, BRADFORD, SHEFFIELD, HULL, & MANCHESTER, STOCKPORT, WARRINGTON, WIDNES, WIGAN, LIVERPOOL, BOLTON, BLACKBURN, OLDHAM, GUIDE BRIDGE, STALYBRIDGE, and other large towns in the Cheshire and South Lancashire Districts, and provides a new and continuous Railway from the East to West Coast.
Facilities are also afforded for the more rapid conveyance of traffic between the places named above and YORK, STOCKTON, MIDDLESBORO', DARLINGTON, SUNDERLAND, WEST HARTLEPOOL, AND THE NORTH EASTERN DISTRICT generally.

GEO. H. TURNER, General Manager.
Derby, May 22nd, 1894.

Bemrose & Sons, Limited, Printers, Derby and London.

This is an advertisement for through carriages in the short period between the commencement of through services and the start of the local service. The previously declared intent of capturing traffic from the north east is demonstrated here.
Glynn Waite collection

A first day first class excursion ticket between Manchester Central and Sheffield return dated 16 May 1894.
Glynn Waite collection

13 May 1894. The Midland engineering notices of late May stated that at 6.00 am the Dore South Curve (the title had now been shortened) and Chinley South Curve would open and the rest of the line was authorised to open for through passenger traffic. The maximum speed on Dore south curve was set at 15 mph. Sidings at all stations were henceforth to be used only by Midland men and vehicles sent to those stations must be worked direct to them. The use of Dore south curve for stabling wagons was to cease and the stations were not to be opened to passengers for the time being. Notices to engine men, guards and signalmen were issued for the opening of the line.

15 May 1894. The first passenger class train was an excursion to Southport under the aegis of Thomas Cook and organised by the Ellesmere Tents of the Independent Order of Rechabites. It started at Rotherham Westgate at 05.00. The fifteen coaches quickly became overcrowded following a stop at Brightside. When it reached Sheffield Midland, at 05.15, one thousand excursionists were assembled on the platform. Shortly after, a second train drew up to take the Sheffield passengers, twelve or thirteen passengers being packed into each compartment. It took six and a half minutes to pass through Totley tunnel and Chinley was reached in forty five minutes. The outward journey to Southport took three hours and the return fifteen minutes longer. Villagers and farm lads and lasses waved to the trains as they passed. It was said to have been a smooth journey.

16 May 1894. The line officially opened for through excursion passenger traffic. For the rest of the week excursion trains ran from Rotherham to Manchester Central leaving Westgate at 10.45 and arriving at 12.45.

15/16 May 1894. A grand fete was held at the Victoria Gardens in Totley. There were stage performances including acrobats and Trojan athletes and the Prince of Wales brass band performed in the evening. The gardens were opened in 1883 and were located on Sheffield Road. Kelly's directory of 1891 records that there were ten acres of grounds, well laid out with a cricket ground, lawn tennis courts, archery grounds, a lake with pleasure boats and a large pavilion which was well lighted and decorated. They could admit up to 10,000 visitors but did not last the decade out, mainly because the gardens could not get a drinks license.

1 Jun 1894. The line opened for all through passenger traffic.

25 Jun 1894. The stations were opened for all traffic and local passenger services commenced. This was later than projected as mid April or, at the latest, Whitsuntide had been expected. The Chinley South Curve was already open and was sanctioned to carry through passenger services to and from Buxton.

The cover of the opening timetable for through passenger traffic from 1 Jun 1894.
Glynn Waite collection

Edward Bradbury comments, 'There are in this last decade of the nineteenth century plenty of people in the Peak District who have never taken a railway journey. Their life is one of vegetation – a mere process of eating, working and sleeping. They resemble the agriculturist, who, when he was told by Mr Roebuck (the local MP) that the great Duke of Wellington was dead, replied, 'Aw be sorry for he; but who wur he?' They are, moreover, as prejudiced against steam locomotion as people were against Lucifer matches and gas illumination'. Fortunately the more enlightened embraced the railway as we shall see.

The *Sheffield Telegraph* reported that from 'early morning until evening trains were running over the new line from Sheffield, Manchester and Buxton, leaving and taking up passengers at all the intermediate wayside stations. Every station was thronged with enthusiastic gatherings of the village residents greeting the visitors, who had come from the crowded centres of industry… The service of trains was fully taken advantage of and over 5,000 excursionists reached Castleton from Hope station where Mr Ross the station master and his staff were there to greet them and the accommodation facilities were overwhelmed. Parties picknicked on the grass and as each of the numerous trains steamed in they raised a lusty cheer. At Castleton the brass band, headed by Mr S. Hardy, turned out in fine style before eight o'clock to meet the first train from Buxton and gaily played the arrivals all the way to the village. They repeated this performance on the arrival of the 8.24 am from Sheffield and at several of the succeeding trains which arrived at 12.28, 2.12, 3.13, 5.36, 7.07, 8.40 and 8.50 pm. In addition two excursion trains, one in the morning and one in the afternoon, were run with the afternoon one requiring a

HALL HOTEL, HOPE.

MATTHEW ROBINSON

(Late Coach Driver for 14 years from Tideswell to Sheffield) begs a call from his old friends from Sheffield at the

HALL HOTEL,

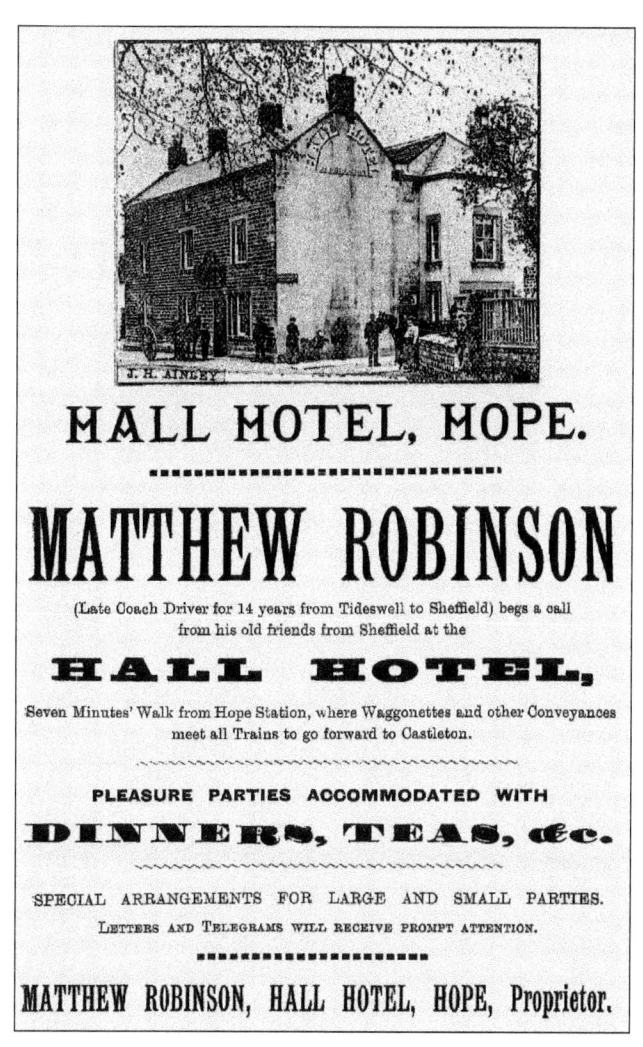

Seven Minutes' Walk from Hope Station, where Waggonettes and other Conveyances meet all Trains to go forward to Castleton.

PLEASURE PARTIES ACCOMMODATED WITH

DINNERS, TEAS, &c.

SPECIAL ARRANGEMENTS FOR LARGE AND SMALL PARTIES.

LETTERS AND TELEGRAMS WILL RECEIVE PROMPT ATTENTION.

MATTHEW ROBINSON, HALL HOTEL, HOPE, Proprietor.

The *Hall Hotel* at Hope advertises its services. It was and still is located at the junction of the roads to Castleton and Edale.

relief train. The Bradwell Brass Band met this train. Brakes and wagonettes and omnibuses from Bradwell, Castleton and Tideswell were in waiting at Hope station and were fully used to take the visitors to the various hostelries. Mr Hardy bore off with great pride the first ticket holder from Buxton and later captured the first ticket holder from Sheffield. Banners were hung from the prominent buildings and were suspended side to side of the roads. Prominent among the inhabitants who lined the route were the vicar of Hope, the Rev Henry Buckstone, and at Castleton the Rev R. J. C. Orde, Mr Edward and Mrs Loxley Firth of Birchfield House. Marquees were erected for the excursionists and entertainment was provided. Mr Matthew Robinson, who had been the coach driver from Tideswell to Sheffield for fourteen years, kept open house at the *Hall Hotel*. He roasted two lambs for visitors and residents. Truswells brewery, who had only recently bought the pub for at least £4,000, supplied the beer. They roasted lambs and sheep whole and had not too much to spare. All the children at Castleton aged under fourteen were allowed a day's holiday and were invited to tea'.

'All the villages fairly divided the celebrations. At Hathersage, the vicar the Rev C. S. Cutler, Mr J. S. A. Shuttleworth of Hathersage Hall, Mr George Henry Cammell of Broookfield Manor and Mr J. B. Howell entertained the school children, who were taken on the first train through to a wet Edale where the station master, Mr Wright, was there to greet them. They received refreshments and then went through the village in procession, led by the Hathersage Brass Band, and returned a couple of hours later. For many of the children it was their first ride on a train. The children of Edale were given a half day (not a full day) holiday. At Bamford both schools were closed for the day.'

Mr J. Ollerenshaw, a retired farmer and past chairman of Bakewell NFU and a member of Bakewell RDC for forty years, when 96 years old in 1982, recalled 'I can remember the railways coming to Hathersage. When the first train went up the valley, all the school children were invited to enjoy a free ride and back but our parents would not let us go because they thought the journey too dangerous'!

The first ticket from Chesterfield was bought by Mr J. E. Manlore of Belmont House, Edale, who travelled back to his home. Mr John Lane, another Edale resident, won the scramble for the first ticket at Edale and travelled to Hope. He is said to have been so overjoyed he went to the pub and drank too much. Alderman Henry Robert Crossland, a magistrate, who lived at Nether Padley Farm, bought the first two tickets from Grindleford to Sheffield. The now famous *Nags Head* pub at Edale was kept by Mr Isaac Walker for sixty three years but he died over two years before this life changing event for the village. One wonders how he felt about the arrival of the navvies and the prospect of change.

Bradbury records a pub discussion as follows:

'When does the railway open for passenger traffic?' I enquire, passing around my Navy Cut. 'It'll be no earthly good to us!' simultaneously exclaim the wheelwright and the village carrier. 'They's bringen goods by th' line and take 'osses to Sheffield to be shodden for nowt just to encourage th' Company. It'll ba th' ruin on us!' A head shaking, sympathetic 'Aye! Aye! Ah!' comes from the assembled conscript fathers. 'Aw've only bin by treen once,' volunteers another member of this village parliament. 'One get's no ride for one's money. Aw bought a bit of pasteboard, which cost thray and four, and a mon in brass buttons, with a pea whistle in his mouth, bawls out, 'Are you all in?' and then, afor aw had gotten fairly down, and wor just thinking one thing or another and fumbling in ma pocket for ma smoking tackle, the pea whistle mon shouted, 'All out!' Before that th' treen had stopped, and a mon in buttons pinched a piece of my bit o' pasteboard on th' sly. Hay thought aw wor a country gawby, and wouldna heed on't. When aw left th' treen aw saw some owd neeburs cottages had been ta'en away and used up to make th' steetion. Another mon in buttons wor a standin' at th' little gate. 'Tickets please!' hay shouted. Aw sez aw want no ticket. But hay sez 'the reelway ticket from where you started. Aw sez am not goin'; to be made a fou by thcc as by that other mon. Thou wants a bit 'o my ticket to sell it, dost thee? Well, mester I chucked it through th' winder. The mon in brass than caws th' constable up, and if it hadna bin for he a knowing a half cousin of mine, aw would have had to have peed afresh.'

Thank yer sir, it is very kind of yer. 'Could aw drink half-a-pint? Could I drink a quart, sir?' I give the son of the soil sixpence, with which he seems prodigiously pleased, for he places the silver coin in the bowl of his pipe, which it just fits, and as I bid him good night he proceeds to liquidate the money at the inn, where no doubt:

Village statesmen talk with looks profound,
And news much older than their ale goes round.

(I am glad I disabled my spell check for these paragraphs by Edward Bradbury!)

CONTEMPORARY REPORTS

It is well worth quoting from some contemporary writers to get a flavour of how the line was seen at the time, picturesque language and all.

J. Pendleton in his two volume book 'Our Railways', published in 1894, gives a graphic account, which was first recorded in the *Manchester Guardian*, of a visit to the works on 11 Nov 1891.

'Through the kindness of the general manager of the Midland and of Messrs Parry engineers I was enabled to penetrate to the heading from the Totley end. 'I shall be glad' wrote Mr Parry to those in charge of the new line 'if you will allow the bearer to go through the tunnel and ride upon the engines. He, of course, has taken upon himself all liability for accidents.' With this suggestive note of introduction, I reach Dore station and am cordially welcomed by Mr Percy Rickard, the resident engineer. 'You have chosen a wild day to go over the new line' he says sympathetically, as he clutches the rim of his hat with one hand and wipes the rain off his face with a handkerchief in the other. 'It certainly is a wild day. The rain does not come down in torrents. It is driven against you horizontally by the fierce gusts of wind that sweep across the country from the moors, so that you soon have a wet bedraggled look. The riot of wind and rain is such that even Ariel might find it difficult to direct the storm. But we are well equipped to brave the weather, with thick watertight boots, leggings and mackintoshes, and soon strike the Dore end of the new railway before striding resolutely along the track, through pools and over slippery sleepers, by the screen bank that hide Abbeydale Park from the line. The tunnel opens its mouth in a deep cutting just below Totley Rise. The bank is very high at the entrance to the underground way and has yielded so much owing to the rain that men are busy planking it up. On the line there is the shriek of engine, the rattle and jolt of wagons, and the shouts of workers. 'Is he going in sir?' asks one of the officials. 'Oh yes' replies the engineer in a brisk encouraging tone 'he's come many miles to go though the tunnel'. 'I'll get the lamps then' says the man, moving away; and a grimy Hercules, sludged to the thighs, and with his face clay splashed like an American Indian, advises me in a whisper to 'take that fancy thing off' meaning my waterproof. I am, with considerable kindness, provided with another overcoat, thick and stiff as buckram and with a railway lamp in my hand and speedily slipping, sliding, jumping, stumbling, splashing along the rude road into the darkness. The way is not unlike the main road from the bottom of the shaft to the far workings in a coal pit. Here it is bricked; there it is propped with great timbers. Now we are in the deepest gloom then, through a thick, almost choking vapour that makes your lamplight feeble, we can just discern the shadowy forms of men who look like gigantic phantoms fighting as they strike, not at each other, but at the rock. One is startled by a hoarse cry that sound something like 'Howd up!' and dragged into a refuge hole, dug, like a watchman's box, in the tunnel side while a train of laden wagons clatter by to the tunnel mouth. The last flicker of daylight from the fourth shaft has been passed and we are in the depths of the tunnel. Although air is continuously pumped into the subterranean road, the atmosphere as we get further away from the last shaft becomes dense and oppressive. The brick lined arched part of the tunnel is now behind us. There the way is twenty seven feet wide and twenty two feet six inches high. Here it is at present narrow, rough hewn and low roofed. The road, only just wide enough to enable the wagons to come down, is being dug and cut through the coal measures. The black shale is easy to deal with; but the intersecting rock requires more patient working. Watching the drillers and strikers at their toil, one is inclined to think that to delve three and a half miles of track beneath the moorland from Totley Rise to the Derwent valley is almost a hopeless task. Yet considerable progress has been made with the work. There is still a mile of heading to pierce; but men are driving at both ends of the tunnel and are looking forward with pleasure to shaking hands with each other in the underground junction. A useful friend in tunnel making is found in gelignite, an explosive, which blasts away the most obstinate bulk of rock with scant ceremony; but the men have an annoying enemy in water. In the earlier lengths of the tunnel they were much embarrassed by it. Every man seemed to be possessed of the miraculous powers of Moses. Wherever he struck water sprang out of it. Water dripped from the roof and flowed from the rock and sprang from the tunnel floor. The flow became so constant that the men had to work in mackintosh suits, and looked like divers wading through deep pools and torrents. At the faults particularly the inrush of water was considerable – at one time not less than 1,200 gallons a minute. The men were never in danger; but the flow was too great for their liking, and for the reasonable progress of the undertaking. A head wall of bricks and cement, four feet six inches thick, was at last run up not far from the fourth shaft to keep the water back. Behind this wall the water rose and dashed ominously, but the gangs in the meantime made a drain in the tunnel bed, and ultimately through this drain and along the culvert by the railway side the flood water was carried into the River Sheaf. The water in the Totley length has been successfully coped with by the diversion of the underground stream that now flows beneath the line; but the irruption in the Padley heading was recently gauged at 5,000 gallons per minute. The flow was so great that the men had to go to work on a raft. Then the water rose so high that they could not get in at all without fighting a subterranean flood that almost rivalled the underground torrent Jules Verne evolved from his fancy. I learn all this piecemeal and haphazard, as I stumble along in the uncertain lamplight at the heels of my friend. Now we pause to watch the men – by the light of candles stuck in their caps or in the interstices of the rock – toiling and drilling, or penetrating by means of ladders into the breakups; then we climb over wagons that obstruct our progress. By and by we reach the heading, the most distant point excavated from the Totley end. The rock and shale is as dry as tinder. There is not a drop of water here. The air is hot and heavy. Perspiration bursts from every pore and trickles in fantastic courses down your face. The men, great muscular fellows, perspire too; but they pick and dig on. The shale is steadily shovelled down to the wagons. At the face a sturdy tunnel hewer inserts his pick in a crevice and brings down a great mass of rock that threatens to crush him as it gives way and thuds on the floor; but he leaps aside, reels and comes on his back on the shale heap, causing some diversion. From the soles of his boots, your eyes, with scarcely perceptible effort, have roamed to the tunnel roof. It is altogether a surprising roof – a huge flat, smooth faced slab of shale, many yards in length, that completely covers in the tunnel way; a vast natural roof that may not be a curiosity in geology but is certainly rare enough in tunnel making. Since I emerged from the tunnel by the deep shaft, bathed in perspiration and splashed with mire, the measurement of the natural roof has been taken. It stretches 121 yards along its first length, then after a break continues for another ten yards, and beyond a further break it has been worked for an additional forty five yards, without its edge being reached. My experience of tunnel making was, as it happened, obtained on an extraordinary day. There were comparatively few men in the workings. In the places furthest from the shafts one felt a weight on the chest, and gasped for breath. The oppressiveness of the atmosphere was almost disquieting, and it did not seem surprising that tunnel makers were difficult to get, if they were required to work under such conditions.

Some days after I had returned again to the bustle and whirl of city life, and the deep shafts and the tunnelled way, and the gloom of the underground workings had become scarcely more than a picture in the brain, I received a letter from the resident engineer on the Totley tunnel length that revived my interest in the subterranean work for it said 'Your experience of railway tunnel works here was made during a remarkable depression of the barometer. I wondered, as we went along, how it was there were so many empty working places; and I afterwards ascertained that a large proportion of the workmen were laid up, owing to the bad air, and that this exceptional occurrence accounted for the small number of drillers at work when we were going through. The weather on the day was a meteorological curiosity. The gale rioted throughout the land, buildings were blown to the ground, trees uprooted and houses flooded for the rain fell in torrents for hours, and rivers spread far beyond their banks. The reading at noon was 28.456 inches and the depression had been exceeded only five times in thirty four years; so there was some excuse for the tunnel hewers at Totley, working a mile underground, breaking away from their toil with drill and hammer and pick in the stifling air.'

From the same writer:

'The line, which enters into competition with the MSLR from Sheffield to Manchester pierces a very rugged country, and the work, now completed, has been very heavy. In the past no one would have dreamed, unless he desired to kill time, of travelling from Sheffield to Manchester by the Midland, for he would have had to journey by Chesterfield and Ambergate, southward; then change trains, and travel north-westwards by Matlock and Peak Forest. The loss of traffic to the company and the annoyance of the trader were considerable, for the MSLR had practically a monopoly of the carrying-trade between the two cities with the Great Northern, and did not always succeed in pleasing their customers……The line gives the workers amid the smoke of furnace and the din and clatter of steel-plate easier access to many a pretty Derbyshire valley. The project originated with a number of Sheffield manufacturers, but the Midland finding competition creeping in on all sides, undertook to absorb the scheme in their system and to construct the line, although the estimated cost was one million sterling.'

W. M. Ackworth in the 'Railways of England', 5th edition, 1900 relates:

'The Midland have, however, just undertaken a new piece of tunnel construction on a very different scale. To anyone but those who are well up in the geography of the British Isles – and there are not many people who can honestly claim this distinction – it sounds rather startling to be told that the Company is going to spend about £1,000,000 in order to connect the insignificant village of Dore with the equally insignificant village of Chinley by a line twenty miles in length, and traversing on its course five and a half miles of tunnel. But when we come to realise that Dore means Sheffield, and Chinley Manchester, the matter assumes a somewhat different complexion…. Now the Midland system resembles in shape an open pair of scissors. The handles are at Bristol and London, they meet at Derby, and the blades point, the one towards Manchester and Liverpool; the other to Sheffield and Leeds and the north. The handles are so far apart that a Midland line to unite them is an impossible dream. But not so the blades. Sheffield is 41 miles from Manchester by the existing Manchester, Sheffield and Lincolnshire road. By the new Midland one the journey will be only five miles further. And it need not be said that there is a good deal of traffic worth fighting for between the two towns, in both of which the Midland is already well established.'

Edward Bradbury in 'Over the Dore and Chinley Railway: the New Route to Peakland', published by Richard Keene of Derby in 1895, wrote:

'For many years the wild moorlands that stretch in sharp ridges and deep hollows from the borders of Sheffield to the frontiers of Manchester, across the north east of Derbyshire, has been the despair of constructive engineers. In the board-rooms of the competing railway companies, the directors scrutinised the military maps that are hung from the walls, as big as a schooner's mainsail from Sheffield to Manchester, and from Stockport to Derby, like the 'feelers' of a gigantic iron octopus. The map in this Derbyshire district resembled a gridiron or a cobweb, so interwoven and intersected were the line of rails. But one remarkable stretch of country defied the invasion of the railway engineer – a region so surprising in its scenic beauty as to make a new holiday ground for English tourists, so full of underdeveloped mineral resources as to arouse the avarice of commercial speculators, so advantageous to traffic managers as to upset the strategy of rival routes. This blank space was the grave of railway hopes. The schemes of the Midland, LNWR and MSLR were entombed in the caverns of Castleton. The LNWR directors at Euston consulted their boardroom map and wept – wept not because they had no more worlds to explore, but because the Peak seemed an insuperable difficulty. The voice of the charmer whispered 'You are at Buxton: why not get into Sheffield, from which you are shut out?' The great map was lowered on its pulleys, but 30 miles of line with 10 miles of tunnel frightened even the owners of the Menai Straits tubular bridge. The MSLR whose chairman Sir Edward Watkin is prepared, by means of the Channel Tunnel, to abolish the only good thing between England and France, was frightened at the Peak District of Derbyshire. The astute administrators of the Midland Railway Company watched the timidity of their competitors. They saw it as a waiting game, there was an interval of suspense.' This introduction then covers the 1872 scheme and the birth of the Dore and Chinley Railway.

He later writes:

'The new line opened out a poetical district hitherto monopolised by artists and anglers, cyclists, picknickians, cameranians and coaching parties. It opens nature's recreation ground for street-stricken Sheffield and Manchester, and a picturesque residential country for the traders of the cities of steel and cotton, supplying too, an alternative route for the transit of their merchandise. It will stimulate decaying industries and develop mineral resources for the district is rich in lead and lime and will drive that monster of misapplied mechanics – the traction engine – off the highway, and attract to the Derbyshire Highlands the wealthy class who have preferred foreign spas to English health resorts, who know every inch of Baden Baden, but have never been to Buxton, who have scaled the peak of Tenerife, but have never bestowed a day upon the Peak of Derbyshire.' He then gets completely carried away in favourably comparing the Peak District with Switzerland!

The same writer in 'The New Derbyshire Railway', had an article in 'The Land We Live In', published by Chesterfield Public Library:

'The Dore and Chinley line, with its gigantic works and pretty railway stations, has passed through all the stages that greet great enterprises: that of sheer ridicule, that of virulent resistance, that of passive acceptance, and finally that of enthusiastic welcome. It was derided as the 'Bilberry and Besom' line on account of the moorland character of the country which it crosses: 'The Flue Line' in reference to the tunnels that perforate the hills; and 'The High Pique Line' because of its competition with the MSLR. Those, however, who come to scoff remain to praise, for the Dore and Chinley line is now a fact of very substantial proportions, ballasted with something more solid than bombast, and is the latest completed addition to the new routes to Peakland.'

John Ruskin, that progenitor of the environmental movement and supporter of Sheffield's labouring classes and lover of the Peak District should perhaps have the last say. He wrote a letter to the *Manchester City News* in Sep 1895 regarding the extension of railways in Derbyshire where he admits that if driven out of Brantwood, his Lake Coniston home, he would still set up his rest where:

'He could see the lamb leap and hear the windhover cry... learned travellers, gentle and simple – but above all English paterfamilias – think what this little piece of mid England has brought into so narrow a compass, of all that should be most precious to you. In its very minuteness it is the most educational of all the districts of beautiful landscapes known to me. The vast masses, the luxurious colouring, the mingled associations of great mountain scenery, amaze, excite, overwhelm, or exhaust – but too seldom teach; the mind cannot choose where to begin. But Derbyshire is a lovely child's alphabet: an alluring first lesson in all that's admirable, and powerful chiefly in the way it engages and fixes the attention. On its miniature cliffs a dark ivy leaf detaches itself as an object of importance: you distinguish with interest the species of mosses on the top: you count like many falling diamonds the magical drops of its petrifying well: the cluster of violets in the shade is an Armilla's garden to you. And the grace of it all! And the suddenness of its enchanted changes, and terrorless grotesque – Grotesque par excellence. It was a meadow a minute ago, now it is a cliff, and in an instant is a cave – and here was a brooklet, and now it is a whisper underground: turn but the corner of the path, and it is a little green lake of incredible crystal: and if the trout in it lifted up their heads and talked to you, you would be no more surprised than if it was in the Arabian nights. A half days' work of half a dozen navvies, and a snuff full of dynamite, may blow it into Erebus and diabolic night for ever and ever!'

John Ruskin (1819-900) by Herbert Rose Barraud in 1882.
Author's collection

CHAPTER 4
FROM OPENING TO NATIONALISATION 1894 TO 1947

INTRODUCTION

The time line theme which I have used for the previous chapters is continued. However many events that happened in this period are covered in some depth in Vol. 2 which covers the infrastructure. However they are mentioned in this chapter in order to give a sense of how they fit with what else was going on. Some items such as Royal visits are covered in some depth. Included are significant events that happened on connecting lines that impacted on the line. The number in the far right column shows in which volume the event is featured. Operations on the line and motive power are covered in the next chapter and are also recorded in a time sequence.

CHRONOLOGY OF EVENTS

1894 TO 1900

DATE	DETAILS	VOL
25 Jun 1894	The stations on the line opened for passengers and goods	1
16 Aug 1894	The Board of Trade announced that the line is complete except the shafts at both tunnels	1
1894	During the year the Wicker Goods depot was remodelled and rebuilt at a cost of £100,000	1
13 Jan 1895	Signal box opened in Totley tunnel to protect work on shaft No. 5. Closed by the end of the year	1
14 Mar 1895	Ventilation shaft at Totley tunnel completed	1
Mar 1895	Trafford Park engine shed opened for the Cheshire Lines Committee. The Midland shared the facilities with the GNR and MSLR. It was located on the west side of Manchester on marshy ground alongside the Bridgewater canal. It was a twenty road straight shed	1
1 Nov 1895	Both Totley and Cowburn tunnels had electric communications put in	1
1895	The LNWR gained a foothold in Sheffield when a goods shed at Nunnery was opened	1
11 Jun 1896	Ventilation shaft at Cowburn tunnel completed	1
Oct 1896	A 50 ft turntable put in at Hope	2
1896	During the year Holmes Curve was put in which allowed trains from Sheffield to directly access the 'Old Road' and Masborough Sorting Sidings South were opened	1
8 Feb 1897	The LDECR Chesterfield to Lincoln line opened in its entirety	1
21 May 1897	Royal train carrying Queen Victoria passed down the line hauled by new 4-4-0s 2208 and 2210	1
6 Aug 1897	Midland Railway Act for the New Mills and Heaton Mersey line passed	1
Early 1898	Goods shed erected at Grindleford	2
17 Feb 1898	Plans to extend platforms towards Edale at Hope station with additional waiting rooms added	2
May 1898	Act authorised the widening of the Dore to Sheffield line to four tracks and redevelopment of Sheffield Midland station	2
1 Jul 1898	GNR Deansgate, Manchester goods shed and yard opened. First fitted freight ran from Kings Cross	1
15 Sep 1898	An eight road fitting shop was approved at Grimesthorpe shed	1
9 Mar 1899	The GCR London extension opened from Annesley to London Marylebone	1
9 Aug 1899	The Derwent Valley Water Act received Royal Assent. Provided for formation of Derwent Valley Water Board and provision for six reservoirs in the upper Derwent and Ashop valleys	2
2 Nov 1899	First fitted freight ran from Kings Cross to Deansgate via the Hope valley	1
27 Nov 1899	The Midland plans and sections for the Chinley to New Mills widening completed	1 2
5 May 1900	Edward Sandemann was appointed engineer to the DVWB scheme	2
May 1900	The Sheffield District Railway opened. It was a three mile line from Treeton to Brightside Junction	1
18 Oct 1900	Chinley to New Mills Widening Act passed	1 2
19 Nov 1900	Canklow, Rotherham engine shed opened	1
1900	Railway (Prevention of Accidents) Act passed	1

1901 TO 1910

15 Apr 1901	Eccleshall, Sheffield engine shed opened	1 2
30 Apr 1901	The contract for the building of the Bamford & Howden Railway awarded to Walter Scott and Middleton Ltd	2
13 May 1901	Building of the Bamford & Howden Railway commences	2
16 Jul 1901	Excavations begin for Howden dam's foundations	2
26 Jul 1901	Second Derwent Valley Water Act receives Royal assent	2
Summer 1901	Erection of Birchinlee workmen's village starts	2

Date	Event	Ref
4 Sep 1901	Chinley North Junction to New Mills South Junction widening contract awarded to Walter Scott and Middleton Ltd.	2
19 Sep 1901	The foundations of Ashopton viaduct put in	2
1 Oct 1901	Cheadle Heath station to Heaton Mersey Station Junction opened for passengers	1
4 Nov 1901	Midland agreed to build a siding for the DVWB at Hathersage	2
Nov 1901	DVWB bought fifty two acres of land for Bole Hill quarry	2
9 Dec 1901	Agreement between the Midland and DVWB to build Water Works Sidings	2
1901	During the year agreement reached with DVWB to put in a siding at Bamford	2
1901	During the year a new 60 ft turntable was installed later enlarged to 65 ft at Grimesthorpe shed	1
1901	Platforms at Grindleford extended	2
Jan 1902	DVWB and Midland agree on sidings and signalling at Grindleford sidings	2
6 Feb 1902	Water Works Sidings signal box opened	2
13 Mar 1902	Board of Trade inspection passed connection of Water Works Sidings and main line at Grindleford	2
Apr 1902	Work on Bole Hill incline and Grindleford sidings started	2
4 May 1902	New Mills South Junction to Heaton Mersey and Liverpool curve opened for goods	1
1 Jun 1902	New Chinley station opened	2
1 Jul 1902	New Mills to Heaton Mersey line opened for passengers	1
28 Jul 1902	Ashopton viaduct brought into use	2
Jul 1902	Foundations of Derwent Reservoir started	2
6 Sep 1902	Bamford & Howden Railway became operational	2
19 Oct 1902	The widened lines from Chinley North Junction to Chinley Station South Junction opened	2
26 Oct 1902	Chinley North Junction signal box replaced by a new box	2
23 Jan 1903	Bamford & Howden Railway completed to Howden	2
Feb 1903	The LNWR consolidate their foothold in Sheffield with the opening of their City Goods shed and yard on Broad Street	1
1 Mar 1903	Gowhole up sidings at Gowhole Goods Junction opened	2
19 Mar 1903	The widened lines from Chinley Station North Junction to Gowhole opened	2
30 Mar 1903	Dore to Sheffield widening opened throughout	2
11 May 1903	Gowhole down sidings opened	2
25 May 1903	The first wagon load of stone despatched from Bole Hill quarry	2
May 1903	Grindleford Sidings of the DVWB opened	2
May 1903	The Midland Hotel, Manchester opened	1
1 Jul 1903	Through coach from Manchester to Harwich via Lincoln introduced	1
16 Jul 1903	Work on Rivelin Tunnel started	2
21 Jul 1903	Grindleford, Baslow and Bakewell Railway received its Act	1
Summer 1903	During the spring and summer a military camp of over 5,000 men were billeted in the Edale and Castleton valleys for exercises	2
7 Feb 1904	Collapse of Dove Holes tunnel. Traffic diverted over Hope valley. Re-opened on 17 Mar 1904	1
26 Apr 1904	The Hope & Castleton Light Railway Order granted	1 2
18 Jul 1904	Norman's Bank signal box opened permanently	2
4 Aug 1904	Joel Lean resident engineer for the Rivelin tunnel project died age 46	2
12 May 1905	King Edward VII and Queen Alexandra visited Sheffield and stayed in Hathersage sidings overnight	1
30 Jun 1905	Bus service from Manchester Mottram Street to Hollingworth started by GCR	1
17 Oct 1905	Electric communication put in to Cowburn and Totley tunnels	2
1905	Sheffield Midland station enlargement completed	2
5 Jan 1906	Goods train ran into another from rear between Chinley station and Chinley North Junction	2
May 1906	Work started on the Bamford filter beds	2
Dec 1906	Additional sidings and 60 ft turntable installed at Chinley station	2
1 Jan 1907	The GCR takes over the LDECR	1
21 Jun 1907	Record stones laid at Derwent and Howden reservoirs	2
9 Oct 1907	Serious derailment at Dore and Totley station	2
25 Nov 1907	Wath Yard opened by the GCR which gave the company significantly increased capacity to handle its coal traffic	1
1907	Midland locomotive renumbering scheme introduced	1
1 Apr 1908	Installation of additional water columns at Chinley agreed	2
30 Jul 1908	The LNWR reached a co-operation agreement with the Midland	1
2 Nov 1908	Agreement with LNWR at Buxton regarding trains from Sheffield to Llandudno and return	1

1908	The powers to build the Grindleford, Baslow and Bakewell Railway lapsed	1
4 Jan 1909	Centralised Train Control introduced between Cudworth and Toton which improved the men's hours of work and used resources more efficiently	1
20 Sep 1909	Rivelin tunnel ends meet	2
13 Feb 1910	The powers to build the Hope and Castleton Light Railway lapsed	1
Mid 1910	Bamford filters completed	2
Aug 1910	Lining of Rivelin tunnel completed	2
15 Dec 1910	Main quarrying at Bole Hill quarry finished.	2

1911 TO 1922

11 Jul 1911	National Railwaymen's strike	1
1 Jan 1912	Howden reservoir starts to fill	2
22 Jul 1912	Howden reservoir water first overflows dam's crest	2
5 Sep 1912	Howden reservoir formally opened	2
Sep 1912	Rivelin tunnel finished	2
Dec 1912	Demolition of Birchinlee village begins	2
13 Sep 1914	Bole Hill quarry closed. Grindleford sidings cleared	2
1914	By the end of the year the lifting of the Bamford & Howden Railway from Howden begins	2
1914	Hospital opened in Hathersage to treat injured Belgian, British and Commonwealth soldiers	2
1914	Kings Cross to Deansgate fitted freight via Peak line discontinued and transferred to Hope valley line	1
19 Nov 1915	The filling of Derwent reservoir begins	2
8 Jan 1916	Derwent reservoir water first overflows the crest	2
22 Jun 1916	The Midland bought Grindleford sidings and the land from the DVWB	2
1916	During the year Derwent reservoir opened without any ceremony	2
1 Jan 1917	Dore South Curve and Chinley South Curve open only for goods traffic and occasional excursion trains	2
1 Jan 1917	Hazel Grove station closed for passengers	1
8 Apr 1919	Water Works Sidings signal box closed	2
19 May 1919	King George V and Queen Mary visited Sheffield and stayed overnight at Hathersage	1
26 Sep 1919	National strike to 6 Oct	1
1919	Yorkshire Bridge mechanical filter plant opened	2
4 Aug 1920	The Derwent Valley Calver and Bakewell Railway received its Act	1
4 Aug 1920	Eccleshall shed renamed 'Millhouses'	2
Jul 1921	Bridge 3 Halls Private Road at Dore West Junction superstructure removed and piers taken down	2
1921	Work started on the Ashop and Alport diversion scheme. 2 ft gauge tramway used.	2
9 Oct 1922	The first bus service between Sheffield and the Peak District run by C. H. Battey	1
24 Dec 1922	Water Works sidings cleared and signal box removed	2
31 Dec 1922	The Midland Railway ceased to exist after seventy eight years	1

1923 TO 1947

1 Jan 1923	The newly formed London Midland & Scottish Railway absorbed the Midland Railway	1
2 Jun 1924	Chapel-en-le-Frith station renamed 'Chapel-en-le-Frith Central'.	2
May 1925	The long tenure of Harry Thompson as station master at Hope commenced	2
3 Sep 1925	Head on collision at Hope station. Three killed	2
1925	Peak Forest Tramway closed	1
1 Mar 1928	Contract for building Earle's branch from the works to the main line siding let to Fred Mitchell & Sons of Manchester	2
27 Mar 1928	King Amanullah and Queen Soraya Zarfi spend a night in Edale sidings	2
25 Jun 1928	First bus service between Sheffield and Manchester via Woodhead run by W. T. Underwood	1
12 Aug 1928	A new ground frame put in at Earle's sidings	2
18 Oct 1928	Ashop and Alport water diversion brought into use	2
1 Jan 1929	The Sheffield Joint Omnibus Committee formed by the Sheffield Corporation, LMS and LNER	1
7 Mar 1929	Incline track from quarry face to Hadfield's crushing plant became operational	2
14 Apr 1929	Earle's sidings signal box opened	2
15 Sep 1929	First quarry blasting took place at Earle's and railways laid down in quarry became operational	2
Oct 1929	LNER ran its first bus service from Sheffield to Manchester via Woodhead	1
15 Nov 1929	Earle's Cement works and branch officially opened	2
21 Nov 1929	Earle's Cement new sidings inspected by the Board of Trade	2
4 Jun 1930	Bugsworth station renamed 'Buxworth'	2
Jun 1931	The Longshaw Estate purchased by the National Trust	2
24 Apr 1932	Kinder mass trespass took place	2
24 Apr 1932	Edale Mill closed	2
1933	Work commenced on Ladybower reservoir	2

Date	Event	Ref
Jul 1934	The LMS sold its Blackpool coach service to Sheffield United Tours	1
8 Aug 1934	A fire destroys Forge Mill at Chinley	2
Sep 1934	Contract for building Ladybower reservoir awarded	2
19 Aug 1935	Buxton Midland shed closed	1
19 Aug 1935	Design of Water Board sidings approved by the Chief Engineer's Office of the LMS	2
Sep 1935	Baillie's of Haddington awarded contract to build Ladybower reservoir. Building commenced soon after	2
2 Dec 1935	Water Board sidings and new Water Board Sidings signal box opened and re-laid line to Yorkshire Bridge opened	2
2 Dec 1935	Hasland shed new coaling plant opened	1
Late 1935	Hadfield's quarry at Hope became part of the Derbyshire Stone Company	2
May 1936	Bridge 55 across Mirey Lane at Edale received a new steel centre girder and was part reconstructed	2
15 Jun 1936	60 ft turntable at Chinley fitted with vacuum tractor	2
24 Jun 1936	60 ft turntable at Gowhole fitted with vacuum tractor	2
1936	New five track carriage sidings opened at Dore and Totley	2
1936	New bridge 36A at Thornhill built alongside Midland bridge 36 by DVWB	2
1936	Hathersage open air baths opened	2
1937	New ash handling plant opened at Grimesthorpe shed	1
Mar 1938	Over following two months bridge 105 strengthened between Chinley South and North Junctions	2
Jun 1938	Ban on 'Jubilee' class locomotives in Manchester Central station lifted after bridge strengthening on approaches to the station	2
20 Nov 1938	Grindleford signal box replaced and located 270 yards west of the entrance to the goods yard rather than at the end of the down platform	2
29 Dec 1938	Dore and Totley East up distant replaced by a colour light signal	2
Dec 1938	Now preserved Hudswell Clarke locomotive *Nunlow* was ex works awaiting delivery to Earle's to join *Pindale* and *Winhill* which had been delivered new for the works opening	2
Apr 1939	Plan to relocate one of Brown Bayley's, Sheffield special finishing departments, to land near the closed Edale Mill	2
11 Jul 1939	Emergency passenger timetable into operation	1
Aug 1939	Northern Command militia units guarding entrance to Totley tunnel	2
Jan 1940	Severe snowstorms close the line	1
27 Jan 1940	A Trafford Park to Rowsley double headed goods derailed at Chinley South Junction in the snow	1
May 1940	Hathersage taken over by Anti-Aircraft Unit. Stayed for two months	2
12 Dec 1940	Over three nights blitz Sheffield South No. 1 signal box demolished and houses behind damaged	1
1940	Baker's Accommodation footbridge No. 40 between Hope and Norman's Bank removed	2
Mar 1941	Decision taken to cease using narrow gauge railway for building Ladybower wall and replace by road transport	2
18 Mar 1943	Valves opened to fill Ladybower reservoir	2
1944	Gowhole up sidings 60 ft articulated turntable ordered	2
25 Sep 1945	King George VI and Queen Elizabeth open Ladybower reservoir. Royal train at Bamford station	2
1946	By the end of the year the standard gauge line was mainly or wholly lifted between Water Board sidings and Yorkshire Bridge	2
26 Jan 1947	Serious snow storms arrive	1
23 Feb 1947	Hulleys' bus stranded in snow on Grindleford to Eyam road. Not released until 3 Mar	1
24 Feb 1947	Fifty wagons of ice taken out of Cowburn tunnel. Some icicles 20 ft long, 3 ft thick and weighing over half a ton were removed	1
Dec 1947	Harry Thompson station master at Hope since 1925 retired	2
31 Dec 1947	The last day of the London Midland and Scottish Railway after forty four years. It became the largest constituent of the nationalised British Railways	3

GUIDES TO THE NEW RAILWAY

Following the opening of the line in its entirety and the full range of services, including local and through freight and passenger services the line settled into a routine.

Two different guides to the area accessible from the new line were issued by two different publishers. The author of both was Edward Bradbury who used the pseudonym 'Strephon'. Bradbury was born at Derby in 1853 and worked for the Midland from 1870 to 1888 when he resigned due to ill health. He died in Buxton in 1905 at the age of fifty one. The first was 'The Dore & Chinley Railway Gossiping Guide: The Sheffield Independent Gossiping Guide to the District' price 4d. This ran to three editions, the third in 1895 being enlarged. It was illustrated by photographs. The other was 'Over the Dore and Chinley Railway: The New Route to Peakland' and was published by Richard Keene Limited, All Saints, Derby in 1895. They were printers, publishers and stationers with premises on Irongate. It is illustrated by lithographs. The latter is more comprehensive with twice the number of pages but there is some duplication between them but both are well written and give a good feel of the period and the area.

ADVERTISEMENTS FROM THE 'GOSSIPING GUIDE'

THE Dore & Chinley Railway

THE Sheffield Independent's GOSSIPING GUIDE TO THE DISTRICT

PRICE FOURPENCE

MIDLAND RAILWAY.

OPENING OF THE NEW DORE & CHINLEY LINE.

The Dore and Chinley Line is now OPEN for

Local and Through Passenger and Merchandise Traffic.

Passenger and Goods Train Services are in operation, calling at *Grindleford* (for Eyam, Calver, Stoney Middleton, and Baslow), *Hathersage*, *Bamford*, *Hope* (for Castleton and Bradwell) and *Edale*.

THROUGH PASSENGER & GOODS TRAINS

ARE NOW RUNNING BETWEEN

SHEFFIELD AND BUXTON,

AND

SHEFFIELD AND MANCHESTER, LIVERPOOL, &c.

GIVING CONNECTION WITH

PRINCIPAL TOWNS IN LANCASHIRE, CHESHIRE, YORKSHIRE, & THE NORTH-EASTERN DISTRICT.

The Opening of the line affords a new and quick route from
THE EAST TO THE WEST COAST FOR MERCHANDISE AND MINERAL TRAFFIC.

For Particulars of the Passenger Service see Time Tables, Bills, Cards, &c. Pocket Time Tables, giving the complete service, may be had on application to the Station Masters, or to Mr. W. L. Mugliston, Superintendent of the Line, Derby.

All information as to Goods Rates and arrangements may be obtained from Mr. W. E. Adie, Goods Manager, Derby.

GEO. H. TURNER,

Derby, 1895. GENERAL MANAGER.

MIDLAND RAILWAY.

OPENING OF THE NEW DORE AND CHINLEY LINE,

FOR

LOCAL AS WELL AS THROUGH

PASSENGER TRAFFIC.

Commencing on

Monday, June 25th,

and until further notice, a

SERVICE OF PASSENGER TRAINS,

will be run between

Sheffield & Buxton,

and intermediate Stations as shewn herein.

GEO. H. TURNER,

Derby, June, 1894. General Manager.

MIDLAND RAILWAY,

GENERAL CARRIERS

TO AND FROM ALL PARTS OF THE

UNITED KINGDOM AND THE CONTINENT.

The NEW LINE between DORE & CHINLEY

AFFORDS A

NEW AND QUICK ROUTE

between LEEDS, BRADFORD,

SHEFFIELD, HULL, & MANCHESTER,

STOCKPORT, WARRINGTON, WIDNES, WIGAN, LIVERPOOL, BOLTON, BLACKBURN, OLDHAM, GUIDE-BRIDGE, STALEYBRIDGE, and other large towns in the Cheshire and South Lancashire Districts, and provides a new and continuous Railway from the East to West Coast.

Facilities are also afforded for the more rapid conveyance of traffic between the places named above and YORK, STOCKTON, MIDDLESBRO', DARLINGTON, SUNDERLAND, WEST HARTLEPOOL, AND THE NORTH EASTERN DISTRICT generally.

Goods Stations have been provided at GRINDLEFORD, HATHERSAGE, HOPE, BAMFORD, and EDALE.

For information as to Rates, &c., application should be made to the Station Masters, or to W. E. ADIE, Goods Manager, Derby.

CHEAP WEEK-END & OTHER TICKETS

are issued to the Dore and Chinley Line from MANCHESTER, LIVERPOOL, LEEDS, BRADFORD, DERBY, LEICESTER, NOTTINGHAM, and other Stations on the Midland Railway. See the Company's Time Tables and Bills for particulars.

GEO. H. TURNER,

GENERAL MANAGER.

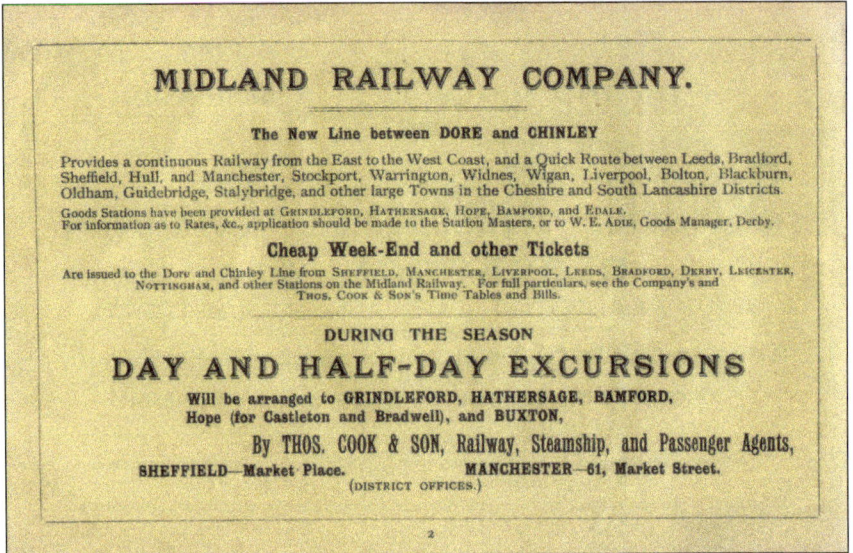

This is the cover and first page of a small booklet issued by Thomas Cook in conjunction with the Midland in 1898 for excursions to the attractions on the line and beyond. The booklet sings the praises of all the locations on or near the line and outlines the opportunities for fly fishing on the Upper Derwent. Note that Edale is not included in the destinations for excursions, probably because there was no access to Kinder Scout for walkers *Laurence Knighton collection*

This is the ornate cover of a Midland pamphlet for express trains run by the company for winter 1894/5 which includes a special mention of the new Dore and Chinley line.
Laurence Knighton collection

The public and working timetable for 1894 is analysed in the next chapter. See page 232

FROM OPENING TO THE FIRST WORLD WAR

VOLUMES OF TRAFFIC

There was a steep increase in passenger traffic nationally in this period from 800 million in 1890 to 1,100 million in 1900 to 1,300 million in 1910 and 1,400 million in 1914. This had been significantly boosted by the Midland abolishing second class travel in 1874 and the improvement in comfort in third class carriages although the other companies followed. First class travel also became for an increasingly smaller proportion of the travelling public.

RAILWAY RATES

The Railway and Canal Traffic Act of 1888 attempted to tackle long held grievances by traders that the railways were overcharging them by offering more favourable rates for transporting imported goods. This Act stopped the companies from increasing their rates in the future. To compensate for problems ahead the companies raised their rates to the maximum provided by the Act which caused uproar among its customers. They had done it to cushion themselves against future vagaries of market conditions. It also caused the companies to harden their stand against claims for improved wages and conditions for its workforce because they would have to carry the entire financial burden it would cause. Following the national railway strike in Aug 1911 the unions achieved improvements in wages for some of the railwaymen. As a result of this the government allowed the railways to raise their charges to meet the additional costs. The railway companies received most of the blame for freight rates on British railways being generally higher than those in the major industrialised countries in Europe and the USA. This was not entirely just. The 600,000 privately owned railway wagons of the collieries, iron works and other companies, lacking as they did any standardised pattern of construction or capacity, cluttered up the tracks, slowed the pace of goods trains and generally raised railway industry costs.

CENTRALISED TRAIN CONTROL

The Midland Railway was the pioneer of a centralised train control system, which began with a small experiment at Masborough in 1907. It was originated by J. H. Follows, who in that year was promoted to the staff of the new general superintendent, Cecil Paget. The Masborough office collected all information about the booking on times of trainmen and found that in that year there were more than 20,000 cases of men working excessive hours. Four years later there were none.

So well did the Masborough telephonic control work that Paget proposed an extension of the central control of train movements and on 4 Jan 1909 the most congested section of line on the whole system between Cudworth and Toton was selected for the expansion. Paget brought all goods and mineral trains under the supervision of central controllers. Constant touch was kept with one another at Cudworth, Masborough, Staveley, Westhouses and Toton. It was as successful as the original pilot at Masborough had been and so it was extended to the entire network of the Midland.

The first end in view was the improvement of heavy coal workings. Much of the task was in the hands of Follows, who investigated the workable capacity of the various sections and prepared large diagrams showing used and optional paths for the various classes of train. It was in connection with the new control system that from 1905 the engines were classified by power and had their numbers painted in large figures on tender or tank side thus making them easily identifiable from distance. At the same time, the handsome armorial devices of the company were transferred on to the cab side. Booked timings were carefully scrutinised and revised where necessary to give maximum utilisation of line capacity, and train diagrams were prepared. The entire Midland system was mapped in line diagrams, with superimposed enlargements of station layouts, showing cranes, single line tablet or staff, stations and water troughs. Slow lines were shown in red and goods lines in green. The railway system was divided into forty two sections, covering over 1,500 miles of route. Separate working books were prepared for goods and passenger train movements, and originally, various symbols were used to describe different classes of train. The use of path diagrams resulted in a remarkable improvement in the standard of punctuality throughout the railway. Central Control was placed at Derby and this became the hub of the system. There had been improvements earlier in the century, but the punctuality of Midland trains now became exemplary, a far call from the eccentric waywardness of the 'nineties.

LOCOMOTIVE RENUMBERING

In 1907 the Midland had a route mileage of nearly 1,500 miles. It had 2,796 engines in 1905, achieving an annual train mileage of 47,920 each engine in all classes of traffic. Since the opening of our line there had been a huge increase in traffic, to which our line had contributed and this had resulted in a steady new build programme. In the spring of 1907 a complete renumbering of engines began abolished the distinction of duplicate stock by dividing classes by wheel arrangement, age and power rating as detailed in the table below.

TYPE	WHEEL ARRANGEMENT	NUMBERS	NO OF ENGINES
Passenger Tender	Four coupled	1 on	544
Passenger Tender	Single driver	600 on	95
Passenger Tender	Four coupled	700 on	116
Passenger Tank	Four coupled	1200 on	231
Goods Tank	Four coupled	1500 on	28
Goods Tank	Six coupled	1600 on	359
Goods Tender	Mogul 2-6-0	2200 on	40
Goods Tender	Six coupled double framed	2300 on	568
Goods Tender	Six coupled	2900 on	815
Total			2,796

RIGHTS FOR RAILWAYMEN

We have seen the appalling neglect by the contractors of the men who built the line to provide safe working conditions and sufficient proper accommodation. The Midland Railway studiously avoided any interest in the working practices of its contractors. In 1875 one in every 334 men employed by the railway companies was killed while at work. The 1897 Workmen's Employment Act gave rights to railway employees to seek redress through the courts rather than through the railway's own inadequate provisions. This Act contributed to an improvement by 1899 to one in 1,006 deaths.

Another piece of regulation was the Railway Regulation Act of 1893 which brought the working hours of some of the staff more into line with those in other industries. Those in the railway workshops and clerical workers were not covered by this improvement and it took until just before the outbreak of the First World War before substantial gains were made.

In 1911 the average weekly wage of all railwaymen was £1/5/9 a week which was a penny less than it had been in 1907 although prices had been rising. The companies refused to recognize the trade unions whose memberships were continually rising and used conciliation boards to settle wage and conditions of service issues. These excluded union representatives and this injustice led directly to the 1911 national strike. Under pressure from the government, the companies at last agreed union officers should be eligible for membership of the men's panels on the Boards. Although formal union recognition had yet to come a big step forward had been taken towards collective bargaining on the railways.

ACCIDENTS

Gruesome railway accidents over the preceding years forced a reluctant Parliament to legislate in order to improve railway practices. The Regulation of Railways Act of 1889 made it compulsory to introduce the block signalling system with interlocking signals and points and continuous brakes on passenger trains. These enforced improvements quickly changed accident rates.

Accidents to railwaymen, particularly shunters, were commonplace and in 1900 the Railway (Prevention of Railway Accidents) Act was passed. This required the railway companies to reduce or eliminate dangerous practices. This resulted in the better lighting of shunting yards, the introduction of side brakes on both sides of wagons, better labelling of goods wagons and the protection of point rods and signal wires. Fatal accidents to shunters fell from 1 in 156 in 1894 to 1 in 444 in 1913.

However the Midland's reputation was seriously damaged by several serious accidents. Bad accidents at Cudworth in 1905 and Sharnbrook in 1909 were only the precursor of two more serious accidents on the Settle and Carlisle line. The first was on Christmas Eve 1910 near Hawes Junction at Garsdale. It was a pitch dark morning and pouring with rain. No less than five locomotives were waiting to be turned on the famous stockade turntable. The signalman then decided to put two of the engines bound for Carlisle on to the down through road. The signalman then forgot all about them and accepted the midnight express from St Pancras to Glasgow. As the signals for the express were pulled off the light engines for Carlisle thought the signals were for them and set off north-west. The inevitable collision took place north of Moorcock tunnel at Grisedale crossing. All the carriages of the express were eight wheelers, except for two twelve wheeled sleepers. The impact resulted in the fitted gas cylinders igniting which set the coaches on fire. Twelve passengers were killed. Lax conduct in following the rules, allied with criticism of the Pintsch gas lighting system, was made at the enquiry.

The second happened on 2 Sep 1913 near Ais Gill. The engine on the Glasgow to St Pancras sleeping car train was steaming poorly and loosing time. The driver blamed the problem on the small coal provided. He finally came to a standstill half a mile before Ais Gill signal box just before the summit. Neither was all well on a following train from Edinburgh which was having similar difficulty with poor steaming due to small coal. The driver's preoccupation with this problem and going out on to the framing to oil an axle box caused him to miss a caution signal and then a stop signal at Mallerstang. The Edinburgh train then ran into the rear of the standing Glasgow express. Fire from the stricken engine caused the gas cylinders to become alight which in turn set the last three carriages on fire. Sixteen passengers were killed. It was the worst accident in the Midland's history.

On the Hope valley line there were minor accidents but none major except for that of Sep 1925 near Hope station when there was a head on collision which caused the deaths of three railwaymen. There was a bad derailment in 1907 at Dore station and further ones around Chinley in the 1900s all covered in more detail in Vol 2.

ROAD TRANSPORT

Motor transport was virtually non-existent when the line opened. The roads were a dust bowl in summer and a muddy quagmire in winter. Horse and steam power were the only available forms of motive power. The growth of the motor vehicle industry in Britain was small scale and mainly bespoke and was well behind American and European practice. As a result, motor transport's impact on the railways was limited. As late as 1913, of the 33,000 motor vehicles produced in Britain, only about 11,000 were for commercial use. When the British Expeditionary Force left for France in 1914 it possessed only 827 motor cars, mostly hastily requisitioned but that was to change rapidly as the war went on. This increase in commercial vehicles was a great benefit as it allowed the distribution of merchandise from the railway's goods yards to be improved.

However the electrification of urban tramways in the early years of the twentieth century caused a marked decline of suburban rail traffic.

FURTHER MIDLAND RAILWAY EXPANSION

On the Midland, the Dore and Chinley Railway, was the penultimate major building of a new line. During 1901 the New Mills to Heaton Mersey line was built and is dealt with shortly. In 1904 the Heysham Harbour and branch was opened. Previously on 1 Jul 1903 the company had acquired by amalgamation the Belfast and Northern Counties Railway comprising a main line from Belfast to Derry and another short line from Belfast to Larne with numerous branches. When all the lines had been acquired the Midland had 265 route miles under its control. For its Irish traffic the company acquired the fleet of the Barrow Steam Navigation Company, and by 1910, had six steamers serving Belfast, Douglas and Scotland. During 1908 the Lancaster, Morecambe and Heysham line was very successfully electrified.

In 1912 the very busy London Tilbury and Southend Railway was vested in the Midland with which it merged completely in 1920.

INCREASING LINE CAPACITY

The rapid increase in traffic meant the Midland had to expand its lines to cope. The sudden expansion of the coal industry in south Yorkshire, north Derbyshire and Nottinghamshire caused particular problems. On the whole line from St Pancras to Leeds there was extensive widening from two to four tracks; usually two were for passenger trains and two for goods. There were widenings from Trent to Alfreton, Clay Cross to Chesterfield and on to Tapton Junction. The line from Dore to Sheffield was widened and is covered more thoroughly in Vol. 2. North of Sheffield there were widenings toward Rotherham and to Swinton, Cudworth and Royston as far as Chevet Junction. Also, Wath to Darfield was widened and extended.

At the western end of Midland territory there was little opportunity to widen the Peak line but a major widening was undertaken between Chinley North Junction and New Mills South Junction. This included the complete remodelling of Chinley station, which changed it from a sleepy two platform wayside station of little importance to a major hub with five through platform faces and a bay at the east end. Enlarged goods facilities with engine turning and water facilities completed the picture. Controlling all this was no less than five signal boxes. Beyond Chinley quadrupling of the lines through Bugsworth (Buxworth from 1930) station, the demolition of Bugsworth tunnel and the building of the extensive Gowhole sidings on both sides of the main line was undertaken. The Act for all this activity was obtained in 1900 and it was all opened during 1902 and 1903. Vol. 2 will cover this widening in detail.

NEW MILLS AND HEATON MERSEY LINE

THE REASON WHY IT WAS BUILT

As we have seen, the Midland's drive to access Manchester was an all embracing ambition of the company over many years. Although it had achieved that up to a point, it was constrained by congestion and slow running on the Sheffield & Midland Company's joint line which started at New Mills and ran via Marple to Romiley Junction. Here passenger traffic and all traffic for Merseyside turned westwards to join the Cheshire Lines Committee's line at Bredbury Junction, and continued through Stockport Tiviot Dale to Heaton Mersey. From there trains for Manchester took the curve from Heaton Mersey East Junction and ran along the Midland's Manchester South District line to Chorlton Junction and then over the CLC into Central station. On the whole of this section the Midland did not have total control due to the shared arrangements which were entered into with other companies. Traffic proceeding directly to Merseyside from the south continued on the CLC from Heaton Mersey to Glazebrook East Junction and then on to Liverpool Central for passengers and for goods to the marshalling sidings at Halewood or to the goods depots at Brunswick, Huskisson, Sandon & Canada Dock and Alexandra & Langton Docks. Mineral traffic for Northwich and Hartford branched off the CLC at Skelton Junction between Heaton Mersey and Glazebrook, and passed over a short section of the 'Manchester South Junction & Altrincham Railway' before running onto the CLC's line to Chester.

Some Midland traffic used the same lines from Chinley and ran beyond Romiley Junction, through Belle Vue to Ashburys East Junction, then over Great Central metals through Ashburys station to Ashbury West Junction followed by Midland tracks to Ancoats Junction for the branch to the Midland's main Manchester goods depot at Ancoats and similarly for traffic to Ashton Road. Passenger trains for Manchester Victoria used the connection from Ancoats Junction to the LYR line from Ardwick to Phillip's Park and Miles Platting at Midland Junction. The trains to Blackpool used this route.

By the mid-1890s the traffic congestion between Chinley and Heaton Mersey via Marple and Stockport was becoming intolerable. During the day the lines were heavily used by passenger and some freight traffic. The nights were little better. There was keen competition with the LNWR for the London to Manchester and London to Liverpool passenger traffic. The GNR in partnership with the GCR also competed for the London to Manchester traffic via Retford and Sheffield, and by 1899, the GCR had their extension to London up and running. This put Nottingham and Leicester on the Great Central's new main line to Manchester via Sheffield and Godley and directly threatened the Midland's monopoly of the Manchester and Liverpool traffic from those towns. On the CLC separation of Manchester Victoria or Liverpool Central portions from the main train to Manchester Central took place at the constricted station at Marple or occasionally at Tiviot Dale.

It was not possible to widen the lines via Marple and Stockport because of the tunnels, viaducts, bridges and steep gradients; indeed there was a lack of space to quadruple the lines on many sections.

These problems drove the Midland to consider alternative solutions which resulted in a new direct though line from New Mills South Junction to Heaton Mersey, which was authorised by an Act of 6 Aug 1897. It was able to bypass Stockport through open country to the south and although it was only nine and three quarter miles long it was expensive to build because it required the boring of the 3,866 yard Disley tunnel. This became the second longest tunnel on the Midland system after Totley and demoted Cowburn from second to third place. The line was laid out for high speed running by avoiding the conflicting junctions, gradients, sharp curves and speed restrictions on the route that it replaced.

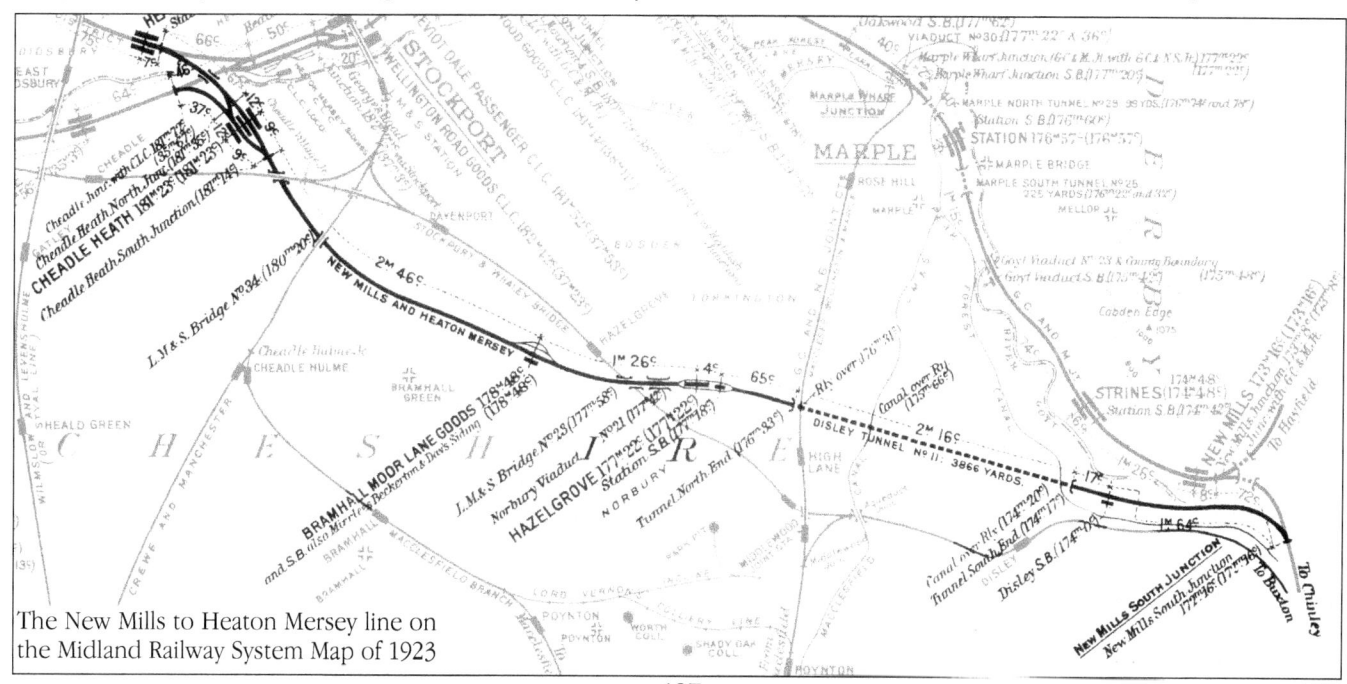

The New Mills to Heaton Mersey line on the Midland Railway System Map of 1923

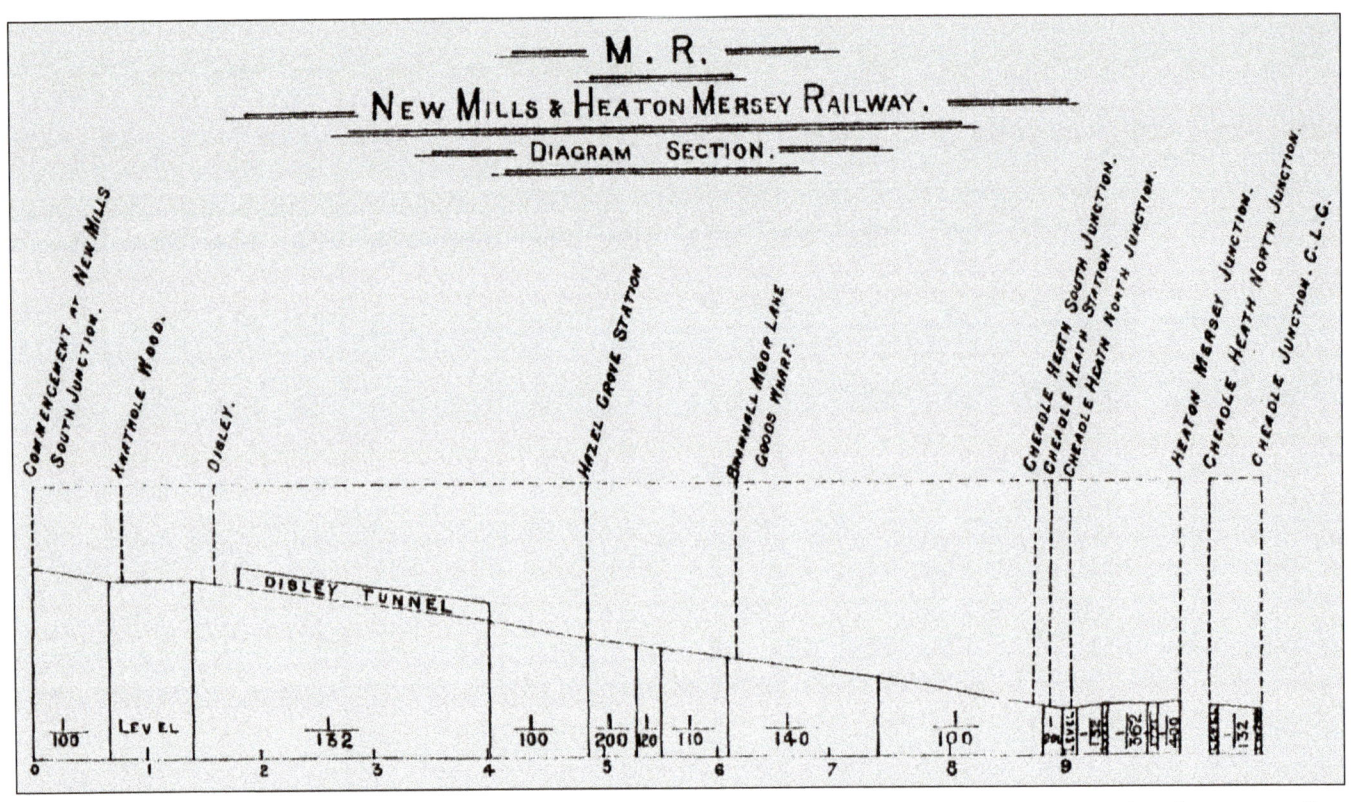

The official Midland Railway gradient profile which clearly shows that the line was built on a descending incline from New Mills.

Newtown viaduct around 1916 from a colour postcard. A lovely view with the River Goyt winding toward it. *Valentine*

Below: Newtown viaduct at an early date. All 13 arches can be seen and a signal controlled by New Mills Goods Junction signal box is on the left.
Hyde Stationer, New Mills

On 16 Jun 1898 the difficult contract No. 1 was awarded to Walter Scott & Co who bid £468,362/9/4. It was to start at a junction with the Derby to Manchester line at New Mills and finish in the parish of Norbury in Cheshire a distance of five miles 797 yards. From Hazel Grove to Heaton Mersey the contract was in the hands of H. Lovatt.

NEW MILLS SOUTH JUNCTION TO DISLEY TUNNEL

The cut off line ran from New Mills South Junction over the graceful, curved, thirteen arch 350 yard long Newtown viaduct. Each arch was 45 ft wide, two of which went over the River Goyt.

The line, now dropping at 1 in 132, passed high retaining walls flanking the ninety yard Newtown tunnel (or covered way) under Albion Road, a busy part of New Mills where the Brunswick Mill was situated. It then headed towards Disley tunnel passing a short lived block post at Knat Hole Wood. At Newtown a large number of newly erected houses and a rope manufacturing works were knocked down to accommodate the line. The residents of New Mills petitioned for the line to start at a station in New Mills so that the town of 20,000 people could have quicker access to Liverpool and Manchester but they were unsuccessful.

DISLEY TUNNEL

Disley Tunnel south end at an unknown date. Surmounting the crown is the Midland Wyvern and on the wing walls the legend 'M.R.' on the left and '1901' on the right.
F. Moore.
Locomotive Publishing Company

Disley Tunnel north end when new. It is of brick construction and is surmounted by the legend 'MR TUNNEL 1901'. A wooden notice board on the right gives the length as 3,866 yards. Above right is an over bridge of the Great Central and North Staffordshire Railways joint line from Marple Wharf Junction to Macclesfield Central.
Ernest Pouteau
John Alsop collection

The tunnel still on the 1 in 132 gradient is two miles 346 yards long. It was driven from both ends with eleven shafts down from the moorland above, making twenty four working faces. Ten of the shafts, surmounted by large blue brick towers remain as ventilation shafts. There were also temporary shafts outside the tunnel. Just before the tunnel there were up and down lie by sidings which had a sixty and fifty wagon capacity, controlled by Disley signal box. Shortly after entering the tunnel, the Peak Forest Canal, and towards the northern end, the LMS owned Macclesfield Canal ran over it.

Because of the length of the tunnel, in mid 1904 special instructions were issued and equipment installed to deal with any emergency or accident. Telephonic instruments were put in at the signal boxes at Hazel Grove and Disley and a further one in a manhole on the up side of the line about 1,000 yards from the Disley end and another one on the down side about 1,000 yards from the Hazel Grove end of the tunnel. By pressing a button on the instrument a horn was sounded in the signal box and a spring in the handle pressed. The person in the tunnel was required to say 'Are you there Hazel Grove' or 'Disley' as appropriate.

In Aug 1913 this arrangement was superseded by the signalman at either end being able to receive notification of problems in the tunnel by the cutting of special telegraph wires which activated warning indicators and bells. The wires were located on the walls of the tunnel on the up and down sides. Similar equipment was also installed in Totley and Cowburn tunnels.

DISLEY TUNNEL TO CHEADLE HEATH

On leaving the tunnel the falling gradient steepened to 1 in 100 and the line then reached the passenger station at Hazel Grove, five mile form New Mills South Junction.

The platform was reached by a subway after a substantial walk along a track from the direction of High Lane, a settlement already served by a station on the Macclesfield Committee's line as well as a better sited LNWR station on the Stockport to Buxton line. Takings were poor and it closed in 1917 as a First World War economy and never reopened.

The line then crossed Norbury viaduct, which consisted of eleven blue brick arches flanked at each end by high metal bridges over main roads, and then over the LNWR Buxton branch. A mile further at Bramhall Moor Lane there were sidings on the up side holding fifty six wagons, and on the down side a signal box. It also had a goods shed, cattle pens and a crane.

The line continued to descend on gradients of 1 in 110, 1 in 140 and then at 1 in 100, before reaching Cheadle Heath station, nine miles from New Mills South Junction.

The line now passed under the LNWR Crewe to Manchester and Stockport to Northenden Junction lines. Two pairs of lines diverged at Cheadle Heath South Junction and passed through the station. The western most pair continued as the Liverpool Curve. This joined the CLC line from Heaton Mersey West Junction to Skelton Junction at Cheadle Junction (CLC) and also gave access to the new Cheadle Exchange Sidings alongside the CLC line.

REFERENCES

Brettle, Roger – A New Midland Route to Manchester and Liverpool: The Centenary of the New Mills & Heaton Mersey Line. *Midland Railway Society Journal* No.18 Winter 2001

Johnson, E. M. – Scenes from the Past 16 (Part Two): The Midland Route from Manchester Cheadle Heath to Chinley. Foxline Publications (1992)

One of the very few pictures of Hazel Grove station which is hardly surprising considering its early closure. We are looking in the up direction towards Disley tunnel. The station consisted of a single island platform with a central office block and an overall canopy, stepped to take account of the rising gradient. The signal box is just beyond the island platform. The sidings on the down side held thirty wagons on the back road and fifty inside whilst on the up side a single siding had a sixty wagon capacity. A Midland Belpaire boiler 4-4-0 is on the far left entering the station.
Manchester Locomotive Society collection

Not far beyond Bramhall Moor Lane was, Garner Occupation bridge No. 29. It has a wing on the right and two arches with spans of 28 ft 0 in each. Work was just under way on the other running line and a contractor's water tank can be seen through the left hand arch. This view was taken during Aug 1900 when new.
Author's collection

Cheadle Heath station was on the western edge of Stockport and had a central island platform and two side platforms serving the four through lines, all protected by platform canopies. There was also a bay platform on the up side. The station offices were at the top of the cutting on the up side with an approach road from the Stockport to Cheadle road. Access to the platforms was by an overbridge. It had goods and carriage sidings before the station, a large impressive goods shed, a 60 ft turntable and watering facilities. This view is looking toward Heaton Mersey with the huge goods shed on the left of the canopied platforms, the typical Midland vee-shaped station name facing both ways, the water column with the built in lighting system on the top and an exquisite lamp. The date is 25 Feb 1903 when it was nearly new.   *Author's collection*

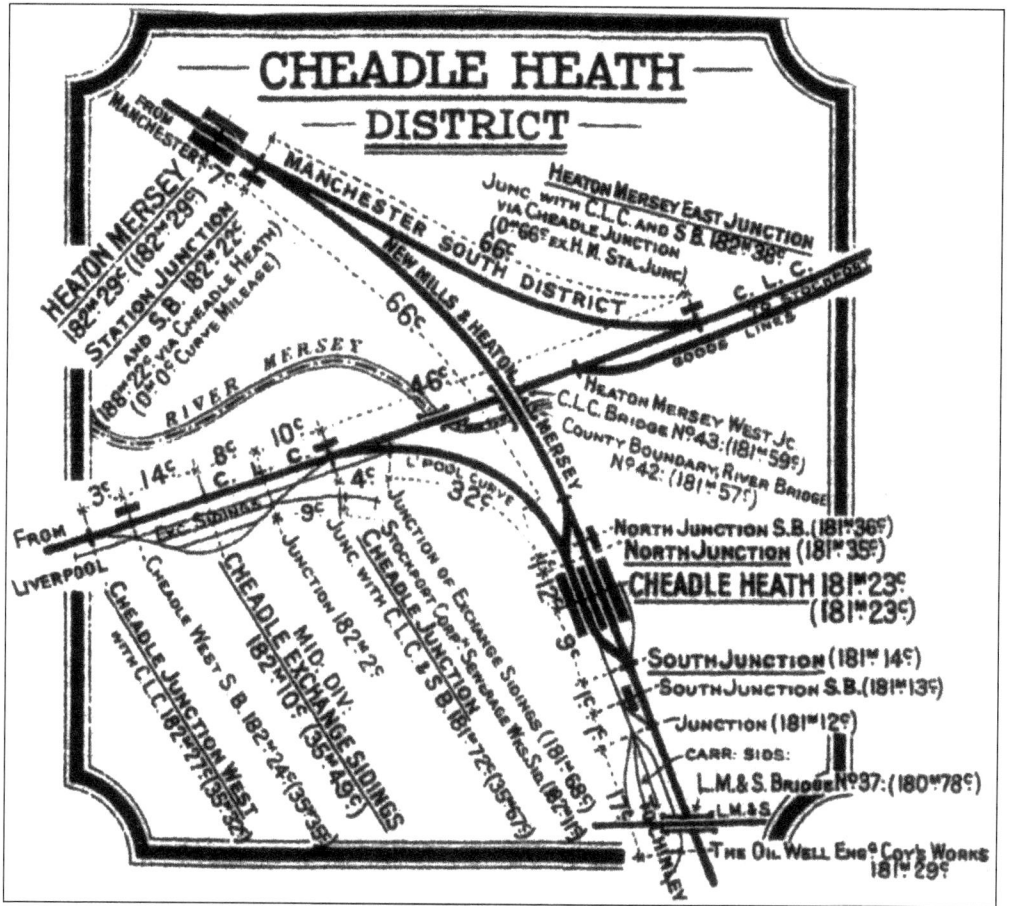

The Midland System map of 1923 showing the complicated connections. Note the Cheadle Exchange Sidings which are featured regularly in the freight timetables and how the Liverpool Curve interacts with Cheadle Heath station.

Heaton Mersey station about 1905 looking back toward Cheadle Heath station. It was opened in 1880 by the Manchester & South District Railway. This was the point where the New Mills to Heaton Mersey link line finished; it can be seen on the right of the train beyond the bridge. The long lattice footbridge on the left dipped down to become the bridge over the line. The station was accessed through a substantial cutting. The buildings on the up platform have a solid grandeur about them and the short gas lamps are embedded in the retaining wall. Heaton Mersey had an out of the way location and a steeply graded access road which made it an unpopular station with passengers. The train may be a suburban working to Manchester Central with its matching clerestory stock and with the Midland tank engine boasting its ownership on the coal tender.
John Alsop collection

LOOK WHO'S COMING DOWN THE LINE

The official photograph of Queen Victoria for her Diamond Jubilee celebrations which were three weeks later.
Author's collection

On a sunny Fri 21 May 1897 anybody watching traffic at Grindleford station would have observed an amazing scene for they would have noticed that (as at every station) all the staff were on duty and each one was looking at his very best. During the early evening the platelayers, who had been busily checking every inch of the line placed clips on all the turnouts to prevent any signalling mistakes and then stood at the side of the line, each within hailing distance of the other. As the light began to wane activity on the line ceased for half an hour and no trains passed either way until, at 19.45, a light engine emerged from Totley tunnel and passed through Grindleford station at a sedate speed. Fifteen minutes later a mind boggling scene was witnessed as the Royal train emerged from the tunnel with none other than Queen Victoria and her entourage of two hundred assistants and officials in eleven LNWR Royal carriages with a carriage truck and brake vans at each end. The train was hauled appropriately, by two of the Midland 4-4-0 locomotives of the '2203' class especially built for the opening of the line, numbered 2208 and 2210. Peering from the footplates to catch every signal were senior drivers Edward Townson and Henry W. Lilburn from Grimesthorpe shed. Climbing on to the tender of the train engine after its emergence from the tunnel was a lookout man who would face the rear of the train watching for any signal given by the rear guard. The train was fitted with continuous brakes and had electrical communication between the compartments of each saloon and carriage and between the guards at front and rear but there was no such connection between all the carriages.

The train was travelling at a leisurely pace as the Queen would not allow it to average more than thirty six miles per hour. She would have been able to observe the lovely evening views of the Hope and Edale valleys and may have been knitting which she habitually did to occupy herself on long journeys.

The event was remarkable because she was known by this time as 'The Great Unknown' having only recently been persuaded to take on some public duties after many years of self imposed hibernation following the death of her beloved Prince Albert in 1861. Hardly anybody remembered her accession to the throne in 1837, or Coronation a year later, and few of her subjects had ever seen her, and certainly none of her billions of subjects overseas. She was just three days off her seventy eighth birthday, increasingly infirm and suffering from heart trouble. Her remarkable Diamond Jubilee celebrations in London were only three weeks away and she had stopped in Sheffield, for no less than a formal state visit, on her way from Windsor to Balmoral. The whole visit started when most people would normally be going home from work for tea and was all over two hours later.

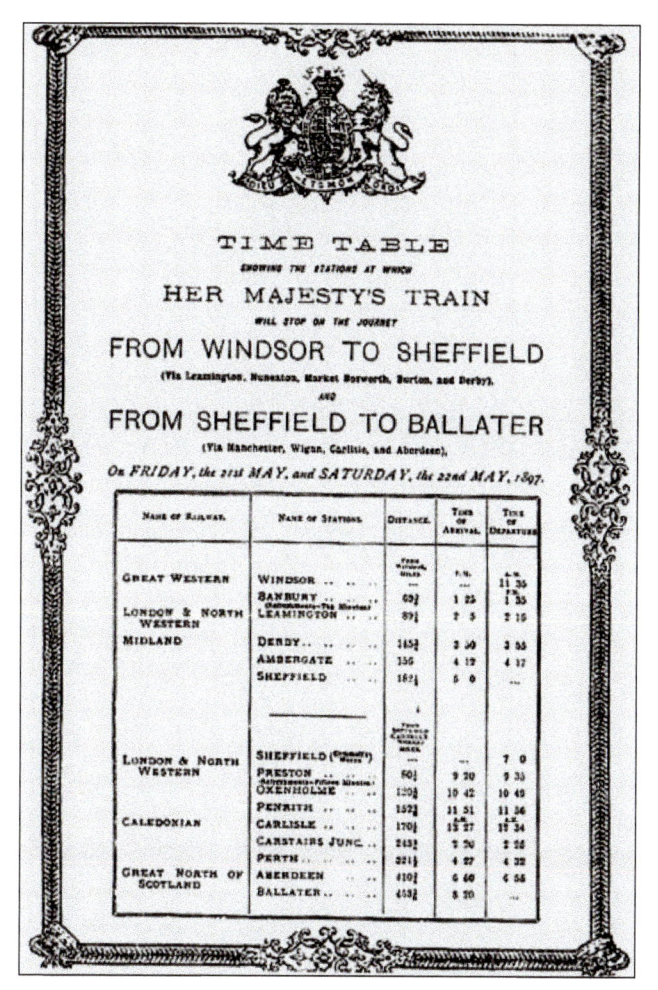

The front cover of the Midland Royal Train Notice.
Laurence Knighton collection

The Queen had left the GWR Windsor station, watched by several hundred spectators, at 11.30 accompanied by her daughter, Princess Christian, and son, the Duke of Connaught, together with officials of the GWR, LNWR, the general manager of the Caledonian Railway and the Home Secretary of the day. The train was in charge of the Great Western for the seventy miles to Banbury where it arrived at 13.25, where refreshments were served (there was no on board catering facilities) and after a ten minute stop the journey continued a further twenty miles to Leamington, where the train was handed over to the LNWR at 14.05 for the fifty six mile journey to Derby. LNWR 2-2-2-2 Compound 2053 *Greater Britain*, was appropriately in charge of the train when it left at 14.15 and travelled via Burton on Trent.

Edward Talbot in his book on LNWR engines describes the livery applied to 2053 at Crewe Works, together with sister engine No. 2054 *Queen Empress*, which was painted white, would you believe, as having been 'given such elaborate and expensive liveries that they were probably the most magnificently finished locomotives ever to run in this country or indeed anywhere on earth. It was painted scarlet with gold leaf and dark blue edging. Smokebox, frames and wheels were dark blue, and the tyres were white whilst the front buffer beam was lined out in gold. The leading splasher and the tender had the LNWR coat of arms and the trailing splasher had the Royal arms.'

On arrival in Derby at 15.50 large crowds gathered but the blinds of the Royal carriage were closely drawn and Her Majesty was not to be seen, but as a consolation they would have been astonished at this apparition from the Midland's fiercest rival in their midst.

The train was handed over to the Midland and locomotives 157 and 158, with Derby drivers John Lomas and Francis Jordan together with Guards B. Ellis and B. Cook, the latter two staying with the train until it was returned to the LNWR again. This quick turnaround was all achieved in five minutes. This must have seemed like a Formula One tyre change in slow motion, getting the LNWR engine off and the two Midland engines hooked up.

The ten miles to Ambergate were covered in twenty two minutes and here again refreshments were served. The exact point at which the front buffers of the leading engine were required to be brought to a stand at Derby, Ambergate and Sheffield were indicated by a man showing a red flag and drivers had to stop within an eighth of an inch of the designated place. The Royal saloon stopped opposite a 'charming little pavilion gay with part-coloured cloth' at the

LNWR *Greater Britain* was a divided drive compound 2-(2-2)-2. It was built in Oct 1891 and had a short life before being scrapped in July 1907. To the end of the century the train remained a collection of more picturesque than convenient saloons, old fashioned sleeping cars and ordinary first class passenger coaches. The carriages had an arcane look and never had complete connections as the Queen would not permit a new train to be built at this time. The train consisted of a brake van, a carriage truck containing the Royal fourgon, a composite carriage for the railway directors and officials, a saloon for the railway directors, a saloon for the Queen's Indian attendants, a saloon for the Gentlemen of the Household and her medical attendants, a saloon for Her Majesty's suite, Her Majesty's saloon, a day saloon for her maids of honour, a day saloon for dressers and ladies' maids, a day saloon for pages and upper servants, a sleeping carriage for the male servants and a further brake van. With the engines, thirteen carriages and brake vans the train was over 600 ft long.
LNWR official postcard

north end of the line on platform No. 3. It was reported that Mr Towle, manager of the Midland catering department, interested himself personally in providing the refreshments. A number of tables covered with 'snowy drapery', had the tea equipage on them but, in addition bronze stands were placed at intervals of ten yards along the platform to enable the refreshments to be served without delay into each carriage.

The train restarted promptly at 16.17 and covered the twenty six miles to Sheffield Midland station arriving three minutes early at 16.57. A report said that the station master, Mr Wheen, and his staff had strove against trying conditions to make the departure platform as nice as possible' (It was a mucky 'oil!) As the train steamed into the station the packed crowds outside the then unrebuilt station knew of the arrival when a twenty one gun salute was fired from Hyde Park by the 4th West Riding Volunteer Artillery. The Queen disembarked on a slightly sloping ramp close to the Rotherham Dock just north of the booking hall. By demolishing the railings that divided the station from Sheaf Street it was possible for the Royal carriage to be driven onto the platform quite close to the train and so avoid the booking hall. Among all the dignitaries who were presented to the Queen was Mr G. E. Paget, the chairman of the Midland Railway, in court dress and Mr J. H. Turner J.P. the general manager in the uniform of the Railway Engineers Volunteer Corps who were to sit in the third of the eleven carriages that traversed the city.

The Royal carriage and the others that carried the rest of the parade, the horses and all the accoutrements required were brought from London by a special train and were returned as soon as the visit was completed.

The leading light among all the multitude of dignitaries present was the Duke of Norfolk who was the Lord Mayor. He successfully master minded the extensive arrangements that were required for such a massive event.

The visit included the ceremonial opening of the new Town Hall, the stone for which was acquired from Stoke Hall quarry and would have been carried from Grindleford by the Midland in the preceding years.

Ambergate where refreshments were served was a triangular station. Curving round to the right is the Peak line. In the rear platform No. 3 is an express for either Sheffield or Leeds and it is near to where the Royal train stopped. In the foreground at platform No. 6 is a three coach down Pye Bridge local. In the foreground is a temporary incline built to serve a new reservoir construction. This crossed the Cromford Canal. The date is 20 May 1911.
Author's collection

Queen Victoria leaves the decorated part of the Midland station on her journey through the crowded streets to the Town Hall. The Royal train is in the background and the railwaymen are standing on the roofs of some carriages behind.
*Picture Sheffield.
Sheffield Libraries*

There was then a visit to Norfolk Park where over 40,000 children sang to the Queen, including some from the school at Derwent village where the Duke of Norfolk had a seat.

Then the Royal parade made its way down to the east end of the city where the Royal carriage drew up under a large canopy and without getting out of her carriage the Queen was shown armour plating being rolled at Cammell's Cyclops works on Carlisle Street. *The Times* correspondent described the scene as follows: 'The furnace lay to her right hand, the rolling mill before her; then at a signal the men gave three lusty cheers and distributed themselves between the rollers and the furnace. There is no place for an explanation of the details of the wonderful process by which a huge ingot of steel at white heat is converted into armour plate of such impenetrability as Sheffield boasts that she alone can produce. Let us rather regard it as a spectacle of fiery splendour and irresistible force submitted to the Queen of a nation depending for its position principally on the ships for which these huge armour plates are made. This particular plate is for Her Majesty's ship 'Ocean'. When it came glowing from the furnace it weighed fifty six tons and was forty two inches in thickness. It passed between the rollers to and fro several times, being pressed each time at a pressure of 6,000 tons until it had lost nearly half of its thickness and a great deal of its weight. And all the while, as the metal grew flatter and thinner and wider, the Queen gazed intently at the fiery mass through a special glass and watched with intent and manifest interest the operation of the machinery.'

Walking with a stick and supported by an Indian servant, she moved from her carriage into the Royal saloon. The special platform was substantially built and arranged so she could move between her horse carriage and the Royal

The Queen did not get out of her coach to open the Town Hall because of her infirmity. She was given a golden key which when she pressed a button the gates swung open. Unfortunately it did not work and workmen laid on their stomachs so they were not seen pulled the gates open manually, a fact that did not emerge until sometime after.
Picture Sheffield.
Sheffield Libraries

This incredible view was taken at Cammell's rolling mill. The Queen again did not have to get out of her carriage and was protected from the searing heat by a glass screen. Banks of bushes are in the background and everything is clean and tidy, a far cry from how it would have normally looked. The furnace men must have been bemused.
Picture Sheffield.
Sheffield Libraries

The rolled plate was destined for *HMS Ocean*, one of six 'Canopus' pre-Dreadnought class battleships launched in 1898. She was sunk by a mine in Mar 1915.
Author's collection

The empty stock of the Royal train is seen in the Wicker goods yard. The unidentified engine would have been put on the rear of the train at Grimesthorpe Junction to bring it into the goods yard. The first carriage is the rear brake van and next is the carriage truck for the Royal fourgon.
Laurence Knighton collection

Another photograph at Wicker goods yard with the two locomotives, 157 and 158, which brought the train from Derby. They were two of six engines of the '2183' class of slim boilered 4-4-0s with 7 ft 0 in driving wheels which were new to traffic in Aug 1896. They were allocated to shed 18, Nottingham and were there for many years. We are looking towards the Wicker with Saville Street on the left. The two locomotives' last task was to bring the Royal train into Cammell's sidings where presumably the engine which drew it into Wicker goods yard in the picture above would have been detached. When the Royal party re-joined the train 157 and 158 would have taken the train the short distance to Grimesthorpe Junction where they were detached. At the same time the two '2203' class engines would be attached at the other end of the train to meet the seven minutes time allowed for the manoeuvres. The only significant difference between the '2183' and '2203' classes was that the latter had smaller 6 ft 6 in driving wheels.
Laurence Knighton collection

The Royal saloon was rebuilt in 1895 from the original twin saloons, dating from 1861. It was mounted on a long frame to form a single twelve wheel carriage with bogies. It was a very beautiful example of nineteenth century styling at its best as well as being an extremely comfortable vehicle. It was 60 ft in length and had a carmine lake body with white upper panels picked out in gold and had a gilded lion's head at each corner. It was lit by oil and candles because the Queen did not approve of gas lighting, let alone electricity. There was a day compartment with a sofa, two easy chairs, two occasional chairs, footstools and a table. The night compartment had two beds. It is now in the National collection.
Author's collection

saloon without the slightest ascent. Rows of trees lined the improvised carriage drive to the Cyclops works and the platform.

After the Royal party had alighted at the station the train proceeded to Grimesthorpe Junction and was then taken down the old Sheffield and Rotherham Railway branch to the Wicker goods yard. Here a detailed check by the LNWR fitters, lamp men and greasers, who travelled on the train throughout its long journey, their work including the oiling of axle boxes and checking the lamps. Everything that they may have needed was carried on the train. Eight or nine additional men from the train's home base at Wolverton, under the carriage superintendent C. M. Park, also travelled with it and were also involved in the checking.

After the Queen alighted, the train was far from empty as most of the retinue of 200 servants remained on the train along with the Queen's young grandsons Prince Leopold age 8 and Prince Maurice age 5½ years. Their father, Prince Henry of Battenberg, had died a year earlier. Their mother was Princess Beatrice, the Queen's youngest daughter. Prince Leopold was a haemophiliac, a condition he had inherited from his mother. He served in the Army from 1912 to 1920 but could not continue after that due to ill health and died age thirty three during a hip operation. Prince Maurice had an even shorter life as he was killed in 1914 at the Ypres salient where he was buried age twenty three years.

They were in the care of their attendants and were seen watching the proceedings at the station out of the windows of the carriage next to the Royal saloon. They were fair haired, had blue eyes and were dressed simply in plain sailor costumes with short cut hair parted at the side and brushed down flat. A reporter had a chat with their lady attendants who spoke with strong German accents as did nearly all the servants and attendants. They and their German attendants missed all the excitement outside the goods yard. It was Leopold's birthday which he duly celebrated in the hardly memorable Wicker goods yard.

As the visit to Cammell's drew to a close the Royal train was moved the short distance to a specially built platform in Cammell's goods sidings where the Queen embarked en route to Balmoral leaving at 19.27, twenty seven minutes late. At Grimesthorpe Junction the two Royal engines of the '2203' class were attached and the train passed through the thronged platform No. 4 at the Midland's Sheffield station at 19.36 as it initially headed south before heading west through the Hope valley. It is not known why this route was chosen as a more logical route would have been via Leeds to the Settle and Carlisle line which the Queen had traversed previously. Perhaps the Midland wanted to show the Queen their new line! From Chinley the train travelled through New Mills, Marple, Reddish, Belle Vue, Ashburys, the Midland curve at Ashton and Phillip's Park to Ardwick Junction which was reached in eighty three minutes at 20.50. Here the train was handed back to the LNWR and the Midland engines came off. No doubt everybody connected with the Midland Railway breathed a huge sigh of relief that everything had gone according to plan. All traffic was suspended for a considerable length of time at the incredibly busy Victoria station in Manchester whilst the pilot engine, followed by the Royal train headed by the white liveried *Greater Britain* (sister of the earlier *Queen Empress*) passed through at six miles per hour, half an hour later there being an interval of 30 minutes between the pilot and the actual train.

The train arrived at Preston station via Wigan at 21.41, twenty one minutes late, where dinner was served in the Royal saloon. Strict security precluded any view except for the privileged few before the train restarted after fifteen minutes. The next forty miles saw a stop made at Oxenholme for seven minutes and Penrith for five minutes before Carlisle was reached, 170 miles from Sheffield at 00.50, here seven minutes was allowed to change engines and hand over to the Caledonian Railway.

The train continued via Carstairs Junction, where there was a further five minute stop, and Perth, where it arrived at 04.55 for an additional five minute stop, before reaching Ferryhill Junction, Aberdeen at 06.50, 240 miles from Carlisle. Here breakfast was served and the train was passed on to the Great North of Scotland Railway.

The problems the lack of connections between the coaches caused was described by G. Neele, the LNWR superintendent, who wrote in his book Railway Reminiscences; 'It was always a satisfaction to find Her Majesty requesting the Lady in Waiting to join her at Perth (on the return journey from Balmoral) as then, in all probability, the change back to the vacated carriage would be made at Greenhill, or later at Larbert, where platforms existed. Otherwise, this transfer had to be made at Beattock summit, where there was no platform whatever to assist the ladies in descending from the Queen's saloon or in climbing up into their own vehicle. The Queen's saloon had no footboard or steps of the ordinary character; it was fitted with a pair of folding steps similar to those in old fashioned post-chaises. The descent from the saloon was thus facilitated; but to gain the other vehicle presented the difficulty, and Mr Christopher Johnstone, the Caledonian manager, a very short, sturdy man, highly amused us by relating his struggles to push up Lady Augusta Bruce into her saloon on one of these journeys'. (I wonder where he put his hand!)

Thirty minutes later it set off again to cover the final forty three miles to Ballater where it arrived at 08.50, thirty minutes late. The Royal party reached Balmoral in a closed coach at 11.00, to be met with raw misty weather and snow still lying on the hills, in stark contrast to the warm sunny weather encountered at Windsor and Sheffield. The whole massive 635 mile journey was covered in eighteen hours and fifty minutes at an average speed of 37 miles per hour (after stops had been allowed for). It is interesting to note that no attempt was made to make up lost time. The Royal train went to Ballater on at least 110 occasions during Victoria's reign but it was the only known occasion that it travelled through the Hope valley.

An estimated one million people were in Sheffield for the Royal visit. Although the Midland had the glory of running the Royal train, all the railway companies benefited hugely from the occasion. The movement of the Royal carriages and horses from Buckingham Palace, over 2,500 troops and police plus their horses and equipment required the commissioning of ten special trains which were equally shared between the MSLR and the Midland. Additionally, over twenty special trains were run for visitors to the city, including one from Buxton which called at all stations. The newspapers reported that 'on both the MSLR and Midland lines the traffic was remarkably heavy, and the greatest difficulty was experienced in dealing with the enormous numbers of persons who came to Sheffield yesterday. The traffic far exceeded that of any Bank Holiday and was heavier than any of the local companies have had for several years past. Until a late hour last night the platforms of both the Midland and Victoria stations were packed with travellers who wished to return home, and it is satisfactory to know that no hitch of a serious kind occurred. The trains on both lines were fairly punctual considering the abnormal traffic.'

The Midland representatives on the train were G. Ernest Paget (chairman), S. W. Johnson (locomotive superintendent), C. H. Jones and W. H. Adams (assistant locomotive superintendents), W. Longdon (telegraph superintendent), T. G. Clayton (superintendent of the carriage department), J. A. McDonald (chief civil engineer) and W. L. Mugliston (superintendent of the line) who was in charge of the Royal train.

Messrs Richard Keane Ltd, the Derbyshire publishers, took advantage of the Royal train travelling over the Dore and Chinley line by presenting a beautifully bound and specially illustrated copy of Mr Edward Bradbury's ('Strephon') work 'Over the Dore and Chinley Railway' to the Queen.

REFERENCES

Knighton Laurence – *Two hours in Sheffield Fri 21st May 1897*. Midland Railway Society Journal No. 11 Summer 1999

Brettle Roger – *Queen Victoria's Visit to Sheffield, 1897*. Midland Railway Society Journal No. 50 Autumn 2012

Midland Railway Train Notice

Sheffield Daily Telegraph and *Sheffield Independent* newspaper reports

Ellis C. Hamilton – *Royal Journey: A Retrospect of Royal Trains in the British Isles*. British Transport Commission 1953

Talbot Edward – *An Illustrated History of LNWR Engines*. Oxford Publishing Co. 1985

THE DOVE HOLES TUNNEL COLLAPSE

Between midnight and 01.00 on Sun 7 Feb 1904, the difficult to maintain, Dove Holes tunnel, between Peak Forest and Chapel en le Frith on the Peak line, fell in at the Manchester end. The line did not re-open for goods traffic until 00.05 on Mon 21 Mar. A supplementary working timetable was issued which shows that most of the traffic was diverted from Ambergate via Chesterfield and the Dore curve on to the Hope valley line where it re-joined the Peak line at Chinley North Junction. This included an enormous amount of freight traffic and passenger traffic but also the magnificent St Pancras to Manchester expresses.

The coaching stock employed on Midland trains had an enviable reputation for comfort, especially for first class passengers, and for internal and external cleanliness. All were painted in a rich shade of crimson lake lined out in black and gold and embellished with the company's coat of arms. The night trains had specially built first class sleeping cars.

Dining cars had already become de-rigeur on the best trains and in 1897 the Midland introduced magnificent first and third class dining cars on its Manchester services. They were 60 ft long with six wheeled bogies and had handsome clerestory roofs. Coaches now had lavatories connected by short internal corridors and each had steam heating which replaced the old foot warmers. C. Hamilton Ellis in his book on the Midland Railway states 'all carriages were very magnificently furnished and decorated: even the upholstery was richer in colour and pattern than that of other railways ….one recalls rich walnut and mahogany, and grandly patterned ceilings.' These state of the art trains were mainly hauled by Johnson thee cylinder compound 4-4-0s, significantly larger and more powerful than the previous 4-4-0s and 'Spinner' 4-2-2s. This increase in locomotive size was prompted by the increasing weight of the carriages being provided. These magnificent trains graced our route for six weeks although finding a path for them was problematic as the line would have been at saturation point. Most of the trains usually seen on the Hope valley route had eight wheeled coaches, with old six wheelers on stopping trains

ROYAL TRAIN IN THE HOPE VALLEY IN 1905

At 10.00 on a bright sunny Fri 12 Jul 1905, the new LNWR Royal train hauled by two Midland engines eased out of St Pancras station for Sheffield carrying King Edward VII and Queen Alexandra with their entourage. Its route was via the Trent and Erewash valley. Arriving at the enlarged Sheffield Midland station at 13.00, having averaged fifty three miles an hour, it had been preceded by the 09.45 express from St Pancras to Sheffield, which ran non-stop in two hours forty nine minutes.

The King and Queen alighted just in front of the station's main entrance hall with its draped walls, carpeted floors, comfortable furniture and a profusion of ferns. Outside the station they were greeted by 10,000 assembled children and a twenty one gun salute.

They drove through crowded streets to the Town Hall and then went to Western Bank and Weston Park to open the extension to the university. Then to Brightside and the River Don works of Vickers, Sons and Maxim Ltd. where they saw the gun shops, in which the machining of heavy ordnance was being undertaken. They then went to the armour plate rolling mill where an armoured plate was being rolled, and finally the steel melting house where several furnaces were being tapped, each containing forty three tons of molten steel.

The day was not without its humorous moments. The *Derbyshire Times* report was less deferential than the national press. 'Flanking the entrance to the Town Hall were banks of children, who beguiled the tedium of waiting by singing. But the youngsters were too excited to pay much attention to the gentleman with the baton perilously perched at the top of some high steps who by the vigour of his efforts more than once narrowly escaped his own discomfiture. The children would not keep in time and those on the station side of the entrance were the worst sinners in this respect. A stout man, with a straw hat, tried to improve matters by energetically acting as deputy choirmaster with the aid of a walking stick for a baton, but he only succeeded in making

The crowds that greeted the Royal couple on Sheaf Street.
SWSR

On 12 Jul 1905 a Sheffield tram specially decorated and illuminated for the visit stands inside the wheel shop at Queens Road depot although it took its first trip from the Nether Edge works and thousands watched it go by. Tram No. 167 carried 2,445 lights and, when in motion, consumed 200 horse power (sic) of current. The busts of the King and Queen were above the driving position and were brought into relief by the lights.
Helland Photographs

himself very hot and uncomfortable and providing a good deal of amusement for the crowd who were not slow to make him the butt of good tempered Yorkshire wit.'

'Amongst the civil and military dignitaries who brought up the rear of the procession into the Town Hall was a Major in brilliant uniform bearing, no means in triumph, two paper parcels. We were a good deal interested in the content of those parcels. Whatever they contained those parcels were highly important, even if they were badly wrapped in brown paper. Judging by the gingerly way the major carried them, he did not enjoy the task. His air was sheepish in the extreme, and his sword had an uncomfortable knack of getting between his legs. The last we saw of the officer was his stalwart form climbing the Town Hall steps with those precious parcels in his charge'.

'As the Royal carriage disappeared from Weston Park, there was a stampede for the refreshment tents and young and old jostled and fought in a manner that reminded one very much of a football scrum for strawberries and cream tea.'

A special platform was erected in the Vicker's sidings near Upwell Street Junction from where the King and Queen left on the Royal train at 17.00. On joining the Midland main line the train went through the thick of Sheffield's muck and grime before receiving 'a last ringing cheer as the train dashed through the Midland station, the platforms of which were crowded with passengers'.

The train went over the Hope valley line on which the Royal couple had not travelled before. They would have been able to enjoy the early evening sunshine in the Hope and Edale valleys.

From Chinley the train travelled via New Mills, Marple, Romiley, Bredbury, Reddish, Belle Vue, Ashburys and then round the curve at Ashton to Midland Junction and Ardwick Junction, just before Miles Platting, where the train was handed over to the LNWR. It proceeded to Huyton on the original Liverpool & Manchester Railway where the Royal couple disembarked to stay with the Earl of Derby at Knowsley.

The following day the Royal couple visited Manchester arriving from Huyton at Victoria station. Among their engagements was the opening of the new dock on the Manchester Ship Canal at Salford. They returned to Knowsley from the same station later in the day.

The visit has many echoes of Queen Victoria's 1897 visit; the use of the LNWR Royal train although it was a new set, the arrival at the Midland station to a gun salute and a visit to a steel works. However the King was happy to be transported at the prevailing speeds of the day and the Midland station had been considerably extended and improved by this time with a concourse more fitting of a Royal visit. It was not as elaborate as the previous visit but was still celebrated with enthusiasm, but did not resonate in the same way because of Queen Victoria's mystique caused by her reclusive behaviour over a forty year period. In reality her presence was one associated with a powerful nation and overseas dominance rather than her physical presence. A the Diamond Jubilee celebrations one later commentator suggested that she looked like a little old lady who was going to the post office to collect her pension.

The Royal train leaving Millhouses station at the end of the visit. Note the spectators in Hutcliff Wood on the right. Consisting of five saloons, a carriage for servants and two brake vans with a tare weight of 250 tons it was 467 ft in length. Following Queen Victoria's death the LNWR was keen to build a new Royal train and the new King gave his permission. Two superb twelve wheel saloon carriages were designed by the LNWR's carriage superintendent C. A. Park and built at Wolverton works in 1903. They were the ultimate expression of the wooden clerestory carriage and were magnificently designed and finished. Firmly rooted in the Victorian era the coaches had silver plated bedsteads, large over stuffed chairs and sofas amongst polished tables, white enamel panels and mouldings. The new development gave provision for bathrooms with silver plated baths in strictly classic wooden casings. Ancient practices were retained with golden lions' heads decorating the headstocks, the leather covered folding steps and the painting of the Royal Arms and the insignia of the senior orders of chivalry on the lower panels. They were accompanied by a new rake of saloons and service coaches. A twelve wheel diner was a new innovation although restaurant cars had been provided on service trains for many years. These coaches were retained in use until new steel cars were built in the early years of the Second World War.

SPC

The train was photographed in several locations. Here it is leaving Bredbury station and is crossing over the CLC Stockport and Woodley line. The leading engine is one of the '2203' class some of which were built for the opening of the Dore and Chinley line. However, by this time, Johnson had retired and his successor Deeley had set about modernising the fleet and that included this class. This is a rebuilt version with Deeley's short cab, round topped dome cover, flowerpot chimney and a dished smokebox door with locking wheel and handle. It carries Deeley's simplified livery. The train engine has a Belpaire boiler which was introduced by Johnson and continued by Deeley, the same flowerpot chimney and a fluted safety valve. *AMC*

This original postcard shows the train a little further on crossing the River Tame just beyond Reddish Junction.
G. Dawson

THE FIRST WORLD WAR

Unlike the Second World War, when normal services were seriously disrupted, this war saw normal services retained at pre-war levels although excursion traffic ceased. Within four months of the declaration over 7,500 railwaymen had joined the forces, which was approximately 10% of the workforce and manpower shortages began to affect the quality of services. Late running became more common and trains had to be cancelled to accommodate troop trains and the increased freight traffic, carrying munitions and supplies for the forces, which had priority.

The Midland 1916 working timetable has a different feel from the febrile summer of 1914. Freight workings had increased to such an extent that trains from Grimesthorpe sidings to Gowhole required a separate timetable. There was a new working, on Mondays only, from Broadheath LNWR (the junction between the LNWR Liverpool line to Manchester line via Widnes and Arpley and the CLC line from Glazebrook to the Liverpool curve at Cheadle) to Rotherham Masborough. The excursions to the Hope valley and through trains to Blackpool have gone and excursion trains to Liverpool for onward travel by steamer to Llandudno and the North Wales coast, New Brighton, Southport, Isle of Man and Ireland had also disappeared to be replaced by the transport of army divisions arriving initially from Ireland and the Empire. In 1917, after the USA entered the war, 2,333 special trains were run nationally to the south coast embarkation ports, some of which the Midland handled via the Peak line with the Hope valley line probably relieving some of the pressure. The Easter Rising in Dublin in 1916 required the diversion of two divisions to Ireland involving sixty four troop trains and it would be surprising if our line was not used for some of those trains.

On the whole system passengers carried in 1914 were 430,635 in the summer months and 381,249 in the winter months. By 1917 these had dropped by over 50% and were only marginally higher in the following year. It was not until 1922 that passenger numbers recovered to somewhere like pre-war levels they being 84% in summer and 93% in winter.

Ordinary passenger fares increased to 50% above the third class rate of 1d per mile on 1 Jan 1917 and to 75% above that rate on 20 Aug 1920. A reduction of 50% above the pre-war level was introduced at the time of the Grouping on 1 Jan 1923, due to a reduction in inflation.

In the Edale valley there were large army camps and the fields were scattered with tents and temporary barracks. One of the largest camps was at Barbers Booth, near to the entrance to Cowburn tunnel.

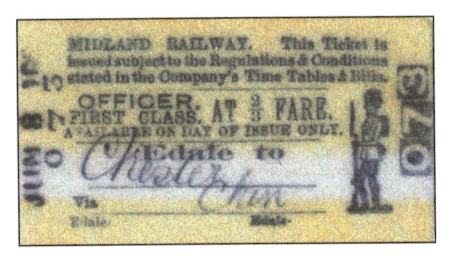

A ticket for an officer to travel first class at two thirds the standard fare from Edale to Chester via Chinley. Although the date is not complete it will almost certainly be in connection with the Army training camp. *Glynn Waite collection*

At Hathersage an auxiliary hospital for wounded soldiers was set up in 1914 in the Wesleyan Institute on the site of the old Atlas works opposite Brookfield Manor Lodge. It cared for Belgian and then British and Commonwealth troops and all were issued with bright blue hospital suits. It had thirty five beds and by the end of the war had 200 to 300 patients a year passing through.

In 1915 the Royal train ran up the valley and stopped at Hathersage where the patients well enough to reach the station and staff met King George V and Queen Mary. The Royal couple were to be seen again at Hathersage in 1919 in more propitious circumstances.

Several fully equipped ambulance trains were built by the Midland during the war, for the British and later the American Expeditionary forces.

By the end of the war 30% of the entire British workforce had joined the forces, initially voluntarily, but later by conscription and a third of these were killed. To fill the gap women were recruited and undertook jobs that had always been seen as work that only men could do.

Because railway works had become munitions factories and locomotives, wagons and carriages were commandeered for the war effort maintenance and repairs to track, stations, engines and rolling stock fell into arrears. By 1918 one fifth of all the engines of all the railway companies were awaiting repair. Fares rose by 50% and by 1917 further cuts were made in passenger services leaving a basic service of local and semi-fast long distance trains. Overcrowding became severe and running times slow. Through workings to Liverpool, Blackburn, Southport and Blackpool were no more and had been replaced by troop and munitions trains which ran at all hours.

The Midland, however, came out of the war with some credit. It kept its trains smart, handsome and clean. They did not reach the state of war time shabbiness which unfortunately came to distinguish many other lines. It kept its dining facilities going as far as possible when its neighbours on either side simply dropped them.

Accidents during the war were serious, 1915 being the worst year with the Great Eastern, London and North Western and North Eastern all having major accidents, but these were capped by the well known Quintinshill disaster on the Caledonian Railway. The Midland avoided anything comparable, but as the war was reaching its final year in 1918, another serious accident occurred on the Settle and Carlisle route. On 19 Jan 1918 a St Pancras to Glasgow express entered a cutting just beyond Little Salkeld and ran into a land slip at 55 mph. Compound No. 1010 turned on its side and two coaches telescoped into it killing seven passengers.

The Sheffield Volunteer Defence Corps (the equivalent of the Home Guard in World War Two) have arrived at Dore and Totley station before being marched off, probably to the rifle range on 16 Apr 1915. Note the footbridge and station name board.
*Picture Sheffield.
Sheffield Libraries*

Fourteen women are shovelling coal and two men are not at Derby in 1917. Back breaking work for anybody.
Author's collection

POST-WAR TO GROUPING

After the war nothing was ever the same again. The halcyon days were over, unemployment was rife, the economy was weak with the cost of the war effort and the country was grieving its dead. A large number of women faced bleak futures as widows or as nurses of physically and mentally wounded husbands and sons as they returned home to a land that was not fit for heroes. To add to the misery, a Spanish flu epidemic in 1919 killed even more of the population than were lost in the war.

All the railway companies were financially weakened by the war effort and a return to pre-war profligacy was not to be continued. In 1921, owing to labour troubles in the coal industry, there was an acute shortage of coal. The Midland equipped some of its 4-4-0 express engines with oil burning equipment which had two prominent cylindrical tanks on the tender. The alteration was carried out quickly and efficiently.

Labour unrest over wages and conditions of employment came to a head when at midnight on Fri 26 Sep 1919 a national strike was called. This lasted until Mon 6 Oct when the union leader J. H. Thomas secured a settlement with the agreement of the Prime Minister David Lloyd George.

THE 'RED ARROWS' OVER HATHERSAGE

However one event did take place that temporarily lifted the gloom for on Mon 19 May 1919 King George V and Queen Mary visited Sheffield for another Royal visit. The mood and atmosphere was very different from the King's father and grandmother's visits before the war. The King and Queen were sensitive to the changed national mood post war and realized that extravagant displays of wealth and prestige would not be well received when there was so much poverty and misery all around. Furthermore there was a mutinous undercurrent after the Bolshevik revolution of three years earlier and the fall of several Royal houses in Europe. The King had earlier refused an invitation to attend the Cutlers' Feast in Sheffield because he felt it was too ostentatious.

The departure from St Pancras illustrated the point. The *Sheffield Daily Telegraph* London representative reported 'The departure of the King and Queen to Sheffield this evening was another of those gracious and considerate actions which distinguish our reigning house. So as to cause no inconvenience by crowds gathering in the streets, the time of the Royal departure was kept a carefully guarded secret. When I reached St Pancras station no one had any knowledge of what time the Royal train would leave. Indeed, the station presented a normal aspect. The only indication that anything unusual was happening was the exhibition of a notice that the 5.35 pm train to Sheffield would not depart from its customary platform, for there drawn up to it was the London & North Western Royal train, resplendent in ivory, white and gold.

Yet it attracted little or no notice. A group of soldiers hurrying on leave gave it but a cursory glance. By ten minutes to six a small crowd, of whom railway officials predominated, had gathered at the bottom end of the platform. Two minutes later a Royal motor car sped by containing the King in naval uniform and the Queen. This was followed by another car in which was Countess Fortescue, Lieut. Col. Clive Wigram, Sir Charles Cust and the Earl of Cromer. The cars pulled up immediately before the crimson baize carpet and upon His Majesty alighting he shook hands with Mr Charles Booth, the chairman of the Midland. A few seconds later, the Royal party had taken their seats in the train, and at five minutes to six the train left St Pancras for Hathersage, where the Royal party will stay the night in the sleeping coach. Dinner is to be served on the train. Mr J. Henry Fellows, the general superintendent of the Midland, and Mr James Briggs, the chief engineer travelled with the Royal party.'

In a separate report the paper noted 'Hathersage was reached shortly before nine o'clock. There was still sufficient light for their Majesties to see the magnificent scenery of the district and the King and Queen spent some time admiring the magnificent panorama which was opened out before them. They spent the night in the sleeping coach of the train'. Another report stated 'the train stopped near Hathersage station'. The most likely place for the train to be stabled would have been at the old Water Board sidings which were behind the main sidings.

The same newspaper reported 'The King and Queen had another glimpse of the beauties of Hathersage before commencing their journey to Sheffield yesterday morning. The village people were out early: they wanted to see the King and Queen, and large numbers of children cheering and waving tiny Union Jacks assembled in the fields and lanes near where the Royal train was standing. The start for Sheffield was made soon after half past nine and at a few minutes before ten o'clock Sheffield was reached'.

(You may think that this section's title is the result of the author burning too much midnight oil but no!) As the Royal train left Hathersage in beautiful sunny weather, six 'Avro' aeroplanes flew over the train and escorted it in formation to the Midland's Sheffield station. They would have had to quickly gain height to clear Totley moor as the train went through Totley tunnel. (Even these dare devils would not have contemplated going through the tunnel!) and once the station was reached were reported to be circling overhead. The planes had been specially sent from RAF Hendon and been based at RAF Coal Aston (which is now covered by the Jordanthorpe and Batemoor housing estates). 'Six of our most daring pilots had been rehearsing over the city in the previous few days.'

The *Sheffield Daily Independent* on the day before the event reported 'First they will accompany the Royal train into the Midland station, and during the whole of the day until his Majesty's departure they will hover around. During the interval they will be looping the loop, spiralling, banking, diving and upside down flying of the most daring description. Not singly will the machines carry out these manoeuvres but in line, in flight, in triangle formation, simultaneously. For instance to see a single machine loop the loop once or twice is astounding to the uninitiated but what will be the feelings of the waiting crowds on seeing six machines rise, all drop their noses and turn over two or three times successively, the whole with the precision and timing of a single machine'.

A risk assessment had obviously not been made for on the morning of the visit the same newspaper reported 'In the morning, owing to engine trouble, one of the machines was obliged to land on the bowling green at Crookesmoor recreation ground and was smashed. The pilot, however, was uninjured, and he pluckily ascended in another machine in the afternoon and took part in the most attractive portion of the exhibition near the Town Hall during the march past'. (Today this accident would have totally overshadowed the main event, with the site becoming the scene of an accident investigation. The other planes would have been grounded sparking a major enquiry resulting, months later, with the conclusion of the inevitable report that all and sundry were to blame and that 'lessons had been learned'.) Back then it was reported in one paragraph under the heading 'A Smash'. However the flying display was described as a 'stunning success' and as 'wonderful, sensational and exhilarating'

Back to the more prosaic. The Royal party travelled by car to visit Walker & Hall, the famous silversmiths, the Town Hall where a military march past took place and finished up at Cammell Laird's works on Carlisle Street just as the King's grandmother did.

The Royal party returned to the Midland station by car at 16.35 to re-join the Royal train, instead of travelling direct from the works. Leaving on time at 17.15 the train travelled via Derby, Burton on Trent, Gresley and Moira Junction where the Ashby & Nuneaton Joint Committee line was joined. Then on to Shackerstone and Market Bosworth before terminating for the night at the small wayside station of Shenton. This was the same route Queen Victoria took on her journey from Windsor to Sheffield.

REFERENCES

Sheffield Daily Independent various issues
Sheffield Daily Telegraph various issues
www.rafmuseums.org.uk

The aeroplanes were described as being Avro Manchester types, each fitted with 100 hp 8 cylinder mono engines'. The Manchester reference can only be to show that the machines originated at Avro's works in Manchester. They were most likely the 504 type which kept the firm busy at its four Manchester factories, and further afield, building as many as 10,000 between 1913 and 1932. It was a biplane with a total length of 29 ft 5 in, a wingspan of 36 ft and had a maximum speed of 90 mph. It was used in a combat role at the beginning of the First World War but was succeeded by better aircraft and became the favoured plane for training purposes, thousands of pilots learning to fly in them. There were numerous variations but the ones used over Sheffield were probably the 504K variant which had a universal engine mounting position so that it could take a variety of engines. The one fitted to the 504K was the 100 hp Gnome rotary Monsoupage engine.
Author's collection

This is the 4,000 tons armour plate forging press at Cammell Laird's steel and ordnance works on 18 Nov 1919 from the brochure of the King and Queen's visit.
Picture Sheffield. Sheffield Libraries

THE END OF THE MIDLAND RAILWAY

After the successful devolved control of the railways by the government during the war, it became clear that the old wasteful competition of the pre-war era was not in the nation's best interest and nationalisation was seriously considered. However it was finally decided to group virtually all the companies into four large undertakings within the private sector.

On 1 Jan 1923 the Midland became part of the London Midland and Scottish Railway (LMS) and was joined by its previous bitter rival the LNWR and the LYR which had amalgamated with the LNWR a year earlier. Its other main rival, the GCR, became part of the London & North Eastern Railway (LNER) and as a result the Woodhead line remained in competition with the LMS Hope valley line for business. However the LYR and LNWR cross-Pennine lines further north became part of the LMS.

31 Dec 1922 saw the end of the Midland Railway as an independent concern after seventy eight years. C. Hamilton Ellis recorded its passing as follows. 'The old spacious ways of running a great and good railway, with single crewed engines working a relatively low daily mileage, and a great deal of time spent on keeping up appearances was gone for ever. Such a railway had been our Midland, and unlike some railways it maintained a great measure of its old dignified elegance right through the lean years of 1914 to 1918, and the labour upheavals which followed them. St Pancras stood firm, though bombs battered it in that war as well as the one that came after. The London & North Western Railway had called itself the 'Premier Line', which for all its several virtues, it was not. The Midland, with a more carefully studied conceit, styled itself 'The Best Way'. In many respects, in the comfort and convenience afforded to its passengers, in its steady conveyance of enormous quantities of coal and wool into the great metropolis, and its peculiar stateliness, its claim is as well justified as those of any other railway company, and more so than the claims of most. For, indeed, the Midland was a very great railway'.

THE GROUPING PERIOD

INTRODUCTION

In many respects, the Midland was the winner when the LMS was formed because most of the top posts went to Midland men. Sir Guy Granet became chairman, J. H. Follows general superintendent, R. W. Reid was given head of the carriages and wagons department. On the motive power front George Hughes (ex LYR) became Chief Engineer with Sir Henry Fowler his deputy. However Hughes retired in 1925 and Fowler succeeded him which clinched the Midland's control of the new company. When it is considered that the LMS was the largest joint stock company operating a railway anywhere in the world this was no mean feat.

The period up to the Second World War was difficult for the railway industry. The new railway companies were still required to be common carriers, ie being obliged to carry any merchandise to any destination irrespective of commercial considerations. Railway rates, the prices that could be charged, were fixed by a tribunal. The wages and working conditions of railwaymen also became protected by legislation. None of this applied to the burgeoning road transport industry which allowed it to undercut the railways at every turn. Road transport with its flexibility took a lot of short haul business away and the growth of urban passenger transport systems resulted in a loss of suburban passengers eg, at Heeley, Millhouses and Beauchief. On the wider passenger front the railways fought back by reducing fares and by 1938 85% of passenger receipts were collected this way. This resulted in the railways slightly increased the number of passengers compared with 1913 levels. This was particularly so in the Hope valley where efforts to attract passengers resulted in a plethora of excursion fares. Declining freight receipts were also a feature of this period. Road hauliers took over a lot of the merchandise traffic up to seventy five miles and other mineral and bulky goods traffic decreased due to the decline in business activity. In 1913, 225 million tons of coal was carried on the railways but by 1933 this had declined to 165 million tons. Coal traffic was a major part of the Hope valley traffic and this level of decline had a serious effect.

OMNIBUS SERVICES

In the first two decades of the century road transport mainly operated as feeders to and from valley stations. The Midland although operating bus services in a few areas did not introduce any in the immediate Derbyshire area. The GCR only ran one service over the whole of its system and that was from Mottram Street Manchester to Hollingworth and Tintwistle although it never reached Tintwistle because of the state of the road. The service started on 30 Jun 1905 with a 20hp Milnes-Daimler bus seating eighteen passengers. It broke its back axle twice on the dreadful roads and was out of service for long periods. It celebrated the New Year in 1906 by knocking down a pillar in Market Street, Hollingworth. Before the end of that year the 'service' had terminated. In 1914 Sheffield Corporation started a service to Totley although a horse bus service had operated from Dore and Totley station to Cross Scythes since at least 1911.

After the war, with the release by the War Office of thousands of heavy motor vehicle chassis and with many well trained heavy motor vehicle drivers and mechanics being demobbed, road began to rival rail for the carriage of passengers and goods. The unregulated nature of road transport and the lower overheads meant that road transport could undercut the railways at almost every turn.

However, it was not until 9 Oct 1922 that a bus service was started between Sheffield and the Peak District. This was provided by C. H. Battey who started a daily service three times a day between Millhouses tram terminus and Bakewell via Baslow. On 10 Oct 1924 Sheffield Corporation Underwood started their service to Manchester on 25 Jun 1928 with two Gifford 26 seater buses running from Exchange Street, Sheffield three times a day with fares of 3/6 single and 5/- return. This is Underwood's advertised timetable for Winter 1929 which shows that the service frequency had doubled. All the journey times were two hours fifteen minutes.

took over the service and five months later switched it from being a feeder service to the trams to a city centre departure from Moorhead. The Corporation inherited two 24 and 25 seater charabancs from Battey one painted grey and the other light brown which did not survive much longer.

In Jun 1924 a new bus service was started by Bakewell man Murdoch Mackay from Bakewell via Ashford, Longstone, Calver, Froggatt and Ecclesall to Sheffield Moorhead. By Apr 1925 he had changed this circuitous route to run via Hassop and Calver and the same year Sheffield Corporation took it over.

From Aug 1926 Sheffield Corporation numbered the routes 37 Bakewell via Baslow, 38 Baslow, 40 Bakewell via Calver and 41 Calver.

After World War One A. F. Hancock, who had operated road haulage and weekend excursion trips from as early as 1910 from his Bamford garage, saw the need for a regular service to connect outlying villages in the Peak District with the major towns. On 4 Jun 1921 he decided to provide five journeys a day each way between Castleton and Moorhead, Sheffield. On 22 April 1922 he started a second service from Sheffield to Calver, Stoney Middleton, Foolow, Tideswell and Buxton. On 6 Oct 1927 he added a thrice weekly service from Grindleford station to Ashopton and Sheffield. However a week later he sold all these services to Sheffield Corporation who acquired one 28 seat Daimler and three 26 seat Karrier buses. Another one went to the Northern Western Road Car Co. All the Sheffield buses had gone by Sep 1928. Hancock's decision was based on a desire to concentrate solely on tours and excursions in which he was highly successful. By 1932 he was running services to Blackpool in season along with many other holiday places. The firm became part of Arthur Kitson Ltd. who in turn became Sheffield United Tours although it retained its name for some time after. In 1932 these services became a joint operation with the North Western Road Car Co. They were seen as very progressive as some other areas were still regarding the bus as having no great future.

In Nov 1927 the bus company W. T. Underwood, a long term thorn in the side of Sheffield Corporation, on the eastern side of the city, was granted a licence to operate long distance services to Manchester via Woodhead. Then in Apr 1929 Underwood started a daily service via Manchester to Blackpool, without seeking a licence. The Sheffield Watch Committee refused a later application by Underwood.

The railway companies became alarmed that the growth of road services was undermining their previous monopoly. This resulted in them legalising their position in 1928 by gaining powers under the Railways (Road Transport) Act. This coincided with the maximum speed of buses on pneumatic tyres being raised from 12 mph to 20 mph to 30 mph by 1931. The Act empowered each of the big four railway companies including the LMS and LNER to provide road transport services. It particularly allowed them and any local authority operating public service vehicles to enter into working agreements along routes on which the local authority possessed the necessary powers and this was the option that the railways took. It had the advantage that railway companies did not need to set up the infrastructure necessary to house and service buses as they could negotiate with the local authority bus operators to use their facilities.

On 1 Jan 1929 the LMS and LNER entered into such an agreement with Sheffield Corporation which created the Sheffield Joint Omnibus Committee (SJOC). The agreement created three categories of operation.

Cat. A covered all services within the city boundary which were to be the property of the Corporation alone.

Cat. B covered services operated within a defined area from Sheffield, extending various distances up to about twelve miles, plus one or two routes extended beyond that distance, to be jointly owned in equal shares by the Corporation and the railways.

Cat. C covered services operating to points outside the Cat. B area to be wholly the property of the railway companies. In fact these services were operated by the Corporation as agents for the railways.

The Bakewell via Calver service became Cat. B at the request of the Corporation.

The Cat. C services operated by the LNER and LMS were agreed amicably, the LNER operating a service to Gainsborough and to Manchester via Woodhead and the LMS operating to Bakewell, Buxton, Castleton and Manchester via the Snake.

The LNER service to Manchester via Woodhead started in Oct 1929, the LNER working from the Sheffield end and the North Western Road Car Co. from the Manchester end. They were in direct competition with Underwood Express as they were now known, and provided six trips a day to equal Underwood's service. By Feb 1930 the service,

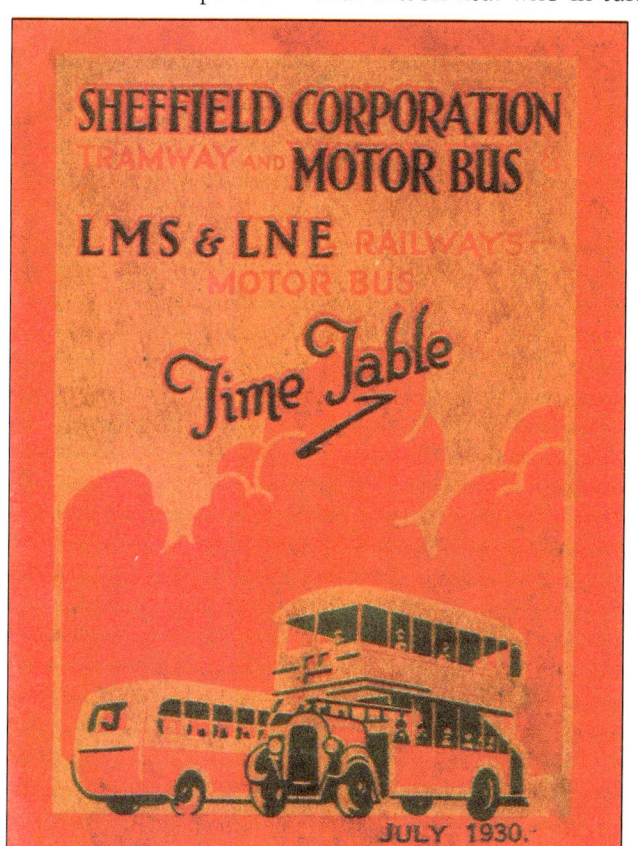

This is the attractive cover of the three partner's timetable booklet for Jul 1930. *Author's collection*

unsurprisingly, was making a loss and so Underwood's were bought out together with their Blackpool service. This became a purely railway service operated from Sheffield LMS station on Fridays, Saturdays and Mondays with connections to Blackpool from Manchester on other days. Essentially it was designed not to damage their rail services and to deter potential bus competitors.

On 18 May 1929 the North Western Road Car Co. extended their portion of the Sheffield to Castleton service through Glossop to Manchester.

In 1930 a joint service with the North Western was begun via the Snake but only in the summer months. This ran under an arrangement similar to that on the Woodhead route and ran to Manchester. In early 1931 a new bus

The Cat. C fleet was increased by the addition of four Leyland Lions from the LMS which had been built at their Derby works. They were single deck 32 seaters and were numbered 14F, 16F, 17F and 24F and were painted in railway maroon and cream. One of them is pictured in Queen's Road works with two Corporation owned Leyland Titan double deckers.
Charles C. Hall collection

Later in the year four AEC coaches joined the fleet and were used mainly on the Manchester route. They were very comfortable and far in advance of any buses then being operated. This is LMS bus No. 51F, registration number UR 3767 with the bodywork constructed by Craven's of Darnall and painted maroon with gold lettering.
Charles C. Hall collection

Leyland Tiger No. 216 registration number WJ 3556 with a Craven body had thirty seats. It was in service from 1932 to 1938.
Leyland Bus & Truck

service emerged, without a licence called 'International Express' between Nottingham and Liverpool via Mansfield, Sheffield and Manchester. In the first year of operation it proved very popular, carrying 26,000 passengers, but despite that, in Apr 1932 its application for a licence was refused. In 1938 the LMS started a service to Bamford via Ashopton and this was later extended to Bakewell in 1951.

When the SJOC was formed Sheffield Corporation drafted 14 buses to the Cat. C fleet.

In 1933 a Leyland single deck coach was acquired, fitted with a diesel engine, and it achieved phenomenal mileage on the Manchester route without overhaul, although it had a fuel consumption of only 10 mpg.

The LNER had some Thorneycroft single deckers with Vickers full fronted bodies on order and six of those, with Nos. 183-188, came to Sheffield. The driver sat with the engine in a completely enclosed front, the area being unbelievingly hot in summer. They were replaced in 1935.

In Apr 1934 two new AEC Regals were purchased to replace the LMS vehicles then in use on the Manchester service. By the end of Jul 1934 the LMS decided that, rather than invest in new vehicles, they would sell the Blackpool service and existing vehicles to Sheffield United Tours (SUT) for £685. All the coaches were elderly and only one was used by SUT.

The Cat. C routes to Bakewell via Baslow, Buxton and Manchester by both routes continued in the control of the LMS and LNER until 1948 when they were transferred to the newly formed British Transport Commission. By 1935 the only vehicles left belonging to the LMS and LNER were those working from Sheffield and these were replaced by the end of the year. SJOC acquired four AEC, four Leyland and one Albion from the railway companies and on Cat. C routes one Reo, eleven Albion's and six Thorneycrofts. Four of these buses from the Manchester route were sent to London in 1940.

REFERENCES

Jenkinson K.A. – *Sheffield United Tours 1935-1985*. Autobus Review Pub 1985

Humpidge C.T. – *The Sheffield Joint Omnibus Committee: It's Origin and Development*. Sheffield Transport Department 1963

Hall Charles C. – *Sheffield Transport*. The Transport Publishing Company Glossop 1977

Cummings J. – *Railway Motor Buses and Bus Services in the British Isles 1902-1933 Vol. 1*. Oxford Publishing Company 1978

CHANGES TO THE SIGNALLING ARRANGEMENTS

As we have seen the Hope valley line was worked by the block telegraph system with block posts at which manual signal boxes were provided.

On 12 Aug 1928 a ground frame was put in at Earle's Sidings and on 14 Apr 1929 Earle's Sidings signal box was opened to control access to the soon to be opened Hope valley cement works.

2 Dec 1935 saw a new signal box of LMS design opened named 'Water Board Sidings' for controlling the reopened sidings that linked to the Ladybower reservoir building.

There were no further changes until 20 Nov 1938 when Grindleford signal box was moved from the end of the down platform to a new location near the entrance to the goods yard where it has remained ever since.

On 29 Dec 1938 Totley Tunnel East up distant signal was replaced by a colour light signal.

CAMPING COACHES

In the 1930s holidays in camping coaches became popular. They were old coaches which had been withdrawn from service and converted for holiday use and were located in the sidings at beauty spots around the country, 142 being available in 1937. Some were located in the Hope valley. Hathersage had two in 1934 and 1935 and one from 1936 to 1939. Grindleford had two between 1935 and 1938 and Edale two between 1935 and 1939. During the winter they were removed to Cheadle Heath for storage – ten coaches from various locations found their way there. During February and March 1935 a sample coach was taken on tour to Mansfield, Chesterfield, Sheffield, Rotherham and Barnsley to attract bookings. The coaches were withdrawn when the war started but re-appeared in the 1950s and early 1960s. By today's standards they were very basic being gas lit, without running water and no toilets, the conveniences on the station being used. A photograph of one in the stations yards has eluded me.

BANK HOLIDAY VISITORS

It is interesting to record the changes regarding visitors to the valley just before the war. As will be seen there were record numbers in the months before war was declared as if people recognized that it might be the last time they would have the chance of visiting the Peak District with the war clouds gathering.

On Whit Monday 1939 'There were record crowds in the Hope valley at Whitsuntide, 15,000 visiting by train from Sheffield. Grindleford and Hope dealt with 5,000, Hathersage 4,000 and Bamford 1,000. The number of visitors from Sheffield was so large that it became necessary to run additional trains in addition to the thirty which had been scheduled. The area was a favourite haunt of campers. Over 1,000 scouts camped in the Derwent valley where the Sheffield Youth Council had established more camps than ever before. This is probably the last Whitsuntide that campers will be allowed in the Derwent and Ashop valleys (before they become flooded) in any great numbers. The Edale valley became a great attraction to thousands of visitors and many came to watch the gliding at Great Hucklow. Monday's crowd at Castleton consumed all the liquid refreshments obtainable at several of the hotels, and late in the evening many people were unable to obtain a drink. On Tuesday 7,000 visitors visited the valley by train. The crowds at Hathersage were the largest on record for Whit Monday and the demand on the hotels and refreshment caterers was such that by early afternoon many of their commodities were completely sold out. 4,000 passengers arrived at the station and their numbers were increased by hikers returning home by train. Twenty five special trains were laden on the return journey to Sheffield, in addition to trains to other centres. The swimming pool at the King George Memorial Field was fully taxed and the gate receipts were close on £20. Other attractions including the bowling green, which

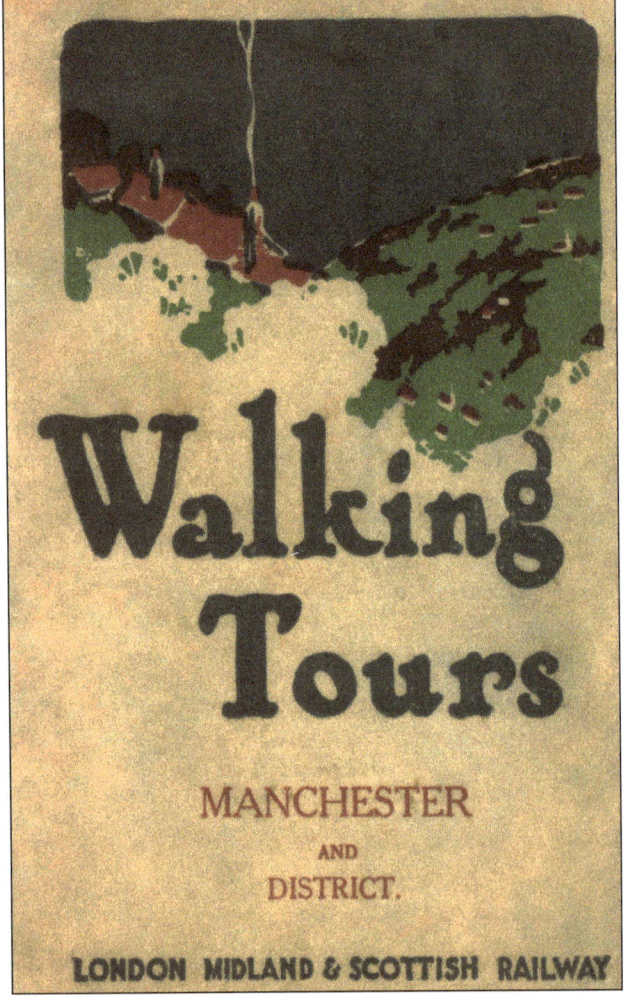

The front cover of a booklet of walking tours from the Manchester area. *Author's collection*

was occupied all day whilst a large crowd witnessed the cricket match at the Baulk Lane ground. Two special trains from Manchester and Sheffield brought several hundred excursionists to the village on Tuesday morning. *Derbyshire Times* 2 Jun 1939

On August Bank holiday 1939; 'Although the number of visitors at the weekend was not as large as on the two previous Bank holidays, the Hope valley had its share of visitors. One feature was the number of London people visiting the Peak District. Many more than usual spent the weekend under canvas, almost every camp site in the district having been booked up in advance. The Ashop and Derwent valleys were two favoured camp sites, although it is most likely the last Bank holiday that camping in large numbers will be allowed. Sunday traffic was heavy, and Monday's crowd numbered 8,000, forty eight special trains being run into the valley from Manchester, Sheffield, Birmingham, Doncaster and other places. The train service was remarkably punctual and the bus services also maintained good time. *Derbyshire Times* 11 Aug 1939

As an example the booklet of walking tours offered Tour 46 from Edale and return from Buxton. The walk described is vaguely to go via Harden Clough or Chapel Gate to Lord's Seat and the old track leading to Bettfield Clough, so as to descend to Chapel en le Frith and proceed via Combs and White Hall to Buxton. About 14 miles. Ticket return prices were 5/4d first and 3/3d third class.

This ticket is for a CLC walking tour. It is a cheap third class ticket but the tour number is not given. It is valid on the day of issue only from Manchester Central to Edale and then return from Buxton to Manchester Central.
Glynn Waite collection

THE SECOND WORLD WAR

Just as in the First World War, the railways were brought under the control of a Railway Executive Committee, consisting of the four general managers of the grouped companies and a representative of London Passenger

The significance of this image of the west portal of Totley tunnel is the soldier with his shiny boots, 303 rifle with bayonet, guarding the entrance. He was with the Northern Command Militia and the date is late 1939. There is another photograph of a soldier guarding shaft No. 5 on Totley Moor.
Sheffield Newspapers

220

On 27 Jan 1940 a heavy goods train from Trafford Park to Rowsley became derailed at Chinley South Junction. For two days the crews of the double header and their guard took it in turns to struggle through steep snow from the shelter of the South Junction signal box to obtain food from a shop in Chinley. Eventually a relief crew reached the stranded train which allowed the men to move to the Princes Hotel in Chinley for three days until the line to Manchester was cleared. They then managed to return to their shed at Rowsley via Crewe and Derby This grainy shot is looking towards Chinley with the south curve to the right.
Author's collection

Transport Board. All wagon resources were taken under the REC's control including the requisition of 563,000 privately owned and 689,000 company owned wagons.

Comparing nationally 1944 with 1938, freight traffic rose by nearly 50% and passenger traffic by 68% although the number of locomotives only rose by 2.3% and many of them were engines that would have normally been scrapped but were kept running for the duration of the war. Locomotive works were taken over for ammunition production which dramatically reduced engine maintenance. Passenger coaching stock decreased by 8.6%, restaurant cars were almost completely withdrawn. Nearly all trains were packed with military personnel going home or returning from leave together with many civilian workers away from their home areas. Train loads rose significantly. Because of the threats faced by east coast ports there was a switch of imports to west coast ports.

At the outbreak of the war there was a perceived threat of invasion so it was decided to protect important transport and important utilities.

The government feared that bombing of British cities was imminent with the resulting frightful casualties and damage to homes and industry. They therefore decided that three million people should be evacuated to safer rural areas. Children were prioritised and made up the majority of the total, they being escorted by 100,000 teachers. An order was made on 31 Aug 1939 that the evacuation should be done in a week and was called 'Pied Piper'. Local authorities in the receiving areas had to do their best to accommodate everybody but in reality they were dependant on the good will of its residents being able to take the children in. This was a massive undertaking for the railways and it was executed with surprising success.

Writer Vera Brittain of Buxton fame grumbled; 'before nightfall the blinds are drawn and the railway carriage, if lighted at all, is illuminated by a blue pinpoint of light not strong enough to enable me to distinguish the features in a pale oval which are my neighbours' faces'.

SURVIVING 1940

As if there were not enough problems in Jan 1940 one of the country's worst snow storms all but paralysed the Peak District. The temperature fell to eighteen degrees the lowest recorded for nearly fifty years. In one week 3 ft of snow fell with drifts up to 20 ft. The result was that there were many trains not available to move essential war supplies.

Another train of empty coaches became entombed in a cutting half a mile further on towards Chapel en le Frith. It took a week for troops from Lancashire to reach and then to dig it out. Local people are said to have brought the soldiers buckets of strong tea.

Peter Clowes writing in 1962 describes being a pupil at New Mills Grammar School in 1940 and catching the train to New Mills from the Hope valley. His memories are of 'stamping numb feet on cold snow covered platforms as we warmed our red knuckles at the side of the brazier that wheezed and spluttered to keep the station water towers free from ice. In exceptionally severe winters the 07.15 from Sheffield would be delayed by frozen points at Hope or giant icicles dangling in Cowburn tunnel. Sometimes in fact it meant no school for two days. The line would be completely blocked by drifts, and there was even less chance of getting out of the valley by road. In 1940 the weather was particularly atrocious. Troops were summoned to help dig out two goods trains buried under huge drifts at Chinley. One engine had escaped, leaving its wagons behind. The other, its fire drawn for safety, had been abandoned by its crew. Icicles festooned its black boiler and tender. A sorry spectacle indeed. One day a couple of years later a few scholars from Chapel en le Frith, Chinley and Buxworth managed to reach New Mills in the guard's van of a mail train that had forced its way through snowdrifts covering the line near Buxton. Crowded into the van with them were a dozen forlorn passengers who had been marooned all night in a train outside Chinley station. No one from the Hope valley attended school that day. The return train after school left New Mills at 16.52, the narrow up platform at New Mills Central was a seething mass of

Hundreds of girls from Westcliff High School in Southend arrive at Chapel en le Frith station in Jun 1940. A fleet of buses wait to take other children to nearby villages. The teachers and children are all bright and smiling which seems at odds with their circumstances, it being a journey into the unknown with parents left behind and no knowledge of what was to be their fate. Sixty arrived at Hathersage. It was said that most had a good experience, particularly those escaping the city slums to a life in the countryside but because there was no vetting there were some dreadful experiences which were mainly kept hidden.
Author's collection

blue and green caps, blazers and coats. The locomotive in charge was usually one of the Midland 2P 4-4-0s.'

Enemy bombing in the last months of 1940 resulted in more damage to the railways than the rest of the war put together. Transport planning improved after this and resulted in higher load factors for railway wagons and greater availability of locomotives although time spent in the workshops increased as many locomotives were kept running beyond the end of their life span. Much doubling and quadrupling of tracks on busy routes was done and the construction of loop lines and sidings, stations and halts serving new war factories also took place.

Canadian troops began to arrive in Dec 1939 and USA forces in large numbers from May 1942 with all their armaments and supplies. Their movements including leave traffic was mainly handled by the railways. The Dunkirk evacuation in 1940 and the crushing heavy burden of the Overlord programme for the D-Day landings in Normandy with thew consequent follow up supplies stretched the nation's railways to the absolute limit.

EVACUEES TO THE AREA

When the battle raging around Dunkirk was at its height the girls of Westcliff High School in Southend had heard the sound of falling bombs and gunfire as the German air force attacked ships in the Thames estuary. On 2 Jun 1940, 500 teenage girls and their teachers from the school arrived at Chapel en le Frith station from Derby after an eight hour journey from their homes. The local education authority had only been informed the day before that the children were on their way. An appeal was put out for residents to take the girls in and miraculously, before midnight, they had all been fixed up. Most stayed in the Chapel area but the rest were dispersed to Chinley where 100 were welcomed, fifty to Dove Holes and the rest to Peak Dale and the Hope valley.

Younger children had been evacuated from the cities at the beginning of the war in 1939. In three days one and a half million children and adults were herded on to trains and despatched to unfamiliar areas around Britain.

Parents of girls attending Notre Dame Catholic school in Sheffield agreed in Aug 1939 that some of their children should be evacuated to Derwent Hall which had been a youth hostel and was doomed to demolition when Ladybower reservoir was filled. Even Chatsworth House took some girls from a boarding school. Most of the children had returned to their homes by 1942 as the danger reduced.

WARTIME CHANGES IN THE VALLEY

Christie's hospital in Manchester had more radium for the treatment of cancer than all of Europe put together and it was decided to store it safe from air attack in the Blue John mine at Castleton.

In May 1940 at Hathersage, an anti-aircraft unit of 283 Field Battery 123 Field Regiment, Royal Artillery arrived. Soldiers were billeted all round Hathersage, their vehicles and guns parked on the field where Moorland Road is now. They stayed for two months.

On 12 Dec 1940 during the Sheffield Blitz the LMS station was damaged at the south end. One signal box was demolished and one damaged as well as houses behind the station. Further destruction was caused in 1941 at Little London Road, Heeley when Stokes paint facility at the side of the line was bombed and some coaches were wrecked.

There are said to have been secret movements of cement from Earle's for the D-Day preparations and it was also despatched abroad. There was a Monday to Saturday train from Earle's Sidings to Water Board Sidings in the mid-afternoon delivering cement for the Ladybower works.

Many thousands of tons of grain and cereals together with a vast quantity of foodstuffs were unloaded at Hope station and taken to secret store houses in the valley.

Searchlights were set up near Cowburn tunnel. As we will see in Vol. 2 there was the massive works involved in the building of the Ladybower reservoir. Although road transport played a major part in delivering the materials needed the railway had a part to play.

REFERENCES

The Book of Edale – The Edale Society, Halsgrove 2003
Buxton Barbara A. – *Hathersage in the Peak: A History*. Phillimore 2005
Clowes Peter – *The Peak District at War*. Churnet Valley Books 2001

DISASTER AVERTED BY CHINLEY SOUTH JUNCTION SIGNALMAN

There was a near disaster when a double headed heavy down Birmingham bound train loaded with ammunition snapped its couplings at Peak Forest in 1944. The train without its engines and with the guard unable to brake the train sufficiently ran backwards on the 1 in 90 incline through Dove Holes tunnel and Chapel en le Frith but through the quick thinking of the signalman at Chinley South Junction he diverted it on to the Chinley East Curve. After travelling more than five miles the train came to a halt safely on the rising 1 in 100 gradient near Cowburn tunnel. Had it not been diverted it could have run all the way down the Manchester line as far as Cheadle!

BANK HOLIDAY VISITORS

We have seen that there were large numbers of visitors just before the war and although the number of excursion trains were much reduced people from the towns around found ways of enjoying a break in the Peak District.

'During the August Bank Holiday in 1941 there was a large influx of visitors to the Hope valley and the number staying in the district exceeded anything since the last war. Many spent the period in caravans and tents. On Monday the LMS ran a few special trains into the valley and these were heavily loaded, as were the large number of buses. Castleton, Edale, Ashop and the Derwent valleys were the favourite haunts. Ramblers were more numerous than at any previous holiday this year, hotels and boarding houses did well. There was a shortage of beer in some districts, but several enterprising landlords established coffee stalls. Large crowds assembled during the weekend and sleeping accommodation was taxed to the utmost. The Hathersage playing fields and gardens were packed before noon on Monday. Hundreds of people waited in queues for buses to Sheffield and only a few visitors remained in the village after six o'clock.' *Derbyshire Times* 8 Aug 1941

The Hope valley is enjoying a holiday boom, and visitor's who are expecting to find accommodation and have not already booked will, in the majority of cases, be unlucky. Every boarding house and hotel is full and could have booked twice the number of people had the accommodation been available. *Derbyshire Times* 31 Jul 1942

With the war in Europe over there was a great desire to pick up on pre-war pursuits despite the rationing, lack of fuel etc. as the report below shows.

'For the August Bank Holiday crowds in the Hope valley equalled any year before the war. Every village had its full quota of visitors – holiday homes, youth hostels, boarding houses and hotels being full to capacity. The number of Boy Scouts, Girl Guides and youth organizations under canvas exceeded many previous years. Monday saw the greatest number of visitors. Four special trains were run to Hope, but it was from the Manchester area that most people came. At Castleton fifty boys whose fathers have died in the war were the guests of the Rotary Club. Record figures were reached at Hathersage bathing pool, 1,500 persons paying for admission on Thursday week. A break in the weather conditions reduced the number of visitors on Bank Holiday Monday and the bathing pool was practically deserted throughout the day. One prominent gardener found several roots of his potatoes had been pulled up and these no doubt formed the menu at one of the several camping parties. A local shopkeeper reported the loss of a large sunblind from his premises on Sunday evening, this evidently providing additional cover during the cold nights. *Derbyshire Times* 10 Aug 1945

NEW WAR TIME MOTIVE POWER

The United States Army Transportation Corps S160 class were 2-8-0 locomotives designed for use in Europe for heavy freight work. A total of 2,120 were built and worked on railways all around the world. They were designed on austerity principles and built using methods which created efficient and fast construction speeds over a long life span. These engines included axle box grease lubricators and rolled plates instead of castings. They were built between 1942 and 1946 by the American Locomotive Company (755), Baldwin locomotive works (712) and Lima locomotive works (653). The one depicted here, No. 2245, was built by Baldwin's in 1943. No. 2245 was one of the first batches of 400 shipped to South Wales and despatched from the GWR locomotive depot at Ebbw Vale Junction near Newport. It was one of fifty acquired by the LMS, the rest going to the other main line companies. They were allocated under the guise of 'running in' but in fact replaced damaged stock and increased the capacity of the system to allow for shipping of military pre-invasion equipment and troops. Another batch of 400 was prepared for storage at Ebbw Junction in the immediate run up to D-Day. After the invasion those loaned to the railway companies were recalled and refurbished at Ebbw Junction for shipment to Europe. This rare wartime view, in 1943, shows No. 2245 on a mineral empty approaching Avenue Sidings in the down direction. It may have worked from Gowhole but might also have arrived by the 'Old Road' from Rotherham and beyond.   *J. C. Naylor*

This engine is a train spotter's dream because of its extreme rarity particularly at this location. It has just emerged from Dore tunnel on the South Curve heading for the Hope valley. The War Department had over 900 locomotives built cheaply to a simple but rugged design which met the difficult requirements of the railways on the continent and beyond. Most of them were 2-8-0 heavy freight engines and there were also some 0-6-0 tanks. However this is one of the smaller number of the longer 2-10-0 wheel arrangement which proved to be highly successful. Only twenty five finished up in BR ownership after the war and all were shedded in Scotland. They were all built at the North British Locomotive Works in Glasgow – this one emerging at the same time as the D-Day landings in Jun 1944 and was immediately loaned to the LMS. Of the four pre-nationalisation companies the LMS took only a few of the WD's because they already had a large modern fleet of the Stanier 8F 2-8-0s. The engine was only with the LMS until Oct 1944 before returning to the War Department. It was initially numbered 3737, which is the number carried here, but was soon renumbered 73737. Sixteen of the class went to Greece, four to Syria, forty three to Belgium and sixty to Holland, which included this one. All the Belgian locomotives were transferred to Holland by Jun 1946. No. 73737 was eventually sold to the Netherlands State Railways where it became No. 5051 and was withdrawn in Jul 1950. Note the Westinghouse brake apparatus on the side of the smokebox, an American design. To see this engine was quite remarkable but to get a photograph of it when film was almost unobtainable and using it to film railways could lead to being arrested is remarkable.

J. C. Naylor

POST-WAR TO NATIONALISATION
REMINISCENCES

Ken Stokes, a Grimesthorpe engine driver, records what he considered his roughest ever night for weather. 'In the winter of 1937, we left Sheffield at 11.28 pm for Liverpool and, as we climbed Norman's Bank, the elements excelled themselves! A howling gale, snow and rain driving by the 4F cab in parallel lines, although fortunately we were, in railway parlance 'right way for the weather'. Vivid flashes of violent lightning lit up the surrounding countryside and, on that wild night, I witnessed a queer phenomenon. At the top of the safety valves, along with a white feather of steam, played a nine inch high blue flame, an eerie companion which stayed with us all the way up the bank until Cowburn tunnel. It was static electricity or 'St Elmo's Fire'. It was I suppose a scientific curiosity which I have not seen since that night.'

The following story keeps recurring and is possibly apocryphal. 'On one occasion while turning a light engine on the Chinley triangle at Chapel Milton a young fireman was asked by his driver if he had changed the lamps and when he replied in the affirmative, the driver enquired which side of the engine he had walked. 'I walked on the platform' replied the lad. Judge the driver's feelings when he realized that his mate had walked along the parapet of the (Chapel Milton) viaduct in order to carry the necessary change of lamp code.'

THE WINTER OF 1947

Your author has vivid memories of this time as a boy living in the lofty heights of Crookes in Sheffield. I recall going to Lydgate Lane school (never missed a day) through drifts which were well over my head, of a sledging track down our road which became unusable to vehicles for over two continuous months and which became so icy that Old King Cole the coal merchant could not get his lorry up the hill. All the fit men in the road commandeered our sledges to bring the lifesaving bags of fuel up the road to our houses and deposited them in the cellars. In May when the snows finally melted we made huge dams to hold the water. To my uninformed mind it was a wonderland of fun but to everybody else it was sheer misery after the travails of the war. With power cuts meaning night time hours lit only by candles, men having to walk long distances to work, bread rationing and other food shortages life was hard.

Two snow plough locomotives stand by for further snow clearance duties on the east side of the Buxton triangle with the station to the left. The line to Ashbourne is behind the photographer. The first engine is an LMS built 4F 0-6-0 and behind is an 8F 2-8-0. To the right is what appears to be an LMS built 7F 0-8-0 on the line down to Buxton East Junction. *Author's collection*

This caption states that this is the Peak main line being used as a footpath as the men approach from Buxton. However the telegraph posts suggests it is a road. It serves the purpose of showing the exceptional state the Peak District was in.

Author's collection

The exposed village of Sparrowpit caught the full force of the weather in 1947. *Derby Daily Telegraph collection*

The snow started in the south of England towards the end of January and swept north a few days later. On the railways, points froze and had to be thawed by blow lamps, whilst water columns had to be warmed by braziers. Lubricating oil was unusable without being warmed first so locomotive preparation took longer than usual. Vacuum and steam hose connections on rolling stock were routinely thawed out before use. Signals were also affected; one mile of signal wire could contract by 2 ft in only twelve hours of sub-zero temperatures.

Feb 1947 started with a burst of sunshine but no more was seen for three weeks. On 3 Feb there was continuous snow for twenty four hours in the Peak District with passengers stranded overnight in the cutting at Dove Holes. Scotland was as yet snow free. On 10 Feb power cuts were imposed because of the difficulties of getting coal from the pitheads to the power stations. In the first week of February nearly 20,000 movements of coal deliveries had to be cancelled or postponed nationwide at a time when 75% of the nation's coal was moved by rail. By the end of the month, traffic managers were able to restore services to the extent that 3.3 million tons of coal was moved in an eight day period. By mid-February, with conditions described as Arctic, the LMS experienced no fewer than forty three blockages to running lines of which the Peak District had a high share.

Mid-March brought warmer air which thawed the snow on the ground. This snow melt rapidly ran off the frozen

A group of men pause from their shovelling to look at the photographer as a 3F 0-6-0 on the left and the tender of an 8F 2-8-0 wait for release from the snow at Chinley North Junction. It is said that the workers had originally gone to fix temporary lighting inside Dove Holes tunnel for the never ending maintenance that was required in this difficult to maintain tunnel but had been cut off when the line became blocked by the heavy snow. The date is almost certain to be around 4 to 6 Feb 1947.

Mrs P. Cannon.
Picture the Past.
Derbyshire Libraries

The same group of men are now in front of the 8F.
*Mrs P. Cannon.
Picture the Past.
Derbyshire Libraries*

Inside Chinley North Junction box not a single lever has been pulled off which indicates nothing is running. Understandably, the men have come in for a warm. The signalman is on the right and on the left is Harold Goodey. The time is 15.55.
*Mrs P. Cannon.
Picture the Past.
Derbyshire Libraries*

The men's hard work in freezing conditions seems to have paid off for the lines here in front of Chinley North Junction box are sufficiently clear to allow some running
*Mrs P. Cannon.
Picture the Past.
Derbyshire Libraries*

ground into rivers which caused widespread flooding. 100,000 properties were affected across the country. On 17 and 18 March there were strong gales as well as snow melt. The River Trent overtopped its banks in Nottingham. Large parts of the city and surrounding areas were flooded, 9,000 properties and nearly a hundred industrial properties were affected, some to first floor height. The suburbs of Long Eaton, West Bridgford and Beeston suffered particularly badly.

A scouring of the local newspapers brings home the length and severity of the snow and the responses to it. There has been nothing as extreme as that winter. Many men would have been exhausted through hard physical labour, day after day, in extremely cold temperatures and in exposed places with inadequate clothing. The worst of the disruption to the railways in the Peak District was on the west side of Hope, the Peak main line from Millers Dale north to Chinley, and rail access to Buxton, including the line to Ashbourne. The Woodhead line was badly affected and, of course, the Woodhead and Snake roads were closed for long periods which included a severe land slip on the Snake. The roads from Sheffield and Chapel en le Frith over the moors to the Hope valley presented a continuous challenge to the snow clearance teams.

The newspapers of the period reported as follows:

'Blizzards raged through the Peak. All roads to Edale have become impassable.' *Derby Daily Telegraph* 26 Jan 1947

'Road conditions improved today but a road at Hathersage is blocked by drifts and snowploughs are at work. The thaw expected today has been delayed. The forecast is for east winds, occasional slight snow, very cold, and frost by day and night.' *Derby Daily Telegraph* 1 Feb 1947

'There was an eight hour blizzard in Derbyshire, the worst of the winter so far. Edale is cut off by drifts but during the weekend it had the largest number of winter sportsmen. Drifts are 20 ft deep on Kinder. There is no rail access to Buxton.' *Sheffield Daily Telegraph* 3 Feb 1947

'The blizzard was the worst for forty years. Woodhead and Snake roads are both closed and by nightfall the Moscar road to the Hope valley was impassable at Hollow Meadows. The Hope to Chapel road is blocked by 8 ft deep drifts for 400 yards. Snowploughs aided by prisoners of war, tried to force a way through a huge drift blocking the Chapel road but had to abandon the effort as the road behind them became blocked. Drifts on the Snake Pass defied the efforts of a bulldozer. The road over Owler Bar has been blocked since Sunday morning. Buxton remains cut off and trains cannot get through. Dozens of Peakland farms are isolated and some have not seen a newspaper since Thursday. A driver, conductor and one passenger were stranded and spent the night at the *Fox House Inn*, Longshaw, last night, when their bus was bogged down on the Grindleford road. It took them an hour to walk the half mile to the inn.'

Sheffield Daily Telegraph Tue 4 Feb 1947

'Trains between Sheffield and Manchester were held up at Hope. At Chinley gangs of men were hurriedly brought in to dig out stranded trains.'

Lancashire Evening Post Tue 4 Feb 1947

8F 2-8-0 No. 8341 with Chinley North Junction signal box behind looking toward Chinley station. The engine is on the Dore line and had become snowbound after all the wheels were derailed on 8 Feb 1947. On 16 Feb the men have just finished digging the engine out of the snow ready for re-railing.
Harold D. Bowtell.
Frank Berridge collection

'Access to Buxton has now been achieved. The blizzard was still raging this morning. Troops of the Manchester Regiment have been rushed by rail to reinforce the weary snow clearers.' *Derby Daily Telegraph* Thu 6 Feb 1947

'There are drifts up to 14 ft in the Peak. Telephone lines are down, coal is in short supply, gas pressure is low and electricity subject to cuts. On Sunday Edale was cut off. The collieries are short of men. Their yards are full of coal but wagons are unable to move.'
Derbyshire Times Fri 7 Feb 1947

'In the Peak District the Woodhead line was closed near the tunnel. The Hope valley line opened at 10.00 yesterday to allow the first train to pass over a single line. The line through Cowburn re-opened for freight at 19.45.' *Yorkshire Post* 10 Feb 1947

'Heavy rain thawed lasts night's fall of snow. With temperatures barely above freezing a thick bed of ice remains beneath the surface water on rural roads. Conditions are still very dangerous. The LMS announced the cancellation of some long distance expresses to assist coal traffic movements from Monday next. There are restricted services on the Hope valley line. All the other Derbyshire lines are clear. On Wednesday the LMS moved 20,200 coal wagons and 202,000 tons of coal compared with 18,187 wagons and 182,000 tons on Tuesday.' *Derby Daily Telegraph* Thu 13 Feb 1947

'There were more severe blizzards last Sunday. Many villages were cut off again. Thousands of sheep are buried on the moors. One farmer near Hathersage has found thirty dead sheep. Only half of the marooned sheep have been reached so far. German POWs are getting supplies to the farms. Sixty ramblers on Sunday went on to Bamford Edge to rescue sheep. Edale has been cut off by road for nearly a fortnight with drifts 20 feet deep. Bread is being brought in by rail, the station having become a distribution centre. Milk is not getting out as there are no churns available. From Thursday several main line passenger trains have been withdrawn. Others have had their timetables altered including through trains. The weather forecast is for temperatures on Fri 28/23°, Sat 28/23°, Sun 32/27°, Mon 32/27°, Tue 30/27° and Wed 31/28°F.'
Derbyshire Times Fri 14 Feb 1947

'Thirty trains each carrying 360 tons of coal passed through Cowburn tunnel while 100 men worked in the tunnel to clear the icicles which are as thick as a man's body. Coal is now being despatched from south Yorkshire pits at the rate of 60,000 tons a day. A 'Keep the Coal Moving' campaign has been launched over the weekend.' *Dundee Courier* 17 Feb 1947

'Following further blizzards it took three days to clear the Snake road which had been blocked by a landslide. A twenty four hour watch is being kept to watch for ice and icicles in Cowburn tunnel. Hundreds of sheep are buried in snowdrifts 20 ft deep. Most of the ewes are lambing. Foxes have killed scores of sheep.'
Western Daily Express 22 Feb 1947

'Workmen toiled for twelve hours breaking ice formations from the Cowburn tunnel walls. Fifty wagons of ice were removed. Many were 20 ft long and 3 ft thick weighing over half a ton.' *Dundee Courier* 24 Feb 1947

'A snow plough carrying a Rolls Royce Derwent jet engine left Derby this morning to clear snowdrifts blocking the Buxton to Ashbourne line between Hurdlow and Alsop en le Dale. The line has been blocked for three weeks. There have been further landslides on the Snake road with earth, snow and ice up to 50 ft blocking the road. It is not expected to be re-opened for another month.'
Sheffield Daily Telegraph Sat 1 Mar 1947

'By 10.00 pm on Saturday all routes to the Hope valley were blocked by snow. At Cowburn men have been on duty for hours to keep a passage through drifts 7 ft high and twenty yards long. One train that became snowbound was a fast goods taking foodstuffs to Manchester and Liverpool.' *Derbyshire Times* 3 Mar 1947

'Another blizzard has hit the Peak District. The Derby to Manchester and Buxton to Ashbourne line are blocked. Trains from Manchester have been diverted over the Dore and Chinley line. Engines and wagons are stuck at Tissington and cannot be moved. The Woodhead line is blocked at Dunford Bridge.' *Derby Daily Telegraph* 5 Mar 1947

'Storms were experienced for thirty hours non-stop yesterday. The main Manchester to Derby line was blocked but was cleared following all night work. The Ashbourne to Buxton line is closed. An LNER train from Manchester to London is not expected to reach its destination until twenty one hours after it set out. The 10.35 from Manchester is lost somewhere near Nottingham.'
Derby Daily Telegraph Thu 6 Mar 1947

'Blizzards blocked the roads again. A Hulleys' bus, which had been stranded on the Grindleford to Eyam road since 23 Feb, was released on Monday afternoon. Snow started falling on Monday at 9.00 pm and every road into the valley is blocked. After being held up for five weeks twenty three lorries left Earle's Cement works on Tuesday for Lancashire and Staffordshire. Sixteen became stranded, some around Chinley. The temperatures ahead are a touch warmer (not at night!): Thu 40/29°, Fri 33/23°, Sat 34/21°, Sun 39/9°, Mon 40/11°, Tue 36/29° and Wed 34/21°F.'
Derbyshire Times Fri 7 Mar 1947

'A thaw is slowly setting in but this did not stop further dislocation on the Hope valley line on Wednesday and new snowfall blocked the Peak Forest to Millers Dale line for some hours.' *Derbyshire Times* Fri 14 Mar 1947

'Many ramblers again joined in the weekend roundup of Peakland sheep, marooned in deep drifts. Sheep losses are believed to be as high as one in three among some flocks. During the weekend the LMS moved nationally 293,020 tons of coal from the collieries, a record since the crisis began.' *Derby Daily Telegraph* Sat 8 Apr 1947

'Farmers, ramblers, prisoners of war, gamekeepers, DVWB employees assisted shepherds over the Easter weekend find dead sheep and bury them as it was thought that rotting carcasses could contaminate the water supply. Dead sheep were found on tree tops where they had climbed deep snow drifts to eat the top branches. In one gully 100 dead sheep were found laying four deep.'

Derby Daily Telegraph Sat 8 Apr 1947

'Sheep losses in the Peak District were between fourteen and fifteen thousand beasts as well as 300 horses, forty pigs and 2,000 poultry.' *Derby Daily Telegraph* 31 May 1947

NATIONALISATION

THE RAILWAYS ON THEIR KNEES

By the end of the war there had been a net disinvestment in the railways which, when the excessive wear and tear and the huge arrears of replacing stock was taken into account, showed that the railways were in very poor shape to face the challenges of peacetime. One Labour minister described them as 'a poor bag of assets'. However, the railways had demonstrated what Ludendorff had concluded in 1918 'there comes a time when locomotives are more important than guns'.

The LMS, like the other grouped companies, came out of the war in a very run down condition. 50% more freight was carried during the war years than in 1938. This abnormally large wartime traffic with the excessive and huge arrears of replacement meant the company was in poor shape to take on the re-introduced road competition. In 1945 124,000 wagons were undergoing or awaiting repair. Two years later it was worst with 203,000 wagons or 16.6% of the total. Track maintenance in 1945 was running at less than a third of pre-war levels, 2,500 route miles needed attention.

However in the latter part of the war the Ministry of War had complete control of inland transport in a manner that was unparalleled and had made a pronounced success of it. Thus it became clear that the companies as constituted did not have the assets or finance to tackle the maintenance and renewal backlog.

'Cheer Churchill – vote Labour' was the landslide election winning slogan in 1945. Labour campaigned on nationalising the railways and many other utilities This resulted in nearly all the railway system being brought into public ownership by the Transport Act of 1947.

Rail nationalisation meant the end of the LMS on 31 Dec 1947 after twenty four years and a new dawn broke on 1st January 1948 with the enterprise becoming the London Midland Region of British Railways.

CHAPTER 5
OPERATIONS

INTRODUCTION TO THE WORKING TIMETABLES

The timetables examined here cover first the Midland Railway and later the Midland Division of the LMS and were instructions from management to drivers, signalmen and other staff working on the line. Studying these timetables in detail reveals the complexity of tracing particular train movements and is a far from trivial exercise. Trains are arranged chronologically based on the time of their first appearance on a particular table. A train may appear on several tables within one volume and is only cross referenced between tables on the basis of starting time and place. Still more difficult is relating trains between one operating district and the geographically adjoining one; a train may suddenly appear or disappear at a junction. Signalmen and platelayers only needed to know what time a train passed their location but drivers and guards were required to know the line before running the trains as timetabled. Knowing the road was crucial.

Many railway histories merely print relevant timetables which does not encourage detailed study. I have chosen to group trains around one locality in the Hope or Edale valleys over a twenty four hour period thus making it possible to know what passed both ways on that particular day. There won't be too many quiet moments.

Initially passenger and freight times were collated together but by the 1920s published working timetables had been split into freight and passenger workings. Passenger services are easier to trace because the company published both working and public timetables and there is always a 'Bradshaw' to turn to. Also local timetables, which would include railway, bus and tram information were printed by the railway and bus companies. In addition newspapers and other local publications listed passenger services. Nevertheless, working timetables are always the most instructive because these have additional information such as empty carriage movements and light engine workings.

PASSENGER OPERATIONS
TRAIN FORMATIONS

Until at least 1925 express trains in the valley consisted of just three coaches weighing about seventy tons; the report into the 1925 accident at Hope in Vol. 2 illustrates this. The carriages were light Midland ones, probably non-corridor lavatory stock, and only some compartments had access to a lavatory. In the twenties and thirties a strengthener was added, possibly due to increased traffic but also because corridor stock came into use which seated fewer passengers. The strengthener was usually at the Sheffield end of the trains.

Most expresses stopped at Dore and Totley and then a station in the valley, which was usually Hope, and then Chinley. The expresses were discontinued at the outbreak of the war, and were never reinstated. The trains consisted of what the LMS called an 'inter-district set' consisting of brake third, composite and another brake third. The strengthener could be any third class coach, corridor or vestibule, but never with a brake compartment. Some of the stock used may have been Pre-Grouping but be the mid-thirties clerestory stock was becoming rare, none having been built since 1915.

Ordinary local passenger trains were made up in much the same way; a strengthener could be added at either end however. Lavatory stock was still in use until at least 1949. Sometimes a passenger train could consist of just three vehicles in which case the brake vehicle would be the middle one.

The other class of trains that used the line were the scheduled and additional excursion trains to Llandudno and Blackpool in particular, often worked by a Grimesthorpe 4F or 'Crab'. These could load up to ten coaches.

I am grateful to the late Chris Croft, member of the LMS Society and long time Peak District resident for these details.

FROM THE OPENING

Some of these trains commenced from Rotherham and called at Attercliffe Road. A local service preceded the departure from Sheffield and stopped at Heeley, Mill Houses & Ecclesall, Beauchief and Abbey Dale to Dore to connect with the 08.20, 11.00 and 18.55 trains to Marple although the 08.20 also called at Heeley some fourteen minutes after the local. Passengers from Chesterfield changed at Dore for the 08.31, 11.08 and 19.03 trains to Marple. The 13.21 and 15.50 trains went directly to Sheffield where passengers connected with the 14.00 and 16.55 non-stop service to Marple which took around fifty minutes. The Dore South Curve was not opened for passenger services for another ten years.

Marple was the junction station at the western end of the line because Chinley was still a small wayside station. Marple, however, was also ill-equipped to cope with this extra traffic and had no room for expansion. It was particularly busy because it shared its traffic with the MSLR. To illustrate this point on a typical day well over a hundred trains were booked to call from twenty two different places, ranging from Bristol to Blackburn, Southport to Lowestoft and Leicester to Blackpool. Including non-stop expresses and goods trains, about 240 trains had to pass through Marple every twenty four hours, an average of one every six minutes night and day. The station employed forty staff of which fifteen were on duty at any one time.

From Marple the service into Manchester took twenty five minutes with a stop at Stockport on the 09.20, 11.55 and 19.52 trains. The 14.59 and 17.48 trains ran non-stop although there was a separate local service. Altogether five trains ran between Rotherham via Sheffield to Manchester Central taking around eighty five minutes. From Manchester Central connections could be made

The timetable for the start of through passenger trains to Manchester's Central and Victoria stations on 1 Jun 1894.

to Liverpool Central and Southport. All the trains that reached Marple had a connection to Manchester Victoria and ran non-stop in around twenty minutes, the route being via Romiley where it headed northwest via the Sheffield & Midland Committee (MSL/MR) joint line to Bredbury, Reddish Junction, Belle Vue, Ashburys and then the Midland Curve at Ashton Road where it gained Lancashire & Yorkshire metals. This line went via Beswick Junction and Phillip's Park Junction where a left curve gained the Ashton branch to Miles Platting and then into Victoria station. Here there were connections to LYR trains to Blackburn and Blackpool. It thus became possible to reach Blackpool from Sheffield in three hours and forty two minutes. Trains from Manchester to Sheffield and Rotherham followed a similar pattern, although three trains stopped at Heeley where passengers to Chesterfield changed.

PASSENGER SERVICES IN WINTER 1894/1895

As we have seen there was much advertising promoting the new line whose passenger service had started only four months earlier. When compared with later timetables the passenger services were sparse, the number in 1914 being over double in both directions. Buxton was coming to its zenith as a fashionable watering place and, as a result, there was a regular service from Sheffield, there being three through trains via the Chinley South Curve from Sheffield in early morning, noon and evening and from Buxton early morning and late afternoon. To Manchester Central there were six trains with two stopping at all stations. In the opposite direction there were five trains but only one was all stations. There was one train to Manchester Victoria in the down direction with a stop at Marple and an up train at lunchtime all stations with a connection from Blackpool. There was also a Sheffield to Hope and return and a Dronfield to Hope in the down direction. In total there were twenty two trains.

The physical confines of Marple station are well seen in this 1900 view looking towards New Mills. The station's confined track layout must have taxed the signalmen controlling the lines to the limit and is seen in its almost final condition before the addition of the later platform signal box. The black roundel on a white background for the reverse of the stop signal was abandoned in 1912 by the Midland. The joint influence of the MSLR can be detected by the style of the lamp posts.
Author's collection

WORKING TIMETABLE OF PASSENGER TRAINS MAY 1898

This timetable covers Section E of the Midland Railway WTTs which did not include before or beyond Dore and Totley. Therefore the times at Sheffield and intermediate stations are not available although adding or subtracting ten minutes from the Dore times will give a rough time for Sheffield and about twenty five minutes to and from Chesterfield. The times of arrival and departure from Buxton are not included either. The Dore South Curve and Chinley South Curve were both open at this time. Edale has been chosen for the freight timetable because it was the exchange point for through freights at this time although it was not the most frequented station for passengers. The format shows the days operated and the 'Detail' column starts with the departure stations and the time of departure and the end station, with times if available. It then lists the stations where the train stopped, with arrival and departure times. If there is no arrival time then the train does not stop. The day(s) the trains ran are notated below the arrival and departure times. Trains that worked on the line but did not reach Edale are also included for completeness.

The beautifully designed cover of the public timetable for the summer of 1894 featuring the new Dore & Chinley line.
Laurence Knighton collection

TIME ARR DEP DAY	EDALE DOWN TRAINS 1898 DETAIL
08.14 / 08.15 / Mon	**Sheffield to Buxton** Dore 07.41 Grindleford 07.52 Hathersage 07.57 Bamford 08.01 Hope 08.05 Chapel 08.24/ 08.28
08.36 / 08.39 / Not Mon	**Sheffield to Buxton** Dore 07.59 Grindleford 08.09 Hathersage 08.14 Bamford 08.19 Hope 08.24 Chapel 08.50/ 08.53 Peak Forest 09.02
08.59 / 09.00	**Sheffield to Manchester Cen 09.46** Dore 08.36 Hope 08.51 Marple 09.17/ 09.20 Stockport TD 09.30/ 09.32
09.11 / 09.12 / Sun	**Sheffield to Buxton** Dore 08.35 Grindleford 08.45 Hathersage 08.50 Bamford 08.55 Hope 09.00 Chapel 09.21/ 09.23 Peak Forest 09.31/ 09.34
11.09 / 11.10	**Sheffield to Buxton** Dore 10.36 Grindleford 10.47 Hathersage 10.52 Bamford 10.56 Hope 11.00 Chapel 11.19/ 11.21
12.30	**Express Sheffield to Manchester Cen 15.15** Dore 12.04 Grindleford 12.12 Hathersage Bamford Hope 12.21 Edale stops at these five stations when req to take up for beyond Marple. 5 mins in booking to allow for stops. Marple 12.48/ 12.51
13.04 / 13.05	**Sheffield to Buxton** Dore 12.29 Grindleford 12.39 Hathersage 12.44 Bamford 12.49 Hope 12.55 Chapel 13.16/ 13.18 Peak Forest 13.26/ 13.28
Sun	**Sheffield to Hope 13.58** Dore 13.31 Grindleford 13.42 Hathersage 13.47 Bamford 13.52
15.04 / 15.06	**Sheffield to Buxton** Dore 14.29 Grindleford 14.39 Hathersage 14.44 Bamford 14.49 Hope 14.53/ 14.55 Chapel 15.15/ 15.17 Peak Forest 15.24/ 15.27
17.39	**Express Sheffield to Manchester Cen 18.27** Hope 17.30 Edale stops to set down when req, Marple 18.00/ 18.02
18.15 / 18.16	**Sheffield to Buxton** Dore 17.39 Grindleford 17.49 Hathersage 17.54 Bamford 17.59 Hope 18.04 Chapel 18.25/ 18.27
19.05 / 19.06 / Sun	**Sheffield to Manchester Cen 20.00** Dore 18.26 Grindleford 18.36 Hathersage 18.41 Bamford 18.46 Hope 18.51/ 18.54 Chinley 19.15 New Mills 19.23 Marple 19.28/ 19.30 Didsbury, Withington, Chorlton stops at these 3 stations to set down passengers as req, Five minutes in booking allowed for stops. Stockport TD 19.39/ 19.42
19.47 / 19.48	**Express Sheffield to Manchester Cen 20.38** Dore 19.12 Grindleford 19.22 Hathersage 19.27 Bamford 19.32 Hope 19.37 Chinley 19.53 New Mills 20.06 Marple 20.11/ 20.13 Stockport TD 20.22/ 20.24
	Sheffield to Hope 20.44 Dore 20.18 Grindleford 20.29 Hathersage 20.34 Bamford 20.39
Sat	**Empty Coaching Stock Heeley to Grindleford 20.36** Dore 20.26
21.14 / 21.19 / Sun	**Grindleford 20.40 to Manchester Cen 22.45** Hathersage 20.44/ 20.46 Bamford 20.50/ 20.53 Hope 20.58/ 21.04 New Mills 21.45 Marple 21.51/ 22.08 Heaton Mersey 22.18 Didsbury 22.23 Withington 22.29 Chorlton 22.35/ 22.37
21.31 / 21.34	**Sheffield to Manchester Vic 22.22** Dore 20.45 Grindleford 20.54/ 20.56 Hathersage 21.00/ 21.02 Bamford 21.06/ 21.08 Hope 21.12/ 21.19 Marple 21.56/ 22.00

EDALE UP TRAINS		
TIME ARR DEP DAY	DETAIL	1898
07.37 07.38	**Buxton to Sheffield** Chapel 07.26/ 07.27. Hope 07.49 Bamford 07.53 Hathersage 07.57 Grindleford 08.02 Dore 08.10	
09.07 09.08	**Buxton to Sheffield** Hope 09.17 Bamford 09.21 Hathersage 09.25 Grindleford 09.30 / 09.33	
10.02 10.03	**Marple 09.40 to Sheffield** Chinley 09.51 Hope 10.11 Bamford 10.15 Hathersage 10.19 Grindleford 10.24 Dore 10.32	
11.16 11.17 Sun	**Manchester Cen 10.10 to Sheffield** Chorlton 10.17 Withington 10.22 Didsbury 10.25 Heaton Mersey 10.29 Stockport TD 10.34/ 10.36 Romiley 10.43 Marple 10.46/ 10.48 New Mills 10.56 Chinley 11.03 Hope 11.29 Bamford 11.34 Hathersage 11.39 Grindleford 13.15 Dore 13.25	
12.15	**Manchester Cen 11.30 to Sheffield** Marple 11.51/ 11.56 Edale stops to set down pass from Marple & beyond	
12.25 12.26	**Buxton to Sheffield** Peak Forest 12.10/ 12.11 Hope 12.35 Bamford 12.40 Hathersage 12.44 Grindleford 12.50 Dore 12.59	
Sun	**Hope 13.00 to Sheffield** Bamford 13.05 Hathersage 13.10 Grindleford 13.15 Dore 13.25	
Sat	**Empty Coaching Stock Hope 14.03 to Sheffield** Dore 14.25	
14.24 14.25	**Manchester Vic 13.43 to Sheffield** Miles Platting 13.44/ 13.46 Hope 14.35 Bamford 14.39 Hathersage 14.44 Grindleford 14.49 Dore 14.58	
14.35 14.37 Sat	**Stockport TD 13.55 to Grindleford 15.02** Marple 14.07/ 14.09 New Mills 14.16 Hope 14.47 Bamford 14.52 Hathersage 14.57. Empty coaching stock to Heeley Carriage Sdgs	
15.08 15.10	**Manchester Cen 14.25 to Sheffield** Marple 14.46/ 14.50 Edale when req to set down Hope 15.18	
15.36 15.37 Sat	**Buxton to Sheffield** Peak Forest 15.18 Chapel 15.25/ 15.26 Hope 15.46 Bamford 15.50 Hathersage 15.55 Grindleford 16.00 Dore 16.08	
Sun	**Hope 15.55 to Sheffield** Bamford 16.00 Hathersage 16.05 Grindleford 16.10 Dore 16.20	
17.08	**Express Manchester Cen 16.20 to Sheffield** Marple 16.44/ 16.49 Edale stops to set down Grindleford 17.23 to set down Dore 17.34	
18.23 18.24	**Express Manchester Cen 19.40 to Sheffield** Marple 18.01/ 18.05 Hope 18.32 stops when required to pick up passengers for Mansfield	
18.37 18.38	**Buxton to Sheffield** Chapel 18.26/ 18.27 Hope 18.50 Bamford 18.55 Hathersage 19.00 Grindleford 19.06 Dore 19.15	
19.57 19.59 Sun	**Buxton to Sheffield** Peak Forest 19.38 Chapel 19.45/ 19.47. Hope 20.10 Bamford 20.16 Hathersage 20.22 Grindleford 20.28 Dore 20.38	
	Hope 21.02 to Sheffield Bamford 21.08 Hathersage 21.13 Grindleford 21.20 Dore 21.31	

REFERENCE
Midland Railway Working Time Tables Liverpool, Manchester, Dore and Totley, Buxton, and Rowsley May 1898. Dragonwheel Books Reprint 2008

PASSENGER SERVICES IN THE SUMMER OF 1903

The widened lines at the Sheffield and Chinley ends were only recently opened and the public timetable for the summer shows, that on a weekday, there were nineteen passenger trains in the down direction and seventeen in the up direction including trains originating in the valley. The direct Sheffield to Buxton service had ended and now required a change at Chinley's new station although Chinley South Curve was available for passenger trains. Most of the services to Manchester had been cut to one or two a day in each direction. However, there were well co-ordinated connections at Chinley to Buxton, Manchester Central and Manchester Victoria.

THROUGH COACH FROM MANCHESTER TO HARWICH

There was an interesting, but short lived, through coach working between Manchester Central and Harwich Parkeston Quay which was introduced by the Midland on 1 Jul 1903. It was included on a fast Sheffield train from Manchester via the Hope valley and then attached to a new through express to Lincoln via the Sheffield District Railway and Lancashire Derbyshire & East Coast Railway. From Lincoln the Great Eastern included the coach on the same train that carried through Great Central coaches from Liverpool and Manchester London Road.

REFERENCE
Joy D. – *Regional History of the Railways of Great Britain Vol 8: South and West Yorkshire.* David & Charles 1975

LANCASHIRE DERBYSHIRE& EAST COAST TRAFFIC

In 1897 the Lancashire Derbyshire & East Coast Railway opened from Chesterfield Market Place to Pywipe Junction with running powers into Lincoln. It also had a link to Beighton and Treeton where it had running powers over the Sheffield District Railway into Sheffield Midland. In 1906 the *Railway Magazine* noted that the Midland was controlling the traffic from Lincoln to Sheffield and that through connections had been arranged to and from Manchester via the Hope valley.

PASSENGER SERVICES IN 1910

Bradshaw's timetable shows that the Hope valley saw thirty two trains a day, starting with the 06.22 Sheffield to Edale which returned to Sheffield at 08.18 all stations. Four trains a day ran each way between Liverpool, Manchester and Sheffield, the Liverpool portions being attached at Chinley, with a further fourteen trains from Manchester Central.

PASSENGER SERVICES IN SUMMER 1914

In the down direction there were seven fast trains and four all stations to Manchester Central plus one to Manchester Victoria. Four all station trains went to Buxton with an additional one on Sunday that ran non-stop as at this time the Chinley South Curve was open. Additionally five all stations and one non-stop finished at Chinley and would have afforded more connections to Buxton. There was a Saturday and Sunday service to Hope from Sheffield and one from Chesterfield. There was an odd service, that was not repeated again, to Cheadle Heath which called at all stations.

In the up direction there were markedly fewer trains from Manchester Central and Buxton to Sheffield but more from Chinley which suggests that some Manchester and

Buxton travellers would have changed there. There were a number of trains from Blackpool Talbot Road to Sheffield, Chesterfield and one to Nottingham, mainly on Saturdays. There was an unusual working from Manchester Victoria to Grindleford calling at all the stations in between which would have been a connection for Blackpool passengers. Ignoring those that ran on stipulated days there were in total thirty passenger trains a day. The best times were Sheffield to Manchester sixty five minutes, Chinley forty two minutes, Blackpool Talbot Road to Sheffield two hours fifty minutes and Nottingham three hours one minute.

PASSENGER TIMETABLE AT HATHERSAGE FROM JULY 1914 UNTIL FURTHER NOTICE

This timetable covers the last throes of the Midland in all its pomp but it was to become seriously disrupted by the overriding requirement to provide troop trains. A special mobilisation timetable had been in preparation for some time, war being finally declared on 4 Aug when all excursion traffic was immediately cancelled and the railway came under the control of the Railway Executive Committee. This was directly responsible to the government but had a free hand to manage and co-ordinate the nation's railways. In addition to the peak tourist traffic the Midland, along with other railways, moved Territorial Army units to their annual training camps. One of these trains used on our route is detailed in the following timetable extract. When the international situation became critical on 3 Aug it was decided to cancel the camps and, with no notice at all, the railways were required to return all Territorial units to their home depots on 3rd and 4th Aug. General mobilisation began on 5 Aug. This was followed by the complex task of moving the Expeditionary Force to the south coast for embarkation to France including horses, baggage and equipment.

The following is what the observer would have seen at Hathersage in that fateful summer before everything was turned on its head by the needs of wartime.

Where the 'Day' column is left blank then services ran Monday to Saturday. Times in brackets at Hathersage indicate trains which did not stop.

DOWN TRAINS		
TIME AT HATH	DAY	DETAIL 1914
(05.03)		**Empty Carriages Leeds 03.08 to Cornbrook Carriage Sdgs 06.15** Sheffield 04.30. Leeds & Sheffield to provide 25 carriages & train must be charged with gas
(05.21)		**Empty Carriages Manningham 03.00 to Cornbrook Carriage Sdgs 06.47** Sheffield 04.48. Bradford & Sheffield to provide 25 carriages & the train must be charged with gas
07.00		**Sheffield 06.30 to Chinley 07.35** Heeley 06.36 Dore 06.43/ 06.44 Grindleford 06.55 Bamford 07.05 Hope 07.10 Edale 07.22
(07.47)		**Express Sheffield 07.30 to Liverpool Cen 09.28** Heeley 07.36 Chinley 08.19/ 08.23 Warrington 08.58/ 09.01
08.02	Mon	**Sheffield 07.35 to Chinley 08.35** Dore 07.45/ 07.46 Grindleford 07.57 Bamford 08.07 Hope 08.12 Edale 08.24

DOWN TRAINS		
TIME AT HATH	DAY	DETAIL 1914
08.34		**Sheffield 08.05 to Manchester Cen 09.59** Heeley 08.10 Dore 08.17/ 08.18 Grindleford 08.29 Bamford 08.39 Hope 08.44 Edale 08.56 Chinley 09.07/ 09.09 Strines 09.16 Marple 09.21/ 09.22 Stockport T.D. 09.34/ 09.39
08.51	Sun	**Sheffield 08.15 to Manchester Cen 10.39** Heeley 08.21 Millhouses 08.27 Dore 08.31/ 08.35 Grindleford 08.46 Bamford 08.56 Hope 09.01 Edale 09.12 Chinley 09.23/ 09.35 Bugsworth 09.38 New Mills 09.45 Marple 09.50/ 09.55 Romiley 10.01 Stockport T.D. 10.06/ 10.11 Heaton Mersey 10.18 Didsbury 10.22 Withington 10.25 Chorlton 10.29/ 10.32
(08.52)		**Express Sheffield 08.35 to Chinley 09.20** Heeley 08.41
(09.08)	Sat 8 Aug to 12 Sep	**Express Chesterfield 08.20 to Blackpool Talbot Road 11.46** Chinley 09.28
(10.06)		**Express Sheffield 09.40 to Blackpool Talbot Road** Heeley 09.45 not Saturday 25 Jul to 5 Sep Dore 09.51/ 09.54 Tue Thu only when req to pick up passengers from Chesterfield, Grindleford 10.01 Chinley 10.27/ 10.30 Tue Thu, Midland Jcn 10.50/ 10.53 to change engines, Manchester Vic 11.00 to set down passengers as req
(10.48)	Sat 25 Jul	**As below** but must call at Marple. Two thirds to be attached at Sheffield next to the engine and must be kept empty for Marple passengers
(10.58)	Sat only	**Express Sheffield 10.25 to Blackpool Talbot Road** Millhouses 10.32 Dore 10.40/ 10.42 Chinley 11.16/ 11.18 Midland Jcn 11.44/ 11.47 to change engine
11.01	Sun	**Sheffield 10.25 to Hope 11.10** Heeley 10.31 Millhouses 10.37 Beauchief 10.41 Dore 10.44/ 10.45 Grindleford 10.56 Bamford 11.06
11.04		**Sheffield 10.28 to Chinley 11.41** Millhouses 10.34 Beauchief 10.40 Dore 10.44/ 10.49 Grindleford 11.00 Bamford 11.10/ 11.12 Hope 11.16/ 11.18 Edale 11.30
(11.36)		**Sheffield 11.05 to Manchester Cen 12.23** Heeley 11.11 Dore 11.18/ 11.20 Chinley 11.54/ 11.58
12.56		**Express Sheffield 12.28 to Chinley 13.29** Dore 12.39/12.40 Grindleford 12.51 Bamford 13.01 Hope 13.06 Edale 13.18
13.42	Sat	**Express Sheffield 13.15 to Buxton** Grindleford 13.37 Bamford 13.47 Hope 13.52
13.56	Not Sat	**Sheffield 13.20 to Chinley 14.29** Heeley 13.26 Millhouses 13.32 Beauchief 13.36 Dore 13.39/ 13.40 Grindleford 13.51 Bamford 14.01 Hope 14.06 Edale 14.18
13.56	Sat	**As above** but Edale 14.28 **Chinley 14.37**
(14.34)	Not Sat 1 Aug	**Express Sheffield 14.15 to Manchester Cen 15.24** Millhouses 14.20 Chinley 14.56/ 15.00
(14.38)	Sat 1 Aug	**Additional Train 83 Sheffield 14.15 to Chinley 14.59** to connect with 15.05 to Midland Jcn 15.40 for Blackpool. Load 14 vehicles
(14.43)	Sat 1 Aug	**Express Sheffield 14.20 to Manchester Cen 15.32** Chinley 15.03/ 15.07. Load 12 coaches
14.50	Thu Sat	**Sheffield 14.20 to Hope 15.00** Heeley 14.26 Dore 14.33/14.34 Grindleford 14.45 Bamford 14.55
14.55	Sun	**Sheffield 14.25 to Hope 15.04** Heeley 14.31 Dore 14.38/14.39 Grindleford 14.50 Bamford 15.00

235

\multicolumn{3}{c}{DOWN TRAINS}	
TIME AT HATH	DAY	DETAIL 1914
15.12		**Sheffield 14.35 to Cheadle Heath 16.07** Millhouses 14.42 Beauchief 14.48 Dore 14.52/ 14.56 Grindleford 15.07 Bamford 15.17 Hope 15.22 Edale 15.34 Chinley 15.45/ 15.47 Bugsworth 15.50 Hazel Grove 16.00
15.16	Sun	**Sheffield 14.40 to Chinley 15.49** Heeley 14.46 Millhouses 14.52 Beauchief 14.56 Dore 14.59/ 15.00 Grindleford 15.11 Bamford 15.21 Hope 15.26 Edale 15.38
16.39	Thu Sat	**Sheffield 16.10 to Hope 16.48** Heeley 16.15 Dore 16.22/ 16.23 Grindleford 16.34 Bamford 16.44
(16.51)		**Express Sheffield 16.35 to Manchester Cen 17.42** Dore 16.43 when req for passengers to Liverpool Cen, Chinley 17.16/ 17.19
17.46		**Express Sheffield 17.22 to Manchester Cen 18.54** Grindleford 17.41 Bamford 17.51 Hope 17.57 Edale 18.09
(18.11)	Sat	**Express Sheffield 17.47 to Buxton**
18.38		**Sheffield 18.05 to Buxton 19.45** Heeley 18.11 Millhouses 18.17 Dore 18.21/ 18.22 Grindleford 18.33 Bamford 18.43 Hope 18.48 Edale 19.00 Chinley 19.11/ 19.18 Chapel 19.23/ 19.25
18.47	Sun	**Passenger Sheffield 18.12 to Manchester Cen 20.17** Heeley 18.20 Millhouses 18.26 Dore 18.30/ 18.31 Grindleford 18.42 Bamford 18.52 Hope 18.57 Edale 19.09 Chinley 19.21/ 19.24 New Mills 19.32 Marple 19.37/ 19.40 Romiley 19.45 Stockport T.D. 19.51/ 19.52 Didsbury 20.00 Withington 20.03 Chorlton 20.07/ 20.10
	Sat	**Empty Carriages Heeley Carriage Sdgs 18.23 to Grindleford 18.48**
19.12	Sun	**Express Sheffield 18.45 to Chinley 19.40** Grindleford 19.06 Hope 19.20
(19.25)	Sun	**Empty Carriages Heeley Carriage Sdgs 19.03 to Hope 19.35**
19.28		**Express Sheffield 18.58 to Manchester Cen 20.32** Dore 19.12 Grindleford 19.23 Bamford 19.33 Hope 19.38 Edale 19.50 Chinley 20.01/ 20.05
	Sat to 29 Aug	**Empty carriages Heeley Carriage Sdgs 19.43 to Grindleford 20.06**
20.15	Sat to 29 but not 1 Aug	**Grindleford 20.10 to Manchester Vic 21.50** Bamford 20.23 Hope 20.28/ 20.31 Edale 20.46/ 20.48 New Mills 21.08 Marple 21.14/ 21.18 Miles Platting 21.46 to set down at last 3 stns
	Sat to 25 Jul	**Empty Carriages Heeley Carriage Sdgs 20.10 to Grindleford 20.30**
20.38	Sat to 25 Jul	**Grindleford 20.33 to Manchester Cen 22.30** Bamford 20.45/ 20.47 Hope 20.52/ 20.56 Edale 21.11/ 21.13 Chinley 21.27/ 21.30 Marple 21.43/ 21.45 Stockport T.D. 21.58/ 22.00 Heaton Mersey 22.08 Didsbury 22.12 Withington 22.15 Chorlton 22.19/ 22.22
	Sat to 25 Jul	**Empty Carriages Heeley Carriage Sdgs 20.20 to Grindleford 20.43**
21.03	Not Sat 1 Aug	**Sheffield 20.32 to Chinley 21.36** Heeley 20.38 Dore 20.45/ 20.47 Grindleford 20.58 Bamford 21.08 Hope 21.13 Edale 21.25
21.03	Sat 1 Aug	**Sheffield 20.32 to Manchester Cen 22.08** as above but leaves Chinley 21.40
22.33	Not Fri Sat	**Sheffield 22.05 to Hope 22.42** Dore 22.16/ 22.17 Grindleford 22.28 Bamford 22.38
23.35	Fri Sat	**Sheffield 23.05 to Hope 23.44** Heeley 23.11 Dore 23.18/ 23.19 Grindleford 23.30 Bamford 23.40

\multicolumn{3}{c}{UP TRAINS}	
TIME AT HATH	DAY	DETAIL 1914
07.50		**Chinley 07.20 to Sheffield 08.16** Edale 07.33 Hope 07.41 Bamford 07.45 Grindleford 07.54 Dore 08.02/ 08.03 Beauchief 08.06 Millhouses 08.09 Heeley 08.11/ 08.13
08.27		**Chinley 07.55 to Sheffield 08.49** Edale 08.09 Hope 08.16/ 08.18 Bamford 08.22 Grindleford 08.32 Heeley 08.43/ 08.46.
08.55		**Express Buxton 08.25 to Sheffield 09.20** Heeley 09.14/ 09.17
09.15		**Express Manchester Cen 07.48 to Sheffield 09.36** Cheadle Heath 08.01/ 08.02 Hazel Grove 08.12 Bugsworth 08.27 Chinley 08.30/ 08.44 Edale 08.58 Hope 09.06 Bamford 09.10 Grindleford 09.20 Heeley 09.31/ 09.33
09.30	Wed	**Express Chinley 09.13 to Sheffield 09.54** Two minutes allowed at each station in valley to set down if req, Dore 09.46/ 09.48
09.55	Sun	**Manchester Cen 08.15 to Sheffield 10.22** Chorlton 08.23 Withington 08.28 Didsbury 08.31 Heaton Mersey 08.35 Stockport T.D. 08.41/ 08.43 Romiley 08.52 Marple 08.56/ 08.59 New Mills 09.07 Bugsworth 09.16 Chinley 09.19/ 09.25 Edale 09.38 Hope 09.46 Bamford 09.50 Grindleford 09.59 Dore 10.07/ 10.08 Beauchief 10.11 Millhouses 10.14 Heeley 10.16/ 10.19
10.32		**Chinley 10.02 to Sheffield 10.57** Edale 10.15 Hope 10.23 Bamford 10.27 Grindleford 10.37 Dore 10.45/ 10.46 Heeley 10.51/ 10.54
(12.00)		**Express Chinley 11.40 to Sheffield 12.19** Dore 12.11/ 12.13
(12.20)	Sun 31 May	**Empty carriages Liverpool Cen 10.00 to Heeley Carriage Sdgs 12.35** Chinley 11.09/ 11.16
12.48		**Express Manchester Cen 11.20 to Sheffield 13.17** Chorlton 11.27 Withington 11.32 Didsbury 11.35 Heaton Mersey 11.39/ 11.45 Marple 11.58/ 12.00 Chinley 12.14/ 12.17 Edale 12.31 Hope 12.39 Bamford 12.43 Grindleford 12.53 Dore 13.01/ 13.03 Beauchief 13.06 Millhouses 13.09 Heeley 13.13/ 13.14
(13.39)	Sun	**Express Chinley 13.15 to Sheffield 13.57** Hope 13.33 Heeley 13.51/ 13.54
13.49	Sun	**Hope 13.40 to Sheffield 14.17** Bamford 13.44 Grindleford 13.54 Dore 14.02/ 14.03 Beauchief 14.06 Millhouses 14.09 Heeley 14.11/ 14.14
	4 Jul	**Empty Carriages Grindleford 13.37 to Heeley Carriage Sdgs 14.53**
(14.41)		**Manchester Cen 13.50 to Sheffield 15.01** Chinley 14.26
15.06		**Chinley 14.35 to Sheffield 15.32** Edale 14.49 Hope 14.57 Bamford 15.01 Grindleford 15.11 Dore 15.19/ 15.20 Heeley 15.25/ 15.28
15.26	Sat to 29 Aug except 1 Aug	**Manchester Vic 13.43 to Grindleford 15.31** Miles Platting 13.48/ 13.51 Belle Vue 14.06/ 14.08 Marple 14.21/ 14.24 New Mills 14.32 Chinley 14.44/ 14.46 Edale 15.02/ 15.04 Hope 15/13/ 15.15 Bamford 15.20
	As above	**Empty Carriages Grindleford 15.33 to Heeley Carriage Sdgs 15.49**
15.39	Sat to 25 Jul	**Manchester Cen 13.53 to Grindleford 15.46** Chorlton 14.02 Withington 14.07 Didsbury 14.11 Heaton Mersey 14.16 Cheadle Heath 14.19/ 14.20 Hazel Grove 14.34 Chinley 14.55/ 14.58 Edale 15.14/ 15.17 Hope 15.26/ 15.29 Bamford 15.34

UP TRAINS			
TIME AT HATH	DAY	DETAIL	1914
	Sat to 25 Jul	Empty Carriages from Grindleford 15.48 to Heeley Carriage Sdgs 16.01	
(15.56)	Sun 19 Jul	**Additional Express Buxton Mid 15.17 to Sheffield 16.16** 8 vehicles added to 16.45 from Sheffield Mid to Scarborough	
(16.17)	Not Thu	**Express Manchester Cen 15.25 to Sheffield 16.45** Chinley 16.01 Dore 16.28 Wed. Stops to set down passengers only at any station beyond Chinley. 2 mins allowed	
(16.26)	Thu	**Express Manchester Cen 15.25 to Sheffield 16.45** Chinley 16.01. Worked by goods engine	
17.00	Thu Sat	**Hope 16.50 to Sheffield 17.27** Bamford 16.54 Grindleford 17.06 Dore 17.14/ 17.16 Heeley 17.22/ 17.24	
17.09	Sun	**Hope 17.00 to Sheffield 17.37** Bamford 17.04 Grindleford 17.13 Dore 17.21/ 17.23 Beauchief 17.26 Millhouses 17.29 Heeley 17.31/ 17.34	
(17.20)		**Express Chinley 16.59 to Sheffield 17.43** Dore 17.30/ 17.32 Heeley 17.37/ 17.40	
(17.27)	Sat 8 Aug to 12 Sep	**Express Blackpool Talbot Road 14.45 to Chesterfield 17.52** Manchester Vic 16.10 Midland Jcn 16.19 to change engine, Chinley 17.00/ 17.04 Dronfield 17.44	
18.00		**Chinley 17.29 to Sheffield 18.25** Edale 17.43 Hope 17.51 Bamford 17.55 Grindleford 18.05 Dore 18.13/ 18.14 Heeley 18.19/ 18.22	
18.34		**Chinley 18.04 to Sheffield 19.00** Edale 18.17 Hope 18.25 Bamford 18.29 Grindleford 18.39 Dore 18.47/ 18.49 Heeley 18.55/ 18.57	
(18.48)	Sat	**Blackpool Talbot Road 15.58 to Nottingham 20.03** Midland Jcn 17.35/ 17.40 to change engine, Pye Bridge 19.29/ 19.32 Ilkeston Jcn & Cossall 19.44/ 19.47	
(19.11)	Sun	**Express Blackpool Talbot Road 16.50 to Sheffield 19.40** Midland Jcn 18.12/ 18.17 to change engine Chinley 18.52/ 18.58 Heeley 19.32/ 19.37	
20.01	Sun	**Hope 19.50 to Sheffield 20.32** Bamford 19.55 Grindleford 20.05/ 20.07 Dore 20.15/ 20.17 Beauchief 20.20 Millhouses 20.23 Heeley 20.25/ 20.29	
20.18	Sun	**Manchester Cen 18.45 to Sheffield 20.50** Stockport T.D. 19.01/ 19.03 Chinley 19.32/ 19.45 Edale 19.59 Hope 20.07 Bamford 20.12 Grindleford 20.22/ 20.24 Dore 20.32/ 20.34 Beauchief 20.37 Millhouses 20.40 Heeley 20.42/ 20.47	
20.29	Thu Sat	**Hope 20.20 to Sheffield 20.57** Bamford 20.24 Grindleford 20.34 Dore 20.42/ 20.43 Beauchief 20.46 Millhouses 20.49 Heeley 20.51/ 20.54	
20.38		**Chinley 20.15 to Sheffield 21.05** Hope 20.28 Bamford 20.33 Grindleford 20.42 Dore 20.49/ 20.51 Beauchief 20.54 Millhouses 20.57 Heeley 20.59/ 21.02. To be formed of engine & carriages of 14.20 Sheffield to Hope	
(20.45)		**Express Manchester Vic 19.10 to Sheffield 21.15** Marple 19.36/ 19.41 New Mills 21.47 stops Sat only, Chinley 19.55/ 20.15 Edale 20.28 Hope 20.36 Bamford 20.40 Grindleford 20.50 Dore 20.58/ 21.00 Beauchief 21.02 Millhouses 21.05 Heeley 21.07/ 21.10	

UP TRAINS			
TIME AT HATH	DAY	DETAIL	1914
21.37		**Express Manchester Cen 20.23 to Sheffield 22.05** Withington 20.33 Didsbury 20.36 Heaton Mersey 20.40 Chinley 21.05/ 21.07 Edale 21.20 Hope 21.28 Bamford 21.32 Grindleford 21.41 Dore 21.49/ 21.50 Heeley 21.55/ 21.58	
(22.39)	Mon Sat	**Express Liverpool Cen 21.00 to Sheffield 22.58** Warrington 21.28/ 21.31 Cheadle Heath 21.53/ 21.55 Chinley 22.17/ 22.18 Heeley 22.52/ 22.55	
(22.54)	Mon to Thu	**Empty Carriages Hope 22.47 to Heeley Carriage Sdgs 23.16**	
(23.59)	Fri Sat	**Empty Carriages Hope 23.53 to Heeley Carriage Sdgs 00.22**	

EXCURSION TRAINS ON WHIT MON 1 JUN 1914

Included is a sample of the more interesting excursion trains in the month of Jun 1914 which is not the period covered in the summer timetable tabulated above. I have particularly chosen Mon 1 Jun because, along with August Bank Holiday Mon 1 Aug, these days would have been two of the busiest days of the year for passenger traffic. The logistical problems of running day trips to the valley are well highlighted here. This was because of the difficulty of finding stabling space for the carriage stock which resulted in a constant movement of empty stock back to Sheffield. I was expecting to see Heeley carriage sidings being the specific destination but just 'Sheffield' is named. Perhaps carriages were stabled wherever space could be found such as in the station yards on the line as well as Heeley. Dore carriage sidings were a later addition. Hope was a terminal point for most trains from Sheffield, because of the access to Castleton and the caves, although there was a train through to Edale and the stock for that train was stabled at Chinley. It points up the fact that the hills around Edale did not have the pull that they later had as the populace were educated to see moors and peat hag as being unattractive which, alongside the prohibitions going on to the moors reduced the attraction of the area. Excursions from the Manchester area all terminated at Grindleford with the stock being stabled around Sheffield.

Most of the Sheffield to Hope specials originated at Rotherham Westgate and ran as ordinary trains as far as Sheffield. Additional Hope trains were run as required. Empty trains between Sheffield and Hope were not shunted for excursion or ordinary stopping trains to pass. Although many freight trains did not run on this day there would have been a number of late evening and overnight trains which included the movement of empties. Although some normally timetabled trains are included there would also be through trains which are not included. Especially noteworthy was the Hull & Barnsley Railway trip from Hull to Matlock Bath, with the HBR coaches working right through after the handover to the Midland at Cudworth. Although the HBR had just acquired a rake of excellent Pickering built coaches for its flagship passenger service from Hull to Sheffield Midland it is certain that, for the excursionist from Hull, the notoriously ramshackle coaches owned by that company would have been pressed into service on this nine hour return journey if the complete trip to Matlock Bath was endured.

TIME AT HATH	DETAIL	1914
07.06	**Express Excursion 249 Leicester 04.46 to Blackpool Talbot Road** Trent 05.22 Clay Cross 06.22 Chesterfield 06.30 Chinley 07.34/ 07.37 Midland Jcn 08.06 to change engine	
07.22	**Express Excursion 217 Rotherham Westgate 06.30 to Liverpool Cen 09.20** Brightside 06.42 Attercliffe Road 06.46/ 06.49 Sheffield 06.52/ 06.56 Heeley 07.02 to pick up passengers from Chesterfield Dore 07.11 Cheadle Heath 08.03/ 08.10 Farnworth 08.49/ 09.02 Tickets issued for Douglas Isle of Man & steamers from Liverpool to North Wales.	
09.05	**Ordinary train Rotherham Westgate 08.08 to Manchester Cen 12.23** Holmes 08.12 Wincobank 08.16 Brightside 08.20 Attercliffe Road 08.25 Sheffield 08.30/ 08.35 Heeley 08.41 to pick up passengers from Chesterfield Dore 08.48	
10.22	**Excursion 205 Hull Cannon St (HBR) to Matlock Bath 12.00** Cudworth 08.43 all stns to Rotherham Sheffield 09.48 all stations to Chinley S Jcn Millers Dale all stns to Matlock Bath. Empty carriage stock to Ambergate 12.20. HBR carriages work throughout.	
10.37	**Special 218 Sheffield 09.36 to Hope 10.43** Heeley 10.01 Dore 10.15 Grindleford 10.28 Bamford 10.44 Hope 11.00	
10.50	**Special 219 Sheffield 10.20 to Edale 11.10** Heeley 10.26 Grindleford 10.45 Bamford 10.55 Hope 11.00	
11.10	*Empty Carriage Stock 218 Hope 11.00 to Sheffield 11.35*	
11.29	**Normal service train Rotherham Westgate 10.30 to Manchester Cen 12.23** Holmes 10.34 Wincobank 10.38 Brightside 10.40 Attercliffe Rd 10.44 Sheffield 10.50/ 11.05 Heeley 11.11 to pick up passengers from Chesterfield Dore 11.20	
11.45	**Special 220 Sheffield 11.15 to Hope 11.55** Heeley 11.21 Grindleford 11.40 Bamford 11.50	
12.15	*Empty Carriage Stock Hope 12.05 to Sheffield 12.40*	
12.30	**Special 221 Sheffield 12.00 to Hope 12.40** Heeley 12.06 Grindleford 12.25 Bamford 12.35	
13.12	**Special 222 Sheffield 12.40 to Hope 13.22** Heeley 12.46 Dore 12.56 Grindleford 13.07 Bamford 13.17	
	Additional Special 223 for 'Esparanto' Party Sheffield 13.40 to Grindleford 14.00	
14.53	**Special 224 Sheffield 14.20 to Hope 15.03** Heeley 14.26 Dore 14.36 Grindleford 14.48 Bamford 14.58	
18.12	*Special 221 Hope 18.02 to Sheffield 18.42* Bamford 18.07 Grindleford 18.17 Dore 18.27 Heeley 18.34/ 18.38	
18.24	*Special 222 Hope 18.13 to Sheffield 18.53* Bamford 18.18 Grindleford 18.28 Dore 18.38 Heeley 18.45/18.49	
(19.02)	**Empty Carriage Stock Heeley Carriage Sdgs 18.47 to Grindleford 19.10**	
19.07	*Special 219 Edale 18.45 to Rotherham Westgate 20.05* Hope 18.55 Bamford 19.01 Grindleford 19.13 Dore 19.25 Heeley 19.32/ 19.36 Sheffield 19.40/ 19.45 Attercliffe Road 19.49 Brightside 19.54 Wincobank 19.57 Holmes 20.02	
19.20	**Relief Passenger Grindleford 19.12 to Manchester Cen 20.59** Bamford 19.25 Hope 19.32 Edale 19.44 Chinley 19.55/ 19.57 New Mills 20.03 Marple 20.12 Romiley 20.20 Stockport TD 20.33 Didsbury 20.46 Withington 20.51 Chorlton 20.57	
19.37	**Empty Carriage Stock 225 Sheffield 19.05 to Hathersage**	
19.50	*Special 225 Hathersage to Sheffield 20.22* Grindleford 19.55 Dore 20.07 Heeley 20.14/ 20.18	
19.50	**Empty Carriage Stock 226 Sheffield to Hathersage**	

TIME AT HATH	DETAIL	1914
20.01	*Special 224 Hope to Sheffield 20.31* Bamford 19.55 Grindleford 20.06 Dore 20.17 Heeley 20.23/ 20.27	
	Additional Special 223 for 'Esperanto' Party Grindleford 20.20 to Sheffield 20.42 Heeley 20.34/ 20.38	
20.30	**Special 226 Hathersage to Sheffield 21.02** Grindleford 20.35 Dore 20.46 Heeley 20.54/ 20.58	
20.45	**Normal Service train Hope 20.36 to Sheffield 21.13** Bamford 20.40 Grindleford 20.50 Dore 20.59 Heeley 21.08	
21.10	**Empty Carriage Stock Sheffield 20.45 to Hope 21.20**	
21.20	*Express Excursion 249 Blackpool Talbot Road to Leicester 23.33* Midland Jcn 20.13 to change engines Chinley 20.48/ 20.56 Chesterfield 21.50 Trent 22.47	
21.37	**Normal Service train Hope 21.28 to Sheffield 22.02** Bamford 21.32 Grindleford 21.41 Dore 21.49 Heeley 21.56	
21.47	**Special 227 Hope 21.35 to Sheffield 22.16** Bamford 21.42 Grindleford 21.52 Dore 22.02 Heeley 22.08/ 22.12	
21.56	**Excursion Matlock Bath 19.58 to Hull Cannon St** (Empty HBR carriages from Ambergate 19.42). All stations to Hassop shunted for 17.35 St Pancras to Manchester Millers Dale 20.53/ 20.56 connect with 20.15 from Buxton Edale 21.35 Hope 21.45 Grindleford 22.03 Heeley 22.19/ 22.23 Sheffield 22.27/ 22.31 Masboro 22.43 all stations to Darfield 23.13 connect with 22.42 from Sheffield to Barnsley 23.25. Cudworth 23.31 through carriages to Hull Cannon St.	

OTHER EXCURSIONS IN THE EARLY SUMMER OF 1914

On the following day **Tue 2 Jun**, four specials were run from **Sheffield** to **Hope** between 10.20 and 14.20 with four return empty stock trains between 17.52 and 20.45. Two empties returned from Hope at 11.20 and 12.05. Five specials and four ordinary trains were run between Hope and Sheffield, all between 17.51 and 21.35. The imbalance reflects that many visitors to the Hope valley had stayed over from Monday or even earlier.

The following are a few examples of special excursions organized by companies and organizations.

Sun 31 May an additional express excursion for a St John's Ambulance Brigade party left **Worksop 09.25** for **Blackpool Talbot Road**. It went via Shirebrook, Mansfield, Pye Bridge and Chesterfield and then by the usual route to Blackpool.

Tue 2 Jun there was an express excursion from **Parkgate & Rawmarsh 06.22**, to **Southport Chapel Street 09.37**. This picked up at Sheffield and Dore where passengers from Sheepbridge and Chesterfield embarked. Its only other stops were at Cheadle Heath and then Birkdale, just before Southport. The return train left **Southport 20.35** and arrived back **Parkgate & Rawmarsh 23.44**, a seventeen hour day. It stopped at Heeley, rather than Dore, for Sheepbridge and Chesterfield connections.

Sat 13 Jun the West Derbyshire and High Peak Unionist Association booked a guaranteed excursion which left **Grindleford 12.57**, all stations to **Buxton 14.08**. Returning from **Buxton 23.15** it arrived back **Grindleford 00.23** the following day.

Thu 25 Jun the Heeley and Norton Central Primrose League's (Conservative party supporters) guaranteed express excursion left **Sheffield 08.45** to **Chester Northgate 11.17** going via Altrincham and Northwich. It returned from **Chester Northgate 19.55**, arriving back **Sheffield 22.17**.

Sat 4 Jul an excursion for the Cemetery Road Baptist Sunday School left **Sheffield 13.50** for **Grindleford 14.15**, and returned **Grindleford 20.35** for **Sheffield 21.01**. Perhaps the most exciting day of the year for those involved!

Sat 11 Jul the Glapwell Colliery owners undertook a massive operation to transport their employees to Liverpool Cen, possibly for a steamer trip to the North Wales coast or for the ferry across to New Brighton on the Wirral. They booked three guaranteed excursion trains, two of which left **Mansfield 03.08** and **04.10** and the other from **Barrow Hill 05.03**. These travelled via Pleasley West, Rowthorn, Glapwell, Palterton, Bolsover, Staveley Town, Barrow Hill and Whittington. At Chesterfield everyone changed trains and travelled on the usual route to **Liverpool Cen 07.00**, **08.00** and **08.10**. The return journeys saw starts from **Liverpool Cen** around midnight which arrived back at **Mansfield 03.50**, a twenty four hour marathon!

Sat 25 Jul another epic was organized by Hoyland Nether Working Men's Club with three trains leaving **Wombwell** between **05.00** and **05.10** and reaching **Liverpool Cen 08.00**. The returns were from **Liverpool Cen 22.30, 22.35, 22.40** and arrivals were at **Wombwell 01.13, 01.23** and **01.39**. A mere twenty hours.

EMIGRANT SPECIAL

These trains ran from Hull to Liverpool and carried people escaping persecution or poverty and seeking a new life in the United States. The fact that they got away before the outbreak of First World War meant they would be escaping the conflagration to come in Europe and certain death for many of the men. The emigrants faced an unknown future with great difficulties ahead but also unbounded opportunity. It was said that at the points where the trains stopped the area was sealed off to prevent any passengers escaping. The discomfort of the journey would have been extreme as the trains only stopped once at Sheffield. This was followed by the long sailing to New York in tough conditions followed by the indignities of Ellis Island and the gross overcrowding encountered once through the immigration process. For many the journey was a frightening experience as most of the emigrants had never travelled much beyond where they were born. In all likelihood they passed through the Hope valley with unseeing eyes.

The North Eastern Railway was required to advise Sheffield and the general superintendent at Derby as early as possible when a special was required at any time except that a passing time of 08.45 at Swinton had to be factored in. Duplicate trains could be run, if required, to carry baggage. This train was called 'Emigrant Special 91' from Hull Paragon which left at 08.45 and arrived at Liverpool Cen at 13.00. It ran as required and stopped at Sheffield at 10.52 for six minutes and Cheadle Heath for five minutes, both for water. The route from Hull was via Selby, Milford, Ferrybridge, Pontefract, Dearne Junction, Swinton and Rotherham. NER engines worked right through to Liverpool. Midland guards and pilot drivers joined the train at Sheffield. When required the Midland provided assisting engines from Sheffield to Chinley which suggests these were often very heavily laden trains. The return empty coaching stock was required to stop at Cheadle Heath for inspection.

TERRITORIAL SPECIAL ON 26 JUL 1914

This special troop train was run for the 6th Nottinghamshire and Derbyshire Regiment Territorials. It comprised eight officers and 337 men and was worked by a Buxton engine and crew departing from Buxton at 09.40 to Milford Junction where it arrived at 12.37 for onward travel on the NER to the annual camp at Hunmanby, near Filey. Stops were made at Millers Dale, Peak Forest, Chapel en le Frith and Chinley at 10.30 where men from New Mills, Hayfield, Birch Vale and Marple had arrived by ordinary train at 10.19. The special left Chinley at 10.36 and stopped at Edale, Hathersage and Sheffield at 11.32 where soldiers from Sheepbridge, Unstone and Dronfield had arrived via an ordinary train at 10.38. Milford Junction was reached via Rotherham and the Swinton and Knottingley Joint line. The empty return carriage working to Buxton left Milford Junction at 18.13 and worked from Rotherham to Chesterfield via the 'Old Road' going on to Ambergate and the Peak Line.

Six trains arrived at Milford Junction between 11.10 and 15.51, one of which originated from Buxton (another Buxton engine working) via Ambergate, The others came from Derby, Butterley, Melbourne, Mansfield and Stretton which combined at Pye Hill. Another ran from Mansfield via Nottingham. The GCR also provided trains to Ferrybridge.

When the international situation became critical on 3 Aug it was decided to cancel the camp and so, with virtually no notice at all, the railways were called upon to return all the Territorial units to their home bases during 3 and 4 Aug. This was an early illustration of the adaptability that became essential in the succeeding war years.

PASSENGER SERVICES IN 1922

Bradshaw's timetable for 1922 shows the passenger services offered by the Midland in the last summer of its existence. The day started at Sheffield Midland at 06.18 with an all stations, except Millhouses and Beauchief, to Edale which arrived at 07.16. The first Manchester train left from Rotherham Westgate at 07.20 and called at all stations, except Beauchief, to Chinley. The stop at Hope was eighteen minutes to allow for the exchange of engines and crews. Stops at Marple and Stockport followed with an arrival at Manchester Central at 10.05, a very leisurely two and three quarter hours journey. The following 08.00 from Westgate ran non-stop from Sheffield to Hope where the same engine and crew exchange took place and arrived at Manchester Central at 09.32, a respectable hour and a half journey time. A further train left Masborough at 08.31 with a similar timing. On Mondays and Fridays an interesting working was the 09.13 from Masborough with stops at

Sheffield and Heeley to Chinley and then to Manchester Exchange via Marple, where it did not stop, arriving at 11.23. The 09.25 from Westgate stopped at Sheffield, Dore and Chinley where the train divided. The Manchester Central portion arrived via Marple and Stockport at 11.25 while the Victoria portion arrived some thirty minutes later. The final clutch of morning departures was completed by the 10.15 all stations to Manchester Central, which arrived at 12.55.

In the return direction the early morning from Sheffield to Edale returned at 19.24 and reached Masborough at 20.52. The pattern of services and stopping places almost replicates the down services. Mention should be made of a Thursday only train leaving Manchester Central at 15.00 which ran non-stop to Sheffield, arriving at 16.05, the fastest train over the line, and also the Monday and Friday service at 14.55 from Manchester Exchange which stopped only at Chinley and Heeley, arriving in Sheffield at 16.22. On Saturdays there were five additional trains, including the returning Llandudno to Sheffield train and a further train from Hope to Sheffield.

On Sundays there were only two through trains and two trains terminating at Hope. Altogether sixteen trains ran through the valley in the up direction.

A Cook's cheap ticket leaflet for shop workers in the Manchester area just after the Grouping in Feb 1923. Note the heading; the ampersand and 'R' were soon dropped by the new company for the more simple LMS.

Author's collection

SPECIAL TRAFFIC NOTICES FOR 1929

This information has been drawn from the special traffic notices which were issued every fortnight during the year. They were designed to cater for specific dates and particularly holiday periods and list the regular excursion trains which were strengthened on specific dates and also the regular services which were suspended to make way for the special workings which took their timings. The August Bank Holiday weekend has been chosen which not only included special workings but also the Works Weeks traffic. I have centred our observations on this busy period, when the company was stretched to the limit, to what would be seen and not seen in a twenty four period on each day at Hope. If a train did not stop it has a bracket and up trains are in italics. On some trains the loadings have been hand written in ink and are included also in brackets.

STRENGTHENED TRAINS

On Sat 3 Aug all the following trains had three additional carriages.

The 07.47 and 10.35 from Sheffield to Chinley, the 12.38 and 17.37 return workings; the 08.56, 10.10, 13.50 and 16.10 from Sheffield to Manchester Cen and 11.38, 14.00 16.57, 18.45 return trains.

EXCURSION TRAINS ON BANK HOLIDAY MON 5 AUG 1929

EXC NO	DETAIL
747	**Clay Cross 06.30 to Blackpool Talbot Road 10.41** Empty Carriage Stock Heeley Carriage Sdgs 05.30 Clay Cross 06.10 Chesterfield 06.38/ 06.41 (321) Sheepbridge 06.48 Dronfield 06.58 Dore S Jcn Edale Chinley 07.47/ 07.52 water (400) Romiley Belle Vue Engine Shed 08.25/ 08.28 to change enginemen Phillips Park 08.55 Manchester Vic fast line, Dobbs Brown Jcn, Horwich Fork Jcn, Chorley Crow Nest Jcn, Hingley No 2, De Trafford Jcn, Whalley Jcn, Standish Jcn, Euxton Jcn, Preston fast line, Kirkham Poulton
749	**Kilnhurst 06.43 to Blackpool Talbot Road 11.17** Empty Carriage Stock Heeley Carriage Sdgs 06.00 slow line Parkgate 06.50 Rotherham Mas 06.57 (50) Wincobank 07.05 Brightside 07.09 Attercliffe Road 07.16 Sheffield 07.19/ 07.24 Heeley 07.31 Dore 07.42 Grindleford 07.55 Hathersage 08.02 Bamford 08.08 Hope 08.15 Chinley 08.44/ 08.49 water (700) Romiley, Belle Vue Engine Shed 09.18/ 09.20 to change enginemen, Manchester Vic, Preston (10.38)
750	**Nottingham 06.17 to Blackpool Talbot Road 11.21** Nottingham (350) Beeston 06.25 Long Eaton Jcn North Erewash Jcn Long Eaton 06.36 Stapleford 06.41 Ilkeston Jcn 06.51 Langley Mill 07.02 Pye Bridge 07.15 Alfreton 07.22 (700) Dore South Curve Chinley 09.00/ 09.04 water (800) Belle Vue Engine Shed 09.25/ 09.26 to change enginemen, Manchester Vic Fast Line, Preston 10.45. Nottingham to provide motive power and carriages
	Millhouses 07.25 to Hope 07.55 Light engine to work empty carriages off 159
159	**Sheffield 07.37 to Hope 08.20** Sheffield (250) Heeley 07.42/ 07.43 Dore 07.52/ 07.53 Grindleford 08.04/ 08.05 Hathersage 08.09/ 08.10 Bamford 08.14/ 08.15

EXC NO	DETAIL	1929
101	**Sheffield 08.12 to Hope 08.55** Sheffield (300) Dore 08.25/ 08.26 Grindleford 08.37/ 08.38 Hathersage 08.43/ 08.45 Bamford 08.49/ 08.51	
161	**Sheffield 08.28 to Hope 09.11** Sheffield (300) Heeley 08.33/ 08.35 Dore 08.43/ 08.44 Grindleford 08.55/ 08.56 Hathersage 09.00/ 09.01 Bamford 09.05/ 09.06	
162	**Rotherham Westgate 08.16 to Hope 09.25** Empty carriages Heeley Carriage Sdgs 07.00 to Rotherham Westgate 07.30 (54) Wincobank 08.25 Brightside 08.30 Attercliffe Road 08.35 Sheffield 08.38/ 08.42 (280) Heeley 08.47/ 08.48 Dore 08.57/ 08.58 Grindleford 09.09/ 09.10 Hathersage 09.13/ 09.14 Bamford 09.19/ 09.20	
163	**Sheffield 09.00 to Hope 09.45** Sheffield (230) Heeley 09.05/ 09.06 Dore 09.16/ 19.18 Grindleford 09.29/ 09.30 Hathersage 09.34/ 09.35 Bamford 09.39/ 09.40	
164	**Sheffield 09.19 to Hope 10.02** Sheffield (240) Dore 09.32/ 09.34 Grindleford 09.44/ 09.46 Hathersage 09.50/ 09.52 Bamford 09.56/ 09.57	
159	**Sheffield 09.35 to Hope 10.21** Sheffield (250) Heeley 09.40/ 09.41 Millhouses 09.47 Dore 09.52/ 09.53 Grindleford 10.05/ 10.06 Hathersage 10.10/ 10.11 Bamford 10.15/ 10.16	
166	**Rotherham Westgate 09.45 to Hope 10.56** Empty carriages Heeley Carriage Sdgs 08.35 to Rotherham Westgate 09.05 Rotherham (150) Wincobank 09.51 Brightside 09.56 Attercliffe Road 09.59 Sheffield 10.04/ 10.07 (280) Heeley 10.17/ 10.19 Dore 10.28/ 10.30 Grindleford 10.39/ 10.40 Hathersage 10.44/ 10.45 Bamford 10.50/ 10.51	
162	**Sheffield 10.33 to Hope 11.17** Sheffield (240) Heeley 10.38/ 10.40 Dore 10.49/ 10.50 Grindleford 11.01/ 11.02 Hathersage 11.06/ 11.07 Bamford 11.11/ 11.12	
165	**Sheffield 12.06 to Hope 12.48** Sheffield (330) Heeley 12.11/12.12 Dore 12.21/12.22 Grindleford 12.33/ 12.34 Hathersage 12.38/ 12.39 Bamford 12.43/ 12.44	
166	**Sheffield 12.57 to Hope 13.40** Sheffield (320) Heeley 13.02/ 13.03 Dore 13.12/ 13.13 Grindleford 13.24/ 13.25 Hathersage 13.29/ 13.30 Bamford 13.34/ 13.35	
161	**Rotherham Westgate 13.15 to Hope 14.35** Rotherham (86) Wincobank 13.24 Brightside 13.27 Attercliffe Road 13.32 Sheffield 13.36/ 13.42 (200) Heeley 13.48/ 13.50 Dore 13.59/ 14.03 Grindleford 14.14/ 14.16 Hathersage 14.20/ 14.22 Bamford 14.26/ 14.28	
159	**Sheffield 14.10 to Hope 14.56** Sheffield (160) Heeley 14.15/ 14.17 Dore 14.27/ 14.28 Grindleford 14.39/ 14.40 Hathersage 14.44/ 14.45 Bamford 14.49/ 14.51	

EXC NO	DETAIL	1929
153	*Stockport 08.49 to Sheffield 10.30* Empty carriage stock Cornbrook 08.20 Stockport 08.47 (120) Romiley 09.01 Marple 09.05/ 09.06 New Mills 09.15 Chinley 09.25/ 09.30 (143) Edale 09.48 Hope 09.56 Bamford 10.00 Hathersage 10.05 Grindleford 10.11	
157	*Manchester Central 09.35 to Sheffield 11.30* Manchester Cen (298) Chorlton 09.43 Withington 09.48 Didsbury 09.51 Heaton Mersey 09.55 Cheadle Heath 09.59 Chinley 10.23/ 10.27 (285) Edale 10.44 Hope 10.55 Bamford 11.01 Hathersage 11.07 Grindleford 11.13	

```
LONDON MIDLAND AND SCOTTISH RAILWAY COMPANY.
                                                    11.29
       PASSENGER DEPARTMENT,
                         ROTHERHAM (Masboro' Station). 46.
                         5th April, 1929.

Ashton Davies Esq.,
    Chief General Supt.,
        Derby (49).

Dear Sir,
              Hope Valley Excursion, Easter Monday 1929.
              ─────────────────────────────────────────

         No. 189 Excursion 8.40am Westgate to Hope, etc.
due Westgate 8.15am.

         This train clashed with the ordinary trains
7.55am Sheffield to Westgate and 8.40am Westgate to
Sheffield.

         Owing to the limited accommodation at Westgate
I suggest in future the excursion be timed to leave
Westgate about 9.0am, empties due to arrive after
departure of 8.40am ordinary train.

         No. 187 Special 12.30pm Westgate to Hope did
not get away until 1.31pm, empties due 12.3pm not
arriving until 1.26pm.

         No. 191 Special 1.15pm Westgate to Hope did
not get away until 1.53pm, empties due 1.3pm not
arriving until 1.46pm.  We had over 200 passengers
for each train and there were many complaints about
the delays.

         It is rather a pity such delays occurred on
the outward journeys.

                             Yours truly,
                              T. Hudston (Sgd).
```

The traffic planners made a complete hash of these Easter Monday excursions by timing them to conflict with normal services. The loading of over 200 passengers for each excursion was excellent considering that an even greater number would board at Sheffield. *Author's collection*

At Rotherham Westgate 2P 2-6-2T No. 41245, a Millhouses engine, on the 17.05 to Manchester Central waits for a 2F 0-6-0 of 1870s vintage which is pulling some mineral wagons from the yard. The date is 3 Oct 1952, three days before the station closed for good. This was the original station of the Sheffield & Rotherham Railway and was opened on 1 Nov 1838. Most excursions used this station as it was much nearer to the town centre than Masborough station.
R. J. Buckley

EXC NO	DETAIL	1929
153	**Sheffield 18.50 to Manchester Cen 21.03** Grindleford 19.12 Hathersage 19.17 Bamford 19.22 Hope 19.28 Edale 19.42 Chinley 19.53/ 20.05 New Mills 20.16 Marple 20.23/ 20.25 Romiley 20.30 Stockport 20.37/ 20.41 Heaton Mersey 20.46	
157	**Sheffield 19.50 to Manchester Cen 21.34** Grindleford 20.12 Hathersage 20.17 Bamford 20.22 Hope 20.28 Edale 20.41 Chinley 20.52/ 20.54 Cheadle Heath 21.09/ 21.10 Heaton Mersey 21.14 Didsbury 21.18 Withington 21.22 Chorlton 21.27	
749	*Blackpool Talbot Road 19.50 to Kilnhurst 00.20* Belle Vue Engine Shed box 21.47/ 21.50 to change enginemen Marple 22.07/ 22.12 water and examination Chinley 22.28/ 22.30 slow line Hope 22.55 Bamford 23.00 Hathersage 23.07 Grindleford 23.13 Dore 23.31 Heeley 23.39 Sheffield 23.44/ 23.49 Attercliffe Road 23.52 Brightside 23.58 Wincobank 00.01 Rotherham Mas 00.08 slow line Parkgate 00.15	
750	*Blackpool Talbot Road 22.15 to Nottingham 02.51* Belle Vue Engine Shed box 00.05/ 00.07 Marple 00.22/ 00.26 water Hathersage 01.05 Alfreton 01.58 Pye Bridge 02.05 Langley Mill 02.14 Ilkeston Jcn 02.21 Stapleford 02.28 Long Eaton 02.33 Beeston 02.45	
747	*Blackpool Talbot Road 22.22 to Clay Cross 02.05* Belle Vue Engine Shed box 00.16/ 00.18 to change enginemen and examination Romiley 00.24 Chinley 00.49/ 00.54 water and examination Sheepbridge 01.50 Chesterfield 01.55/ 01.57	

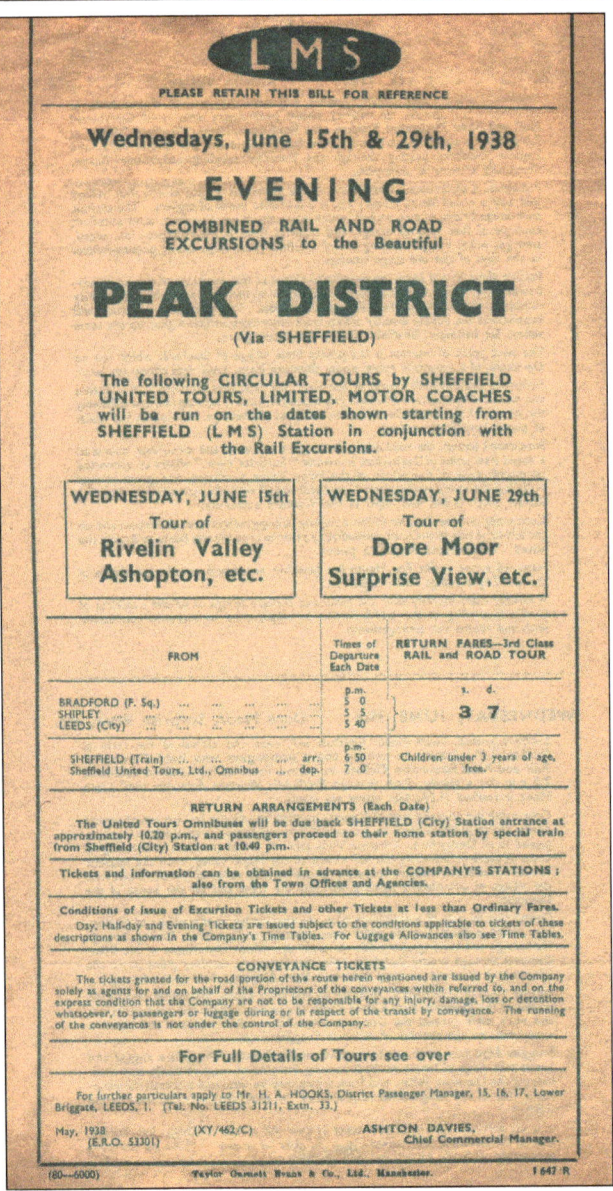

FOOTBALL SPECIALS

These were a regular occurrence and three are detailed here.

DATE EXC NO	DETAIL	1929
Sat 30 Mar 1929 Exc 30	**Everton v Sheffield United Division 1** Kick off 3.00 p.m. Empty coaching stock Heeley Carriage Sdgs 10.28 Masboro 10.50/ 11.00 Sheffield 11.13/ 11.16 Heeley 11.22 Cheadle Heath via Disley 12.16/ 12.20 examination & water, Liverpool Cen 13.06. The return left at 21.25 Cheadle Heath 22.12/ 22.20 water Heeley 23.24 Sheffield 23.28/ 23.32 Masboro 23.42/ 23.52 empty coaching stock to Heeley Carriage Sdgs 00.12. Millhouses engine allocated. Guard and vestibule set of 290 tons provided by Sheffield. The result was 3-2. Everton were relegated with 35 points and Sheffield United finished one place above the relegation zone on goal difference with 36 points from 42 matches at Burnley's expense.	
Sat 30 Nov 1929 Exc 734	**Southport v Chesterfield F.A. Cup 1st Round** Kick off 2.15 Empty coaching stock Heeley Carriage Sdgs 10.02 Clay Cross 10.38/ 10.55 Chesterfield 11.03 Sheepbridge 11.08 Marple 12.17/ 12.21 for examination and water Belle Vue Engine Shed signal box 12.33/ 12.35 to change engine or trainmen Manchester Vic Dobbs Brow Jcn Crow Nest Jcn Wigan Burscough Bridge 13.44/ 13.46 Southport Lord Street 13.50. The return left at 19.08, Belle Vue 20.21/ 20.25 to change engine or trainmen, Marple 20.42/ 20.47 for examination & water, Sheepbridge 21.46 Chesterfield 21.52 Clay Cross 22.00/ 22.10 empty coaching stock Heeley Carriage Sdgs 22.50. Both clubs were in the Third Division North – Southport finishing 9th and Chesterfield 6th. The score was 0-0 with Chesterfield winning the replay 3-2. Chesterfield went out when they were beaten by Middlesbrough in the 3rd round.	
Wed 1 Jan 1930 Exc 35	**Manchester City v Sheffield Wednesday Division 1** Kick off 2.15 p.m. Empty coaching stock Heeley Carriage Sdgs 10.35 Masboro 10.55/ 11.10 Brightside 11.17 Sheffield 11.23/ 11.28 Heeley 11.33/ 11.35 Manchester Cen 12.50. The return left at 22.45 Heeley 23.55/ 23.57 Sheffield 00.02/ 00.06 Brightside 00.12 Masboro 00.17/ 00.32 empty coaching stock Heeley Carriage Sdgs 00.52. Guard and vestibule set of 290 tons provide by Sheffield. The result was 3-3. Sheffield Wednesday became champions on 60 points from 42 games with a ten point advantage over the second place team. Manchester City finished third on 47 points.	

THEATRICAL SPECIALS

These were regular features on the line and moved all the stage props and performers from one venue to another. They were usually routed on fast lines and were dealt with expeditiously on arrival, which might suggest that they sometimes included animals. Here are a few examples.

May 1938 saw the publication of a leaflet for an innovative combination of road and rail using Sheffield United Tours coaches to take passengers on a Peak District evening tour passengers having travelled by the LMS from Bradford, Shipley and Leeds to Sheffield. *Author's collection*

DATE EXC NO	DETAIL	1929
Sun 30 Oct 1929 Exc 823	**'Desert Song' Coy – Blackpool to Sheffield** Light engine Belle Vue 11.40 to Manchester Vic 12.00/ 12.25 Sheffield 14.07. Vehicles must be placed in position for unloading on arrival (camels!) Vehicles included 4 composite, 2 brake standard, covered carriage truck, horse box – 162 tons	
Sun 20 Jan 1929	**'Humpty Dumpty' Coy – Lincoln to Oldham** **'My Son John' Coy – Lincoln to Carlisle** Nottingham 11.00/ 11.05 Long Eaton Jcn, Dore S from where engineering works to Hathersage 12.33, Marple 13.10/ 13.18 for examination and water, Belle Vue Engine shed signal box 11.28/ 11.30 for examination & change engine or trainmen, Manchester Vic. Oldham train included composite, brake standard – 50 tons Carlisle train included composite, brake standard – 50 tons	
Sun 10 Feb 1929	**Exc 64 'Lady Luck' Coy – Sheffield to Manchester** Sheffield 11.53 to Manchester Cen 13.16. Vehicles included 2 composites, brake standard – 110 tons	

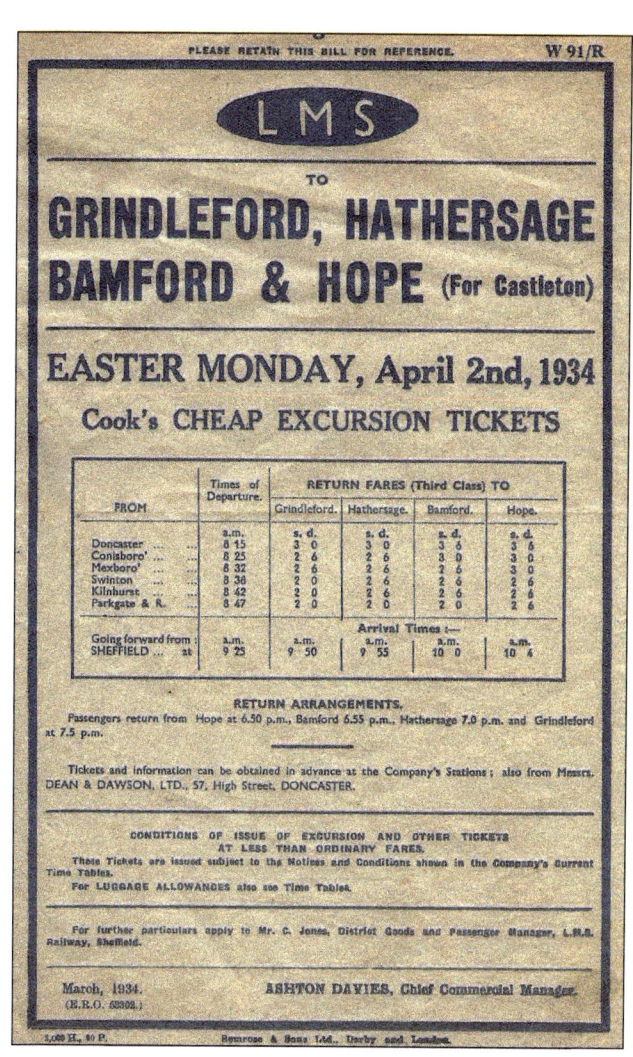

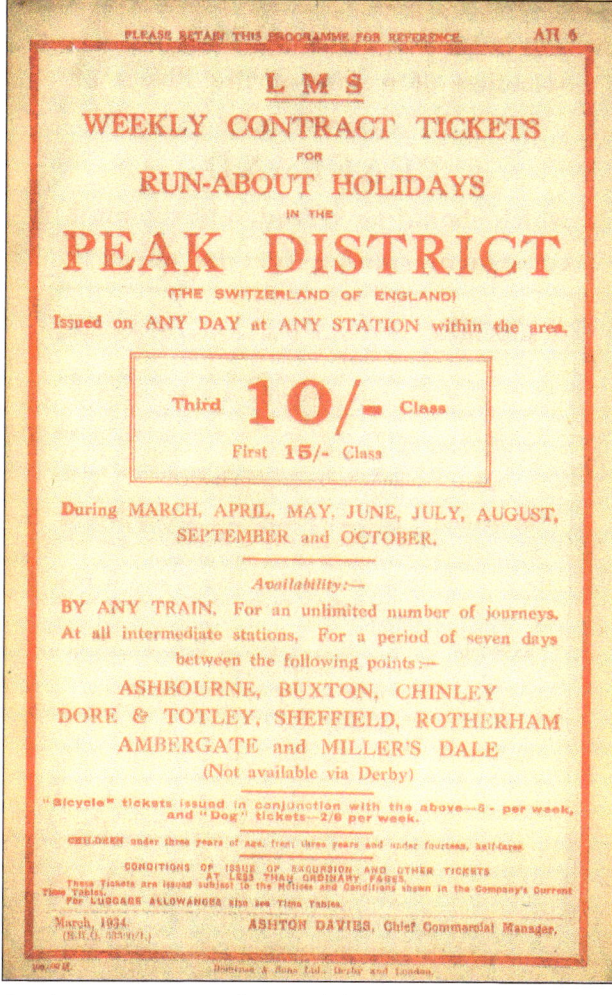

For the summer period in 1934 the complete runabout ticket for one week with no exceptions for ten shillings. Take your bike for another five shillings or your dog for half a crown. If you were in a time warp it would be the dream ticket.

Author's collection

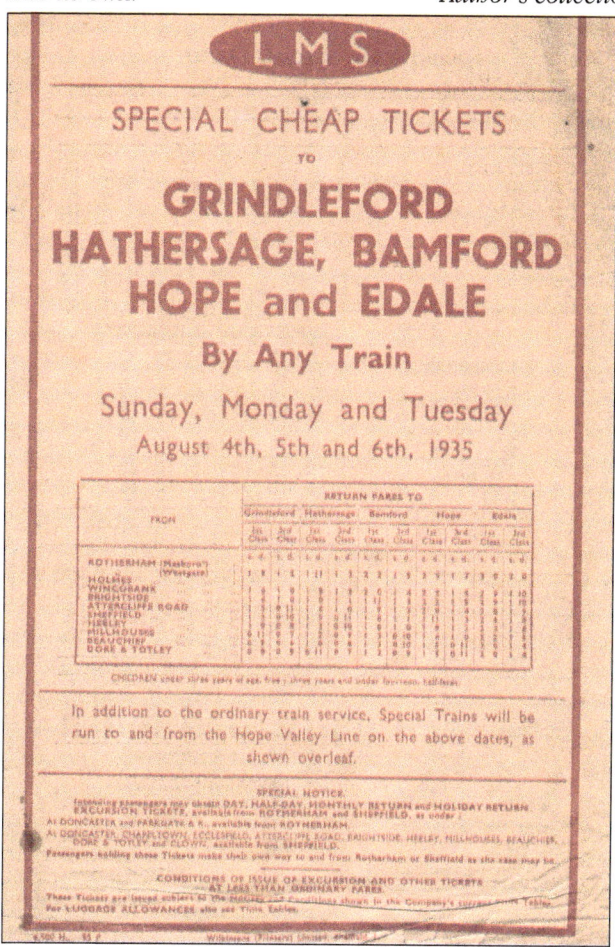

Right: August Bank Holiday weekend in 1935 shows the arrangements for trains starting from Rotherham and all stations to Dore and Totley to all the Hope valley stations and Edale on both ordinary service trains and additional excursion trains. There was the flexibility for additional trains to run according to demand.

Author's collection

The Easter Monday hike was a common feature of the pre and post war calendar. Here is a 1934 fixed time excursion train starting from Doncaster. The stock would have been held in Hope sidings and the turntable at Hope would have come into its own.

Author's collection

PASSENGER TIMETABLE WINTER 1933

The first line shows all trains originating from north of Dore (up) and the second line from south of Dore (down) that would run in the down direction on the Hope valley line.

\multicolumn{4}{c	}{DOWN}	
FROM	**TIME**	**DAY**	**DETAILS**	**1933**
Sheffield	06.09		All stations to Dore 06.20	
Chesterfield	05.56		All station to Dore 06.20/ 06.22 all stations to **Edale 07.00**	
Sheffield	07.47	Sun	All stations to Dore 08.01	
Derby	06.20		Chesterfield 07.28/ 07.34 Dore 08.01/ 08.06 all stations to **Hope 08.32**	
Sheffield	08.25		All stations except Beauchief to Dore 08.36	
Derby	06.45		Chesterfield 07.59/ 08.07 all stations to Dore 08.36/ 08.56, all stations to Chinley 09.51/ 10.00 New Mills 10.12 Marple 10.20 Romiley 10.27 Stockport T.D. 10.34/ 10.37 Cheadle Heath 10.44 Heaton Mersey 10.48 Didsbury 10.51 Withington 10.56 **Manchester Cen 11.00**	
Hope	08.50		Edale 08.59/ 09.03 Chinley 09.14/ 09.16 Marple 09.33 Manchester Cen 09.25/ 10.05 **Liverpool Cen 10.58**	
Sheffield	08.36		Heeley 08.39 Dore 08.48	
Derby	07.48		Chesterfield 08.20/ 08.32 Dore 08.48/ 09.10 Chinley 09.42/ 09.45 Chapel 09.53 Buxton 10.25 Manchester Cen 10.00 **Liverpool Cen 11.15**	
Sheffield	09.00	Sun	Heeley 09.07 Dore 09.21 Grindleford 09.31 Hathersage 09.37 Bamford 09.45 **Hope 09.51**	
Sheffield	09.03	Sat to	Through Exp Heeley 09.07 Dore 09.14	
Chesterfield	08.50	30 Sep	Dore 09.14/ 09.23 all stations to Hope 09.53 Chinley 10.17/ 10.23 **Blackpool North 12.35**	
Sheffield	10.00	Sun to	Heeley 10.03 to Dore 10.09	
Chesterfield	09.42	4 Nov	Dore 10.09/ 10.19 all stations to **Chinley 11.11**	
Sheffield	09.59		Dore 10.08 to set down pass	
Chesterfield	09.40		Dore 10.08/ 10.23 Chinley 10.56/ 10.58 **Manchester Cen 11.22** through carriage to **Liverpool Cen 12.15**	
Sheffield	10.23		All stations to Dore 10.40	
Chesterfield	10.16		All stations to Dore 10.40/ 11.02 all stations to Chinley 11.52/ 12.18 Chapel 12.26 Peak Forest 12.38 **Buxton 13.02** Chinley 12.27 Manchester Cen 12.53 **Liverpool Cen 14.15**	
Hope	11.20	Sun to 4 Nov	Chinley 11.41/ 11.46 all stations to Marple 12.06 all stations to Manchester Cen 12.45 **Liverpool Cen 15.33**	
Sheffield	11.25	Sat to	Through Exp Heeley 11.31 Dore 11.42	
Leicester		30 Sep	Chesterfield 10.46 Treeton Rotherham Sheffield Chinley 12.22/ 12.32 Cheadle Heath 12.48 **Llandudno 15.30**	
Hope	11.40	Sun to 4 Nov	Chinley 12.01/ 12.06 Stockport T.D. 12.32 Manchester Cen 13.05 **Liverpool Cen 15.33**	
Sheffield	12.33	Sat	Heeley 12.36 Sat Dore 12.40	
Chesterfield	12.16		Dore 12.40/ 12.47 all stations to **Chinley 13.38**	
Sheffield	13.14		Heeley 13.17 Dore 13.37	
Derby	12.45		Chesterfield 13.18/ 13.20 Dore 13.37/ 13.45 Chinley 14.17/ 14.19 Cheadle Heath 14.33 **Manchester Cen 14.48**	

\multicolumn{4}{c	}{DOWN}	
FROM	**TIME**	**DAY**	**DETAILS**	**1933**
Sheffield	13.11	Sat	Heeley 13.17 Dore 13.24 all stations to **Chinley 14.28**	
Sheffield	13.37	Sun to	All stations except Beauchief to Dore 13.48	
Chesterfield	13.23	14 Nov	All stations to Dore 13.48/ 14.16 Grindleford 14.28 Hathersage 14.33 Bamford 14.38 **Hope 14.43**	
Sheffield	13.55	Sat to	All stations to Dore 14.08	
Chesterfield	13.49	28 Oct	All stations to Dore 14.08/ 14.27 Grindleford 14.39 Hathersage 14.44 Bamford 14.49 **Hope 14.55**	
Sheffield	14.15	Sun	All stations except Beauchief to Dore 14.23	
Chesterfield	13.23		Dore 14.23/ 14.43 all stations to Chinley 15.29/ 15.40 (For Manchester Vic leave 15.52), Stockport T.D. 16.00 **Manchester Cen 16.30**	
Sheffield	14.22		All stations to Dore 14.38	
Chesterfield	13.44		All stations to Dore 14.38/ 14.41 all stations to Chinley 15.33/ 15.41 all stations to Marple all stations to **Manchester Cen 17.03**	
Sheffield	15.58		Dore 16.09	
Chesterfield	15.45		All stations to Dore 16.09/ 16.20 Chinley 16.53/ 16.55 Manchester Cen 17.22 **Liverpool Cen 18.15**	
Sheffield	16.30		All stations to Dore 16.44	
Chesterfield	16.20		All stations to Dore 16.44/ 16.51 Grindleford 17.01 Hathersage 17.07 Bamford 17.10 **Hope 17.15**	
Hope	17.48	Not Sat	Edale 18.01 Chinley 18.12/ 18.17 Marple 18.37 **Manchester Cen 19.12**	
Sheffield	17.30		Dore 17.30 (Note error)	
Chesterfield	17.10		Dore 17.30/ 17.42 all stations to Chinley 18.35/ 18.47 Cheadle Heath 19.05 Manchester Cen 19.26 **Liverpool Cen 20.52**	
Sheffield	18.10	Sun to	All stations except Beauchief to Dore 18.30	
Chesterfield	17.25	4 Nov	All stations to Dore 17.47/ 18.30 all stations to Chinley 19.23/ 19.28 Chapel 19.39 **Buxton 20.58**	
Sheffield	18.25	Not Sat	Heeley 18.28 Dore 18.36	
Clay Cross	17.14		Chesterfield 17.25 all stations to Dore 17.50/ 18.37 All stations to **Chinley 19.27**	
Hope	18.42	To 4 Nov	Edale 18.54 Chinley 19.00/ 19.07 Marple 19.31 Stockport T.D. 19.39 **Manchester Cen 20.15**	
Sheffield	19.07		Dore 19.17	
Chesterfield	18.53		All stations Dore 19.17/ 19.21 all stations Chinley 20.13/ 20.22 Marple, Stockport T.D. 20.51 **Manchester Cen 21.10**	
Hope	19.32	Sun	Edale 19.45 Chinley 19.56/ 20.02 Manchester Cen 20.30 **Liverpool Cen 22.10**	
Sheffield	19.25	Sun to	Dore 19.35	
Chesterfield	19.18	4 Nov	Dore 19.35/ 19.58 all stations to Chinley 20.51/ 20.53 Marple 21.07 Stockport T.D. 21.19/ 21.21 **Manchester Cen 21.50**	
Sheffield	20.35		All stations Dore 20.44	
Chesterfield	20.25		All stations Dore 20.44/ 20.48 all stations **Chinley 21.37**	
Sheffield	22.05		All stations Dore 22.17	
Chesterfield	21.16	Not Fri Sat	Dore 21.31/ 22.17 Grindleford 22.27 Hathersage 22.32 Bamford 22.36 **Hope 22.42**	

DOWN

FROM	TIME	DAY	DETAILS 1933
Sheffield	23.05	Sat	All stations Dore 23.17
Derby	21.45		Chesterfield 22.38 Dore 23.17 Grindleford 23.29 Hathersage 23.34 Bamford 23.39 Hope 23.45 **Edale 23.58**
Sheffield	22.48	Fri	Dore 23.02
Chesterfield	22.38		Dore 23.02/ 23.17 Grindleford 23.39 Hathersage 23.44 Bamford 23.49 **Hope 23.55**

UP
Each line shows originating train and then onward train from Chinley.

FROM	TIME	DAY	DETAILS 1933
Buxton	07.05		Chapel 07.26 Chinley 07.30
Liverpool Cen	05.05		Manchester Cen 06.05 Stockport T.D. 06.34 Chinley 07.17/ 07.40 all stations to Grindleford 08.21 Heeley 08.35 Sheffield 08.39 Treeton **Chesterfield 09.20**
Edale	08.05	Sun	Hope 08.15 Bamford 08.20 Hathersage 08.26 Grindleford 08.34 Dore all stations to **Sheffield 08.59**
Buxton	08.10		Chapel 08.28 Chinley 08.32
Manchester Cen	07.24		Cheadle Heath 07.47 Chinley 08.14/ 08.38 all stations to Dore 09.24 Heeley 09.30 **Sheffield 09.35**
Liverpool Cen	08.30	Sun to 4 Nov	Manchester Cen 10.15 Stockport T.D. 10.35 Marple Chinley 11.06/ 11.08 all stations to Dore 12.32 (Chesterfield 12.53) **Sheffield 12.42**
Stockport T.D.	09.02	Sun To 4 Nov	Marple Chinley 09.32/ 09.34 all stations to Dore 10.22 Heeley 10.28 **Sheffield 11.01**
Buxton	09.16		Chapel 09.28 Chinley 09.33
Liverpool Cen	08.08		Cheadle Heath 09.02 Chinley 09.26
Stockport T.D.	08.58		Chinley 09.32/ 09.44
Manchester Cen	08.55		Chinley 09.32/ 09.44 Dore 10.15/ 10.44 (Chesterfield 11.03) **Sheffield 10.54**
Manchester Cen	09.08	Sun from 5 Nov	Chinley 09.43
Stockport T.D.	09.14		Marple, Chinley 09.54/ 10.01 Dore 10.48 all stations except Beauchief **Sheffield 11.01**
Manchester Cen	09.12	From 5 Nov	Stockport T.D. 09.32 Marple Chinley 10.05/ 10.12 all stations to Dore 10.58 all stations except Beauchief to **Sheffield 11.11**
Manchester Cen	09.12	Sun to 29 Oct	Stockport T. D. 09.32 Chinley 10.00/ 10.24 Edale 10.39 **Hope 10.46**
Peak Forest	09.35		Chapel 09.43 Chinley 09.48 / 09.55 all stations to Dore 10.41/ 10.44 (Chesterfield all stations 11.03) all stations **Sheffield 10.56**
Manchester Cen	10.15	Sun to 4 Nov	Stockport T.D. 10.35 Chinley 11.06/ 11.08 Edale 11.23 **Hope 11.31**
Liverpool Cen	10.30	Sun	Manchester Cen 12.00 Stockport T.D. 12.18, Marple Chinley 12.45/12.53 all stations to Dore 14.02 (Chesterfield 15.25) all stations except Beauchief to **Sheffield 14.18**
Liverpool Cen	10.30		Manchester Cen 11.44 Chinley 12.14/ 12.21 Dore 12.52/ 13.04 (Chesterfield 13.23) **Sheffield 13.12**
Chinley	12.38		All stations to Dore 13.24/ 13.28 (Chesterfield all stations 13.50) all stations **Sheffield 13.39**

UP

FROM	TIME	DAY	DETAILS 1933
Llandudno	13.35	Sat to 23 Sep	Through express Cheadle Heath 16.20 Chinley 16.49/ 16.54 Dore 17.32/ 18.10 (Chesterfield 18.29) **Sheffield 18.22**
Liverpool Cen	14.00	Sat to 28 Oct	Manchester Cen 15.00 Chinley 15.32/ 15.33 Dore 16.04/ 16.09 (Chesterfield 16.29) **Sheffield 16.22**. Through carriage from Liverpool
Manchester Cen	14.00		Chinley 14.32/ 14.37 Dore 15.09/ 15.20 (Chesterfield 15.34) **Sheffield 15.30**
Manchester Cen	14.00	Sun to 4 Nov	Stockport T.D. 14.30 Marple Chinley 15.08/ 15.11 Edale 15.26 **Hope 15.33**
Chinley	14.45		All stations to Dore 15.31/ 16.09 (Chesterfield all stations 16.19) all stations **Sheffield 16.26**
Hope	17.25	Sat	Bamford 17.29 Hathersage 17.33 Grindleford 17.38 Dore **Sheffield 17.55**
Hope	17.35	Not Sat	Bamford 17.39 Hathersage 17.44 Grindleford 17.50 Dore Heeley 18.07 **Sheffield 18.10**.
Blackpool North	14.50	Sat to 30 Sep	Through express Chinley 17.21/ 17.25 Dore 18.00/ 18.10 (Chesterfield 18.29) **Sheffield 18.16**
Liverpool Cen	16.00		Manchester Cen 16.56 Stockport T.D. 17.09 Chinley 17.34/ 17.36 Dore 18.07/ 18.10 (all stations Chesterfield 18.29) **Sheffield 18.16**
Chinley	17.44		All stations to Dore 18.54/ 19.30 (all stations Chesterfield 19.13) all stations **Sheffield 19.39**
Blackpool North	15.35	Sat to 23 Sep	Through Express Chinley 18.07/ 18.18 Chesterfield 19.05 **Leicester**
Liverpool Cen	15.45	Sun to 4 Nov	Manchester Cen 18.35 Stockport T.D. Marple Chinley 19.23 / 19.30 all stations to Dore 20.19 all stations except Beauchief to **Sheffield 20.33**
Liverpool Cen	15.45	Sun from 5 Nov	Manchester Cen 18.35 Stockport T.D. 18.54 Chinley 19.23/ 19.55 all stations to Dore 20.46 (Chesterfield 21.45) all stations except Beauchief to **Sheffield 21.01**
Blackpool North	15.50	Sat to 23 Sep	Through express Chinley 18.20/ 18.30 Grindleford to set down only **Sheffield 19.22**
Buxton	17.22	Not Sat	Chapel 18.08 Chinley 18.13
Liverpool Cen	16.25		Manchester Cen 17.27 Chinley 17.58/ 18.19 all stations to Dore 19.01 (Chesterfield 19.39) Heeley 19.09 **Sheffield 19.13**
Hope	18.24	Sun	Bamford 18.27 Hathersage 18.37 Grindleford 18.46 Millhouses 18.50 Heeley 18.54 **Sheffield 19.00**
Stockport T.D.	19.11		Chinley 19.51
Buxton	19.30		Chapel 19.51 Chinley 19.55
Liverpool Cen	18.25		Manchester Cen 19.25 Chinley 20.00/ 20.07 all stations to Dore 20.51 (Chesterfield 21.20) all stations to **Sheffield 21.06**

2P 4-4-0 No. 468 leaves Dore & Totley station for the Hope valley on 8 Sep 1938. Three and four coaches were the norm in the inter war years, only being strengthened at holiday times. Note that the signals are on the 'wrong' side because of the curve and the bridge and are still of Midland origin. The other striking thing is the immaculate ballasting of the permanent way. *E. R. Morten*

UP				
FROM	**TIME**	**DAY**	**DETAILS**	**1933**
Buxton	21.30		Chinley 21.59	
Liverpool Cen	19.20		Manchester Cen 20.53 Stockport T.D. 21.10 Chinley 21.47/ 22.07 all stations Dore 22.50/ 23.10 (Chesterfield 23.29) Heeley 22.56 **Sheffield 23.00**	
Chinley	20.30	To 4 Nov	All stations to Dore 21.21/ 21.24 (Chesterfield 21.45) all stations except Beauchief **Sheffield 21.35**	
Buxton	21.30		Chinley 21.59	
Liverpool Cen	19.20		Manchester Cen 20.53 Stockport T.D. 21.10 Chinley 21.47/ 22.07 all stations Dore 22.50/ 22.52 (Chesterfield 23.29) Heeley 22.57 **Sheffield 23.00**	

OH! I DO LIKE TO BE BESIDE THE SEASIDE

LLANDUDNO TRAINS

Llandudno was widely known as the 'Queen of Welsh resorts'. Developed from the mid-1800s as a seaside resort, the station was opened in 1858 with a modest two platforms. In 1876 the building of the pier began and by the 1890s it had developed into a major holiday town in a wonderful setting. The station was rebuilt in 1892 with five platforms and a massive glass canopy and at peak times it was said that a train arrived every four minutes. There were twenty sidings for stabling empty coaches and a servicing point for the locomotives. It had two further attractions namely the ever popular Great Orme Tramway, opened in 1902, followed by the Llandudno and Colwyn Bay Tramway which opened in 1907 and closed in 1956. I vividly remember riding on a 'toast rack' which were open single deckers.

No. 22 a 'toast rack' tram on the Llandudno & Colwyn Bay Tramway in 1956, the year of its closure.
Author's collection

Looking east towards Buxton East Junction on the Midland's Buxton branch in 1937. Had the signal been like this when the through train ran the right hand arm would have controlled the line on to No. 1 Junction. The original signal was a Midland type gantry across both tracks.
Mike Bentley collection

On 30 Jul 1908 the LNWR and the Midland Railway concluded an agreement which provided for closer working and the elimination of wasteful competition at locations served by both companies. Buxton was one of those places. The Buxton agreement was initiated on 2 Nov 1908 when Samuel Pitt, the Midland's station master and goods agent, became responsible for both passenger stations and also the LNWR facilities at Higher Buxton. A facing connection at Buxton East Junction, which allowed running to the LNWR line, was brought into use on 17 May 1908, shortly before the agreement was signed.

The route from Buxton to Llandudno was via Northenden, Cheadle Village Junction and Davenport Junction to Warrington Arpley. Stops were included at Rhyl and Colwyn Bay. It is known that a regular, rather than excursion, service actually ran via Buxton in the summer of 1910 and other years. This was not an independent train, the Llandudno portion being detached at Chinley from a Sheffield to Manchester Central train and then running independently to Buxton via Ashwood Dale. On the LNWR section the portion was attached at Cheadle Village Junction to a Leeds to Llandudno train.

The 1910 timings were; Sheffield depart 11.05 with stops at Heeley and Dore and then non-stop to Chinley, which was reached at 11.53 and departed five minutes later. Chapel was left at 12.04 and Buxton LNWR reached at 12.25. The destination times were Rhyl 14.55, Colwyn Bay 15.17 and Llandudno 15.42; four hours thirty seven minutes in total. The return left Llandudno at 15.45 and collected passengers at Colwyn Bay 16.05, Rhyl 16.27 and arrived at Buxton at 18.45. Chinley was reached at 19.04 where there was a twelve minute wait before a further stop at Dore. Arrival at Sheffield was 19.55. four hours and ten minutes in total.

There were no scheduled workings to Llandudno in the summer of 1914 but there were excursions, an example being the two organized by the Sheffield & Ecclesall Co-Operative Society on Thu 2 Jul which departed from Sheffield at 05.27 and 05.50 respectively. Handover at Buxton Junction was at 06.55 and 07.19. The return workings arrived at Buxton to hand over to the Midland at 23.20 and midnight arriving in Sheffield at 00.42 and 01.21.

On Mon 13 Jul 1914 an excursion ran from Rotherham Westgate at 05.12; from Sheffield it had similar timings to the previous excursions. It is known that a Grimesthorpe engine was used and that the carriages came from Heeley. The return service was handed over to the Midland at Buxton at 00.50 and Westgate was finally reached at 01.40.

Moving on to 1929 the special traffic notices throw light on additional services to Llandudno above the normal scheduled trains. Trains from the Leicester and Nottingham areas invariably went over the Peak line or via Burton and Stoke to Crewe. However, there were exceptions when the Hope valley line was used. Unlike Blackpool, where the season was extended by the illuminations to late October, the season at Llandudno started at Easter and finished by late September.

The old Pre-Grouping arrangement via Buxton had finished but the practice of attaching coaches to Leeds to Llandudno trains lingered on. On Thu 28 Mar, the day before Good Friday, an additional express third class left Sheffield at 11.50 with 185 passengers and picked up more at Heeley and Dore. It arrived at Chinley at 12.42 where it picked up a further ninety passengers. Cheadle Heath was reached at 12.59 from where it ran to Skelton Junction and Broadheath and on to Warrington Arpley, arriving at 13.30. Here it was attached to a Western Section excursion from Leeds. Motive power was provided by Millhouses and worked through to Arpley with a Western Section pilot-driver from Cheadle Heath. The engine returned light, leaving Arpley at 14.30, passing Cheadle Heath at 15.17, arriving at Millhouses at 16.36.

On Whit Sat 18 May 1929 a repeat train left Sheffield at 12.56 with only sixty passengers and arrived at Chinley at 13.47 where it picked up a further 128 passengers. Arriving at Arpley at 14.35 it was attached to the train from Leeds. However, the engine ran light to Cheadle and then to Belle Vue shed to work the 18.47 to Heeley.

The first through train on Whit Mon 20 May 1929 No. 949 left Masborough at 08.45 with 112 passengers and another 479 passengers boarded at Sheffield. After further stops at Heeley and Dore it ran non-stop to Cheadle Heath, where it was allowed five minutes for a water stop and

Ex-Midland 4F 0-6-0 No. 3927 passes Gowhole sidings on a return nine coach excursion M87 from Llandudno to Sheffield on 12 Aug 1939.
R. D. Pollard. Manchester Locomotive Society collection

examination, before leaving at 09.38. Running non-stop via Arpley, Frodsham Junction, Chester and Saltney Junction it arrived at Rhyl at 11.30 where there was an eight minute stop. Colwyn Bay followed at 12.00 and Llandudno at 12.20, a four hour journey. The return working left Llandudno at 22.00 and took water at Cheadle Heath at 00.33 arriving in Sheffield at 01.57 and Rotherham Masborough at 02.10. The empty coaching stock left at 02.55 and came back to Heeley carriage sidings at 04.42. A Grimesthorpe engine (almost certainly a newish 'Crab' 2-6-0) worked through.

One unusual working that did not use the Hope valley route was a staff outing, No. 896 from Sheffield, which left at 05.40 and picked up at Dore, Chesterfield, Ambergate, Belper, Duffield, Derby, Egginton, Tutbury, Stoke and Crewe. It then ran non-stop to Llandudno, arriving at 10.55, a lengthy five hour fifteen minute journey. Grimesthorpe provided a 'Crab' 2-6-0. The return left at 19.08 and arrived in Sheffield at 00.17.

On Sat 15 Jun Arthur Balfour's booked a guaranteed excursion again No. 896, which left Sheffield at 08.36 and ran non-stop to Arpley where it had five minutes for water and examination before running non-stop to Rhyl 10.14, Colwyn Bay 10.33 and Llandudno 10.52, a four hour twenty seven minute timing. The return, which left at 20.38, had an identical schedule except that it took water at Cheadle Heath as well as Arpley.

On the same day J. Pickering & Sons booked a guaranteed excursion No. 900, from Attercliffe Road which left at 05.35 and picked up at Sheffield and Heeley before running non-stop to Cheadle Heath and Arpley, stops being made for water at both places. It reached Llandudno at 09.47. The return left at 22.30 and retraced its steps, with the same stops, arriving at Attercliffe Road at 02.28. The empty coaching stock returned to Upwell Street, arriving at 02.37. A week later Spear & Jackson booked a restaurant car train with a similar schedule which started at Rotherham Masborough.

Another excursion to Llandudno on Sat 6 Jul and booked by Cammell Laird, started at Millhouses and was routed via Sheffield all stations to Rotherham, Cudworth, Royston Junction, Thornton Midland Junction, Mirfield, Huddersfield, Marsden and Stalybridge.

A further alternative route was chosen for excursion No. 152 on Bank Holiday Mon 5 Aug, from Rotherham Masborough via the Hope valley to Chinley, Romiley and Midland Junction where the engine and trainmen were changed. The route beyond was not detailed after it had passed Manchester Exchange. This was a well patronised train as 280 passengers boarded at Sheffield and 360 at Chinley.

The winter 1933 timetable (see page 244) shows one train each way from and to Sheffield on Saturdays to 30 Sep outward and 23 Sep inward. Another started at Leicester and combined with the Sheffield train at Dore.

REFERENCE
Midland Railway Society Journal Issue 1 Jun 1996 and *Issue 2 Sep 1996*

TRAINS TO BLACKPOOL

In the 1890s Blackpool had grown to the extent that it had a permanent population of 35,000, serving 250,000 visitors annually. The attractions were further improved when the iconic Blackpool Tower opened during the decade. Central station was said to be the busiest station in the world in 1911 so how did Blackpool's two stations cope when trains were arriving from all over the country? In 1898 Talbot Road was rebuilt and enlarged with six platforms for all year round use, all under cover, with an additional nine open platforms for summer use. Central station was literally just behind the Tower and its disembarking passengers spilled into the streets right in the centre of things. Rebuilding followed in 1900 when the station was enlarged to fourteen platforms. Although excursion trains through the Hope valley usually changed engines and trainmen at Belle Vue it is also likely that many engines worked through to Blackpool which was noted for receiving engines from all the northern and Midlands railway companies. The LYR simply did not have enough motive power available to cover the immense traffic. An observer at the two stations in the Edwardian period would have had an unforgettable experience.

Blackpool was the most popular seaside resort during this period and attracted holiday makers and excursionists from all over the country but particularly from the northern industrial towns. Trains to Blackpool were commonplace through the Hope valley. Regular timetabled trains ran throughout the season to late October, when the

The promenade at Blackpool in about 1898 when the Tower was only recently opened. The tram is electric, note the conduit between the rails. This type of operation was ended in 1899 when overhead wires were installed. As the Big Wheel had only opened in 1896 this allows us to date the picture between 1896 and 1898.
Author's collection

illuminations finished. These were supplemented by numerous excursion and additional trains scheduled by both the Midland or privately chartered by community groups, religious denominations or companies for employees.

The route to Blackpool went from Chinley via Marple, Romiley, Bredbury, Reddish Junction, Belle Vue, Ashburys West Junction and Midland Junction where engines and trainmen were changed as the trains entered LYR territory. This practice continued deep into LMS days even though the companies were no longer independent of each other. The route then went via Phillips Park Junction and Miles Platting to Manchester Victoria. All trains to Blackpool in the nineteenth century required a change there but through trains became the norm thereafter. From Victoria the lines were either LYR owned or jointly worked with the LNWR. After Manchester Victoria, the route proceeded by Dobbs Brown Junction, Horwich Fork Junction, Chorley Crow Nest Junction and Euxton Junction where the LNWR West Coast Main Line was accessed as far as Preston. Then the route ran via Kirkham North Junction to Poulton Junction, which had a new curve added in 1896, to Blackpool Talbot Road station – renamed 'Blackpool North' in 1932. The other station was 'Central', which closed in 1964 as part of the Beeching cuts, although the original recommendation had been the closure of Blackpool North.

During the winter of 1894/5 and the summer of 1898 there was one train from Sheffield to Manchester Victoria and return. By summer 1903 there were no scheduled trains at all. However, by summer 1914 there were two through trains from Sheffield, one from Chesterfield and one all stations from Grindleford to Manchester Victoria. The number of return trains was the same but there was an additional working to Nottingham. On Whit Monday of that year there was an excursion from Leicester return and on August Bank Holiday Monday 1914 there were three return excursions from Clay Cross, Kilnhurst and Nottingham.

However it is the 1929 STNs which give the most illuminating information.

The date, Sat 27 Jul, has been chosen because it was the start of the Works weeks, when the factories closed for the holiday and maintenance was undertaken on the machinery and furnaces.

19A Grimesthorpe 'Crab' 2-6-0 No. 2760 is on Excursion No. 816 for Blackpool from Sheffield and is passing Dore West Junction during the Whit weekend of 1938. Note the coal piled high on the tender and the black exhaust as it comes toward the end of the six mile 1 in 100 flog from Sheffield to Totley tunnel. However, No. 2760 still has steam to spare as it is feathering round the steam valves.
A. G. Ellis

These trains are listed but without further details.

EXC NO	DEP	TO BLACKPOOL FROM	DEP	FROM BLACKPOOL TO
683	13.31	Nottingham		
745+	06.50	Sheffield	21.30	Chesterfield
747	06.18	Mansfield*	13.00	Nottingham*
748	08.25	Sheffield	14.10	Mansfield*
749			14.50	Sheffield
750			15.10	Leicester*
751	09.07	Sheffield	15.50	Sheffield
752	10.40	Leicester*	16.40	Leicester*

* No information on which route was used for these trains

+ This train was scheduled from Chesterfield at 05.50 and then via the 'Old Road' stopping at Whittington, Barrow Hill, Eckington and Killamarsh to Sheffield to form this excursion. The return train was scheduled to stop at Marple, New Mills, Chinley, Heeley, Sheffield, Attercliffe Road, Killamarsh, Eckington, Barrow Hill, and Whittington to Chesterfield where it arrived at 01.50. The empty carriage stock departed at 02.10 to Heeley carriage sidings where it arrived at 02.40. The train guard from excursion 745 outward to Blackpool fulfilled the same duty on the return train.

The first three of these services were booked by individual companies and the fourth was an excursion laid on by the LMS.

EXC NO	FROM & TO WITH DETAILS	27 JUL 1929
845	**Guaranteed Excursion T. Wragg & Sons Sheffield 05.52 to Blackpool Talbot Road 09.20** Sheffield to provide guard & power. Chinley 06.45/ 06.50 water & change enginemen Marple 06.59/ 07.04 water & examination Belle Vue Engine Shed Box to change engine or trainmen 07.18/ 07.21 then non-stop **Blackpool Talbot Road 21.25 to Sheffield 00.43** Belle Vue Engine Shed Box 23.10/ 23.12 to change engine or trainmen & examination Chinley 23.45/ 23.50 water & examination Heeley 00.37/ 00.38	
848	**Guaranteed Excursion Brightside Foundry Ecclesfield 06.00 to Blackpool Talbot Road 10.05** Brightside 06.08 Attercliffe Road 06.14 Sheffield 06.16/ 06.24 to provide guard & power, Heeley 06.29/ 06.32 Millhouses 06.37 Dore 06.43 Marple 07.41/ 07.46 water & examination Belle Vue Engine Shed Box 08.04/ 08.06 to change engines or trainmen then non-stop. **Blackpool Talbot Road 22.50 to Ecclesfield 02.30** Belle Vue Engine Shed Box 00.27/ 00.29 to change engine or trainmen & examination, Marple 00.48/ 00.53 water & examination Dore 01.51 Millhouses 01.56 Heeley 02.00/ 02.02 Sheffield 02.05/ 02.14 Attercliffe Road 02.18 Brightside 02.25	
834	**Guaranteed Excursion Bitterlings Nottingham 05.25 to Blackpool Central* 10.17** Nottingham to provide guard & power, Chinley 07.36/ 07.40 water & examination Belle Vue Engine Shed Box 08.10/ 08.12 change engine or trainmen Phillips Park No 1 08.48 for examination then non-stop. **Blackpool Central 22.15 to Nottingham 02.50** Belle Vue Engine Shed Box 00.42/ 00.46 to change engine or trainmen & examination then non-stop * The only train noted that started and terminated at Blackpool Central.	
837	**Advertised Period Excursion Chesterfield 07.05 to Blackpool Talbot Road 11.17** Sheepbridge 07.11 Dronfield 07.23 Grindleford 07.42 Hope 07.55 Chinley 08.20/ 08.27 water & examination Belle Vue Engine Shed Signal Box 08.58/ 09.00 to change engine or trainmen inc guard from Sheffield for guard from Manchester Phillips Park No 1 09.23 for examination then non-stop	

Some more Blackpool trains can be found tabulated under specific dates.

The fastest of these trains took three hours and eighteen minutes.

When normal timetabled trains are considered it is likely, that about thirteen passenger trains passed through the Hope valley each way from very early morning. The excursion carried eager excited families westward and returned in the early hours of the following morning with exhausted children and parents longing for home on this exceptionally busy day on the railways.

The 1933 winter timetable (see page 244) details that there were two Blackpool trains from Sheffield and one return which ran until either 23 or 30 Sep. Additionally there was a train to Leicester which left mid-afternoon and ran until 23 Sep.

TRAINS TO SOUTHPORT AND MORECAMBE/ HEYSHAM

No regular timetabled trains to Southport have been traced although there were excursions booked by organizations, one at least being tabulated later in this work.

There were no trains of any description that ran to Morecambe and Heysham for the Belfast ferry. Trains starting from south of Dore as well as those from Sheffield, either joined the LYR at Thornhill Junction or later worked over the Midland via Cudworth, Leeds, Whitehall Junction, Keighley, Skipton, Hellifield, Settle Junction, Clapham, Wennington and Lancaster.

FREIGHT OPERATIONS

PRESENTATION OF TIMETABLES

These timetables contain an almost bewildering mass of trains of many varieties and classifications which had been developed on the basis of agreement and heritage. In the routing of traffic commercial choices predominated although the exchange of traffic from a Pre-Grouping company to another still persisted even though they had now become part of the LMS.

The freight business was largely divided between coal/mineral traffic moved at the dictates of collieries, coal factors and industrial users and was initiated outside railway management but still incurred a very considerable railway workload. Merchandise, and more particularly what the railway termed 'smalls' traffic, revolved around London and the large provincial centres such as Sheffield and Manchester. The key group of freight trains started mainly from London and radiated out to all areas of the country, mostly worked overnight. The second group of services combined merchandise and particularly coal. These linked a multitude of marshalling yards and exchange sidings set up by the Pre-Grouping companies. Trip workings between yards in areas such as Manchester and Sheffield were legion. There remained what the railway called the company traffic which carried a variety of commodities and mainly served industrial complexes with raw materials and finished or semi-finished products. These also included meat, fresh vegetables, cattle, milk etc. Whenever frequency justified it the trains were timetabled and resourced by a 'conditional' pathway which was put into the timetable; this is why it became common to note trains suspended or only running as required. Priority of movement was determined by the classification of traffic, a fully brake fitted freight having a high priority for example. In the Derby trains office protractors were shaped to help plot a path on the paper graph for the different trains.

Planning for freight growth was a positive experience but planning for decline was far more difficult. Negotiations were needed with other areas of the business to remove services and matters such as the effect on personnel had also to be taken into consideration.

The shifting sands of day to day operations eventually became clear. The greater part of traffic intelligence was largely historical and in many cases the planner's day was spent solving yesterday's problems. The main timetables were changed twice a year to reflect seasonal changes between winter and summer with fortnightly STN notices being issued to amend, delete or add information. These mainly centred round the cancellation of some passenger services, the strengthening of other trains and the wholesale cancellation of freight traffic in favour of excursion traffic at busy holiday periods.

The marshalling yards and exchange sidings were a key part of the operations network but no two were alike. A yard such as Toton was designed on a huge scale to segregate coal traffic but was quite unsuitable for passing trains to call or to handle merchandise traffic. Many yards were cramped, antiquated and awkward to operate with all sorts of movements conflicting with one another.

STARTING AND FINISHING POINTS

Here are a selection of sidings. All of these sidings are long gone and are fading from memory; there will be a detailed consideration of Gowhole sidings in Vol. 2.

ADSWOOD SIDINGS – An LNWR facility to service the huge Co-Operative Society warehouse and coal depot near Edgeley, Stockport.

ARPLEY JUNCTION – The place where trains for north Wales were handed over to the LNWR from the CLC. It also had sidings which were enlarged in 1890.

ANCOATS – An official Midland photograph of 15 May 1922 shows Ancoats, the Midland main warehouse in central Manchester. It received and despatched many trains through the Hope valley. Opened on 2 May 1870, it was located on the end of a more than one mile branch which ran from Ashburys West Junction on the MSLR main line. The first part of the branch later formed the connection which was to be called the Ancoats Junction line to Midland Junction, the hand over point for trains accessing the LYR from 1889. The Sheffield & Midland Joint line of 1875 ran south east from Ashburys East Junction to Romiley and Chinley. From the joint line, junctions at Reddish and Brinnington gave access to the CLC system westwards via Stockport. This view shows the approaches to the yard leading up to the main warehouse with the line curving from Ashburys East and Ancoats Junction. Great Ancoats Street can be seen in the foreground with its cobble surface and tram tracks.
Eddie Johnson collection

AVENUE SIDINGS – Located south of Chesterfield just beyond Hasland shed which provided and serviced the motive power. This was the collection point for coal from Avenue, Bonds Main, Grassmoor, Holmewood, Williamthorpe and Pilsley collieries. The GCR also had lines running into some of these collieries.

A mixed freight including an empty low loader passes Avenue sidings in the up direction hauled by Normanton's 3F No. 43321 during Jun 1957. The sidings stretch into the far distance.
Author's collection

A later view on 2 Sep 1978 looking north. Whilst still active the yard looks dishevelled and tired.
M. A. King

2F No. 58153, a Hasland engine, leaving Williamthorpe colliery in 1955. The tipping mechanisms for the three slag heaps form the backdrop. The colliery buildings are top right. *Gordon Coltas*

BRINDLE HEATH GOODS YARD – An LYR facility located near Bolton and next to Agecroft shed which provided and serviced the motive power.

BLACKWELL SIDINGS – The collection point for Tibshelf, Sutton, Butcherwood, Pleasley East, New Hucknall and Winning Collieries.

BRINSLEY JUNCTION – The GNR freights from London to Manchester Deansgate and Liverpool transferred from the GNR line at Brinsley Junction to the Midland Railway on the Codnor Park branch at Great Northern Junction, just south of Codnor Park and Ironville station.

CARLTON EXCHANGE SIDINGS – These were jointly owned by the Midland Railway and the Hull & Barnsley Railway Pre-Grouping and were located between Cudworth and Royston. There were the north sidings which had a fan of sixteen lines and the separate south sidings which had a fan of thirteen lines. The LMS built Royston shed was just north.

EDGE HILL GOODS YARD (LNWR) – Recorded below is a regular working from the main LNWR goods yard in Liverpool to the same company's City Goods in Sheffield. In this view, on 12 Jun 1959, some of the yard complex can be seen. The 'gridirons' and sorting sidings are on the north side of the main line. The sidings on the right led down to Downhill carriage sidings and the CLC goods station. On the far left is Edge Hill goods station. At this time the yard was still handling over 2,000 wagons a day including over half of the traffic of the Port of Liverpool. 'Princess Royal' 4-6-2 No. 46209 *Princess Beatrice* is on the 07.45 express from Euston.
Ben Brooksbank

GRIMESTHORPE SIDINGS – A large amount of traffic down the Hope valley emanated from these sidings. This official 1912 view graphically captures the pollution that created an almost permanent gloom in the east end of Sheffield. We are looking toward Rotherham with Grimesthorpe Junction No 1 signal box guarding the entrance to Grimesthorpe sidings on the right. Cammell Laird's works are on the left. *Author's collection*

GLAZEBROOK SIDINGS – A CLC facility near Warrington located where the line to Godley diverged. These were one mile south of the Manchester Ship Canal, which opened in 1893 and from that date the sidings handled coal workings from the canal. In 1910 the Partington Steel & Iron Co opened at Irlam and attracted additional traffic.

MOLD JUNCTION (LNWR) – Located at Saltney Ferry near Chester, it was the principal freight yard for north Wales coast traffic.

MORTON COLLIERY SIDINGS – These were located on the up side of the Trent to Chesterfield line between Tibshelf and Clay Cross. The colliery was sunk between 1865 and 1874 and closed in 1965. It was owned by the Clay Cross Iron Co until the nationalisation of the coal industry.

HEATON MERSEY SIDINGS – Heaton Mersey sidings figure prominently in the timetables. On 30 Jul 1952 K3 No. 61862 has a load of slack and is on the down main line passing Heaton Mersey West box. The engine shed is behind the signal box although the coaling stage and a stabled engine can just be seen. The lines behind the engine's dome brought goods traffic in the down or westbound direction around the back of the sidings. The main sidings are in the centre distance.
Norman Preedy

HUNSLET LANE GOODS SHED – Hunslet Lane, Leeds goods shed entrance in an official view of 21 Dec 1921. Along with Stourton this was the main Midland goods yard. The location was the original station of the line from Derby before it moved to the more central Wellington station in 1846. The site is now occupied by the Crown Point Retail Park.
Author's collection

MASBOROUGH STATION SIDINGS – Despite the rapid adoption of petrol driven vehicles at the time this fascinating view shows a steam lorry in 1920.
Author's collection

ST. PANCRAS GOODS YARD – Although most of the London traffic originated at Somers Town the station itself had extensive goods facilities which went mainly unremarked. This 1933 view shows horses still being used as two men hand load bricks.
Author's collection

SHEET STORES JUNCTION – Located on the western point of the triangle which still has Trent station to the north and Trent Junction to the south.

STORRS MILL SIDINGS – Could be found between Wath and Cudworth and held up to ninety five wagons. This was the collection point for Grimethorpe colliery.

WINNINGTON – On the CLC near Northwich. A branch ran from just before Hartford & Greenbank station to Winnington & Anderton Goods Depot, a collection point for soda ash.

WICKER GOODS DEPOT – This was built on the site of the original Sheffield station which became the end of a branch when the direct line to the new station on Sheaf Street was opened in 1870. We see the interior of the goods shed in 1898. Note the destination boards which include Bradford, Keighley and Derby and the small crane on the left.
Author's collection

THE WORKING TIMETABLES

In the following section are freight workings over the line detailed from the working timetables for May 1898, Jul 1914, Jul 1927, Sep 1938 and May 1945. Also included is a comparison with traffic in 1916. From these has been recreated the operational rationale and an assessment of what freight demand was being addressed. There is also a comparison with the volume of traffic over the rival Woodhead route of the LNER for the summers of 1936 and 1944.

WORKING TIMETABLE OF FREIGHT TRAINS AT EDALE FROM MAY 1898

Edale has been chosen because it was the traffic exchange point for trains before Gowhole was opened.

Quoted below are three notes from the Appendix to the Working Timetables relevant to these trains.

'Fully loaded down goods and mineral trains worked with a single framed engine and a 15 ton brake may contain the same loading as when worked with a single framed engine and a 20 ton brake or two ten ton brakes but must not exceed a speed of 25 miles per hour between Peak Forest and Romiley, the running time for this speed being thirty five minutes. Also the same trains must be stopped at Romiley in order that the guard may pin down as many wagon brakes as necessary before descending the incline to Stockport.'

'All trains starting from Ancoats and having to attach wagons at Ashton Road Sidings must leave Ancoats without waiting for the booked time. Goods and mineral trains booked to run to Ancoats arriving at Ashton Road between 18.00 and midnight must detach all Ancoats traffic at Ashton Road and not run to Ancoats. Cattle and timber traffic labelled to Ancoats is dealt with at Ashton Road and must be detached at that point.'

'Traffic over the Dore & Chinley line for Hyde and Guide Bridge arriving at Edale during the day must be sent forward to the destination on the 19.40 Hasland to Ancoats (not found) and after that train has left this traffic will be sent to Chapel by the 01.15 Hope to Buxton to be worked forward by the 04.40 ex Rowsley and trains arriving after the above will be sent forward to Chinley to connect with the 09.15 ex Rowsley.'

Up traffic is in italics and where there is no entry in the 'Day' column trains run Mon to Sat.
A single time indicates the passing time at Edale.
Blanks in the 'Arrival' column are for trains that originated or terminated before Edale.

ARR DEP	DAY	DETAILS 1898
00.06 00.20	Sun	**Goods Sheffield to Heaton Mersey Sdgs 01.15** Dore 23.23 Romiley 01.01
(00.19)	Not Sat	**Express Goods Leeds 18.45 to Huskisson 03.05** Dore 23.20 Hope 00.05 Chinley N Jcn 00.33 to change from Class B to C & change lights, Halewood Sdgs 02.25 Walton 02.45/ 03.00
00.20 01.00	Not Sat	*Express Goods Heaton Mersey 23.20 to Queens Road & Staveley Edale changes from Class C to Class B. Dore 01.40. Runs as Through Goods when conveying salt traffic*
(00.49)	Sat	**Express Goods Sheffield to Huskisson 04.30** Dore 22.57 Hope 00.20/ 00.40. New Mills Goods Jcn 01.42 Heaton Mersey Sdgs 02.36 only if req examination Halewood Sdgs 03.40/ 03.50 Walton 04.10/ 04.25
01.20		*Engine & Brake Ancoats 00.30 to Edale*
01.25 01.45	Not Mon	**Freight Hope 01.15 to Buxton** Chinley S. Jcn 02.05
01.26 01.46	Not Sat	*Express Goods Huskisson 22.15 to Sheffield Halewood Sdgs 22.40/ 23.05 Heaton Mersey Sdgs 00.10/ 00.25 water Edale change from Class C to B and change lights Dore 02.21*
02.08 03.35	Not Mon	**Express Goods Bradford to Ancoats 04.45** Through Goods to Edale then Class C. Bredbury 04.15 (when Bredbury signal box closed traffic for Bredbury must be taken through to Ashton Road) Reddish 04.30 Ashton Road 04.40

ARR DEP	DAY	DETAILS 1898
02.08 03.20	Sun	**Express Goods York to Ancoats 04.45** Dore 01.20 Bredbury 04.15 Reddish 04.30 Ashton Road 04.40
02.10 02.30	Sun	*Goods Ancoats 00.35 to Avenue Ashton Road 01.00 Dore S Jcn 03.18*
02.17 02.30		*Express Goods Huskisson 22.30 to Sheffield Huskisson attaches traffic at Hartley's Sdgs detached by Alexandra pilot when req Halewood Sdgs 23.20 Farnworth 23.48 Heaton Mersey 00.45/ 01.07 water New Mills Pass 01.43 pick up one wagon Chinley 01.58 pick up one wagon Dore 03.10*
02.28 02.45	Sun	*Express Freight Leeds to Huskisson 06.15 Dore 01.40 Heaton Mersey Sdgs 03.45/ 04.10 Halewood 05.18/ 05.35 Walton 05.55/ 06.10*
02.30	Not Mon	**Express Goods Ancoats 00.35 to Sheffield** Ashton Road 01.05 Romiley 01.30 Marple 01.35/ 01.45 when req Engine runs to Hope to turn. Engine leaves shed coupled
02.34 02.45	Not Mon	*Express Goods Leeds to Huskisson 06.15 Dore 01.51 Heaton Mersey Sdgs 03.35*
02.35	Mon	**Express Goods Edale to Ashton Road 03.30** Romiley 03.12
02.50 03.25	Sun	**Goods Sheffield to Walton 07.15** Dore 01.27 Hope 02.34 Chinley N Jcn 03.47 Halewood Sdgs 06.30/ 06.50
	Not Mon	**Mineral Empties Hope 03.00 to Avenue Sdgs** Grindleford 03.30 to attach only. Worked by engine & men of 19.40 ex Ancoats
03.01 03.20	Not Mon	*Express Goods Bradford to Ancoats 04.00 Detaches Liverpool & CLC traffic at Edale when carrying less than 30 loads to make up. Engine & Brake to Heaton Mersey*
03.02 03.30		*Express Goods Huskisson 21.20 to Leeds Walton 21.40 Halewood Sdgs 22.05/ 22.30 Warrington 22.55/ 23.15 attaches traffic for Sheffield as well as Leeds & beyond Heaton Mersey Sdgs 23.59/ 00.04 water Edale traffic for Sheffield detached & changes from Class C to Class B, Dore 04.09*
03.28 03.40	Sun	**Express Goods Bradford to Ancoats 04.50** Dore 02.45 Ashton Road 04.45
03.40	Sun	*Express Goods Ancoats 02.00 to Edale Ashton Road 02.15 New Mills Goods Jcn 03.05 Chinley 03.25*
04.13 04.30		*Express Goods Heaton Mersey Sdgs to Leeds New Mills Pass 03.40 attaches only, Dore 05.12*
04.46. 05.15	Not Mon Sat	**Mineral Avenue to Heaton Mersey Sdgs 06.55** Dore W Jcn 03.50 Chinley N Jcn 05.45 Portwood Sdgs 06.50
(05.30)	Mon As Req	**Express Goods Heaton Mersey Sdgs 04.20 to Sheffield** Hope 06.20 to attach cattle, Dore 06.52
06.00	Sun	**Express Goods Edale to Ancoats 07.20** Romiley 06.36 Heaton Mersey Sdgs 06.50 when req Ashton Road 07.15
06.13 06.45		**Express Goods from Leeds to Heaton Mersey Sdgs 08.00** Dore 05.30 Edale runs as 'through goods' when conveying mineral traffic Chinley N Jcn 07.00 to change from Class B to Class C & change lights Chinley 07.20 to detach Manchester line wagons
(07.05)	Sat	**Mineral from Tibshelf to Northwich 11.35** Dore 05.48 Hope 06.45 Chinley N Jcn 07.20 New Mills Goods Jcn 08.00 Heaton Mersey Sdgs 08.45/ 09.20 Hartford 11.05/ 11.30
06.43 07.05	Sun	**Express Goods Leeds to Heaton Mersey Sdgs 08.20** Dore 06.00 Chinley 07.30 New Mills Goods Jcn 07.50 to detach

256

ARR DEP	DAY	DETAILS 1898
19.20 19.45		**Mineral Empties Huskisson 12.10 to Wharncliffe Sdgs** Linacre Gas Works 12.25 Halewood 13.15 Heaton Mersey Sdgs 14.30/ 15.20 Gowhole Goods Jcn 16.26 Edale where detaches Sheffield traffic. Runs one hour later on Mon
07.30 08.05	Not Mon	**Mineral Staveley to Heaton Mersey Sdgs 09.44** Dore 06.35 New Mills Goods Jcn 08.50 to detach wagons if req, Portwood Sdgs 09.37
09.21 09.35	Mon	**Mineral Tibshelf to Ancoats 10.55** Dore W Jcn 08.05 Hathersage 08.50 water Chinley N Jcn 10.00
09.45 09.55		**Mineral Tibshelf to Hartford 13.25** Dore W Jcn 08.50 Romiley 11.00 detaches at Portwood Sdgs on Mon if req Heaton Mersey Sdgs 11.30 Northwich 12.30/ 12.45
12.35 13.10		**Pick up Goods Sheffield to Buxton** Dore 10.40 to change lights to stopping goods Grindleford 11.05 Hathersage 11.26 Bamford 11.40 Hope 12.15 Chapel 13.28/ 14.15 Peak Forest Stn 15.30 Peak Forest Jcn 16.00
13.36	Sat	**Mineral Hasland to Edale** Dore W Jcn 11.47 Grindleford 12.00 Hathersage 12.20 Bamford 12.52 Hope 13.10
13.50	Not Mon	**Pick up Goods Buxton to Sheffield.** Buxton call Central Lime Co Sdgs & Peak Forest Jcn if req 11.08 Peak Forest Station 12.15 Chapel 12.26/ 13.25 weighs and shunts on Mon Wed Fri Edale detaches all of its wagons for Sheffield and beyond & shunts Stockport to Grindleford passenger Sat only Hope 14.30 Bamford 14.50 Hathersage 15.08 detaches all wagons except those to Grindleford & adds brake tariff van & any odd wagons & runs forward to Grindleford. Grindleford 15.35 shunts yard & returns to Hathersage with all traffic loaded at Grindleford and works all wagons to Sheffield. Any wagons for stations on Manchester line to be left at Hathersage
15.53 17.20	Not Mon Sat	**Mineral Empties Ancoats 14.40 to Hasland** Romiley 15.00 Dore 18.12
16.15 17.40	Mon Sat	**Mineral Empties Ancoats 13.20 to Blackwell Sdgs** Ancoats works ice and vegetable traffic for Buxton to Ashton Road when req Guide Bridge 13.30/ 14.41 Hyde 15.05 Woodley Jcn 15.10/ 15.19 Romiley 15.22 Dore S Jcn 18.32/ 18.48. Works with a 15 or 20 ton brake
17.37 18.09	Not Mon	**Empties Hartford 13.50 to Blackwell Sdgs** Northwich 13.53/ 14.10 Skelton Jcn 14.55 Heaton Mersey Sdgs 15.10/ 15.35 Romiley 16.44 shunts as req for more important trains, Dore 19.02. Runs via Dore & Chinley line when practical
20.17 20.35	Not Sat	**Mineral Tibshelf Jcn to Hartford 23.15** Dore S Jcn 19.21 Chinley N Jcn 20.52 New Mills Goods Jcn 21.17 Heaton Mersey Sdgs 22.00 water Northwich 22.58/ 23.10 detaches when req
20.38 21.00	Not Mon	**Goods Sheffield to Huskisson 00.50** Dore W Jcn 19.41 Chinley N Jcn 21.18 New Mills Goods Jcn 21.41 Heaton Mersey Sdgs 22.25 Skelton Jcn 22.40 Halewood Sdgs 00.05 Walton 00.25/ 00.45. Runs to Aintree Jcn when req Wed to Sat mornings to fetch traffic
(20.40)		**Express Goods Heaton Mersey Sdgs 19.15 to Staveley** Chinley 20.21 Dore 21.20
20.55 21.02		**Mineral Peak Forest Stn 19.50 to Sheffield** Chapel 20.02/ 20.30 Chinley S Jcn 20.40 Hope 21.16 attaches when req Dore 21.47

ARR DEP	DAY	DETAILS 1898
21.00 21.17	Not Sat	**Express Goods Huskisson 17.35 to Sheffield** Engine leaves Walton shed at 17.00 with guard who signs in at 16.35 and runs light to Alexandra. Halewood Sdgs 18.25 attaches important traffic for Midland system at Knotty Ash when req Warrington 18.58 Heaton Mersey Sdgs 19.40/ 19.52 water Romiley 20.15 Edale where becomes Class B & changes lights and marshals as follows – brake, wagons for Leeds & beyond, wagons for Sheffield, Doncaster and other stns, engine. Dore 21.57 conveys wagons for north of Sheffield, York and North east line in preference if less than 30 wagons of north traffic on leaving Halewood will be made up with Sheffield's
21.25 21.46	Mon	**Mineral Staveley to Heaton Mersey Sdgs 23.15** Dore 20.29 Gowhole Goods Jcn 22.25 to detach coal for New Mills
21.26 21.40	Not Mon	**Mineral Staveley to Heaton Mersey Sdgs 22.45** Dore 20.29 Gowhole Goods Jcn 22.10 to detach coal for New Mills
21.46 22.00		**Mineral Chapeltown to Huskisson 01.50** Dore 20.49 Heaton Mersey Sdgs 23.05 water. Stops when req Sat to unload and attach traffic for Walton only. Glazebrook 23.55 Halewood Sdgs 00.40/ 01.00 Walton 01.25/ 01.45
22.27	Sat	**Express Goods Hyde to Edale** Romiley 20.55 New Mills Pass 21.14 attaches only New Mills Goods Jcn 21.35 Chinley 22.10 attaches north wagons only
22.40 22.50	Sat	**Express goods Leeds to Huskisson 02.10** Dore 21.57 Stockport 23.36 Heaton Mersey 00.00 Warrington 00.40/ 00.50 Halewood Sdgs 01.30 Walton 01.50/ 02.05
23.00 23.40	Sat	**Express Goods Huskisson 19.05 to Leeds** Halewood Sdgs 19.30/20.20 Heaton Mersey Sdgs 21.30/ 21.55 water Romiley 22.17 Dore 00.20
23.04 23.23	Not Sat	**Express Goods Heaton Mersey Sdgs to Leeds** Waits when req for arrival of Leeds & Bradford meat on 18.35 from Birkenhead & when conveying this train or fruit runs passenger line New Mills to Gowhole Jcn. Limited to 25 wagons. Runs under meat regulations to Chinley E Jcn when become Class A regulations and does not stop at Edale. When Mr Wignell, Stockport is advised that there are 6 wagons or more of meat for Leeds & Bradford on 18.35 or special from Birkenhead 21.55 ex Heaton Mersey leaves to time with traffic which has left Birkenhead up to and including 17.45 train and a special is run with meat off 18.35 & a special from Birkenhead under same regulations as 21.55 ex Heaton Mersey not stopping en route to attach, Dore 23.55
23.15 23.40	Not Sat	**Express Goods Huskisson 20.00 to Leeds** Halewood 20.50 Heaton Mersey Sdgs 22.00/ 22.15 water Edale change from Class C to B, Dore 00.20
23.27	Not Sat	**Express Goods Ancoats 22.10 to Bradford** Engine leaves shed coupled to 22.30 Rowsley & 22.45 York engines. Ashton Road attaches only for Leeds & Bradford 5 mins allowed Bredbury attaches for Leeds & Bradford if req Cowburn Tunnel West 23.15 for examination Edale changed from Class B to C & change lights, Dore 02.07
23.46 23.55	Sat	**Express Goods Sheffield to Huskisson 03.05** Dore 22.57 Heaton Mersey Sdgs 00.55 Warrington 01.43/ 01.50 Halewood Sdgs 02.25 Walton 02.45/ 03.00

ARR DEP	DAY	DETAILS	1898
23.48	00.30	**Express Goods Ancoats 22.45 to York** Engine leaves shed coupled to engine of 22.10 Bradford and 22.30 Rowsley. Ancoats advises Pontefract by wire immediately it is known there is Pontefract skin traffic so that special arrangements can be made for receiving wagons. Wagons for D&C line to be placed next to engine, Romiley 23.05 Edale change from Class C to B. Dore 01.10	
23.52 00.05		**Goods Buxton to Edale** Peak Forest Station 22.35 Chapel 22.45 Edale Engine & Brake only run to Hope. On Sat engine runs light to Hope to turn	

PRIVATE OWNER WAGONS

Most of the freight traffic flow consisted of westbound coal and empties eastbound. Mineral trains could also convey 'other traffic'. Don Rowland, some thirty five years ago, said that the mix of wagons on the line would be LMS forty three, LNER thirty nine, GWR twelve and a half and SR five which leaves one half for 'other'. Another source who worked on the LNER pre-war said that they very rarely had a GWR or SR wagon in the yard. Coal was largely carried in private owner wagons. There is photographic evidence of private owner wagons from Barrow, Barnsley, Birley, Bolsover, John Brown, Clay Cross, Co-Operative Wholesale Society Manchester, Davies Coal & Coke Co (Llandudno), Firbeck Main, John Hadfield & Sons (Hope), Lowe Bros (Birch Vale), Markham Main, Pilsley, Stanton, Staveley and Thrutchley. Firbeck and Markham Main were part of Doncaster Amalgamated Collieries Ltd and so it is reasonable to suppose that Brodsworth, Bullcroft, Hickleton Main and Yorkshire Main also appeared, the wagons of these collieries being common user within the group. George Cooper of Hope, Noblett of Edale and Froggatt of Hathersage also had wagons at various times of which a drawing of a Cooper wagon appears in Vol. 2.

Dearne Valley Collieries are also reported to have sent coal over the line. In addition it is also reasonable to assume that Blackwell, New Hucknall, Shireoaks, Oxcroft, Grassmoor, Hardwick, Eckington and Sheepbridge collieries would also have been seen. The lime traffic from Peak Forest would have been in ICI and, perhaps, Dowlow wagons. A Webb wagon, from Cheltenham, is known to have gone to or from Hatfield Main Colliery to Colwyn Bay and was photographed at Buxton. It must have gone over the Hope valley line.

FREIGHT TRAFFIC PASSING THROUGH HATHERSAGE BETWEEN JULY AND SEPTEMBER 1914

Hathersage is the location chosen because many up and down freight trains stopped for water and to be examined, Hathersage being the main place where water was available between Dore and Chinley. Five minutes was the allowance for taking water and another three minutes for train examination although times could vary depending on the traffic requirements. Trains starting or terminating at Sheffield station or Grimesthorpe Sidings were not required to stop. The time stated is the arrival time. W = Water and * = examination. As before, a single time indicates the passing time at Hathersage. All mineral trains terminating or calling at Gowhole had to be

This is why Hathersage was the favoured watering hole for steam locomotives. Here is the pillar water column on the down side, just off the end of the wooden platform looking toward Chinley. A standard Midland design although the top does not have the shallow pointed cap which was more common. Set in brickwork it has the brazier for preventing the water from freezing when the temperature fell below zero still present in this post steam view from Jun 1969. Another non-standard feature is the suspended gas light as many were built with a gas lamp moulded at the top. The column's colour in the 1907 to 1922 period was a light canary yellow. Another one of identical design was located at the east end of the up platform. They were not located in lie by sidings which explains why the sharp timing of five minutes was allowed for watering since the main line was occupied whilst it was taking place. *M. A. King*

marshalled with wagons for the LYR, Liverpool, Partington, other CLC stations and Belle Vue locomotive department in that order. Gowhole was closed on Sundays from 14.00 to 06.00 on Monday and mineral trains had to be made up with through traffic only between these times. All trains that finished at Grindleford from Sheffield and finished at Edale, Hope or Bamford from Chinley are included for completeness. Also included are seasonal trains but excursion traffic has been listed separately. Information for June (before this timetable became operative) and Jul 1914 has been traced and excursions ceased from August onwards because of the threat of war.

ARR DEP	DAY	DETAILS	1914
(00.04)	Not Sat	**Through Freight Staveley 20.50 to Cheadle Ex Sdgs 07.47** Gowhole 00.49/ 05.00. Cheadle Heath 07.28/ 07.42	
00.05 *	Sat	**Empties Cheadle Ex Sdgs 21.30 to Staveley** Gowhole 22.05/ 22.50 Queens Road 00.43/ 01.20 Wincobank Sdgs 02.25 Holmes 02.30 by 'Old Road'	
00.25	Sat	**Through Freight Huskisson 20.00 to Hunslet Sdgs 05.06** Walton 20.07/20.20 Halewood 20.53 Warrington 21.22/ 21.40 Edale 23.55 Queens Road 00.53/ 01.32 Engine Shed Sdgs 02.05 to attach & detach Wincobank Sdgs 02.30 Masboro 02.35/ 02.47 where becomes mineral Carlton Ex Sdgs 03.29/ 03.47 Oakenshaw 04.09/ 04.29	
(00.27)	Sat	**Mineral Grimesthorpe Sdgs 23.30 to Gowhole 01.21**	
00.40 W	Not Sat	**Express Freight Huskisson 20.00 to Hunslet Sdgs 03.14** Walton 20.07/ 20.20 Halewood 20.53 Padgate Jcn 21.21/ 21.25 Cheadle Ex Sdgs 22.01/ 23.15 water New Mills S Jcn 23.48 via Chapeltown & Cudworth Carlton Ex Sdgs 01.40/ 02.36	
01.02 *	Not Mon Sat	**Express Freight Ancoats 22.45 to York Goods 04.15** Gowhole 23.20/ 00.10 Bamford 01.07 Masboro 01.36/ 02.00 water, Bolton on Dearne 02.55 Frickley 03.06	
01.06 W	Not Mon	**No 2 Fitted Freight Somers Town 20.15 to Ancoats 02.25** Dore W Jcn 00.46 Gowhole 01.43/ 01.53 Romiley 02.02 Ashton Road 02.20	
01.15 *	Not Sat	**Through Freight Trafford Park Sdgs 22.00 to Masboro 02.35** Cheadle Heath Sdgs 22.35/ 22.40 Chinley 23.25/ 23.35 Bamford 01.02 Dore 01.35/ 01.45 Queens Road 01.55/ 02.20. Runs Light Engine & Brake to Grimesthorpe shed from Masboro	
01.29 *	Not Mon	**Express Freight Stourton 20.12 to Huskisson 05.20** Cudworth 22.56 attaches fruit & veg from Hull (HBR) & import fruit from Dewsbury, Dore 00.41/ 00.59 Gowhole 02.38/ 02.55 Cheadle Heath Sdgs 03.00/ 03.10 Cheadle Ex Sdgs 03.13/ 03.19 Walton 04.47/ 05.15	
01.42 W	Not Mon Sat	**Through Freight Cheadle Ex Sdgs 23.00 to Horns Bridge 06.31** Gowhole 23.36/ 00.43 Queens Road 02.13/ 05.00 when req Runs Engine & Brake to Pond Street to work fitted vans off express parcels St Pancras 21.40 to Queens Road, Millhouses 05.15 Beauchief 05.38 Dronfield 06.13 Runs passenger line from Tapton Jcn to Horns Bridge where crosses over to goods yard	
01.46 W *	Not Mon	**Express Freight Manningham 20.55 to Ancoats** Cudworth 23.43 water, Sheffield Stn 00.26/ 00.36 Gowhole 02.38/ 02.55	
02.40 W	Inc Sun	**Empties Buxton 00.05 to Blackwell Sdgs 05.10** Peak Forest Stn Sun only, Chesterfield 03.30/ 04.10 Avenue 04.45	
02.53 W	Sun	**Empties Hartford 22.25 to Kirkby** Northwich 22.35/ 23.10 Skelton Jcn 23.55/ 00.05 Cheadle Ex Sdgs 00.15/ 00.20 water Chesterfield 03.42/ 04.15 Avenue 04.50 Pye Bridge 05.25	
03.01 W	Not Mon	**No 2 Fitted Freight Somers Town 22.15 to Brunswick 05.50** Carries No. 3 head lamps to Gowhole 03.38/ 04.05 water now Express Freight Cheadle Ex Sdgs 04.30/ 04.40	
03.10 W	Not Mon	**No 2 Fitted Freight Somers Town 22.30 to Ancoats 04.20** These two trains above could be combined when total not more than 40 wagons & double headed to Gowhole where train split into two parts for Brunswick and Ancoats	

ARR DEP	DAY	DETAILS	1914
03.10 *	Not Mon	**Empties Buxton 01.00 to Blackwell Sdgs 05.10** Bamford 02.55 Chesterfield 03.52/ 04.40 Clay Cross 04.55	
03.16 *	Sat	**Mineral Tibshelf Sdgs 00.40 to Heaton Mersey Sdgs 06.10** Chesterfield 01.10/ 01.46 water, Gowhole 04.20/ 05.10 Portwood Sdgs 06.05	
03.28 *	Wed Thu Fri	**Through Freight York Goods 22.40 to Ancoats 07.05** Masboro 01.37/ 01.42 water Dore 02.35/ 02.58 Gowhole 04.28/ 06.20	
	Sat	**Through Freight York Goods 22.40 to Wicker 02.10** Masboro 01.37/ 01.42 water	
03.30	Not Mon	**Through Freight Gowhole 02.35 to Chesterfield 04.10** Hathersage detaches traffic for north. Engine & Brake to Hasland 04.55	
03.47 *	Not Mon	**Mineral Staveley 02.20 to Gowhole 04.45** Dore W Jcn 03.05/ 03.15	
03.53	As Req	**Mineral Roundwood 02.15 to Brunswick 08.00** Gowhole 04.55/ 05.03 water, Cheadle Ex Sdgs 05.35/ 05.43 Halewood Sdgs 07.40	
04.05 *	Sun	**Through Freight Manningham 21.05 to Ancoats 06.05** Normanton 00.01 Carlton Ex Sdgs 00.21/ 02.05 Grimesthorpe Sdgs 03.17 Gowhole 04.50/ 05.18 Ashton Road 06.00	
04.06	Sat	**Mineral Pond Street 03.00 to Trafford Park Sdgs 06.20** Gowhole 05.05/ 05.20 Cheadle Heath 05.50	
04.10	Not Sat	**Through Freight Huskisson 22.15 to Wicker Goods 05.05** Walton 22.35 Halewood 23.05/ 23.55 Cheadle Ex Sdgs 01.02/ 01.35 water Gowhole 02.12/ 03.12 Hope 03.55 Queens Road 04.18/ 04.42 Engine Shed Sdgs 04.55	
04.11 W		**GNR Fitted Freight Brinsley Sdgs 02.55 to Deansgate 05.35** Chinley 04.48/ 04.49 where becomes Class 'A' Goods	
04.27 *	Not Mon	**Through Freight Cheadle Ex Sdgs 01.00 to Hunslet Sdgs 07.14** Gowhole 01.35/ 03.20 Edale 03.50 Hathersage attaches north traffic Masboro 05.10/ 05.25 to attach, Carlton Ex Sdgs 06.02/ 06.35	
04.31 *	Not Mon	**Mineral Sheffield 03.30 to Gowhole 05.35**	
04.47 *	Sun	**Through Freight Stourton Sdgs 02.00 to Huskisson 09.45** Normanton 02.25 Grimesthorpe Sdgs 03.52/ 04.07 Gowhole 05.43/ 06.30 Cheadle Heath Sdgs 07.05/ 07.20 Warrington 08.10/ 08.20 Halewood Sdgs 09.00 Walton 09.20/ 09.40	
05.00	Not Mon	**Mineral Grimesthorpe Sdgs 04.05 to Gowhole 06.00**	
05.03	Sun	**Through Freight Cheadle Heath Sdgs 03.05 to Hunslet Sdgs 08.44** Gowhole 03.40/ 04.10 Engine Shed Sdgs 06.05 Masboro 06.15/ 06.35 water Carlton Ex Sdgs 07.20/ 07.45 where becomes Mineral	
(05.19)	Sun	**Empties Gowhole 04.30 to Engine Shed Sdgs 06.10**	
05.25 *	Not Mon	**Mineral Morton Sdgs 03.20 to Cheadle Ex Sdgs** Clay Cross 03.42 to attach, Chesterfield 03.57/ 04.07 water, Queens Road 04.18/ 04.42 Gowhole 06.30/ 07.00	
05.31 05.40 *	Tue	**Through Freight York Goods 00.55 to Ancoats 07.35** Church Fenton 01.19 Swinton 03.35 Masboro 03.47/ 04.00 water Wincobank Sdgs 04.29 Wicker 04.46 Gowhole 06.35/ 06.51	
06.12 *	Not Mon	**Through Freight Heaton Mersey Sdgs 00.30 to Avenue Sdgs 07.45** Gowhole 01.10/ 04.15 Dore S Jcn 06.28/ 06.55 Chesterfield 07.10/ 07.35	
06.25 *	Not Mon Sat	**Mineral Tibshelf 03.30 to Heaton Mersey Sdgs 09.10** Clay Cross 03.47/ 03.55 Avenue Sdgs 04.05 to attach & detach Chesterfield 04.25/ 05.05 water Dore W Jcn 05.55/ 05.57 Gowhole 07.23/ 08.15 Portwood Sdgs 09.00	

259

ARR DEP	DAY	DETAILS	1914
07.05 *	Not Mon	**Mineral Avenue Sdgs 05.00 to Water Works Sdgs 07.19** Chesterfield 05.10/ 05.35. Returns Engine & Brake to work further trip if necessary	
07.05	Mon	**Mineral Avenue Sdgs 07.00 to Water Works Sdgs 09.19.** Runs to Heeley if required	
07.05 *	Sun	**Mineral Stourton Sdgs 03.00 to Cheadle Ex Sdgs 09.20** Oakenshaw 03.55/ 04.05 Carlton Ex Sdgs 04.24/ 04.44 Masboro 05.27/ 05.42 Grimesthorpe Sdgs 06.02 Gowhole 08.04/ 08.45	
07.05 W	Mon	*Empties Cheadle Ex Sdgs 05.30 to Chesterfield 10.15* Sheffield Stn 07.40/ 07.44 Wincobank Sdgs 08.30 Masboro 08.40/ 09.05 Barrow Hill 09.40/ 10.00 Chesterfield 10.15/ 10.30. Light engine to Hasland 10.35	
07.24 W	Mon	**Mineral Morton Sdgs 05.10 to Cheadle Ex Sdgs 09.25** Gowhole 08.20/ 08.50	
07.25 *	Sun	**GNR Class 'B' Goods Brinsley Jcn 06.10 to Brunswick** Dore W Jcn 06.50/ 06.55. Load 34 wagons	
07.33 W	Not Mon	**Through Freight Stourton 03.25 to Cheadle Ex Sdgs 10.25** Gowhole 08.25/ 09.45	
07.33 W	Sat	**Through Freight Stourton 03.25 to Gowhole 08.40**	
08.06 *	Mon	**Mineral Clay Cross 05.30 to Gowhole 09.00** Avenue Sdgs 05.50 Chesterfield 06.00/ 06.25 Dore W Jcn 06.53/ 07.22	
08.20	Mon	**Empties Grimesthorpe Sdgs 06.40 to Buxton LNWR 10.55** Sheffield Stn 06.50/ 07.05 Hope 08.56 to detach Chapel 09.45/ 10.10 Peak Forest 10.35	
08.20 *	Sun	**Mineral GNR Class 'B' Goods Brinsley Jcn 07.08 to Deansgate 10.15** Cheadle Ex Sdgs 09.26/ 09.46	
08.30 W	Not Mon	*Empties Gowhole 07.15 to Wincobank Sdgs*	
08.38		**GNR Class 'B' Goods Brinsley Jcn 07.10 to Deansgate 10.15**	
08.45 *	Not Mon	*Empties Gowhole 07.25 to Staveley 11.18* Bamford 08.30 Grindleford 09.46 Dore 10.01 Dronfield 10.17 Dunston & Barlow to detach, Chesterfield 10.37/ 11.08	
09.19	Mon	**Mineral Grimesthorpe Sdgs 07.45 to Buxton LNW 11.53** Grimesthorpe Jcn 07.55/ 08.05 Dore 08.20/ 08.55 Edale 09.50 to detach Chapel 10.07/ 10.20 water Peak Forest Stn 11.25 Topley Pike to detach empties	
09.45	Not Mon	**Mineral Staveley 06.50 to Gowhole 11.05** Dore W Jcn 08.39/ 09.13. On Sat follows Chesterfield to Blackpool passenger	
09.47	Mon	**Mineral Grimesthorpe Sdgs 08.55 to Gowhole 11.05** Bamford 10.06	
10.00 W		*Empties Gowhole 08.40 to Engine Shed Sdgs 10.57* Edale 09.25 Dore 10.23/ 10.30 Sheffield Stn 10.47/ 10.50	
10.30		**Stopping Freight Grimesthorpe Sdgs 07.12 to Edale 12.50** Millhouses 08.45 Dore 08.53/ 09.31 Grindleford 10.00 Bamford 11.36 as req Water Works Sdgs 11.41/ 11.51 Hope 12.30	
10.55 *	Not Mon	**Mineral Tibshelf 08.15 to Gowhole 12.30** Avenue 08.47 Chesterfield 08.57/ 09.10 Dronfield 09.27 Dore 09.33 Queens Road 09.48/ 10.05 Dore 10.20 Hope 11.42	
10.55	Mon	**As above but Dore 10.00 then direct to Gowhole 11.25**	
11.52		**Mineral Grimesthorpe Sdgs 09.35 to Gowhole 12.50** Sheffield 09.45/ 10.00 Dore 10.17/ 10.28. Double headed if req	
12.10		**Mineral Grimesthorpe Sdgs 10.30 to Gowhole 13.10** Dore 10.55/ 11.46. Double headed Tue to Sat	

ARR DEP	DAY	DETAILS	1914
13.14		**Mineral Wicker Goods 11.20 to Gowhole 14.13** Dore 11.45/ 12.50 Grindleford 13.08 Bamford 13.18 Hope 13.23 Edale 13.43 Chinley 14.03	
13.20		**Mineral Wicker Goods 12.30 to Buxton** Dore 12.54/ 13.06	
13.35	Not Mon	*Mineral Buxton 11.30 to Engine Shed Sdgs 14.28* Peak Forest Stn 12.07 Bamford 13.30 Sheffield 14.11/ 14.20	
14.10	Mon	**Mineral Buxton 11.50 to Engine Shed Sdgs 15.08** Peak Forest Stn 12.45 Chapel 13.00/ 13.05 water, Bamford 14.05 Sheffield 14.47/14.55	
14.12	Mon	**Express Freight Broadheath LNWR 12.00 to Masboro Stn 15.11** Cheadle Ex Sdgs 12.25/ 12.45 water Queens Road 14.35/ 14.48 Chesterfield traffic is worked by shunter from Queens Road to Sheffield Stn thence by 16.50 passenger, LNWR brake works through to Masboro	
14.21 W	Not Mon	*Empties Gowhole 13.20 to Staveley 15.30* Bamford 14.04 Unstone 14.58 Chesterfield 15.09	
14.30		*Empties Gowhole 13.30 to Holmes 16.05* Bamford 14.25 to attach, Grindleford 15.14 Sheffield 15.38/ 15.44 Engine Shed Sdgs 16.00	
14.38 *		**Mineral Staveley 12.00 to Heaton Mersey Sdgs 17.30** Chesterfield 13.20 Dronfield 13.45 Dore 14.07 Gowhole 15.33/ 16.25 Portwood Sdgs 17.20. Follows 11.45 from Avenue on Sat (below)	
14.45		**Mineral Avenue 11.45 to Gowhole 16.23** Chesterfield 11.55/ 12.40 Dore 13.10/ 13.51 Grindleford 14.20 carries stopping freight to Edale, Bamford 15.05 Hope 15.30 Edale 16.00. Precedes 12.00 from Staveley (above)	
15.21 *		*Empties Gowhole 13.50 to Blackwell Sdgs 16.30*	
15.41 W		*Empties Heaton Mersey Sdgs 12.00 to Staveley 16.42* Portwood Sdgs 12.45 Gowhole 13.15/ 14.10 Edale 14.53 Bamford 15.24 Dore S Jcn 15.56/ 16.08 Tapton Jcn 16.32. All wagons marshalled in proper order with Staveley wagons next to engine	
15.50	Mon	*Empties Gowhole 14.30 to Engine Shed Sdgs 16.40* Edale 15.15 Grindleford 15.58 Sheffield Stn 16.28/ 16.33	
16.10		*Stopping Freight Edale 13.10 to Grindleford 16.15* Hope 14.00 Bamford 14.50	
16.12 *		**Mineral Tibshelf 13.00 to Gowhole 17.10** Avenue 14.00 Chesterfield N Sdgs 14.10/ 14.45 Dore W Jcn 15.25/ 15.40. Double headed	
16.40	Not Mon	**Mineral Buxton LNWR 13.40 to Engine Shed Sdgs 17.40** Peak Forest 14.45 Chapel 15.00/ 15.05 water Bamford 16.35 Dore 17.03 Sheffield 17.19/ 17.30	
16.42	Thu Sat	**Mineral Grimesthorpe Sdgs 15.50 to Buxton** Bamford 16.58. Follows 16.10 passenger from Sheffield	
17.25		**Stopping Freight Grindleford 17.20 to Hathersage** Shunts at Grindleford	
17.33		*Empties Gowhole 15.15 to Wincobank Sdgs 18.40* Bamford 16.52 Sheffield 18.08/ 18.25. Shunts as req Thu & Sat for 16.50 passenger Hope to Sheffield	
18.05		*Stopping Freight Hathersage 18.05 to Wincobank Sdgs 21.20* Millhouses 18.38 Sheffield 20.47/ 21.00	
18.08		**Mineral Grimesthorpe Sdgs 16.30 to Gowhole 19.35** Grindleford 17.43 Edale 19.08 Chinley 19.23	
19.04 *		**Mineral Staveley 18.08 to Cheadle Ex Sdgs 21.52** Tapton Jcn 17.38 Dronfield 18.20 Dore W Jcn 18.28/ 18.36 Edale 19.56 Gowhole 20.20/ 21.15	

260

ARR DEP	DAY	DETAILS	1914
19.41		***Empties Gowhole 17.30 to Avenue 20.50*** *Edale 18.45 Hope 19.00 for cattle, Grindleford 19.46 Chesterfield 20.37/ 20.45*	
19.49	Not Mon	**Mineral Grimesthorpe Sdgs 18.30 to Trafford Park Sdgs 00.35** Dore 19.10/ 19.25 Gowhole 20.47/ 23.40	
20.01 *	Sat	***GNR Class B Goods Deansgate 18.02 to Brinsley Jcn*** *Chinley 19.01/ 19.18 Dore 20.20*	
20.29		***Empties Gowhole 19.00 to Blackwell Sdgs 22.20*** *Chinley 19.08/ 19.23 Hope 20.15 Dronfield 21.10 to attach, Chesterfield 21.25/ 21.40 Clay Cross 21.55 Coney Green Sdgs 22.00*	
21.11 *	Not Mon	**Mineral Grimesthorpe Sdgs 19.50 to Huskisson 02.25** Bamford 21.27 Gowhole 22.30/ 23.20 Cheadle Ex Sdgs 23.55/ 00.10 Halewood Sdgs 01.20/ 01.35 Walton 02.20	
21.11	Mon	**As above** but terminates at **Cheadle Ex Sdgs 23.55**	
21.49	Not Sat	***Mineral Avenue 20.30 to Gowhole 22.50*** *Chesterfield 20.40/ 21.00*	
21.50	Sat	***Express Freight Ancoats 20.10 to Manningham 04.47*** *Romiley 20.37 Chinley 21.06/ 21.10 Edale 21.26 Masboro 22.25/ 01.00 when becomes mineral, Carlton Ex Sdgs 011.45/ 02.03 detaches wagons for Oakenshaw and Normanton, Hunslet Sdgs 03.00/ 03.55 Shipley 04.37 where detaches skins when required*	
22.08 W		***GNR Class 'A' Goods Brunswick to Brinsley Sdgs*** *23.21 Heaton Mersey Sdgs 20.25 Romiley 21.00 Dore S Jcn 22.20/ 22.26 Clay Cross 23.00. 33 wagon limit, 34 on Sat*	
22.16	Not Sat	**Express Freight Huskisson 17.35 to Hunslet Sdgs 01.30** Walton 17.40/ 17.50 where picks up 10 wagons of soap, Cheadle Ex Sdgs 19.25/ 20.45 Gowhole 21.25 Sheffield Stn 22.42/ 22.45 Masboro 22.57/ 23.55 where marshals train and detaches York line traffic, Carlton Ex Sdgs 00.26/ 00.43 Normanton 01.13	
22.16	Sat	**As above** but terminates **Masboro 22.57**	
22.35 W	Not Sat	***GNR Class 'A' Goods Deansgate 20.46 to Brinsley Sdgs 23.40*** *Gowhole 21.34/ 21.38 Chesterfield 23.13 Clay Cross 23.20*	
22.48	Sat	***Empties Gowhole 21.30 to Engine Shed Sdgs 23.45*** *Edale 22.10 Hope 22.37 Sheffield 23.27/ 23.35*	
23.08	Not Sat	**GNR Express Freight Deansgate 21.18 to Brinsley Sdgs 00.11**	
23.12 W	Sat only	***Through Freight Staveley 21.25 to Cheadle Ex Sdgs 01.02*** *Gowhole 00.10/ 00.30*	
23.12		***Empties Gowhole 22.20 to Engine Shed Sdgs 00.00*** *Grindleford 23.23*	
23.18	Not Sat	**Express Freight Ancoats 21.30 to Manningham 04.44** Romiley 22.08 Edale 22.50 Sheffield 23.45/ 23.50 Cudworth 00.29/ 00.32 Carlton Ex Sdgs 00.36/ 01.23 St John's Colliery 01.50 Normanton 01.54 detaches Hull traffic Hunslet 02.14/ 03.50 Wortley Jcn 04.13	
23.41 W *	Not Sat	***Fitted Freight No. 3 Brunswick 19.35 to St Pancras Goods 05.10*** *Warrington 20.15/ 20.34 Cheadle Ex Sdgs 21.15/ 22.00 Cheadle Heath 22.03/ 22.13 New Mills S Jcn 22.50 Dore S Jcn 23.55/ 00.05 Clay Cross 00.26/ 00.30 Pye Bridge Jcn 00.48 Trent 01.10/ 01.17 Leicester 01.50/ 01.58 Irchester 02.58 Bedford 03.19/ 03.27 West End Sdgs 04.44/ 05.00*	
23.49	Not Sat	**Through Freight Wicker Goods 22.15 to Huskisson 07.20** Grimesthorpe Sdgs 23.08 Gowhole 00.34/ 04.34 Cheadle Heath Sdgs 05.00/ 05.15 Warrington 05.58/ 06.08 Walton 06.54/ 07.15	

ARR DEP	DAY	DETAILS	1914
23.49	Sat	**As above** but terminates **Gowhole 00.34**	
23.53 W*	Not Sat	***Express No. 3 Fitted Freight Ancoats 22.05 to St Pancras Goods 05.35*** *Ashton Road 22.35 Dore S Jcn 00.17/ 00.23 Chesterfield 00.38 Clay Cross 00.45 Trent 01.21/ 01.23 Leicester 01.56/ 02.04 water, Irchester 03.06 Bedford 03.14/ 03.38 St Albans 04.26/ 04.36 West End Sdgs 05.13/ 05.25*	

FREIGHT TRAFFIC PASSING THROUGH HATHERSAGE FROM 11 JUL 1927 UNTIL FURTHER NOTICE

Again Hathersage has been chosen because of its location as a watering hole. The Sectional Appendix instruction regarding Hathersage was – 'All up and down freight, mineral and empty wagon trains, except those starting from or terminating at Sheffield or up trains that have been examined at Grimesthorpe Sidings, must stop at Hathersage for the purpose of greasing but between 15.15 and 18.30 guards must look round their trains and do what greasing is necessary.' Under the arrival time 'W' indicates a stop to take water, five minutes being allowed. An asterisk '*' indicates the train will stop to shunt for or follow other trains. If only one time is listed for Hathersage then this is the passing time. Trains starting at Grindleford in an easterly direction and Bamford, Hope and Edale in a westerly direction are included for completeness with the time at the respective station in brackets. The type of train eg 'Express Freight', starting place with departure time and destination with arrival time are listed first and highlighted. Days not run between Monday and Saturday and specific days are listed; trains that only ran as required 'As Req' and services that are suspended 'Susp' are also included. Stops on the way are then listed, together with motive power arrangements eg double heading. Two different times indicate arrival and departure times and entries in italics are up (eastbound) trains and in normal font down (westbound) trains. As before a single time indicates the passing time at Hathersage.

It is noticeable that a number of trains are suspended, usually on specific days, and as many as eighteen workings only run as required which indicates that the dramatic increase in road haulage during the 1920s was taking its toll.

ARR DEP	DAY	DETAILS	1927
00.10 00.25 W	Not Mon Sat	**Express Freight Huskisson 20.00 to Hunslet Sdgs 03.02** Queens Road 00.48/ 01.02 Cudworth 01.46/ 01.51 water	
00.10 00.25 W	Sat	**Express Freight Huskisson 20.00 to Masboro Stn 01.28** Walton 20.07/ 20.25 to attach, Sankey Jcn 21.08/ 21.28 Cheadle Ex Sdgs 22.20/ 22.45 water, Queens Road 00.48/ 01.02	
(00.10)	Sun	**Through Freight Grimesthorpe 23.28 to Huskisson 06.32** Sheffield 23.36 New Mills S Jcn 02.45 Cheadle Ex Sdgs 03.18/ 03.53 water, Walton 06.22/ 06.27	
00.10 00.26 W	Mon	**Express Freight Huskisson 20.00 to Masboro Stn 01.28** Queens Road 00.48/ 01.02	
00.18 00.47 * W	Sat	***Empties Cheadle Sdgs 21.30 to Staveley*** *New Mills S Jcn 22.08 Gowhole 22.13/ 23.15*	
00.22 00.29 W	Sun	***Empties St Mary's 22.05 to Brunswick*** *Trowell 22.41, Heanor Jcn 23.00 New Mills S Jcn 23.28. Conveys empty vans. Signalled 'Express Freight'*	

ARR DEP	DAY	DETAILS 1927
00.30 00.40 *W	Not Sat	**Fitted Freight Ancoats 22.45 to St Pancras** Gowhole 23.25/ 23.30 Chesterfield 01.11 Toton 01.53
00.30 00.40 *W	Sat	**Through Freight Staveley 21.58 to Heaton Mersey Sdgs 04.25** Masboro S Jcn 22.20 Grimesthorpe Sdgs 22.38/ 23.12 Queens Road 23.23/ 00.00 Gowhole 01.36/ 03.55 becomes Mineral, Romiley 04.13
00.58 01.06 *W	Sat Susp	**Express Freight Huskisson 19.20 to Hunslet Sdgs 03.15** Walton 19.27/ 19.48 to attach Cheadle Ex Sdgs 21.17/ 21.45 water New Mills S Jcn 22.22 Gowhole 22.25/ 00.10 Cudworth 02.09
00.59	Sun	**Empties Gowhole 00.12 to Staveley**
01.05 01.13 W	Sun	**Mineral Stourton 21.45 to Cheadle Ex Sdgs 04.30** Gowhole 02.15/ 03.45
01.13 01.21 *W	Not Mon	**Express Freight Trafford Park Sdgs 23.35 to Masboro Stn 02.50** Queens Road 01.44/ 02.32
01.16 01.24 *W	Not Mon	**Mineral Peterborough Spital Bridge 16.20 to Heaton Mersey Sdgs 03.10** Wisbech W. Jcn 16.30/ 16.50 Stamford 17.38/ 17.44 water Pilton Sdgs 18.06/ 18.38 Melton 20.02/ 20.12 Toton 21.40 Sandiacre 21.46/ 21.56 water Chesterfield N Sdgs 23.27/ 23.32 Totley Tunnel E 00.30/ 00.53 Dore W Jcn 01.15/ 01.24.
01.28 01.36 *W	Sun As req	**Empties Gowhole 00.25 to Wincobank Sdgs 02.30**
01.50 01.58 W	Sun	**Mineral Dronfield 01.10 to Gowhole 03.05** Light Engine 03.25 to Belle Vue Engine Shed box 04.00
01.51 01.59 *W		**Express Freight Edge Hill 21.15 to Sheffield City 05.17** Manchester Vic 23.59 Romiley 00.42/ 00.48 for examination Queens Road 02.24/ 04.52 Nunnery Main Line Jcn 05.01 Nunnery Yard 05.10/ 05.12
02.06 02.18 *W	Not Mon As req	**Special Mineral Storrs Mill 00.05 to Brunswick 07.10** Holmes Jcn 00.40/ 00.50 to attach assisting engine when req Harrison & Camms 00.55 Sheffield Stn 01.08/ 01.18 water Cheadle Heath Sdgs 04.05/ 04.15 Cheadle Ex Sdgs 04.20/ 04.45
02.06 02.14 *W	Not Sat	**Through Freight Cheadle Ex Sdgs 23.00 to Queens Road 02.40** New Mills S Jcn 23.38 Gowhole 00.03/ 00.45 Bamford 01.34/ 02.00 Engine & Brake 03.00 Sheffield Stn 03.05
02.24 02.32 *W	Sun	**Express Freight Huskisson 20.58 to Hunslet Sdgs 04.32** Gowhole 00.36/ 01.36 Chapeltown 03.17 Cudworth 03.35
02.28	Sun	**Through Freight Gowhole 01.40 to Stanton Gate 04.55** Hasland 03.40/ 03.42 to change trainmen Stanton Gate N 04.38. Light engine to Toton 05.05
02.44 02.52 *W	Not Mon	**Express Freight Stourton 00.15 to Huskisson 07.50** Cudworth 01.19 Chapeltown 01.42 Sheffield Stn 02.01/ 02.06 water, Gowhole 03.40/ 04.25 becomes Through Freight, Cheadle Heath Sdgs 04.53/ 05.03 Cheadle Ex Sdgs 05.07/ 05.22 water, Walton 07.13/ 07.43
02.46 02.53	Sun	**Through Freight Toton 00.35 to Gowhole 03.53** Trowell 00.47 Chesterfield 01.50 to change engines or enginemen
02.48 02.56 *W	Sun	**Mineral Stourton 23.15 to Cheadle Ex Sdgs 06.05** Holmes Jcn 01.35/ 01.43 Gowhole 03.53/ 04.28 New Mills S Jcn 04.33

ARR DEP	DAY	DETAILS 1927
02.46 02.54 *W	Not Mon	**Express Freight Cheadle Heath Sdgs 00.40 to Hunslet Down Sdgs 05.32** Light engine Heaton Mersey shed 00.10 Masboro Stn 03.31/ 03.35 water, Carlton Ex Sdgs 04.35/ 04.50
02.49 02.56 W	Sun	**Through Freight Cheadle Ex Sdgs 00.42 to Carlton Ex Sdgs** Gowhole 01.30/ 02.00 Sheffield 03.25/ 03.42 water Grimesthorpe Jcn No. 1 03.52/ 03.54 to change engine or trainmen Masboro Stn 04.30
02.59 03.04 *W	Wed As req	**Express Freight Ship Canal Sdgs 00.15 to Queens Road 03.30** Manchester Vic 00.36 Phillips Park Sdgs 00.48/ 01.08 Midland Jcn 01.15/ 01.25. Midland Engines & men
03.12 03.22 W		**Fitted Freight Somers Town 22.00 to Ancoats 04.35** Dore W Jcn 02.56 Gowhole 03.59/ 04.10
03.22	Sun	**Through Freight Gowhole 02.30 to Chesterfield**
03.26 03.34 *W	Not Mon Tue As req	**Empties Brunswick 01.55 to Storrs Mill Jcn 05.36** Halewood Sdgs 02.45/ 02.48 Dore 03.57 Sheffield Stn 04.30/ 04.42 water Holmes Jcn 04.57
03.26 03.34 *W	Sun As req	**Empties Brunswick 23.25 to Masboro Stn 04.50** Halewood Sdgs 00.00/ 00.03 Cheadle Ex Sdgs 01.28/ 01.48 water Sheffield Stn 04.12/ 04.17 water, Harrison & Camm 04.38/ 04.45
03.33 03.39 *W	Not Mon	**LNER Fitted Freight Kings Cross 20.30 to Deansgate** Dore S Jcn 03.18 Chinley 04.14 for examination when becomes Class 'A' freight
03.42 03.50 W	Sun	**Mineral Wincobank 02.40 to Gowhole 04.55**
03.52 03.57	Not Mon	**Mineral Holmes Jcn 01.48 to Gowhole 04.58** Light Engine Masboro Stn 01.17 to Holmes Jcn 01.44
03.52 03.57 *W	Not Mon As req	**Light Engine Chinley 03.11 to Grimesthorpe**
03.58 04.35 *W	Sun	**Through Freight Gowhole 02.55 to Hasland**
04.12 04.22 *	Not Mon	**Mineral Staveley 02.20 to Gowhole 05.25** Totley Tunnel E 03.48
04.15 04.25 W		**Through Freight Huskisson 21.45 to Wincobank Sdgs 05.47** Walton 21.52/ 22.13 Cheadle Ex Sdgs 23.48/ 00.25 water Gowhole 01.05/ 03.28
04.17 04.25 *W	Not Mon	**Through Freight Huskisson 21.45 to Engine Shed Sdgs 05.40** Queens Road 04.50/ 05.32
04.18 04.28 *W	Sun	**Express Freight Somers Town 22.00 to Ancoats 06.10** Fitted Freight to Syston
04.22 04.30	Sun	**Through Freight Huskisson 21.45 to Engine Shed Sdgs 05.10** Walton 22.30/ 22.48 Halewood Sdgs 23.15/ 23.30 Cheadle Ex Sdgs 00.50/ 01.18 water, Gowhole 02.02/ 03.30.
04.33 04.41 *W	Not Mon	**Through Freight Gowhole 03.05 to Chesterfield 05.55** Bamford 04.03/ 04.26 Tapton Jcn 05.37. Engine & Brake to Hasland 06.03
04.33 04.41 *W	Sat	**As Above** but Dronfield Colliery Sdgs 05.31 Tapton Jcn 05.44
04.52 05.00 W	Sun	**Fitted Freight Somers Town 22.00 to Ancoats 07.00** Gowhole 06.15/ 06.20. Express Freight from Gowhole.

ARR DEP	DAY	DETAILS	1927
05.03 05.13 *	Not Mon	Mineral Grimesthorpe 04.00 to Gowhole 06.18	
05.03 05.08 * W	Not Mon As req	**Empties Heaton Mersey 02.55 to Staveley** Bamford 04.35/ 04.55 Chesterfield 05.40. Engine & Brake to Hasland 05.48	
05.10	Sun	Mineral Grimesthorpe 04.17 to Buxton	
05.27 05.35 * W	Not Mon Susp Fri	**Through Freight Heaton Mersey 01.40 to Avenue 07.10** George's Rd 01. 45 Romiley 02.00 Gowhole 02.42/ 03.45 Edale 04.20/ 04.30 Hope 04.45/ 05.04 Bamford 05.11/ 05.21 Chesterfield 07.00	
05.32 05.45 W	Not Mon	Mineral Stourton 02.00 to Cheadle Ex Sdgs 08.30 Cudworth 03.27 Elsecar & Hoyland 03.52/ 03.55 Grimesthorpe Sdgs 04.28/ 04.38 double headed when req Hathersage to detach only Gowhole 06.45/ 07.40 Cheadle Heath Sdgs 08.15/ 08.25	
05.34	Sun	**Through Freight Toton 03.25 to Brindle Heath Down Sdgs 07.59** Trowell 03.38 Chesterfield 04.41 water Belle Vue Engine Shed Box 07.04 Colyhurst Street 07.22/ 07.27 Manchester Vic 07.34/ 07.42	
05.47 05.52 * W	Not Mon As req	**Light Engine Gowhole 05.05 to Grimesthorpe** After assisting 01.48 Holmes Jcn to Gowhole	
05.55 06.05 * W	Not Mon Susp Sat	Mineral Morton Sdgs 03.35 to Heaton Mersey Sdgs 10.15. Horns Bridge 05.23 Gowhole 07.10/ 09.30	
06.13 06.21 * W	Sun As req	**Empties Brunswick 01.55 to Masboro Stn 07.50** Chinley 05.18 Sheffield Stn 06.58/ 07.30 water	
06.15 06.21 * W	Not Mon As req	**Empties Brunswick 01.55 to Storrs Mill** Cheadle Ex Sdgs 04.10/ 04.35 Sheffield Stn 06.58/ 07.08 Holmes Jcn 07.26	
06.18	Not Mon	**Empties Ashton Road 02.50 to Hathersage** Romiley 03.30/ 03.45 New Mills Goods 04.20/ 04.25 Hope 05.37 Bamford 06.11	
06.30 07.00 * W	Not Mon	Mineral Tibshelf 04.50 to Heaton Mersey Sdgs 09.28 Horns Bridge 05.23	
06.30 07.00 * W	Sat Susp	Mineral Tibshelf 05.00 to Heaton Mersey Sdgs 09.28 Horns Bridge 05.23 Hope 07.15/ 07.30 Portwood Sdgs 08.46 Stockport 09.20	
06.30 07.00 * W	Mon	Mineral Morton Sdgs 05.00 to Heaton Mersey Sdgs 10.15 Gowhole 08.06/ 09.30	
06.33	Sun	*Mineral Gowhole 05.30 to Avenue 07.30*	
06.35 06.40 * W	Not Mon As req	**Light Engine Gowhole 05.28 to Staveley** After assisting 02.20 Staveley to Gowhole	
06.35	Sun	**Express Freight Toton 04.20 to Ancoats 08.40** Gowhole 07.52/ 07.55 to change engines or trainmen	
	As req	**Engine & Brake Bamford 06.40 to Gowhole 07.45** Hope 06.45/ 07.05 turn engine	
06.50	Sun	*Mineral Buxton Jcn No. 1 05.00 to Engine Shed Sdgs 07.31* Chinley E Jcn 06.05/ 06.10 to change trainmen	
07.10 07.20 * W	Mon Sat Susp As req	**Special Mineral Houghton Main Colliery 05.15 to Glazebrook Sdgs 11.35** Swinton 05.34 Holmes Jcn 05.55/ 06.05 water, Disley 08.35/ 09.12 Hazel Grove 09.28/ 09.58 Cheadle Ex Sdgs 10.18/ 11.00 water Skelton Jcn 11.18 Partington Jcn 11.30. Runs to Brunswick & double headed when req	

ARR DEP	DAY	DETAILS	1927
07.30 07.35 * W	Not Mon As req	*Light Engine Gowhole 06.17 to Grimesthorpe 08.28* New Mills S Jcn 06.50. After assisting 02.00 Leeds to Cheadle freight	
07.37 07.47 *	Not Mon	Mineral Staveley 06.27 to Gowhole 08.50 Double headed if req	
(07.57)	Sat Susp	Mineral Grimesthorpe Sdgs 07.05 to Gowhole 09.40 Edale 09.08	
08.03 08.24 * W	Not Mon Susp Sat	*Empties Gowhole 06.50 to Staveley*	
08.05 08.10 W	Sun	Light Engine Earle's Sdgs 07.50 to Hasland 08.56	
08.38	Sun	*Mineral Gowhole 07.35 to Engine Shed Sdgs 09.30*	
08.46 08.51 * W	Mon Susp	**Express Freight Adswood Sdgs 04.35 to Sheffield City 10.20** Peak Forest 07.48/ 07.53 Chapel 08.04/ 08.09 water Chinley E Jcn 08.14 Western Section 'A' engine and men to Queens Road 09.18/ 09.45 Midland men to City Goods, Sheffield Stn 09.49/ 09.54 water, Nunnery Main Line Jcn 09.59 Nunnery Yard 10.06/ 10.10.	
09.00 09.20 *	Mon	**Empties Gowhole 07.30 to Wincobank Sdgs 10.40** Bamford 08.30/ 08.52 Queens Rd 09.55/ 10.17 Sheffield Stn 10.22/ 10.27	
09.05	Sat Susp	Grimesthorpe 07.50 to Buxton LNW 12.15 Sheffield Stn 08.00/ 08.19 Bamford 09.13/ 09.28 Topley Pike 11.47/ 12.05 to change trainmen. Double headed when req	
09.14	Sun	Mineral Clay Cross 08.03 to Gowhole 10.16 Horns Bridge 08.53	
09.29 09.34 * W	As req	**Light Engine Chinley N Jcn 08.22 to Grimesthorpe 10.15** Hope 08.55/ 09.18. After assisting 05.15 Special Mineral Houghton to Glazebrook.	
09.35 09.42 * W	Mon	**Empties Cheadle Ex Sdgs 05.45 to Hasland 11.30** Gowhole 06.30/ 07.30 Edale 08.08/ 08.18 Hope 08.33/ 09.10 Bamford 09.17/ 09.27 Chesterfield 11.23. Worked by Heaton Mersey engine	
09.46 09.51 * W	Not Mon As req	*Light Engine Gowhole 08.57 to Staveley* Chinley 09.14. After assisting 06.27 Staveley to Gowhole	
09.53	Sun As req	Mineral Westhouses 08.20 to Gowhole 11.00 Light Engine 11.05 Belle Vue Engine Shed Box 11.38	
10.03 10.11 *		Mineral Tibshelf 08.20 to Gowhole 11.35 Bamford 10.22/ 10.40	
10.15 10.21	Sat As req	Mineral Tibshelf 08.20 to Gowhole 11.35 Bamford 10.28/ 10.40	
10.20 10.26 W		Mineral Grimesthorpe 09.25 to Gowhole 11.06 Chinley change engine or trainmen 11.00/ 11.02	
10.22 10.40 * W	Not Sat As req	Mineral Staveley 08.52 to Heaton Mersey Sdgs 12.50 New Mills S Jcn 12.12	
10.43	Sun	*Mineral Gowhole 09.40 to Avenue 11.50*	
10.46 11.06 W	Not Wed	**Stopping Freight Grimesthorpe 07.18 to Hope 12.00** Millhouses 07.38/ 08.40 Grindleford 09.34/ 10.40 Bamford 11.12/ 11.53	

263

ARR DEP	DAY	DETAILS	1927
10.46	Sat	**Stopping Freight Grimesthorpe 07.18 to Hathersage** Millhouses 07.38/ 08.40 Grindleford 09.34/ 10.40 wagons to beyond Hathersage detached & worked forward on 11.10 from Hasland later	
10.58		**Mineral Grimesthorpe 09.25 to Gowhole 12.15** Grindleford 10.32 Edale 11.30/ 11.46	
11.05	Not Sat	**Stopping Freight Hathersage to Wincobank Sdgs 12.50** Queens Road 11.35/ 12.05 Engine Shed Sdgs 12.20/ 12.40.	
11.26	Sun	*Mineral Gowhole 10.15 to Staveley*	
11.34 11.42 * W	Not Mon	*Empties Gowhole 10.30 to Staveley*	
11.38 12.08 * W		**Mineral Grimesthorpe 10.25 to Gowhole 13.10** Double Headed when required	
11.48	Sun	*Engine & Brake Gowhole 11.00 to Hasland 12.33*	
12.21 12.40 * W	Sat Susp	**Empties Gowhole 10.45 to Frickley Colliery Sdgs** Bamford 11.44/ 12.14 Sheffield Stn 13.17/ 13.23 Masboro Station 13.50	
12.22	Sun	*Mineral Gowhole 11.20 to Staveley* Dore South Jcn 13.16/ 13.47	
12.25 12.30 * W	Mon	**Mineral Tibshelf 10.20 to Heaton Mersey 14.08** Totley Tunnel E 12.00/ 12.02	
12.25 12.30 * W	Not Mon Susp	**Mineral Staveley 11.06 to Gowhole 13.34**	
12.30 12.40 * W	Sat	**Through Freight Staveley 09.58 to Heaton Mersey Sdgs 16.30** Masboro S Jcn 10.20 Grimesthorpe Sdgs 10.38/ 11.12 Queens Road 11.23/ 12.00 Gowhole 13.36/ 15.55 becomes Mineral	
12.32	Sun	*Mineral Staveley 11.13 to Gowhole 13.35*	
(12.38)		**Mineral Grimesthorpe 11.35 to Gowhole 13.42** Sheffield Stn 11.45/ 11.49 Hope 12.50/ 12.52 to change trainmen	
12.50	Sun	**Mineral Grimesthorpe 11.55 to Gowhole 14.05** Chinley 13.46/ 13.51 to change engine or trainmen	
13.07	Sun	*Mineral Gowhole 12.00 to Avenue 14.20* Light Engine Belle Vue Engine Shed Box 11.05 to Gowhole 11.45 Dore S Jcn 13.28/ 13.37	
13.18 14.05	Not Thu Sat	**Through Freight Hasland 11.10 to Gowhole 17.05** Grindleford 12.44 / 13.10 Bamford 14.15/ 14.27 Hope 14.35/ 17.50 Edale 16.20	
13.18 14.05	Thu Sat	**As Above** but Bamford 14.15/ 15.42 Edale 16.10/ 16.20	
13.36 13.55 *	Not Sat	**Mineral Staveley 12.00 to Gowhole 15.00** Double headed when req	
13.42 13.50 *	Not Sat	*Empties Gowhole 12.35 to Blackwell Sdgs 15.48* Dore S Jcn 14.13 Hasland 15.15/ 15.20	
13.50	Sun	**Mineral Avenue 12.45 to Earle's Sdgs 14.10** Engine & Brake Earle's Sdgs 14.50 to Gowhole 15.40	
13.51 13.59		*Express Freight Edge Hill 09.15 to Sheffield City Goods 17.17* Manchester Vic 11.59 Midland Jcn 12.17 Romiley 12.42/ 12.48 Queens Road 14.24/ 16.52 Nunnery Main Line Jcn 17.09 Nunnery Yard 17.10/ 17.12. Worked by Midland & LNW engines and men alternately	
14.06 14.14	Not Sat	*Through Freight Cheadle Sdgs 11.00 to Queens Road 14.40* Gowhole 12.03/ 12.45 Bamford 12.34/ 14.00	
14.10	Sun	**Mineral Staveley 13.00 to Gowhole 15.25**	

ARR DEP	DAY	DETAILS	1927
14.10 14.16 * W	Sat As req	**Mineral Buxton 11.45 to Grimesthorpe 15.03** Bamford 13.52/ 14.02	
14.10 14.16 * W	Not Sat As req	**Stopping Freight Hope 13.20 to Masboro Sorting Sdgs 16.45** Bamford 13.26/ 14.02 Grindleford 14.21 Dore 14.40/ 15.27 Wincobank Sdgs 15.55/ 16.30 Harrison & Camm 16.36	
14.15 14.25 * W	Sat Susp	**Staveley 12.00 to Gowhole 15.25** Double headed when required	
14.30 14.46 *	Sat Susp	**Mineral Avenue 13.15 to Gowhole 16.12** Bamford 14.54 / 15.16	
(15.10)	Thu	**As above**	
14.52 15.30 * W	Sat As req	**Light Engine Gowhole 13.48 to Grimesthorpe Shed** Edale 14.18/ 14.30. After assisting 10.25 Grimesthorpe to Gowhole	
15.08 15.38 *		***Empties Gowhole 13.30 to Frickley Colliery Sdgs 18.29*** Hope 14.20 Bamford 14.26/ 15.00 Hathersage Light Engine coupled to Grimesthorpe 16.22, Wincobank Sdgs 16.34 Harrison & Camms 17.10 Masboro Stn 17.20 water Wath Road Jcn 18.03	
15.12	Sun	**Mineral Empties Gowhole 14.00 to Wincobank Sdgs 16.05**	
15.21 15.26 * W	Not Mon	**Mineral Grimesthorpe 14.25 to Huskisson 21.50** Double headed to Gowhole 17.00/ 18.20 Cheadle Ex Sdgs 19.00/ 19.27 Partington traffic marshalled next to engine and detached Walton 21.18/ 21.43	
15.48 15.56 *		**Mineral Tibshelf Sdgs 13.40 to Gowhole 17.32** Edale 16.30/ 16.48 Chinley 17.10/ 17.12	
15.53	Sun	**Mineral Grimesthorpe 15.00 to Gowhole 17.08** Chinley 16.48/ 16.53 to change engines or trainmen	
16.06 16.11 * W	Sat	**Mineral Grimesthorpe 15.10 to Peak Forest S 17.22** Hope 16.26/ 16.43	
	Sat	**Mineral Grimesthorpe 14.40 to Grindleford 16.15** Bernard Road Sdgs 14.50/ 14.55. Uses Sheffield trip engine. The 'Muck' train	
16.22 16.50 *	Sun	*Mineral Empties Gowhole 15.15 to Staveley*	
(16.45)		*Empties Gowhole 15.00 to Wincobank Sdgs. 18.43* Cowburn Tunnel W 15.25/ 15.42 Hope 15.52.	
(16.45)	Mon	**As Above** but Edale 15.19 Bamford 16.18/ 16.38 Queens Road 17.50/ 18.28. Double headed	
16.53 17.14 *	Not Sat	**Mineral Grimesthorpe 15.38 to Gowhole 18.30** Totley Tunnel E 16.15/ 16.30. Double headed Tue	
16.53 17.00 *	Sat	**Mineral Grimesthorpe 15.38 to Trafford Park Sdgs 20.50** Totley Tunnel E 16.15/ 16.30 Gowhole 1830/ 19.40 New Mills S Jcn 19.45. Partington traffic marshalled next to engine	
17.02	Sun	**Mineral Avenue 15.55 to Gowhole 18.05** Light engine 18.35 Belle Vue Engine Shed Box 19.05	
		Empties Grindleford 17.20 to Grimesthorpe 18.43 Queens Road 17.50/ 18.28. The 'Muck' train	
17.20	Sun	**Mineral Empties Gowhole 16.15 to Wincobank Sdgs 18.10**	
17.22 17.30 *	Sat	*Empties Gowhole 16.20 to Staveley* Assisting engine of 12.00 Staveley to Gowhole returns coupled to this train	
(17.40)	Sat	*Engine & Brake from Gowhole 16.45 to Staveley*	

ARR DEP	DAY	DETAILS	1927
17.41 18.08		**Mineral Grimesthorpe 16.45 to Buxton 19.33** Hathersage change trainmen with 14.10 Buxton to Wincobank Sdgs, Chinley S Jcn 19.03	
17.50 18.20		**Mineral Buxton 14.10 to Wincobank Sdgs** *19.16* Hope 16.50 Bamford 17.43 Hathersage change trainmen with 16.45 Grimesthorpe to Buxton	
18.25 18.33 *	Not Sat	**Mineral Staveley 17.00 to Heaton Mersey 22.40** Gowhole 19.35/ 19.58 New Mills S Jcn 22.03. Double headed when req	
18.25 18.33 *	Sat	**Mineral Staveley 17.00 to Gowhole 19.35** Double headed when req	
18.27	Sun	**Mineral Empties Gowhole 17.20 to Staveley**	
18.48	Sun Susp	**Mineral Empties Gowhole 17.45 to Avenue 19.55**	
19.03 19.20	Sat Susp	**Empties Gowhole 17.35 to Sherwood Colliery Sdgs** Bamford 18.35/ 18.55 Hasland 20.23/ 20.26 to change engine or enginemen or both, Tibshelf S Jcn 20.56	
(19.10)		**Light Engine Gowhole 18.10 to Grimesthorpe** Coupled to 18.10 Gowhole to Avenue to Dore W Jcn 19.32/ 19.34. After assisting 15.10 Grimesthorpe to Huskisson	
(19.10)	Sat	**Engine & Brake Gowhole 18.25 to Hasland** Coupled to Light Engine Gowhole 18.10 to Grimesthorpe. Uncouples Dore W Jcn 19.30/19,36	
(19.10)	Sat Susp	**Empties Gowhole 18.10 to Avenue** Dore S Jcn 19.30/ 19.34	
19.27 19.46 * W	Not Mon Sat Susp	**Empties Brunswick 14.35 to Wincobank Sdgs** *20.38* Cheadle Ex Sdgs 16.22/ 16.50 water, Hazel Grove 17.13 New Mills S Jcn 18.14 Chinley N Jcn 18.39. As Req	
19.50 19.55 * W	As req	**Engine & Brake Gowhole 18.50 to Blackwell Sdgs** Edale 19.16/ 19.29. After working 13.40 Tibshelf to Gowhole	
20.00 20.10 * W	Not Mon Sat	**Mineral Grimesthorpe 19.05 to Trafford Park** *23.40* Gowhole 21.20/ 21.25 double headed to Gowhole as req, New Mills Goods 22.45 Throstle Nest S Jcn 23.31	
20.11 20.16 * W	Sat	**Mineral Grimesthorpe 19.05 to Gowhole 21.20** Double headed when req	
20.04 20.48 *	Tue Wed	**Empties Gowhole 19.00 to Blackwell Sdgs**	
20.11 20.48 *	Not Tue Wed	**As above** but Bamford 19.56/ 20.06.	
20.18	Sun	**Mineral Empties Gowhole 19.15 to Wincobank Sdgs 21.15** Sheffield 20.53/ 20.58	
20.50 21.00 * W	As req	**Light Engine Gowhole 19.46 to Staveley** Hope 20.11/ 20.24 Bamford 20.38 Grindleford 21.06/ 21.42. After assisting 17.00 Staveley to Heaton Mersey Sdgs	

ARR DEP	DAY	DETAILS	1927
21.10 21.20 W	Not Thu Sat	**Mineral Peak Forest 19.10 to Kilnhurst** Bamford 20.17/ 21.02 Queens Road 21.58/ 22.40 Sheffield Stn 22.46/ 22.53 water, Wincobank Sdgs 23.07/ 23.40 Harrison & Camm 23.45	
21.03 21.20 W	Thu Sat	**As above**	
		Empties Cheadle Ex Sdgs 19.00 to Bamford 21.05 Cheadle Heath Sdgs 19.08 Disley 19.54	
21.41 21.49 *	Sat As req	**Mineral Grimesthorpe 20.45 to Brunswick** *03.10* Disley 22.58/23.19 Cheadle Heath Sdgs 23.43/ 23.56 Cheadle Ex Sdgs 00.00/ 00.48 water, Halewood Sdgs 02.18/ 02.48 Hunts Cross W 02.51	
(21.48)		**Empties Gowhole 20.15 to Wincobank Sdgs** Bamford 21.25/ 21.40	
22.06 22.12 * W	Not Sat	**LNER Class A Goods Deansgate 20.25 to Brinsley Jcn Sdgs 23.40** New Mills S Jcn 21.17. Limited to 33 wagons	
	Not Sat	**Engine & Brake Bamford 22.10 to Gowhole 23.00**	
22.20 22.44 * W	Mon to Thu	**Through Freight Grimesthorpe 21.30 to Edge Hill** Gowhole 23.40/ 23.46 where picks up trainmen & sets them down at Belle Vue Engine Shed box 00.22/ 00.25, Midland Jcn 00.33 where becomes Express Freight Phillips Park Sdgs 00.38/ 00.43. Worked by Western & Midland Section engines & men alternately	
22.00 22.15 * W	Fri Sat	**As above** but Grimesthorpe 21.05 when required for season excursions	
22.37 22.42 * W	Not Mon As req	**Light Engine Gowhole 21.27 to Grimesthorpe** Cowburn Tunnel W 21.54/ 22.09 Dore 23.04. After assisting 19.05 Sheffield to Trafford Park	
22.54 23.12	Not Sat	**Through Freight Huskisson 17.15 to Wincobank Sdgs 00.04** Walton 17.22/43 Cheadle Ex Sdgs 19.20/ 20.15 Gowhole 20.55/ 21.50 Edale 22.28/ 22.42 where shunts when req for seasonal excursions	
23.12 23.20 *	Sat	**Empties Gowhole 22.10 to Staveley** Dore S Jcn 23.43	
23.26 23.38	Sat	**Empties Gowhole 23.30 to Engine Shed Sdgs**	
23.32 23.42 * W	Mon Susp	**Mineral Grimesthorpe 22.25 to Longsight** Sheffield Stn 22.40/ 22.45 Chinley S Jcn 01.13 Chapel 01.17/ 01.24 Buxton LNW 01.51. Worked by Western Section engine & men throughout	
23.50 23.58 * W		**Mineral Avenue 22.30 to Gowhole 01.00**	
23.50 00.03 *W	Not Sat	**Express Freight Ancoats 21.50 to Masboro 00.53** Gowhole 22.31/ 22.35 Queens Road 00.18 Sheffield Stn 00.39	

Ex-Midland 3F 0-6-0 No. 3742 of a class that first appeared in 1885 passes through Dore and Totley station heading for the Hope valley on 30 Apr 1932. Coal wagons predominate but mixed in is a covered wagon next to the engine a ventilated cattle van and an oil tanker. The home signals on the right await the arrival of an up train from Dore West Junction.
E. R. Morten

FREIGHT TRAFFIC PASSING THROUGH HATHERSAGE FROM 26 SEP 1938 UNTIL FURTHER NOTICE

ARR DEP	DAY	DETAILS 1938
00.03	Not Sat	**Empties Gowhole 22.30 to Engine Shed Sdgs 00.50** Chinley North Jcn 22.47 Edale 23.05 Bamford 23.26/ 23.56
00.03	Sat	**As above** but Chinley North Jcn 23.10 Edale 23.30. No stop at Bamford
00.07	Not Sat	**Express Freight Engine Shed Sdgs 23.20 to Huskisson 05.57** Gowhole 01.02/ 02.42 becomes Mineral but not on Mon, Cheadle Ex Sdgs 03.20/ 03.38 water, Skelton Jcn 03.58 Walton 05.20/ 05.50
00.18 00.50 *W	Sat	**Empties Cheadle Ex Sdgs 21.30 to Staveley**
00.46 00.51 *W		**Mineral Chesterfield 23.15 to Gowhole 01.52** Light Engine Hasland to Chesterfield 22.15. Dore West Jcn 23.50/ 00.20 Edale 01.23
01.05	Not Mon	**Through Freight Staveley 20.20 to Heaton Mersey Sdgs 03.50** Totley Tunnel East 22.30/ 00.42 Gowhole 02.08/ 03.12. Mineral from Gowhole
01.06 01.12 *W	Sat	**Through Mineral Freight Stourton 21.39 to Cheadle Sdgs 04.10** Storrs Mill where ceased to be Through Freight Holmes Jcn 23.37/ 23.39 Grimesthorpe Sdgs 23.50/ 00.50 water & shunt Chinley Stn 02.17/ 02.25 Gowhole 02.35/ 03.35 New Mills South Jcn 03.40
02.00	Not Mon	**Express Freight Edge Hill 21.45 to Sheffield City** Manchester Vic 00.09 Midland Jcn 00.19/ 00.28 Ancoats Jcn 00.32 Dore 02.16/ 02.19 Queens Road 02.28/ 02.44 as req Sheffield Stn 02.50/ 03.00 water Nunnery Main Line Jcn 03.03. Four fitted freight vehicles connected to next engine. Worked alternately by Midland & Western Divn engines & men
02.06 02.14 *W	Not Sat	**Through Freight Cheadle Ex Sdgs 23.00 to Queens Road 02.43** Light Engine leaves Heaton Mersey 22.30 Gowhole 00.03/ 00.45 Bamford 01.34/ 02.00 Queens Road 02.43
02.17 02.22 W	Susp Sat	**Mineral Westhouses 00.45 to Gowhole 03.22**
	Not Mon	**Mineral Buxton 23.10 to Hope 02.22** Peak Forest 00.20/ 01.10 Chapel 01.25/ 01.40
02.29	Sun	**Express Freight Edge Hill 21.15 to Queens Road 02.54** Manchester Vic 23.59 Phillips Park Sdgs 00.12/ 00.25 Belle Vue Engine Shed Box 00.38/ 00.40 change engine or men Gowhole 01.18/ 01.45. Light Engine 03.25 to Grimesthorpe Jcn 03.40
02.46 02.52 W	Not Mon Sat	**Through Freight Heaton Mersey Sdgs 00.02 to Carlton Sdgs** Gowhole 00.45/ 02.00 changes to Express Freight Sheffield Stn 03.19/ 03.30 water Masboro Stn 03.44/ 03.55
02.46 02.52 *W	Sat	**As above** but terminates **Hunslet Sdgs 06.22** Freight from Carlton Sdgs
02.46 02.54 *W	Sun	**Through Freight Cheadle Ex Sdgs 00.45 to Carlton Sdgs 05.12** Gowhole 01.25/ 02.00 changes to Express Freight Masboro Stn 03.54
	Not Mon	**Engine & Brake Edale 02.50 to Gowhole 03.35** After working ex Buxton 23.10. To work 05.10 Gowhole to Buxton
02.52 03.00 *W	Not Mon	**LNER Fitted Goods Kings Cross 20.30 to Deansgate 04.28** GN Jcn 01.40 Codnor Park Stn Jcn 01.43 Morton Sdgs 01.58 Chesterfield 02.12 Dronfield Colliery Sdgs 02.27 Throstle Nest South Jcn 04.20. Limited to 37 wagons

ARR DEP	DAY	DETAILS 1938
02.59 03.04 *W	Wed As Req	**Empty Freight Ship Canal Sdgs 00.15 to Queens Road 03.30** Manchester Vic 00.36 Phillips Park No 2 00.48/ 01.08 Midland Engines & Men Midland Jcn 01.15/ 01.25 Buxworth 02.14
03.14 03.20 *W	Not Sat	**Fitted Freight No 1 Somers Town 22.00 to Ancoats 04.36** St Pancras 22.05/ 22.25 Luton 23.17/ 23.25 Syston N Jcn 01.39 Toton 02.02 Gowhole 03.56/ 04.11
03.14 03.20 *W	Sat	**As above** but starts **St Pancras** & runs Express Freight from Syston
03.42	Not Mon Susp	**Mineral Avenue 02.30 to Gowhole 05.22** Hope 03.56/ 04.35
04.00	Not Mon	**Mineral Masboro Stn 01.35 to Gowhole 05.02** Wincobank Sdgs 01.42/ 02.40 Grimesthorpe Jcn No 1 02.52/ 02.56 to change engine Totley Tunnel E 03.32/ 03.38
04.00 04.10 W	Sun	**Through Freight Gowhole 03.05 to Engine Shed Sdgs 05.20** Queens Road 04.37/ 05.05
04.10 04.15 *W	Sat As Req	**Express Freight Cattle Peterborough 22.40 to Bolton** Saxby 00.42/ 01.00 Melton 01.20/ 01.25 water, Tibshelf S Jcn 02.58/ 03.03 water Gowhole 05.03/ 05.25 Ancoats 06.14/ 06.25 Phillips Park Sdgs 06.36/ 06.42 Ardwick Jcn 07.25 Colyhurst St 07.34 to shunt or follow other trains Manchester Vic 07.40
04.10 04.18 *W	Not Mon	**Express Freight Huskisson 21.45 to Engine Shed Sdgs 05.25** Cheadle Ex Sdgs 23.50/ 00.35 where becomes Through Freight Gowhole 01.18/ 03.00 Hope 03.45/ 04.00 Queens Road 04.45/ 05.10
04.22 04.27 W	Sun	**Fitted Freight No 1 Somers Town 22.00 to Ancoats 06.13** St Pancras 22.05/ 22.25 Wellingborough 00.11 Kettering 00.22/ 00.34 for examination Trent Jcn 01.34 Toton 02.40 Chinley Stn 05.13/ 05.23 to detach only Belle Vue Engine shed Box 06.04 to change engines and men. Express Freight from Syston
04.30 04.40 *W	Not Mon Sun	**Through Freight Gowhole 03.25 to Chesterfield 05.40** Dore S Jcn 05.00/ 05.05 Dronfield Stn 05.18/ 05.22 Tapton Jcn 06.05 Light Engine to Hasland 05.48
04.50 04.57 *W	Not Mon	**Empties Cheadle Ex Sdgs 03.00 to Staveley 06.33** Dore S Jcn 05.20/ 05.50 Tapton Jcn 06.20
05.02	Not Mon	**Mineral Grimesthorpe Sdgs 04.00 to Buxton** Hope 05.54 change trainmen Chinley E Jcn 06.21/ 06.38
05.20	Not Mon	**Mineral Avenue 04.15 to Gowhole 06.25** Chinley N Jcn 06.08/ 06.13
05.45 05.50 *W	Sat Susp	**Through Freight Gowhole 04.22 to Blackwell Sdgs 07.35** Edale 04.45/ 05.15.
05.52 06.04 W	Not Mon	**Mineral Carlton Sdgs 03.15 to Cheadle Ex Sdgs 08.20** Grimesthorpe Jcn No 1 04.30/ 04.45 water & examination Gowhole 07.08/ 07.42. Assisting engine runs light from Gowhole 08.08 to Grimesthorpe
06.17 06.45 *W	Not Mon	**Mineral Buxton 03.42 to Wincobank Sdgs 08.45** Bamford 05.25/ 06.00 to change trainmen Sheffield 07.25/ 07.48 Engine Shed Sdgs 07.57/ 08.35
	Not Mon	**Empties Ancoats 02.32 to Bamford 06.18** Bredbury 02.58/ 03.10 Romiley 03.15/ 03.35 Marple 03.40/ 04.18 New Mills Goods 04.23/ 04.32 Gowhole 04.40/ 05.00 Edale 05.32/ 05.42 Hope 05.57/ 06.11
06.23 06.44 *W	Not Mon	**Mineral Staveley 05.00 to Gowhole 07.55**

ARR DEP	DAY	DETAILS	1938
	Not Mon	**Engine & Brake Bamford 06.35 to Earle's Sdgs 06.40** Hope 07.08 to turn engine	
07.20	Mon	**Mineral Grimesthorpe Jcn 06.15 to Buxton** Edale 07.54/ 09.10 change enginemen Chinley S Jcn 09.25/ 09.28 Chapel 09.28/ 09.32 water Millers Dale 10.38/ 11.08 Buxton Jcn 11.12	
07.22	Not Mon Susp	*Mineral Gowhole 06.25 to Avenue 08.25*	
	Not Mon	**Mineral Earle's Sdgs 07.50 to Hazel Grove 10.35** Gowhole 08.42/10.10. Engine & Brake 10.50 to Gowhole 11.10	
07.52 08.00 * W	Not Mon	**Express Freight Edgeley to Sheffield City** *Chinley 07.14/ 07.19 Queens Road 08.30/ 09.20 Nunnery Main Line Jcn 09.27. Western Divn Engine & Men*	
	Mon	**Engine & Brake Chapel 08.10 to Earle's Sdgs 08.42**	
09.12 09.25 W	Not Sat As req	**Mineral Grimesthorpe Jcn 08.02 to Buxton** Sheffield Stn 08.08/ 08.19 Earle's Sdgs 09.43/ 10.05 Chinley S Jcn 10.41 Chapel 10.45/ 11.14 water Buxton Jcn 11.43	
09.19 09.25 * W	Mon	**Mineral Buxton 05.47 to Wincobank Sdgs 10.14** Cowburn Tunnel West 07.29/ 07.52 Edale 08.09/ 08.26 to change trainmen	
09.20 09.25 * W	Not Mon	**Light Engine Gowhole 08.08 to Grimesthorpe Sdgs** Chinley N Jcn 08.18/ 08.22 Hope 08.55/ 09.10. After assisting 03.15 Carlton Sdgs to Cheadle Ex Sdgs	
09.36 10.12 W	Not Sat	**Stopping Freight Grimesthorpe Sdgs 07.15 to Earle's Sdgs 12.10** Millhouses 07.38/ 08.04 Grindleford 08.47/ 09.30 Bamford 10.18/ 11.30 Water Board Sdgs 11.34/ 11.44 Hope 11.49/ 12.04	
10.15 10.40 W	Sat As req	**As above** but Sheffield S 07.15/ 07.19 Millhouses 07.40/ 08.04 Totley Tunnel East 09.37 Grindleford 09.51/ 10.10 Bamford 10.46/ 11.30	
	Mon	**Mineral Earle's Sdgs 09.32 to Gowhole 10.25**	
09.37 09.42 * W	Not Mon	*Engine & Brake Gowhole 08.30 to Avenue 10.27*	
09.58 10.03 * W		**Mineral Westhouses 08.10 to Gowhole 11.40** Avenue 08.30/ 08.53 Chesterfield 09.02 Chinley Stn 11.24	
10.22 10.38 * W	Not Sat	**Mineral Staveley 09.04 to Heaton Mersey Sdgs 12.50** Totley Tunnel East 09.54/ 09.58 Gowhole 11.47 New Mills S Jcn 11.55/ 12.12. New Mills 12.16/ 12.18	
10.36	Not Mon	*Empties Gowhole 09.00 to Staveley 12.00* Tapton Jcn 11.48/ 11.50	
10.58	Susp	**Mineral Grimesthorpe Jcn 09.32 to Gowhole 12.18** Edale 11.30/ 11.48	
11.03 11.11 *		*Empties Gowhole 09.50 to Staveley 12.14* Tapton Jcn 11.59/ 12.00	
11.50 11.54 *	Not Mon	**Mineral Grimesthorpe Jcn 11.12 to Gowhole 13.30** Chinley N Jcn 13.10/ 13.13	
12.21 12.47 * W	Susp	*Empties Gowhole 10.45 to Masboro Sorting Sdgs 16.12* Bamford 11.44/ 12.14 Sheffield 15.26/ 15.30 Grimesthorpe Jcn 15.38/15.40	
12.38		**Empties Avenue 11.10 to Earle's Sdgs 12.58** Totley Tunnel East 12.15. Light Engine works back to Hasland	
13.18 14.04		**Mineral Chesterfield N Sdgs 12.02 to Gowhole 17.05** Grindleford 12.46/ 13.10 Bamford 14.10/ 14.20 Water Works Sdgs 14.24/ 14.42 Hope 14.47/ 15.23 Earle's Sdgs 15.30/ 15.55 Edale 16.12/ 16.20 Chinley Stn 16.44/ 16.48	

ARR DEP	DAY	DETAILS	1938
13.35	Not Sat	**Mineral Staveley 12.08 to Gowhole 15.00** Dore W Jcn 13.00 Hope 13.50/ 14.08 Chinley N Jcn 14.45/ 14.48	
14.20 14.26 * W	Sat	**As above** but Dore W Jcn 13.56, no stop at Hope, Chinley N Jcn 15.14/ 15.17 **Gowhole 15.25**	
13.42 13.50 *	Not Sat	*Empties Gowhole 12.35 to Blackwell Sdgs 15.40* Earle's Sdgs 13.17/ 13.38 Dore S Jcn 14.18/ 14.23 Hasland 15.13/ 15.20 water	
14.12		*Light Engine Earle's Sdgs 13.55 to Hasland 15.13*	
	Not Mon	**Mineral Grimesthorpe Sdgs 12.35 to Grindleford 14.13** Bernard Rd Sdgs 12.42/ 12.58 Totley Tunnel E 12.38/ 13.58. 'Muck' train	
	Sat From 23 Oct	**Mineral Grimesthorpe Sdgs 12.40 to Grindleford 14.30** Sheffield 13.02/ 13.13 Millhouses 13.20 Totley Tunnel E 13.39/ 14.15.' Muck' train.	
	Sat To 22 Oct	**As above** but Totley Tunnel East 13.39/ 14.54 **Grindleford 15.10**. 'Muck' train.	
14.30 14.47 * W	Susp	*Empties Gowhole 13.30 to Masboro Sorting Sdgs*	
14.33 15.05 W	Not Sat	**Mineral Avenue Sdgs 13.10 to Gowhole 16.10** Hasland 13.13/ 13.16 to change engines	
15.35 15.53		*Mineral Gowhole 14.40 to Masboro Sorting Sdgs 17.36*	
15.40 16.28		*Stopping Freight Earle's Sdgs 13.05 to Wincobank Sdgs 18.04* Hope 13.11/ 14.05 Water Board Sdgs 14.11/ 14.28 Bamford 14.32/ 15.32 Grindleford 16.35/ 16.50 (Sat 17.08) Sheffield 17.23/ 17.48 Grimesthorpe Jcn 17.56/ 17.59	
15.45 15.53 * W		**Mineral Westhouses 13.40 to Gowhole 17.32** Avenue Sdgs 14.07/ 14.45 Tapton Jcn 14.58 Edale 16.28/ 16.48 Chinley Stn 17.10/ 17.22 to change enginemen	
16.02 16.08 * W		**Mineral Grimesthorpe 15.00 to Peak Forest S 17.48** Earle's Sdgs 16.28/ 16.46 Chinley S Jcn 17.18 Chapel 17.22/ 17.30	
17.12		*Empties Gowhole 16.10 to Staveley 19.18* Grindleford 17.22/ 18.00 Dore S Jcn 18.17/ 18.33 Dronfield Stn 18.43/ 18.46 Tapton Jcn 19.06	
		Mineral Empties Grindleford 17.20 to Grimesthorpe 18.47 Queens Road 17.50/ 18.28 Sheffield 18.33/ 18.37. 'Muck' train	
	Not Sat	**Express Freight Cheadle Sdgs 15.50 to Bamford 17.20**	
17.21 18.10		**Mineral Buxton Up Sdgs 13.55 to Wincobank Sdgs 19.05** Chinley E Jcn 15.48/ 15.54 Bamford 16.40/ 17.15. Double headed when required	
17.41 18.08 W		**Mineral Grimesthorpe Sdgs 16.45 to Buxton Midland 19.56** Chinley S Jcn 19.03/ 19.22. Changes trainmen at Hathersage with 13.55 Buxton to Wincobank Sdgs. Double headed when required	
18.23 18.31 * W	Not Sat	**Mineral Staveley 16.15 to Heaton Mersey 22.57** Earle's Sdgs 18.47/ 19.15 Gowhole 22.02/ 22.13 Romiley 22.38	
18.23 18.31 * W	Sat	**As above** but terminates at **Gowhole 22.02**	
18.39	Not Sat	*Empties Gowhole 17.28 to Avenue Sdgs* Bamford 18.18/ 18.34 Dore S Jcn 19.06/ 19.35	

267

ARR DEP	DAY	DETAILS	1938
	Not Sat	Light engine to Bamford 18.50/ 19.10, Engine & Brake to Hope 19.16/ 19.30 to turn engine Earle's Sdgs 19.35 **Mineral Earle's Sdgs 20.00 to Widnes WD Jcn 00.43** Gowhole 20.50/ 22.20 New Mills S Jcn 22.25 Hazel Grove Ex Sdgs 22.40/ 22.50 Cheadle W 23.08/ 23.28 for water & examination Skelton Jcn 23.44	
19.23 19.30		**Empties Gowhole 18.25 to Avenue Sdgs 20.30** Chesterfield 20.19	
19.33 19.46 *W	Sat Susp	**Light Engine Gowhole 18.35 to Avenue 20.40** Hasland 20.45	
20.00 20.10 *W		**Mineral Grimesthorpe Jcn 19.05 to Gowhole 21.12**	
20.24 20.28 *W	Sat As req	**Fitted Freight No. 1 Ancoats 18.23 to St Pancras** Follows Blackpool to Leicester passenger. Belle Vue Engine Shed Box 18.32/ 18.35 Gowhole 19.05/ 19.50 Dore S Jcn 20.44 Toton 21.42 Bedford South 01.05 West End Sdgs 02.54. Express Freight from Wigston	
20.47 20.53 *W	Not Sat	**Empties Gowhole 19.00 to Blackwell Sdgs 23.12** Earle's Sdgs 19.47/ 20.12 Hope 20.17 Bamford 20.24/ 20.42 Tapton Jcn 21.37/ 22.00 Chesterfield 22.05 Blackwell S 23.07/ 23.09	
21.00 21.05 W	Sat	**As above** but Earle's Sdgs 19.47/ 20.34 Bamford 20.42/ 20.55 Tapton Jcn 21.44/ 21.51	
21.15 21.23 *W	Not Thu Sat	**Mineral Peak Forest 19.10 to Masboro Stn 23.50** Chinley E Jcn 19.38 Edale 19.55/ 20.28 Bamford 20.48/ 21.07 Sheffield 22.02/ 22.20 Grimesthorpe No 2 22.30/ 22.32 Grimesthorpe Sdgs 22.40/ 22.53	
21.04 21.23 *W	Thu	**As above** but Bamford 20.48/ 20.56	
21.08 21.23 *W	Sat	**As above** but Chinley E Jcn 20.36 Edale 19.55/ 20.36 no stop at Bamford	
21.20 21.25 *W	Not Sat As req	**Fitted Freight No. 2 Garston Dock 18.15 to Masboro Stn 22.35** Skelton Jcn 19.25 Cheadle Ex Sdgs 19.40/ 20.05 water Queens Road 21.48/ 22.10. Worked by Western Divn engines & men	
21.53 21.58 W	Not Sat As req	**Mineral Grimesthorpe No. 1 Sdgs 20.48 to Cheadle Ex Sdgs 23.33** Sheffield 20.58/ 21.06 New Mills South Jcn 23.00	
22.06 22.12 *W	Not Sat	**LNER Class 'A' Goods Deansgate 20.22 to Colwick** Dore S Jcn 22.32/ 22.42 Chesterfield 23.03 Great Northern Jcn 23.42. Limited to 33 wagons	
22.48 22.53 *W	Sat	**Mineral Staveley 21.40 to Heaton Mersey Sdgs 04.35** Cowburn Tunnel E 23.31/ 23.50 Chinley E Jcn 23.25 Chinley N Jcn 23.53 Gowhole 00.22/ 04.00 Romiley 04.19	
23.03	Sat	**Empties Gowhole 21.30 to Staveley** Cowburn Tunnel W 21.55/ 22.20 Dore S Jcn 23.23/ 23.34	
23.17	Inc Sun	**Express Freight Grimesthorpe Sdgs 22.30 to Edge Hill** New Mills S Jcn 00.10/ 00.21 for examination Midland Jcn 00.52 Colyhurst St 01.02/ 01.07 Manchester Vic 01.14/ 01.18. Worked alternately by Midland & Western Divn engines & men	
23.37 23.42 *W	Not Sat	**Fitted Freight No. 1 Leicester Bell Lane 20.42 to Ancoats 00.44** Syston N Jcn 20.50 Nottingham New Sdgs 21.20 then as Fitted Freight No 2 Trent Jcn 21.24 Lenton South Jcn 21.34 Trowell 21.40 Pye Bridge Jcn 22.36 Chesterfield 23.00 Dore S Jcn 23.20 New Mills S Jcn 00.18 Ashburys 00.39	
23.43		**Fitted Freight No. 2 Ancoats 21.50 to Masboro Stn 00.36** Romiley 22.12/ 22.13 to pick up guard Gowhole 22.35/ 23.05 Dore Stn Jcn 23.55/ 00.18 Queens Road 00.03/ 00.20	

HANDLING THE FREIGHT

Gerald Jacobs started his career in an LMS Freight Control Office and finished his career forty years later as a senior freight planner on the operational side at British Railways' headquarters. This is a précis of an article written about his experiences but with particular reference to operations in the Hope valley.

'Handling freight was the bread and butter business. Day to day control occupied a great deal of management and supervisory time. At the end of the Second World War, in 1945, the system of operations developed by the Pre-Grouping companies was perpetuated by the four mainline companies. Although during the war the systems of operation were amended by the Railway Executive Committee it was still largely in force in 1945, though operating under great difficulties. However, things were to get worse very quickly. A large number of requisitioned private owner wagons had to be withdrawn and elderly freight locomotives, rescued from the scrap heap in 1939, took their final retirement. Rapid replacements were therefore needed for these locomotives and wagons but there was a critical time lag. In addition labour supply became critical. Hours of work for young people were restricted and more congenial work was available elsewhere, particularly in the growing motor industry. Thus the railways entered a boom period for traffic, which continued beyond Nationalisation, but were in no fit state to cope.'

FREIGHT TRAFFIC PASSING THROUGH HATHERSAGE FROM 7 MAY 1945 UNTIL FURTHER NOTICE

ARR DEP	DAY	DETAILS	1945
00.05 00.06	Sat	**Through Freight Chesterfield 23.05 to Gowhole 01.22** Earle's 00.20/ 00.35	
00.17	Not Sat	**Fitted Freight No 2 Leicester Bell Lane 20.52 to Ancoats 02.00** Trowell 22.49 Tibshelf S Jcn 23.12/ 23.17 water Chesterfield 23.38 Gowhole 01.00/ 01.20 from where becomes Express Freight	
00.17 00.25 W	Not Mon	**Express Freight Ancoats 22.30 to St Pancras 06.10** Gowhole 23.20/ 23.40 where becomes Fitted Freight Trowell Jcn 01.35 Syston N Jcn 02.07 Leicester Stn 02.15 Wigston N Jcn 02.23 Glendon N Jcn 02.58 Kettering 03.05/ 03.25 for examination, Wellingborough 03.37 Luton 04.40 Hendon 05.16 West End 05.28/ 05.58	
00.22 00.29 W	Sun	**Empties St Mary's 22.05 to Brunswick 04.25** Trowell 22.41 Heanor Jcn 23.00 Pye Bridge Jcn 23.11 Chesterfield 23.46 Cheadle Ex Sdgs 02.34/ 02.45 water. Conveys empty vans	
00.32 00.40 W	Not Mon	**Empties Beeston NE Divn Sdgs 22.10 to Brunswick 04.25** inc empty vans Cheadle Ex Sdgs 02.00/ 02.45. Leaves **St Mary's 22.05** Tue & Thu only	
00.34		**Empties Gowhole 23.45 to Engine Shed Sdgs 01.05**	
00.59	Sun	**Empties Gowhole 00.12 to Staveley**	
01.05 01.13 W	Sun	**Mineral Stourton 21.45 to Cheadle Ex Sdgs 04.30** Gowhole 02.15/ 03.45.	
01.24 01.25	Mon	**Empties Grimesthorpe 00.35 to Walton 04.30** Cheadle Ex Sdgs 02.40/ 02.50	
01.50 01.58 W	Sun	**Mineral Dronfield 01.10 to Gowhole 03.05** Light Engine 03.30 to Belle Vue Shed 04.00	

ARR DEP	DAY	DETAILS	1945
01.52	Not Mon	**Through Freight Grimesthorpe 01.00 to Heaton Mersey 04.40** Gowhole 02.55/ 03.55	
02.28	Susp Sat from 23 Jun	*Through Freight Ancoats 00.10 to Toton 04.28* Gowhole 01.05/ 01.40 water Morton Sdgs 03.35 Ilkeston S Jcn 04.10 Stanton Gates S 04.19	
02.28	Sun	**Through Freight Gowhole 01.40 to Stanton Gates 04.55** Dore S Jcn 02.51/ 03.12 Hasland 03.40/ 03.42 to change trainmen. Light Engine 05.05 to Toton	
02.40	Not Mon	**Through Freight Toton 00.30 to Gowhole 03.35** Chesterfield 01.45/ 01.47 water	
02.45 02.53 W	Sun	**Through Freight Toton 00.35 to Gowhole 03.53** Trowell 00.47 Chesterfield 01.50 to change trainmen	
02.49 02.56 W	Sun	**Through Freight Cheadle Ex Sdgs 12.42 to Carlton Sdgs**	
02.52 02.57	Not Mon	**Through Freight Heaton Mersey Sdgs 00.15 to Hunslet Down Sdgs 07.05** Gowhole 00.56/ 02.05 Sheffield Stn 03.26/ 03.34 water, Grimesthorpe Jcn 03.41/ 03.43 to change trainmen, Masboro Stn 03.55/ 05.00 Cudworth Stn 05.33 W Riding Jcn 06.22	
02.55 03.03	Not Mon	**LNER Fitted Goods Colwick 01.03 to Deansgate 04.15** Brinsley Jcn 01.37 Codnor Park 01.50. Limited to 37 wagons.	
02.55	Not Mon	*Mineral Buxton 23.00 to Earle's 02.08* Chinley S Jcn 01.38. Light Engine 02.50 to Hope 02.55	
03.13	Not Mon	*Through Freight Gowhole 02.25 to Chesterfield*	
03.22	Sun	*Through freight Gowhole 02.30 to Chesterfield*	
03.32		**Mineral Clay Cross 02.20 to Gowhole 04.42**	
03.42 03.50 W	Sun	**Mineral Wincobank 02.40 to Gowhole 04.55**	
03.50 04.00 W	Not Mon	**Mineral Wincobank 02.40 to Gowhole 05.20**	
03.51 03.59 W	Not Mon	*Through Freight Huskisson 22.20 to Engine Shed Sdgs 05.21* Walton 22.30/ 22.48 Halewood Sdgs 23.15/ 23.32 Cheadle Ex Sdgs 00.50/ 01.18 Gowhole 02.02/ 03.00 Queens Road 04.30/ 05.15	
04.25 04.33 W	Not Mon	*Through Freight Trafford Park 02.23 to Tibshelf Sdgs 05.52* Cheadle Ex Sdgs 02.51/ 02.54 Buxworth Jcn 03.33/ 03.35 for guard Clay Cross N Jcn 05.33	
04.48 04.55 W	Not Mon	*Empties Heaton Mersey 03.10 to Staveley.*	
04.50 04.57 W	Not Mon	**Mineral Grimesthorpe 03.55 to Buxton** Earle's Sdgs 05.15/ 05.35 where changes trainmen with 03.30 Buxton to Engine Shed Sdgs Chinley S Jcn 06.15	
04.52 05.00 W	Sun	**Fitted Freight No 2 Somers Town 22.00 to Ancoats 07.00** Toton 03.27 Chesterfield 04.14 Gowhole 05.43/ 06.15 where becomes Express Freight	
	Not Mon	**Earle's Sdgs 04.55 to Buxton** Chinley S Jcn 05.34	
05.04 05.12 W	Not Mon	**Fitted Freight No 2 Somers Town 22.00 to Ancoats 06.50** Toton 03.27 Chesterfield 04.22 Gowhole 05.55/ 06.10	
05.10	Sun	**Mineral Grimesthorpe 04.17 to Buxton** Chinley East Jcn 06.00/ 06.10 to change trainmen	

ARR DEP	DAY	DETAILS	1945
05.29 05.37 W	Mon	**Mineral Avenue 04.18 to Gowhole 08.20** Earle's Sdgs 05.58/ 07.25	
05.34	Sun	**Through Freight Toton 03.25 to Brindle Heath Down Sdgs 07.59** Trowell 03.38 Chesterfield 04.41 water Chinley 06.27 Belle Vue engine shed box 07.04 to change trainmen Midland Jcn 07.10 Miles Platting 07.20 Colyhurst St 07.22/ 07.27 Manchester Vic 07.34 / 07.42	
05.42 05.50 W	Not Mon As req	**Mineral Avenue 04.35 to Winnington 11.30** Earle's 06.12/ 07.25 Gowhole 08.20/ 09.10 Cheadle Ex Sdgs 09.55/ 10.05 water Skelton Jcn 10.22 Knutsford 10.45 Northwich 11.08 Hartford East 11.17	
05.50 05.58 W	Not Mon	*Mineral Buxton 03.30 to Engine Shed Sidings 07.15* Chinley E Jcn 04.40/ 04.43 Earle's Sdgs 05.12/ 05.33 to change trainmen with 03.55 from Grimesthorpe Bamford 05.45 Queens Road 06.36/ 06.55 Sheffield Stn 07.00/ 0705 water	
06.03 06.23 W	Not Mon As req	**Mineral Carlton Sdgs 04.05 to Glazebrook Sdgs 10.50** Masboro Stn 04.59 water Edale 06.59/ 07.01 to change trainmen Gowhole 07.35/ 08.55 Cheadle Ex Sdgs 09.36/ 10.20. Runs to Partington when req	
06.33	Sun	*Mineral Gowhole 05.30 to Avenue 07.30*	
06.36	Sun	**Express Freight Toton 04.20 to Ancoats 08.40** Trowell 04.32 Chesterfield 05.29 water Gowhole 07.52/ 07.55 to change trainmen	
06.36	Not Mon	**Express Freight Toton 04.10 to Ancoats 09.55** Stanton Gates 04.22 Chesterfield 05.23 water Edale 07.15/ 08.15 Gowhole 08.50/ 09.00. Susp from 23 Jun	
06.46	Not Mon	*Empties Gowhole 05.05 to Avenue 07.37* Hope 05.51/ 06.17 Bamford 06.25/ 06.40	
06.50	Sun	**Mineral Buxton Jcn No 1 05.00 to Engine Shed Sdgs 07.31** Chinley E Jcn 06.05/ 06.10 to change trainmen with 04.17 Grimesthorpe to Buxton	
06.51	Sun	**Mineral Clay Cross 05.20 to Gowhole 08.05** Avenue 05.28/ 05.50 Earle's Sdgs 07.10/ 07.20. Double headed to Earle's from Avenue	
06.56		**Mineral Staveley 05.38 to Gowhole 08.00**	
06.59		*Empties Gowhole 06.00 to Avenue 08.02* Edale 06.38/ 06.40 to change trainmen Dore S Jcn 07.18/ 07.32	
07.12 07.19 W	Mon	**Mineral Grimesthorpe 06.10 to Buxton** Bamford 07.28/ 07.55 to change trainmen Earle's Sdgs 08.40/ 08.43	
07.23	Sun	**Mineral Staveley 06.05 to Gowhole 08.35**	
07.47	Sun	**Mineral Staveley 06.35 to Gowhole 09.00**	
08.05 08.10 W	Sun	*Light Engine Earle's Sdgs 07.50 to Hasland 08.56* After assisting 05.20 Clay Cross to Earle's Sdgs	
08.23 08.31 W	Mon	**Mineral Buxton 05.10 to Engine Shed Sidings 09.17** Bamford 07.24/ 08.15 to change trainmen	
08.27 08.45 *W		**Mineral Staveley 06.48 to Gowhole 09.50**	
08.50 09.35 W		**Stopping Freight Grimesthorpe Sdgs 07.10 to Earle's Sdgs 11.47** Grindleford 08.07/ 08.40 Bamford 09.45/ 10.47 Hope 11.00/ 11.40	
09.14 09.22 W		**Mineral Blackwell Sdgs 07.00 to Gowhole 10.30**	
09.42		*Empties Gowhole 08.55 to Avenue 10.42* Dore S Jcn 10.03/ 10.08	

ARR DEP	DAY	DETAILS
10.07 10.15 W	Not Sat	**Mineral Staveley 08.50 to Heaton Mersey 11.59**
10.20 11.06 W	Sun	**Mineral Grimesthorpe Sdgs 09.25 to Gowhole 12.15** Chinley 12.02 to change engines or enginemen
10.24 10.37 W	Mon	*Through Freight Heaton Mersey Sdgs 08.30 to Toton* Hope 09.55/ 10.13
10.28		**Mineral Grimesthorpe 09.32 to Gowhole 12.43** Hope 10.45/ 10.48 where relief men set down Sat
10.30 10.37 W	Not Mon	*Through Freight Heaton Mersey 09.00 to Toton 13.20* Tibshelf S Jcn 11.45/ 12.02 Stanton Gates Jcn 13.10. Susp from Fri 13 Jul
10.43	Sun	*Gowhole 09.40 to Avenue 11.50*
10.52 11.00 W		**Mineral Avenue 09.38 to Earle's Sdgs 11.20**
11.06 12.25 *		*Goods Buxton Jcn No 1 08.45 to Queens Road 13.05* Chinley S Jcn 10.20. Hathersage change enginemen, Heeley 13.00. Light Engine 13.40 to Grimesthorpe shed 13.55
11.14 11.58 W		**Mineral Grimesthorpe 10.05 to Buxton** Change trainmen at Hathersage with 08.45 Buxton to Queens Road
11.20	Sun	**Mineral Gowhole 10.15 to Staveley**
11.21		*Empties Gowhole 10.25 to Staveley*
11.29 11.35 W	Tue Thu	**Mineral Toton 09.10 to Gowhole 12.45** Hasland 10.24/ 10.26 to pick up trainmen Dore W Jcn 11.02/ 11.05 to change trainmen
11.45	Not Sat	**Mineral Grimesthorpe Jcn No 1 10.32 to Mold Jcn** Hope 12.00/ 12.02 to drop off trainmen Earle's Sdgs 12.07/ 12.25 Cheadle Ex Sdgs 13.38/ 15.15 Northenden 15.24 Skelton Jcn 15.33. Double headed when req
11.48		*Engine & Brake Gowhole 11.00 to Hasland 12.33*
12.12		*Empties Gowhole 11.25 to Staveley*
12.20		**Mineral Storrs Mill 10.30 to Gowhole 13.35** Holmes Jcn 11.08
12.22		*Mineral Gowhole 11.20 to Staveley* Dore S Jcn 13.16/ 13.47.
12.32	Sun	**Mineral Staveley 11.13 to Gowhole 13.35**
12.38		**Mineral Staveley 11.20 to Gowhole 13.45**
12.50		*Empties Gowhole 11.45 to Blackwell Sdgs 14.40* Earle's Sdgs 12.24/ 12.40 Dore S Jcn 13.11/ 13.16 Chesterfield Hollis Lane 14.00
13.07	Sun	*Mineral Gowhole 12.00 to Avenue 14.20* Light Engine Belle Vue 11.05 to Gowhole 11.45
13.27	Not Mon	*Empties Mold Jcn 09.13 to Roundwood* Cheadle Heath Sdgs 11.48/ 12.00 water, Holmes Jcn 14.05
13.32 14.00	Mon Sat from 14 Jul	**Stopping Freight Chesterfield N Sdgs 12.02 to Gowhole 17.10** Grindleford 12.45/ 13.24 Bamford 14.10/ 14.30 Water Board Sdgs 14.36/ 15.16 Hope 15.26/ 15.37 Earle's Sdgs 15.44/ 15.57 Edale 16.14/ 16.34
13.38 13.46 W	Not Mon	*Empties Cheadle Ex Sdgs 12.10 to Staveley* Light engine leaves Heaton Mersey 11.35 to Cheadle Ex Sdgs 11.40
		Mineral Grimesthorpe 11.48 to Grindleford 13.43 (13.40 Sat) Mill Race Jcn 11.55/ 12.40 Bernard Road 12.44/ 12.55. The 'Muck' train
14.10	Sun	**Mineral Staveley 13.00 to Gowhole 15.25**

ARR DEP	DAY	DETAILS
14.16		*Empties Gowhole 13.30 to Wincobank Down Sdgs 15.50* Sheffield 14.42/ 14.47 Grimesthorpe Jcn 14.54/ 14.56 to change trainmen. Engine & Brake leaves Wincobank 16.20
14.18	Not Fri Sat	**Mineral Avenue 13.15 to Gowhole 15.22**
14.28 14.33 W	Not Sat	*Empties Earle's Sdgs 13.35 to Chesterfield* Hope 13.42/ 14.15 to turn engine Dore S Jcn 14.50/ 15.02
14.30 14.35 W	Sat	*As above* but Dore S Jcn 15.02
14.47 15.37	Not Sat	*Stopping Freight Earle's Sdgs 13.03 to Wincobank Sdgs 16.50* Hope 13.10/ 13.35 Water Board Sdgs 13.43/ 13.58 Bamford 14.03/ 14.38 Grindleford 15.45/ 16.10
14.59 15.37 W	Sat	*As above* but change of times at Hathersage
15.02 15.03		*Freight Trafford Park Sdgs 12.40 to Tibshelf Sdgs 16.40* Gowhole Goods Jcn 13.48/ 13.55 water, Chinley N Jcn 14.10/ 14.25 Chesterfield 16.00 to change trainmen. Light Engine Tibshelf to Toton 17.45
15.12	Sun	*Mineral Empties Gowhole 14.00 to Wincobank Sdgs 16.05*
15.16	Not Sat	**Gowhole 14.30 to Wincobank Sdgs 16.05** Sheffield 15.42/ 15.47 water Grimesthorpe Jcn No. 1 15.55/ 15.57
15.31		*Empties Gowhole 14.45 to Staveley*
15.52		**Through Freight Grimesthorpe 15.03 to Peak Forest South 17.33** Earle's Sdgs 16.10/ 16.30 changes trainmen with 13.45 Buxton to Queens Road. Chapel en le Frith 17.09/ 17.14 water
15.53	Sun	**Mineral Grimesthorpe 15.00 to Gowhole 17.08** Chinley 16.48/ 16.53 to change trainmen
15.55	Sat	*Empties Gowhole 15.10 to Wincobank Sdgs 16.45*
16.17	Not Fri Sat	*Empties Gowhole 15.20 to Tibshelf Sdgs 17.58* Dore S Jcn 16.40/ 16.52 Hasland 17.28/ 17.30 to change trainmen. (See 17.08 at Hathersage)
16.22		**Mineral Blackwell Sdgs 14.45 to Gowhole 17.36** Horns Bridge 15.19
16.22 16.50 *	Sun	*Mineral Empties Gowhole 15.15 to Staveley*
16.43 16.55 W		*Mineral Empties Buxton Up Sdgs 13.45 to Queens Road 17.25* Earle's Sdgs 16.17/ 16.30 to change trainmen with 15.03 Grimesthorpe to Peak Forest. Double headed when required
17.02		**Mineral Avenue 15.55 to Gowhole 18.05** Light Engine Gowhole 18.35 to Belle Vue engine shed 19.05
17.08	Fri Sat	*Empties Gowhole 16.05 Tibshelf Sdgs 18.20* Hasland 17.51/ 17.53 to change trainmen. (See 16.17 at Hathersage)
17.08	Tue Thu	*Express Freight Langton Dock 13.40 to Sheffield City 18.35.* Brunswick 13.50 when req Cheadle Heath 15.32/ 15.43 water Queens Road 17.45/ 1822 water Nunnery Main Line Jcn 18.29. Light Engine 21.00 to Nunnery Main Line Jcn 21.05/ 21.07 Mill Race Jcn 21.12 Grimesthorpe 21.15
17.20	Sun	*Mineral Empties Gowhole 16.15 to Wincobank Sdgs 18.10*
17.33 18.15 W		**Mineral Grimesthorpe 16.30 to Buxton** Chinley S Jcn 19.05. Changes trainmen at Chapel. Double headed when req

ARR DEP	DAY	DETAILS	1945
17.41	Not Sat	**Empties Mew Mills Goods 16.57 to Avenue 19.25** Dore S Jcn 18.10/ 18.15	
17.41	Sat as req	**As above** but New Mills Goods Jcn 17.25 Dore S Jcn 18.38/ 18.49	
17.56 18.03 W		**Express Freight Cheadle Ex Sdgs 15.50 to Bamford 17.12** Light engine to Hathersage for water then to Grindleford	
		Mineral Empties Grindleford 18.08 to Grimesthorpe 18.48 'Muck' train	
18.27	Sun	**Mineral Empties Gowhole 17.20 to Staveley**	
18.29	Wed	**Express Freight Nunnery 17.30 to Langton Dock 22.48** Nunnery Main Line Jcn 17.35 Cheadle Ex Sdgs 20.08/ 20.50 Fazakerley S Jcn 22.35 Linacre Gas Sdgs 22.40	
18.43		**Mineral Avenue 17.25 to Gowhole 19.50**	
18.48	Susp Sun	**Mineral Empties Gowhole 17.45 to Avenue 19.55**	
18.57 *		**Mineral Toton 16.05 to Earle's Sdgs 19.15** Hasland 17.30/ 17.32 to change trainmen. Chesterfield 17.40 Dore W Jcn 18.25 /18.35	
	Not Sat	**Mineral Earle's Sdgs 20.10 to Widnes WD Jcn** Light Engine 19.05 to Bamford 19.10/ 19.20 Chinley N Jcn 20.38/ 20.46 New Mills South Jcn 21.08. Engine & Brake to Hope 19.26/ 19.42 where engine turns Earle's Sdgs 19.46	
	Sat	**As above** but runs to **Arpley**. New Mills South Jcn 21.08/ 21.18	
19.32 19.38		**Empties Gowhole 18.35 to Avenue 20.35** Hasland 20.28/ 20.30 to change trainmen	
19.45 19.52 W	As req	**Empties Cheadle Ex Sdgs 18.20 to Staveley** Light engine leaves Heaton Mersey 17.50	
19.46	Not Sat	**Empties Washwood Heath to Huskisson 23.10** for Sandon. Dore W Jcn 19.15/ 19.22 Cheadle N 21.00/ 21.06 Cheadle Ex Sdgs 21.16/ 21.25. Conveys common user wagons	
20.05 20.12 W	Not Sat	**Mineral Staveley 19.20 to Heaton Mersey 23.34** Earle's 20.38/ 21.06 Gowhole 21.58/ 22.50	
20.20 20.28 W	Sat	**Mineral Staveley 19.03 to Gowhole 21.58** Earle's 20.47/ 21.06	
20.30 20.50 * W		**Empties Gowhole 19.35 to Avenue 22.02** Light Engine 22.22 to Westhouses 22.45	

ARR DEP	DAY	DETAILS	1945
21.05 21.13 W		**Empties Earle's Sdgs 20.45 to Avenue 22.20** Engine & Brake Earle's Sdgs 19.50 Hope 19.54/ 20.10 to turn engine Earle's Sdgs 20.15	
21.13		**Mineral Grimesthorpe 20.18 to Gowhole 22.15**	
21.25 21.35 W		**Mineral Peak Forest S 18.55 to Wincobank Down Sdgs 22.45** Earle's 20.00/ 21.00 Grimesthorpe Jcn No 1 22.32/ 22.34 to change trainmen	
21.59 22.06 W		**LNER Class 'A' Goods Deansgate 20.22 to Colwick** Codnor Park Jcn 23.22. Limited to 40 wagons	
22.28		**Empties Halewood Sdgs 19.15 to Tibshelf Sdgs 23.45** Cheadle Heath 20.37/ 21.00 water Chinley 21.44/ 21.46 change trainmen Clay Cross N Jcn 23.20	
22.37		**Through Freight Toton 20.20 to Buxworth Jcn 23.28** Conveys Brindle Heath traffic	
22.50	Sat As req	**Mineral Staveley 21.33 to Cheadle Ex Sdgs 00.37** Dore W Jcn 22.25/ 22.27 to change trainmen Buxworth Jcn 23.53	
22.50	Not Mon	**Empties Heaton Mersey Sdgs 21.20 to Kilnhurst 23.55** Gowhole 22.04 Sheffield Stn 23.17/ 23.22 water Holmes Jcn 23.35	
23.08	Not Sat	**Through Freight Grimesthorpe 22.18 to Edge Hill** Chinley 23.55/ 00.02 water Midland Jcn 00.50 Ashton Bch Sdgs 00.58 Miles Platting 00.59 Colyhurst St 01.01/ 01.06 Manchester Vic 01.15	
23.08 23.14 W	Sun	**Light Engine Belle Vue 21.30 to Dronfield 23.43** Gowhole 22.15/ 22.30 to attach brake. To work 01.10 Mineral Dronfield to Gowhole	
23.37	Not Mon	**Express freight Grimesthorpe 22.48 to Huskisson 06.30** Gowhole 00.30/ 02.30 from where becomes mineral, Halewood Sdgs 04.55/ 05.30 Walton 05.58/ 06.23	
23.45	Not Mon	**Mineral Gowhole 22.40 to Avenue 00.55**	

The Supplement to the Fortnightly Notice for Sat 25 Aug to Fri 31 Aug 1945 informs trainmen that from Thu 30 Aug until further notice preparing and relaying of track is being undertaken in between trains in Totley tunnel from 07.30 to 17.00 (Sat 11.45). Speed is not to exceed 15 mph day and night. An indicator is fixed at the limit of the work.

8F 2-8-0 No. 8167 awaits a signal to join the Hope valley line on Dore South Curve. This is one of a batch built at Crewe in 1943. The photographer took a number of photographs in this year and it is likely that this image was taken when the engine had just entered into traffic, it has a 19C Canklow shed plate. The posing driver has taken the opportunity to check his engine and has a white cloth in his hand for the purpose.
J. C. Naylor

LMS built 7F 0-8-0 No. 9578 leaves Gowhole on an up mineral empties train on 9 May 1931.
R. D. Pollard Manchester Locomotive Society collection

RUNNING POWERS FOR THE GREAT NORTHERN RAILWAY

By the late 1880s, the Great Northern Railway's finances were in decline due to the expense that it had incurred in developing joint lines with other companies. With the threat of the MSLR having its own line to London the GNR needed to strengthen its position in Manchester and had obtained running powers over the MSLR route from Sheffield to Manchester via Woodhead in 1892. This was achieved because the GNR dropped its opposition to the MSLR's London extension. Having achieved these running powers the GNR built the huge Deansgate goods depot and yard in central Manchester, from which the first train departed on Fri 1 Jul 1898.

The Great Northern pioneered the development of express and perishable services with fully braked wagons to provide quick transit and the number of these trains expanded rapidly between 1901 and 1904.

At the outset the GNR ran four express goods trains from Deansgate to Kings Cross via Retford. They operated on weekdays only and departed at 17.39, 18.50, 19.30 and 21.15. Further, because of its own joint ownership of the Cheshire Lines, the GNR was also able to run three trains from the Liverpool area.

However, the MSLR began to use delaying tactics to GNR freights north of Nottingham and to the west of Sheffield. To alleviate the problem the GNR approached the Midland to obtain running powers from the Nottingham area. An agreement was reached and the GNR built a connection from its Codnor Park ironworks branch at Brinsley Junction to the Midland's Erewash valley line at what became known as 'Great Northern Junction'. Running powers were granted to run night freights from this junction to Clay Cross, Chesterfield and via the Dore South Curve on to the Hope valley line. The first service ran on 2 Nov 1899. The GNR also obtained powers to run over the Peak line, which it accessed via Ironville Junction and Crich Junction to Ambergate.

The *Sheffield & Rotherham Independent* of 23 Oct 1899 reported the new arrangement but speculated that the extension of the GNR Leen valley route to Langwith would allow them access to the LDECR line to the Sheffield District Railway at Treeton This would then permit access to Sheffield's Midland station under the latter company's running powers into the station – from there the Dore and Chinley line would be used to access Deansgate without any of the Great Central's lines being used at all. There is no evidence to show that this unlikely course of events happened or that the Great Eastern Railway, which had an interest in the Sheffield District Railway exercised their same powers. It was thought that a through train by the same route from Langwith could be run from Lincoln to Manchester and Liverpool without changing trains.

The potential complications of running other companies engines over LMS lines is highlighted in the Sectional Appendix of 1937 which details what would happen in the event of an LNER engine failing between New Mills and Codnor Park. In that circumstance the LMS would provide an engine to work up trains to Brinsley Junction and down trains forward to Deansgate. Five different control offices were itemised to make the arrangements, depending on where the breakdown took place, namely Gowhole, between New Mills and Hathersage; Masborough, between Hathersage and Dronfield; Staveley, between Dronfield and Broad Oaks Sidings and Alfreton between Alfreton and Great Northern Junction. In the up direction the LNER Control Officer at Nottingham would be required to supply an engine to work the train forward from Brinsley Junction but not before the LNER driver of the disabled engine had conducted the LMS driver from Great Northern Junction to Brinsley Junction. In the case of down trains the LNER Locomotive Department at Trafford Park would provide a conductor from Great Northern Junction to Deansgate. If the engine failed whilst working an up or down train between Deansgate and New Mills South Junction via Cheadle Heath and Stockport, Trafford Park shed would be required to provide a relief engine.

The running via Ambergate continued until 1914 when all the Midland workings were transferred to the Hope valley. In that year there were two trains each way to Deansgate with an additional working, both ways to Brunswick via the Cheshire lines. This transfer is reflected in the number of trains through the valley. In the down direction there were workings from Brinsley Junction at 02.55 and 07.10 to Deansgate which arrived at 05.35 and 10.15. The latter was the only example of daylight running. The returns left Deansgate at 20.46 and 21.18 and arrived at Brinsley Sidings at 23.40 and 00.11. There was also a working from Brinsley Junction at 06.10 to Brunswick which, on its return arrived at Brinsley Sidings at 23.21.

By 1916 there were still two workings each way but with two extra workings on Saturdays from Deansgate and an up working from Brunswick. In the inter war years there was just one working each way. By 1945 there was still only one working each way but this originated at Colwick and cleared Brinsley thirty four minutes later in the down direction. By 1952 the working was still the same with revised timings in the down direction.

During the Grouping period there were three daily braked goods trains between Kings Cross and Colwick, two of these ran to Deansgate and Huskisson via Woodhead with the third running to Deansgate via the Hope valley.

From 1948, under British Railways, there were no significant changes until 1953. After that year the few trains that were left ran once again exclusively over the Woodhead route. Deansgate warehouse and sidings finally closed on 29 Mar 1954 as a rail connected depot, the remaining traffic being moved to the myriad of other depots in the Manchester area. The junction at Brinsley was taken out on 4 Jul 1954. So ended fifty five years of continuous operation over the Hope valley from that original agreement of 1898.

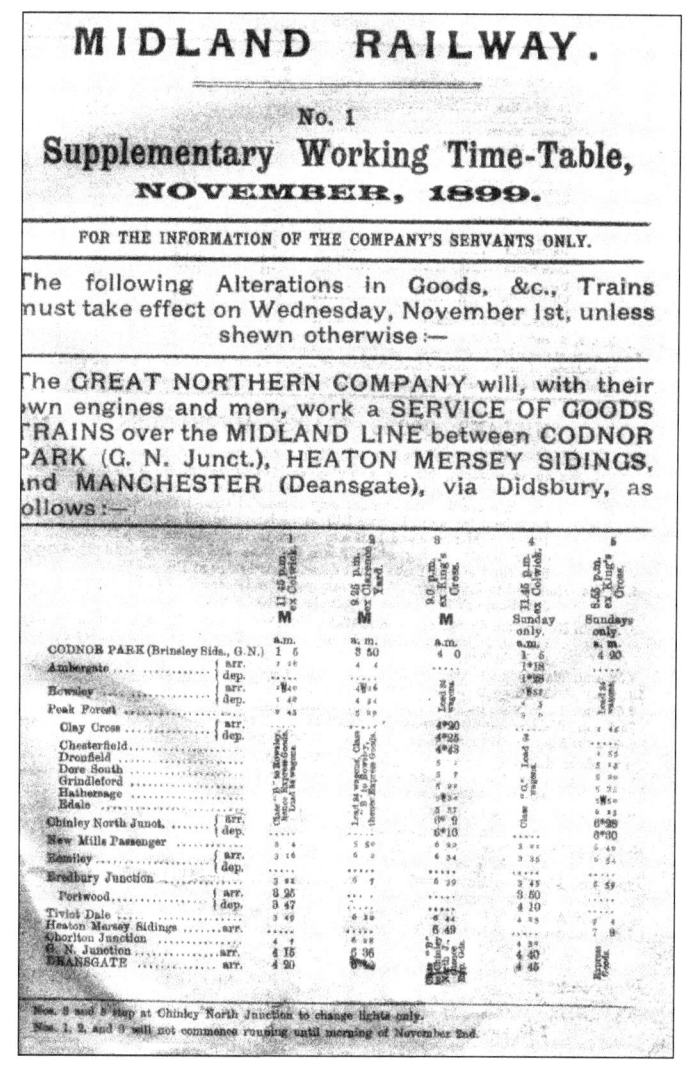

The Midland Railway Distance Diagram of 1921 shows the connection between the Midland and Great Northern located below Codnor Park and Ironville station on the Erewash Valley line. Note that all but the first few hundred yards were owned by the GNR.

This is the original working timetable of the GNR goods trains which started on 2 Nov 1899. It shows two workings left Brinsley Junction at 01.05 and 03.50 on Mondays with a further train at 01.05 on Sundays – these ran via the Peak line and at 04.00 on Mondays and 04.20 on Sundays over the Hope valley route. The 04.00 Hope valley working was Class 'B' to Chinley North Junction where it was allowed one minute to change lights to show the change to 'Express Goods'. The maximum permitted loading was thirty four wagons.

Laurence Knighton collection

273

GREAT NORTHERN AND LNER MOTIVE POWER

With the arrival of the fitted freights many were hauled by Stirling 2-4-0s and even the remaining Eight Foot Singles but they were all proving inadequate for the task. As a result, H. A. Ivatt set about modernising the locomotive fleet by providing more powerful engines, some of which were used to work the Deansgate trains.

Six nearly new D2 4-4-0s 1341-1346 were transferred to Trafford Park shed, which the GNR shared with the Midland and the GCR. Later in the GNR period 1396 to 1399 (4396-9) were also used on the night freights from Deansgate to Kings Cross via Ambergate or the Hope valley. During the 1933 to 1935 period 1361 (4361), 1378 (4378) 1393 (4392) and 1399 (4399) were at Trafford Park. Colwick had a continuous allocation of D2s from 1924 through to the post war period. Many of them were withdrawn for scrapping from the shed in the period to 1951 although by then they had been superseded by more modern engines.

Just before Gresley succeeded Ivatt at Doncaster works, there was an urgent need for new engines to work the fast braked goods trains between York and London and also between Peterborough and Manchester. To meet these requirements a small class of fifteen mixed traffic 0-6-0s was built in 1908 and designated Class J21. As a result the D2s at Trafford Park moved elsewhere although, as we have seen, they returned later in the GNR period. Three engines numbered 4 to 6, were allocated to Colwick shed for working to Peterborough and Manchester. In 1912 Colwick received another three numbered 1 to 3. All six became Class J1 at the Grouping and were renumbered 3001 to 3006. Although all six reappeared during 1941 and 1945, together with a number of the later engines of the class, they were not involved in the Deansgate workings during this period. The class were saturated engines whereas later designs were superheated which considerably improved performance.

However, despite this provision in 1911, just as Gresley was actually taking over the reins from the retiring Ivatt, there again was an urgent need for additional power. As a result Gresley introduced a design identical with the previous engines and retaining the same J21 classification, although these were fitted with superheaters and piston valves. Ten were built and numbered 71-80, four of which, 75 to 78, went to Peterborough from where they worked to Deansgate. With the advent of Gresley's 2-6-0 design Peterborough's allocation increased to seven although one, No. 77, was immediately transferred to Trafford Park. Just after Grouping period Nos. 76 and 78 were at Colwick by now designated Class J2. Colwick retained an interest in the J2s until the last was withdrawn, No. 78, by now BR No. 65022. It was the very last at Colwick being withdrawn by 14 Dec 1953.

D2 4-4-0 No. 1341 was built in 1898 and rebuilt to D3 in 1915. It became No. 4341 at the Grouping when the class was designated D4 and it was withdrawn in 1937. In fact only one of the class reached Nationalisation. Here No. 1341 is seen after rebuilding.
R. K. Blencowe collection

Here is J21 (LNER J1) 0-6-0 No. 3005. It was renumbered No. 5004 in 1946 and survived into BR ownership, being withdrawn in 1952 as No. 65004. *Photomatic*

GNR J21 (LNER J2) 0-6-0 No. 75 was built in Sep 1912 and renumbered No. 3075 in Oct 1926. It was further renumbered No. 5019 in Jun 1946 and was withdrawn in Mar 1953. It is seen in its last years on 21 Sep 1952 at Colwick shed, it having worked the Deansgate trains from Peterborough when new.
Ken Boulter © Ted Hancock

J6 0-6-0 No. 3538 is seen at Colwick shed in 1932 and was one of the engines that worked over the Hope valley as GNR No. 538. It was built in Nov 1912 and was renumbered No. 3538 in Feb 1926, No. 4187 in Sep 1946 before being withdrawn by BR in Jan 1958 as No. 64187. They were sometimes called 'Knick Knacks' from the peculiar noise made when running with steam shut off. It was one of the seven at Trafford Park in the Pre-Grouping period.
Gordon Coltas

The continued increase in traffic resulted in the J22 Class (LNER J6) 0-6-0s being built in large numbers between 1911 and 1922. The first seventy five engines were built between 1911 and 1914 and twenty three were allocated to Peterborough, eighteen to Colwick and three to Manchester. They took over the duties of the earlier J21s. The three based at Manchester replaced the Ivatt 4-4-0s on the fast goods turns to and from Colwick while some of the large allocation at Colwick worked to Manchester on Midland lines and also the Great Central trains and over the CLC lines to Liverpool. By the Grouping, Colwick had a massive forty engines at the shed and Manchester eight but they were seen less on main line duties by this time.

Gresley next designed and built, between 1913 and 1921 the H2 and H3 2-6-0s, the later ones having larger boilers. They were known as 'Ragtimers' because they had a sharp turn of speed. They were numbered 1630 to 1639 (H2) and 1640 to 1704 (H3). Colwick received six of the first batch which increased when the larger engines arrived. By 1920 Colwick had H2s 1630, 1631, 1633, 1639 and Peterborough had nineteen of the class. At the Grouping, Colwick had the same engines with the addition of Nos. 1635 and 1638, and Peterborough had an increase to twenty five. All of the Colwick engines would have worked over the Hope valley.

When seventy five of the larger H3 Class were built between 1914 and 1921, six were initially allocated to Colwick. By 1920 they had all gone although Peterborough's allocation had swollen to sixteen. At the Grouping, Peterborough had twenty five and Colwick three, Nos. 4630 (1720), 4631 (1721) and 4633 (1723).

In the first years after the Grouping the K2s, as they became known, monopolised the Deansgate workings from Kings Cross to Colwick. There were three workings; one to Huskisson via Woodhead, the second to Deansgate via Guide Bridge and the third via the Hope valley but from 1925 the ex-GCR B8 4-6-0s shared these duties.

In 1938 there were seven K2s numbered 4641 (1731), 4643 (1733), 4646 (1736), 4651 (1741), 4660 (1750), 4680 (1770) and 4683 (1773) at Colwick. In 1942 there were thirty two of the class at four sheds with Colwick having five. On 27 Apr 1947 eight were transferred out on the same day but that still left fifteen at the end of the LNER period. Soon more were allocated back to Colwick to cater for traffic diversions because of the rebuilding of Thurgoland tunnel on the Woodhead route. It is likely that the Deansgate workings would have been transferred to the Hope valley. On 13 Apr 1948, Colwick K2 No. 1741 worked the 23.20 Colwick to Deansgate goods. It then went to Trafford Park and worked a filling in turn which was the 17.43 Manchester Central to Guide Bridge passenger, usually the duty of a J39 off a Colwick to Deansgate freight. It then ran light engine to Dewsnap to work the 19.10 braked goods to Colwick.

Between 1926 and 1941 289 J39 0-6-0s were built. The first to arrive at Colwick in Mar 1932 was No. 2976 (4837) when it was brand new. Up to 1936, others were there for short periods but in 1936 engines numbered 1828 (4908), 1854 (4909), 1856 (4910) and 1857 (4911) arrived new to join No. 2976 as permanent replacements for withdrawn ex-GNR 0-6-0s. By 1939 Colwick had twelve J39s and eighteen by 1947.

Trafford Park first received members of the class in 1933 when Nos. 1233 (4721) and 1265 (4725) arrived. Altogether nine were shedded there before the war but none of them stayed for more than two years. During the war, Nos. 1263 (4723), 1265 (4725), 1290 (4740) and 2691(4744) arrived in the early years and settled until after the war ended. After 1945 another five arrived but did not have long tenures. Brunswick had two during 1925 to 1927, one in 1930 and 1939 and two in 1947. There is no evidence that the Brunswick engines ever worked over the Hope valley.

Eleven ex-GCR 'Glenalmond' 4-6-0s were built by the GCR between 1913 and 1915. They were designated B8 by the LNER. They took over some of the Deansgate duties from 1925.

The original B1s, later LNER B18, of which there were only two, had very short stays at Colwick except for 5195 which was there for three years during the war. They may have worked the Deansgate freights but there is no evidence that they did. The B7s were at Colwick for a very short period in the mid 1920s but there was only one by the late 1930s. All the class were shedded at Gorton during the war from where some were loaned out to CLC sheds, including Trafford Park, but there is no indication that they worked the Deansgate trains. As can be seen between 1926 and 1928 eleven B8s moved to Colwick for the first time, the rest of the class being at Annesley. The two sheds housed the whole class for the next twenty years. By 1943 the entire class was at Annesley and none returned to Colwick. The B8s worked the fitted freights to Kings Cross and back and Colwick to Deansgate, including those routed via the Hope valley. They shared the workings with the K2s and J39s.

EX-GCR 4-6-0 CLASSES AT COLWICK

CLASS	GCR NO	LNER NO	FROM	TO
(B18) B1	5195	1479	03.03.40	05.04.43
			04.07.43	16.01.44
			26.06.47	21.09.47
	5196	1480	03.03.40	26.05.40
			05.05.46	20.10.46
			26.06.47	21.09.47
B7	5036	1363	04.03.26	01.04.26
	5037	1364	28.10.25	07.04.26
	5458	1366	09.02.26	01.04.26
	5470	1378	04.03.37	05.01.38
	5034	1386	30.11.25	27.03.26
			16.03.37	13.12.37
B8	5004*	1349	09.06.26	08.11.26
			16.01.28	15.08.43
	5439	1350	29.03.26	10.08.43
	5440	1351	12.10.27	04.01.33
	5441	1352	27.03.26	09.08.43
	5442	1353	09.07.26	15.10.28
	5443	1354	27.03.26	09.08.43
	5444	1355	16.06.27	12.10.27
			02.04.28	15.06.43
	5445	1356	14.11.28	15.08.43
	5446†	1357	29.03.26	06.06.26
	5279§	1358	31.03.26	08.11.26
			06.03.28	09.10.33
	5280	1359	10.06.26	31.03.27
			02.04.28	08.06.28

* Sutton Nelthorpe
† Earl Roberts of Kandahar
§ Earl Kitchener of Khartoum

EX-GCR 4-6-0s AT TRAFFORD PARK

CLASS	GCR NO	LNER NO	FROM	TO
B5	6068	1679	06.10.46	24.08.47
	6069	1680	06.10.46	08.01.47
	5153	1686	06.10.46	24.08.47
B9	6105	1469	24.11.27	19.03.30
			04.06.30	30.05.32
			04.03.33	13.07.34
			17.03.33	05.08.38
			30.09.38	11.10.41
			22.04.45	06.05.45
	6106	1470	07.06.26	08.08.28
			27.08.28	04.06.30
			09.09.30	29.08.32
			27.10.32	11.10.33
			17.06.35	19.01.37
			13.10.37	27.09.39
			06.06.41	21.09.41
	6107	1471	18.03.30	09.09.30
			06.01.32	14.07.33
			19.06.36	13.10.37
			06.04.41	21.09.41
	6108	1472	08.08.28	24.08.28
			24.11.30	11.07.32
			29.08.32	27.10.32
			03.11.32	02.02.35
			19.07.35	01.09.36
			04.03.37	02.06.47
	6109	1473	15.04.29	25.10.29
			11.07.32	23.03.34
			21.06.41	31.12.47
	6110	1474	01.08.21	15.04.29
			13.08.29	06.01.32
			30.04.32	03.11.32
			23.03.34	01.04.36
			27.09.39	21.09.41
			22.03.42	07.10.47
	6111	1475	25.11.27	13.08.29
			25.10.29	30.04.32
			02.02.35	09.06.36
			05.08.38	30.09.38
	6112	1476	28.05.32	04.03.33
			31.05.40	06.11.42
			13.08.44	19.01.48
	6113	1477	14.07.33	19.07.35
			31.03.36	04.03.37
			13.04.40	25.08.47
	6114	1478	18.07.34	17.06.35
			13.04.40	06.11.42

From 1927 Trafford Park started an association with the B9s which was to last virtually throughout their lives. In 1927 four engines went there and that number remained almost constant until World War Two. They had two main duties – the evening Deansgate goods to Colwick and the Ardsley goods, both worked overnight.

The B5s were only at Trafford Park for a short period after the war before returning to Mexborough. They worked CLC trains with no mention of working eastwards. The B9s were there from 1927 and lasted nearly to the end of their lives.

Over the fifty five years 4-4-0s, 0-6-0s, 2-6-0s and 4-6-0s from the GNR, GCR and the LNER worked the Deansgate fitted freights.

K2 2-6-0 No. 1652 was built in May 1916 at Doncaster and was renumbered No. 4652 in Aug 1924. Renumbered again as No. 1742 in Mar 1946 and then No. 61742 in Sep 1949 it had a forty six year life, being withdrawn in May 1962. No. 4652 is seen at an unknown location in between the wars.
A. G. Ellis

J39 0-6-0 No. 1255 was built in May 1927 at Darlington and was the twenty third of this large class to be built. It was renumbered No. 4722 in Apr 1946 and lasted until Feb 1960 as No. 64722. It is seen at the east end of Sheffield Victoria station on 30 Nov 1929.
W. Leslie Good

Because the Deansgate trains ran at night photographs are very rare. Here J39 No. 1298 passes under the Manchester Road bridge just outside Chorlton cum Hardy station with the 20.22 up Deansgate to Colwick fitted goods around 1938. The engine was built in Sep 1927 and renumbered No. 4743 in May 1946 and withdrawn in Jan 1961. The engine was shedded at Immingham until 20 Feb 1928 when it was transferred to Gorton, its home at the time of this photograph. Note that there were only about ten vans which shows that business at this time was poor. This section of line was reinstated in May 2013 as part of the Manchester Metrolink system.
Eddie Johnson collection

Ex-GCR B8 'Glenalmond' No. 1350 *Sutton Nelthorpe* was built in Jul 1914 and became LNER No. 5439 in Oct 1925 and No. 1350 in Dec 1946. Here it is recorded on the scrap line at Annesley on 22 Jun 1947, after it had left Colwick, and was officially withdrawn in August of that year.
Ken Boulter © Ted Hancock

REFERENCES

Midland Railway Working Timetable:
  Supplement Nov 1899
  Jul to Sep 1914
  14 Jul 1916 until further notice
LMS Working Timetables:
  11 Jul 1927 until further notice
  26 Sep 1938 until further notice
  7 May 1945 until further notice
Henshaw A. – *Great Northern Railway in the East Midlands No 3.* RCTS 2000
Groves N. – *Great Northern Locomotive History*
  Volume 3a: 1896-1911 – The Ivatt Era. RCTS 1990
  Volume 3b: 1911-1922 – The Gresley Era. RCTS 1992

Locomotives of the LNER
  Part 2B: Tender Engines – B1 to B19. RCTS 1975
  Part 3B: Tender Engines Classes – D1 to D12. RCTS 1980
  Part 5: Tender Engines Classes – J1 to J37. RCTS 1966
  Part 6A: Tender Engines Classes – J38 to K5. RCTS 1982
Yeadon W. B. – *Yeadon's Register of LNER Locomotives*
  Volume 11: Gresley J39 Class. Challenger Press 1996
  Volume 18: Gresley K1 K2 Thompson K1/1 & Peppercorn K1. Book Law/Railbus 2000
  Volume 19: Class D1 D2 D3 D4 & the M&GN. Book Law/Railbus 2001
  Volume 22: Class B1 (B18) to B9 the GC 4-6-0s. Book Law/Railbus 2001
  Volume 37a: Class J1 J2 J3 J4. Book Law Publications 2005
  Volume 37b: Class J5 J6 J7 J40 & J42. Book Law Publications 2006
Johnson E. M. – *Scenes from the Past 48: Manchester Central Station and the Great Northern Goods Warehouse.* Foxline Publications 2005

LOCOMOTIVE AND TRAFFIC SUMMARIES

WEEKLY SUMMARY OF FREIGHT TRAINS INCLUDING THOSE THAT STARTED AND TERMINATED AT THE HOPE VALLEY STATIONS

	1914 DOWN	1914 UP	1927 DOWN	1927 UP	1938 DOWN	1938 UP	1945 DOWN	1945 UP
DAILY	117	78	138	60	90	114	138	132
TUE – SAT	65	45	74	65	35	55	64	80
MON – FRI	10	45	5	40	40	20	6	5
TUE – FRI	14	4		4			4	
TUE – THU							2	3
MON ONLY	6	4	2	2	2	2	1	2
TUE ONLY	1							
WED ONLY						1		
SAT ONLY		5	3	8	1	6	2	2
SUN ONLY	5	5	2	7	2	3	21	17
NO OF TRAINS IN A 7 DAY PERIOD	1,105	948	1,234	918	920	1,016	1,212	1,263
TOTAL NO OF TRAINS	2,053		2,152		1,936		2,476	

SUMMARY OF TRAINS BETWEEN DORE AND CHINLEY BY STARTING AND FINISHING POINT

The table does not include places where the trains stopped en route and therefore does not give a full picture; as an example many of the trains for Sheffield first called at Queen's Road.

Trains that were run as required are included but trains that were suspended are not.

\multicolumn{7}{c	}{DOWN DIRECTION}
FROM	TO	1894	1914	1927	1938	1945
BIRMINGHAM						
WASHWOOD HEATH	HUSKISSON					6
CHESTERFIELD						
AVENUE	ANCOATS	5	6			
	EARLE'S				7	13
	GOWHOLE		13	22	13	19
	WATER WORKS SIDNGS		7			
	WINNINGTON (CLC)					6
CHESTERFIELD NORTH SIDINGS	GOWHOLE				14	3
CLAY CROSS	GOWHOLE			1	1	14
DRONFIELD	GOWHOLE				1	1
DUNSTON & BARLOW	ANCOATS	6				
STAVELEY	CHEADLE EXCH SIDINGS		14			
	GOWHOLE		20	21	14	25
	HEATON MERSEY			20	19	12
DERBY						
ST MARY'S	BRUNSWICK			1		1
LEEDS/ BRADFORD						
BRADFORD	ANCOATS	1	7			
	HEATON MERSEY	6				
LEEDS	HEATON MERSEY	6				
	HUSKISSON	6				
MANNINGHAM	ANCOATS		7			
STOURTON	CHEADLE EXCH SIDINGS		7	7		1
	HUSKISSON		7	6		
LEICESTER						
BELL LANE	ANCOATS				6	6
LONDON						
KINGS CROSS (GNR)	DEANSGATE (GNR)			6	6	
ST PANCRAS	ANCOATS				1	
SOMERS TOWN	ANCOATS	6	12	8	7	7
	BRUNSWICK		6			
NOTTINGHAMSHIRE						
BEESTON NE DIVN SIDINGS	BRUNSWICK					6
BRINSLEY SDGS	BRUNSWICK		1			
	DEANSGATE (GNR)		15			
BLACKWELL	GOWHOLE					14
COLWICK (GNR)	DEANSGATE (GNR)					6
MORTON SIDINGS	CHEADLE EXCH SIDINGS			7		
	HEATON MERSEY			6		
TIBSHELF	GOWHOLE			14	15	
	HEATON MERSEY	6	6	11		
	NORTHWICH	5				
TOTON	ANCOATS				1	6
	EARLE'S					7
	GOWHOLE				1	13
WESTHOUSES	GOWHOLE			1	13	7
PEAK DISTRICT						
EARLE'S SIDINGS	ARPLEY (LNWR)					1
	BUXTON					6
	GOWHOLE				1	
	HAZEL GROVE				6	
	WIDNES WD JCN (CLC)				6	6
EDALE	ANCOATS	1				
	HEATON MERSEY	5				
PETERBOROUGH						
SPITAL BRIDGE	HEATON MERSEY				6	1
ROTHERHAM						
HOLMES JCN	GOWHOLE				6	
MASBOROUGH STN	GOWHOLE					6

| DOWN DIRECTION |||||||
FROM	TO	1894	1914	1927	1938	1945
SHEFFIELD						
ENGINE SHED SIDINGS	HUSKISSON				6	
GRIMESTHORPE	BRUNSWICK			1		
	BUXTON (LNWR)		2	6		
	BUXTON		2	8	20	22
	CHEADLE EXCH SIDINGS		1		6	
	EARLE'S				7	7
	EDALE		7			
	EDGE HILL (LNWR)			7	7	6
	GOWHOLE		30	33	13	22
	GRINDLEFORD			7	6	7
	HEATON MERSEY					6
	HOPE			7		
	HUSKISSON		6	6		6
	LONGSIGHT (LNWR)			6		
	MOLD JCN (LNWR)			14		
	PEAK FOREST SOUTH			1	7	7
	TRAFFORD PARK		5	7		
	WALTON					6
NUNNERY	LANGTON DOCK (LNWR)					1
POND STREET	GOWHOLE		6			
	TRAFFORD PARK		1			
SHEFFIELD	HEATON MERSEY	11				
	GOWHOLE		6			
WICKER	BUXTON		7			
	GOWHOLE		8			
	HUSKISSON		6			
WINCOBANK	GOWHOLE			1		7
WEST RIDING						
CARLTON	CHEADLE EXCH SIDINGS				6	
	GLAZEBROOK (CLC)					6
HOUGHTON MAIN COLLIERY	GLAZEBROOK (CLC)			5		
ROUNDWOOD	BRUNSWICK		7			
STORRS MILL	BRUNSWICK			6		
	CHEADLE EXCH SIDINGS				1	
	GOWHOLE					7
YORK						
YORK	ANCOATS	5	4			
TOTAL		69	248	255	199	296

| UP DIRECTION |||||||
FROM	TO	1894	1914	1927	1938	1945
CHESHIRE						
HARTFORD (CLC)	KIRKBY	1				
MOLD JCN (LNWR)	ROUNDWOOD					6
MANCHESTER TO CHINLEY						
ADSWOOD SDGS (LNWR)	SHEFFIELD CITY (LNWR)			6		
CHEADLE SDGS	AVENUE			1		
	CHESTERFIELD		6			
	HUNSLET			5		
	QUEENS ROAD				6	
CHEADLE EXCH SIDINGS	CARLTON			7	6	7
	STAVELEY					7
EDGELEY (LNWR)	SHEFFIELD CITY (LNWR)				1	
GOWHOLE	AVENUE		6	1	5	7
	BLACKWELL		14	8	20	7
	CHESTERFIELD		6	1	5	7
	ENGINE SHED SIDINGS		16	1	8	7
	FRICKLEY COLLIERY			13		
	GRIMESTHORPE			7		
	HOLMES		14			
	MASBORO SORTING SDGS				7	
	SHERWOOD COLLIERY			6		
	STANTON GATE			1		1
	STAVELEY		12	25	14	42
	TIBSHELF					7

UP DIRECTION						
FROM	TO	1894	1914	1927	1938	1945
MANCHESTER TO CHINLEY (cont.)						
HEATON MERSEY	AVENUE		6	5		
	BRADFORD	6				
	KILNHURST					6
	SHEFFIELD	6				
	STAVELEY		7	6		6
	TOTON					7
NEW MILLS GOODS	AVENUE					8
LIVERPOOL						
BRUNSWICK	BRINSLEY JCN		7			
	ST PANCRAS		6			
	STORRS MILL			11		
	WINCOBANK			5		
EDGE HILL (LNWR)	SHEFFIELD CITY (LNWR)			7	6	
	QUEENS ROAD				1	
GARSTON DOCK	MASBORO STATION				6	
HALEWOOD	TIBSHELF					7
HUSKISSON	ENGINE SHED SIDINGS			7	6	7
	HUNSLET	7	6	6		
	LEEDS	14				
	MASBORO		1			
	SHEFFIELD	7				
	WICKER	6				
LANGTON DOCKS (LNWR)	SHEFFIELD CITY (LNWR)					2
MANCHESTER						
ANCOATS	AVENUE	5				
	BAMFORD				6	
	BRADFORD	7	7			
	EDALE	7				
	MASBORO			6		
	ST PANCRAS		6	6	7	6
	TOTON					7
ASHTON ROAD	HATHERSAGE			6		
DEANSGATE (GNR)	BRINSLEY JCN (GNR)		13	6		
	COLWICK (GNR)				6	7
SHIP CANAL SIDINGS	QUEENS ROAD			1	1	
TRAFFORD PARK	MASBORO			6		
	TIBSHELF					13
PEAK DISTRICT						
BUXTON	BLACKWELL	13				
	EARLE'S				7	
BUXTON JUNCTION NO 1	ENGINE SHED SIDINGS				1	
	GRIMESTHORPE			6		
BUXTON MID	HOPE				6	
BUXTON NO 1 SDGS	QUEENS ROAD					7
BUXTON UP SDGS	QUEENS ROAD					7
	WINCOBANK				1	
EARLE'S SIDINGS	AVENUE					7
	CHESTERFIELD					7
	WINCOBANK				7	6
EDALE	GRINDLEFORD		7			
GRINDLEFORD	GRIMESTHORPE			7	7	7
HATHERSAGE	WINCOBANK		7	6		
HOPE	MASBORO			6		
PEAK FOREST	KILNHURST			7		
	MASBORO STN				7	
	SHEFFIELD	7				
PEAK FOREST SOUTH SIDINGS	WINCOBANK DOWN SIDINGS					7
TOTAL		86	147	192	147	222

CONCLUDING ANALYSIS OF THE FREIGHT TIMETABLES

The total volume of trains between Dore and Chinley showed an increase in each year from 1914 with the exception of 1938 when it dropped. In the up direction there was a small increase between 1914 and 1927 followed by a decrease in 1938 and a 20% increase in 1945.

The 1914 and 1927 timetables show more trains heading west but this was reversed in 1938 and 1945. The 1945 excess of eastbound traffic may be explained by the fact that nearly all imports arrived on the west coast for onward transmission by rail to the eastern counties. Given that the Woodhead route was working to capacity the LMS would have been in a better position to handle this increased traffic.

It is interesting to compare freight traffic with that carried on the Woodhead route. In 1936 the Woodhead line carried 73 trains a day from east to west on weekdays ie 438 trains between Monday and Saturday compared with 168 on the Hope valley. In the opposite direction the figures were 81 daily and 486 on Monday to Saturday compared with 198 on the Hope valley. The Woodhead line occupancy was at a maximum of about four trains an hour in each direction as against just over one an hour on the Hope Valley.

In 1944 the Woodhead line carried 75 trains a day in the east to west direction on weekdays ie 450 trains Monday to Saturday compared with 214 on the Hope valley. In the other direction the figures were 86 daily and 516 Monday to Saturday as against 228 on the Hope Valley. The line occupancy was about the same on the Woodhead with an increased three trains every two hours on the Hope valley. Passenger train numbers would have obviously swelled the above numbers.

MOTIVE POWER

It has not been possible to give any great detail of engines that ran on the line during the Pre-Grouping period although there is more detailed information on the '2203' Class 4-4-0s which worked the line when it opened.

After the Grouping there was no immediate change in the classes working through the Hope valley. The 'Spinner' 4-2-2s were coming to the end of their useful lives; a few were at Nottingham and would have occasionally worked over the line but all were withdrawn by 1928. The Midland built 'Compound' 4-4-0s were the backbone of the main express workings at the Grouping and were supplemented by the LMS built Compounds which started to appear in 1924. The panoply of Midland rebuilt 4-4-0s were also well represented. From 1926 to 1932 the well liked Hughes mixed traffic 'Crab' 2-6-0s came on stream and were long linked to excursion traffic, Grimesthorpe shed receiving an allocation. By 1928 the LMS built 2P 4-4-0s of Midland design were appearing and took their place on the line. Freight workings were still in control of the myriad 0-6-0s of Midland origin and were supplemented by Fowler's LMS 4F 0-6-0s built between 1924 and 1928, which were still of pure Midland origin. Between 1927 and 1930 the mighty Garratts started to arrive, and, although primarily designed to haul the heavy coal trains from Toton to Brent they gradually worked to places such as Saltley, Peterborough and York and from Avenue and Toton to Gowhole.

The appointment of William Stanier as Chief Mechanical Engineer in 1932, he having come from the GWR allowed for a disinterested outsider to have a clean sheet and the massive restocking of the LMS with standard classes was soon reflected on the Hope valley. The Jubilees appeared in 1935 and took over the main London express workings, allowing the Compounds to be demoted to secondary services such as the Hope valley.

On passenger services 'Black Five' 4-6-0s started to appear with the occasional 'Jubilee' after 1934 although the embargo on the class running into Manchester Central was not lifted until Jul 1938 because of bridge weight restrictions. After the war Charles E. Fairburn, who succeeded Stanier in 1944, brought out the 2-6-0s Nos. 6400 to 6419, in 1946 and 1947 and with more being built after nationalisation this class was to become important players in the following years on passenger services. In 1947, forty more powerful 2-6-0s, Nos. 3000 to 3039 with high running boards to ease maintenance access, appeared and were regular performers although they did not sit easily with the beautiful environment of the valley.

On the freight side Fowler designed the 7F 0-8-0s which appeared from 1929. They were not highly regarded and were not dominant on the line. The revolution in freight motive power came with the introduction of Stanier's 8F 2-8-0s, which started to appear in 1935. They were built continuously until 1945. The 8Fs became the heavy freight engine of choice for the whole system during the war and many were used overseas. The class became the mainstay of freight workings on the Hope valley line until the end of steam.

A number of engines of American design, the 'S160' Class, were used during the war before leaving for work in mainland Europe. There is in existence a photograph of one near Hasland working a freight which might have been bound for the Hope valley (see page 223).

Mention also needs to be made of the ex-LNWR G1 and G2 'Super D' 0-8-0s mainly based at Buxton which regularly worked to Sheffield Grimesthorpe. The Midland men at Grimesthorpe hated them. Ken Stokes records 'More often than not, the trains to and from Buxton changed over en route at Hope, so we did not have the pleasure of a Super Ds for very long. They were extremely uncomfortable on which to work: a poor cab, a poor tender, which never seemed to hold enough coal: a flat fire grate of good size but a fire-hole much the same size as on the detested L&Y tanks, and a teaspoon sized shovel: a regulator that operated the opposite way to those of the Midland: a straight vacuum brake handle situated very high up, made of brass which got very hot in service. I remember once, when driving one of these Super Ds, we were dropping down to Chinley en route to Gowhole sidings. It was a very heavy train and I was reaching high up for the brake handle, on, off, on, eased and the palm of my hand became redder and redder by having constant contact with the burning heat of the brass handle. I was greatly relieved when we eventually stopped at Chinley North Junction advance starter and I was able to immerse my hand in the water bucket. One advantage was

Here is one of the '18 inch' Class, No. 8801, working a mineral empties in the up direction at Hasland on a windy day in 1943. *J. C. Naylor*

that the valve gear was of the Joy variety, so at least there was plenty of room in which to oil around. Moreover, as long as you kept at the firing, they would steam, whilst the best feature was the injectors. Both were situated below the footplate so you could not see the overflow and had to go by the sound to know that everything was working alright. They were strong engines and would amble along with a heavy train with the beats at the chimney random and all over the place – sometimes a loud one followed by three small ones, sometimes a small one, then a really big one and then two small ones – and so on.'

Talking of unattractive engines, the War Department 2-8-0 Austerity locomotives were built in large numbers for home and overseas use and became a common sight on the line right into the 1960s.

Back to ex-LNWR engines fireman Mike Stokes relates having an ex-LNWR '18 inch' 4-6-0 mixed traffic loco No. 8801 on a 09.00 special train Liverpool and lodge turn from Grimesthorpe to Liverpool Aintree with 35 wagons of Frickley steam coal. Neither he nor his driver had been on one before. He records that 'all the engines shunting in the sidings stopped work for a moment for their crews to watch our 'Premier Line' representative wheeze its way on to the up local line. If anyone did not see us at first they were soon made aware of our presence by its extraordinary beat – *peff, peff, peff, peff*. My mate remarked it sounded as if we had a wooden leg! But I soon found out that uneven beats or not, there was nothing wrong with the firebox's appetite for coal and I began steadily plying the shovel. We passed through platform No. 6 at Sheffield station with a couple of Millhouses men on their Compound looking with some amusement at our progress. The 18 inch liked neither the load nor the gradient but it was a dry day and she kept her feet admirably up the long pull to Dore and Totley.

Good progress was made to Hathersage where water was taken. On the downgrade through Bamford a good speed was reached but at Earle's Sidings we were pulled off to let a couple of other freights pass. At Edale, the same happened but this time for a slow passenger. On checking the tender it was found that coal stocks were low although we had only covered 20 miles. I climbed onto the top of the first wagon and soon lumps of the Frickley best were being pitched forward on to the tender. The eighteen mile descent from Cowburn tunnel presented a different problem. 'Without any prejudice, the vacuum brake compares badly with a steam brake on a loose coupled train. However with the tender brake screwed hard on, plus heavy applications of the power brake, allied to the hand brake being applied by the guard in the rear, we were just about in control of the train. At Aintree a couple of 'Lanky' men relieved us and took the train on to the docks.' The following day, Ken was booked on a train to Gowhole and, much to his disgust, it was the same engine.

| CLASSIFICATION OF TENDER FREIGHT ENGINES 1945 ||
No.	CLASSES
2	Midland 2F 0-6-0 2987-3177, 22567-22863, 22900-22984 LNWR 18in 4-6-0 8801, 8815, 8824, 8834, 8858, 28768
3	Midland 3F 0-6-0 3191-3834
4	Midland 4F 3835-4026, LMS 4F 0-6-0 4027-4606 LMS 'Compound' 4-4-0 900-939, 1045-1199 one seventh less load than 4F
5	'Crab' 2-6-0 2700-2794 LMS Stanier 2-6-0 2945-2984 'Black 5' 4-6-0 5000-5494 5X 'Jubilee' 4-6-0 5552-5742
6	LNWR G1 0-8-0 8892-9391
7	LMS 7F 0-8-0, LNW G2 & G2a 0-8-0 8893-9454
8	LMS 8F 2-8-0 8000-8684, USA 2-8-0, WD 2-8-0 loaned
UN-CLASSIFIED	Garratt 2-6-6-2 7967-7999. Load equal to one 4F 0-6-0

A working instruction stated – 'All mineral trains must as far as possible be worked by a 20 ton brake van. Between 04.00 and 22.00 the maximum numbers of wagons authorised in both directions for full and empty mineral trains between Chinley East Junction and Hathersage is 43 wagons (because of the limits of the lie by sidings)'.

Another consideration for trains accessing the Hope valley from the south was that sometimes trains were put inside at Dronfield Colliery sidings which could only hold 39 wagons, an impediment to using the 8Fs full potential. A retired goods guard is reported to have claimed to have worked the first Hope valley Garratt hauled train, 50 wagons of Dunston slack, in about 1942. However it is known that Garratts worked over the line before the war. He said that 'once Tapton Junction was cleared you knew you had right of way all the way to Gowhole as there was nowhere you could be put inside before Chinley.'

MOTIVE POWER SEEN ON THE LINE

Of the thirty three built the following Garratts were shedded at Hasland in the LMS period and would have worked over the line from Avenue to Gowhole.

THE HASLAND GARRATTS				
ORIGINAL No.	1938/9 No.	BR No.	FROM	TO
4968	7968	47968	28.05.38	10.08.57*
	7971	47971	15.02.41	16.04.56
	7973	47973	01.10.38	23.03.57*
4980	7980	47980	28.05.38	26.01.57*
4983	7983	47983	28.05.38	01.01.56*
4984	7984	47984	08.32	16.04.54
	7990	47990	29.03.41	16.04.54
	7992	47992	29.03.41	25.02.56*
	7993	47993	29.03.41	06.11.53
4997	7997	47997	13.08.32	24.11.50
* = date of withdrawal.				

Two arrived in 1932 with four more allocated in 1938 followed by a final four in 1941. All remained until after Nationalisation.

Toton had a larger allocation and they were occasionally to be seen in the valley as well.

OBSERVATIONS

Chris Crofts provided notes of sightings on the line on 4 Jul 1939 at Grindleford:-

4-4-0s – 351, 447, 461, 462, 485, 543,

2-8-0s – 8054, 8055

0-6-0s – 3771, 3882

The ex-Midland 4-4-0s were in black livery with red shading to the letters and numbers and red lining. The two ex Midland 0-6-0s had Belpaire boilers and were painted black with coal rails on the Fowler tenders.

That doyen of all things Midland, David Tee, made meticulous notes of his observations and the following are extracts concerning the Hope Valley and connecting lines.

24 DEC 1945			
WHEEL ARR	No.	DESCRIPTION & LOCATION	TIME
		GRINDLEFORD	
2-8-0	8099	Down mixed freight	10.06
0-6-0	3343	Shunting the yard	10.24
2-6-2T	113	Chinley to Sheffield stopper	
		EDALE	
2-8-0	8208	Down mixed freight	20.06
		DIDSBURY	
2-6-2T	95	Manchester Central to Sheffield stopper. Six coaches	08.45

25 APR 1946			
WHEEL ARR	No.	DESCRIPTION & LOCATION	TIME
		DORE	
2-8-0	8697	Up mixed freight from Hope valley	10.36
0-6-0	3334	Up mixed freight from Hope valley	11.25
4-6-0	5268	Sheffield to Manchester Cen stopper	19.10
		EDALE	
2-8-0	8124	Down coal train	09.59

The imposing bulk of Garratt No. 4998 (7998), when new, on 21 Jul 1927 at Cricklewood. It was the second of the first three built by Beyer Peacock in Manchester. The overall wheelbase was seventy nine feet with a total weight of 149 tons when carrying seven tons of coal and 4,500 gallons of water. Note the squat chimney of the first batch. They had screw couplings because they were vacuum braked rather than the three link more common to freight engines. This one, and No. 4999, retained the original bunker with the coal rails at the top edge when all the rest acquired rotating bunkers which assisted in accessing the coal for the fireman. When new, No. 4998 was shedded at Toton. After a four month spell at Wellingborough in 1930/1 it was at Westhouses until Apr 1935 and then Toton on 10 Feb 1940 where it stayed until withdrawal in Aug 1956 having covered 551,315 miles over twenty nine years. *Photomatic*

25 APR 1946 (cont.)

WHEEL ARR	No.	DESCRIPTION & LOCATION	TIME
		HATHERSAGE	
2-6-0	2901	Up coal empties	
		CHINLEY	
4-4-0	468	Chinley to Dore	
0-6-0	4418	Chinley to Hope valley mineral empties	09.44
4-4-0	545	Chinley to Sheffield stopper	20.10
4-4-0	693	Sheffield to Chinley stopper	
2-6-2T	113	Chinley to Sheffield stopper	17.45
4-6-0	5621*	Manchester to Sheffield stopper	
4-4-0	1075	Manchester to Sheffield stopper	
		* Northern Rhodesia	

12 Oct 1946

WHEEL ARR	No.	SHED	DESCRIPTION & LOCATION	TIME
			HEATON MERSEY	
4-4-0	419	16A	Sheffield to Manchester express 10 coaches including dining car	09.12
4-4-0	468		Chinley to Dore	
0-6-0	4826	22B	Sheffield to Manchester express 10 coaches	11.22
4-4-0	438		Manchester to Sheffield stopper 6 coaches	13.24
4-4-0	693		Sheffield to Chinley stopper	
0-6-0	4826	22B	Manchester to Sheffield stopper 6 coaches	15.13
4-6-0	5621*		Manchester to Sheffield stopper	
4-4-0	1052	19G	Manchester to Sheffield stopper 6 coaches	16.16
2-6-4T	2371	19B	Sheffield to Manchester stopper 5 coaches	19.28
			DIDSBURY	
4-4-0	693	9D	Sheffield to Manchester stopper 4 coaches and one van	16.42
4-4-0	468		Manchester to Sheffield	
4-4-0	419	16A	Manchester to Sheffield express	17.01
4-4-0	564	19B	Sheffield to Manchester express	17.35

Howard Turner, Sheffield's well known transport raconteur and photographer, recalled, that as a schoolboy he visited along with his brother an uncle who lived at Hathersage. This list is the 'cops' he made. The engines that he had seen before are not included.

Howard's juvenile notes comment 'Eighteen locomotives from eight classes including one Garratt, one LMS 7F and no less than six 'Duck eights' (ex-LNWR G1, G2)'.

3 May 1947

WHEEL ARR	No.	SHED	WHEEL ARR	No.	SHED	WHEEL ARR	No.	SHED
4-4-0	1052	19G	4-6-0	5263	19B	0-8-0	9214	9D
4-4-0	1076	19G	2-6-6-2T	7984	18C	0-8-0	9245	3A
0-6-0	3219	18C	2-8-0	8011	18B	0-8-0	9326	9D
0-6-0	4141	20C	2-8-0	8053	18D	0-8-0	9376	9D
0-6-0	4334	19A	2-8-0	8111	18D	0-8-0	9428	2D
0-6-0	4365	9D	0-8-0	9085	8B	0-8-0	9551	25G

MOTIVE POWER FROM PHOTOGRAPHS

From photographs and the observation lists above the following engines certainly worked over the line. These should just be seen as a sample as they represent only a fraction of the engines in the fifty year period covered by this volume. The GNR engines that worked the Deansgate to Colwick night fitted freights are not included.

CLASS	No.	SHED	DATE
3P 2-6-2T	89	9F	
	95	19D	24.12.45
	113	19B	24.12.45 25.04.46
2P 4-4-0	342		
	346		
	351	19A	04.07.39
	353	19A	05.34
	373		
2P 4-4-0	382	19A	25.07.32
	384	19B	03.09.25
	386		
2P 4-4-0	401	19A	07.08.37
	419	16A	12.10.46
	438	2B	12.10.46
	446	20C	1934
	447	9D	04.07.39
	461	5C	04.07.39
	462	3C	04.07.39
	468	19A	25.04.46
	478	16A	07.08.37
	479		07.08.37
	485	19B	07.09.39
	490		
	494		
	543	15C	07.09.39
	544	19D	
	545	19B	25.04.46
2P 4-4-0	564	19B	12.10.46
	623		
	693	9D	25.04.46 12.10.46
MIDLAND COMPOUND 4-4-0	1016	19A	
	1020		
	1040		

285

CLASS	No.	SHED	DATE
LMS 'COMPOUND' 4-4-0	1052	19F	03.05.47
	1057	19B	
	1063	19A	18.06.32
	1075	19B	25.04.46
	1076	19B	03.05.47
	1089	19A	
	1090	2A	15.05.38
	1144	20A	
1P 0-4-4T	1396 (58076)	19B	
	1398		
4P 2-6-4T	2371	19B	12.10.46
5F 2-6-0 'CRAB'	13069 (2739)		31.07.32
	2752		
	2760	17D	1936
	2761	19A	1938
	2769	17B	
	2787		
	2797	19A	
	2901	26A	25.04.46
3F 0-6-0 MID	3219	18C	03.05.47
	3274	9D	
	3334	19A	25.04.46
	3336		
	3343	19A	24.12.45
	3468	16C	
	3533	19C	
	3574	19E	24.07.43
	3575	18D	
	3622	19A	06.08.47
	3660	19C	
	3731	19A	
	3749	19A	04.05
	3771	18C	
	3793	18A	
4F 0-6-0 MID	3842	9D	03.09.25
	3863	18D	
	3865	17C	
	3882	18B	07.08.37
	3892	18A	
	3927		
	3981		
	3983	16D	
	3984	19A	
	4017	17D	12.03.39
	4018	17D	09.38
	4019	9D	
4F 0-6-0 LMS	4053	18C	
	4107	16A	
	4141	20C	03.05.47
	4162		
	4287	15C	
	4294	18C	

CLASS	No.	SHED	DATE
4F 0-6-0 LMS (cont.)	4323		
	4334	19A	03.05.47
	4365	9B	03.05.47
	4418	19A	25.04.46
	4426	19A	07.08.37
	4428	17B	07.08.37
	4550	19A	21.09.45
	4572		
	4573	19A	08.38
	4826	22B	09.45
5MT 4-6-0	4884	12A	09.45
	4886	12A	09.45
	5180	17A	1937
	5263	19B	03.05.47
	5268	21A	25.04.46
5XP 4-6-0 'JUBILEE'	5621	19B	25.04.46
2-6-6-2T GARRATT	7967	18A	
	7968	18C	
	7984	18C	03.05.47
	7990		
8F 2-8-0	8011	18B	03.05.47
	8053	18D	03.05.47
	8054	18D	
	8055	18B	07.09.39
	8067		
	8082	18B	
	8099		24.12.45
	8111	18D	03.05.47
	8124	18D	25.04.46
	8167	14A	
	8208	19D	24.12.45
	8314	19A	
	8341	18D	16.02.47
	8616	16C	11.07.46
	8697		25.04.46
	8748	8C	
G1 0-8-0 LNWR	9085		03.05.47
	9134	10B	11.07.46
	9214	9B	03.05.47
	9245	3A	03.05.47
	9326	9B	03.05.47
	9376	9D	03.05.47
G2a 0-8-0 LNWR	9428	2D	03.05.47
	9505	27B	
	9551	19A	03.05.47
LNWR 19 in 4-6-0	8801		
2F 0-6-0 MID	22940 (58134)	20C	
	22951 (58140)	19A	

In the Midland period each area had a main engine shed which was identified by just a number. Satellite sheds had the same number but with the addition of a small letter. In 1935 under the LMS the shed codes were revised with all sheds having a number and capital letter grouped round a parent shed. The codes quoted here are from the 1947 list.

2A	Rugby	17B	Burton
2B	Bletchley	17D	Rowsley
2D	Nuneaton	18A	Toton
3A	Bescot	18B	Westhouses
3C	Walsall	18C	Hasland
5C	Stafford	18D	Staveley
8B	Warrington Arpley	19A	Grimesthorpe
8C	Speke Junction	19B	Millhouses
9B	Stockport	19C	Canklow
9D	Buxton	19D	Heaton Mersey
9F	Heaton Mersey	19E	Belle Vue
10B	Preston	19F	Trafford Park
12A	Carlisle Kingmoor	20A	Holbeck
14A	Cricklewood	20C	Royston
15C	Leicester	21A	Saltley
16A	Nottingham	22B	Gloucester
16C	Kirkby	25G	Farnley Junction
16D	Mansfield	26A	Newton Heath
17A	Derby		

And so on to Vol. 2 which will cover in detail the stations and infrastructure, the widening of the lines from Sheffield to Dore, and Chinley North Junction to New Mills South Junction. Also, the reservoir railways and Earle's Cement history and branch and much more.

REFERENCES

Stokes Ken – *Both Sides of the Footplate*. Bradford Barton 1985

Hobson Dennis – *Hobson's Choice: Recollections of a North Country Engineman*. OPC 1986

Locomotives Illustrated 165 – The Midland Railway 1907 Renumbering. RAS Publishing 2007

Ellis C. Hamilton – *The Midland Railway*. Ian Allan 2nd imp 1974

Bagwell Philip S. – *The Transport Revolution 1770-1985*. Routledge 2nd ed 1988

APPENDIX 1
NUMBERS OF MEN, HORSES AND ENGINES EMPLOYED ON BUILDING THE LINE

The information is taken from the engineers reports to the directors. The period December 1893 until June 1896, when the reports finished, does not record these figures. The numbers of engines would have included stationary as well as locomotive engines.

DATE	CONTRACT No.1 MEN	HORSES	ENGINES	CONTRACT No.2 MEN	HORSES	ENGINES
18.12.1888	300	n/k	n/k	240	n/k	n/k
16.01.1889	430	n/k	n/k	386	n/k	n/k
12.02.1889	425	8	16	414	50	6
12.03.1889	400	16	2	467	45	5
13.04.1889	420	10	19	484	51	6
11.05.1889	510	18	22	600	60	7
15.06.1889	481	23	23	584	57	10
16.07.1889	520	10	22	502	57	11
06.08.1889	540	15	24	675	60	13
12.09.1889	596	17	26	681	61	14
10.10.1889	621	19	28	714	66	16
12.11.1889	572	14	28	813	50	19
17.12.1889	591	29	14	916	50	16
09.01.1890	598	27	29	844	50	25
28.02.1890	696	31	29	1,066	50	25
13.03.1890	647	26	30	1,048	50	30
10.04.1890	662	34	39	986	50	27
08.05.1890	809	80	36	947	47	35
12.06.1890	844	98	38	921	67	26
10.07.1890	806	87	40	916	90	28
05.08.1890	707	70	39	902	98	27
13.09.1890	690	76	39	974	96	29
11.10.1890	725	80	38	1,350	97	30
15.11.1890	861	84	38	1,406	54	31
13.12.1890	938	80	40	1,310	75	32
10.01.1891	1,001	78	40	1,078	74	24
14.02.1891	967	84	40	1,318	94	35
14.03.1891	936	85	41	1,454	110	39
09.04.1891	984	73	41	1,407	119	39
07.05.1891	1,057	74	42	1,506	130	38

DATE	CONTRACT No.1 MEN	HORSES	ENGINES	CONTRACT No.2 MEN	HORSES	ENGINES
11.06.1891	*1,056	90	43	1,308	126	38
09.07.1891	1,230	91	36	1,179	89	28
01.08.1891	1,185	94	27	1,200	93	25
10.09.1891	1,399	92	26	1,473	51	18
10.10.1891	1,486	93	27	1,472	64	20
12.11.1891	1,472	83	29	1,513	65	21
10.12.1891	1,408	87	29	1,557	66	21
09.01.1892	1,330	155	29	1,417	57	21
11.02.1892	1,381	132	26	1,413	57	21
10.03.1892	1,401	135	29	1,513	57	21
07.04.1892	1,444	135	28	1,637	57	21
12.05.1892	1,568	104	24	1,646	57	21
09.06.1892	1,533	85	28	1,671	51	21
09.07.1892	1,703	93	28	1,647	53	20
06.08.1892	1,690	91	31	1,591	53	20
15.09.1892	1,840	85	30	1,582	45	20
13.10.1892	1,841	105	29	1,553	27	13
10.11.1892	1,746	129	29	1,520	18	7
08.12.1892	1,815	145	32	1,292	45	20
12.01.1893	1,798	159	28	813	34	12
09.02.1893	1,715	171	26	831	25	10
09.03.1893	1,673	117	25	903	25	10
13.04.1893	1,694	118	23	821	25	10
11.05.1893	1,530	93	21	861	16	15
10.06.1893	1,309	126	21	787	15	15
15.07.1893	1,192	71	18	829	15	18
03.08.1893	923	75	19	809	15	18
14.09.1893	783	39	19	780	7	13
12.10.1893	933	24	16	696	2	8
09.11.1893	295	18	16	432	12	21

* These figures are further broken down into 608 men in Totley tunnel and 448 outside.

APPENDIX 2
NAVVY ACCIDENTS AND DEATHS
Contract No. 1

MEN KILLED

NAME	AGE	DATE	ADDRESS	NOTES
George Griffiths		22.12.1888	Whittington Moor	Miner. Killed Totley tunnel
John Sorrell	14	25.06.1889	Hathersage	Navvy. Buried in Hathersage churchyard
Frederick Herbert		14.08.1889	Totley	Resident engineer. Killed by train Totley
Richard Green	43	05.11.1889	Padley	Killed in Totley tunnel
Thomas Spencer Cook	51	28.04.1890		Navvy. Killed in tunnel
John Johns	51	22.06.1890	Hathersage	Navvy. Buried in Hathersage churchyard
Henry Stevens Wilcox	24	16.08.1890		Navvy. Killed in tunnel
Moxon Slandford	51	11.03.1891	Padley	Navvy. Buried in Hathersage churchyard
John Marriner	32	02.05.1891	Hathersage	Navvy. Buried in Hathersage churchyard
Edward Green	51	11.07.1891	Hathersage	Navvy. Buried in Hathersage churchyard
Thomas Hunt	63	02.09.1891	Padley	Navvy. Buried in Hathersage churchyard
Albert Schofield	22	04.12.1891	Hathersage	Navvy. Killed by cutting collapse Padley Wood. Buried in Hathersage churchyard
Herbert Turner	18	10.12.1891	Hathersage	Navvy. Crushed between two wagons at Padley Wood. Buried in Hathersage churchyard
Thomas Lynch	27	14.12.1891	Padley	Navvy. Buried in Hathersage churchyard
Joseph King - 'Lincoln Joe'	45	15.01.1892	Padley	Navvy. Killed by wagon in tunnel. Buried in Hathersage churchyard
Amos Webb	21	23.03.1892	Hathersage	Navvy. Buried in Hathersage churchyard
Robert Bird	35	30.03.1892	Padley	Buried in Hathersage churchyard
Charles Ronksley	21	22.04.1892	Hathersage	Navvy. Killed at Padley. Buried in Hathersage churchyard
John Morley		07.05.1892	No fixed abode	Civilian. Killed by engine Totley Bents
Frederick Walter Spafford	30	17.06.1892		Killed in Totley tunnel. Buried in Dore churchyard
George Wood	43	02.09.1892	Bakewell Union	Navvy. Buried in Hathersage churchyard
George William Ellis	25	28.09.1892	Hathersage	Navvy. Buried in Hathersage churchyard
John Clayton	43	10.01.1893	Newtown	Navvy. Buried in Hathersage churchyard
George Hunt	13	25.01.1893	Dore	Locomotive boy assistant. Killed in cutting
William King	31	31.03.1893	Padley	Navvy. Buried in Hathersage churchyard
John Thomas Lavers	21	25.04.1893	The Huts No 4 shaft	Killed. Buried in Dore churchyard
Richard Cullen	48	08.05.1893	Newtown	Navvy. Buried in Hathersage churchyard
William Wainwright	20	16.05.1893	Padley	Navvy. Killed in Totley tunnel Buried in Hathersage churchyard
Arthur Ford	35	31.05.1893	Bakewell Union	Navvy. Buried in Hathersage churchyard
James Hodge	64	09.08.1893	Hathersage	Navvy. Buried in Hathersage churchyard
Richard Jones	51	16.01.1894	Hathersage	Navvy. Buried in Hathersage churchyard
George Sanson	23	?	Padley	Navvy. Working in a cutting

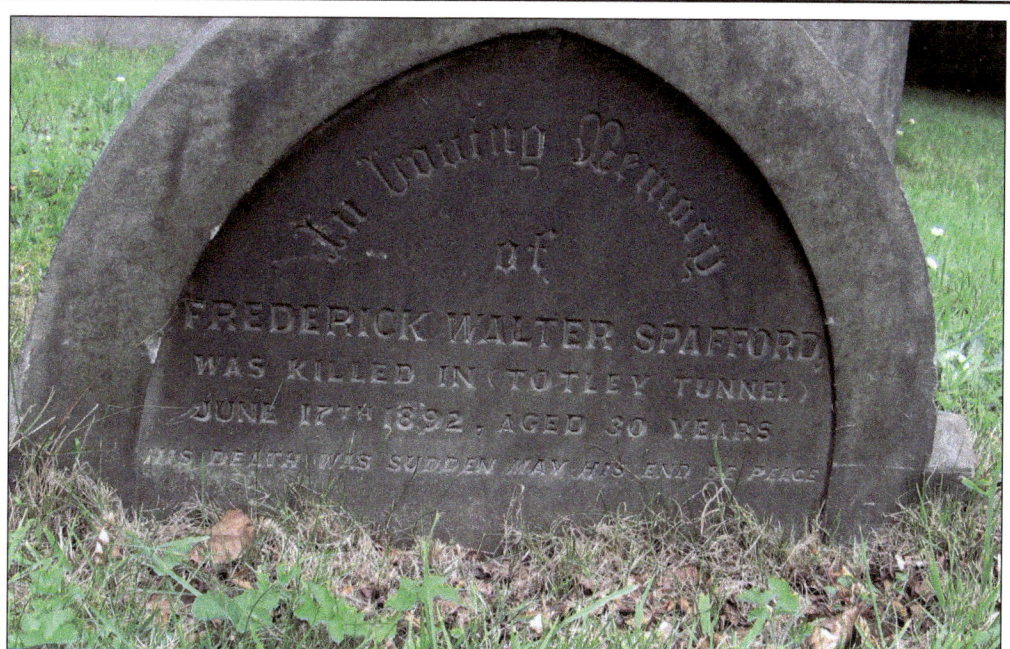

The headstone of Frederick Walter Spafford in Dore churchyard. There are only two identifiable navvy headstones in the churchyard, the other being John Thomas Lavers. The latter's headstone is identical, including the verse, but does not mention the tunnel. Compared with other headstones nearby this is small and is near the small-pox headstones. The details of Frederick Spafford's death can be found on page 141.

Author

OTHER DEATHS

16 Feb 1890. **William Thorpe**, age 41, a navvy was found dead in bed.

19 Jun 1890. An **unnamed** man, was found dead on the road in the parish of Hope and conveyed to a burial at Hathersage on this date. He may have been a navvy seeking work.

30 Apr 1891. **John Marriner** was a navvy from Tugby in Leicestershire who had been drinking very heavily. On Sun 26 Apr, at Schofield's lodging house at Hathersage, he attempted to cut his throat with a pocket knife. The wound, which was not very serious, was stitched up and he was kept under surveillance overnight by PC Irwin. The following day Irwin took him to Bakewell workhouse infirmary. There he was watched until the following Thursday by the local police, to whom he was speaking when he rolled over, groaned and, within a short time, died. At the inquest the verdict was that 'the deceased died from apoplectic convulsions brought on in consequence of a wound to the throat which wound was self inflicted whilst the deceased was in a state of temporary insanity'.

Sun 31 Jul 1891. **'Bandy Wheeler'** was found early in the morning dying under a haystack at Totley Bents. He was removed to a hut nearby but died within a few minutes. He had been in the neighbourhood for about three weeks during which time he had been drinking and sleeping out.

MEN INJURED

4 Sep 1888. **Samuel Weir**, engineer of Totley, was recovering the machinery of the Rock Mining Co when, having fixed a large chain to remove the steam pump from the bottom of the shaft, the tub being drawn up with some small castings caught the large chain, which took it up the shaft a distance of several feet. The tub then fell and severely injured Weir, rendering him unconscious. The man at the top descended the shaft and put him in a tub and brought him up to the surface.

23 Mar 1889. **'Devon Jack'** age over 50, who lived in one of the No. 4 shaft huts started work at 06.00 at the shaft. Shortly afterwards a large piece of shale fell down the shaft and struck him on the head, cutting him across the scalp and rendering him unconscious. Although little hope was entertained of his recovery he did, in fact, recover.

25 Mar 1889. An **unnamed** man who was working in the cutting between Dore station and the tunnel was near the 'steam jubilee navvy' when a large stone fell off the bucket and struck him on the head, severely cutting him.

15 Apr 1889. **'Dick'** was sinking a shaft near the tunnel entrance when a piece of bind fell down the shaft and cut him severely across the top of the head. He was taken to the surface where his injuries were treated.

20 Apr 1889. **'Gunner'** was on scaffolding near the bottom of Shaft No. 1 when he fell off and landed on his head and face which was cut in a dreadful manner. Medical assistance was summoned and he was taken home. He was recovering but would not be back at work for some considerable time. (Is the nick name 'Gunner' linked to the saying that somebody is always 'gunner' do something but never does or is it more likely linked to a military connection or a gunpowder charge?)

Wed 22 May 1889. Two months later **'Devon Jack'** survived another accident. He was standing on some scaffolding at the entrance when he fell off it to the ground. He was seriously injured by coming into contact with loose bind and shale.

Wed 22 May 1889. On the same day **George Pethers**, age 17, of Green Oak, Totley, who was employed to grease the tip wagons, went under one of the wagons when a horse was attached to them. His right knee was under the wheel of the wagon when it moved and he was seriously injured.

Wed 29 May 1889. **James Thorpe**, a miner, was working on some scaffolding when he accidentally fell to the level of the line. He was taken to the surface where he was found to have a broken leg. This was the same leg as the one broken whilst previously working on a tunnel at Halifax.

Sat 1 Jun 1889. **Frank Ball**, age 18, of Green Oak, Totley, was working with the tip wagon which removes spoil from the steam navvy at Totley Brook to the tip at Totley Bents when he got the elbow of his left arm between two of the wagons and was crushed. He was taken to Sheffield Infirmary for treatment and was discharged later in the day. Tragically his father, Andrew Ball, died suddenly the following day.

Wed 12 Jun 1889. **'Linton Charlie'** or **'Little Charlie'** had a large quantity of soil fall on his back, sending him with full force against a wagon. His head was cut four inches in length and was stitched up by a medical man.

9 Aug 1889. **Thomas Rodgers** was working on a crane with the stonemasons at the Dore end of the tunnel when he slipped and accidentally let go of the handle. This struck his left arm with great velocity and broke it just below the elbow.

23 Nov 1889. **'Rattening Charlie'** of Totley had a quantity of loose bind fall on his head and back. He was taken to the surface and conveyed to his home.

Nov 1889. **'Yorkie'** was hit on the head by a fall of bind.

Thu 5 Dec 1889. **James Dyson**, who lived in Campo Lane, Sheffield, broke his leg when a fall of earth fell on him. He was sent to Sheffield station by train where a policeman rendered first aid before taking him by ambulance to hospital.

Fri 6 Dec 1889. **Petterford**, of Bradway, was working with two others in the crane shaft (No. 4). A shot had been set and fired, the refuse of which had been cleared away. The men were again at work when suddenly a quantity of bind fell from the side and pierced three inches into Petterford's thigh, which was crushed. Another unnamed man had two fingers broken and the third man hurt his leg but not seriously.

Fri 6 Dec 1889. On the same day **Taylor**, of Holmesfield, was injured by a brick falling down No. 4 shaft. He was conveyed home.

Fri 6 Dec 1889. This was a bad day on the works. **Jones**, of Dronfield Woodhouse, was returning for his coat after a charge had been laid when a premature explosion severely cut his head and face.

Thu 12 Dec 1889. A number of men were working in the cutting near Dore station when a quantity of earth fell down the embankment on to an **unnamed** man. His legs were severely crushed. He was sent by rail to his home at Heeley where he received attention.

Wed 8 Jan 1890. A man named **Williams** was working in No. 3 shaft when a huge piece of wood fell and cut off two of his toes.

Sat 11 Jan 1890. **Harry Sloper** was working in Shaft No. 1 when a large piece of wood, used as a prop, fell and struck him on the head, cutting his scalp a considerable length and also damaging his shoulder. A medical man was summoned who stitched the head wound.

Sat 11 Jan 1890. On the same day an **unnamed** man was in the crane shaft (No. 4) near the tunnel mouth when a piece of bind fell on his head and cut it badly.

Sat 11 Jan 1890. On the same day a man known as **'Little Punch'**, a Norfolk man, was working in the tunnel at No. 3 shaft. A scaffold had been erected near the head of the tunnel and several shots had been fired off. Upon the men resuming work a large piece of bind, which had been resting on the scaffold from shots, fell down ten feet and caught 'Little Punch' on his head, cutting a gash from which blood flowed freely. He was taken to his home, where he grew weak from loss of blood and became unconscious. A medical man was sent for and found that he was suffering from a fractured skull and was given little chance of recovery. Another **unnamed** man was similarly injured.

Feb 1890. **J. Hall**, an engine driver, together with **James Dayer**, a rope runner, were taking a locomotive from the shed near Dore station to the tunnel mouth and as it crossed a temporary bridge over the River Sheaf the structure gave way. Dayer and a youth who was on the engine jumped out into four feet of water but Hall courageously stayed on the engine as it turned over. He quickly climbed on top and opened the safety valves, thus preventing an explosion. Hall escaped with a ducking and a small scald on one arm.

5 May 1890. **John Hall**, a labourer at Shaft No. 3 fell eighteen feet off a scaffold onto his face. His nose was cut off, his mouth was cut and all his front teeth knocked out. He was moved to his lodgings.

4 Jun 1890. **John Parry** had his right arm severely crushed whilst working at Shaft No. 2. He was taken to see a doctor.

Mid 1890. **Harry Sloper**, again, was hit by a wooden prop which fell down Shaft No. 1. It cut open his scalp again and injured his shoulder. A doctor stitched his wound.

4 Aug 1890. **William Farmer**, an engine driver, was working at Shaft No. 4 and was trying to get an air compressing engine to start when he slipped into the flywheel. He was taken on a stretcher to his lodgings for medical aid in a critical state.

Wed 20 Jun 1891. **'Prince'**, a miner, drilled and charged two holes. He fired one shot but a second did not go off. He went back to check when there was an explosion and he was struck by a rock. His right eye was very badly damaged. He was taken to his home.

Sat 23 Jun 1891. **Richard Howard**, while working at Totley Bents, fell backwards off a scaffold in the tunnel. First aid was promptly rendered by Mr Williams, a member of the St Johns Ambulance Society, who had him moved to his home.

Sat 30 Jul 1891. **William Sheldon**, age 37, of Dronfield, a stone mason, was injured in the erection of a new tunnel face. With a number of other men he was putting in the foundations when a large piece of timber fell from the side of the cutting and struck him on the forehead. He was rendered unconscious and remained in that condition for an hour and a half. He was then removed to his home.

28 Aug 1891. **Thomas Smith** was working in No. 5 cutting at Kettle (between Grindleford and Hathersage) when a fall of earth and stones left him partially buried. His right leg was broken. He was moved to Hathersage for treatment.

1 Feb 1892. An **unnamed** rope runner was on a locomotive at Totley. He was seriously injured to his left foot when a wagon ran over it.

4 Apr 1892. **'Punch'** of Dronfield Woodhouse fell through a scaffold. He was taken home where he was examined whereupon it was decided to move him to Sheffield Infirmary.

20 Oct 1892. **Isaac Bower** was in charge of three horses hauling ten trucks of earth. One of the horses knocked him down and three trucks ran over him. Several of his ribs were broken and he had other serious injuries He was taken to Sheffield Infirmary.

12 Nov 1892. **Charles Short**, a rope runner on the contractor's locomotives, was seriously injured while conducting shunting operations. A wagon got off the metals and Short got between the buffers of the engine. He received serious injuries about the chest and was removed to the hospital at Sheffield.

8 Dec 1893. A report stated that there was an explosion of gas in Totley tunnel. 'The bore hole, which had been put down shaft No. 4 to release the water accumulating in the shaft above, became blocked. Attempts to velar (cover) the obstruction above the heading having failed, the fireman of the gang of men working at the heading conceived the idea of pushing rods from the bottom. The idea was attempted and was partially successful and allowed some water to be released. However, a large quantity of gas had accumulated in the bore hole which escaped into the heading. It came into contact with the men's candles and caused an explosion. The heading was temporarily illuminated with great brilliance and then the workers were thrown and rendered insensible. A huge stone hit one man and his side was hurt and all the men received burns to their hands and faces. The balcony and ladder under the bore was blown away. Dr Allred had one of the men removed to Sheffield Infirmary, others who were suffering from burns and shock were sent home and one or two were able to return to work later in the day. There was considerable alarm in the neighbourhood but the consequences were not as bad as first feared.' Interestingly none of the men involved were named.

SMALLPOX DEATHS

BURIALS AT DORE CHURCH 1893

NAME	AGE	DATE	ADDRESS
Arthur Blakemore	30 years	12.03.1893	Totley Bents
Mary Anne Blakemore	12 years	13.03.1893	Totley Bents
Kate Blakemore	2 years	18.03.1893	Totley Bents
Elizabeth Jane Carter	5 days	14.03.1893	Shaft No. 4
James Williams	24 years	05.04.1893	Green Oak Totley
Benjamin Gittens		11.04.1893	Hill Side Totley
Florence Bishop	2 weeks	04.04.1893	Totley Moor
Elizabeth Martin	10 years	24.04.1893	Green Oak Totley
John William Holthan	2 years	24.04.1893	Hill Side Totley
George Frederick Lockett	5 months	25.04.1893	Totley
Alice Martin	11 years	26.04.1893	Green Oak Totley
Thomas Leach	47 years	30.04.1893	Totley Rise
Joseph Preston	3 days	05.05.1893	Green Oak Totley
Walter Holthan	5 months	05.05.1893	Totley
Thomas Fuller	38 years	15.05.1893	Green Oak Totley Died at Smallpox hospital Totley
Frederick Russell	n/k	31.05.1893	Green Oak Totley Died at Smallpox hospital Totley
Emily Bird	1 year	16.06.1893	Smallpox hospital (late Heeley)

BURIALS AT HATHERSAGE CHURCH 1888-1893

NAME	AGE	DATE	ADDRESS
Thomas Grinnell	7 years	06.12.1891	Hathersage
Samuel S. Godley	1 year	14.12.1891	Hathersage
Arthur Sydney Ince	3 years	15.12.1891	Outseats
John Vickers Perrson	9 months	19.12.1891	Outseats
Edith Frost	4 years	27.12.1891	Booths
Agnes Isabella Truscott	2 years	30.12.1891	Hathersage
Emily Elworthy	2½ years	15.01.1892	Hathersage
George William Ellva	25 years	28.09.1892	Hathersage
Henry Mills	52 years	09.01.1893	Padley
Albert Bird	9 months	28.01.1893	Hathersage
Winifred Sorrell	17 years	22.02.1893	Hathersage
Emily Robinson	3 years	18.03.1893	Padley
Samuel James Robbins	9 months	08.04.1893	Padley
Harry Garfield	20 years	10.04.1893	Bakewell Union
George Ingram	28 years	11.04.1893	Bakewell Union
James Alvis	5 weeks	22.04.1893	Padley
George Page	42 years	23.04.1893	Hathersage
Beatrice Powell	4 years	12.05.1893	Padley
Hector Froggatt	11 years	15.05.1893	Sunny Bank
John Froggatt	39 years	16.05.1893	Sunny Bank

These are specifically recorded in the burial register of Hathersage church as being of railway families. On 9 Aug 1893 it was noted in the burial records that fifty six navvies and railway people had died since the work began. Forty one were specifically noted in the register as navvies or family members – thus another fifteen people died but are not recorded as being related to the railway.

DEATHS NOT SMALLPOX RELATED

AT TOTLEY

NAME	AGE	DATE	ADDRESS
Robert Pinder Booth	4 months	19.10.1888	Totley Bents
Frederick Taylor	3 weeks	01.05.1889	Totley Rise
Ella Stone	2½ months	10.08.1889	Totley Bents
Edward Dalton	45 years	29.08.1889	Totley Bents
Annie Reed	4 months	19.09.1889	Green Oak
Thomas Vaughan	9 weeks	20.02.1889	Totley Bents
John Roberts Williams	3 years 4 months	13.03.1889	Totley Bents
Ambrosine Barrett	9 years	22.03.1890	Green Oak
Edgar Davies	5 months	27.04.1890	No 1 shaft
Ernest Roberts	7 years	15.06.1890	Totley Bents
Emily Bastow	18 days	12.07.1890	Totley Bent
Nell Udall	2 months	19.07.1890	Totley Rise
Wilfred Wolstenholme	11 months	04.08.1890	Totley Rise
Nettie Mint	2 years 3 months	19.10.1890	Totley Rise
Elizabeth Wolstenholme	28 years	02.02.1891	Totley Rise
Mabel Beatrice Davis	7 months	26.03.1891	Totley Bents
Ivan Jones Noon	9 months	29.03.1891	Totley Rise
John William Williams	1 month	29.05.1891	Totley Rise
James Taylor	3 weeks	18.06.1891	Totley Rise
Ernest Edward Colson	4 months	28.06.1891	Totley Rise
Bernard Ramkin Clark	9 months	29.06.1891	Totley Moor
Frank Taylor	7 weeks	04.07.1891	Totley Rise
John James Dalton	5 months	23.10.1891	Totley Rise
Frank Barnett	2 years	05.11.1891	Totley Moor
William James Williams	7 months	23.11.1891	Totley Moor
Mary Jones	35 years	07.01.1892	Totley Rise
John Norman	7 months	18.01.1892	Totley Rise
Thomas Bishop	72 years	30.01.1892	Brick Houses
Alfred Barnett	5 years	21.05.1892	Totley Bents
Olive Brown	7 weeks	18.08.1892	Totley Rise
Mary Reeve	24 years	14.09.1892	Totley Bents
Jim Reeve	11 days	16.09.1892	Totley Bents
Elizabeth Mountain	58 years	08.10.1892	Totley Rise
Lily Roberts	8 days	17.10.1892	Oldway Huts
Walter Russell	6 months	16.12.1892	Totley Rise
Lily Williams	7 days	17.02.1893	No 4 shaft
Mary Fox	75 years	03.05.1893	Totley Bents
Walter Jackson	9 months	27.05.1893	Totley Bents
Jenny Heer	2 years	06.06.1893	Totley Rise
Elizabeth Freeman	18 days	09.06.1893	Red Huts, Totley Lowe
Lily Elizabeth Agatha Goodgroves	4 months	05.07.1893	Totley Bents
Daisy Davis	2 days	05.09.1893	Totley Rise
Rosetta Law	14 years	07.09.1893	Totley Bent
Ellen Russell	2 years 2 months	28.12.1893	No 4 shaft
Thomas Davy	5 weeks	29.12.1893	Totley Rise
Florence Blanche Davis	5 weeks	17.01.1895	Totley Bents
Thomas Wright	6 days	20.03.1895	Totley Bents

HATHERSAGE CHURCH

NAME	AGE	DATE	ADDRESS
Edith Bond	2 years	21.05.1890	Padley
Violet Annie Astill	2 years	01.12.1890	Hathersage
Edward Green	7 years	02.12.1890	Hathersage
Lucie Marie Nelson	3 years	28.12.1891	Hathersage
Harriot Mary Preston	6 weeks	08.02.1892	Padley
James Fuller	15 months	10.02.1892	Padley
John Benjamin Schofield	3 days	30.30.1892	Hathersage
Elizabeth Ann King	6 months	10.04.1892	Padley
Lydia Clark Wolstencroft	5 months	11.05.1892	Hathersage
Lionel Perkins	1 year	11.05.1892	Hathersage
Ann Palmer	84 years	15. 06.1892	Padley Wood
Annie Rodgers	5 years	27. 01.1893	Hathersage
Elizabeth Isabella Ball	32 years	27. 03.1893	Padley
Violet Juite*	24 years	30. 03.1893	Booths
Alice Painter	23 years	09.04.1893	Padley
John William Elworthy	2 months	15. 8.1893	Hathersage
Grace Elliott	27 years	27. 8.1893	Sunny Bank

* Spelling uncertain

Because of the recorded addresses the following are likely to be relatives of railway workers noted in Dore church burial register.

Contract No. 2

Men Killed

NAME	AGE	DATE	ADDRESS	NOTES
Hamar or James Lane	46	02.11.1889	Hathersage	He was leading a horse drawn wagon loaded with bricks. On entering Cowburn tunnel the horse bolted and Lane was found dead, with his left arm smashed, and his head nearly severed from his body
William Carey	45	08.01.1890		An Irishman killed at 02.30 when a beam of timber fell on him in Cowburn tunnel. Two other men were 'somewhat seriously injured'
Jonathon Thomas Millward	49	27.02.1890	Railway huts Edale	Buried in Edale churchyard
Sidney John Rosewall	28	18.06.1890	Edale	Killed at Cowburn tunnel mouth
Edward Bishop	19	08.07.1890	Chapel	Killed in tunnel
William Slinn		03.12.1890		Killed by machinery at Edale
Walter Mosby	28	10.01.1891	Edale	Killed in tunnel
Roger Hall	50	19.02.1891	Little Hucklow	Killed at Normans Bridge
Johnson		08.1891		Horse driver. Killed in tunnel
Joseph Hynds	50	09.10.1891		Signalman. Killed in tunnel
Anthony Potter	27	30. 05.1892	Castleton	Horse driver. Killed in tunnel
Whitfield Watson	30	15.06.1892	Edale	Platelayer. Run over by engine at Edale
William Buck	49	10.10.1892		Killed in tunnel
Samuel Slater	14	02.08.1892		Point turner. Killed in tunnel
John Evans		14.11.1892		Killed in tunnel
Herbert Hall	34	18.08.1893	Chapel	Inspector of works. Killed in tunnel

OTHER DEATHS

15 Dec 1889. **Eli Robins**, age 39, died after a short illness. He left a widow and eight young dependant children unprovided for.

2 Feb 1892. **Herbert Wilson**, age 31, a married man from Chapel Milton was working on the viaduct as a stonemason when he experienced chest pains and fell down dead.

15 Jun 1892. **John Watson** from Skipton was killed while trespassing on the line at Edale.

MEN INJURED

Jan 1889. The first reported accident was at the Chinley entrance when a fall of dirt badly bruised the legs of an **unnamed** man who had been working at the site for about a week.

28 Jan 1889. An **unnamed** man suffered the shattering of one arm and an injury to an eye when material exploded after a large stone had been bored and charged with dynamite. He was taken to the surgery of Dr Jones and his injuries were attended to.

8 Aug 1889. A bricklayer called **Beech** fell from scaffolding at the Chinley end of tunnel and dislocated his shoulder and broke his arm.

20 Aug 1889. **Samuel Driver** a ganger was seriously hurt by a fall of earth in the tunnel.

Sep 1889. An **unnamed** man jumped from scaffolding and was 'badly hurt' when he fell on a wagon.

29 Nov 1889. A large block of stone had been bored for blasting and was charged with dynamite. It exploded before the men got clear. An **Unnamed** man had his arm shattered. He was attended by Dr Jones at his surgery.

12 Feb 1890. During the afternoon there was an explosion at Chapel Milton. A large steam crane, which was used for winding large blocks of stone, exploded. The crane was smashed and the jib fell. **Joseph Allen** was below and was knocked down and cut about the head and face and scalded by boiling water and steam. Nobody else injured.

Early Mar 1890. An **unnamed** man received severe head injuries from a 'heavy weight unexpectedly falling on him'.

11 Apr 1890. **John Dunn** was caught between the buffers of two wagons and badly crushed. Taken to workhouse hospital where reported to have died 'but this was not so'. It is not known whether he survived. I have been unable to find a coroners' report so may have.

18 Jun 1890. This particular afternoon was wet and when the men had finished their dinners some of them stood just within the entrance of the tunnel at the Edale end to shelter from the rain when the roof where they were standing, which was supported by timber fell in and two of the men **Sidney John Rosewall** and **William Lawrence** were completely buried. Rosewall died of his injuries and Lawrence suffered such serious injuries that his life was despaired of.

10 Dec 1890. An **unnamed** horse driver was knocked down when his horse shied at a lighted candle. He was treated at the workhouse hospital for a bruised knee.

10 Jan 1891. Six men were working at the Edale heading. One of them **Walter Mosby** was putting a gelignite cartridge in a hole. The charge was too large and it exploded killing him. **James Boyles** right arm and hand was seriously injured and also his head and he was taken to Sheffield Infirmary. His injuries were not considered to be of a serious nature. Others injured were **Edward Anthony** and **John James**.

23 Jan 1891. **Benjamin Garrett** was seriously injured by a stone falling from the roof.

8 Mar 1891. **George Smith** and **Thomas Griffiths** were about to start work for the first time, having only been taken on the previous day and were walking from the Edale end of Cowburn tunnel when their lights went out. Some laden wagons were coming in the opposite

direction. They were unable to get out of the way in the total darkness and suffered serious injuries. They were moved in a cart to the Chapel workhouse infirmary where on examination it was found that Smith had suffered serious internal injuries and several ribs were fractured while Griffiths was badly cut about the head.

26 Aug 1891. Ganger **Abraham Brickwood** and a labourer were working at the Edale end when some bind fell. Brickwood had a 3½ inch wound to his head.

26 Aug 1891. A man called **Jackson** was severely crushed between the buffers of two wagons in Cowburn tunnel.

29 Jan 1892. **Alfred Jones,** age 19, who lived at Chinley was a rope runner in Cowburn tunnel. He was uncoupling some wagons when he was knocked down and a wheel passed over his arm. It was amputated at Chapel workhouse infirmary.

21 Apr 1892. An **unnamed** man broke both legs following a roof fall. He was moved to Chapel workhouse infirmary.

25 May 1892. A man called **McKee** or **M'Vee** working at the Edale end of the tunnel became jammed between moving trucks and sustained a broken jaw and other facial injuries. He was moved to Chapel workhouse infirmary. He had only started work the previous day.

On the same day two **unnamed** men working at the Chinley end fell through scaffolding and were badly hurt.

30 Jun 1892. At the Chinley end of the tunnel an engine came into contact with a prop which supported some scaffolding on which some men were working causing it to fall on to them. **James Lawns**, a labourer of Chapel had several ribs broken and had to be conveyed in a cart to the Chapel workhouse infirmary. **Samuel Locks** the engine driver had one of his shoulders dislocated and a youth called **Martin** was badly cut and bruised around the head and shoulders.

17 Nov 1892. Another accident of **unnamed** man who had to be carried home.

18 Nov 1892. An **unnamed** man was run over by an engine. He was moved to Chapel workhouse infirmary.

29 May 1893. **Gregory Waterhouse**, who lived at Chinley was blown off a platform by a strong wind and fell to the floor at the Chinley end of the line. He was badly injured internally and became confined to his bed.

23 May 1896. **Charles Clayton** a platelayer of Chapel was riding on a lurry (sic) on which were some steel rails. One of the rails fell on his leg crushing it. He was admitted to Buxton hospital where his leg was amputated. It was probably linked to the completion of No. 2 Shaft.

TRESPASS ON THE RAILWAY

26 Apr 1893. **William Morris** had just been discharged from a workhouse having recovered from an attack of 'delirium tremens'. He walked from Glasgow to Cumberland and then to Preston. He then caught a train to Chinley where he arrived in the evening. He wandered on to the railway works and walked through Cowburn tunnel. On emerging at the Edale end he was caught by a policeman who had him medically examined. He was sent to the Chapel workhouse.

| BURIALS AT EDALE CHURCH ||||
NAME	AGE	DATE	ADDRESS
Arthur Wood	4 months	18.09.1888	Railway Huts
Charles Barnicott	3 months	18.06.1890	Railway Huts
Mary Fowler	79 years	18.11.1890	Railway Huts
Isaac Barnes	57 years	11.01.1891	Railway Stores
Harry Tidmarsh	2 months	27.10.1891	Railway Huts
Samuel Clark	5 months	14.01.1892	Railway Huts
Joseph Bertie Cookson	3 years	23.04.1892	Railway Huts
Ada Hatcliffe	9 months	23.04.1892	Railway Huts
William Hugh Hughes	3 years	29.04.1892	Railway Huts
Harriet Latham*	12 years	24.06.1893	Railway Huts

*This child may have died of smallpox because the date she died was during the smallpox outbreak.

The only way to distinguish between the permanent residents of the parish and the temporary railway workers and their families is the address. Those who lodged in the area and died may be listed but cannot be confirmed as temporary residents.

BURIALS AT CHAPEL-EN-LE-FRITH

It is known that the smallpox hospital was at the workhouse. The burial records give the workhouse address as 'Union Workhouse'. It is not possible to differentiate between those who were railway workers and local residents in the establishment.

IN PREPARATION

VOLUME 2

The tunnels, stations and bridges and the branches
built for the reservoir constructions and Earle's Cement.

VOLUME 3

The British Railways period from 1948 to 1993
including the Beeching Report

In Volume 2, I will be covering the infrastructure. This early picture of the bridge to Padley chapel and the western end of Totley tunnel will appear under the Grindleford station section. I will also be covering staffing, passenger experiences, accidents, newspaper reports and more at all the stations.
Author's collection